# Table of Contents

- Course Outline .................................................................
- Rules and Policies ...........................................................
- Introduction To Viticulture And Vinification ................................... 5
- Champagne & Sparkling Wine ................................................. 23
- Burgundy .................................................................... 38
- The Loire Valley ............................................................ 51
- Alsace ...................................................................... 57
- Jura and Savoie ............................................................. 69
- The Rhône Valley ............................................................ 72
- Provence .................................................................... 78
- Languedoc-Roussillon ........................................................ 80
- Southwestern France ......................................................... 99
- Bordeaux .................................................................... 113
- Spain ....................................................................... 118
- Portugal .................................................................... 130
- Italy ....................................................................... 136
- Germany ..................................................................... 168
- Austria ..................................................................... 178
- South America ............................................................... 190
- Chile ....................................................................... 192
- Brazil ...................................................................... 197
- Uruguay ..................................................................... 197
- Bolivia ..................................................................... 198
- Peru ........................................................................ 198
- Colombia, Venezuela, Ecuador ................................................ 198
- Argentina ................................................................... 199
- California .................................................................. 203
- Napa Valley ................................................................. 210
- Sonoma County ............................................................... 214
- Mendocino ................................................................... 217
- Lake County ................................................................. 218
- Sierra Foothills ............................................................ 218
- The Central Coast ........................................................... 219
- The Bay Area ................................................................ 222
- The South Coast ............................................................. 223

| | |
|---|---|
| Oregon | 224 |
| Washington State | 227 |
| New York State | 231 |
| Virginia | 232 |
| Texas | 233 |
| Canada | 234 |
| Australia | 236 |
| New Zealand | 250 |
| South africa | 258 |
| Beer | 266 |
| Sake | 271 |
| Spirits, Dessert & Fortified Wines | 279 |
| Appendix A: Latitude | 291 |
| Appendix B: Grape Pages | 294 |

# Course Outline

## Viti 1

| | |
|---|---|
| Class #1 | Component Tasting and Grape Growing |
| Class #2 | Pinot Noir |
| Class #3 | Chardonnay |
| Class #4 | Cabernet Sauvignon & Blends |
| Class #5 | Sauvignon Blanc & Blends |
| Class #6 | Grenache, Syrah, and Tempranillo |
| Class #7 | Riesling |
| Class #8 | Chenin Blanc & Pinot Gris |
| Class #9 | Sangiovese & Nebbiolo |
| Class #10 | Champagne & Sparkling Wine |

Students should already have a very basic understanding of how to taste. Students should have a basic understanding of how grapes are grown and wine is made.

## Viti 2

| | |
|---|---|
| Class #1 | Viticulture & Vinification |
| Class #2 | France I: Burgundy & Bordeaux |
| Class #3 | France II |
| Class #4 | Italy I: Piedmont & Northern Italy |
| Class #5 | Italy II: Tuscany & Central/Southern Italy |
| Class #6 | Spain |
| Class #7 | Germany & Austria |
| Class #8 | USA |
| Class #9 | Southern Hemisphere |
| Class #10 | Beer & Spirits |

## Viti 3

| | |
|---|---|
| Class #1 | Barolo |
| Class #2 | Burgundy |
| Class #4 | Bordeaux Red |
| Class #5 | Northern Rhone Syrah |
| Class #6 | Napa & Sonoma Cabernet Sauvignon |
| Class #7 | Willamette Valley Pinot Noir and Columbia Valley Cabernet Sauvignon |
| Class #8 | Riesling |
| Class #9 | Cabernet Franc |
| Class #10 | Central Otago Pinot Noir |

# Rules and Policies

1. Please arrive on time as quizzes are distributed promptly at 6:00 p.m. and collected at 6:20 p.m. Anyone arriving after the quizzes are collected will not have an opportunity to take or make up the quiz.
2. Students not able to attend a class due to illness or jury duty will be asked to provide a doctor's note or summons notice and you will have an opportunity to make an appointment with the AS office within one week (7 days) of the missed class to take the quiz.
3. Students who will be unable to attend a class due to travel, work or other such engagements may make an appointment with the AS office to take the quiz in advance of the missed class.

## Class Etiquette
*Extends to all American Sommelier events, tastings, and seminars*

1. Please refrain from wearing strong scents (perfume, aftershave, cologne, etc.) or carrying in strong scents (cigarette or cigar smoke, etc.) to class, as it interferes with the sensory aspect of the tasting portion of class.
2. Please empty your wine glasses into the provided spit buckets after each flight and before the end of the class and discard any tissues or napkins used.

## How to Use This Book

Welcome to the Viti Series: an intensive course on the theory of viticulture and vinification, winemaking regions, laws, and classification systems.

Each week you will hear a lecture and taste flights of wine. The following week you will be quizzed on the lecture and homework readings. This textbook is designed to follow and go hand-in-hand with the lecture series laid out for the course. For example, the first class is Introduction to Viticulture and Vinification, for which you will be required to read chapter one, as well as the corresponding pages in the Sotheby's Wine Encyclopedia. Supplemental reading from books like the World Atlas of Wine or from the internet is encouraged, but not mandatory. You are not required to bring the texts to class.

We strongly recommend that you read the relevant chapter before class so that you are able to participate in class and focus on the additional information provided by the educator.

## What to Study

Each quiz is designed by that lecture's instructor and is based on three main sources of information:

- American Sommelier course pack
- Sotheby's Wine Encyclopedia
- Lecture

We recommend that students do <u>a minimum</u> of two hours of reading for each hour of lecture (approximately five hours of studying each week); however, feedback from students who successfully complete the course shows that it is highly advantageous to spend additional time reviewing provided materials and seeking out supplementary readings and tastings. American Sommelier has a small library of books, which is available to students and members who wish to come into the office (books are not permitted to be taken out).

In general, it is expected that for each winemaking region students have a solid grasp of the following (this list is NOT complete):

- Climate
- Any pronounced and influential geographical feature(s) and how it (they) impact wine and winemaking

- History and significant figures who have impacted the wine industry
- Classified winemaking areas (AOCs, AVAs, etc.)
- Varieties grown
- Styles of wine and the laws that apply to them

# Introduction To Viticulture And Vinification

To understand the final product, you must first understand the base material: grapes! To understand grapes, we should begin with the vine: the vine is a plant, and a plant's life's mission is to reproduce. To do that, it must create seeds. These seeds grow within the berry that eventually becomes the wine.

## The Vine

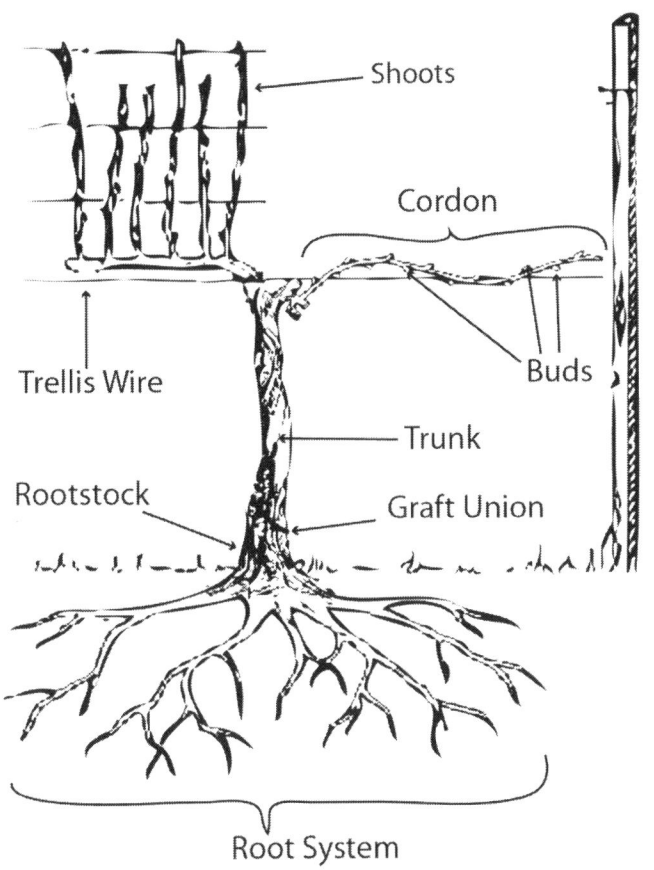

Each vine has an underground root system that digs deep to find water and minerals to help the plant grow. Above ground we find a trunk, from which will grow arms that vintners call "cordons". These cordons develop buds that grow into shoots with leaves, referred to as the "canopy". The leaves in turn use photosynthesis to convert light, carbon dioxide and water into the sugar that is used as energy to continue the plant's growth.

When we talk about "vines" in the study of wine, for the most part we are referring to a specific botanical species called *Vitis vinifera*. Native to Europe, this species encompasses all of the most well-known grape varieties like Chardonnay and Cabernet Sauvignon. In fact, most commercially produced wine is made from *vinifera* grapes, mainly because they taste good as wine. There are other species, including American natives *Vitis labrusca*, *Vitis rupestris* and *Vitis californica*. While these species generally don't produce grapes that are as desirable for winemaking, they have the huge advantage of being more resistant to certain widely-devastating pests and diseases.

To fully understand the anatomy of vines in most commercial vineyards, you must understand this: most are *Vitis vinifera* budwood grafted to a more disease-resistant species of rootstock. You can see where the grafted budwood (called the "scion") joins the rootstock near the ground. Grafting allows us to benefit from the desirable flavor profile of *vinifera* grapes in addition to the disease-resistance of the rootstock's species. While there are exceptions—which we will discuss in future chapters—grafting is typically the rule.

## The Grape

The grape's purpose is to protect the seed as it grows and, when the time is right, aid in the seed's dispersal by attracting birds and other creatures. Vintners want to focus a lot of the plant's energy on creating physiologically ripe grapes.

A grape, which is attached to its cluster by a "pedicel" (a.k.a., stem), has three basic components:

1. Seeds or "pips"
2. Flesh or "pulp" that contains water, sugar and acids, and
3. Skin that contains compounds called "phenols" that impart flavor, aroma and color.

The general consensus is that there are thousands of different grape varieties. Additionally, there are often a number of different clones of each variety (in some cases, hundreds). Some berry-related factors that differentiate the varieties and clones include:

- The number of seeds per berry
- The size of each berry
- The size and shape of each grape cluster
- The naturally occurring levels of sugar, acid and phenols
- The types of phenols present
- How long it takes ripen the berries

These factors will all have an impact on the wine that ends up in your glass. Varieties and clones also differ in things like leaf shape, disease susceptibility, tolerance for heat or cold and the amount of clusters and leaves they produce.

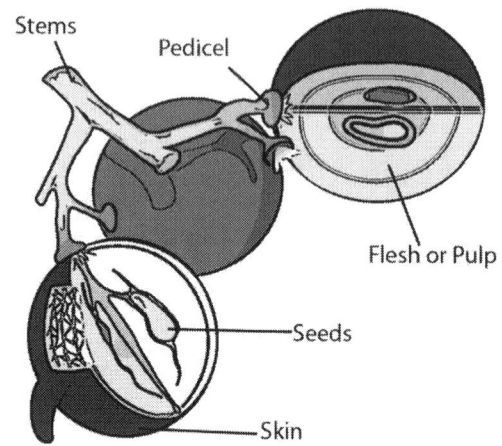

## THE VINTNER'S TOOLS

For quality wine-making, the grower doesn't necessarily want his vine to produce as *many* grapes as possible. Too many grapes will spread the plant's energy too thinly, creating grapes (and wine) with undesirably diluted levels of sugars, acid and phenols. As such, grape growers must limit the "yield" of their vineyard. This is one major difference between growing grapes and other agricultural crops. Let's say you are growing wheat—you will look for fertile soil with abundant water and minerals so that you can grow a large and profitable crop. When growing grapes, you *don't* want the most fertile of soils or the largest of crops—you want the vine to struggle just enough that it focuses all of its energy into producing a smaller number of higher-quality grape clusters.

To limit yield and focus the vine's energy on quality grape development, grape growers must choose their vineyard site carefully and manipulate the vine in such a way as to (hopefully) give it an ideal balance of sun, water, nutrients and warmth. The ideal balance will vary based on the grape variety, and achieving that balance will require different manipulations in different regions. For example, Cabernet Sauvignon has different needs than Pinot Noir, and grape growers face different environmental challenges in Germany than they do in Argentina.

Tools at the vintner's disposal for regulating his crop include things like:

- Vine spacing: altering the distance between plants will affect how much or how little the roots must compete for water and minerals, the circulation of air, and even the exposure of grapes and leaves to the sun.
- Vineyard orientation: planting in rows aligned North to South, East to West, or some degree in between will affect the amount of light shed on the plants by the sun as it travels throughout the day.
- Cover crops: planting certain crops between the rows of the vines can have an impact on the nutrient content of the soil.
- Irrigation: to control the amount of water received by the vines. In a dry climate this may be essential, though in others it may actually be banned.
- Vine "training": referring to the practice of using posts and wires to control the way that the trunk and cordons grow. Training gives order to the vineyard, but also controls the distance between the ground and the cordons, which impacts the amount of heat—reflected up from the soil—that reaches the shoots and grapes.
- Canopy management techniques including pruning and "trellising". There are many different trellising methods, employing wires to control how the shoots and canopy grow. Trellising can affect circulation, as well as sun exposure.

The blend of complex science and art used to balance all of these variables in the vineyard is called viticulture.

## SEASONS OF THE VINE

The season of the vine is approximately 120 days long and includes seven major steps.

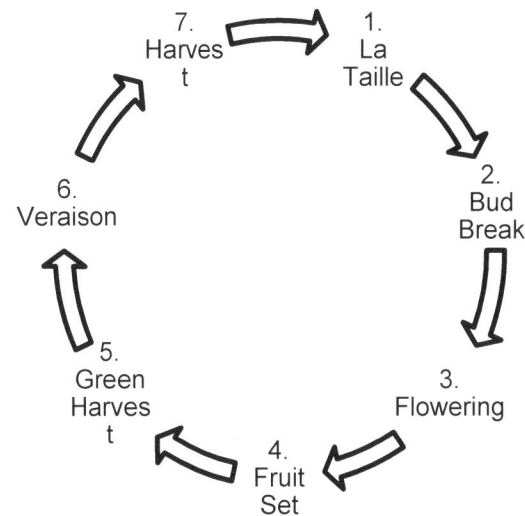

1. ***La Taille*** is the process of cutting away the previous year's wood growth, trimming down the plant for the new season; it is usually done between February and March (in the northern hemisphere).
2. **Bud break** occurs in the spring when the vine comes out of dormancy and shoots begin to push out of the cordon, now trained to a wire.
3. From bud break the vine moves into **flowering**. Flowering is a critical step, as it is the flowers that are fertilized and eventually become grapes. Flowers are delicate and can easily be destroyed by a freak hail storm—thus destroying your crop for the year! Throughout flowering and the steps that follow, shoots and leaves are growing.
4. **Fruit set** follows; this is when the flowers become tiny, hard, green berries. In the course of the following month, the berries will slowly grow in size, but remain bitter, with very little sugar in the grape.
5. As the clusters develop, the vintner is presented with an additional tool to help control the vineyard's yield. If he decides that there are too many clusters—that the vine's energy is being spread too thinly—he may decide to "**green harvest**". This simply means to "drop" (or remove) some clusters, leaving the vine to focus its energy on the remaining grapes.

\* From the time the vine begins to develop leaves and grow its canopy, the vineyard manager must decide how much he wants to keep it in check. Pruning or "**leaf pull**" allows better air circulation around the vine and more sun exposure for the grapes. Care must be taken to avoid pulling too many leaves, as extreme sun exposure can cause the fruit to burn.

6. Four to six weeks prior to harvest, there will be a spike in sugar levels within the grape and green fruit will turn red. This is called **veraison**. Now the vintner waits for the magic moment when sugar and acid levels are ideal and all the components of the grape have reached physical maturity. His timing must be precise, as the acid level will plummet should he wait too long. At long last, it's time to…
7. **HARVEST**! In the northern hemisphere, harvest can begin toward the end of August (in warmer regions) and continue through the end of October. For "late harvest" wines, which will be discussed later, picking takes place as late as the end of December. In the southern hemisphere, harvest usually occurs in the February–March time frame, with the latest harvests taking place in May or even June.

From the time that the vine passes bud break, the vineyard manager begins to lose sleep. The onset of cold weather is of great concern. Should a frost set in before the grapes are ripe enough to pick; the crop could be either severely reduced or destroyed altogether. If you spend time at a winery at this time of year you may bear witness to sleepless nights and the occasional frost alarm going off in the darkness.

Water is also very important. Too much causes rot on the grapes and doesn't force the vine to struggle. Not enough can cause the vine to stress too much, which may lead to it shutting down. A stressed vine that shuts down stops its physiological development.

In the winter, the vineyard manager is back in the field pruning back the branches preparing for the next season. The degree to which a vine is cut back in the winter will determine the potential quantity of grapes for the following season. Different regions and grape varieties are treated differently.

## WHERE TO PLANT

Most quality winemaking regions are situated between the $30^{th}$ and $50^{th}$ parallels both north and south of the equator. In general, it is too cold at latitudes higher than 50 degrees and too hot at those lower than 30—though there are exceptions. Centuries of winemaking has helped us hone in on which regions on the globe have proven most successful for grapegrowing. This vast experience has also helped winemakers determine which varieties grow best in which regions.

Climate, geography and soil all have a major impact on a vine's development and thus play a big part in the characteristics of wine.

## CLIMATE

Here's how NASA differentiates climate and weather:

"The difference between weather and climate is a measure of time. Weather is what conditions of the atmosphere are over a short period of time, and climate is how the atmosphere "behaves" over relatively long periods of time."[1]

Weather changes vintage to vintage, climate does not. When discussing viticulture, you'll hear climate classifications like:

- **Continental**: hot summers, cold winters, lower average precipitation
- **Mediterranean**: warm/hot dry summer, mild wet winters
- **Maritime**: relatively cooler summers and warmer winters, a smaller variance in temperature from summer to winter, higher average precipitation levels throughout the year

Within a climate zone you might find microclimates different from their surroundings created by particular geographical features.

## GEOGRAPHY

Geographical features like mountains, hills, valleys, lakes and rivers can affect the climate and weather of a region. In many areas mountains act as a barrier, protecting the region from precipitation. Weather systems heading for the vineyards may be stopped in their tracks by mountains, leaving the other side sunny and dry—for example the Cascade Mountains in Washington State prevent rainy weather coming in from the Pacific Ocean from reaching the vineyards in the east of the state.

Mountains and hills also provide slopes on which to plant vines. Slopes can promote drainage below the surface of the earth and circulation above (warm air rises, cold air sinks). The direction of the slope (or "**aspect**") of a vineyard will not only affect the sun exposure. Slopes facing east will catch morning sun but may be shaded from the intense afternoon light. A westerly aspect will have the opposite effect.

Planting a vineyard up a mountain will put it at a higher elevation. This can have different effects based on the particular region. Planting at an altitude can put the vineyard above a fog line, meaning it will get more sunlight than the vines below. As you go up the mountain, in general, the average temperature will drop (approximately four degrees Farenheit per 1,000 feet) and winds may pick up. In a hot region like northern Argentina (at a latitude of about 25 degrees South) this can cool an area enough to allow for successful viticulture.

Bodies of water can help warm or cool a region, in addition to creating fog or increased humidity. The Finger Lakes in New York State gather heat throughout the summer and help keep surrounding areas warmer during the winter as this heat slowly dissipates. Conversely, as the land heats up during the summer, the lakes are slow to catch up, remaining cool longer and helping moderate the temperature in the other direction. Fog cover rolling in off the ocean can reduce sun exposure and cool a region down.

## SOIL

Soil around the world varies greatly. Soil from wine region to wine region and even within each region also varies dramatically. Considering the soil when choosing a vineyard site is critical, as it can have a significant impact on the development of the grape and vine—it can also impact the final flavor and aroma characteristics of a wine.

---

[1] (National Aeronautics and Space Administration. (2005, February 5). *What's the Difference between Weather and Climate?* Retrieved Janaury 10, 2013 from NASA: http://www.nasa.gov/mission_pages/noaa-n/climate/climate_weather.html

Why does soil affect the vine's development? Different types of soil will drain and retain water at different rates, which affects how much water the vine's root system has access to. Remember, the vine needs enough water to stay nourished, but little enough that it is required to struggle a little. Large particles of soil with bigger spaces between them allow water to drain much faster than small particles with smaller spaces between them. Imagine pouring water through a bucket of large rocks versus pouring water through a bucket of garden soil…in which situation will the water reach the bottom of the bucket first?

Soil particles are divided into three broad size categories: **sand**, **silt** and **clay** (from largest to smallest). All soil is made up of some percentage of these three particle types. Sand, being the largest particle, has the most space between particles; it will drain water the quickest and also lose nutrients the quickest. **Loam** is a soil that is composed of equal parts sand, silt and clay.

In the study of viticulture you will hear terms like slate, shale, limestone, schist and granite. These are types of bedrock—a parent material for soil. Consider a vertical cross section of the earth: the layer closest to our feet is the top soil. This layer often contains a larger percentage of broken down organic material, which can enhance the nutrient profile of the soil. Under the top soil is the subsoil. And under the subsoil is the bedrock. Because of the topography of the land and how it has developed, bedrock can be near or even at the surface.

Different soils and bedrock vary in pH level. The scale ranges from 0 to 14 with 0 being acidic, 7 being neutral and 14 being aklaline (or "basic"). Grape vines tend to like to grow in soils that are slightly acidic, though the range can vary from about 6 to 7.5.

Soil is formed by various physical and chemical weathering processes that break up a parent material like bedrock. Soil from the tiniest particles to gravel to large boulders can then be transported and deposited by lakes and rivers, the wind, glaciers, volcanoes, and movement of the tectonic plates of the earth. As you can imagine, the 4.5 billion year history of our planet has led to an incredibly complex global soil map!

## TERROIR

As a vintner, not only do you have to choose the particular variety of grape to plant, the clone of the variety and the type of rootstock, you must weigh carefully the choices of location. Hundreds if not thousands of years of experimentation with these variables has given rise to a theory of *terroir*, which is necessary in understanding and appreciating wines. The French word has no direct translation to English, but expresses, instead, a notion. Terroir is the effect the vine's specific surroundings upon its fruit as expressed through the grape in the resulting wine. It encompasses both the physical (soil type, geography, climate) and spiritual—the sense of place and history derived from generations of winemakers honing their craft.

## THE MAKING OF WINE

Fermentation is what turns grape juice into wine. The formula for fermentation is:

$$\text{Sugar} + \text{Yeast} \xrightarrow{\Delta} CO_2 + \text{Alcohol}$$

Sugar is naturally found in grapes. One of the determining factors that tell a winemaker exactly when to harvest is the amount of sugar in the grape. Yeast is also naturally found in the vineyard, though for the most part winemakers will kill the natural yeast present and (when the time is right) inoculate their grape juice with lab-developed yeast strains. Some winemakers do use the indigenous yeast for fermentation, but it can be less reliable and predictable. The fermentation process takes place as the yeast reacts with the sugar, creating heat (symbolized by delta in the formula above) and in turn yielding alcohol and carbon dioxide as byproducts.

There are as many variables in the winery as there are in the vineyard. In fact, the environmental factors already discussed will necessarily impact which techniques are used in the winery. For example, cooler growing areas generally produce grapes with higher acidity levels and proportionately lower sugar levels. The inverse is true in hotter growing areas where sugar levels are elevated and naturally occurring acidity levels are lower. As a result, **chaptalization** (the process of adding sugar to fermenting juice in order to increase the final alcohol level) is not allowed in southern France but adding acid to compensate for naturally lower levels is. The opposite is true in the north. In warm California, winemakers rarely have a potential alcohol problem so there is no need for chaptalization. However, due to the warm growing season, there may be a lack of natural acidity in the fruit; therefore, winemakers regularly acidify to balance their wines.

## UNDERSTANDING THE PROCESS

So, how is wine made? The basic process is simple.

**HARVEST**: As grapes near maturity, the vineyard is sampled in order to measure the sugar and acid concentrations in the berries. Sugar may be measured in two ways:

1. By its refraction of light (using a refractometer) which is expressed as the percent of sugar by weight or degrees Brix
2. By the density of the juice (using a hydrometer)

Acid is measured by titration and by pH (both which the measure of the acidity or basicity of a solution).

The decision to harvest is dependent upon the style of wine to be made. Varietal character is extremely important at this step. Winemakers wait until they feel the fruit is in full expression of its potential flavor and until the fruit has the components necessary to produce the desired level of alcohol after fermentation is complete.

The potential alcohol may be estimated by multiplying the sugar concentration in the fruit by 0.55. So in the vineyard, if your refractometer measures 23° Brix, you would calculate your potential alcohol (the level of alcohol after fermentation is completed) as:

(23) X (0.55) = 12.65%

Alcohol is expressed as % by volume on the bottle label. Most American-made table wines are in the 12-14% alcohol range.

Many vineyard managers and winemakers use no equipment at all, using only their senses and knowledge based on years of experience to tell them when to pick. They taste the berries every day and determine when to pick based on the flavors and textures of the skins and seeds.

Grapes may either be harvested by hand or by machine. The benefits of machine harvesting are:

- Easy
- Fast
- May be done any time of day (or in the middle of the night when it's much cooler)

The disadvantages of machine harvesting are:

- Less gentle on the grapes than hand harvesting (crushes them prematurely)
- Obtain a mixture of "good" and "bad" clusters
- May get material other than grapes (leaves, sticks, other debris)
- Harvesting by hand is beneficial for the following reasons:
- It is more gentle on the grapes; skins are kept intact
- Pickers can be selective on which clusters to cut from the vine
- Leaves and other debris are left out

Conversely, the disadvantages of harvesting by hand include:

---

**Chemical Formulas in Winemaking**

Sugar
$C_6H_{12}O_6$

Carbon Dioxide
$CO_2$

Sulfur Dioxide
$SO_2$

Tartaric Acid
$C_4H_6O_6$

Citric Acid
$C_6H_8O_7$

Malic Acid
$C_4H_6O_5$

Lactic Acid
$C_3H_6O_3$

- Expensive
- Slower than machine harvesting
- Lower yield (by being selective, many clusters are left behind)

**CRUSHING**: The grapes are picked either manually or by machine and are then brought into the winery, destemmed and crushed. The product of crushing is called **must**, which consists of approximately 80% juice, 16% skins and 4% seeds. In order for fermentation to begin, it is necessary for the juice to come in contact with yeast. Wild yeast, as mentioned previously, is naturally present on the skin of grapes; this yeast is able to convert sugar to ethanol, which is called natural fermentation, however wild yeast present certain disadvantages including a lack of predictability of the fermentation with regard to timing and formation of off-character flavors. Some winemakers prefer a natural fermentation because native flora may add complexity to the flavor of the wine).

**PRESSING**: At this point in the production of WHITE wine, juice from the grapes is pressed off the skins. Unlike red wine (where the pigment is found entirely in the skins), the juice for white wine is almost never fermented in the presence of skins or seeds. Several types of presses exist, but currently the most popular is the pneumatic press.

Once this apparatus is filled with grapes, a balloon inside the cylindrical press expands, creating pressure that crushes the berries against the side of the container. The perforated walls of the press allow the juice to escape while containing the solids.

After the berries are crushed, the juice is transferred to another vessel so fermentation may begin. At this point $SO_2$ (sulfur dioxide) is usually added to prevent oxidation (browning) and to inhibit undesirable microorganisms from contaminating the juice.

The type of container used for fermentation depends on the style of wine desired by the winemaker. There are three primary choices, each of which contributes particular characteristics to the final product:

- small oak barrels (white wine only)
- large oak barrels (does not impart any flavor to the wine)
- stainless steel tanks (does not impart any flavor to the wine)

So, white wine grapes are pressed immediately after they are crushed, prior to the start of fermentation, while red wine grapes are pressed after they are fermented. This is because red wine remains on the skins and seeds in order to extract color and tannin. The red color comes from the skins, and tannin comes from skins and seeds.

**MUST ADJUSTMENTS**: Once the juice is in the fermentation vessel, yeast is added to jump start the fermentation process. There are many choices to make at this stage; as yeast will impart flavor to the final product, it is necessary to select a strain that will accentuate the flavors a wine derives from oak, from malolactic fermentation or from terroir. The temperature of fermentation and presence of increasing alcohol concentration are also factors in determining which yeast strain to select.

There is even a strain of yeast referred to as "killer yeast", which pushes the sugar/alcohol fermentation to the conversion of every last gram of sugar to alcohol.

If the potential alcohol of the must is too low, it may be enriched by the addition of concentrated grape juice, or in some places sugar, which is called chaptalization. This practice is permitted in cool climates such as Western Europe where grapes may attain phenolic ripeness (skins, seeds) but do not reach sugar levels needed for desired final alcohol (remember that sugar is in the juice of the grape). Chaptalization is prohibited in California; the nature of ripening is such that usually with appropriate phenolic ripeness, high sugar concentrations are naturally attained (hence a style of wine somewhat more full-bodied).

The acidity may also be adjusted by the addition of citric or tartaric acid.

In some regions, this is also the point of production when nutrient additions are made. These include nitrogen (which is the most limiting nutrient, but vital for yeast survival), yeast "ghosts" (dead yeast cells that help feed the viable yeast), malic acid (which helps to stimulate malolactic fermentation), plus other amino acids and vitamins.

**MANAGING THE FERMENTATION**: After making the desired adjustments, it is crucial to monitor the temperature of the must. Every 1° Brix that is fermented produces a temperature increase of approximately 2.3°F. The temperature must be kept down because hot environments may kill the yeast or create off-flavors in the resulting wine. Temperature can be managed using refrigeration jackets that surround the fermentation tanks.

$CO_2$ (Carbon Dioxide) is naturally produced during fermentation; it must be safely released from the fermentation vessel without permitting the entry of excess oxygen. "Fermentation locks" are attached to the vessel to allow for this process.

**MALOLACTIC FERMENTATION**: The process whereby grape acid, or "malate", is converted to lactate by lactic acid bacteria.

This fermentation process:

- Occurs naturally, but is often induced by the addition of lactic acid bacteria
- May occur simultaneously with alcoholic fermentation but usually occurs after
- Generates $CO_2$
- Is responsible for the production of a compound called **diacetyl**, which can lead to a creamier texture to the wine and, in a hot climate, aromas and flavors of butter
- Reduces acidity
- Increases the stability of wine, because once it is completed it cannot occur in the bottle (this is undesirable as the formation of $CO_2$ in the bottle will create fizziness and a cloudy appearance)
- May be prevented if the wine is clarified immediately following fermentation, along with the addition of high levels of $SO_2$, which kills lactic acid bacteria

**FINING & FILTRATION:** In order to further clarify or stabilize the wine or to reduce any excess tannin in the wine, winemakers may decide to fine and/or filter. Fining is the process of adding a substance to the wine to which unwanted particles and solids will adhere via "adsorption" and then proceed to "fall out" or fall to the bottom of the container holding the wine. Examples of such substances are egg whites, casein (a milk based product) or gelatin, but bentonite (a natural clay) is most commonly used. After the addition of any of these products, the wine must then be racked. Racking a wine means carefully moving the liquid to another vessel while leaving the undesired solids at the bottom of the tank. This process may need to be done several times throughout the winemaking process.

Filtration is a process by which wine is passed through a fine mesh or porous medium (somewhat similar to the notion of a coffee filter) in order to discard unwanted solids. Diatomaceous earth (a natural product) is a commonly used filtration agent.

Sterile filtration is another type of filtration, which may be used if the wine has not yet undergone malolactic fermentation and is not intended to—sterile filtering is another method of killing off lactic acid bacteria which leads to malolactic fermentation. It is also used for wines that are meant to have residual sugar, "RS" because leftover sugar serves as a substrate for remaining viable yeast cells: fermentation would continue or restart after bottling.

As with excessive fining, excessive filtration may remove flavor and complexity. Some winemakers do not exercise either, some use both. In fact, some producers feel that if a wine has gone through malolactic fermentation, is clear and has the concentration of tannin that the winemaker is looking for, filtration is often considered an unnecessary step.

**TARTRATE STABILIZATION**: This step is very important in winemaking, and requires little more than chilling the wine to extremely low temperatures. When wine is chilled, potassium and tartaric acid in wine form a crystalline precipitate called Potassium Acid Tartrate (KHT). This is a natural byproduct of a severe drop in temperature, and while it resembles broken bits of glass stuck to the cork or at the bottom of the wine, is absolutely harmless; however, it is undesirable for the consumer and almost totally preventable by a process called cold stabilization. After fermentation, wine should be chilled to below 32°F for up to several weeks, or run through a cooling system. Cold stabilization should be followed by racking in order to leave the behind the solid "tartrates".

Cold stabilizing is an expensive step in wine processing; many winemakers choose alternative methods of keeping the temperatures cool. Sometimes an ice bath and garden hose are fashioned into make-shift cooling systems.

It should be noted that even if a wine is cold stabilized, tartrate crystals may still precipitate later on in the bottle if the wine is stored at cool temperatures.

**AGING**: Barrel maturation may be the next step, depending on the style of wine the winemaker is looking for. Part of the art of winemaking is to utilize barrels of different ages to arrive at the perfect expression of fruit and terroir. Barrel aging is not necessarily a measure of quality. It is used to further enhance the stylistic approach of the winemaker, to compliment the natural flavors of the fruit grown in a particular area. Barrels will be discussed in more detail in a following section.

**BOTTLING**: Wine is ready to be bottled when the winemaker decides it has finished aging in the winery. The wine will continue to age in the bottle and is released to the market at the winemaker's discretion. Before bottling, the wine is transferred to a holding tank where it will often receive one final treatment of SO2 to prevent instability or premature browning in the bottle. Empty bottles may be spurged with Nitrogen or another inert gas in order to displace the oxygen within, which is another step to help prevent oxidation. A cork (synthetic or natural), screw cap or glass closure is immediately inserted into the bottle once filled.

## WHITE WINE PRODUCTION

A key difference between red a white winemaking occurs almost immediately after pressing. The grapes for white wine are immediately pressed in order to separate the juice from the skins, seeds and stems, all three of which would otherwise impart bitterness and astringency. The juice is forced from the press into a separate receptacle where it is kept cold, protected from oxygen and allowed to settle. This settling period is called débourbage, a process which serves to clarify the juice prior to the beginning of sugar/alcohol fermentation and may last from 8-12 hours.

That said, often in Germany and Austria white grapes are not pressed right away to separate the juice from the skins and seed, rather the juice is left in contact with the skins in order to attain complexity in lieu of later having to use oak. This is called skin contact fermentation (maceration of lightly crushed berries before pressing) and commonly practiced with German Rieslings and Austrian Chardonnays.

Once the juice has completed this stage of clarification, the juice is racked into a different vessel for fermentation, leaving behind unwanted solids that were still present after pressing. Next, fermentation begins. Here winemakers have yet another tool at their disposal to further enrich the wine's flavor at this point in the process called *bâtonnage*, which is the **stirring of the lees**. Lees are the solids that are produced by dead yeast cells toward the end of fermentation. Stirring the lees adds richness to the wine through the extraction of glycerol and can be detected in a wine by increased mouth feel and silkiness on the teeth.

It should be understood that there are gross lees, which constitute the initial thick layer of lees that settles at the bottom of the vessel after fermentation. Depending on fruit quality and whether enzymes were used by the winemaker in order to assist in the further breaking down of berries (sometimes a tool used to increase quantity), this could be a very thick layer. Most producers will rack off the gross lees, because letting the wine sit on them could potentially cause formation of H2S (Hydrogen Disulfide) which has the distinct odor of rotten eggs. However, there is always the exception, and again, depending on the region, the grapes and the winemaker's own personal style he/she may decide to not only let the wine sit on the gross lees, but stir them occasionally to incorporate their flavor and richness into the wine. Some winemakers even filter the lees, in order to acquire as much wine as possible; this fraction is later used to top off.

After the initial racking off of the big lees, there still exist some solids in solution, which will eventually settle to the bottom as well. This second layer of settled solids is much thinner and finer than the big lees, and is referred to as fine lees. It is common for winemakers to leave this layer in the wine for an extended period of time and through malolactic fermentation, because fine lees add complexity and creaminess to the wine. They also serve as a nutrient substrate for the lactic acid bacteria which are, at this point, underway in converting malic acid to lactic acid.

Overall, the process of stirring on the lees is typically used for wines undergoing barrel fermentation and helps limit the extent to which the wood tannins and pigments are passed into the wine.

Malolactic fermentation is often induced following the completion of "primary" or alcoholic fermentation. This is also classified as another tool of winemaking. The conversion of malic acid (most closely related to green apple acid) to lactic acid (found in milk products) results in a creamy texture and flavor, which may reduce the perception of acidity on the palate. This fermentation does not need to occur to 100%, which means the winemaker has the ability to manipulate the wines final flavor profile.

After the fermentation is complete and the lees have served their purpose, the wine is racked to separate the solids from the liquid. If the winemaker chooses to barrel age his white wine (very common with a variety such as Chardonnay) they often let the wine age sur lies (aging on the lees) in order to obtain the full potential of flavor. The final steps of cold stabilization, fining, filtration and bottling then occur.

White wine is typically fermented at low temperatures (55-70°F) to maximize fruit flavors. This low temperature and scarcity of nutrients (there are no skins or seeds) will result in a fermentation time of roughly 10 to 30 days. This depends on the temperature, strain of yeast used (if any), nutrient limitations or enhancements, pH, grape quality and microbial interactions.

White wine can be made dry or sweet. A wine is considered dry when it is fermented to completion (~0°Brix), where there is no detectable residual sugar in the final product.

Sweet wine may be made by arresting the fermentation by either chilling, sterile filtration (use of a 0.45 micron nominal filter pad) or by fermenting to dryness and then adding sterile juice concentrate.

## RED WINE PRODUCTION

When the grapes for red wine are received to the winery from the vineyard, they are either destemmed by machine and sometimes further sorted through by hand, a process called triage, in order to select only the best berries and also to discard any unwanted matter before they enter the fermenting vessel. Or, the red wine grapes are fermented as whole clusters, which include the stems.

Fermentation takes place before pressing (the opposite of white wine) because the juice of red grapes is actually clear. The color is found in the skins and the tannins are found in the skins and seeds so it is important that they stay in contact with the juice to ensure good color and flavor extraction. Some winemakers also utilize a cold soak, which is a pre-fermentation maceration at low temperatures to allow the marc (stems, skins, seeds) to steep/rest in the juice of the crushed grapes prior to the beginning of fermentation. This process is usually done in a stainless steel tank so that the temperature can be carefully monitored. By keeping the temperature low, the wine will not ferment. Cold soaking the wine aids in the extraction of color and aromatic compounds from the marc. The duration of a cold soak is based entirely on the grapes involved and the desired result.

Once this period is over, yeast (and sometimes other nutrients) is introduced to the marc and fermentation begins. As the must ferments, $CO_2$ is released into the atmosphere, which causes a solid layer, or cap, of grape skins and seeds to form on the surface of the wine. In order to further extract color and tannin from the solids, the winemaker begins the practice of pump-overs (large vessels, requires a pump and hoses) or punch downs (small fermenters, done by hand), which breaks up the solid surface and incorporates it into the juice.

Punch-downs require a person to stand on a platform (or ladder, or sometimes anything he/she can find) and, using a tool, physically push the cap down to the bottom of the vessel. In large, closed-topped fermenters, the person uses a hose and pump set-up. A hose would be attached to a valve at the bottom of the fermenter with the other end attached to a pump; another hose would be connected from the pump to the opening in the top of the vessel which would create a circular mixing system. The force of the juice being suctioned from the bottom of the tank and through the pump would break through the cap at the surface, thereby mixing the wine.

Another more infrequently used practice, pigeage, actually requires a person to enter an open-topped fermenter while holding on to a rope that is suspended from the top. The individual moves through the fermenter, breaking through the cap and mixing the wine, which is thought to be a more gentle method than punch-downs or pump-overs; however, due to the lack of oxygen in the tank and presence of $CO_2$, this practice is extremely dangerous and becoming less popular among winemakers.

The practice of mixing the wine and breaking the cap is carried out 2-3 times a day during fermentation. As the sugar is converted to ethanol and the release of $CO_2$ is reduced, the skins and seeds begin to sink to the bottom; the cap becomes less and less solid. Fermentation time for red wines ranges from 8 to 21 days, again depending on the yeast strain, the quality of the grapes, microbial activity and temperature (often higher than that for whites, to ensure sufficient color and tannin extraction). Maximum color extraction peaks after roughly 5 to 8 days of skin contact, while tannin extraction will continue to increase should the juice be left in contact with the skins and seeds for a prolonged period of time. The winemaker must take care not to let the wine become overly tannic or astringent.

Following primary fermentation, red wines also go through malolactic fermentation (ML). As red wine is never fermented in small oak barrels, ML can occur in a "pièce" or "barrique". (The characteristics brought on by ML are not as apparent in red wines as they are in whites, but red wine having not gone through this process would be undrinkable). Here, the winemaker must make the decision whether to use new or used barrels, and which kind. This decision is based on the grapes being fermented, the style of wine desired and of course the finances of the winery.

Carbonic Maceration is a red wine processing technique where whole berries or whole clusters (not yet crushed) are covered with a blanket of $CO_2$ and left for up to ten days in a near-closed container. By covering them with $CO_2$, there is no exposure to oxygen. The juice inside the berries will begin to ferment and eventually explode, splitting open the skins. But without the initial pigment extraction from the skin, the wine produced is much lighter, fruitier and less tannic than wine made from grapes that were crushed immediately. After the skins break down naturally during carbonic maceration, the must is pressed and inoculated and allowed to ferment normally.

This method is used in nouveau wines that are released a few weeks after harvest and meant to be drunk immediately.

Following fermentation the wine is racked off the marc and is separated into two categories: the *vin de goute*, or free run juice is the liquid that runs off the grape skins without the harshness of pressing. The second category is called the *vin de presse*, or press wine, which is the liquid obtained from pressing the skins, seeds and lees. This fraction is often quite higher in tannin than the free run juice and may be used to increase the power of the other cuvées.

Barrel maturation is often the next step in red wine processing, though not always employed. The length of maturation is at the winemaker's discretion, which depends on the variety being fermented. When this period is over, the wine will be racked again and perhaps followed by fining and/or filtering, then bottled.

## Rosé Wine Production

There are two ways to produce rosé wine:

- As a "blush" wine of a red variety
- As a blend of a white wine with a red wine

The scope of this course will only explore the first way of producing rosé. There are two methods of obtaining a "blush" wine from red grapes. They are:

- Beginning just as one would for the white wine making process, by crushing the red grapes and pressing them after a very short period of time in contact with the skins (up to 3 days). The skins are pressed and discarded, resulting in juice of a pink hue and tannin concentration closer to a white wine than a red.
- Saignée (French for "bleeding") is applied when the winemaker is intending to actually increase the color and tannin of his/her red wine. By bleeding off a portion of the juice, the ratio of juice to skins for the red wine is now lower, thus creating a higher concentration of tannin, color and flavor. The portion that was initially bled

off has a pink color since it was briefly left in contact with the skins. This will ferment separately and be bottled as rosé.

Rosés are almost always fermented in stainless steel, and there is usually no wood contact or aging; they are meant to be drunk young.

## SPARKLING WINE PRODUCTION

Sparkling wine is legally defined in the U.S. as that which contains greater than 0.392 grams $CO_2$ per 100 ml. This is approximately 1 atmosphere of pressure. However, sparkling wines often have much more $CO_2$ than this, near 5 or 6 atmospheres of pressure.

Sparkling wine is made by a second fermentation which occurs in a closed container so that the $CO_2$ produced may not escape. A wine cannot legally be called "sparkling" if $CO_2$ is added artificially by carbonation instead of by natural fermentation in the bottle, although some sparkling wine is made this way. The bubbles are a result of dissolved $CO_2$ in the bottle that is released when opened.

The production begins with a base wine (or vin de base) called the cuvée. The grapes are picked early, usually between 11-18° Brix (and high acidity) in order to achieve a low final alcohol, less than 9%. Sugar will be added after fermentation is complete, in order to induce a second fermentation that will occur in the bottle, which produces $CO_2$ and increases the concentration of alcohol just as the primary fermentation does.

There are different methods of producing sparkling wine: Méthode Champenoise, Crémant, Charmat Method (Cuvée Close), Transversage Method and Carbonation.

These methods will be further discussed as we explore the regions in which they are practiced.

Other styles of wine production include late harvest, ice wine and fortified (Port, Madeira, Vin Doux Naturel, Sherry) which will be discussed in detail when we examine the regions in which they are made.

The winemaking process is similar to wines from all over the world. During the next 24 weeks, this course will examine the wines of the world from a viticultural and vinification perspective.

## OAK & STEEL

As you now know, a winemaker makes many choices throughout the vinification process that will influence the resulting wine. One of these choices is whether to use oak or steel during fermentation and/or aging—a decision that can have a significant effect on the final product.

The following table illustrates the (simplified) differences between steel and oak:

| STAINLESS STEEL TANK | OAK BARREL |
| --- | --- |
| Cheaper | More expensive |
| One tank can be used for many years | Each barrel has a relatively limited usage |
| Easy to clean | Can be cleaned, but not sterilized |
| Easy temperature control | Harder to control temperature |
| Anaerobic environment | Allows very small amounts of oxygen to interact with the wine |
| Will not impart flavor or aroma characteristics to the wine, but will allow a pure, fresh expression of the grape varietal | Will impart distinct flavor & aroma characteristics, and will chemically interact with components of the wine to alter the existing structure |

Economics can play a part in the winemaker's decision to use steel or oak. One steel tank can be much cheaper than the number of barrels that would be required to contain an equivalent volume of wine. A stainless steel tank will give consistent results year after year; a barrel will impart fewer characteristics to a wine with each subsequent use. Labor costs of maintaining wine in a barrel will be greater than those of keeping wine in a tank, as barrels often need topping up due to evaporation. These expenses will have a direct effect on the final price of the wine. Because of the cost, oak is typically used more in the making of higher end wines, while mass produced wine is more often made in steel vats. Of course, there are exceptions to every rule, and cost is not the only thing to consider when choosing between steel and oak.

The winemaker will also consider which grape variety he is working with and what qualities he wants in the final product. Certain grapes are more often oaked than others—you are more likely to find a Chardonnay that has spent time in oak than a Riesling, for example. A grape's suitability to oak depends on its naturally occurring physical composition. Components like pH and tannins are factors in how a grape variety will stand up to the characteristics that oak brings to wine.

If the winemaker wants a crisp, fresh, angular wine that will bring grape- and terroir-driven characteristics to the foreground, he may be more likely to choose stainless steel. A stainless steel tank allows the winemaker to keep oxygen out of the process. Oak, on the other hand, will affect wine by imparting certain aromas, tannins and flavors to the final product and by allowing a slight amount of oxygen to come in contact with the wine—this in turn will affect the color and structure of the wine.

Tannin refers to compounds that are found in both grape skins and wood. While grape tannins are felt on the top of your tongue, wood tannins are perceived as a dryness between your lip and gum.

## CHOOSING A BARREL

The art and science of selecting *which* oak container to use can be as complex as the process of making wine itself. There are many variables to consider, including:

- Size or volume of the barrel
- Where the tree came from
- How the barrel was "seasoned"
- The degree of "toast"
- How many times the barrel has been used already

Winemakers have experimented with types of wood other than oak, like chestnut, redwood and acacia, but in general all are considered inferior. Oak is watertight, easily bent into shape, and comes with desirable flavor attributes—a combination that no other type of wood possesses.

The size of container used will significantly affect the degree to which oak characteristics are imprinted on the wine. There is a wide range of sizes to choose from. The term "cask" is often used as an umbrella term for all sizes of containers. A "barrel" is a cask that is transportable, and a "vat" is a larger container that is fixed in place. Barrels and vats come in a plethora of styles, each with their own name. For example:

| NAME | VOLUME | REGION |
|---|---|---|
| Barrique | 225 L / 59 gallons | Bordeaux |
| Pièce | 228 L / 60 gallons | Burgundy |
| Feuillette | 132 L / 35 gallons | Chablis |
| Foudres | Very large, exact size varies (~1000 L) | Alsace |

In a smaller barrel, more wine will come into contact with the surface area of the wood. Using several *barriques* will impart more characteristics to 1,000 liters of wine than one *foudre*.

The specific characteristics imparted can depend on the geographic origin of the tree. The most commonly used oaks are French and American, though there are others. Slavonian oak, for example, is popular in Italy, and Russian oak has been explored as a cheap alternative to French.

French oak generally has a more subtle effect on wine; it is naturally lower in aromatic compounds and its tight grain allows for a more gradual integration of flavors. Because of the wood's properties and the traditional cooperage (barrel-making) techniques often used to make these barrels, French oak will impart qualities of toast, caramel, vanilla, and butterscotch.

American oak can often be recognized by aromas and flavors of dill and coconut. It can have a more intense effect on wine than French oak and has significantly more naturally occurring aromatic compounds. Also, American oak barrels are often made using different techniques, which also affects the impact of the barrel on wine.

A new French oak barrel from a reputable cooperage will cost approximately $1,100. An American-made barrel is about two thirds of that price. One 225 liter barrel can hold roughly three hundred 750 ml bottles. The math is simple in terms of how the cost of one bottle of wine is affected by the use of a new barrel.

## Cooperage

Barrel-making is an art and a science. First, the oak tree is cut into staves, which then need to be "seasoned" in order to reduce the moisture in the wood and remove some of the stronger bitter or astringent compounds. The traditional method of seasoning staves is to leave them outside for up to 2-3 years. To speed the process up, coopers use kilns that dry the staves, but don't have the same chemical effects on the wood (this is the technique often used to make American oak barrels).

After seasoning, the staves are heated and bent into the barrel shape, using iron rings to hold them together. The staves are heated by being held over an open flame, which will also toast or char the wood. The level of toasting is controlled by the cooper and will affect the characteristics that will be imparted to the wine. A light toast will allow more of the natural oak characteristics to be passed on to the wine, while a medium toast will increase the vanilla, spice, smoke, and roasted qualities of a wine. A heavy toast will give a lot of smokiness and is often used to age whisky and distilled spirits. The head of most barrels is often marked with information on the origin of the oak, the degree of toast, the time the staves spent seasoning and whether the head was toasted in addition to the staves.

Once assembled, the new barrel is complete and ready to be purchased by the winemaker.

## Barrels in the Vinification Process

Not every winemaker wants to age their wine in *new* oak barrels—some prefer barrels that have been used to store wine a few times already. New oak has a stronger effect on wine. The aromatic and flavor characteristics will be more intense and the tannins more evident. The dryness between your lip and gum will be pronounced. With each use, these properties are leeched from the barrel and a layer of deposits forms on the inside that acts as a buffer between the oak and wine. Used oak has a subtler effect on wine. Fewer flavor characteristics and wood tannins will be passed to the wine—you may barely feel the dryness. The winemaker can choose to use 100% new oak, 100% used oak, or some combination of the two. This decision depends on what the producer wants to achieve.

Other choices that the winemaker needs to make include:

> Will the wine *ferment* in oak?
> Or simply *age* in oak?
> Should the *lees* be stirred?
> How long should the wine stay in oak?

Red wines generally are not fermented in oak, as it is hard to remove the marc from the barrel following fermentation. Barrel fermentation *is* a better option for white wine. Fermenting in barrels has a more subtle effect on wine than aging in barrels. The yeast involved in fermentation attaches to the aromatic compounds and both are removed when the wine is racked off its lees. Some whites are left on their lees to age, which the winemaker may choose to stir every so often. As mentioned previously, stirring the lees adds richness to a wine, and acts as a buffer between wine and wood.

For the most part, the decision of how long to age a wine is a winemaker preference. In certain regions of the world—Italy in particular—the local regulatory body requires a certain length of aging in barrel for the wine that is released with a specific appellation on the label. During the aging period, a very small amount of oxygen will enter the barrel through the wood's pores and interact with the wine (not enough to cause oxidation). Oxygen is what causes the wine to "age" and what softens tannin over time. However, just as oxygen molecules can get INto the barrel, other molecules can also get OUT of the barrel. A small amount of evaporation will happen over time, requiring the barrels to be topped up every so often. It is very important to eliminate air space or "head space", which can lead to the formation of volatile acidity (VA) (acetic acid and ethyl acetate by acetobacter. In other words, leaving the wine in the presence of air is damaging). Volatile acidity has the aroma of paint thinner and is detrimental to the wine.

## BARREL ALTERNATIVES

Deterred by the high cost of barrels, winemakers have tried to come up with ways to replicate the barrel-aging process. Some will put oak chips or staves into a steel tank to impart flavor to the wine as a teabag would. While this practice may give some of the same flavor characteristics as a barrel, it doesn't replicate the gradual oxygenation effect of the barrel. Microoxygenation—the process of gradually, mechanically introducing oxygen to the wine in tank—was invented for just that purpose.

To keep costs down, some have tried shaving the inside of used barrels and inserting a thin layer of new oak. There has even been experimentation with oxygen-permeable polyethylene vessels, which are cheaper than oak barrels and do not allow evaporation (so there is no topping up!).

The choice between steel and oak depends on many factors, and has a significant impact on the resulting product. Knowing the potential effects of each material will give you yet another tool to help navigate the wine world.

## Tasting Components

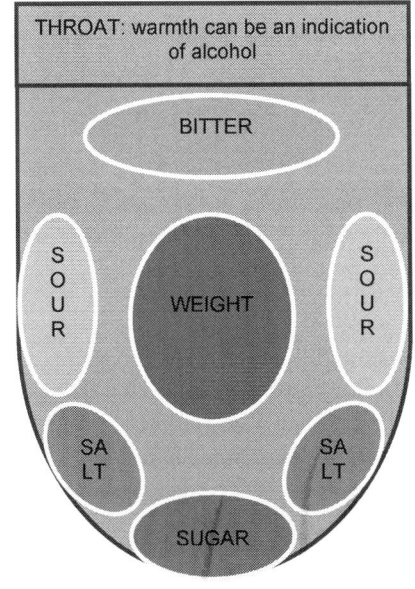

Your tongue helps you perceive several different characteristics of a wine—sweetness, acidity, bitterness, and weight. The sensations that occur in the different regions of your tongue can tell you volumes about what you are drinking.

**Sugar** – all grapes have glucose and fructose as a result of photosynthesis. Fermentation converts sugar to alcohol. Stopping fermentation prior to the conversion of all sugars leaves Residual Sugar (RS). The RS is most profoundly felt on the tip of the tongue. Less than 2 grams of sugar per liter is considered imperceptible. Growing areas with warmer climates create grapes with more sugar and thus higher potential alcohol.

**Salty & Sour** – the prickly feeling along the side of your tongue is your mouth's recognition of acid in the wine. Your physiological response will be salivation. Andrew likes to call it "Liberace playing up and down the sides of your tongue." Growing areas with cooler climates typically create grapes with higher acidity.

**Weight** – the center of your tongue is a dead zone where you do not experience taste. The sensation here is what will lead you to describe a wine as being light, medium, or full bodied. The body of a wine is usually a function of its alcohol level. Texturally on your tongue, you will also feel grape-based tannins.

**Bitter** – the last area of perception, the back of your tongue, is the bitterness zone. It is normal for the last sensation after tasting to be bitterness, as it is the last sensory location on the palate. All wines can have a note of bitterness.

**Balance** is where these different aspects play on the palate in harmony to the individual consuming the product.

## Classification

Most wine growing countries have instituted some system of wine classification that denotes regional typicity, "quality" or even grape ripeness level. Some countries have more than one classification system—applied to either the entire country simultaneously or separately to different regions. Some systems are regulated by the federal government, some are instituted by voluntary grape-growers' associations. Some systems are very involved—with lots of regulations and requirements—others are more hands-off.

Perhaps the most well-known system is France's national AOC system. AOC stands for *Appellation d'Origine Controlée* and generally refers to a demarcated growing region. Wines labeled with the name of an AOC must meet standards and requirements that are specific to that particular appellation. The basic concepts at the heart of the AOC system were informally passed down from generation to generation over the centuries, but it is now formally governed by an organization called the INAO (formerly the *Institut National des Appellations d'Origine*, now the *Institut National de l'Origine et de la Qualité*). Similar systems are also seen in other countries in Europe and, more recently, in the United States.

In many systems, viticultural areas must meet minimum requirements to attain the relevant appellation designation. There are differences from country to country, but the basic requirements are:

1. Minimum alcohol levels or ripeness at harvest
2. Delimited geographical area
3. Grape varieties permitted and blending percentages
4. Allowable yields
5. Viticulture: training system, vine density, irrigation
6. Vinification: chaptalization, acidification, aging requirements, and fortification
7. Ageing minimums

In France, regions receive "AOC" status based on having a distinguishing style and constant quality level from wines produced using the above criteria. Every year, winemakers must submit their wines to a group of impartial tasters. These tasters are given each of the wines blind to assess whether they are representative of the region. Wines that are rejected by the group are kept from being labeled with the name of the AOC and are thus *declassified*.

Below the AOC status, historically there were two other classifications within each geographic area reserved for such wines: *Vin de Pays* (country wine) and *Vin de Table* (table wine). In 2011, France instituted a few changes:

1. Added AOP or *Appellation d'Origine Protegée,* which is the European Union's version of AOC
2. Added *Indication Geographique Protegée* or IGP, which is the EU's version of VdP
3. Both AOC and VdP still exist and are used in addition to AOP and IGP
4. *Vin de Table* became *Vin de France*

Regulations in other countries also allow for similar declassification.

Even with centuries of information and trial and error, picking growing locations is still an inexact science. Quality discrepancies can occur when cultivating the same variety in two vineyards that are located right next to each other. One theory suggests that this is so due to the differences between the nutritional balances of the soils. One vineyard may have more organic matter in its soil, which breaks down into the ammonia and nitrate ions, benefiting the plant-feeding process and producing higher-quality grapes.

| COUNTRY | MAJOR CATEGORIES | |
|---|---|---|
| France | IGP | Indication Géographique Protégée |
|  | AOP | Appellation d'Origine Protégée |
| Italy | VdT | Vino di Tavola |
|  | IGT | Indicazione Geografica Tipica |
|  | DOC | Denominazione di Origine Controllata |
|  | DOCG | Denominazione di Origine Controllata y Garantita |
| Spain | DO | Denominación de Origen |
|  | VdP | Vino del Pago |
|  | DOCa | Denominación de Origen Calificada |
| Portugal | DO | Denominação de Origem |
|  | DOC | Denominação de Origem Controlada |
| Germany | QbA | Qualitätswein bestimmter Anbaugebiete |
|  | QmP | Qualitätswein mit Prädikat |
| United States | AVA | American Viticultural Area |

# Champagne & Sparkling Wine

By Kelly Magyarics

*I drink [Champagne] when I'm happy and when I'm sad. Sometimes I drink it when I am alone. When I have company I consider it obligatory. I trifle with it if I am not hungry and drink it when I am. Otherwise I never touch it—unless I'm thirsty.*

–Lily Bollinger: La Grande Dame du Champagne

No other beverage elicits such a response of unabashed delight as a flute of Champagne. Champagne is loved the world over, and with good reason. Its effervescence trails up the glass like a string of pearls and dances on the palate. Its enticing aromas range from green apple and lemon, to honey and hazelnuts, and mouth-watering bakeshop smells of bread dough, brioche and toast.

Champagne is synonymous with life's special events and celebrations: weddings, birthdays, anniversaries, promotions. But thankfully, more oenophiles are beginning to realize that Champagne needs no special occasion, it *is* the occasion. A glass on a Tuesday night with takeout can be as perfectly apropos as one on the eve of an elegant wedding reception, and so comes the realization that Champagne, and sparkling wine in general, is an amazing food partner. The bubbles wake up the taste buds and serve as "palate scrubbers" to wash away rich and fatty dishes. The crisp apple and citrus flavors are akin to a lemon wedge squirted on a piece of fish adding a zesty, mouthwatering acidity. The complexity of French Champagne holds its own against a variety of flavors, textures and culinary styles.

Champagne has always possessed a regal quality. Reims was, after all, the site of the coronation of French kings, and Champagne was the official drink at the celebrations of the new monarchies. It's undeniable that its presence over the years at events full of pomp and circumstance has done wonders for Champagne's reputation as *the* bottle to uncork to mark noteworthy occasions.

And let's not forget about the bubbles themselves, which give the sipper a brazen carte blanche to act giddy, light-headed and even, well, bubbly. As Brillat-Saverin descriptively stated, "Burgundy makes you think of silly things; Bordeaux makes you talk about them, and Champagne makes you do them."

Champagne is produced with one or several of three permitted grape varieties: Chardonnay, Pinot Noir, and Pinot Meunier, grown in one of five sub-regions. Offerings can be unique and *terroir*-driven like Grower's Champagne and Vintage Champagne; or show a consistency from year- to- year, as in non-vintage examples from the top Champagne houses. Most Champagne is ready to be consumed as soon as it's bottled, but the highest quality vintages continue to evolve in the bottle for years. During this time the *mousse* (fizziness/bubbles) softens in intensity, and flavor notes take on fascinating multi-dimensional tones of nuts, truffles and honey.

Champagne offerings are generally more expensive than traditional method sparkling wines made elsewhere in the world. No other bottles contain the tradition, history, or complexity found in a bottle of Champagne. Overcoming viticultural obstacles also factor into the price of Champagne. As the northernmost wine growing region in France, Champagne is prone to spring frosts. Grapes struggle to ripen in the cool climate and the nutrient poor soil requires constant fertilization. But the hard work and attention of the vignerons allows magic to happen, resulting in one of the most famous, celebrated and adored wines in the world.

The wine inside each bottle of Champagne is waiting patiently in suspended animation until it's opened, admired, sniffed and tasted. Every bottle of Champagne is both alive, and is a celebration of life itself. As author Jared M. Brown declared, "Champagne is the great equalizer. It makes anyone feel like royalty."

# HISTORY

There are references to effervescence in wine in literature and historical texts that date back to the ancient Greeks and Romans, but the first recorded sparkling wine production occurred in 1531. Benedictine monks from the Abbey of St. Hilaire, in southern France's Limoux region, intentionally produced a sparkling wine called *Blanquette de Limoux*. It is still made today in the same region. A century later, the English scientist and physician Dr. Christopher Merret wrote about the process of adding sugar to a finished wine, which kicks off a second fermentation that renders wine effervescent. This is part of the process now referred to as the **méthode champenoise** (or **méthode traditionnelle** outside of the Champagne region)—the method by which Champagne and other quality sparkling wine is produced.

*Indeed, in the seventeenth century, prior to the british invention of coal-fired glass, when second fermentation in the bottles could result in exploding bottles, and popping corks in the cellar—the cause of which was often attributed to the full moon(!)—people described champagne as "sauté-bouchon" or "vin-diable." Perhaps this served as a convenient excuse for naughty behavior, à la "the devil made me do it."*

Benedictine monk **Dom Pérignon** (1639-1715), though erroneously believed to have invented Champagne, is owed much credit for the success of the Champagne region and the improvement of its wine production methods. Pérignon became cellar master at the Abbey of Hautvilliers in 1668, and was the first person in Champagne to make white wine from black grapes. He was not fond of white grapes due to their tendency to re-ferment, and dedicated his life to improving the still—not sparkling—wines of the region. Pérignon insisted on aggressively pruning vines to produce lower and more concentrated yields. He recommended harvesting early in the day and pressing grapes as soon as possible to retain fresh aromas and flavors using a vertical press he created called the ***pressoir coquard***. Perhaps most significantly, Pérignon created the art of **assemblage**—a scheme for blending lots from different varieties and vintages to add complexity and dimension to wines, which is still the basis for Champagne production today.

Some historians assert that sparkling wine was actually an English invention. As mentioned above, recent historical research has unearthed evidence that self-taught British scientist Christopher Merret documented a technique to induce a wine's second fermentation and therefore the bubbles. In a paper submitted to the Royal Society in 1662 he described how adding sugar and molasses to French wines made it taste "brisk and sparkling."

Merret also had a particular interest in glass making. British furnaces began to use coal for their fuel instead of timber (which had been earmarked for the British army to build a stronger fleet), and furnace temperatures were much higher. This allowed for the production of stronger glass bottles, which helped prevent exploding bottles caused by the pressure that develops as wines undergo secondary fermentation within. However, it is Sir Kenelm Digby who is considered to be the father of the modern wine bottle. In the 1630s, Digby's glassworks used a coal furnace with a wind tunnel to manufacture wine bottles that had a high, tapered neck, a collar, punt and a translucent green or brown color to protect the contents from the light. In 1662, the British Parliament recognized his claim to this invention.

In the early nineteenth century, the practice of **riddling** or *remuage* (the dislodging of the yeast sediment from a Champagne bottle) was invented by Nicole Barbe Ponsardin Clicquot. The famed Widow or *Veuve* Clicquot used her own kitchen table to make the first riddling rack, known as a ***pupitre***. She proved herself to be a shrewd businesswoman during the reign of Napoléon by establishing her Champagne brand throughout Europe, including Imperial Russia.

The British have always been a major market for Champagne. For many years they imported Champagne in casks, then upon its arrival in Britain placed it in glass bottles and sealed it with cork stoppers. In 1830, legislation was passed that allowed the transport of Champagne in bottles within France, thus revolutionizing the Champagne trade.

The process of ***dégorgement à la glace*** or disgorgement (freezing the neck of the bottle to more easily remove the yeast sediment) was invented in 1884 and put into commercial use by Moët & Chandon and Perrier-Jouet in 1891. *Dégorgement* allows for cleaner tasting wines and less wine loss per bottle during the process of removing the sediment.

Champagne's popularity continued to grow until it was threatened by several major setbacks in the late nineteenth and early twentieth centuries. Frost and rain severely reduced yields, and the **phylloxera** epidemic that had destroyed vineyards across France finally made its way to the region. Harvests from 1902 to 1909 were riddled with hailstorms and flooding. Almost 96 percent of the 1910 crop was lost. World War I and II saw the ravage of Champagne's wineries and vineyards, which became battlefields and were destroyed. The loss was particularly devastating during World War I's Battle of the Marne in 1918, which left the vineyards of Champagne suffused with the blood of 139,000 soldiers killed or wounded. A by-product of the two World Wars was France's loss of the American and Russian markets for its wine, including Champagne.

Champagne sales rebounded after World War II and sales have quadrupled since 1950. Today, about 20,000 growers sell their fruit to approximately 300 production houses. The popularity of other sparkling wines that mimic or are inspired by Champagne is increasing, including Cava and California wineries affiliated with French houses.

## Regulation & Classification

In 1927, Champagne's vineyards were legally delimited by the French government; permitted grape varieties (Chardonnay, Pinot Noir and Pinot Meunier) were identified; and strict regulations for yields, pruning, vine height, spacing and density were instituted. Vines in Champagne are high density (6,000-10,000 vines/ha) and have relatively high yields (10,400 kg/ha, making 66 hl/ha). For context, in Bordeaux vine density is also high (about 8,000-10,000 in the Médoc's classified growth areas), but yields are lower 9,800 kg/ha, making 60 hl/ha). Only four pruning methods are permitted in Champagne: ***Taille Chablis***, ***Cordon de Royat***, ***Guyot*** and ***Marne Valley***, and two are preferred.

***Taille Chablis* (spur trained)** is the preferred pruning method for Chardonnay grown in Champagne. It looks like a slanted bush vine but without the support of a central post. This technique uses three, four or five permanent branches. Once the oldest branch encroaches on the next vine, it's removed and a new one is cultivated from a bud on the main trunk.

***Cordon de Royat* (spur trained)** is used for Pinot Noir and Pinot Meunier. This system uses a single cane that's horizontally trained. An extension of the main branch may have up to four more buds. Once pruned, each shoot is usually allowed two buds. Both pruning systems allow the vine to retain permanent wood, which assists with frost resistance.

*Le **Comité Interprofessionnel du Vin de Champagne (CIVC)*** is the umbrella organization for Champagne growers, cooperatives and merchants. It was created by the French government in 1941 and is responsible for regulating the production and trade of Champagne. Until 1990, it set the price for grapes and currently it regulates the size of harvest and wine production.

The ***Institut national de l'origine et de la qualité (INAO)*** was founded in 1935 to oversee France's appellation system made up of the ***Appellation d'Origine Contrôlée*** (**AOC**) ("controlled designation of origin"). AOC is a certification that specific French products (including wine, cheese, butter and other agricultural products) are produced in a particular geographic region and adheres to specific criteria. The ***CIVC*** and ***INAO*** assure that anything labeled "Champagne" comes only from the Champagne region, under specific regulations for viticulture and viniculture.

As of 2009 the AOC classification for wine is being replaced by a new quality system with the top step being **AOP (Appellation d'Origine Protégée)**. In theory, this AOP concept is to be adopted by all countries in the European Union.

The new quality rating system includes:

- Appellation d'Origine Protégée (AOP - top step)
- Vin Délimité de Qualité Supérieure (VDQS)

**Grand Cru Villages in Champagne**

Ambonnay

Avize

Ay

Beaumont-sur-Vesle

Bouzy

Chouilly

Cramant

Louvois

Mailly Champagne

Le Mesnil-sur-Oger

Oger

Oiry

Puisieulx

Sillery

Tours-sur-Marne

Verzenay

- Indication Geographique Protegée (IGP - replacing VdP)
- Vin de Table (VdT) will become Vin de France and will be allowed to show both vintage and variety

The sparkling wine from the entire region of Champagne is enclosed in a single AOC. Unlike many other regions in France—like Bordeaux or Burgundy—there are no sub-appellations within the Champagne AOC. To be called Champagne, all of the grapes used must be grown within this region.

There are several other requirements that must be adhered to in order for a sparkling wine to legally be called Champagne. This includes:

- Pruning and yield regulations
- Grapes must be hand harvested
- Only Pinot Noir, Chardonnay, and Pinot Meunier may be used
- For 375 ml bottles, 750 ml bottles, Magnums and Jeroboams, the wine's secondary fermentation, which gives the sparkling wine its bubbles, must occur in the bottle from which the wine is consumed. For bottles larger than a Jeroboam, the wine is transferred from smaller-sized bottles to a tank, chilled, rebottled and corked.

## ÉCHELLE DES CRUS (LADDER OF GROWTH)

Villages in Champagne are rated for quality. This rating system, known as *Échelle des Crus*, was originally introduced by the CIVC in the mid-twentieth century to establish grape prices based on the source of the fruit. At the time, a kilogram of grapes was assigned a fixed price and each grower's grapes would be valued at a certain percentage of that price based on the rating of the village in which the fruit was grown. The EU now forbids price fixing.

Today, the *Échelle des Crus* is used as a guideline in determining pricing for grapes, as well as an aid in determining quality in the bottle. But as Daniel Thibaud, chief winemaker at Charles Heidsieck and Piper Heidsieck explains, "The *échelle* has little bearing on the final quality of Champagne in the bottle. The system gives an indication of grape quality, but the important elements that determine the quality of Champagne are threefold: grape quality, the vinification process and the blend."[2]

A debate exists today on the merit of the scale, but the *Échelle des Crus* is still set up as follows:

- 17 Grand Cru villages are given a value of 100%
- 43 Premier Cru villages receive a score of 90-99%
- Some Villages outside of the Marne département are valued at 80-89%
- No village receives a score of less than 80%

## LABELING

Champagne is unique as a French wine region in the sense that most producers do not grow grapes but buy the fruit from a ***récoltant*** or grower. Producers also heavily rely on ***cooperative-manipulants*** (cooperative producers) which are groups of growers who pool resources and share profits. Cooperatives play a large role in Champagne and are responsible for helping to process over half of the wine produced. Most Champagne producers are at the mercy of growers for their base material. Growers have used this to their advantage over the years.

Roughly 70% of Champagne is sold by ***négociants*** or merchants. The négociant buys wine or grapes from growers, bottle it under their own label, and sell the wine to retailers for wholesalers. The number of ***récoltants-manipulants*** (grower-producers) has traditionally been small in the region, though their number is slowly increasing. According to the most recent data from the ***CIVC*** and ***Syndicat Général des Vignerons de la Champagne (SGV)***, in 2008 there were 15,594 ***vignerons*** (growers) in Champagne, 293 Champagne houses, 66 coopératives and 329 négociants.

---

[2] http://www.thewinenews.com/decjan0102/cover.html

Special terminology is used on Champagne labels to provide information about the origin of the grapes and the wine's production. The following are terms found on the label:

| | Stands For | Description |
|---|---|---|
| NM | Négociant-Manipulant | Commercial house that buys grapes and *vins clairs* from cooperatives, growers or other houses; also called a Champagne house |
| CM | Coopérative-Manipulant | Cooperative producer; makes and sells Champagne under its own brand(s) |
| RM | Récoltant-Manipulant | Grower-producer; not allowed to buy grapes from other sources, but some allowance is made for purchasing small amounts of a variety not grown on the RM's own vineyards, for blending needs |
| MA | Marque-d'acheteur | Brand name not owned by the producer, but the purchaser (restaurant, wine merchant, supermarket, etc.) |
| RC | Récoltant-Coopérative | Grower working with a cooperative who delivers grapes in return for Champagne that is already made; then sold under grower's own label |
| SR | Société de Récoltants | Grower partnership: two or more growers that share facilities to produce and market Champagne under several labels |
| ND | Négociant-Distributeur | Distributor label: a company that sells Champagne (but does not make it) |

Other details about Champagne's labeling and bottling include:

- The word 'Champagne' must be printed on the section of the cork inside the bottle
- Champagne is the only AOC wine in France that does not have to bear the words 'Appellation Contrôlée' on the label
- **Blanc de Blancs** on a Champagne label means the wine was produced from 100% Chardonnay grapes. These wines tend to be drier and lighter in body than other styles.
- **Blanc de Noirs** on the label signifies that the wine was produced only from black grapes (Pinot Noir and/or Pinot Meunier grapes), resulting in a fuller-bodied wine that is a deeper yellow-gold in color
- **Rosé** on the label signifies that the Champagne was either produced with black grapes that saw some skin contact or that the wine was blended with a small amount of red wine
- **Non-vintage (NV) Champagne** accounts for 85-90% of all Champagne produced. Each year, producers are required to allocate 20% of their wine for use in future NV Champagne. This assures a consistent house style from year-to-year. NV Champagne is aged for a minimum of 15 months.
- **Vintage Champagne** is produced with grapes from a single harvest. Producers decide each year, based on vintage quality, if they will release a vintage offering. Producers can use no more than 10-15% of their wine for vintage Champagne. Its minimum ageing time is three years, though producers often age it much longer.
- **Prestige Cuvée** refers to a Champagne house's highest-quality Champagne. Roederer's Cristal, Moët & Chandon's Dom Pérignon and Veuve Clicquot's La Grande Dame are three examples of prestige cuvées.
- **Grower's Champagne**, identifiable by RM (Récoltant-Manipulant) on the label, is terroir-driven and varies widely by vintage and producer. Currently, there are about 5,000 grower-producers in Champagne.

Non-vintage Champagne is often a consistent "house style" that offers a similar aroma and flavor profile from year-to-year. There is much more variability in vintage and *prestige cuvée*, as they are more dependent on unpredictable and uncontrollable factors like rain, temperature, etc. Vintage and prestige cuvée champagnes may offer the opportunity of interesting and atypical characteristics in the wine, but it also comes at an increased expense.

# TERROIR

Lying approximately between the 48th and 49th parallel, Champagne is France's northernmost wine-growing region and grapes often struggle to ripen here. The area's cool climate is influenced by its proximity to the English Channel, which is in turn affected by the Atlantic Ocean. The rolling hillsides of the Reims Mountain (*Montagne de Reims*) and the Marne River with its tributaries create unique microclimates. Champagne is prone to early frost in the spring, especially along the low-lying Marne Valley and on the slopes of the Montagne de Reims. Average rainfall for the entire region is about 25 inches. For context, Bordeaux gets closer to 35 inches per year.

The soil in Champagne is characterized by a thin layer of topsoil above a chalk base composed of the fossils of belemnites and micrasters (extinct marine mollusks). This geography stretches north into England and the stark brightness of the White Cliffs of Dover gives a good comparison to what is underground in Champagne. The presence of chalk here is crucial, as it provides an appropriate balance of drainage and water retention. Cellars are carved out of the chalk and the resulting cool temperatures are ideal for ageing Champagne. Calcareous soil is also present in areas, which is comprised of chalk, marl and limestone with some clay.

The combination of the northern latitude, poor soil, and potential for frost makes the region seemingly inhospitable for growing grapes and producing wine. However, because the grapes used in Champagne require a high level of acidity to balance the effervescence and flavors imparted by the yeast, their struggle to sufficiently ripen actually works in the wine's favor. Overripe grapes would not have the crisp, tart-fruit flavor desirable in finished Champagne, and could potentially lead to out of balance alcohol levels.

## VARIETIES

Since 1927, three primary grape varieties have been used in the production of Champagne: **Pinot Noir, Pinot Meunier,** and **Chardonnay**. Each grape makes its own contribution to the Champagne blend and specific districts of Champagne are best suited to grow certain varieties. There are a few other varieties (Arbanne, Petit Meslier, Pinot Blanc Vrai) also allowed, though they are not permitted to be replanted.

|  | Pinot Noir | Pinot Meunier | Chardonnay |
|---|---|---|---|
| Varieties | Buds early and ripens late; prone to spring frosts and **coulure** (failure of grapes to develop after flowering) | Late budding and early ripening suited to a northern climate with spring frosts and summer rains | Buds early (just after Pinot Noir); prone to spring frosts and coulure |
| Characteristics | Red fruit flavors, body, length on palate and backbone. Develops biscuit-like flavors with age. | Easy drinking; provides freshness and fruitiness. Well-suited for Champagne that is best consumed in its youth. Attains spicy, earthy, mushroom-like complexity when aged. | Gives acidity, floral & mineral notes and citrus fruit, as well as light-body, elegance & finesse |
| Percentage of acreage under vine | 39% | 32% | 29% |
| Current Production | In 2010, there were 315 million bottles of Champagne produced | | |

# REGIONS

The Champagne region is located 90 miles (145 kilometers) northeast of Paris and covers about 35,000 hectares or 86,500 acres. Five sub-regions exist within Champagne, each with its own predominant grape variety. The 17 *Grand Cru* villages are located in the **Montagne de Reims**, **Vallée de la Marne** and **Côte des Blancs**. The **Côte de Sézanne**, and the **Aube** (Côte des Bar) do not have any *Grand Cru* vineyards.

| Region | Terroir | Major Grape Variety | Grand Cru Vineyards |
|---|---|---|---|
| Montagne de Reims | Large, fairly flat plateau. Best vineyards (though counterintuitive) are on north-facing slopes. | Pinot Noir | Ambonnay, Beaumont-sur-Vesly, Bouzy, Louvois, Mailly-Champagne, Puisieulx, Sillery, Verzenay, Verzy |
| Vallée de la Marne | Extends from Saâcy-sur-Marne in the département of Seine-et-Marne to Tours-sur-Marne beyond Epernay. Vineyards line edges of the valley that slope toward the river. | Pinot Meunier | Aÿ, Tours-sur-Marne |
| Côte des Blancs | A cliff at right angles with the Montagne de Reims south of Epernay. | Chardonnay | Avize, Chouilly, Cramant, Le Mesnil-sur-Oger, Oger, Oiry |
| Côte de Sézanne | Ten miles south of the Côte des Blancs. | Chardonnay | None |
| Aube Vineyards | Extends the region to the south, mainly clustered around Bar-sur-Seine and Bar-sur-Aube, with a small amount of plantings to the east in the department of the Haute-Marne. | Pinot Noir | None |

# VINIFICATION

The method for producing Champagne is officially referred to as the *méthode champenoise*. Today other sparkling wines are also produced using the same method as Champagne (such as Cava, Franciacorta, other French sparklers called Crémant and certain American sparkling wines), occasionally with the same grape varieties. In 1994, the EU forbade the use of the term *méthode champenoise* on labels of wine produced outside the region of Champagne and replaced it with *méthode traditionelle* or **traditional method**.

Simply put, while all Champagne is sparkling wine, not all sparkling wine is Champagne. The use of the term "Champagne" on a bottle's label defines a specific wine, traditional method sparkling wine from the demarcated Champagne region, and not just a specific style. The term "*méthode traditionelle*" or "traditional method" on a label indicates that no matter where the wine was crafted or with what grapes, its contents were produced with the same method as Champagne.

**Harvest** in Champagne usually begins in mid-October and **is done by hand**, as mechanical harvesters are not permitted in the region. **The grapes are kept in whole bunches and are not de-stemmed.** Both techniques allow the juice to more easily flow when the grapes are pressed, and also allows for a gentle extraction of juices.

**Pressing** traditionally occurs in a ***pressoir coquard***, a large vertical press whose shallow base permits only a thin layer of grapes to be squeezed. Because the layer of grapes is so shallow, the juice drains away quickly before coming in contact with the skins, which would impart color and phenolics. The *pressoir coquard* holds 4,000 kilograms of grapes from which a total of 2,550 liters of juice can be obtained. The first 2,050 liters is considered superior juice and called the *cuvée,* which contains a higher sugar level and retains the most acidity. The remaining 500 liters is considered inferior juice and is called the *taille*. Recently, there has been a move towards using **horizontal pneumatic presses**, which allows more control than a vertical press. Pneumatic presses are horizontal cylinders that contain a balloon that is inflated to press the grapes against the side of the cylinder. The cylinder rotates and has slits that allow the juice to flow out.

The first **fermentation** is usually done quickly in a temperature-regulated tank, although a few producers use barrel fermentation. The end product is a highly acidic, dry wine. Chaptalization—or the addition of sugar to the fermenting must in order to increase the final alcohol level—is allowed in vintages where grapes do not ripen sufficiently. Fermentation is maintained for 12 to 48 hours, at a low temperature between 54 to 77 degrees Fahrenheit (12°-25°C).

**Malolactic fermentation (ML)**, the process by which highly acidic malic acid is converted to a softer lactic acid, almost always occurs in the production of Champagne to tame high acidity levels due to the cool climate, and give a softer mouth feel. However, Bollinger and Krug are two well-known houses that block ML.

**Clarification** of the wine removes any sediment by **fining** (the process of coagulating particles so they may be removed from the wine) and **filtering,** assuring a clear final product.

*Assemblage* or **blending** is the key to the art of Champagne production. House, non-vintage styles maintain their consistency year-to-year by blending many base wines from different vineyards, parcels and grapes, as well as blending in reserve wine from other vintages. A non-vintage *cuvée* can potentially contain up to 70 base wines in its blend.

To produce **rosé Champagne**, two methods exist:

1. Maceration (skin contact) for a brief period with either of the two permitted black grapes, Pinot Noir or Pinot Meunier; or
2. Blend in red wines to obtain color during *assemblage*

The **second fermentation**—also referred to as ***Prise de Mousse*** or "capturing the sparkle"—occurs after the wine goes through a final racking. (**Racking** is draining wine off of its sediment or lees.) *Liqueur de tirage*—a mixture of reserve wine, sugar, yeast and a clarifying agent— is added to the wine in tank or cask (at 0° C to prevent fermentation) to set the stage for the second fermentation. The wine is then bottled and sealed with a temporary **crown cap** (like a beer cap). Bottles are placed *sur latte*—stacked on their sides between thin layers of wood—or *sur pointe* (fully inverted). As the temperature slowly rises from 0°C, the second fermentation begins. As the yeast converts the present sugar to alcohol, carbon dioxide is produced. Cooler temperatures, due to the wine's placement in either chalk or refrigerated cellars, will slow down the second fermentation, creating smaller bubbles and a more consistent bead. This fermentation can last from four to eight weeks and will produce a pressure of 5-6 atmospheres of $CO_2$ and an additional 1.2-1.3 percent Alcohol By Volume. The second fermentation comes to an end when the yeast has no more sugar to digest and, as such, begins to decompose. The decomposition of the dead yeast cells, known as **autolysis**, is what gives Champagne its trademark yeasty, toasty, bread dough aromas and flavors.

**The aging clock for Champagne begins immediately with bottling.** It cannot be bottled before January 1st of the year following harvest. The minimum aging period for non-vintage Champagne is 15 months (including at least 12 months on the lees), although most age for 18-30 months. Vintage wines must be aged for at least three years but most are held for a much longer period of time.

*Remuage,* or riddling, is the process of shifting all the yeast sediment to the neck of the bottle by slowly rotating and inverting the bottle. Two methods can be used. The traditional more time consuming method involves a ***remueur*** or *riddler*. An experienced riddler can turn about 30,000 bottles per day. The riddler manually turns the bottles (in very small increments) while they are stored in wooden racks, or *pupitres*. Over a six-week period the bottles gradually stand in a fully inverted position. A faster and more modern way is to use a *gyropalette*, a computerized riddling machine that is automated, accomplishing the same goal in about a week.

**Disgorgement**, or *dégorgement*, is the act of removing the collected yeast sediment from the bottle. The neck of the bottle (now containing all the yeast) is submerged in a very cold (-27° C) brine solution, freezing the sediment in an ice plug. The crown cap is then removed and the pressure in the bottle pushes out this plug. It is then turned upright quickly to avoid losing much wine.

The final step, known as **dosage**, tops up the bottle to account for the loss of volume during *dégorgement*. The winemaker adds a ***Liqueur d'Expédition***, which is a mixture of wine and sugar solution. This step determines the ultimate sweetness of the Champagne. The sidebar lists the various styles of Champagne and their corresponding Residual Sugar levels. Except for Brut Nature, Dosage Zero and Pas Dose wines, the dosage always contains some sugar. In the 1990s zero dosage Champagnes were popular for a brief time. As it is challenging to create wines that are completely balanced without the addition of a sweetener, bottles were often harsh and austere. For the most part this style of Champagne has fallen out of favor.

Finally, a cork is inserted and secured with a capsule and wire cage. It is then dressed with a deep foil around the neck of the bottle. The cork has two sections that are highly compressed, allowing it to expand and take on the familiar mushroom shape assuring a tight seal.

***Styles of Champagne and Corresponding Residual Sugar Levels***

| Style | Residual Sugar |
|---|---|
| Brut Nature | <3 grams/liter |
| Extra Brut | < 0-6 g/l |
| Brut | < 12 g/l |
| Extra-Sec | 12-17 g/l |
| Sec | 17-32 g/l |
| Demi-Sec | 32-50 g/l |
| Doux | >50 g/l |

Champagne is bottled in a wide range of bottle sizes:

| Name | # of Bottles | Liters |
|---|---|---|
| Standard | 1 | 750 ml |
| Magnum | 2 | 1.5 L |
| Jeroboam | 4 | 3 |
| Rehoboam | 6 | 4.5 (no longer used) |
| Methuselah | 8 | 6 |
| Salmanazar | 12 | 9 |
| Balthazar | 16 | 12 |
| Nebuchadnezzar | 20 | 15 |

Large format bottles are mostly named for ancient Kings of Israel, though no one is sure exactly why. Winemakers in Bordeaux have used the term Jeroboam for their four-bottle size since 1725. Jeroboam ruled from 931-920 BC and was seen as a "man of great worth," perhaps a nod to the worth of the larger-sized bottles?

Extremely small bottles (175 ml) and bottle formats larger than the double magnum (Jeroboam) are bottled using the **Transversage Method**. The second fermentation is carried out in the same way as it is in the traditional method. The wine is then removed from the bottle, placed in a tank, and chilled. The dosage is added to the tank and the wine is then re-bottled.

Most Champagne is ready for consumption upon its release. However, the highest quality Champagne (especially vintage) continues to evolve in the bottle. Bubbles become creamier and less aggressive, and the wine can develop complex notes of bread, toast and biscuits from the remnants of yeast autolysis.

## HOT TOPICS & TRENDS

- Champagne makes up 12% of the sparkling wine market
- In 2009, there were 293.3 million bottles of Champagne sold (181 million sold in France, 112 million exported); in 2009, exports of Champagne fell by 28%
- The top exporters of Champagne are Moët & Chandon, Veuve Clicquot, Piper Heidsieck, Laurent Perrier, Pommery, Mumm, Nicholas Feuillatte, Lanson, Taittinger and Perrier Jouët
- Traditional brands account for 90% of sales outside France but are less dominant in the domestic market, where half of the sales are wines made by growers, co-operatives and co-operative unions
- Lighter bottles (835 grams vs. 900 grams) are now available to Champagne producers in order to reduce the region's carbon footprint. The CIVC encourages all houses and co-operatives to use them, though it is not enforced.
- In 2008, Grower Champagne (*récoltant-manipulant*) accounted for less than 3% of Champagne sales, but it is a rapidly growing section of the market and a favorite among many sommeliers

## Champagne: The Essentials

| | |
|---|---|
| Parallel (Latitude) | Vineyards to the north of Reims are at 49.5° N, and the southernmost are at 48° N |
| Regions at the Same Latitude | British Columbia, Germany |
| Area Under Vine | 35,000 ha |
| Volume Produced | 300,000,000 bottles (750 ml) / 2,325,000,000 L |
| % White | .005% |
| % Red | .1% |
| % Sparkling | 99% |
| Top Export Markets | UK, US, Germany, Belgium, Japan, Italy, Switzerland, Spain Australia, Netherlands |
| # Growers | 20,000 (many own less than 1 ha) |
| # Producers | 300 total; 140 co-operatives represent over half the growers, 7 biggest houses account for 70% of production. |
| Stats Related to USA | Most purchased are Moët & Chandon, Veuve Clicquot, Perrier Jouët, Piper Heidsieck and Nicolas Feuillatte; 4.5 million bottles are annually exported to the United States. |
| Climate | Cool Continental climate, very dry, affected by both the Atlantic Ocean and English Channel. Frost poses a threat in the early spring, especially in the Vallée de la Marne. |
| Average Temperature | 10 °C / 50 °F |
| Hours of Sunlight Per Year | 1,600 |
| Rain Per Year | 630 mm / 25 inches |
| Soil | Thin layer of topsoil above a chalk base composed of the fossils of belemnites and micrasters. The chalky soil aids in the retention of water. |
| Major Cities | Reims, Épernay |
| Major Geographical Features | Most Grand Cru villages are in the east-facing Côte des Blancs or on the Montagne de Reims. Best vineyards are on slopes in the area. |
| Primary Grapes | Pinot Meunier, Pinot Noir, Chardonnay |
| Local Governing Body | Comité Interprofessionnel du Vin de Champagne (CIVC) |
| Ageing Regulations | Minimum 15 months for non-vintage; 3 years for vintage |
| Quality/Rating Levels | 17 *Grand Cru* vineyards; 43 *Premier Cru* vineyards; *Village* |

# Côteaux Champenois

Not all of the wine produced in the Champagne region is sparkling. The **AOP Côteaux Champenois** covers the same area as sparkling wine production but is reserved for still white, red and rosé wines. The grapes included in the wine are the same as those for Champagne: Chardonnay for white wines, and Pinot Noir and Pinot Meunier for red wines. There is a very small amount of rosé wine produced that is labeled Rosé de Riceys. As most of the grapes grown in Champagne are reserved for sparkling wine production, the amount of Côteaux Champenoise produced is very small. To put it in perspective, for every bottle of still white Côteaux Champenois produced there are about twenty of still red Côteaux Champenois made, and 16,000 bottles of Champagne.

# French Sparkling Wines

Champagne is not the only sparkling wine produced in France. The category of **Crémant** was created in 1975 by the French government, and with it, controls on permitted grape varieties, yields and ageing. Like Champagne, Crémant is produced using the *méthode traditionelle*. Because it is made outside the Champagne region the minimum time on the lees is nine months instead of fifteen. The grapes included are typically those used to create the best still wines of that particular region. Crémants are often viewed as great value alternatives to Champagne, as many are less well known. They can either mimic the style of their more expensive counterparts, or show the expression of the grapes and the region in which they are produced.

The following are types of Crémant produced in France:

## Crémant d'Alsace

| Region: | Alsace |
|---|---|
| Grapes Permitted: | Pinot Blanc, Pinot Noir, Pinot Gris, Auxerrois, Chardonnay and Riesling. Note: Muscat, Chasselas and Gewürztraminer are not permitted. |
| Soils: | Varied; grapes for Crémant are often grown on limestone and/or chalk. |
| Wine Style: | High acidity, fine mousse, light body. Higher percentage of Riesling will render wines with stronger flavors. |

## Crémant de Bourgogne

This appellation/term replaced *Bourgogne Mousseux*, which is now used solely for sparkling red wines from Burgundy.

| Region: | Usually Auxerre and Côte Chalonnaise (Rully). |
|---|---|
| Grapes Permitted: | Mainly Chardonnay and Pinot Noir. Gamay can be used but may not comprise more than one fifth of the blend. |
| Soils: | Calcareous |
| Wine Style: | Those made in northern Burgundy are light in body and high in acidity. Those produced in the south can be full and soft (a less expensive alternative to Champagne). |

## CRÉMANT DE DIE

This appellation replaced the term *Clairette de Die Brut*. *Crémant de Die* is not to be confused with *Clairette de Die Tradition*, which is a slightly sweet, slightly sparkling wine made mostly from *Muscat Blanc à Petits Grains*.

| Region: | Eastern Rhône, on the Drôme tributary between Valence and Montélimar. |
|---|---|
| Grapes Permitted: | 100% Clairette |
| Soils: | Chalky, argilliferous, clay and iron soils. |
| Wine Style: | Dry, with flavors of green apple. |

## CRÉMANT DE LIMOUX

*Blanquette de Limoux* is similar to the *Crémant* produced here, except that it includes more Mauzac in the blend. However, do not confuse either with *Blanquette de Limoux Méthode Ancestrale*, which is produced with 100% Mauzac. It is not disgorged so it's cloudy, slightly sweet, and less sparkling than Crémant de Limoux.

| Region: | Southern Languedoc |
|---|---|
| Grapes Permitted: | Chenin Blanc (20-40%), Chardonnay, Pinot Noir and Mauzac (Chenin Blanc and Chardonnay together must comprise at least 90% of the blend). |
| Soils: | Calcareous |
| Wine Style: | Designed for the international market; less rustic than Blanquette de Limoux. |

## CRÉMANT DE LOIRE

Note that other sparkling wines are produced in the Loire. Sparkling Vouvray is produced with Chenin Blanc, and *Saumur Mousseux* may use Chenin Blanc and/or Cabernet Franc.

| Region: | Anjou, Saumur and Touraine in the Loire Valley. |
|---|---|
| Grapes Permitted: | Chardonnay, Chenin Blanc, Cabernet Franc. |
| Soils: | Calcareous (Anjou and Saumur); clay, sand, tuffeau and gravel (Touraine). |
| Wine Style: | Persistent mousse, nutty and slightly honey aroma due to Chenin Blanc. |

## CRÉMANT DE BORDEAUX

| Region: | Bordeaux |
|---|---|
| Grapes Permitted: | Semillon, Sauvignon Blanc, Muscadelle, Ugni Blanc and Colombard; reds are Cabernet Sauvignon, Cabernet Franc, Carmenere, Merlot, Malbec and Petit Verdot. |
| Soils: | Gravel, sand, clay. |
| Wine Style: | Declining sector of the Crémant market; no clear style or identity. |

## Crémant de Jura

| Region: | Eastern France, between Burgundy and Switzerland. |
|---|---|
| Grapes Permitted: | Usually 100% Chardonnay; can also use Pinot Noir and Poulsard (Ploussard). |
| Soils: | Limestone and clay, with some marl. |
| Wine Style: | Lighter bodied, flavors of soft apples, good aperitif sparkling wine. |

## Other Production Methods

In addition to the Traditional Method and the Transfer Method, some sparkling wine producers also use the **Charmat Method.** Also known as *Cuve Close* or the **Tank Method**, this is the vinification process used for most of the sparkling wine produced in the world. With this method, the secondary fermentation takes place in a sealed tank rather than in a bottle. Sediment is removed with filtration under pressure and then the wine is bottled. It costs less than the traditional method and produces wines with larger, uneven bubbles that are not as persistent as in wines produced with the traditional method. Wines made with the Charmat method tend to lack the subtle complexity brought on by yeast autolysis, which can make it a desirable method for aromatic varieties such as Muscat and Riesling and fruity sparkling wines like Prosecco.

Sparkling wines made with **carbonation** are the cheapest to produce. Here, effervescence is pumped into a still wine, leading to large bubbles that dissipate quickly. In France, wines produced with this method must have ***vin gazéifié*** on the label. Carbonation is not used for any high quality sparkling wines.

Sparkling wines made in other countries will be discussed in depth the chapters covering those regions.

## Sparkling Wines Around The World

### Germany

Sekt sparkling wines are made from grapes grown in Europe, usually Italy and the Loire Valley. Deutscher Sekt sparklers are made from 100% German grapes.

**Grapes**: Sekt is made from a variety of grapes from other countries. Deutscher Sekt is made from German varieties including Riesling and Muller-Thürgau.

**Production Method**: cuvée close or charmat

### Italy

#### Asti DOCG (previously known as Asti Spumante)

**Region:** Piedmont

**Grapes**: Moscato bianco

**Production Method**: cuvée close or charmat

## Franciacorta DOCG

**Region:** Lombardy

**Grapes:** Chardonnay, Pinot Bianco (Pinot Blanc), Pinot Nero (Pinot Noir)

**Production Method:** Franciacorta DOCG was the first and only DOC/DOCG region to stipulate that its wines must be made by *metodo classico* (*méthode traditionelle*).

**Aging:** 25 months on lees, 37 months for Riserva

## Prosecco

Region: Veneto

**Grape:** Prosecco, a late-ripener native to Fruili

## Spain

### Cava DO (a region and a style – means "cellar")

**Region:** The majority is produced in Penedés within Catalonia and San Sadurni d'Anoia near Barcelona.

**Grapes:** Macabéo for fruit; Xarel-lo for strength and body; Parellada for softness and aroma

**Production Method:** méthode traditionelle

**Aging:** 9 months in the bottle

## United States

The United States has gone through an evolution. First wine makers used the generic champagne name for inexpensive non–*méthode traditionelle* sparklers, then moving on to add *méthode Champenoise* to the label. Now wine makers are using the new term *méthode traditionelle*.

New York uses traditional Champagne varieties for its sparklers as well as **Riesling** and **Seyval Blanc.**

California produces good sparkling wines in three main regions—Napa, Sonoma, and Mendocino (specifically, Anderson Valley). **Pinot Noir, Chardonnay, Pinot Meunier,** and **Pinot Blanc** are used.

Washington produces good value sparkling wines using **Chardonnay, Pinot Noir,** and **Chenin Blanc.**

# BURGUNDY

| AREA UNDER VINE | 29,500 hectares | |
|---|---|---|
| GRAPE VARIETIES | | |
| RED | Pinot Noir, Gamay | |
| WHITE | Chardonnay, Aligoté | |
| CLIMATE | Continental | |
| SOIL | Heavily striated soil system | |
| CÔTE D'OR | Limestone, clay and marl | |
| BEAUJOLAIS | Granitic schist | |
| GEOGRAPHICAL FEATURES | Saone River<br>Yonne River | Loire River<br>Canal of Burgundy |
| REGIONS | Chablis<br>Côte de Nuits<br>Côte de Beaune | Côte Chalonnaise<br>Mâconnais<br>Beaujolais |

## HISTORY

Burgundy is the most fragmented region of France, and its structure is directly related to its history. Romans are thought to be the first individuals to plant vines in Burgundy as evidenced by the writings of Roman agriculturist, Columella, and Greek geographer, Strabo. The two studied the region around the time of Christ and both make reference to existing vineyards in the region. The region survived the decline of the Roman Empire in the 5th century and viticulture was preserved by the rise of Christianity that followed.

Throughout the Middle Ages, the vineyards were largely owned by the Church and later by the nobility. The abbey of Cluny (built in 909AD) was responsible for cultivating vines and producing wine in the Mâconnais and Chalonnais areas, while the abbey of Citeaux (built in 1098 AD) developed and tended to vineyards in the Côte d'Or and the Cistercian monks did so to the north in the Chablis area. Monks and priests developed and studied vineyards and mapped the land according the soil type and quality. The monks also experimented with varieties, planting various grapes in various plots to test the relationship between vineyard site and the quality wine that it produced. These studies were the foundation of the notion of "terroir" and of "cru". The Church undoubtedly helped buttress the reputation of fine wine in Burgundy and viniculture in general. This is clear today as the areas and theories that were established during the medieval period when the vineyards of Burgundy were under the auspices of the Church and aristocracy continue to exist today.

In the 14th and 15th centuries, the dukes of Burgundy, who referred to themselves as the "Grand Dukes of the West and Lords of the finest wines in Christendom", continued the proliferation of viticulture and vinification study and practice in Burgundy via their dominance over the ranks of society. The Duke's power enabled them to extend the reputation of Burgundian wine and mandate winemaking policies. In 1395, Philip the Bold stated that Pinot Noir was superior to the high-yielding prolific grape Gamay and that only the former was able to produce high quality wine. From then on Pinot Noir gradually dominated the Côte d'Or. And those that followed Philip the Bold, including the three following Dukes—John the Fearless (1404-1419), Philip the Bold's grandson Philip the Good (1419-1467), and Charles the Bold (1467-1474)—continued to promote the wines of Burgundy and develop ordinances governing viticulture and vinification.

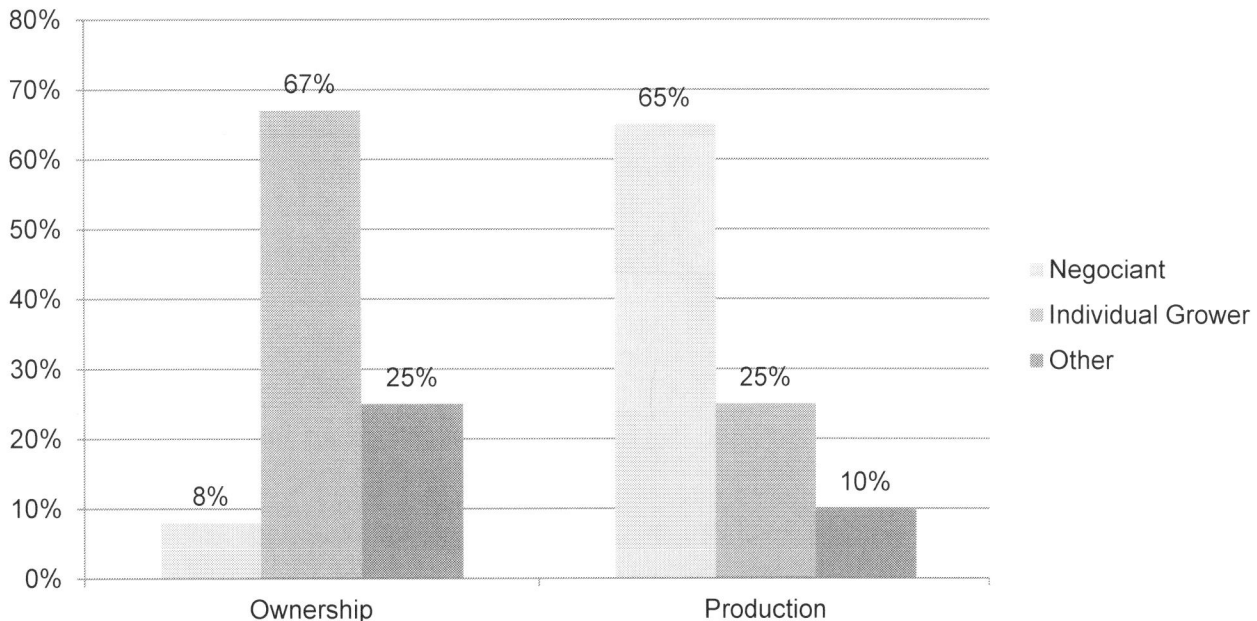

Burgundian wine began to infiltrate society as a direct result of the promotional campaign lead by the Church, the dukes, and those that followed them. In medicine doctors prescribed a glass to cure certain ailments in their patients while economically wine was directly traded to surrounding regions. In science the *Age of Reason (18$^{th}$ century)* questioned the mystery of terroir and why Burgundy was a phenomenal viticultural area. Finally, the literary world welcomed the first book wholly dedicated to Burgundian wine which was written by Claude Arnoux in the early 1700s.

The French Revolution (1789-1799) marks one of the most significant periods in Burgundy's wine history as it is largely responsible of the current layout of the famous region. After the overthrow of the monarchy (that had extended feudal privileges to the Church and nobility) all possessions belonging to the Church and the aristocracy essentially became national property including their large estates and valuable vineyards. Such properties were quickly divided up and redistributed through auction by the revolutionaries.

In the early 19$^{th}$ century the fragmentation of Burgundy's vineyards was exacerbated by the Napoleonic Laws of Succession. These laws mandated that parents' holdings were to be divided equally among their surviving children. Such inheritance laws exist today and contribute to Burgundy's uniqueness as a wine producing region. These laws are the reason why we find single domaines producing an array of wines from different vineyards each marketed under a different label and why a single vineyard can have multiple owners—for example, the Grand Cru Clos de Vougeot whose 450 hectares have 80 owners.

The structure of the wine industry is directly related to the Napoleonic Laws of Succession, laws that over time have resulted in severe fragmentation of Burgundy's vineyards into tiny plots owned by different farmers and domaines. In fact, the BIVB, Bureau Interprofessionnel des Vins de Bourgogne, reports that 85% of the 4,300 domaines in Burgundy own only about 6.5 hectares. Because such inheritance laws combined with AOC law prevent the expansion of classified vineyards, available land is extremely rare and incredibly expensive. Combined with the great expense of owning and running a winery, many of Burgundy's farmers prefer to sell their production either as grapes, juice, must or unfinished wine to a négociant, or merchant, who then blends and bottles the wines in his/her own name. In other words, individual growers own approximately 67% of the land under vine in Burgundy but produce only about 25% of the wine and the 115 négociants who produce the largest quantity of wine only control 8% of the land.

Other groups also exist and share the control of the land as well as the production of wine. Cooperatives operate under a similar principle as négociants like Maison Louis Jadot or Louis Latour or the Drouhin family. However, in a cooperative like La Chablisienne or Co-Operative de Buxy the growers combine their production, finish the product as a group, and sell the wine under the name of the cooperative. If, however, a grower decides to produce his own wines and sell them under his own name then the wine is domaine bottled.

Négociants are a special part of Burgundy's history and continue to have a significant presence in the wine trade today but their rise has not been a smooth ride. Although they dominated the region's wine trade until the 1960s, since their inception in the 1800s they have long been reputed to be merchants more concerned with their financial success than with the quality of the grapes. (It should be noted here that depending on the négociant, some fruit or must can technically be sourced not only from the farmers the négociant represents but also from the négociant's own land. This fact may seem small but we will mention here and will revisit the point later in the chapter.) And it wasn't until recently within the last two decades that their reputation has changed and improved.

After powdery mildew (1850s) and phylloxera (1870s) ravaged the vineyards of Burgundy and the first harvests capable of producing quality wines were cultivated (1890s), négociants controlled the wine trade. They were responsible for building export, establishing direct trade to other regions within France and Europe, and increasing shipments to England and the United States. However, with a focus on wealth and not on the quality and reputation of Burgundy's wines, questionable business practices helped to build a slanderous reputation. Throughout the beginning of the 20th century négociants were seen as greedy businessmen disrespectful of the region's devotion to building a high quality serious industry; they were exploiters of the region often taking advantage of the peasant farmers from whom they bought fruit or must, and in fact, examples can also be found referencing the importation of foreign grapes into that were then sold as true Burgundian wine. In the 1930s, in response to such blatant exploitation, well respected people like the Marquis d'Angerville began to encourage buyers to buy wine from the growers directly rather than through corrupt négociants (and of course their effort was aided when the AOC system was officially created in 1935).

Local efforts combined with official AOC law helped turn négociants away from a goal of wealth to a goal of lawfully continuing to cultivate a top wine industry that had long been in development in the region. And by the 1960s, while négociants were still in control of the wine trade, they had by that time developed a reputation of an oenology- and quality-oriented agent for farmers. The modern négociant had now become a respectable position; today, he is an agent with solid relationships with farmers he respects and trusts and he is as involved in the process as he can be without stifling the skill and expertise of his growers from whom he will buy fruit or must before finishing the wine in his winery and releasing the quality product to the market. While négociants improved their practices and gained a better reputation, so too did tiny domaines up and down the valley.

During the 1960s, 1970s, and 1980s small domaines popped up who were producing outstanding wine and began to compete with négociants. By the 1980s, a major change had occurred in the marketplace and we began to see a significant increase in the availability of domaine bottled Burgundies as opposed to négociant labels. As previously touched upon, it is important to note, however, that négociants did not fade altogether. Despite with the trend shifting toward domaine bottled wines, throughout the 20th and 21st centuries négociants have had increasing access to greater wealth and have therefore been acquiring more and more land from which they continue to produce wine. Later in the chapter we will look at how the unique structure of the region's wine trade impacts being a consumer and knowing what to buy.

# AOC Law

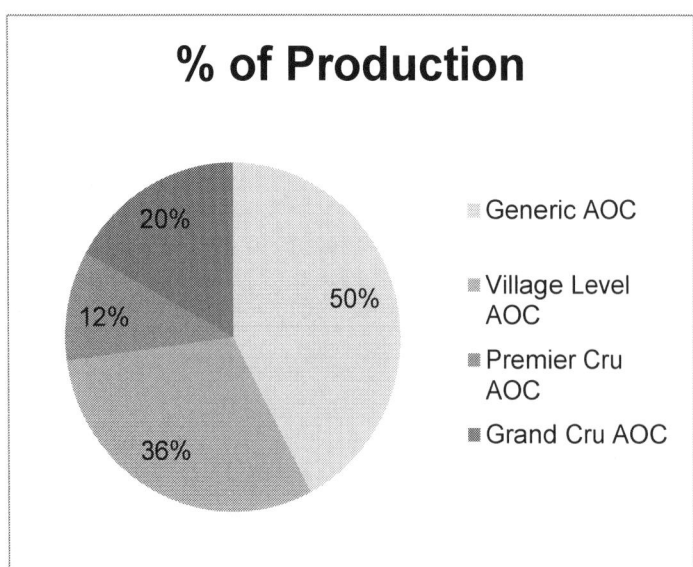

As a result of its history, the AOC structure of Burgundy is fundamentally different than that of, for example, Bordeaux. In Bordeaux, generally speaking a Chateau has a single owner (individual, family, or group) and a single classified vineyard that surrounds it. The entire vineyard is classified by the AOC and, if all AOC laws are upheld for that classification, a single wine is produced and sold under a single label (some Chateaux will bottle a second wine using declassified fruit that was not up to par for their primary wine). In Bordeaux, a Chateau can buy new land and still bottle the production under its own label provided that the land is within the same commune; in Burgundy each vineyard has its own status and cannot be increased in size. In Burgundy the picture is very different.

*The AOC Slope: Where do we find the various AOC levels on the Burgundy Slope?*

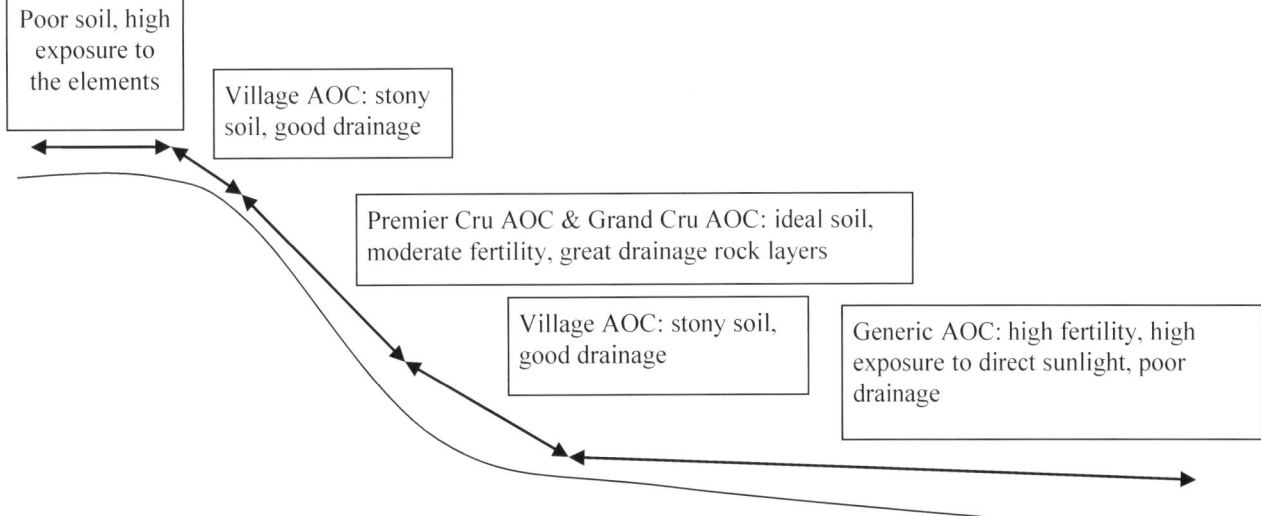

Up and down the valley in Burgundy, the vineyards are classified into Generic AOC, Village or Commune level, Premier Cru, and Grand Cru.

Fifty-two percent of the total production in Burgundy is at the most basic generic or regional level. Wines at this level are sourced from fruit grown in very fertile soil at the very foot of the slope where drainage is poor (we will discuss drainage later in the chapter when discussing soil but, briefly, vines need to be challenged and generally speaking do not perform well when water and nutrients are easily accessible), exposure to the elements is high, and sunlight hits the vines directly from above. (It should be noted here that while at the foot of the slope the soil is too dense and fertile, at the very top of slope where it is flat the soil is usually too sparse to support vines that can produce top-quality wines.) Generic AOC wines have the word Bourgogne in their name, for example, Bourgogne Blanc, Bourgogne Rouge, or Bourgogne Passetoutgrains. There are 23 AOCs at this level and each must abide by yield restrictions of 55hl/ha.

At the second level, the Village or Commune AOC level, there are 44 AOCs. Together they produce 36% of total amount of wine produced in Burgundy. The vineyards at this level are of slightly higher quality sitting above the generic level vineyards with soils that have better drainage and slightly less direct sunlight exposure. AOC law dictates that village level wines must abide by slightly tighter yield restrictions of 50 hl/ha, that 100% of the fruit used must be sourced from within that village's boundaries, and that wines must be labeled with the village or commune they come from, for example, Gevrey-Chambertin or Chambolle-Musigny.

At the third level, the Premier Cru AOC (premier is French for 'first') vineyards are responsible for 10% of the total production in Burgundy. There are 635 Premier Crus each of which is situated higher on the slope than the Village wines in locations with ideal soil, great drainage, moderate fertility, and less exposure to the elements and direct sunlight. At this level AOC law requires that yields are no greater than 45 hl/ha, wines must be made from fruit sourced only from within the boundaries of the premier cru vineyard written on the label which itself must include both the name of the village and the vineyard from which the wine is derived, for example Meursault Les Charmes Premier Cru.

At the highest quality level, responsible for only 2% of the total production in Burgundy, is the Grand Cru AOC. Excluding Beaujolais' Crus (the Beaujolais region does not differentiate between Grand Cru and Premier Cru and classifies its top vineyards as a Cru), there are 33 Grand Cru AOCs in Burgundy and each famed vineyard site must adhere to maximum yields of 35 hl/ha, must source 100% fruit from the boundaries of that vineyard site, and is bottled under the label of the vineyard, for example, Romanée Conti or Montrachet or Charlemagne. Grand Cru Burgundy's site close to and sometimes slightly higher than the Premier Cru vineyards and have moderately fertile soil and moderate drainage elements that challenge the vines that grow and produce fruit.

The four AOC levels guarantee the source of the grapes and, while it is true that a bottle of Clos de Tart Grand Cru may be more expensive and of higher quality than Gevrey-Chambertin Combe du Dessus Premier Cru which may be more expensive and of higher quality than Morey St Denis Village which also may be more expensive and of higher quality than Bourgogne Rouge, they do not guarantee quality. The AOC system should definitely be taken into consideration when selecting a bottle of Burgundy but there are other important, perhaps even more important, factors that must be evaluated.

## Geography and Climate

Just 100 miles south of Paris, Burgundy extends over 200 miles from Chablis in the north to Beaujolais in the south. Although over 750 miles of navigable waterways give the region access to water and keep the area green and lush, vineyards are not found on or near the water's edge as seen in Alsace or Bordeaux. Major waterways such as the Yonne, Loire, and the Saone Rivers sweep through Burgundy but the region is also famous for the Canal of Burgundy which connects the Yonne in the north to the Saone in the south. When construction was completed on the canal in the early 1830s, the Atlantic Ocean and the Mediterranean Sea were joined thereby creating a significant trade route throughout the country and the region. The significance of the waterways is therefore probably more applicable to trade and commerce than for their impact on the vineyards themselves.

Burgundy has a continental climate with four seasons. The winters are cold often with snow-fall; the spring can bring frosts and hailstorms that can pose a threat during the early growing season to the delicate vines that are especially sensitive to the elements (for example, during bud-break such weather can disrupt full budding and can also cause rot); the summers are hot but rain, particularly at harvest where it risks diluting the fruit resulting in a less concentrated wine, can be worrisome for growers; and the autumn is cool with some rain.

Such conditions prohibit many varieties from the region and while chardonnay performs well in most climates they can make it difficult to cultivate pinot noir whose thin-skinned fruit is particularly susceptible to these natural hazards.

# SOIL

The relationship between the region's climate and weather conditions and the microsoils is important and has a significant bearing on the wines being produced at each harvest; in fact, it is here maybe even more than in any other wine region in the world that the impact of soil variations is felt most.

The soil is incredibly varied in Burgundy. The Côte d'Or itself lies on a fault line created by the vertical movement of the earth's plates during the Jurassic period about 145 million years ago. Although the primary soil is rock, more specifically limestone, the tectonic movement resulted in a heavily striated soil system with sedimentary rock of multiple ages and compositions. And all of these variations significantly impact the wine world.

Although much research has been conducted globally as to why a certain variety or variety clone produces better wine in a particular place, a precise theory has not yet been developed and therefore regions worldwide depend on their viticultural history and experience. Here, a winemaking region like Burgundy has an advantage as it is a region with a long rich history of people dedicated to studying soils, aspect, and the relationship between clone type and soil and mapping each plot of land to find the perfect match between vineyard site and variety.

As touched upon earlier in the chapter, let's take a moment to talk about the relationship between soil and vine. A vine, like any other fruit-bearing plant, needs nutrients, sunlight, and water to produce grapes. An ideal situation may seem like a very fertile valley floor that is swimming with nutrients, receives direct sunlight, and has poor drainage thereby allowing easy access to water. While a vine in such a situation may produce fruit it will most likely produce too much fruit that is thin and diluted. Vines need to be challenged; they should be in a situation that is stressful enough to produce fewer grape bunches of increased concentration but not stressful enough to shut down and stop producing fruit because they couldn't access adequate nutrients and water. Generally speaking, in a normal vintage, vines will do well in low to moderately fertile soil with good drainage. At the microbial level, the vine produces substances like cytokinin in the roots that are vital for vine growth; however, these substances will only be produced in balanced quantities if drainage is balanced and the soil is not too wet or too dry. (With this point we are reminded that winemaking in an art with no black and white rules; ideally, in general, in a normal vintage one looks for good drainage, however, in a dry season this would not be ideal as access to water would become limited.) Vines like to have to work to find water digging their roots deep into the soil in their search. Another benefit of such a challenge is that big digging deep in the earth the roots remain in a more stable environment than at shallower levels.

Fertility comes into play simply because the harder it is (to an extent) for a vine to find nutrients, the less fruit it will produce but with less fruit hanging on its branches the more the vine can focus its energies on developing them. A vine

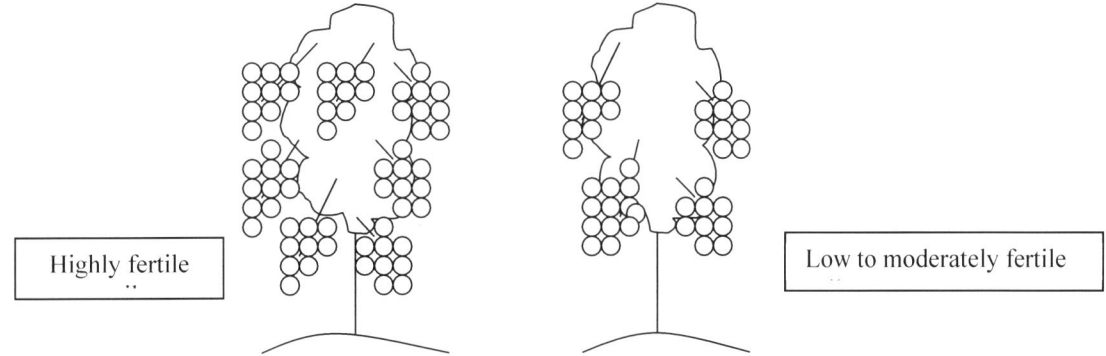

divides its resources, nutrients, and strength among the fruit it yields, therefore a vine producing fewer bunches can devote all of its strength to those bunches resulting in richer more concentrated fruit. Throughout the growing season, farmers further this theory by pruning back bunches to ensure that each vine only needs to devote its strength and power to a limited number of grape bunches. With more concentrated grapes on the vine, the more potential a winemaker has to produce a more concentrated balanced wine.

Having considered the heavily nuanced and vital relationship between soil and vine, we see how in a region with such incredibly varied soils and yet only one red grape and one white grape (in the Côte d'Or) one finds such a wide range of wines. Within each village and even within each vineyard site belonging to that village one finds a unique soil type that produces its own unique wine. There may only be two primary grapes in Burgundy, one red and one white, but the nuances found in a glass of wine from the different villages are profound and are a direct function of the striation in the soil system found throughout the region.

Considering how varied the soil system in Burgundy is, we will discuss soil types further within the context of each region; however, one can say that in very broad terms Chardonnay in Burgundy is grown in limestone, Pinot Noir in marl and clay, and Gamay (in Beaujolais) in granitic schist.

## VARIETIES

Burgundy is famous for Chardonnay and Pinot Noir, its two major varieties; however, the region is also home to Aligoté and Gamay and, although not often mentioned, some Sauvignon Blanc.

Named after the village of Chardonnay in the Mâconnais region south of the Côte d'Or, Chardonnay is one of the most recognized grapes around the globe. Vigorous and prolific, it grows almost anywhere it is planted, however, while it is superbly malleable to different climates, weather conditions, and winemaking techniques it also has a phenomenal inherent ability to express terroir.

Terroir is a French term used to describe a grape's ability to express exactly where it came from taking into consideration factors such as aspect, climate, vintage, soil, and even the history and culture of the region. Planted here in Burgundy's incredibly diverse soil system the phenomenon of terroir as expressed by the grape makes it one of the finest places for Chardonnay. Although the hardy grape is at risk for frost damage at springtime as it buds early, it also ripens early therefore avoiding Burgundy's autumn rains and consequently potential rot. In the winery, Chardonnay responds well to a variety of winemaking styles including different approaches to oak aging. In the glass, due to the high level of pigmentation in its skin (as well as added color if the wine is barrel treated), Chardonnay presents with significant color unlike most white varieties. Notable characteristics of Chardonnay in Burgundy are apple, pear, and quince.

A variety famous for producing elegant red wines, Pinot Noir, unlike Chardonnay, is extremely finicky and difficult to grow. Deriving its name from the French words for "pine" and "black", Pinot Noir prefers specific types of soils particularly those with good drainage, will easily mutate, likes a cooler climate such as Burgundy's, and because of its thin skin can be prone to viticultural issues such as rot. However, like Chardonnay, it too possesses an ability to brilliantly express terroir and reflect even the smallest changes in viticulture and vinification practices. Notable characteristics of Pinot Noir in Burgundy are wild strawberry, raspberry, violet, and cherry with hints of earthiness.

Aligoté, despite being one of the top 30 most widely planted varieties at the turn of the century, is Burgundy's lesser known white variety. As a grape that comes a clear second to Chardonnay, it is often found planted on the poorer soils in the Côte d'Or and is not allowed in most of the AOCs in Burgundy. Aligoté is however tolerant to the cold and produces a very light white dry wine with aromas and flavors of apples, lemons and herbal notes that is to be consumed while young. As a variety with good acidity, Aligoté is often blended with other varieties. For example, Bourgogne Aligoté AOC and Bouzeron-Aligoté AOC (Bouzeron is the most recognized region for the variety within France) permit up to 15% Chardonnay and Crémant de Bourgogne AOC allows a handful of varieties one of which is Aligoté.

Unlike Burgundy's second white variety, its second red variety, Gamay, has a long history in the region that continues today. Historically, Gamay was once the only red variety grown throughout the entire region where it grew prolifically was easy to cultivate and produced a fruity wine in large quantities. However, once the monks and later the dukes began mapping out the land, experimenting with varieties like Pinot Noir and studying the relationship between soil and grape, Gamay quickly lost is place within the Côte d'Or. Noticing that, while more difficult to cultivate, Pinot Noir produced a higher quality wine with elegance that its more acidic counterpart couldn't attain, Gamay was kept out of the Côte d'Or. Although Gamay continues to have a certain reputation today, one could argue that it was simply misplanted in the Côte d'Or and that the granitic soils of the Beaujolais region (as well as some parts of the Mâconnais) to the south were much more suited to the grape. Today, Gamay reigns in Beaujolais.

Sauvignon Blanc is grown in Saint Bris near Chablis in the north of Burgundy where it produces a tart wine with aromas and flavors of lemon, green apple and minerality. In 2003, the AOC of Saint Bris was made official; however, the wine remains obscure and not often discussed.

# REGIONS

Burgundy stretches for over 200 miles north to south. Beginning at its northernmost tip in Chablis and end at its most southern tip in Beaujolais, we will look at its six major regions: Chablis, the Côte de Nuits and the Côte de Beaune (together which comprise the Côte d'Or), the Côte Chalonnaise, the Mâconnais, and Beaujolais.

## CHABLIS

With most of the world's grapes planted within the 30-50 degree latitude lines north and south of the equator, at 47.8°N, Chablis pushes the limits. As one of the most northern wine regions in the world, Chablis has hot summers with long severe winters, a climate that poses challenges to winemakers who over time have come to understand and appreciate the unique location of their vineyards and the wines they produce. The region is very prone to heavy frosts which, as mentioned earlier in the chapter, can cause problems for the vines particularly in the spring (March to May) during bud break when they are exposed and sensitive to the elements. Some producers combat this problem by using fuel burners or more expensive fuel-heating systems to protect the vines from the cold; however, other producers use a technique discovered in the 1970s whereby they spray the vines with water so that, when the temperatures drop below 0°F, a thin protective layer of ice forms around the buds, protecting them from freezing. Although the winter in Chablis is guaranteed it should be noted that the degree of sunlight and amount of rainfall throughout the growing season varies dramatically from year to year and therefore the consumer must pay particular attention to vintage and producer.

As Burgundy's most northern tip, Chablis is famous for its lean minerally dry white wines made from Chardonnay which is known locally as Beaunois, or wine of Beaune (Beaune is Burgundy's capital). The variety is planted in the majority of the vineyards in the region which are divided into four levels:

At the generic regional level, Petit Chablis AOC was created in 1944 and while it has just under 800 hectares under vine, it has recently been on the decline.

At the village level, Chablis AOC was created in 1938. It has over 6,500 hectares, of which about 4,500 are planted.

Chablis Premier Cru AOC has 776 hectares under vine. There are 40 Premier Crus in Chablis although the number 79 is sometimes quoted as each commune is entitled to have one of more climats, or named vineyard sites, within it. There are, however, only 40 recognized Premier Cru vineyards with Vaillons, Vospgros, Les Beauregards, Mont de Milieu and Montée de Tonnerre among the best. While these vineyards can be found on both sides of the Serein River that runs through the region, most are located north of the city near the Grand Cru vineyards. Winemakers producing Premier Cru Chablis much adhere to yields less than 50 hl/ha.

Grand Cru AOC has 103 hectares that produces only about 5% of Chablis' total wine production. There are 7 Grand Crus: Bougros, Les Preuses, Vaudésir, Grenouilles, Valmur, Les Clos, and Blanchot. It should be noted, however, that while the AOC system does not officially recognize it, Burgundy lists an 8th Grand Cru, La Moutonne, a monopole vineyard location between Les Preuses and Vaudésir. Chablis Grand Cru vineyards all lie on a hillside that is covered with a layer of Kimmeridgian limestone clay that dates back over 150 million years. It is a clay soil that is rich with oysters and marine fossils that remind us of when the region was once covered by a sea. Another soil type in Chablis is Portlandian soil which is a sandier form and generally found in vineyards designated as Petit Chablis. There has been some debate over whether Portlandian soil is able to produce fruit as perfect as the fruit grown in Kimmeridgian clay, most of Chablis' best wine is born out of the latter.

Another controversy within Chablis has been the use of oak. Even though the region's wines have traditionally not been oaked, some producers started experimenting with oak barrels especially around the early 1990s. Other producers still prefer the steely, racy unoaked style of Chardonnay that Chablis historically has been known for.

## CÔTE D'OR

The Côte d'Or is one of the most well known regions in the world. The name comes from the French for the Slope of Gold or the Golden Slope which adequately describes both its physical appearance during the autumn as the leaves change color as well as the phenomenal beauty of the wine it produces.

As discussed earlier in the chapter, the soils in Burgundy vary greatly due to fault lines that have shifted and exposed a stunning array of various soil striations; however, in general, the topsoil in the Côte d'Or is composed partly of limestone and partly of marlstone, with a layer of Jurassic limestone beneath. The Premier Cru and Grand Cru vineyards are situated between 800–1,000 feet above sea level. The Côte d'Or is divided into the Côte de Nuits and the Côte de Beaune. In total, the region has 33 Grands Crus.

## CÔTE DE NUITS

The majority of wine production in Côte de Nuits is red made from Pinot Noir, and all of the Côte d'Or's red Grands Crus are found here, except for Corton. There is also only one white Grand Cru in Côte de Nuits, the very rare white Musigny. The most important communes from north to south are Marsannay, Fixin, Gevrey-Chambertin, Morey St.-Denis, Chambolle-Musigny, Vougeot, Flagey-Echézeaux, Vosne-Romanée, and Nuits St Georges.

At the most northern tip of the Côte Marsannay became an official appellation in 1987. It is known for producing good value wine. Its specialty is a rosé made from Pinot Noir as well as an attractive, fruity style of red wine along with some whites. There are no Grands or Premiers Crus.

Further south Fixin became an official designation in 1936. Here there are five Premier Cru vineyards, a few of which are monopoles, with the best ones located closest to Gevrey-Chambertin. While both red and white wines are produced, the region is dominated by Pinot Noir. A typical Fixin wine is said to share the strong structure of a Gevrey-Chambertin with slightly less fruitiness. This difference is thought to be due to the slightly cooler microclimate of Fixin along with the flatter land the commune is built upon. Much of its wine is sold as Côte de Nuits-Villages. The most highly regarded Premiers Crus are La Perrière and Clos du Chapitre.

Gevrey-Chambertin is the largest commune appellation in the Côte de Nuits, and it produces only red wines. The best wines of this commune are known for their power, muscle, richness of bright fruit flavors, and their aging potential. Gevrey-Chambertin has 8 Grands Crus and 27 Premiers Crus. The Grands Crus are Chambertin, Chambertin-Clos-de-Beze, Mazis-Chambertin, Charmes-Chambertin, Chapelle-Chambertin, Griotte-Chambertin, Latricieres-Chambertin, and Ruchottes-Chambertin. And while officially Premier Crus, vineyards such as Les Cazetieres and Clos St. Jacques are thought to match the Grands Crus in quality.

Even though some of the most reliable red wines in Burgundy are produced in Morey-Saint-Denis, the commune is overshadowed by its more famous neighbors Gevrey-Chambertin and Chambolle-Musigny. A typical high-quality Morey-Saint-Denis red is known for is structure and finesse; however, over-cropping the vines combined with over-extracting juice can result in thinner weaker wines. The commune is home to four Grand Cru vineyards, the most famous being Clos Saint Denis. The other three are Clos de la Roche, Clos de Lambrays, and Clos de Tart. The Grand Cru vineyard of Bonnes Mares is shared with the neighboring village Chambolle-Musigny. One oddity from Morey-Saint-Denis is the white wine made in Les Monts Luisants by Domaine Ponsot from Pinot Noir vines, which have mutated into Pinot Blanc.

A fine Chambolle-Musigny is known for its floral elegance and is usually described as being "feminine." Le Musigny, a Grand Cru vineyard of this village, is considered to be one of Burgundy's best sites. The other Grand Cru of Chambolle-Musigny is Bonnes Mares, and as previously mentioned, it is shared with the neighboring village of Morey-Saint-Denis. Among the Premiers Crus, Les Amoureuses is the most sought after, as its wines are very similar in style to those from the adjacent vineyard of Le Musigny. Another Premier Cru, Les Charmes, is also considered to be one of the best.

Vougeot is home to the large Grand Cru vineyard Clos de Vougeot. Although the walled in section of the ancient and famous vineyard is technically classified as Grand Cru, the quality of the wines produced varies a great deal due to the varied subsoils, different levels of drainage, and severely fragmented ownership. A classic example, however, is full with rich fruit. There are four Premier Cru Vineyards: La Vigne Blanche, Clos de la Perriere, Les Cras, and Le Petits Vougeot.

Flagey-Echézeaux has two Grands Crus vineyards, Echézeaux, and Grands-Echézeaux, with the latter being regarded more favorably. Lying towards to the east of most vineyards, all of this commune's Premier Cru vineyards are sold under the Vosne-Romanée label.

Some of Burgundy's most prestigious Grands Crus such as Romanée-Conti, La Tâche, and Richebourg lie within the boundaries of Vosne-Romanée one of Burgundy's smallest winemaking villages. The remaining Grands Crus in the commune are La Romanée, La Romanée-Saint-Vivant, and La Grande Rue, which became a Grand Cru in 1992.

Romanée-Conti is a monopole owned by Domaine de la Romanée-Conti, and its wines fetch the highest prices of all Côte d'Or Grand Cru vineyards.

Nuits-Saint-Georges is home to 41 Premiers Crus but no Grands Crus. Les Saint Georges, Les Cailles, and Les Vaucrains are particularly well known. Nuits-Saint-Georges is an important business center for Côte d'Or. Rather than possessing a homogeneous style of production, the characteristics of its wines depend heavily upon location of the vineyards from whence they come. Some of the wines from this commune have great aging potential, especially the ones from rich years. Very little white wine is produced here from Chardonnay, Pinot Beurot, and from a white grape called that mutated from Pinot Noir. The variety was first discovered by Henri Gouges, and Clive Coates calls the grape Pinot Gouges. The neighboring villages of Premaux-Prissey, Comblanchien, and Corgoloin produce some wines that are labeled under Côte de Nuits Villages AOC. The village of Premaux has the right to the Nuits-Saint-Georges appellation.

## CÔTE DE BEAUNE

The region of Côte de Beaune is nearly twice the size as Côte de Nuits, and most of its production consists of red wines. However, the Côte de Beaune is famous for its whites. Commune appellations from north to south are: Ladoix-Serrigny, Aloxe-Corton, Pernand-Vergelesses, Savigny-lès-Beaune, Chorey-les-Beaune, Beaune, Pommard, Volnay, Monthelie, Auxey-Duresses, St.-Romain, Meursault, Blagny, Puligny-Montrachet, St. Aubin, Chassagne-Montrachet, Santenay, and Maranges. This southern half of the Côte d'Or has more soil variation than its northern counterpart with a variety of limestone and marlstone running through its vineyards.

Sitting at the foot of the Corton hillside, Ladoix-Serrigny produces mostly red wines from Pinot Noir. The wines from the flatter portions of the commune are more frequently sold as Côte de Beaune Villages. The Premiers Crus in Ladoix are: Les Grenchons (white), En Naget (white), Le Rognet (white), Les Buis (red), Les Joyeuses (red), Bois Roussot (red), La Corvee (red and white), Le Clou d'Orge (red and white), La Micaude (red and white), Basses Mourottes (red and white), and Hautes Mourottes (red and white). A portion of the Grand Cru vineyards Corton-Charlemagne and Le Corton of Aloxe-Corton also lie within the boundaries of the commune. One irregularity of the commune is that Ladoix chose to add a neighboring village to its name rather than its most important vineyard.

Reminding us of the highly esteemed Clos de Vougeot in Vougeot, Aloxe-Corton is home to the famous Grand Cru vineyard Corton, the only red Grand Cru appellation in Côte de Beaune. Here we find 22 *lieux-dits,* or a specific plot that does not have Grand Cru status, such as Bressandes, Renardes, Perrieres, and Clos du Roi that are entitled to append Corton to their name. A very small amount of white Corton is also made, with Corton-Charlemagne being the commune's white Grand Cru appellation. Chardonnay is mostly planted in the region's upper slopes that feature a high calcareous content in the soil. Pinot Noir is planted further down the slopes, where iron and clay dominate. A red Corton is meaty and savory, the white rich and buttery. A Corton-Charlemagne usually needs to age at least five years before consumption so it develops into a wine of great richness and structure.

Producing 75% red wine from Pinot Noir, Pernand-Vergelesses has six Premiers Crus, with the best being Ile des Vergelesses. The most sought after wines of Pernand are the ones from vineyards that are close to Corton. Good examples of this commune's Premier Cru wines can be similar to Corton in flavor and can represent good values.

Producing most of the wine from the Cote de Beaune, Savigny-lès-Beaune hosts 22 Premiers Crus that lie on both the northern and southern sides of the Rhoin River. The characteristics of the wines from each side of the river are quite different. Production in the commune is 97% red, and wines from good producers in strong years can be excellent values.

There are no Premier Crus in Chorey-lès-Beaune and much of the wine from the commune is sold as Côte de Beaune Villages. Most of its production is red even though a miniscule amount of white wine from Chardonnay is also made.

Beaune is the third largest commune of Côte d'Or, with Gevrey and Meursault being the first and second respectively. Beaune produces both red and white wines, and almost three-quarters of the commune is Premier Cru vineyards. The soil is sandier, producing wines with medium body and decent aging potential. The most important Premiers Crus are Les Grèves, Les Bressandes, Les Teurons, Les Marconnets, and Les Fèves.

There are 28 Premiers Crus in Pommard. The best are considered to be Les Epenots and Les Rugiens. Pommard's soil has higher levels of clay in it than Volnay's, and it is believed that this is what gives its wines their sturdy character. The commune's wines are well known and quite sought after in the American market.

A classic example of Volnay is perfumed, elegant and "feminine." There are 30 Premiers Crus in the commune, with Cailleret Dessus and Clos des Chenes boasting the best reputations. Red wine from Santenots, Pitures, and Cras is labeled Volnay while white wine from the same vineyards is labeled Meursault. Domaine du Marquis d'Angerville, a Volnay producer, is a pioneer in domain bottling and clonal selection.

Monthelie is home to 11 Premiers Crus, and the best two are extensions of Cailleret Dessus and Clos des Chenes, two Volnay vineyards. The wines from this commune can be great values in good years.

Auxey-Duresses possesses 9 Premiers Crus including Les Duresses and Le Climat de Val. About two-thirds of the commune's production is red. Good examples of its whites are similar in style to Meursault.

St. Romain has been an AOC since 1967; however, there are no Premiers Crus in the region. Almost equal amounts of red and white wines are produced. In warm years the white wines of this village can be a good inexpensive substitute for Meursault.

There are 21 Premiers Crus in Meursault. The Premier Cru vineyards with the best reputations are Les Perrières, Les Genevrières, and Les Charmes. There are also other vineyards in the commune, that while they are not Premiers Crus, they are quite well known, such as Chavalieres, Tessons, and Tillets. Most of the Meursault Premiers Crus can, in theory, be either red or white with the exception of Meursault Les Santenos which can only be white (red wines from this vineyard are sold under the Volnay label). A classic Meursault is intense, rich, and elegant.

Most whites from Blagny are sold either as Meursault-Blagny Premier Cru or as Puligny-Montrachet. Reds from Blagny can be more interesting than reds from Meursault.

There are 17 Premiers Crus and 4 Grands Crus in Puligny-Montrachet. Two of the Grands Crus—Le Montrachet and Bâtard-Montrachet—are shared with Chassagne-Montrachet. However, the other two—Chevalier-Montrachet and Bienvenue-Bâtard-Montrachet—lie entirely within Puligny.

Apart from the two Grands Crus Chassagne-Montrachet shares with Puligny-Montrachet, there is Criot-Bâtard-Montrachet, which lies entirely within Chassagne.

There are 20 Premiers Crus in St. Aubin. White wines from good producers in this commune can be particularly good values.

Les Gravières is one of the best known of Santenay's 11 Premiers Crus. Most of the wine produced in Santenay is red and again, from a good producer, can be a great value wine.

Maranges is a relatively new appellation. In 1989, the AOC replaced three separate regions: Cheilly-lès-Maranges, Dézize-lès-Maranges, and Sampigny-lès-Maranges. The AOC produces medium-bodied red wines.

## CÔTE CHALONNAISE

Beneath the Cote d'Or is the Côte Chalonnaise. Here the soil is very similar to the soil in Côte d'Or; however, vineyards in the Côte are less sheltered from the wind so grapes take longer to ripen. Therefore, Côte Chalonnaise is colder than Côte d'Or, even though the Côte is situated further south. There are five villages in Côte Chalonnaise that are entitled to their own appellations: Bouzeron, Rully, Mercurey, Givry, and Montagny.

Bouzeron is known for its wine from the Aligoté grape. If a wine is labeled Bouzeron, it must be made from Aligoté. Chardonnay and Pinot Noir wines from Bouzeron are bottled as Bourgogne or Côte Chalonnaise.

Rully produces slightly more white wine than red. It is also an important source of sparkling wines.

In Mercurey, about 95% of the wine produced is red. These wines, if crafted by a good wine maker, can be excellent values in good years.

Givry also makes primarily red wine from Pinot Noir. Its whites are made from Chardonnay.

Montagny produces only white wine. Good examples of Montagny are found to be the best whites of Côte Chalonnaise.

## MÂCONNAIS

It is south of the Cote Chalonnais in the Mâconnais that one witnesses the transformation of soil from the limestone found in the lower parts of the Côte d'Or and the Côte Chalonnaise in the north to the granite bedrock of Beaujolais in the south. About two-thirds of the region's production is white wine, while most of the red wine is made from Gamay, rather than Pinot Noir. Here Gamay produces a different style of wine than in Beaujolais. Pinot Noir that is produced in the region is usually bottled under Bourgogne Rouge label, for it brings a higher price than Mâcon. For white wines, communal appellations must be made exclusively from Chardonnay. In generic Mâcon appellations, some Pinot Blanc is permitted. The region also produces a decent amount of Bourgogne Passetoutgrains—a blend composed of a minimum of one-third Pinot Noir and a balance of Gamay.

The primary appellations in the Mâconnais are Mâcon, Mâcon Supérieur (with a higher alcohol level), Mâcon-Villages, or Mâcon (followed by a village name). The village appellations in the region from north to south are Viré-Clessé, Saint-Véran, Pouilly-Loché, Pouilly-Vinzelle, and Pouilly-Fuissé.

In the U.S. market, the most important village from this region is Pouilly-Fuissé. It produces a rather rich, high-alcohol wine from Chardonnay due in part to its warmer microclimate created by the protection of surrounding cliffs. It is not uncommon to encounter new oak in wines from Pouilly-Fuissé, a trait which is rarely seen elsewhere in the Mâconnais.

## BEAUJOLAIS

Located at the most southern tip of Burgundy, the region of Beaujolais produces more wine than all the other regions of Burgundy combined. Ninety-nine percent of the wine produced here is red, primarily from Gamay, with the remaining 1% being comprised of Chardonnay.

Having received its official designation as an appellation in 1937, almost all aspects of wine production in Beaujolais are different than those found in the rest of Burgundy. The climate is warmer, the soil is granitic schist, and the grapes are usually vinified using carbonic maceration. Here, whole grape berries are left to ferment under a blanket of carbonic gas in a closed vat, thus promoting intracellular fermentation that takes place in the absence of oxygen. After a period of 5–15 days, the grapes are pressed, and the resulting juice is transferred to an ordinary vat to complete the fermentation process using the natural yeast from the grape skins. The end product is an easy-drinking wine that has good color and distinct fruity flavors but is not high in tannins. Beaujolais Nouveau is the most famous wine in the world that is produced by carbonic maceration, thanks to the efforts of Georges Dubeouf. This is a wine, which is made especially for early drinking and is released to the market on the third Thursday of November following the vintage. It cannot be sold to the trade after January 31st. However, there are also some red wines from the Rhône, as well as Languedoc-Roussillon that are produced by carbonic maceration.

However, the majority of wine from Beaujolais is produced utilizing a technique called semi-carbonic maceration. In this process, grapes are not put into a tank where oxygen has been completely eliminated. Here, whole berries are put into open tanks where the fruit at the bottom of the vat is crushed due to the weight of the grapes above, thereby initializing fermentation as traditionally seen. This method produces carbon dioxide and causes the berries on the top of the vat to undergo intracellular fermentation. The resulting wine is one that has gone through both carbonic maceration and traditional fermentation in unknown proportions. There are also some producers in cru Beaujolais villages that use purely traditional methods of vinification.

The major appellations of Beaujolais are : Beaujolais, Beaujolais Supérieur, Beaujolais-Villages, Beaujolais Nouveau, and the 10 Crus of Beaujolais. As mentioned earlier in the chapter, Beaujolais does not distinguish between Premier Cru and Grand Cru, only Cru. Its 10 Crus from north to south are: St. Amour, Juliénas, Chénas, Moulin à Vent, Chiroubles, Fleurie, Morgon, Régnié, Côte de Brouilly, and Brouilly.

Of the 10 Crus, Brouilly and Régnié fall at the more flowery, lighter end of the spectrum whereas Moulin à Vent is considered to be the most age-worthy and powerful (it is also usually the most expensive). Thirty nine villages can add their names to the Beaujolais-Villages appellation. All of the cru villages except Moulin à Vent, Brouilly and Côte de Brouilly are among them.

# Burgundy Grand Crus

## Côte de Nuits

ALL FOR RED WINE UNLESS OTHERWISE STATED

| | |
|---|---|
| Gevrey-Chambertin | Mazis-Chambertin |
| | Ruchottes-Chambertin |
| | Chambertin Close-de-Bèze |
| | Chapelle-Chambertin |
| | Griotte-Chambertin |
| | Charmes-Chambertin |
| | Le Chambertin |
| | Latricières-Chambertin |
| | Mazoyères-Chambertin |
| Morey-Saint-Denis | Clos de la Roche |
| | Clos Saint-Denis |
| | Clos des Lambrays |
| | Clos de Tart |
| | Bonnes-Mares (some) |
| Chambolle-Musigny | Bonnes-Mares (most) |
| | Le Musigny (some white wine too) |
| Vougeot | Clos de Vougeot |
| Flagey-Échezeaux | Grands Échezeaux |
| | Échezeaux |
| Vosne-Romanée | Richebourg |
| | Romanée-Saint-Vinvant |
| | Romanée-Conti |
| | La Romanée |
| | La Grand Rue |
| | La Tâche |

## Côte de Beaune

ALL FOR WHITE WINE UNLESS OTHERWISE STATED

| | |
|---|---|
| Ladoix-Serrigny | Corton-Charlemagne |
| | Charlemagne (usually sold as Corton-Charlemagne) |
| Aloxe-Corton | Corton (almost all red) |
| Puligny-Montrachet | Chevalier-Montrachet |
| | Bienvenues-Bâtard-Montrachet |
| with Chassagne-Montrachet | Le Montrachet |
| | Bâtard-Montrachet |
| Chassagne-Montrachet | Criots-Bâtard-Montrachet |

# The Loire Valley

| Area Under Vine | 50,433 hectares |
|---|---|
| Grape Varieties | |
| Red | Gamay, Cabernet Franc, Grolleau, Malbec, Pinot Noir |
| White | Muscadet, Folle Blanche, Chenin Blanc, Sauvignon Blanc |
| Climate | West: maritime, greatly influenced by the Atlantic<br>East: continental—short, hot summers; long, cool winters. |
| Soil | West: Light stony soils, changing to schist, clay, and *Tuffeau* in Anjou-Saumur. Touraine features clay and limestone over *Tuffeau*. Kimmeridgian clay dominates the Central Vineyards. |

White wines of the Loire, both dry and sweet, have an appealing simplicity that is also deceptive, and the reds are anything but green and vegetal in the right hands, defying presumption. The Loire's landscape is just as understated as the wines, with rich countryside justly called the "Garden of France" and humble expressions from more obscure plantings of Gamay, Cot (Malbec), Pineau d'Aunis, and others named after the "Garden" —*Vin de Pays du Jardin de la France*. The most artisanal producers are *vignerons*, or farmers, first, and wine makers second. The Loire is indeed a region in which handfuls of artisanal growers boldly struggle to survive amidst the most industrial, *négociant* productions of wines, whose appellations have benefited from high-profile marketability. Sancerre and Muscadet, for example, are two such appellations.

This tour de force begins with France's longest river (and largest river system) the Loire, which begins in *L'Ardèche*, a *département* in the Rhône Valley. Along its course, the river crosses through a total of 12 *départements*, traveling for more than 1,000 kilometers, through a diversity of landscapes and soil types. In Touraine and Anjou, the heartland of the Loire, vines are found in every commune connected to the river or one of its tributaries. Generally speaking, the bodies of water provide the right microclimate needed to help the fruit ripen at such northerly latitude—similar to the effects of the Rhine and Mosel Rivers in Germany. Vine density in the Loire of 4,000 to 5,000 vines per hectare (1,600 to 2,000 per acre) is not heavy when compared to its eastern neighbor, Burgundy, where 10,000 vines per hectare is common (4,000 per acre).

## History

There is evidence suggesting that wine has been made in the Loire since the 1st century AD by the Gauls. The Bretons (from Brittany) went from plundering the region for wines, to growing grain to pay for it. All throughout the first 11 centuries, this region grew and the wines were used as barter for everyone who traveled the river. Due to the demand for quality wine north of the region, Angers became an important city on the trade route, and in the beginning of the 12th century, the Count of Anjou gave the city of Angers the sole right of transportation of the wines on the Loire and Maine Rivers to the border of Brittany. This coupled with the fact that merchants were forbidden to purchase the wine directly from the producers made for some very wealthy businessmen in Angers. In addition, the wines from Saumur were largely overlooked given the distance of the city from Anjou.

## Geography, Climate, and Soil

Due to the size and various climates in the Loire—ranging from maritime in the west in Muscadet to continental in the east in Sancerre—Geography, Climate, and Soil will be discussed pertaining to the specific wine-growing regions.

## Varieties

Across the Loire, the predominant grape varieties change from region to region. In the West, **Muscadet** reigns in the Pays Nantais. In Anjou-Saumur, **Chenin Blanc** and **Cabernet Franc** rule. In Touraine, **Chenin Blanc** and **Sauvignon Blanc** for whites and **Cabernet Franc** and **Grolleau** for reds dominate. Lastly, in the Central Vineyards, **Sauvignon Blanc** and **Pinot Noir** are the primary varieties planted. More detailed discussions of the variety follows in the major wine region section.

# Major Wine Regions (from West to East)

## The Pays Nantais

The mouth of the Loire River lies in Brittany at St. Nazaire. The next major city it passes through is Nantes, an area fought over as to whether it is in Brittany or Pays de la Loire. The area's importance for us is due primarily to one grape grown in the region—**Muscadet**, also known as **Melon de Bourgogne**, which is used in the production of **Muscadet AOC**. (The **Gros Plant** grape, also known as **Folle Blanche**, is grown in the area as well.) Melon is an interesting variety in that it is relatively neutral. The region's climate is cool, so good acidity levels are a given. While some wine makers harvest early to preserve the acidity amidst uncertain weather, too many often run into the problem of the grapes not being physiologically ripe, especially in cooler, more challenging vintages. This can be seen when the wine has a green sharpness to the fruit, which is often counterbalanced by producers with chaptalization. Hand-harvesting the ripest fruit can obviously yield a wine with better acid-fruit balance, but there are only are a handful of producers that take the care and expense to do so. The AOC of **Muscadet** governs the majority of the Nantais region north and east of the city of Nantes. The most compelling wines from the region, however, come from the **Pays Nantais**—other appellations surrounding the city of Nantes. These wines are also made **Muscadet**, and many of them are bottled *sur lie*.

Most of what we see in America is referred to as **Muscadet sur Lie**. *Sur lie* implies that the wine is left in contact with its lees for one winter after harvest, but technically there is no special language about whether there must be any stirring of the lees. The wine cannot be bottled before the third week in March following the harvest. Some wine makers, looking for a richer style, will do a second bottling in October of the same year. Making wine using the *sur lie* method is a traditional practice of the region—leaving the wine in old barrels during the winter, and then bottling in the spring to preserve clarity and freshness expressed by a slight effervescence. This practice becomes difficult, however, if a grower is not estate-bottling the wine, but rather transporting the must for sale to a *négociant*. In this case, the wine will be racked off its lees for traveling; leaving the wine out of the original contact with its lees by the time the wine is bottled. Muscadet sur Lie can come from any of the following Muscadet AOCs: **Côteaux du Loire, Côtes de Grandlieu,** and **Sévre-et-Maine.**

**Muscadet de Sévre et Maine AOC** is located east of Nantes and extends both north and south of the city. This is considered to be the best of the **Muscadet** regions, with 80% of wines from the area produced here. The region derives its name from the two Loire tributaries that run through it. The soil in this area is lighter and stonier than elsewhere, although there are pockets of sand and clay. There are a few 60- and 70-year-old parcels of vines, which yield Muscadet of austerity in their youth, with natural concentration and aging potential, especially in the strongest vintages. At its best, Muscadet is rich and vibrant with a hint of Atlantic brine—always a natural pair with raw seafood. Unfortunately, at its worst it can make you feel like the enamel is being ripped off your teeth.

The two other Muscadet appellations in this area are **Muscadet Côtes de Grandlieu AOC** and **Muscadet des Côteaux de la Loire AOC**, both considered a step up from basic Muscadet AOC. The **Côteaux de la Loire** is northerly, with chalky soils, and at the limit of Atlantic wine making in France. In very hot years the wines from here can be more balanced than elsewhere. **Muscadet Côtes de Grandlieu** was, up until recently, part of Muscadet AOC. In the first half of the 1990s it received its own AOC designation.

There are three VDQS that complete the Vin du Pays Nantais: **Côteaux d'Ancenis, Fiefs Vendeens,** and **Gros Plant Nantais**. **Côteaux d'Ancenis** is named for its city, which lies between Nantes and Angers. Reds and medium-sweet whites are usually named for the variety here. Red varieties grown include **Cabernet Franc, Cabernet Sauvignon,** and **Gamay**. For whites, the permitted varieties are **Chenin Blanc** and **Pinot Gris**. Sprinkled south of Nantes is **Fiefs Vendeens**. This growing area was upgraded from Vin de Pays in 1984. The vineyards here must be planted with at least 50% **Gamay** and **Pinot Noir** plus **Négrette** (usually found in Fronton in the south), **Cabernet Franc,** and **Cabernet Sauvignon**. The maximum amount of Gamay permitted is 15%. These percentages only apply to the VDQS standards for planting and do not pertain to final blends, so it is not uncommon to find both blends and varietaly-labeled wines produced here.

## Anjou-Saumur

Further east near the city of Ancenis, lies the beginning of the Anjou region. Here in the western extremities of the Central Loire Tufa soil dominates (*Tuffeau* in French). There are some eight wine regions that lie within the confines of Anjou. From west to east the appellations are the generic **Anjou,** to the north and west of Angers; **Anjou Côteaux** de la Loire, to the southwest of Angers), and **Savennières**, which is also southwest of Angers but closer to the city and *north* of the river. As the river continues to wind its way with Savennières to the north, just *south* are the sweet wine appellations of **Côteaux du Layon**, fed by the Layon River; **Côteaux de l'Aubance**, fed by the l'Aubance; **Quarts-de-Chaume**; and **Bonnezeaux**, all especially known for their botrytised **Chenin Blanc**.

There is a break from the eastern limit of L'Aubance along the river that is designated as more generic Anjou AOC prior to arriving in the appellations of **Côteaux de Saumur** and **Saumur-Champigny**. Descending south from the Loire are the Dive, Argenton, and Thouet Rivers, which all feed the appellations of **Saumur** and **Vins du Thouarsais**.

## APPELLATIONS OF ANJOU

Historically, Anjou has been known for its rosés. These wines were never faithful to any one grape and therefore did not promote a specific association. One grape in particular that is used to make much of wines of the **Rosé d'Anjou AOC** is **Grolleau** (Groslot), although **Cot** (Malbec), **Cabernet Franc, Cabernet Sauvignon, Pineau d'Aunis,** and **Gamay** also are allowed. (Pineau d'Aunis is a small, black-berried variety considered by some to be a mutation of Chenin Blanc. It produces lightly-colored wine with a lacy spice expression similar to that of Grenache.) The percentage of rosés being made today has decreased somewhat, and in some cases the remaining pink wine has increased in quality. This is due in part to the replanting of Grolleau (a very prolific grape that is allowed to produce upwards of 70hl/ha) with Cabernet Franc and Gamay. The pink **Cabernet d'Anjou AOC** has also been made for many decades, albeit in smaller quantities than that of Rosé d'Anjou. This wine is usually higher in residual sugar, but complemented by a bracing acidity, making for a brighter, drier finish. Only **Cabernet Franc** and **Cabernet Sauvignon** are permitted in the production of Cabernet d'Anjou.

There are some very promising red wines coming out of Anjou. Between **Anjou AOC, Anjou-Villages AOC**, and **Anjou Gamay AOC**, the reds can prove to be very interesting. Indeed, the spirit of artisanal, progressive wine making can flourish within the more broadly regulated, generic appellations with **Gamay, Cabernet Sauvignon,** and **Cabernet Franc** permitted for the reds, and **Chenin Blanc, Chardonnay,** and **Sauvignon Blanc** permitted for the whites.

In the grand scheme of wine making in Anjou, **Chenin Blanc** is certainly royalty, producing the most remarkable wines—among them, those from the **Savennières AOC**. Formerly a sweet wine–producing area, the AOC laws required very low yields (30 hl/ha) that are still maintained by the best producers. The primary soil type in the area is schist. Within Savennières there are two Grands Crus that were classified during the creation of the appellation in 1952. The first is **Coulée de Serrant AOC**, a monopole owned by Nicolas Joly, who is renowned for being one of the earliest wine makers dedicated to biodynamic viticulture. The second is **Roche Aux Moines AOC**, from which the fruit is used by three producers to make wine. Savennières is considered one of the longest aging white wines in the world. There is an early attraction to the wines before they tend to retreat—characteristic of Chenin Blanc—but, over the next 20–30 years (and sometimes longer); the wines gracefully reveal what many consider to be an unparalleled complexity.

Across the river to the south, lies one of the dessert wine lover's capitals of the world, **Côteaux du Layon.** Similar to their neighbors in Aquitaine, the wines from this area are usually botrytised, but nevertheless always late harvested to meet the requirements of the AOC. It is important to note that **Chenin Blanc** is as susceptible to noble rot as **Sémillon**. The autumns in the region feature misty, foggy mornings and hot afternoons. The region's soil is mostly slate, which retains the heat of the day, keeping the vines warm in the evening and encouraging a gradual ripening process. Chenin Blanc's ability to hang on the vine to extreme ripeness perfectly complements its natural potential for high acidity, resulting in a highly ageable wine.

Within the **Côteaux du Layon AOC** lie many treasures. Twenty percent of the AOC's production is entitled to the **Côteaux de Layon-Villages** appellation, for which there are six villages that may add their names to the label: Beaulieu-sur-Layon, Faye d'Anjou, Rablay-sur-Layon, Rochefort-sur-Loire, Saint Aubin-de-Luigné, and St. Lambert du Lattay. The laws for these wines require a minimum potential alcohol level at harvest of 13%, with 12% in the final product. (This is 1% more than in regular Côteaux du Layon.) **Côteaux du Layon-Chaume AOC**, located in the commune of Rochefort, requires a lower yield due to the higher concentration of clay in its soil (25 hl/ha as opposed to 40 hl/ha). **Quarts-de-Chaume AOC,** which lies across three ridges that hang over the Layon Valley behind the village of Chaume, has historically been considered the site of superior grapes. There are three major and seven minor owners of land in the Quarts-de-Chaume. Yields here are extremely low, 22 hl/ha or 1.2 tons/acre. With 99 ha of vineyards, **Bonnezeaux AOC** is much larger than Quarts de Chaume (56 ha). Although production is higher, yields are just as low. For the dessert wine lover, these two regions cannot be overlooked, especially for their quality-price ratio (QPR).

North of Côteaux du Layon and split by the Aubance River is the appellation of **Côteaux de L'Aubance AOC**. This is probably one of the lesser known AOCs of this region of unknown appellations. However, as the weather conditions here are relatively less favorable and conducive to botrytis, successive *tries*—passes through the vineyard to pick the ripest fruit—are necessary to insure the required minimum alcohol level and a minimum residual sugar level of 17 grams/liter; anything lower than 17 grams/liter must be bottled as **Anjou AOC**.

## APPELLATIONS OF SAUMUR

At the intersection of Anjou and Touraine, lies Saumur, which has it all—dry whites, a rare rosé, the great reds Saumur-Champigny, industrial sparkling wines, underrated sweet whites. In other words, Saumur wines run the gamut, just like every other region in the Loire. Here, the soil is loaded with Tufa—chalk boiled by volcanic action. The two appellations important for quality wine production are **Côteaux de Saumur** and **Saumur-Champigny**. **Côteaux de Saumur AOC** is a botrytised white that in good vintages can yield remarkable wines. **Saumur-Champigny AOC** is one of the homes of the Loire's great **Cabernet Franc**. If that was not enough, Saumur is also responsible for 80% of all sparkling wine made in the Loire, with a considerable amount of it made from **Chardonnay**. In fact, in light of the large amount of sparkling wine produced in the Loire, the bubbly producers of Champagne maintained their preeminence in the field by encouraging the passage of a law in 1985 banning the use of the term *méthode champenoise* for sparklers not produced within the confines of the Champagne region. This had a tremendous effect on the producers of **Saumur Mousseux** and **Petillant AOC**. In the white wines of **Saumur Blanc AOC** there must be a minimum of 80% **Chenin Blanc** and no more than 20% **Chardonnay** or **Sauvignon Blanc**.

## TOURAINE

East of Saumur is the Touraine. As with Anjou, Touraine is both an appellation and a larger area comprising several red, white, and rosé wine appellations. The vineyards wrap themselves around the city of Tours, which was a religious destination back in the 6th century, a center of commerce in the 15th and 16th centuries, and home to the grape **Breton** (the local name for Cabernet Franc) for more than 1,000 years. There is a greater concentration of *Tuffeau* in the soil of the Loire's more eastern regions. In fact, Touraine is the home of the Loire's beautiful châteaux, whose entire edifices were made out of *Tuffeau* from the area. The caves that remained from the excavated *Tuffeau* are still used for the making and aging of wines.

The generic **Touraine AOC** encompasses almost 5,500 hectares of vineyards featuring several different soil types and grape varieties. In addition to *Tuffeau*, which, along with silex, produces the best wines, there is also clay, gravel, and sand making up the soil. In the red grape family, Touraine AOC grows **Cabernet Franc, Gamay, Cabernet Sauvignon, Cot, Pinot Noir, Pinot Meunier, Pinot Gris, Grolleau,** and **Pineau d'Aunis**. White Touraine wines are made with a similar panache of grapes: **Chenin Blanc, Sauvignon Blanc, Chardonnay,** and **Mineau Pineau**—the last being an indigenous variety, with a close genetic relationship to Chenin Blanc. It is also called **Arbois**, but should not, of course, to be confused with the Arbois AOC. Interestingly, the maximum amount of Chardonnay permitted is 20%.

The eastern border of Saumur, north of the Loire River, is home to **Bourgueil AOC**. Here the soil is composed of sand and gravel, producing lighter body wines. However, vines growing on the south-facing slopes of clay and *Tuffeau* produce more full-bodied wines. Grapes growing here can ripen one–two weeks earlier than elsewhere in Bourgueil. Just west of Bourgueil lies **St. Nicolas de Bourgueil AOC** that produces somewhat lighter style wines also from **Cabernet Franc**.

Crossing the Loire to the south and east, 2,100 ha of land open up to **Chinon AOC**. Here **Breton** (Cabernet Franc) once again dominates. Since 1996 this AOC has allowed up to 10% percent of **Cabernet Sauvignon** in the blend. That amount was increased to 25% in 2000. In Chinon the soil is similar to that in Bourgueil and Saumur. The lighter wines come from vineyards with soil composed of gravel and sand whereas the richer, fuller wines come from vines planted in *Tuffeau*.

Upon leaving Chinon there are about 50 long and wide km of Touraine AOC prior to arriving in Vouvray. There are good value wines, both red and white, here, coming from **Sauvignon de Touraine AOC**, **Gamay de Touraine AOC**, and **Cabernet de Touraine AOC**. (As it is throughout the rest of the country, whenever the grape variety is listed on a label, the wine must contain 100% of that grape.) In the area, there are other examples of reds and whites that either list only Touraine on the label or may come from a specific city that has the right to add the name of the village attached to Touraine. East and west of the city of Tours there are several villages that have been permitted to add their name to Touraine. West and south of Tours there is **Touraine Azay-le-Rideau AOC**. Here the tributary Indre-et-Loire runs directly through the village. Good quality whites and rosés come from eight smaller communes on either side of the river produced from **Chenin Blanc**.

Two other villages on the eastern side of Vouvray and Montlouis attach their names to Touraine. Closest to Montlouis and south of the Loire is **Touraine Amboise AOC**. There are eight villages that comprise this area making nervous whites that are often too bracing for most non-local consumers. For the reds however, **Cot** is the primary grape in the blends, along with **Cabernet Franc** and **Gamay**. These are usually richer, fuller wines. Of the three villages that attach their name to Touraine, the third **Touraine-Mesland AOC** is the largest, with 70% of its production devoted to red wines, some of which are considered the best of the reds in Touraine AOC overall. This village lies further east and north of the Loire and **Gamay** comprises 40–50% of the blends.

The two major white wine producing appellations of Touraine are to the immediate east of Tours, north and south of the Loire respectively. **Vouvray AOC** is certainly the more well known of the two, with its vineyards lying closest to the major cathedral city. Today, Vouvray guarantees little in terms of quality wine unless the wine has been bottled by a *domaine* with an address in Vouvray. Because the AOC's fruit can be vinified in such a large range of styles, it takes a conscientious grower-producer to make good decisions with regards to chaptalization, sulfur, etc., especially in more challenging vintages.

Here **Chenin Blanc** is the backbone of the sweet, dry, and sparkling wines, with the best examples reflective of the weather in any given vintage. When possible, Chenin can be infected with botrytis, creating dessert wines (called *moelleux*) capable of doing battle with the best noble rot wines of the world. Vouvray also offers good quality, focused examples of Chenin Blanc that make it a great, diverse grape. (If you are interested in tasting examples of wines where the malolactic fermentation is blocked, Vouvray can be a good place to start as well as Savennières from Anjou).

Vouvray also offers what can be an excitingly flavorful sparkling wine that may be called **Vouvray Pétillant, Brut,** or **Mousseaux AOC**. Made almost exclusively form **Chenin Blanc**, the qualities of ripe Chenin coupled with a small bubble create a sparkling wine of food-friendly character, with the best wines proving to be quite age-worthy.

Across the Loire from and often overshadowed by Vouvray is the 350 ha appellation **Montlouis AOC**. Once again, all expressions of **Chenin Blanc** can be found here. The *Tuffeau* soil so common in this general region is less evident here. More prevalent in this area is sand and gravel, making lighter-styled wines from the early ripening Chenin. When sweet, Montlouis can produce wines of tremendous quality. Examples of dry Chenin can also be found here, depending upon the quality of the specific vintage. Excellent examples of slightly sparkling wines are also made in most all vintages. The wines of Montlouis overall are reasonably priced and usually overlooked by most people outside of France. They are extremely well worth seeking out.

Beyond Montlouis and Touraine AOC there are several satellite appellations, some of which have recently been upgraded from VDQS to AOC. In 1993 **Cheverny AOC** was upgraded. Located south of the river and the city of Blois, the red wines of Cheverny are comprised of **Gamay, Pinot Noir, Cabernet Franc, Cot, Pineau d'Aunis,** and until 2000, **Cabernet Sauvignon**. The white wine of the AOC is a blend of **Sauvignon Blanc** and **Chardonnay**. The appellation should not be confused with the wines of **Cour-Cheverny AOC**, which are made from the indigenous grape **Romorantin**. Romorantin is very high in natural acidity, but it softens and evolves with bottle age. However, it does not blend well with other varieties.

Directly to the north of the city of Tours there are two smaller appellations that are supplied by the tributary of the Loire of a surprisingly similar name—the Loir River. **Côteaux du Loir AOC** and **Côteaux du Vendômois VDQS** are the northernmost vineyards of the Loire. Both of the areas are planted with the same grapes as Cheverny, but they produce wines with a lighter style. The soil is composed of clay, sand, and silex. North of this area, covering 45 hectares of the best south-facing slopes of pure *Tuffeau* within the Côteaux du Loir, is another **Chenin Blanc**–only area, **Jasnières AOC**, which can produce, in good years, very structured and interesting Chenin Blanc.

## THE CENTRAL VINEYARDS

The easternmost area in the Loire Valley is referred to as the **Central Vineyards**. Most of this area is located in the center of France and not the Loire Valley. Here we see a dramatic change not only in soil types but also in grape varieties. While some **Chenin Blanc** is found here, **Sauvignon Blanc** is dominant. Geographically, the region is located in the French *département* of Burgundy, as far as the French Government is concerned, which might explain the plantings of **Pinot Noir**. There is also a band of soil that runs through **Sancerre** and **Pouilly Fumé** and south to **Menetou-Salon** called <u>Kimmeridgian clay</u>. This is the same soil found in some of Chablis' best vineyards.

Surrounding the city of Orleans lie a few small vineyards, which comprise the **Vins de L'Orleannais VDQS** that are producing substantial amounts of **Chardonnay, Pinot Noir, Cabernet Franc,** and **Pinot Gris.** The area typically produces inexpensive, decent quaffing wines that are almost always dry. As the river winds around and heads south from here it leads to a relatively unknown area beginning with the town of Gien. The vines growing on either side of the river are called **Côteaux Giennois VDQS**. **Pinot Noir, Gamay,** and **Sauvignon Blanc** are the major players. Neither the Pinot nor the Gamay may account for more than 60% of the total blend. The wines are good—fruity but dry and drink well young.

The four major appellations of the Central Vineyards are **Sancerre AOC**, **Pouilly-sur-Loire AOC**, **Pouilly-Fumé AOC**, and **Menetou-Salon AOC**, which is influenced by the tributaries Sauldre and Cher. These wines can be some of the raciest whites with a more aromatic appeal in their youth than their Chenin neighbors. Little to no sweet wine is made (although there is a notable Vendange Tardive, or late harvest wine that is made by Lucien Crochet, weather permitting), but reds and very interesting rosés from **Pinot Noir** are available. The reds are light-bodied and bear very little resemblance to Burgundian Pinot. **Pouilly-sur-Loire** wines are made from **Chasselas**.

To the west of the city of Bourges, there are two appellations, **Quincy AOC** and **Reuilly AOC,** which are on the rise due to their similarity to Sancerre and their bargain pricing. **Quincy** is a white wine appellation producing fruity but dry **Sauvignon Blanc** grown in soils with a high concentration of limestone, resulting in higher acidity levels. These wines are typically much less expensive than those from Sancerre. In **Reuilly** there are plantings of **Sauvignon Blanc** and **Pinot Noir.**

# ALSACE

By Sarah Deming

*Let them talk in German. They will fight in French.*

–Napoleon, to an officer complaining about German-speaking Alsatian troops

Think of Alsace as the lovechild of France and Germany. She has always been caught in the middle, her tenuous situation between two possible national borders —the Vosges Mountains to the west and the Rhine to the east— leading to brutal custody battles that would take a toll on her winemaking. In the twentieth century alone she changed hands four times.

It is easy to understand why both nations wanted her. Alsace is ideal winemaking country, sheltered from harsh Atlantic influence by the fir-topped Vosges Mountains, watered by the Ill River and its tributaries, and possessed of an astounding array of soil types and micro-climates that are the dictionary definition of *terroir*.

She takes after both parents. Her most famous grapes, Riesling and Gewürztraminer, are German, as is the tradition of labeling wines by variety rather than village. Yet the dry, rich style of the wines is largely French, and although most of her villages bear German names, French is the official language of Alsace today.

Despite wars, phylloxera, and problems with overproduction, Alsace has always been a survivor. The tenacious Alsatian growers drive her industry, the best of them training their vines on sloping, high-altitude sites with a careful attention to the marriage of variety and terroir. The Alsatians' connection to the land has led them to embrace biodynamic and organic viticulture; their skill makes top Alsatian wine remarkably consistent, even in difficult vintages.

Alsace produces aromatic whites with dazzling fruit, richness and purity of soil expression. Alsatian Rieslings achieve the perfect balance of acidity and ripeness, ageing into their classic petrol nose. Gewürztraminer is indispensable for food pairings— complementing aggressive washed-rind cheeses, foie gras and highly spiced cuisines such as Indian and Thai. The rarer late-harvest wines, Vendage Tardive and Sélection des Grains Nobles, can rival the best *Auslese* and *Beerenauslese* from Germany. The sparkling Crémant d'Alsace is an easy-drinking bargain, and the most widely drunk AOC sparkling wine in France.

The Alsatians have fought hard to carve out a distinct identity amid the ups and downs in their history, an identity that is neither German nor French, but uniquely their own. This fierce commitment to individualism finds its parallel in Alsace's pure varietal wines, which speak with clear voices of their identity and origin. So, too, do famous Alsatian delicacies like *choucroute garni*, Munster AOC, and *kugelhopf*. But you don't have to go to Europe to find the most enduring symbol of the Alsatian spirit; sculptor Frederic Auguste Bartholdi, born in Colmar, Alsace in 1834, left a reminder stateside. The next time you see his Statue of Liberty, raise a glass of Riesling.

# History

Grapes have grown in Alsace since prehistoric times. Winemaking in the region dates back to the second century AD, when records indicate wine was transported along the Moselle and Rhine rivers. Germanic invasion during the fifth century caused winemaking to decline, but it flourished again under Frankish rule, thanks in part to the many monasteries established during the Merovingian (500-751AD) and Carolingian Dynasties (752-987AD).

After the death in 840AD of Charlemagne's son Louis the Pious (also called Louis the Debonaire!), war erupted among his three heirs. In 843 AD, they signed the Treaty of Verdun, dividing their father's holdings into three separate kingdoms. The prized vineyards of Alsace were grouped neither with the bulk of France nor with what would become Germany, but were kept in Middle Francia. It was the least stable of the three kingdoms and soon dissolved. Alsace was ceded to the Holy Roman Empire to its east—which would later be Germany—where it remained for nearly 800 years.

Winemaking in Alsace flourished during this period, reaching its height in the sixteenth century. Riesling, Muscat and Traminer were all cultivated during this time, and Alsace's favorable position along the Rhine facilitated exports throughout Europe. The region prospered until the devastating Thirty Years' War (1619–1648), during which soldiers practicing Cato the Elder's dictum *bellum se ipsum allet* (war feeds itself) depleted the region by rampant violence and looting. The great famine of 1636 added to the hardship, and by the end of the war, Alsace had dropped to one third of its previous population.

The Treaty of Westphalia ended the Thirty Years' War and gave most of Alsace to King Louis XIV of France, who implemented policies to encourage resettling of the war-torn province. Unfortunately, the new settlers often sought quantity over quality in their winemaking, planting productive hybrids in lieu of nobler varieties and working the fertile valley land rather than the hillside sites that were superior for quality grape growing. However, it was also during this post-war period that some of today's most well-known families (Dopff, Hunbrecht and Hugel) began producing wines in Alsace.

The French Revolution (1789-99) dealt quality winemaking another blow when the remaining vineyards were seized from the clergy and nobility by the populace, and divided and sold off. Napoleonic succession laws—parents' landholdings now had to be equally distributed among all surviving children—fragmented vineyard holdings further, just as they did in Burgundy. Modern-day winemaking in Alsace reflects this fragmentation: although there are over 5,000 growers in Alsace, the average size of an individually-owned vineyard is only five hectares. Today, most farmers in the region sell their produce either individually or collectively (through a cooperative) to producers, who then blend and bottle the wine under their own name. Trade associations were also abolished under the French Revolution; the quality of wine fluctuated greatly with the absence of any regional governing body to oversee production standards.

The area under vine in Alsace expanded rapidly during the nineteenth century—partly to assuage the thirst of the massive increase in population there from 1814 to1846—without an accompanying increase in quality. Tensions with Germany and Switzerland brought exports to a standstill, while the domestic market was stifled by high duties and an increased demand for beer. To make things worse, phylloxera and oidium struck in the 1850s and 60s.

The Franco-Prussian War (1870–1871) brought Alsace back under German control, where it remained until the Treaty of Versailles (1919) at the end of World War I. Opinions are mixed regarding the effect of this period on the Alsatian wine trade, some claiming it discouraged quality production, others pointing out that during this period Alsace trade became organized and that wine began being sold in bottle.

The French attempted to legislate quality in Alsace, banning hybrid vines in 1925, and introducing Appellation Controllée laws in 1935 to regulate variety, harvest yields, etc. to the region; but war derailed these efforts with Nazi Germany occupying Alsace from 1940 to 1945. After the war ended, France reclaimed the province, and Alsace has stayed French ever since. In 1962, it became the last major region to be awarded AOC status. Alsace Grand Cru AOC was established in 1975 and Alsace Crémant d'Alsace AOC in 1976.

Wine cooperatives were established with the end of WWII. Alsatian cooperatives are one of the strongest in France. *Négociants* and cooperatives purchase grapes from the over 5,000 farmers in Alsace, and market around 80% of the wine. The remaining 20% is estate bottled.

# Terroir

Alsace, at a latitude of approximately 47.5–49°N, occupies a narrow strip of land in the northeast of France, on the west bank of the Rhine. The vineyards are situated in a valley 100 kilometers long and, at the widest, 4 kilometers in width. As of 2009 15,570 hectares were planted vineyards.

The climate is semi-continental—cool, but sunny with a long, dry growing season. The Vosges Mountains cut Alsace off from the rest of France and act as a climatic barrier against the influence of the Atlantic Ocean; much of the moisture coming in from the west is shed on the Atlantic side of the mountains before it reaches Alsace. As a result of the Vosges' protective influence, Alsace receives abundant sunshine and some of the lowest rainfall in the country, an average of 16-20 inches per year. The chief viticultural hazard is drought, although winters can be cold and bring the danger of frost.

In geological terms, Alsace lies along a rift or *graben* between the raised blocks of the Vosges Mountains to its west and Germany's Black Forest to the east, on the opposite bank of the Rhine. The river helps in creating the autumn humidity that creates a perfect environment for the development of *botrytis cinerea*. Students of terroir adore Alsace, as its location along this important fault line gives rise to an astounding variety of soil types, the most diverse in all of France.

Most of the Grand Cru sites in Alsace run in a narrow strip at 600–1200 feet (182–365m) of elevation along the eastern flank of the Vosges foothills. This location lends vineyards maximum climatic protection from the Vosges with the additional buffer of pine forests at higher altitudes. Top soils here are sufficient for vine health without being overly fertile, as they often can be in the valley below. The vineyards 30–60° slope and southern or southeastern aspect help maximize sun exposure and thus the ripening of the grapes. Slopes with southeastern aspects also assist in shielding the vineyards from winds off the Vosges.

Subsoils of granite, schist, sandstone and volcanic rock predominate on the highest of these sites, giving way to clay and limestone subsoils in the hills. Study the list of Grand Cru vineyards below to get a sense of the tremendous variety present here. The valley soils are fertile, composed of alluvial deposits and loess. While good wines can be produced at these lower elevations, it is here that overproduction of mediocre wine has been most rampant.

In general, Muscat and Pinot Gris, with their strong varietal characteristics, will be less reflective of their soil than Gewürztraminer; Riesling is the most sensitive of them all. Cold limestone soils such as in Rosacker, Altenberg de Bergheim, or Zinnkoepflé produce steely Rieslings with focused acidity and citrus aromas. Warmer soils of sandstone-marl or clay will bring more richness and power, with aromas of stone fruit and flowers. With its excellent drainage, granitic soils such as those of Brand and Schlossberg create wines of great finesse, yet these are particularly vulnerable to vintage variations and suffer in years of drought. The vineyard sites extremely low in lime, such as Froehn and Sporen, are more suited to the lower-acid Gewürztraminer.

# REGULATION & CLASSIFICATION

Alsace has only three AOCs (AOPs under the new EU regulations), all of which are umbrella appellations that cover wines of varying styles from dry, aromatic whites to the sweet, botrytized late harvest wine. There is no Vin de Pays d'Alsace designation, so any wine not satisfying one of the three AOC requirements must be released simply as a Vin de Table de France (new status will be Vin de France).

All Alsatian AOC wines are subject to tasting and analysis tests, and all—except for Crémant d'Alsace—are bottled in the traditional *flûte* or "Rhine wine" bottle, which is long and thin in the German style.

Unusually for French wines, Alsace wines are primarily labeled by grape variety. There is a movement with Alsatian syndicates to have proprietary naming of Alsatian varieties (Riesling. Gewürztraminer, Sylvaner) on their labels only—meaning that only Alsatian winemakers could list these varieties on the new Vin de France category. Presently, nine varieties can appear on the label of Alsatian AOC wine, four of which are considered "Noble".

The Four "Noble Grapes":

1. Gewurztraminer
2. Riesling
3. Muscat
4. Pinot Gris

Five other varieties appearing on labels:

1. Auxerrois
2. Chasselas
3. Pinot Blanc
4. Pinot Noir
5. Sylvaner

The three appellations of Alsace:

| Alsace AOC | 75% of production | Still wines produced and bottled within Alsace. Most are single-variety wines from the nine permitted grapes, but blends are also permitted. |
|---|---|---|
| Alsace Grand Cru AOC | 4% of production | Still wines produced from one of 51 designated Grand Cru vineyards. Most are single-variety wines from the four noble grapes, with some exceptions. |
| Crémant d'Alsace AOC | 21% of production | Sparkling wine produced by the méthode traditionelle. |

## ALSACE AOC

The Alsace AOC is an umbrella appellation that can stand alone on a label, but usually also has one of the nine permitted varieties listed as well. If a variety is listed, however, the wine must be made 100% of the named variety. Similarly, if a village or region is listed, all grapes must be source from the named area.

Blends are allowed. These were once called **Edelzwicker Alsace AOC**, "Edelzwicker" being an old word meaning "noble mixture." But inferior products have caused the term to lose cachet, and many producers now use proprietary/fantasy names, or simply sell their blends under AOC Alsace. The blend can be of two or more of the authorized varieties. The producer does not have to list the varieties in the blend, nor the vintage. Also, the varieties could be vinified separately or together at the discretion of the producer.

**Gentil Alsace AOC** are blended wines subject to regulations: the wines must contain a minimum of 50% Riesling, Muscat, Pinot Gris and/or Gewürztraminer; Sylvaner, Chasselas and/ or Pinot Blanc must make up the remainder of the wine. The varieties must also be vinified separately before blending and the vintage must be listed on the label.

**Klevener de Heiligenstein** is an oddity in Alsace, made from Savagnin Rosé, a variety native to Jura. It is produced in a limited area around the village of Heiligenstein. Replanting is not allowed, and this wine will no longer be entitled to Alsace AOC status after 2021.

At 80 hl/ha, the officially permitted yields are the highest in France—due to the excellent vine health in Alsatian vineyards. But most quality-conscious producers keep their yields lower, to increase the quality of their wine.

| | |
|---|---|
| Date Established (AOC) | 1962 |
| Maximum Yield | |
| White Varieties | 80hl/ha + PLC** |
| Pinot Noir (vinified white) | 75hl/ha + PLC |
| Pinot Noir (vinified red) | 60hl/ha + PLC |
| *Minimum Ripeness for harvest (in degrees potential alcohol)* | |
| Edelzwicker, Muscat, Sylvaner | 9.5° |
| Pinot Blanc, Pinot Noir (white), Riesling | 10° |
| Pinot Noir (red), Klevener de Heiligenstein | 11° |
| Gewurztraminer, Pinot Gris | 11.5° |
| Chaptalization allowed? | Yes** |
| Mechanical harvesting allowed? | Yes** |

*Plafond Limité de Classement* is the legal percentage increase allowed by the INAO in the annual yield in a specified vintage
** Except for the late-harvest Vendange Tardive and Sélection de Grains Nobles wines

# ALSACE GRAND CRU AOC

The Alsace Grand Cru AOC was established in 1975 but the first designated sites were not created until 1983. Theoretically, it was created as a way to distinguish top wines produced from exceptional terroir; but from its inception is has been controversial. (See a detailed discussion under the "Hot Topics" section.)

There are currently 51 delimited sites, which are subject to strict regulations regarding planting density, distance between rows, height of vegetation, and pruning practices (for a list of the 51, see below under Terroir section). Most Alsace Grand Cru wines are single-variety made from one of the four noble grapes—though there are a few exceptions. In 2005, Sylvaner was approved for use in Zotzenberg and in the blended wines of Altenberg de Bergheim. In 2007, blends from Kaefferkopf were also approved.

## THE IMPORTANCE OF THE SYNDICATE IN ALSACE GRAND CRU AOC

The INAO decree of January 24, 2001 reinforced the role of local growers unions in legislating quality within their Grand Crus. The syndicates select local wine experts—Comité Régional d'Experts des Vins d'Alsace (CRINAO)—who are given the power to declare the harvest date for their Grand Cru and late harvest wines. The unions can also establish higher minimum potential alcohol levels, set maximum yields, and either renounce or limit the practice of chaptalization. Yields have decreased significantly since the 2001 decree—some Grands Crus now producing yields in the range of 45 hl/ha. Although restricted yields are associated with higher quality wine, this is not always the case. A lower yield can produce a higher must weight, which, in a sunny region like Alsace, can lead to either overly alcoholic wines or ample residual sugar. The "sweetening" of Alsatian wines is a trend that has drawn criticism from wine writers and consumers alike. The power is now in the hands of the growers to address these concerns and distinguish their Grand Cru wines from the pack.

| | |
|---|---|
| Date Established (AOC) | 1975, but first sites designated in 1983 |
| Maximum Yield* | 55hl/ha + PLC, but never to exceed 66hl/ha |
| *Minimum Ripeness (in degrees potential alcohol)* | |
| Riesling and Muscat | 11° |
| Gewurztraminer and Pinot Gris | 12.5° |
| Sylvaner (Zotzenberg) | 11° |
| Gewurztraminer and Pinot Gris (Altenberg de Bergheim) | 14° |

| | |
|---|---|
| Riesling (Altenberg de Bergheim) | 12° |
| Blend (Altenberg de Bergheim) | 14° |
| Gewurztraminer and Pinot Gris (Kaefferkopf) | 12.5° |
| Riesling (Kaefferkopf) | 11° |
| Blend (Kaefferkopf) | 12° |
| Chaptalization allowed? | Yes** |
| Mechanical harvesting allowed? | No |
| Tasting and Analysis tests required? | Yes |

\* Many local syndicates enforce even stricter yield and ripeness limits

\*\*Except for late harvest Vendange Tardive and Sélection de Grains Nobles, and some syndicates have renounced chaptalization entirely

## The Grand Crus of Alsace[3]

| Grand Cru Vineyard (Village) | Principal Geological Soil Type(s) |
|---|---|
| Altenberg de Bergbieten | Marl-limestone-gypsum |
| Altenberg de Bergheim | Marl-limestone |
| Altenberg de Wolxheim | Marl-limestone |
| Brand (Turckheim) | Granite |
| Bruderthal (Molsheim) | Marl-limestone |
| Eichberg (Eguisheim) | Marl-limestone |
| Engelberg (Dahlenheim and Scharrachbergheim) | Marl-limestone |
| Florimont (Ingersheim and Katzenthal) | Marl-limestone |
| Frankstein (Dambach-la-ville) | Granite |
| Froehn (Zellenberg) | Clay-marl |
| Furstentum (Kientzheim and Sigolsheim) | Limestone |
| Geisberg (Ribeauvillé) | Marl-limestone-sandstone |
| Gloeckelberg (Rodern and Saint-Hippolyte) | Marl-limestone |
| Goldert (Gueberschwihr) | Marl-limestone |
| Hatschbourg (Hattstatt and Voegtlinshoffen) | Marl-limestone & loess |
| Hengst (Wintzenheim) | Marl-limestone-sandstone |
| Kaefferkopf (Ammerschwihr) | Granite and limestone-sandstone |
| Kanzlerberg (Bergheim) | Argilo-marneux-gypseux |
| Kastelberg (Andlau) | Shale |
| Kessler (Guebwiller) | Sablo-argileux |
| Kirchberg de Barr | Marno-calcaire |
| Kirchberg de Ribeauvillé | Marl-limestone-sandstone |
| Kitterlé (Guebwiller) | Sandstone-volcanic |
| Mambourg (Sigolsheim) | Marl-limestone |
| Mandelberg (Mittelwihr et Beblenheim) | Marl-limestone |
| Marckrain (Bennwihr et Sigolsheim) | Marl-limestone |
| Moenchberg (Andlau et Eichhoffen) | Marl-limestone with scree |
| Muenchberg (Nothalten) | Stony-sandstone-volcanic |
| Ollwiller (Wuenheim) | Sandy-Clay |
| Osterberg (Ribeauvillé) | Marl |
| Pfersigberg (Eguisheim and Wettolsheim) | Limestone-sandstone |
| Pfingstberg (Orschwihr) | Marl-limestone-sandstone |
| Praelatenberg (Kintzheim) | Granito-gneiss |
| Rangen (Thann and Vieux-Thann) | Volcanic |

---

[3] Vins d'Alsace. AOC Alsace Grand Cru. www.vinsdalsace.com. Retrieved August 10, 2012, from http://www.vinsalsace.com/IMG/pdf/GrandCrusAlsace_GB-2.pdf.

| Grand Cru Vineyard (Village) | Principal Geological Soil Type(s) |
|---|---|
| Rosacker (Hunawihr) | Dolomitic limestone |
| Saering (Guebwiller) | Marl-limestone-sandstone |
| Schlossberg (Kientzheim) | Granitic |
| Schoenenbourg (Riquewihr and Zellenberg) | Marno-sableux-gypsum |
| Sommerberg (Niedermorschwihr and Katzenthal) | Granitic |
| Sonnenglanz (Beblenheim) | Marl-limestone |
| Spiegel (Bergholtz and Guebwiller) | Marl-sandstone |
| Sporen (Riquewihr) | Stony-clay-marl |
| Steinert (Pfaffenheim and Westhalten) | Limestone |
| Steingrubler (Wettolsheim) | Marl-limestone-sandstone |
| Steinklotz (Marlenheim) | Limestone |
| Vorbourg (Rouffach and Westhalten) | Limestone-sandstone |
| Wiebelsberg (Andlau) | Sandy-sandstone |
| Wineck-Schlossberg (Katzenthal and Ammerschwihr) | Granitic |
| Winzenberg (Blienschwiller) | Granitic |
| Zinnkoepflé (Soultzmatt and Westhalten) | Limestone-sandstone |
| Zotzenberg (Mittelbergheim) | Marl-limestone |

## Crémant d'Alsace AOC

Crémant d'Alsace AOC is a value-priced choice in dry sparkling wine. This is no secret to the French, who have made it their top-selling AOC sparkler at home. Crémant d'Alsace is the fastest-growing appellation in Alsace (sales have multiplied by 14 in 26 years; up from 2.2 million bottles in 1982 to 30 million bottles in 2008).

To ensure the wine's crisp acidity, grapes destined for Crémant d'Alsace are generally harvested early, a few days before the grapes destined for still wines. The bulk of the Crémant d'Alsace blend is the relatively neutral Pinot Blanc, which gives the wine its characteristic softness and delicacy. Riesling and Pinot Gris lend aroma and richness, and Chardonnay adds finesse. Occasionally, Auxerrois is also used. The Pinot Noir grape can be vinified white and used to add structure and body to white Crémant d'Alsace, and it is the only variety in the relatively rare Crémant d'Alsace rosé.

As with all Crémant wines, Crémant d'Alsace is made using the *méthode traditionelle*, in which secondary fermentation takes place in the bottle. The harvest date is fixed by regional committees, usually several days before the harvest of still wines to preserve acidity, and the wine may not be bottled before January 1 following harvest. It must spend a minimum of nine months bottle aging on the lees.

| Date Established (AOC) | 1976 |
|---|---|
| Maximum Yield | 80 hl/ha + PLC |
| Minimum Ripeness (in degrees potential alcohol) | 9° |
| Chaptalization allowed? | Yes |
| Mechanical harvesting allowed? | No |

## Late-Harvest Wines

**Vendange Tardive** (VT) and **Sélection de Grains Nobles** (SGN) are not appellations themselves but are designations that may be affixed to either Alsace AOC or Alsace Grand Cru AOC wines. These wines are only made in years and vineyards where the conditions favor the production of late-harvest wines.

Vendange Tardive wines need not be affected by noble rot. The best show the concentration that comes from being left long on the vine to dehydrate (***passerillage***). Comparable to a German *Auslese*, these wines can range in style from dry to quite sweet. To qualify for the Vendange Tardive designation, winemakers must declare their intention to the local INAO office before harvest so the sugar level in their grapes may be checked. The wine must meet the following requirements:

- Made from one of the four noble grapes (Gewürztraminer, Riesling, Muscat, or Pinot Gris)
- Harvested by hand
- Harvested after a certain date, set annually by the authorities
- Meets minimum ripeness level
- Not chaptalized

**Sélection des Grains Nobles** wines are hand-harvested in several *tries*—a labor-intense process where pickers will move along the vineyard rows and only pick the clusters, and sometimes only the grapes, that are affected by noble rot. Like German Beerenauslese, they are always sweet and have the delicious unctuousness that comes from *botrytis cinerea*. They must meet all the VT requirements, plus:

- A percentage of the grapes must be affected by *botrytis cinerea*
- They must meet an even higher minimum ripeness level

For the 2009 vintage, ripeness levels were as follows:

|  | Vendange Tardive | Sélection de Grains Nobles |
| --- | --- | --- |
| Gewürztraminer/Pinot Gris | 15°3 | 18°2 |
| Riesling/Muscat | 14°0 | 16°4 |

## OTHER APPELLATIONS

To the northwest of Alsace, in the neighboring region of Lorraine, lie two classified winemaking regions. **Vin de Moselle AOC** (elevated from VDQS to AOC in November 2010), in the area around the city of Metz, offers reds from Gamay, Pinot Noir and Pinot Meunier and whites from the usual Alsatian varieties plus Müller-Thurgau. **Côtes de Toul AOC**, elevated to AOC status in 2003, lies west of the city of Nancy, producing Pinot Noir reds, a small amount of Auxerrois-dominated white and, most commonly, a pale rosé made from Gamay, Pinot Meunier, and Pinot Noir. Both wines have limited production and are seldom seen on the export market.

## VITICULTURE & VINIFICATION

Winemaking practices in Alsace are designed to preserve pure varietal characteristics. Much of the entry-level Alsatian wines are chaptalized when grapes do not achieve sufficient ripeness on their own—the winemaker adds sugar to fermenting must in order to increase the resulting alcohol level. The best sites produce grapes of sufficient ripeness to make this unnecessary, and the practice has been prohibited in many Grand Crus. Chaptalization is never practiced for late-harvest wines.

Traditionally, malolactic fermentation is blocked in the winemaking here, as the softening effect of converting malic acid to lactic acid is seen as unnecessary for the bracing, focused wine for which Alsace wine is known. Yet it sometimes happens spontaneously, as it did in 1996 and 2001, and some of the resulting wines were well received. Olivier Humbrecht is one of the producers now favoring occasional natural malolactic fermentation of the small amounts of malic acids that are present in mature grapes. Other producers, such as Trimbach, continue to have a zero-tolerance policy.

The use of new oak is also mostly shunned, as the Alsatians wish nothing to stand in the way of the pure expression of their wines' varietal characteristics and terroir. The overlay of vanilla, caramel and butterscotch leant to wine by new wood ageing would only suppress the individuality that Alsatian growers work so hard to promote. Stainless steel is the rule, or the traditional large wooden vats known as *foudres*, casks used for vinification and storage year after year. The buildup of tartrates on the vats' inner walls creates a protective lining that prevents the transfer of wood flavors onto the wine, preserving its freshness.

Traditionally most Alsatian table wine (outside of the late harvest wines) was fermented dry, leaving no residual sugar. In the past 20 years or so, the trend has been towards sweeter styles—possibly to cater to the tastes of the American export market, more likely because of climate change and changing practices in the vineyard and the winery. As the climate warms, more sugar builds in the grapes as they ripen. As viticultural techniques improve, the yields are lowered and grapes grow more concentrated. To maintain balance, winemakers may elect to leave some residual sugar. Additionally, as more and more producers move towards organic and biodynamic practices, the focus shifts to "hands-off" winemaking and the process of fermentation is allowed to run its course naturally, without intervention. This means that fermentation is allowed to come to a conclusion organically—potentially leaving some residual sugar—and the winemaker does not manipulate the process to force-convert leftover sugar to alcohol.

As of 2012, Alsace does not have an official standardized method for categorizing and identifying levels of sweetness in wine. As such, the consumer for the most part cannot easily tell by the label how sweet or how dry a wine will be.

In 2009 the Conseil Interprofessionnel des Vins d'Alsace (CIVA) proposed following the EU system of classifying all AOC wines as either *sec*, *demi-sec*, *moelleux* or *doux* (dry, medium dry, medium sweet, sweet). Without legislation the system would be voluntary and there would be no guarantee that producers would comply.[4] Some producers have adopted their own unique identification methods—Zind Humbrecht uses indices from 1-5 printed beneath the alcohol level on the label, wherein 1 is dry and 5 is rich and sweet.[5]

## VARIETIES

**Riesling** is currently the most widely planted (around 20% of vineyards) variety in Alsace and, for many, the finest. It is a slow-ripening grape with good acidity that thrives in sheltered sites. Top Alsatian Riesling can be closed when young, taking years to develop its distinctive petrol nose. Riesling is very expressive of the soil, clay yielding fatter and richer wines, granite and limestone producing wines with more finesse, and volcanic soils lending smoke and spice.

**Gewurztraminer** (spelled without the umlaut in Alsace) takes its name from the German word *gewurz* or "spice." It is an early-budding variety prone to spring frosts but can develop quite high sugar levels and is therefore excellent for late-harvest styles. The grape's thick pink skin gives the wine its golden color and opulent nose of lychee, citrus and rose, giving way to gingerbread with age. Current acreage planted is almost the same as Riesling, but with smaller yields.

**Pinot Gris** can produce forgettable wine elsewhere, but in Alsace it reaches its height of spice and richness. Current plantings are about 15% of total hectares cultivated. It can reach high levels of potential alcohol and is thus suitable for both late-harvest and dry styles. The variety was previously known as "**Tokay d'Alsace**," as it was believed to have originated from Hungary, which produces the famous Tokaji wine. Conflicts over the name led to Alsatian producers labeling their wines "Tokay Pinot Gris" as an intermediate step. Since 2007, Alsatian producers may no longer include the word "Tokay" on Alsace Pinot Gris labels.

**Muscat** is the rarest of the four noble varieties and accounts for around 3% of total plantings. The more traditional **Muscat Blanc à Petits Grains** (also called **Muscat d'Alsace**) has both a white and pink strain, and is slowly being replaced by the hardier **Muscat Ottonel**. Muscat wines have a feminine grace, with a characteristic grapey flavor and orange flower bouquet. Slow to ripen, Muscat has lower acidity and alcohol levels and is therefore generally best drunk young, though some of the top wines age well.

**Pinot Blanc** (also known locally as **Clevner** or **Klevner**, not to be confused with Klevener de Heiligenstein) is a vigorous, somewhat neutral grape with good acidity and moderate alcohol. Its plantings are on the rise, driven by growing demand for Crémant d'Alsace, of which it forms the base.

**Auxerrois** is an early-ripening grape from the same family as Pinot Blanc but with greater body and spice. It is often released in a blend with Pinot Blanc that is labeled either "Pinot Blanc" or simply "Pinot." It is also used in Edelzwicker blends. Pinot Blanc and Auxerrois combined total about 19% of the plantings.

**Sylvaner**, although difficult to grow, can produce rich, high-quality wines if grown on very good sites. However, since Sylvaner fetches a lower price in the marketplace, the better acreage is generally allocated to Riesling. Sylvaner is usually planted in the lower vineyards of the Bas-Rhin, where it produces inexpensive, early-drinking wine. Its plantings have declined significantly in the last 30 years, largely being replaced by Pinot Gris and Pinot Blanc.

**Chasselas** is a light, fruity grape that is rarely bottled on its own but is usually blended in Edelzwicker wines. Its plantings are extremely limited and are on the decline.

**Chardonnay** may not appear on the labels of Alsace wine but is grown for use in Crémant d'Alsace.

**Savagnin Rosé** produces the dry, light-bodied Klevener de Heiligenstein, but it is gradually being phased out of Alsace AOC.

---

[4] Style, S. (November 6, 2009). Alsace sweetness levels. In Decanter. Retrieved August 10, 2012, from http://www.decanter.com/people-and-places/wine-articles/484108/alsace-sweetness-levels.
[5] Asimov, E. (October 7, 2008). The Pour - The Sweet and the Dry: Decoding Alsace Wine. In The New York Times. Retrieved August 10, 2012, from http://www.nytimes.com/2008/10/08/dining/08pour.html.

**Pinot Noir** is the only official black grape of Alsace and is notoriously fickle to grow, being susceptible to spring frosts, *coulure* and disease. Alsatian Pinot Noirs tend to be very light, generally lacking the weight and extraction of their German counterparts. The grape is often vinified white and used to give body to Crémant d'Alsace or, occasionally, to produce excellent sparkling rosé. Grand Cru Steinklotz is one of the few regions where Pinot Noir produces deep-colored, perfumed reds. Some growers have been experimenting with aging their Pinot Noir in oak.

## REGIONS

Alsace is divided into two main sub-regions, **the Bas-Rhin** in the north and **the Haut-Rhin** in the south. "Bas" is French for "low" and "Haut" is French for "high", which can be confusing when looking at a map. Haut-Rhin refers to the fact that the area is upriver on the Rhine and Bas-Rhin is downriver. The Rhine River flows north from the eastern Swiss Alps to the North Sea near the Netherlands. The majority of Grand Cru sites are located in the Haut-Rhin, in a narrow strip of hillside vineyards stretching to the north and south of Colmar. In general, the vineyards of the Bas-Rhin are less sheltered by the Vosges and produce lighter wines.

## HOT TOPICS

Grand Cru Alsace AOC has been controversial since its inception. It was created in 1975, but it took until 1983 for a list of the first 25 vineyards to be released. Three years later, 23 more were added, and the current total is up to 51.

Why did it take so long for the first sites to be declared, and why does the number keep changing? This is a lucrative designation. Given the complexities of Alsatian terroir —where soil types can vary literally from row to row within a vineyard— it's easy to imagine the internal politics and haggling over boundaries that must have broken out when the AOC was first announced.

Unlike the 1855 Bordeaux classification, which was based on the prices the wines were fetching in the market, or the Burgundy Grand Cru classification, largely driven by long-standing consumer preference and vineyard reputation, the Alsace Grand Cru classification is young, and many of the wines lack a proven track record. Some of the Grands Crus are indisputably great—names like Schlossberg, Steinert, Goldert, Rosacker, and Rangen have reputations stretching back centuries—while others have yet to show that they can consistently produce great wine. Consumers have been justifiably leery of paying a premium for unproven and inconsistent quality.

Worse yet, many vineyards are large and encompass varying soil types and aspects, some better than others. For this reason, many of the best producers choose not to label their wines as Grands Crus, even when they have the right to do so. Most notably, the house of Trimbach has declined to affix the Grand Cru Rosacker designation to the label of their exquisite Riesling Clos Ste Hune, feeling that not all of Rosacker is on par with their holdings.

The problem of large, diverse vineyards is not unique to Alsace; Grand Cru Clos Vougeot in Burgundy, for example, has been similarly criticized for its vastness and uneven quality. In these cases, when it's often unrealistic to memorize which growers own which parcels, it becomes vital to know the producers who can be relied upon to make wine worthy of the site.

The INAO has attempted to respond to this controversy with changing regulations. They have granted more autonomy to each Grand Cru to dictate yields, harvest dates and sugar levels. They have also relaxed the single-varieties-only rule to allow Grand Cru status to the excellent blended wines from Kaefferkopf and Altenberg de Bergheim and to Zotzenberg's historic Sylvaner. Expect more changes as these wines continue to earn their reputations.

# Jura and Savoie

By Sarah Deming

*A bottle of wine contains more philosophy than all the books of the world.*

–Louis Pasteur, native son of Arbois, Jura

Savoie is a picturesque region in the French Alps, sharing a border with Switzerland. This is skiing country, where vacationers hitting the slopes can relax afterward with the crisp, refreshing whites for which Savoie is most renowned. Savoie is a fascinating region for the student of obscure grapes, with no less than twenty-three distinct varieties, some unique and some reflecting Burgundian, Italian or Swiss influence. The region is quite mountainous and vineyards are dispersed over a wide area, wherever cultivable properties can be found. (The size of the wine producing region is nearly the same as Bordeaux's but only produces about 2% the quantity of wine.) In *The World Atlas of Wine* Vin de Savoie is described as: "more than twice as likely to be white than red or rosé… about ten times more likely to be light, clean and fresh—at one with Savoyard mountain, air, lakes and streams—than it is to be deep and heady…"

The diverse winemaking region of Jura, northwest of Savoie, is located in the mountainous province of Franche-Comté. These vineyards produce crisp whites, too, although much of the still white is in a style called *typé* or *tradition*, bearing a hint of oxidation. Like Savoie, Jura also produces still red, rosé and traditional-method sparkling wine. Jura also produces a fortified wine called Macvin and the delicious Vin de Paille, made from local Savagnin grapes that are left to dry before pressing. After a long, slow fermentation, Vin de Paille ages in small oak barrels for over three years developing into a sweet nectar of great longevity and complexity.

Perhaps the drink that best captures Jura's spirit is Vin Jaune. This unique Savagnin wine is left to age for six years in large oak barrels, without topping off. A coating of yeast forms on the wine's surface, similar to *flor* on Fino Sherry, lending the finished product a distinctly nutty, oxidized flavor. The best examples of Vin Jaune can age up to 100 years.

It makes sense that Jura produces wine in such an ingenious number of styles, for this is a land that seems to breed genius. The list of innovative thinkers hailing from Franche-Comté goes on and on: the filmmaking pioneers Auguste and Louis Lumière; helicopter inventor Etienne Oehmichen; author Victor Hugo; painter Gustave Courbet; and Jura's most famous son, Louis Pasteur, whose investigations into fermentation led to the discovery of the role of yeast in winemaking, effectively founding the field of oenology.

The rustic wines of Jura take patience to make. It may take patience to acquire a taste for them, too, but with all the philosophy contained in Vin Jaune, you can't expect to master it overnight. The deepest things in life are always an acquired taste.

# History

The Jura is one of the oldest vineyard areas in France, dating back to the 6th century BC. The Phoencians brought vine cuttings with them on their way north into battle. The region was a favorite of King Philippe le Bel who introduced Jura's wines to the French court and nobility. Henry IV and Francois I were also supporters of the region's wine. The Jura reached its height in the late 19th century when its plantings surpassed 2,000 ha. The region was home to many artists and poets and the birthplace of Louis Pasteur. Pasteur spent a great deal of time experimenting with fermentation, examining the roles yeast played in the inoculation of grape juice.

# Geography, Climate, and Soil

Jura is situated between Lake Geneva and Burgundy, and Savoie is located slightly south of Jura. The isolation provided by the mountainous environment that surrounds the two regions has furthered the development of traditional winemaking methods and fostered the growth of grapes that differ from neighboring areas.

The climate in both Jura and Savoie is continental—harsher than in Burgundy—as winters can be quite cold. Autumn frosts pose a major threat, especially since some local varieties ripen slowly and are harvested quite late into November. The microclimate of the regions' individual appellations and vineyards depend upon their altitude and proximity to Lake Geneva and the Rhône River, which feeds Savoie. Generally, vintage variations in these regions are considered to be secondary to the differences between the appellations and the producers.

Jura vineyards are found mostly at altitudes between 800–1,300 feet, between the Bresse Plains and Jura Mountains, whereas in Savoie, the vines are situated on lower slopes and are more scattered. Primary soil types are similar to those in Burgundy, with more clay on the lower slopes and limestone at higher elevations. Additionally, there are a variety of different soil types distributed throughout the vineyards.

# Jura Varieties

Two white grapes—**Chardonnay** and **Savagnin**—and three red grapes—**Pinot Noir**, **Trousseau** and **Ploussard**—dominate in Jura. Chardonnay is a popular grape because it is easy to grow, and Pinot Noir is usually paired with Ploussard to add color and structure to the blend. Ploussard is a thin skinned, perfumed grape that yields light-colored red wines that are prone to oxidation. It is also vinified as a white wine within the **L'Etoile AOC**. Plantings of Trousseau have been declining within the region, even though some producers still use it in making varietal wines, which can be likened to Pinot Noir, although somewhat more bitter.

**Savagnin** is the region's signature local variety and is grown almost exclusively in Jura. It is a difficult grape to grow because it ripens very late and is susceptible to *coulure*. It is blended with Chardonnay in many appellations but is the only grape permitted in the production of **Vin Jaune**, a specialty of Jura.

# Jura Appellations and Winemaking

The major AOCs of Jura are **Arbois, Château Chalon,** and **L'Etoile**. These three AOCs comprise approximately 930 hectares of vineyards. The remaining 1,100 hectares fall into the **Côtes du Jura AOC**.

**Arbois** was the first AOC to be named by the INAO on May 15, 1936. It is also the largest AOC in Jura at 800 hectares.

**Château Chalon AOC** is unique in that it produces only one wine, from the Savagnin grape, Vin Jaune. The appellation covers only about 50 hectares.

**L'Etoile** is located further south of Château Chalon and has a surface area of about 80 hectares. The AOC is located at the northern extremity of Lons-le-Saunier.

**Vin Jaune**, after normal fermentation, is left in wooden barrels to age for a minimum of six years without being topped off. A layer of yeast forms on top of the wine that is similar to the *flor* that exists in the production of Sherry. In the Jura it is called the *voile*. The *voile* prevents the wine from oxidating too quickly, and it imparts nutty flavors to the wine, some of which are already naturally present to some extent in **Savagnin**. Vin Jaune is traditionally bottled in 620 millileter bottles called *clavelins*. The 130 milliliter difference between a *clavelin* and a standard wine bottle is an accommodation for the evaporation that occurs while the wine is in barrel.

**Vin de Paille** (French for 'straw wine') is another rather rare wine that is made in Jura, however this is not an exclusive specialty of the region. The production technique is also used in Hermitage and some other regions of the world. The wine is usually made from **Savagnin** and **Ploussard**. After the grapes are picked, they are dried either on a flat surface, usually straw mats, or hanging from a rafter until about late December. The dehydrated fruit is then pressed to yield a very small amount of juice highly concentrated with sugar, which is then used to make a very sweet wine with great aging potential. Fermentation can last for almost one year. The AOC for Vin de Paille requires three years of aging in small oak barrels. The wine is usually only bottled in 375 milliliter bottles.

The last unique wine from the area is **Macvin**, a *vin de liqueur*, made by arresting fermentation of the must by the addition of **Marc de Jura**, a local brandy. The addition of the brandy, which arrests fermentation, results in residual sugar and an alcohol content of about 20%. Macvin was granted its own appellation in 1991.

There are also some sparkling wine appellations in Jura such as Arbois Mousseux AOC, Crémant du Jura AOC, Côte du Jura Mousseux AOC, and L'Etoile Mousseux AOC.

## Savoie Varieties

The primary white grape varieties of Savoie include **Aligoté, Jacquère, Chardonnay, Roussette** (also known as **Altesse), Malvoisie,** and **Mondeuse.** In the Haut-Savoie the whites are **Molette Grignet, Roussette d'Ayze,** and **Chasselas.** The red varieties in Savoie include **Gamay, Pinot Noir, Mondeuse, Persan, Cabernet Sauvignon,** and **Cabernet Franc.** Amongst these **Jacquère** is the most widely planted, and **Roussette** is known to be the highest quality indigenous white variety. About two-thirds of Savoie's wine production consists of crisp beautiful whites. The most famous red is La Mondeuse, which can be peppery and full-bodied.

## Savoie Appellations and Winemaking

The viticultural area of Savoie is comprised of two main regions: Savoie and Haut-Savoie. The appellations are widely dispersed within these two areas.

**Vin de Savoie AOC** is an umbrella appellation to which 17 villages have the right to append their name. These wines are typically of high quality with a lighter style.

**Crépy AOC** grows both Chasselas roux and vert.

Sparkling wines are produced under Vin de Savoie Mousseux and Vin de Savoie Pétillant AOCs.

Roussette has its own appellation, **Roussette de Savoie.** If the wines are comprised of 100% Roussette, four villages are permitted to add their names to this appellation.

Other noteworthy appellations include **Seyssel AOC** and **Bugey VDQS**.

# THE RHÔNE VALLEY

| TOTAL AREA UNDER VINE | 76,330 hectares |
|---|---|

| THE NORTHERN RHÔNE | |
|---|---|
| GRAPE VARIETIES | |
| RED | Syrah |
| WHITE | Viognier, Marsanne, Roussanne |
| CLIMATE | The Northern Rhône has a continental climate, The summers are sunny and hot, and the winters are hard, cold, and wet. The occasional icy northern wind known as le Mistral increases the effect of the cold in springtime but is useful in drying out a wet harvest. |
| SOIL | Shallow granite and slate soils dominate. |

| THE SOUTHERN RHÔNE | |
|---|---|
| GRAPE VARIETIES | |
| RED | Grenache, Syrah, Cinsault, Carignan, Mourvèdre |
| WHITE | Clairette, Grenache Blanc, Bourboulenc, Roussanne, Muscat |
| CLIMATE | This southern half of the Rhône benefits from a true Mediterranean climate with hot dry summers and warm wet winters. The area needs to manage the effects of le Mistral. |
| SOIL | It is mostly clay, limestone, and gravel, or just plain stones in comparison to the north's slate and granite. |

The Rhône Valley is home to wines as distinct and unique as Condrieu, Côte-Rôtie, Tavel, and Muscat Beaumes-de-Venise, making it one of the most difficult viticultural areas in the world to neatly categorize. In the world of winemaking, it is a titan, with almost 190,000 acres under vine. In France, only Bordeaux can claim more Appellation d'Origine Controlée vineyards. The Rhône's approximately 6,000 growers, *négociants*, and cooperatives collectively produce nearly 3 million hectoliters (79 million gallons) of wine each year—95% of which is red.

# HISTORY

While most scholars agree that the Rhône Valley has produced wine for about 2,500 years, the viticultural history of its common grape varieties such as Syrah, Viognier, and Grenache is a matter of debate. Some contend that Roman legions introduced Syrah and Viognier to the Rhône Valley in the late $3^{rd}$ century AD, but its history as a wine-producing region becomes clearer in the early $14^{th}$ century.

Under political pressure from the King of France, Pope Clement V agreed to resettle the papacy at Avignon. This controversial decision, which ushered in the period known in the Catholic Church as the "Babylonian Captivity" (1309-1379), was immeasurably damaging to the prestige of the papacy yet critical in spurring on a new viticultural era in the Rhône Valley. Although some of the popes at Avignon lived modestly, the general atmosphere was one of luxury and extravagance. The local Rhône wines, comprising about three-quarters of the drink consumed at the papal court, were integral to the festive spirit. It was during this time of religious crisis that the Rhône's wines gained fame and prestige, becoming popular in Rome after the restoration of the papacy there in 1378.

Ironically, it was in France that the producers of Rhône Valley wine met with the fiercest and most determined opposition to the proliferation of their product. During the later Middle Ages, as the prestige of Burgundian wine grew, so too did the Burgundians stronghold on the increasingly international wine markets. The government of Burgundy, through tariffs and severe regulatory restrictions, effectively banned the entry of non-Burgundian wine traders along the Saône River. This mid-$15^{th}$-century legislation would debilitate the proliferation of Rhône wines until the latter part of the 17th century, when developments of new routes and easing of restrictions allowed for unfettered access to many of the most desirable trading destinations.

The quality and unique properties of many Rhône wines, especially those from northern Rhône appellations, gradually became more familiar to the rest of France. The strength and muscular characteristics of wines from Hermitage became prized traits to wine makers in Burgundy and even in Bordeaux, where weaker wines would be enhanced by the addition of the more powerful and dense Hermitage. In what would be a precursor to the AOC laws of the early 20th century, a law passed in Châteauneuf-du-Pape in 1727 stated that grapes used to make the wine of the same name must come from a defined area. In the 1920s, Châteauneuf-du-Pape Château Fortia owner Baron Le Roy de Boiseaumarie would continue this tradition, proposing regulations for wine of his region and subsequently providing the inspiration and prototype for the entire French AOC system.

## Geography, Climate, and Soil

The Rhône Valley, lying between the Alps and Massif Central Mountains, spans 125 miles (200 km) in length, from Vienne in the north to Avignon in the south. The Rhône River itself commences as a small body of water in the Swiss Alps, winds its way through Burgundy and the Rhône Valley, before plunging southward and emptying into the Mediterranean—a total journey of more than 500 miles (800 km).

The Rhône is divided into two regions, the *Septentrionales* in the north and the *Meridionales* in the south, with the town of Montélimar serving as the dividing point between the two areas. The northern and southern Rhône have little in common besides the river that names them. The two wine-growing regions are strikingly different from each other in most aspects—climate, soil type, vineyard placement. The northern Rhône's climate is continental with the best vineyards sited on rocky terraces in close proximity to the river. The soil is rich with granite and slate. The Meridionales is strongly influenced by the Mediterranean, with hot summers and warm winters. Its vineyards with clay, limestone, and gravel soil are planted at greater distances from the Rhône on gentler sloping hills.

## Varieties

The varieties grown in the northern and southern Rhône Valley differ greatly and will therefore be discussed in relation to the specific growing areas.

### Northern Rhône

We begin our descent through the Rhône Valley with the appellations of the *Septentrionales* region, as the northern portion of the Rhône is known in France. Many of the Rhône Valley's rarest and most expensive wines are made here. The region begins with Côte-Rôtie, the northernmost appellation, and extends about 50 miles south as far as Cornas and Saint-Péray. In between are five more appellations: Condrieu, Château Grillet, Saint-Joseph, Hermitage, and Crozes-Hermitage.

**Côte Rôtie** ("roasted slope"), situated on the western bank of the Rhône River, is one of the region's better-known appellations. The total area under vine in the Côte Rôtie is approximately 250 ha, with **Syrah** comprising the majority of plantings complemented by small amounts of **Viognier**. The local topsoil is known as arzelle, which is composed of broken mica schist and pebbles. The incredibly steep incline of the vineyards warrants the use of *cheys*, or terraces to protect the soil from erosion.

Within the Côte-Rôtie are two famous slopes, Côte Brune and Côte Blonde. The distinctions in the wine produced on both of these hillsides can be found in the varying soil compositions indigenous to both slopes. The soil on the Côte Blonde is dominated by sand, granulite, and limestone. The Côte Brune's soil is characterized by more clay and iron. As a result, the wines produced from the Côte Brune tend to be significantly more tannic, muscular, darker in color, and cellar worthy. Conversely, wines produced from the Côte Blonde may be less tannic, more approachable in their youth, and more perfumed due to the frequent addition of Viognier. It should be noted that appellation laws in the Côte Rôtie allow for the addition of up to 20% Viognier in the red composition, with most producers choosing to include less than 5%. "Blonde" and "Brune" appear on the labels of wines from both slopes when the two are used separately. However, many producers prefer to blend the two for the ultimate expression of Côte Rôtie.

Just south of Côte Rôtie, on the west bank of the river, lies **Condrieu**, known for arguably the finest white wine of the entire Rhône Valley. With approximately 150 ha under vine, this appellation devotes all its plantings to **Viognier**. As in Côte Rôtie, the most successful vineyards are sloped, though not as dramatically as their northern neighbors, where granite terraces combat the threat of soil erosion and are dominated by arzelle. Viognier is infamous for being an incredibly sensual yet fickle and difficult grape to grow. As a result, growers must be extremely vigilant about the timing of their harvesting. Picking too soon means that under-ripe, overly acidic grapes will dominate, while harvesting too late risks producing Viognier that is impossible to vinify dry due to its potentially high sugar content. It has become increasingly popular for wine makers to allow the grapes to have more prolonged contact with their skins, a process and technique used mainly for white grapes known as *maceration pelliculaire*. It is thought by wine makers that this extended contact between grape and skin lends the unique and prized perfume for which Condrieu is renowned.

Contained as an enclave within the confines of Condrieu is the unique appellation of **Château Grillet**. With just a few hectares in its property, it is one of the smallest appellations in France and the smallest in the Rhône. It is also one of only a few appellations in all of France with a single owner. Like Condrieu, the wines of Château Grillet are produced solely from **Viognier**. However, there are essentially two features that set Château Grillet apart from its neighboring properties in Condrieu. One is that its vineyards are set in what is commonly considered a perfect amphitheater composed of granite, serving to masterfully shelter the grapes from harsh northerly winds. The second is that the grapes, which are grown in a soil higher in mica content, are generally picked at an earlier date than their Condrieu counterparts. The resulting wine will often be more austere, less perfumed and alcoholic, and longer-lived than neighboring Condrieu wines.

Continuing southward, wedged between Condrieu to the north and Cornas to the south lies the longest appellation of the *Septentrionales*, **Saint-Joseph**. Spanning 65 km and with approximately 1,150 ha under vine, Saint-Joseph is the second largest appellation in the northern Rhône. Despite its size, Saint-Joseph is continually and consistently overshadowed by the other more prestigious appellations of Côte Rôtie and Hermitage. As is the case with these two appellations, the overwhelming majority of the wines from Saint-Joseph are red, produced solely from **Syrah**. Small portions of vineyards are devoted to the production of white wines, from the grapes **Marsanne** and **Roussanne**. Although the soil composition of Saint-Joseph (granite, sand, and gravel) differs from the arzelle composition of Côte Rôtie, it is closer in quality to the granite-dominated soil of its more prestigious neighbor, Hermitage. Despite this similar soil composition, the wines of Saint-Joseph tend to have considerably less density, finesse, and potential for long life than those of Hermitage. One possible reason for this is that the vineyards of Saint-Joseph face the east, and as a result, lose the sun up to two hours earlier than vineyards that face south (as they do in Côte Rôtie and Hermitage).

Across the river from Saint-Joseph, on the east bank, lies the comparatively tiny and world-renowned appellation of **Hermitage**. Thought to have had vineyards planted as early as 400 BC, Hermitage has consistently maintained 134 ha of vines (a figure considered unalterable), planted on a hill that faces south and is composed of heat-retaining granite. These factors combine to offer winemakers the advantage of working with grapes that ripen fairly easily. As is the case in Côte Rôtie, soil erosion is a constant threat, requiring a significant number of vineyards to use terraces. Another quality that makes Hermitage unique within the Rhône Valley is the hill itself. Embracing a tradition of terroir similar to that of Burgundy, the vineyards of Hermitage are divided into various *climats*, or individual sites, which can possess diverse soil compositions. Accordingly, the wines produced by *climats* such as Les Bessards, Le Meal, and Les Murets, should represent the individual soil and vineyard characteristics of that particular parcel. Red wines are produced solely from **Syrah** (15% white grapes are permitted, but blending is extremely rare) and white wines from **Marsanne** and **Roussanne**, which combine to comprise 25% of all grape plantings in Hermitage. Strict appellation regulations in Hermitage limit yields to 40 hl/ha, and alcohol levels to 13.5% for red Hermitage and 14% for white.

The largest appellation in the *Septentrionales*, with approximately 1,500 ha under vine, is **Crozes-Hermitage**. Completely surrounding the appellation of Hermitage, Crozes-Hermitage is the undisputed production champion of the northern Rhône, with well in excess of five million bottles of wine produced every year. As in Hermitage, red wines are made from **Syrah** and whites from a blend of **Marsanne** and **Roussanne**. A clay-limestone alluvial soil composition tends to dominate this region. Similarly to Hermitage, appellation laws permit the addition of white grapes (up to 15%) in the final blend of Crozes-Hermitage red wine but, again, such blending is rare. Sites thought to produce the most memorable red Crozes-Hermitage tend to mimic the characteristics of certain Hermitage *climats*. These include vineyards surrounding the northern village of Gervans, with hillsides composed largely of granite, facing south/southwest, and vineyards close to the town of Larange, where soils are more clay-based, resulting in wines with a bit more focus and direct, ripe fruit.

Traveling back to the west bank of the river, one encounters the small (approximately 100 ha under vine) but intense appellation of **Cornas**. Sandwiched between the appellations of Saint-Joseph to the north, and Saint-Péray to the south, Cornas is the southernmost red wine appellation in the *Septentrionales*, producing wines with considerable tannin and power. Derived from the Celtic word for "scorched earth," Cornas enjoys the combination of southern facing slopes and heat-retaining granite soil. Unlike its neighbors to the north and the east, Cornas produces only red wine, made exclusively from **Syrah**, which often manages to find its deepest, darkest, and potentially most long-lived expression in the world.

Just about one mile south of Cornas is one of the great anomalies in the Rhône Valley—the southernmost of the *Septentrionales* appellations, **Saint-Péray**. With 70 ha under vine, devoted almost entirely to **Marsanne** and **Roussanne**, Saint-Péray seems at present to be the only appellation in the northern Rhône in danger of becoming extinct. The majority of wine produced in this appellation, once rumored to be a favorite of Napoleon, is a strangely unknown sparkling white wine made by the *méthode traditionelle*. With slopes of granite characterizing much of the terrain in Saint-Péray, many consider it curious that Syrah is not planted. Instead of vineyard expansion and innovation, Saint-Péray is being subjected to an ever-increasing number of developers, eager to transform the scenic hillsides into valuable, private vacation-style properties.

## SOUTHERN RHÔNE

As we travel south from the town of Valence (considered the southernmost tip of the northern Rhône) to the town of Montélimar (the northernmost tip of the southern Rhône), something curious happens. For the approximately 50 km between these two points and along the Rhône, there are no vineyards.

The major grape varieties of the *Septentrionales* are planted with some regularity in the southern Rhône, known as the *Meridionales*, but with substantially less prominence. Whereas Syrah dominates the composition of northern Rhône red wine, **Grenache** takes center stage in the southern Rhône, with **Syrah** playing a supporting role, along with **Mourvèdre, Cinsault,** and **Carignan. Viognier, Marsanne,** and **Roussanne** are planted as well, but the vast majority of white wines from the south are composed of lesser-known, less glamorous varieties, such as **Grenache Blanc, Bourboulenc,** and **Clairette**. The vineyards become more level in the south, spanning both sides of the river and decreasing the need for terracing. Most importantly, the styles of wine diverge almost completely. In the north, the most sought after wines feature single grape varieties. In the south, the wine that commands the most loyal following—red Châteauneuf-du-Pape—may be composed of up to 13 varieties, both red and white.

Before moving into the southern Rhône, a small ancient region known as the **Die**, requires a brief explanation. It is home to three appellations that are found in the very eastern Rhône between the northern and southern regions, interestingly enough, not on the Rhône River but on the Drome River. The first and most esteemed of these wines, **Clairette de Die**, is a low alcohol (7–8%) sparkling wine, that is older than Champagne and made of **Clairette** and **Muscat Blanc** using the *méthode dioise*. **Crémant de Die** is a brut version, composed of all Clairette, using *méthode traditionelle*. Finally, **Chatillon-en-Dois** is a small appellation (60 ha), producing only still wines that are generally light and made from cooler climate grapes, such as **Gamay, Aligoté,** and **Chardonnay**.

Proceeding southward, one encounters the sprawling appellation of **Grignan les Adhémar** (formerly Coteaux du Tricastin). Granted AOC status in 1973, this area was substantially developed in the 1960s by French natives of North Africa. Known as "pieds noir," the new settlers saw potential for success in planting southern-facing vineyards with traditional southern Rhône varieties. Today, Grignan les Adhémar has more than 2,800 ha under vine with maximum yields preserved at approximately 50 hl/ha. The INAO granted the appellation a name change in 2010 after two years of petitioning by local producers who feared that the name "Tricastin" held negative connotations. In 2008, the Tricastin nuclear plant accidentally leaked uranium into surrounding areas—nearby vineyards were tested for radioactivity and declared safe.

Situated on the west bank of the Rhône in the Ardèche department, opposite Grignan les Adhémar, is the **Côtes du Vivarais**. This large area with 700 ha under vine became a VDQS in 1962 and was awarded the Appellation d'Origine Contrôlée in 1999. Given its mainly limestone soil and comparatively cooler climate, some cooperatives within the Côtes du Vivarais have been successful in planting non-traditional grape varieties, such as **Chardonnay**. The majority of wine produced here is red and made with traditional varieties such as **Grenache, Syrah, Cinsault,** and **Carignan**. The white wines produced here are typically made from **Clairette** and **Grenache Blanc**.

Multiple communes often form larger, generic appellations such as Côtes du Rhône AOC. A relatively frequent occurrence is a single commune being elevated to its own appellation status, thus enhancing its prestige. **Vinsobres** was elevated to AOC status in 2005, producing red wines from at least 50% Grenache, 25% Syrah and/or Mourvèdre, and maximum of 25% other grape varieties.

Another such commune, now appellation, is **Rasteau** (elevated in 2010). Nestled in the heart of the Côtes du Rhône appellation, on the east bank of the river, Rasteau is known for fairly rustic reds, to a lesser degree for rosé, and to a still lesser degree for whites. Rasteau may be labeled as such or have "Rasteau" affixed to the "Côtes du Rhône" label. What Rasteau is probably best known for is its production of **Grenache-based** (at least 90% under appellation law) *vin doux naturel*. The Rasteay Vin Doux Naturel AOC was established in 1944 (See the fortified wine section for more detailed information.)

Like Rasteau, **Gigondas** was once a commune within the Côtes du Rhône AOC—though it was elevated to AOC status nearly 40 years earlier in 1971. This appellation is known primarily for red wine produced from the traditional varieties, with **Grenache** dominating (60-80%). With just over 1,200 ha under vine, Gigondas produces rugged, sometimes age-worthy reds, with small quantities of memorable rosé (approximately 7% of the total production) and no whites. Arguably the second most important appellation in the *Meridionales*, Gigondas benefits from regulations regarding maximum yields similar to those of Châteauneuf-du-Pape (35 hl/ha). The soil composition here ranges from gravel and clay to sand and gravel to limestone and splintered rock. Not surprisingly, the vineyards of Gigondas are situated diversely—along plains, lower-altitude terraces, and sloped hillsides.

Just a few miles south of Gigondas on the east bank of the river is the appellation **Vacqueyras**. This is the third commune to come out of the much larger Côtes du Rhône appellation and be awarded its own AOC status (1990). With roughly 1,450 ha under vine, Vacqueyras is subject to maximum yield regulations similar to those of its neighbor, Gigondas. Red wine represents the vast majority (approximately 95%) of production, with Grenache leading the way (although not as predominately as in Gigondas). In Vacqueyras, **Grenache** generally comprises at least 50% of most blends, with the rest consisting of **Syrah, Cinsault,** and **Mourvèdre**. However, given the comparative lack of diversity in the terroir of Vacqueyras and the relatively consistent red sandy soil, the wines of this AOC tend toward a monolithic style—resembling a highly concentrated Côtes du Rhône Villages, without the grace and finesse of Gigondas.

East of Vacqueyras is the only AOC in the *Meridionales* that grows the **Muscat Blanc** grape, **Beaumes-de-Venise**. This appellation, which produces the only still, sweet white wine from the Rhône Valley apart from the extremely rare *Vin de Paille* (a sweet wine in the northern Rhône, mainly Hermitage, made from dried **Marsanne** and **Roussanne**), also has plantings of traditional red grapes. Its fame and fortune, however, are derived from the production of the *vin doux naturel* known as **Muscat Beaumes-de-Venise**, a luscious, golden-hued wine generally fortified at 21% alcohol.

West of Beaumes-de-Venise lies the most well known and prestigious of all *Meridionales* appellations, **Châteauneuf-du-Pape**. More than 3,000 ha are under vine in this relatively flat appellation where, in its embrace of tradition, yields are kept to a maximum of 35 hl/ha, and chaptalization is not permitted. Winemakers in Châteauneuf-du-Pape range tremendously with regard to technique, grape varieties employed in their blends, technology used, and—most significantly—quality of their final products. Methods range from traditional, as in Château de Beaucastel, where all 13 permitted grape varieties are blended, to an increasingly popular emphasis on modern techniques like carbonic maceration—a tactic used by wine makers to produce wines that are more accessible in their youths. The use of carbonic maceration represents a departure from the traditionally rich and highly-extracted wines that would

### The Châteauneuf 13

Grenache
(including Grenache Blanc)

Syrah

Mourvèdre

Cinsault

Muscardin

Counoise

Vaccarese

Terret Noir

Clairette

Bourboulenc

Roussanne

Picpoul

Picardan

require five to six years of patience from consumers, to easier and more-forward wines designed to be purchased and consumed within two to four years of the vintage.

Châteauneuf-du-Pape can be produced from a blend of 13 permitted varieties. Blends range from Château de Beaucastel, which generally uses 30% Grenache in its blend, to Le Vieux Donjon, employing 80% Grenache, 10% Cinsault, and 10% Syrah, to the celebrated Château Rayas, which uses Grenache as the sole variety in its Châteauneuf-du-Pape. Winemakers also prize the various soils that characterize the diversity of this appellation—heat-retaining pebbles, known as *galettes*, that tend to cover red clay alluvial soils are cherished by some, whereas sand, chalk, and gravel are the favorites of others. It should be noted that although red wine dominates the production of Châteauneuf-du-Pape at approximately 96%, there is a small but significant number of white wines produced, notably a Roussanne-based Châteauneuf-du-Pape from Château de Beaucastel and a Clairette-dominated Châteauneuf-du-Pape from Château Rayas.

Traveling back over to the west bank of the river, we encounter two appellations known for rosé wines. **Tavel** contains soils that are clay-based with substantial levels of heat-retaining stones that lend a relatively full texture to its Grenache-based rosé. With almost 950 ha under vine, Tavel experiences levels of extremely high ripeness in its **Grenache** and **Cinsault** grapes, and as a result must mandate a maximum alcohol level in its rosés of 13.5%.

While Tavel commands some of the world's steepest prices for its rosé, neighboring **Lirac** produces a diverse array of wines at more reasonable prices. In addition to rosé, Lirac makes **Grenache**-dominated reds and **Clairette**-based whites. Unlike Tavel, but similar to Gigondas and Châteauneuf-du-Pape, Lirac imposes maximum yield restrictions of 35 hl/ha.

Across the river, on the east bank and to the south, are two considerably extensive appellations: the **Côtes du Ventoux** and the **Côtes du Luberon**. As with the more northern Grignan les Adhémar, these appellations have received relatively recent elevations to AOC status. Elevated in 1973, the Côtes du Ventoux with roughly 6,400 ha under vine is known for the beneficial presence of Mont Ventoux, which provides some degree of relief from le Mistral as well as the occasionally oppressive Mediterranean climate. Almost immediately to the south, with 3,300 ha planted, is the Côtes du Luberon. Both appellations share a similar limestone-based soil composition and nearly identical grape varieties (**Grenache, Syrah,** and **Cinsault** for the red and rosé wines and **Grenache Blanc, Clairette, Bourboulenc, Marsanne, Roussanne,** and **Ugni Blanc** for the white wine). Two key distinctions in the Côtes du Luberon lie in its increased emphasis on white wine production and the proliferation of single variety wines, sold as declassified Vin de Pays du Vaucluse.

Costières du Gard AOC is designated for wines that are produced in the area between the ancient city of Nîmes and the western Rhône delta. Formerly of the Languedoc region, its wines stylistically resemble more the Rhône's, and so it was made an administrative part of the Rhône Wine Committee. It earned AOC status in 1986 and three years later in 1989 the appellation's name was changed to **Costières de Nimes AOC** to avoid any confusion with Vin de Pays du Gard, a more generic wine from the area. The majority of the wine produced here is red and is made from **Grenache** (must make up 25% of the blend) and **Carignan** (can comprise up to 40%). **Syrah** is being planted to replace the Carignan, which is slowly being phased out.

Finally, there is the simple **Côtes du Rhône** appellation. This AOC is far and away the most prolific producer of Rhône wine, at nearly two million hectoliters and more than 200 million bottles per year. With more than 37,000 ha under vine, Côtes du Rhône encompasses massive plantings on both sides of the Rhône in the *Meridionales*, as well as substantial vineyard sites in the *Septentrionales*. In the north, *négociants* mostly create blends that are **Syrah**-dominated and have a tendency to be slightly richer than the typical Côtes du Rhône offering. Throughout the Rhône, the permissible varieties for Côtes du Rhône include every variety legally accepted in the blends of Châteauneuf-du-Pape, with the addition of **Viognier** and **Carignan**. In the south, **Grenache**, often with the utilization of full or semi-carbonic maceration, is the premier choice for Côtes du Rhône blends.

Distinct from the Côtes du Rhône AOC, **Côtes du Rhône Villages** requires lower maximum yields (42 hl/ha versus 50 hl/ha) and mandates higher minimum alcohol content, thus insuring a degree of richness and texture seldom found in the simpler Côtes du Rhône. With more than 10,000 ha under vine, Côtes-du-Rhône-Villages permits 17 of the best villages within the appellation to affix their commune name to the label of the wine.

# PROVENCE

| AREA UNDER VINE | 26,966 hectares |
|---|---|
| GRAPE VARIETIES | |
| RED | Grenache, Carignan, Cinsault, Mourvèdre, Syrah, and Cabernet Sauvignon |
| WHITE | Ugni Blanc, Clairette, Sémillon, Grenache Blanc, Sauvignon Blanc, and Bourboulenc |
| CLIMATE | Mediterranean with hot, dry summers and warm, wet winters. Region receives a lot of sun. Le Mistral winds influence the region. |
| SOIL | Vineyards closest to the sea are planted in mostly limestone, schist, and quartz with those planted farther inland containing clay and pebbly sand. |

## HISTORY

The practice of making wine in Provence is ancient. The Greeks planted vines here in the 6th century BC and the Romans during the 2nd century BC produced wine here that was good enough to ship back to Rome. Provincia, as it was called long ago, would languish for many centuries in relative viticultural obscurity, being fought over by forces as disparate as the Saracens, Carolingians, the Holy Roman Empire, the rulers of Toulouse, Catalans, and Savoy. However, in the 19th century the area came under the control of Sardinia, which proved to have a direct affect on its wine making. It was not until the 20th century that Provence at last emerged as a remarkably diverse and serious wine region.

## GEOGRAPHY, CLIMATE, AND SOIL

Provence is tucked away in the far southeastern corner of France, with the Rhône Valley to its north, the Mediterranean to its south, Nice to its east, and Languedoc to its west. The region has a classic Mediterranean climate, with hot dry summers and warm, wet winters. Provence is also fortunate to receive a great deal of sunlight—up to 3,000 hours a year. The aggressive wind from the north, le Mistral, plays an important role in helping dry the grapes after an occasional soaking rainfall. The soil in the region varies depending on a vineyard's proximity to the ocean. Inland growing areas are predominantly clay and pebbly sand, while those closer to the water are composed of limestone, schist, and quartz.

## WINE REGIONS

**Côtes de Provence** is easily the most substantial and significant appellation in Provence, with approximately 20,000 ha under vine. Much like the Côtes du Rhône, this region consists of many vast tracts of noncontiguous vineyards, producing wines from numerous terroirs and diverse microclimates. The majority of wine produced in Côtes de Provence (75% of the region's total production) is dry, generally undistinguished rosé. The typical blend includes **Grenache, Cinsault,** and occasionally, a variety indigenous to Provence known as **Tibouren**, which can lend an earthy quality to rosé wines. In addition, most Côtes de Provence rosés must contain a unique ingredient, *saignée* wine, which is essentially run-off juice from grapes that have been recently pressed. The addition of the *saignée* is considered valuable in imparting the characteristic lighter color and juicier texture so common in Provencal rosé.

Awarded full AOC status in 1993, the **Coteaux Varois** has roughly 2,200 ha under vine, with the majority used to produce rosé wine. Roughly 20% of production is devoted to red wines made from a blend of the traditional regional varieties—**Grenache, Cinsault, Syrah, Mourvèdre, Cabernet Sauvignon, Carignan,** and **Tibouren.** Curiously, white wines produced in the Coteaux Varois are a blend of the same grapes from the Côtes de Provence—**Clairette, Ugni Blanc, Rolle,** and **Bourboulenc**—but with the lawful addition of **Grenache Blanc**.

To the west of the Coteaux Varois lies **Coteaux d'Aix-en-Provence,** an expansive appellation with approximately 4,100 ha under vine. As is the case in the Côtes de Provence, dry rosé dominates, with winemakers using essentially the same grape varieties, with the addition of local **Counoise** for both rosé and red wines.

**Les Baux de Provence** is a tiny sub-region of the Coteaux d'Aix-en-Provence at its northwestern edge. Warmer and slightly wetter than its former parent appellation to the east, "Les Baux" is subject to fairly rigid viticultural regulations. Red wines, which comprise four-fifths of the total output, must be composed of at least 60% of **Grenache, Mourvèdre, and Syrah,** with other regional grapes completing the blend. Les Baux produces no white wine, so the remaining one-fifth of production consists only of rosé, in which **Cinsault** replaces **Mourvèdre** as the principal grape in the blend.

The remainder of Provence's wine producing area is composed of four small appellations. Generally considered to be the most serious and prosperous of all the winemaking areas of Provence, **Bandol** is a small seaside region 30 miles southeast of Marseille. With approximately 1,300 ha under vine, the red wines of Bandol make up nearly two-thirds of the total production. These reds are arguably the noblest and most individualistic expression of the **Mourvèdre** grape, which must comprise at least 50% of the blend and age a minimum of 18 months in cask.

The Cap Canaille, one of the highest cliffs in France, fortuitously protects the appellation of **Cassis** from the harsh Mistral winds. Located on the Mediterranean, with 175 ha under vine, Cassis produces mostly white wines using **Clairette, Ugni Blanc, Marsanne,** and **Sauvignon Blanc.** As in Bandol, the primary grape for the reds and rosés is **Mourvèdre.**

Almost due north, located in the hills of Aix-en-Provence, is the microscopic appellation of **Palette.** With only 20 ha under vine, the wine production in Palette is fiercely traditional. It is dominated by the Rougier family–controlled Château Simone, which produces 80% of Palette wine. Rich, full-bodied reds, lush rosés, and to a lesser extent, aromatic whites, all employing the standard indigenous grape varieties, are the trademarks of Château Simone, which essentially shuns modern viticultural techniques in favor of barrel maturation in older wood.

Located in the hills above Nice, in the upper reaches of the Var Valley, is the tiny appellation of **Bellet** with 31 ha under vine. Bellet produces essentially equal quantities of red, white, and rosé wine, although not from the grape varieties typical for the rest of Provence. Its uniquely cooler climate favors whites produced from **Rolle** and **Chardonnay**. Reds are often a blend of **Grenache, Cinsault,** and a little known variety of the south called **Folle Noir**. In the production of rosé, the region's proximity to northern Italy becomes a significant factor. Often these wines are produced from the **Braquet** grape, known in Piedmont as **Brachetto**. It is a light, aromatic red grape, occasionally used to produce sparkling wine under the Brachetto d'Acqui DOCG.

# Languedoc-Roussillon

By Jamal Rayyis

| Latitude | 42.5-44°N |
|---|---|
| Area Under Vine | 270,000 hectares |
| Volume Produced | 12,900,900 hectoliters / year |
| Red | 69% |
| White | 13% |
| Rosé | 18% |
| Grape Varieties: Mediterranean, international, and unique, local varieties | |
| Red | Carignan, Grenache Noir, Syrah, Mourvèdre, Cinsault, Cabernet Sauvignon, Cabernet Franc, Merlot, Pinot Noir |
| White | Piquepoul Blanc, Vermentino (Rolle), Muscat à Petits-Grains, Muscat d'Alexandrie, Macabeu, Mauzac, Marsanne, Roussanne, Clairette, Bourboulenc, Grenache Blanc, Grenache Gris, Viognier, Terret Gris, Terret Blanc, Chasan, Chardonnay, Chenin Blanc |
| Climate | The climate is Mediterranean with many microclimates scattered throughout. |
| Soil | Exceptionally varied, with patches of difference throughout. Predominantly clay/limestone, schist, gravel |

The Languedoc-Roussillon is, quite possibly, France's most anarchic wine region. Its *vignerons* are France's most rebellious, both in terms of their political and social activism. Protests demanding government assistance or against the importation of bulk wines from other places are not uncommon. As is the propensity of some winemakers to ignore official regulations and just make the kind of wines they like. Within the same commune, one will find multi-generation producers growing their grapes beyond permitted yields who sell everything to a local co-op, next to passionate practitioners of biodynamics plowing their soils with the aid of donkeys. This restlessness comes in the face of being France's oldest (with Provence) viticultural region, dating back to the sixth century BC. The Languedoc-Roussillon is also France's (indeed, the world's) largest wine region. Truly, the region is a work in progress.

For decades, the region was known for supplying vast quantities of inexpensive *vin ordinaire*. The wine was so pallid that it had to be beefed up by more powerful wines from North Africa before quenching the thirst of workers in an increasingly industrial France. Demands for better quality wine—especially after France cut purchases of North African wines after Algeria won its independence in 1962— forced the region's producers to rethink their approach. But change took time. Only a fraction of Languedoc-Roussillon sub-regions could claim hallmark AOC status by the end of the 1970s. More than half the region's 40-odd AOCs (some are in the process of being defined) were designated no earlier than the 1980s; seven created since the beginning of the millennium.

Indeed, in the past quarter century, a number of iconoclastic vintners have gone their own way entirely, producing superlative wines in violation of AOC/AOP protocols. Born from sin, these wines were forced to assume lowly Vin de Pays or Vin de Table status, regardless of the fact that some are among the most special wines from the region. And, one of them, Mas de Daumas Gassac, can reasonably be said to have launched the quality renaissance in the region.

High quality and innovation have long been a part of the Languedoc-Roussillon. **Vins doux naturels** (VDN) was first articulated in Montpellier by the Catalan researcher Arnaud de Villeneuve in the late thirteenth century—three centuries before Port wines came into being. Limoux documents (dated 1531) show the oldest, deliberate, production of sparkling wines; predating any stars allegedly tasted by Champagne's Dom Perignon by 150 years. These processes have been kept alive by sweet wines such as Muscat de Frontignan and Banyuls, or sparklers such as Blanquette de Limoux, both long recognized for their excellence.

Because of its large size and diverse terrains and microclimates, the Languedoc-Roussillon is uniquely able to produce commercially significant quantities of all wine types: dry and sweet whites, dry and sweet reds, and sparkling wines, usually for modest prices. Beyond allowing a sommelier or wine buyer to fulfill certain needs within budget, the Languedoc-Roussillon constantly offers surprises. As an ancient region that has been reinventing itself in the last three decades, there are always new producers who are doing things differently than expected—showcasing a forgotten grape variety, applying an ancient method, all for discovery.

# HISTORY

Winemaking in the Languedoc-Roussillon dates back more than two millennia; and there is a dispute as to how close it goes to three. What is known is that Greek settlers were in the wine trade there from at least the sixth century BC; and the Romans expanded production from their provincial capital at Narbo (Narbonne) in the second century BC. After the fall of Rome in the early fourth century AD, viticulture was expanded by the Church—using wine both for spiritual rituals and the rather earthly purpose of making money. Vineyards expanded around monasteries and abbeys. Over time, noted differences between wines from these different religious institutions created a sense of identity, and a nascent appellation system.

Remove the hyphen between Languedoc and Roussillon, and one finds two different regions. In fact, it might be said that the two represent a minimum of three different cultures or identities; sometimes intermingled, sometimes conjoined, sometimes at odds. The eastern part of the Languedoc, the *département of* Gard, is distinctly Provençal. Farther west, in the center, is the land of "oc," the Occitan word for "yes" that gives the Languedoc (Language of Oc) its name. In the far western corner of the region, on the Spanish border, is the département of Pyrénées-Orientales, the Catalan zone of France known as "Roussillon."

These distinct identities have influenced the manner of wines from each zone. The wines of the Gard are very much a part of the Rhône River region, to which it also belongs. Indeed, several administratively Languedocian appellations such as Tavel, Lirac, and Costières de Nîmes, are conventionally considered part of the southern Rhône rather than the Languedoc. Depending on the subregion, the wines of the Languedocian heartland can be Rhône-like, Bordeaux-like, Burgundy and Champagne-like, or even Italian in profile. Those of Roussillon show a distinct resemblance to wines of Spanish Catalonia.

Given the size of the Languedoc-Roussillon, its proximity to Spain, Italy, other parts of the Mediterranean basin, and of course, other parts of France, it isn't surprising that different parts of the hyphenated region have somewhat different historical and cultural experiences. The easternmost portion, in the département of Gard, is Provençal culture and part of the southern Rhône River valley. The installation of a papal court at Avignon in 1309 guaranteed a large market for the region's wines.

In contrast, the Languedoc heartland farther west was the center of the **Cathar** religious movement, which challenged the hegemony of the Roman Catholic Church in the eleventh to thirteenth centuries. The Church declared the movement heretical and called for a crusade against it. Various forces were raised against the Cathars, who were suppressed by the mid-thirteenth century through vicious warfare and inquisition. The conflict devastated the region, killing thousands and ruining the economy for years to come.

Because of a political and religious quarantine and other insecurities caused by warfare against the Cathars, Languedocian merchants were unable to bring their wines or other produce to France or to other markets in Europe without the expense of sailing around Spain. As pro-Cathar leaders were decimated, the resulting power vacuum was filled by James I of Aragon. Signing the Treaty of Corbeil with Louis IX of France in 1258, James (who was born in Montpellier) withdrew some claims against the French crown. This consolidated Roussillon and parts of the Languedoc, including Montpellier, under Catalan suzerainty. Other parts of the Languedoc such as Carcassonne and Béziers went to the French crown. Regardless, the resulting stability helped revive the wine industry.

Research in Montpellier by one of James II's (son of James I) subjects, the **Catalan alchemist Arnaud de Villeneuve**, discovered the process of ***mutage***. Mutage preserves the natural sweetness of a wine by halting the conversion of grape sugars to alcohol by the addition of a spirit part of the way through the fermentation process. The spirit suffocates the yeasts, conserving residual sugars. Villeneuve received a patent for his method in 1299, launching the ***vin doux naturel*** industry in the Languedoc-Roussillon. Less susceptible to spoilage during transport, *vins doux naturels* could be shipped to markets over longer distances.

The Catalan connection to the region cannot be overstated. Roussillon is France's *Pays Catalanes*, and did not formally become a part of France until The Treaty of the Pyrenees in 1659. More than any other part of France, "northern Catalonia," as Roussillon is sometimes called, absorbed and applied many of the technologies of the Moors who ruled large parts of Iberia until the fifteenth century. Much of Villeneuve's research was based on Arab sources; the **alembic still**—a simple distillation apparatus essential for making spirits for mutage— was an Arab invention that Villeneuve is credited with bringing to France.

The seventeenth century brought perhaps a more significant development to the Languedoc-Roussillon: the building of the **Canal du Midi**. Completed in 1681, the canal connected the Mediterranean to the Atlantic, facilitating trade and other exchanges between the Languedoc and other parts of France. In theory, the canal allowed Languedoc wines to be transported to Atlantic ports for distribution to Britain and northern Europe. In reality, protectionists from Bordeaux at the Atlantic end of the waterway restricted access until 1776. Ironically, exchanges between the Languedoc and Bordeaux brought Atlantic grapes to the Languedoc, especially in the northwestern corner of the region in the modern appellations of Cabardès, Malepère, and Limoux. To this day, these three appellations require some percentage of Bordeaux-variety grapes in their red wines.

In the mid-seventeenth century, a surplus of Languedoc wine (and plummeting prices for it) was seen as an opportunity by entrepreneurs —who distilled it into brandy. Eventually, more than one thousand distilleries were installed in the Languedoc. The spirit was sold throughout the region, other parts of France, and exported to northern Europe. Even a group of Louis XIV's financiers got into the business, setting up a brandy exporting firm in Sète from 1676 to 1689. Sète became a major spirits exporter in its day, though the Canal du Midi mentioned above offered easy Atlantic access as well. Growing grapes of undistinguished quality— preferred for brandy— was remarkably easy on the fertile Languedocian plain. Previously, vineyards were mostly restricted to hillsides, and plains were used to grow grain. But high demand for inexpensive raw materials encouraged conversion to large grape plantations, especially of high-yielding, high-potential-alcohol grapes.

The transportation revolution accelerated in the nineteenth century with the building of railways connecting the Midi (south of France) with rapidly growing urban population centers in the north. Demand for brandy and inexpensive wine increased enormously, resulting in the vine plantings doubling in Hérault between 1850 and 1870.

This boom overlapped with the disaster of phylloxera, which was first recorded in France in 1863, in the outskirts of Languedoc's eastern edge. By the mid-1870s huge portions of vineyards had been destroyed without an easy remedy. The only vineyards spared were some on schist soils that were inhospitable to the pest and were often located in terrains too steep for mass exploitation. There was a solution to the crisis: replanting vines grafted to disease-resistant American rootstock. But, this endeavor was too expensive for all but the largest, best capitalized, wine growers. That is, the ones on the plains supplying the brandy industry. As a result, more encouragement was given to planting highly productive varieties like Aramon, Alicante and Carignan vines that could produce over 150 hl/ha (10 US tons/acre).

Initially, high production restored a measure of prosperity to the region. But, over-supply throughout France collapsed wine prices. By the beginning of the twentieth century, pressed by exploitative land owners, workers took to the streets creating nascent labor unions. A series of strikes and protests, which eventually also drew support from large producers suffering from low prices, culminated in legislation to protect distilleries, guarantee a certain level of quality, and to reduce some of the excess land under vine. Vitally, too, these actions facilitated the creation of wine cooperatives, which had profound effects, positive and negative, on industry developments in the last part of the twentieth century.

But, despite official encouragement to cut yields and to improve quality initiatives— such as subsidized vine pulling schemes and conversion to higher quality grape varieties—the mentality toward cutting yields and improving quality was slow to take. French wine consumption continued to rise, past 130 liters (35 gallons!) per person per year, well into the 1950s, inhibiting the move from quantity to quality. And, imports of hardy wine from French-ruled North Africa (starting from the late nineteenth century) helped ameliorate the insipid nature of much of the wine coming from the Midi.

Inevitably, crisis returned. By the beginning of the 1960s, France had entered a period of prosperity that lasted a generation. People were demanding better wine. And, Algerian independence in 1962 ended mass imports of North African wine that had previously masked the poor quality of production from the Languedoc. As a result, the region went into economic decline, and the French government took measures to improve quality. Economic incentives were given to rip out excessive, poor-quality vineyards; to encourage conversion to better quality vines; or to diversify to other crops.

Of vital importance, too, was the establishment of Appellation d'Origine Contrôlée standards that demarcated terroir, defined permitted grape varieties, and established production limits. Standards were established on a region by region basis starting in 1936. In the Languedoc, only one appellation, Muscat de Frontignan was granted AOC status from the start. Indeed, many regions that have AOC status today did not have the capacity to meet all requirements immediately, and went through a sort of undefined "probationary" period during which they were classified *Vin Délimité de Qualité Supérieur* (VDQS). Most of these eventually became AOCs, including quite well-known appellations such as St. Chinian (1982), Minervois (1985) and Côteaux du Languedoc (1985), portions of which are considered especially excellent. It should be stressed that though small, individual producers from these areas receive much of the positive attention, appellation-centered cooperatives played an essential role in defining a region's identity, assuring a consistent level of quality, and for advocating on behalf of an appellation's identity.

AOC-designated wine is only part of the story in the Languedoc. Indeed, the vast majority of wine produced in the region is designated Vin de Pays (VdP)—6,000,000 hectoliters in 2008, compared to just under 2,000,000 hectoliters of AOC-designated wine. The designation was adopted in 1979 to provide standards for wines made outside AOC protocols. (Overwhelmingly, VdP wines have less character than AOC wines.) However, more than a few iconoclastic vintners from the region have taken advantage of the more permissive regulations to make the type of wine they want, rather than wines they are mandated to. Such was the case with the Guibert family's wine, Mas de Daumas Gassac. The wine was made with unauthorized grape varieties, including Cabernet Sauvignon, and grown in an undesignated zone in the highlands of Hérault. Initially overlooked, if not scorned, the first vintage in 1978 (which, being made before the VdP decrees, was designated Vin de Table) garnered superlative praise in 1982 from leading wine critics in France and the UK. The plaudits caused a number of skeptics to rethink their notion of Languedoc-Roussillon wine, and tickled the enthusiasms of several young winemakers with more talent than money who recognized the potential from an undervalued land.

# CLASSIFICATIONS

The AOC system remains the basis of the classification system in the Languedoc-Roussillon. Reforms and harmonization to European Union standards in 2007 were adopted in 2009. Among these changes are the replacement of the label Appellation d'Origine Contrôlée (AOC), with **Appellation d'Origine Protégée (AOP).** Technically speaking, AOC wines no longer exist. However, producers may choose to use "AOC" (or Appellation d'Origine Contrôlée) rather than AOP until some yet undetermined time in the future. Regions formerly designated Vin Délimité de Qualité Superieur (VDQS) can be elevated to AOP status if they agree to certain protocols, or they may become IGPs. The category Vin de Pays (VdP) has been changed to **Indication Geographique Protégée (IGP)**. Wines previously designated Vin de Table will be without geographical designation and now are to be designated **Vin de France**. Unlike the past, these wines are permitted to note vintage and grape variety on their labels.

Perhaps more than any other region in France, the Languedoc-Roussillon is still defining itself. Appellations formerly appended to larger ones are being given their own recognition. For example, Côteaux du Languedoc-Pic St. Loup AOC will become Pic St. Loup AOP. So, too, will other regions hyphenated to Côteaux du Languedoc, such as Grés de Montpellier or Picpoul de Pinet, which are becoming distinct AOPs. And, decisions have yet to be made about some likely candidates for promotion, such as Côteaux du Languedoc-Montpeyroux, which is technically a commune of Côteaux du Languedoc-Terraces de Larzac, despite the distinctive profile of Montpeyroux wines. In fact, some Languedoc producers, who have a touch of anarchy in them, have taken to labeling wines as they please. The proud winemakers of Montpeyroux, for instance, never put the word "Terraces du Larzac" on the label, calling themselves, Montpeyroux-Côteaux du Languedoc. Provided producers don't go too far, regulators are inclined to look the other way. Also, the Languedoc-Roussillon can now officially be referred to as "Languedoc."

Another large change is the creation of a quality pyramid for AOP wines that includes categories of Grand Cru for special appellation terroirs, Grand Vin, and a general Languedoc category, created by the local wine governing authority, the ***Conseil Interprofessionnel des Vins du Languedoc*** **(CIVL)**. The system is in the process of being implemented, and while intended for clarity, some confusion remains. It is important to note that this designation of "Grand Cru" has not yet been approved by the *Institut National des Appellations d'Origine* (INAO), France's governing body for appellations. It is possible that the INAO will forbid the use of "Grand Cru" in the Languedoc entirely, as the process to designate Languedoc Grands Crus is not the same as that used in other parts of France.

Created by the CIVL and effective the 2011 vintage, the scheme works as follows:

**Grand Cru du Languedoc**   On the top of the pyramid the following appellations are considered superior to others: Minervois-La Livinière, Corbières-Boutenac, Saint Chinian-Roquebrun, Saint Chinian-Berlou, Pic Saint Loup, Terrasses du Larzac, La Clape, Pézenas, Grès de Montpellier, and Limoux Blanc tranquille (still).

Wines classified as Grand Cru du Languedoc must:

- Be made from vines harvested at ≤ 45 hl/ha (3 tons/acre) for reds and 50 hl/ha for whites
- Be bottled within the cru
- Be aged for a minimum of twelve months for reds, six months for whites
- Command a retail price of at least 10 euros per 750 ml bottle

**Grand Vin du Languedoc**   The middle tier includes many of the Languedoc's most classic appellations : Cabardès, Corbières, Faugères, Malepère, Minervois, St. Chinian, Limoux rouge, all the sweet Muscats (Mireval, Lunel, Frontignan, St-Jean de Minervois) and appellations or terroir previously hyphenated Côteaux du Languedoc not elevated to Grand Cru status—Picpoul de Pinet, Clairette du Languedoc, Sommières, Terrasses de Beziers, Quatourze, Cabrières, St. Saturnin, Montpeyroux, la Méjanelle, St. Georges d'Orques, St. Christol, St. Drézery and Verargues.

Wines classified Grand Vin du Languedoc must :

- Adhere to the regulations of their individual appellations
- Command a retail price of between 3.5 to 10 euros per 750 ml bottle

**Languedoc**   This basic category is reserved for so-called "easy-drinking," mass-market wines by large producers.

These wines must :

- Adhere to regional protocols regarding grape variety and harvest yields
- Command a retail price of between 3 to 4 euros per 750 ml bottle

Sparkling wines from Limoux are to be classified on a case-by-case basis following the pricing and production guidelines outlined above.

While there is a certain simple elegance to the pyramid, critics of the scheme note the anomaly that certain exceptional producers in appellations not designated "Grand Cru" are superior to many and possibly most producers within the Grand Cru appellations. Moreover, the "Grand Cru" system fails to recognize world class Vin de Pays/IGP wines from the region, such as Mas de Daumas Gassac or Grange des Pères.

The wines of Roussillon are not included in this scheme, though a category of Grand Cru has existed in Banyuls since 1962, and particular communes within the Côtes du Roussillon and Côtes du Roussillon Villages have official recognition as being unique, such as Côtes du Roussillon-Les Aspres, Côtes du Roussillon Villages-Caramany, Côtes du Roussillon Villages-Lesquerde, Côtes du Roussillon Villages-Latour de France, and Côtes du Roussillon Villages-Tautavel.

Other changes in recent years, up to the present, included defined minimal requirements for each appellation, including blending requirements of each wine.  Four basic requirements, often exceeded by particular appellation rules include the following:

- A minimum of two designated grape varieties (exceptions are made for particular AOPs)
- Basic yield: 50hl/ha for reds; 60hl/ha for whites
- Wine alcohol content > 11.5%

- Maturity of grapes harvested: 198g/l sugar in red (190 for whites)

Regulations for Languedoc's Rhône Valley appellations located within the *département* of the Gard, such as Tavel, Lirac and Costières de Nîmes are available in the Rhône Valley chapter. These appellations are governed by the Inter-Rhône agency.

Languedoc appellations are governed by the *Conseil Interprofessionel des Vins du Languedoc* (CIVL). Roussillon appellations are overseen by **the *Conseil Interprofessionel des Vin du Roussillon* (CIVR).** A regional public-private marketing group, Sud de France Export, represents wines from all three jurisdictions.

# TERROIR

The Languedoc-Roussillon is a Mediterranean climate, par excellence; hot in summer, moderate in winter, with nearly year-round sunshine. But stretching more than 170 miles from its easternmost point in the Rhône River Valley to the point France touches Spain on the Mediterranean, and almost 80 miles inland, the Languedoc-Roussillon is home to dozens of microclimates with multiple terroirs and soil types. Many of these are described in the table below. The region's best quality wines are generally made from vineyards on the slopes of mountain ranges that rise almost immediately from the seacoast in parts of Roussillon to no more than a dozen miles inland in central Languedoc. Elevations ranging from 200 to almost 1000 meters (650 to 3250 feet) moderate daytime temperatures somewhat and lower the temperature by as many as 30° F at night, offering vines relief from the sun's damning heat.

So, too, do the region's **five wind systems**, which not only cool temperatures and ward away insects, but also, help prevent molds and funguses from developing in vineyards. **The Tramontane** blows from the northwest, bringing cool northern airs. **The Cers,** from the west, is cold in winter, warm in summer, but always dry. Warm and dry, too, is **the Sirocco** from the south. **The Autan** from the southeast blows cool in winter, warm in summer. And, **the Marin**, from the Mediterranean brings damp, salty air to the region. All these winds are funneled through the region's multiple valleys and canyons, and, regardless of temperature, the winds that run over Languedoc's numerous rivers have a moderating effect on an otherwise hot climate. The northwestern appellations in the Languedoc, Limoux, Malepère, and Cabardès, enjoy temperate influences of Atlantic breezes during much of the year. Not surprisingly, Atlantic grapes such as Merlot, Cabernet Sauvignon, and Cabernet Franc thrive there. The famed **Mistral** winds that bring cold air through the Rhône Valley into Provence, affects portions of the Languedoc in the Rhône River delta, particularly Costières de Nîmes and Clairette de Bellegarde.

The particulars of climate in the Languedoc-Roussillon—warm, dry, with multiple wind systems— offer clement conditions for sustainable, organic, or biodynamic viticulture. Fungicides and insecticides aren't needed in large quantities, as molds and fungi are not generally a problem. Pests, of the insect sort, anyway, are regularly blown away. One problem *vignerons,* particularly those working mountainside vineyards, worry about are pests of a different kind, hungry boars, wild goats, and deer.

The Roussillon region is especially mountainous. Banyuls and Collioure, which nearly completely overlap, are well known for their exceptionally steep vineyards planted on terraced mountains of nearly pure schist. Other parts of Roussillon show similar conditions, as do the mountainous portion of Fitou, marking essentially, the point of hyphenation between Languedoc and Roussillon. In Languedoc proper, rugged vineyards are found in several sections of Corbières. Minervois is not so obviously steep, pushing into the shadows of the domineering Montagne Noire; its vineyards reach an altitude of 450m. Minervois La Livinière, a dry area located on a limestone plateau, is a bit lower in altitude, but it enjoys the relief of cool mountain breezes during the growing season. Its terroir is especially treasured for ***garrigue*-scented (***garrigue* = "wild herb") wines that are robust, but have polished tannin.

Though overstated in parts, the Côteaux du Languedoc openly announces its hilliness. "Côteaux" means "hillsides," with a few sub-appellations climbing high into the Cevennes Mountains against the **Massif Centrale.** This massive elevated mountainous plain occupies a whopping fifteen per cent of the country. Wines from Pic St. Loup and Montpeyroux are especially well regarded. Adjacent to some particularly steep parts of the Côteaux, but not designated an AOP zone, is the uniquely cool area around Aniane where famed Vin de Pays producers such as Mas de Daumas Gassac and La Grange des Pères call home.

Other subregions of Côteaux du Languedoc (though not every) are at considerably lower elevations. Up until Roman times, La Clape was a limestone-rich island. After waters separating it from the mainland receded, it was still limestone rich, but, also a notably dry area for most of the growing season. That is, until August, when fog from the sea blankets its vineyards, giving La Clape's wines a distinct freshness. Its white wines are particularly good. Picpoul de Pinet, occupies a stretch of sand and pebbles next to the Bassin de Thau near the port of Sète. Its wines seem to reflect the salinity of its environs, perfectly.

The far east of the Languedoc is very much part of the southern Rhône Valley. It is hot here, and its wines are very much a reflection of others from the region. One possible anomaly is found at Costières de Nîmes' **galets roulé** (large round pebble) soils that resemble some of the most dramatic parts of Châteauneuf du Pape. At night, these pebbles radiate the heat of the day, which accelerates grape ripening—unless the vineyards are close to the marshlands of the Camargue, which bring cool breezes and fog to the region at night. It is this cooling phenomenon that allows Syrah to thrive in Costières de Nîmes more easily than other parts of the southern Rhône Valley.

Extending over a large area, with multiple topographies, the soils within the Languedoc-Roussillon are exceptionally varied, with patches of difference throughout (and are also summarized in the Essential Table at the end of the chapter).

Within Roussillon, one finds schist, granite, gneiss, clay/limestone. The soil of Banyuls is predominately gray and brown schist. That of Maury, black schist. Fitou, which is composed of two non-contiguous zones shows two distinct soil types: schist in its mountainous portions and clay and limestone by the coast. The Languedoc's largest AOP, Corbières has a diversity of soil types ranging from sandstone in its northern reaches, chalk near the coast, to marl and schist in the mountains. Soils in Corbières-Boutenac are clay and limestone. Minervois shows diversity as well, limestone and pebbles are widespread, with granite and sandstone in parts. Minervois-La Livinière is largely limestone and marl. Limestone is widespread in the "Atlantic" regions of the Languedoc, mixed with clay and granite in Malpère, pebbles, granite, schist, and gneiss in Cabardès, and clay in Limoux. Faugères and bordering portions of St. Chinian are exclusively schist. So too are the AOPs of St. Chinian-Berlou and St Chinian-Roquebrun. Other parts of St. Chinian are clay and limestone and some sandstone. The hillsides appellations —what was formerly called the "Côteaux du Languedoc"—are predominantly clay and limestone, but particularities exist. Grès de Montpellier (for marketing/design purposes, Grès is very often spelled Grés, though it is pronounced "Gress" rather than "Grey" as one might assume with the accent aigu , i.e. –' é'.) is shaley limestone with round alluvium pebbles (grès) Terraces de Larzac is diverse, with sandy, stony soil, red 'ruffes' and layers of varied limestone. Soils in Sommières are stony with a mix of hard and soft limestone with marl. Pic St. Loup is clay and limestone and some limestone marl. Soils in Terrace de Bèziers are sandy marl giving way to brown limestone soil. Pézenas is sandstone alternating with schist, with gravel and stones. Cabrières is almost exclusively schist. La Clape is hard limestone, red stony clay, stones and boulders. Soils in the terraced vineyards of Quatourze are full of round pebbles. Picpoul de Pinet soils are mixed, though sand and pebbles are prominent closer to the coast. Of the Languedoc's Muscat areas, Frontignan is mostly clay and limestone soil, with limestone gravel dominating to the west and north and sandy clay-silt closer to the Mediterranean. Lunel is sandstone soil with red siliceous gravel. Mireval has limestone and clay soils. And, St. Jean de Minervois is very stony, honeycombed limestone.

## Soil

| Region | Soil |
| --- | --- |
| Côtes du Roussillon | Schist, granite, gneiss, clay/limestone |
| Côteaux du Languedoc | Predominantly clay/limestone |
| Picpoul de Pinet | Sand and pebbles, |
| La Clape | Limestone/clay |
| Costières de Nîmes | Large, round pebbles (*galets roulés*) |
| Limoux | Limestone/clay |
| Cabardès | Chalk and pebbles; granite, schist and gneiss |
| Malepère | Chalk and clay with granite |
| St. Chinian | Clay/limestone, sandstone, schist |
| Faugères | Schist |
| Fitou | Schist in hills; clay/limestone near coast |
| Corbières | Varied: sandstone in north, chalk near coast, marl and schist in the mountains |
| Minervois | Chalk and pebbles; granite and sandstone |

## Varieties

The Languedoc-Roussillon grows more than thirty grape varieties, both Mediterranean and "international." Between the plague of phylloxera and the region's renaissance starting in the 1970s, producers privileged quantity over quality, planting high-yielding grapes like Aramon, Alicante Bouschet, Chasan, and Listan, that went into vast quantities of *vin ordinaire*. Encouragement by officials and the market has driven growers to replace lower-quality, high yielding varieties with others of higher-quality, such as Grenache Noir, Grenache Blanc, Mourvèdre, Viognier, and the current darling, Syrah. Carignan Noir, the region's most widely planted grape has the distinction of being a vigorous producer when young and untrained, but can show exceptional quality as vines age, usually marked at forty years or more. Inexpensive land and easy growing conditions encouraged export-minded producers of international varietal wines to plant many of France's major varieties, including Cabernet Sauvignon, Merlot, Pinot Noir, Chardonnay, Sauvignon Blanc, and others. Most of these go into varietally-correct Vin de Pays d'Oc such as Chardonnay Vin de Pays d'Oc. These grapes have shown excellence in certain microclimates, and are even required components in some appellations. Over seventy-five percent of Languedoc wines are red.

## Red

**Carignan Noir** is the region's most widely planted local grape. A hardy variety, it stands up well to the area's heat and sometimes fierce winds, ripens easily, and can be highly productive. Carbonic maceration is often used during fermentation to soften tannins of its thick skin and enliven its fruitiness. It produces purple colored juice and its flavor profile is distinctly red fruit, with some floral notes. Considered an inferior variety by some (including officials), it is being replaced by other grapes. But, old-vine Carignan has been gaining increased favor. (46,250 ha planted/2009)

**Grenache Noir** is found throughout the region, adding power and red cherry notes to blends as well as greater aging potential. (43,800 ha/2009)

**Lledoner Pelut**, also known as "Grenache Pouilu," is closely related to Grenache Noir, but differentiated by its fuzzy leaves. It generally holds acidity better than Grenache Noir. (425 ha/2009)

**Syrah** is the region's current "it" grape. Though long permitted, Syrah is a relative newcomer with most plantings done in the last couple of decades. It thrives on the hillsides of Côteaux du Languedoc and in Costières-de-Nîmes, lending rich dark berry flavors and some smoke, though somewhat less pepperiness than one finds in the northern Rhône. (43,800 ha)

**Mourvèdre** (also, **Mataro**) is also gaining popularity, adding body, dark color, and black fruit flavors to blends. It tends to be less gamey than Mourvèdre grown in Bandol. (5300 ha)

**Cinsault** suffers like Carignan in reputation, but it very much has its charms, and its lighter color is used to good advantage in the making of rosé wines. (12,451 ha)

**Merlot, Cabernet Sauvignon** and **Cabernet Franc** (the "Atlantic grapes") are planted throughout the Languedoc. Logically, they do especially well in Atlantic-influenced sub-regions, as well as higher elevation, and cooler microclimates. (30,550 ha/19,125 ha/3640 ha)

**Pinot Noir** does quiet well near **Limoux**. Stylistically, it falls between Pinot Noir from warmer parts of Burgundy and Russian River Pinot. (1100 ha)

Other grapes grown include **Alicante Bouschet** (4450 ha), **Aramon** (2650 ha), **Côt** (387 ha), **Marselan** (1770 ha), **Aspiron, Fer Servadou,** and **Negrette**.

## WHITE

**Muscat** is the grape that most of the region's sweet, fortified wines are based on. All designated Muscat appellations except Rivesaltes require **Muscat à Pétits-Grains**, known for its small berries, citrus and peach flavors and distinctive floral notes (5665 ha planted in 2009). Rivesaltes demands that **Muscat d'Alexandrie** be blended with Pétits-Grains, the former adding more green fruit and musky herbal flavors (2560 ha). Bone-dry Muscat wines are also being made.

**Mauzac** finds its home mostly near Limoux, where it largely goes into the production of sparkling wines, notably Blanquette de Limoux. It has an appealingly rustic quality, with telltale baked apple flavors. The fuzzy white underside of its leaves inspires its synonym **Blanquette** (1180 ha).

**Macabeu**, a Catalan variety, is a late-budding grape well-suited to areas subject to late frosts, an important consideration at higher elevations. It is lightly perfumed, a touch low in acidity, but resists oxidation (2690 ha).

**Piquepoul Blanc** is the basis of Picpoul de Pinet. Grown in vineyards especially close to the Mediterranean, the variety echoes mineral-laden freshness of a sea breeze. Naturally high in acidity (its name means "lip prickler") it is the ideal companion to the oysters raised a short distance away near the port of Sète (1380 ha).

**Clairette** is most common in the Rhône valley portions of the Languedoc. It tends to be soft in acidity, but offers some light floral and apple flavors (828 ha).

**Grenache Blanc** produces full-bodied wines with some pear and citrus flavors. Surprisingly, unlike its dark-hued kin, it tends to maintain a good level of acidity (3708 ha).

**Grenache Gris** is its pink-skinned sibling, going into white wines and light-tinted rosés alike (1520 ha).

**Vermentino** (also called **Rolle** here as well) is light colored, with citrus and green almond flavors. It is balanced, but tends to be lower in acidity. (674 ha)

**Viognier, Marsanne,** and **Roussanne**, are three Rhône grapes with an increasing presence in the Languedoc. Viognier shows its typical aromas of peach and flowers, but tends to be simpler than northern Rhône versions. Roussanne lends apricot and nut flavors and good acidity. Its frequent partner Marsanne is somewhat lower in acidity, but adds honeyed notes and an attractive waxy texture. (2612 ha/530 ha/830 ha)

**Bourboulenc** (called also **Tourbat** or **Malvoisie**) makes an elegant wine with appealing aromas of citrus and smoke. It ripens late and maintains good acidity. It is required in the white wines of La Clape AOP. (181 ha)

**Chardonnay** is found throughout the region, and it has become a vital part of the white wines of Limoux where it thrives in the calcareous soils and relatively cool temperatures. It goes into sparkling and still wines alike. Limoux Chardonnay from the coolest vineyard sites can be surprisingly Burgundian in style. (11,970 ha)

**Chenin Blanc** is native to the Loire Valley, but, like Chardonnay, has found a welcoming home in the Languedoc, particularly near Limoux. Less aromatic than it is in the Loire, Languedoc Chenin adds body and fresh fruit flavors and good acidity. It is required in Crémant de Limoux. (440 ha)

**Sauvignon Blanc** is another Loire Valley grape that has found a home in Languedoc. Stylistically it falls somewhere between Loire Valley and California Sauvignon Blanc, citrusy and grassy, but exuberant like examples from New Zealand. The grape is used in Vin de Pays/IGP wines, blends and varietal. (6770 ha)

Other white grapes with a presence that usually goes unrecognized include **Terret Blanc** (1525 ha)**, Terret Gris**, **Chasan** (660 ha)**, and Carignan Blanc** (280 ha)**.**

## Summary of Requirements by AOC

| AOC | COLOR | GRAPE REQUIREMENTS | SPECIAL REQUIREMENTS |
|---|---|---|---|
| **Cabardès** | Red | 40 % min of Atlantic grapes: Merlot, Cabernet-Sauvignon, Cabernet Franc, 40% min of Mediterranean grapes: Syrah, Grenache 20% max of Cot, Fer Servadou and Cinsault. | |
| **Malepère** | Red | Combination of Atlantic and Mediterranean grapes. Main grape: Merlot (min 50%), complementary grapes, Cabernet Franc, Cot (min 20%), secondary grapes, Cabernet Sauvignon, Grenache, Cinsault. | |
| | Rosé | Main grape, Cabernet Franc (min 50%) complementary grapes: Cabernet Sauvignon, Cinsaut, Cot, Grenache, Merlot (min 20%) | |
| **Limoux** | Red | Limoux red (still wine): Merlot (50% min), Cot, Syrah Grenache (30% min), Carignan (10% max). | |
| | White | Limoux white (still wine): Mauzac (min 15%), Chardonnay, Chenin. | |
| **Limoux cont'd** | Sparkling | Blanquette de Limoux: 90% Mauzac, Chardonnay and Chenin-Blanc (max 10%) | Aging on lees min 9 months |
| | | Cremant de Limoux: Chardonnay (40% min) Chenin (20 % min), Chardonnay + Chenin (90% max). Secondary grapes: Mauzac + Pinot Noir (20% max), Pinot noir (10% max) | Aging on lees min 12 months |
| | | Blanquette de Limoux Méthode Ancestrale: Mauzac | No secondary fermentation, no disgourgement, no dosage |
| **Faugères** | Red and Rosé | Syrah, Grenache, Mourvèdre, Carignan and Cinsault | |
| | White | Roussane, Grenache blanc, Marsanne, Vermentino | |
| **St. Chinian** | Red and Rosé | Grenache, Syrah and Mourvèdre, Carignan, Cinsault, Lladoner Pelut | |
| | White | Grenache blanc, Marsanne, Roussanne, Rolle | |

| AOC | COLOR | GRAPE REQUIREMENTS | SPECIAL REQUIREMENTS |
|---|---|---|---|
| Coteaux du Languedoc (now Languedoc) | Red and Rosé | Principal grapes: Grenache Noir, Syrah and Mourvèdre (50 % min and 20% min Syrah and Mourvèdre), Cinsault and Carignan. | |
| Sub-appellations<br><br>La Clape, Terrasses de Béziers, Pézenas, Grés de Montpellier, Picpoul de Pinet, Terres de Sommières, Pic Saint Loup, Terrasses du Larzac (including Montpeyroux)<br><br>Note: By the end of 2011, these sub-appellations will be their own AOPs | | For the Pic St Loup: Syrah, black Grenache, Mourvèdre (90 % min)<br><br>For the Clape and the Grés of Montpellier: Syrah, Grenache, Mourvedre (70 % min). | |
| | Rosé | Grenache Noir (60% min), Syrah, Mourvèdre, Cinsault, Carignan | |
| | | Grenache Blanc, Clairette, Bourboulenc, Piquepoul, Roussanne, Marsanne and Rolle (70% min), Viognier (10% max). | |
| | Whites | La Clape: Bourboulenc (min 40%), Grenache Blanc, Clairette, Piquepoul<br><br>Picpoul de Pinet: 100% Piquepoul. | |
| Clairette du Languedoc | White | Clairette | |
| Corbières | Red and Rosé | Carignan 50% max, Syrah, Grenache Noir, Mourvèdre, Lledoner Pelut and Cinsault (20% for red wines, 70% for rosés). | |
| | White | Bourboulenc, Grenache Blanc, Macabeu, Clairette, Marsanne, Roussanne, Rolle or Vermentino. Terret Blanc, Picquepoul and Muscat (max 10%). | |
| Corbières-Boutenac | Red | Carignan, Grenache, Syrah, and Mourvèdre grapes. Carignan accounts for 30 to 50% of planting. The Syrah must not account for more than 30% | |
| Minervois | Red and Rosé | Syrah, Mourvèdre (min 20%). Syrah, Mourvèdre, Grenache and Lladoner Pelut (min 60%), Carignan, Cinsault, Terret, Aspiran, Piquepoul Noir for the red wines (40% max) | |

| AOC | COLOR | GRAPE REQUIREMENTS | SPECIAL REQUIREMENTS |
|---|---|---|---|
| | White | Marsanne, Roussanne, Macabeu, Bourboulenc, Clairette, Grenache, Vermentino and Muscat à Petits-Grains | |
| **Minervois La-Livinière** | Red | Min of 60% Syrah, Mourvèdre and Grenache (thus 40% min Syrah or Mourvèdre), possibly complemented using Carignan, Cinsault, Terret, Piquepoul Noir and Aspiran. | |
| **Fitou** | Red | Carignan (40% min) Grenache, Lladoner Pelut, Mourvèdre and Syrah | |
| **Muscat du Languedoc**<br><br>**Includes: Muscat de Lunel, Muscat de Mireval, Muscat de Frontignan and Muscat de St. Jean de Minervois** | White Vin Doux Naturel | Muscat à Petits-Grains | The alcohol used for mutage must be 96% by volume of wine-based spirit, in a quantity between 5 to 10% of total must volume. The final alcohol content must be between 15 and 18%. |
| **Muscat de Rivesaltes** | White Vin Doux Naturel | Blend of Muscat d'Alexandrie and Muscat à Petits Grains | |
| **Rivesaltes** | Red Vin Doux Naturel | Rivesaltes Grenat<br><br>Grenache Noir min 75%, Grenache Blanc, Grenache Gris, Macabeu, Tourbat (Malvoisie du Roussillon), Carignan Noir, Cinsault, Syrah, Listan. | Conserved in reducing conditions at least 12 months, with 3 months |
| **Rivesaltes cont'd** | | Rivesaltes Tuilés<br><br>Grenache (min 50%), Grenache Blanc, Grenache Gris, Macabeu, Tourbat (Malvoisie du Roussillon), Carignan Noir, Cinsault, Syrah, Listan | Maturation in large vats for 2 years, 3 months in bottle |
| | White Vin Doux Naturel | Rivesaltes Ambré<br><br>Grenache Blanc, Grenache Gris, Macabeu, Malvoisie du Roussillon, Muscats | Maturation for 2 years in barrels |
| | | Rivesaltes hors d'âge<br><br>The term "hors d'âge" can be added to "ambré" and "tuilé" for wines aged wine was matured 5 years. In practice it is applied for wines aged around 20 years. | |
| **Côtes du Roussillon** | Red and Rosé | Blend of three varieties, Carignan Noir, Grenache Noir, Lladoner Pelut, Cinsault, Syrah, Mourvèdre, Macabeu (only for rosé) | |

| AOC | COLOR | GRAPE REQUIREMENTS | SPECIAL REQUIREMENTS |
|---|---|---|---|
| | White | Blend of three varieties, Grenache Blanc, Grenache Gris, Macabeu, Tourbat or Malvoisie du Roussillon, Roussanne, Marsanne, Vermentino | |
| **Côtes du Roussillon Les Aspres** | Red | Blend of three varieties, Grenache Noir, Syrah, Mourvèdre et Carignan Noir | |
| **Côtes du Roussillon Villages** | Red | Blend of three varieties, Carignan Noir, Grenache Noir, Syrah, Mourvèdre | |
| **Côtes du Roussillon Villages – Caramany** | Red | Blend of three varieties, Carignan Noir, Grenache Noir, Lladoner Pelut, Syrah | |
| **Côtes du Roussillon Villages – Lesquerde** | Red | Blend of three varieties, Carignan Noir, Grenache Noir, Lladoner Pelut, Syrah | |
| **Côtes du Roussillon Villages – Latour de France** | Red | Blend of three varieties, Carignan Noir, Grenache noir, Lladoner Pelut, Syrah, Mourvèdre | |
| **Côtes du Roussillon Villages – Tautavel** | Red | Blend of three varieties, Carignan Noir, Grenache Noir, Lladoner Pelut, Syrah, Mourvèdre | |
| **Collioure** | Red and Rosé | Blend of three varieties, Grenache, Syrah, Mourvèdre<br><br>Complementary grapes: Carignan Noir, Cinsault, Grenache gris | |
| | White | Blend of three varieties, Tourbat (Malvoisie du Roussillon), Macabeu, Marsanne, Roussanne, Vermentino | |
| **Maury** | Red | Grenache Noir, Carignan et Syrah | Maury "Vendange," "Récolte" and "Vintage": Min Aging min 12 months |
| | White | Grenache Blanc et Gris, Macabeu, Malvoisie du Roussillon, Muscats d'Alexandrie, Muscat à Petits Grains. | **Maury Blancs:** Min 12 months aging<br><br>**Maury Hors d'Âge:** Five years minimal aging in an oxidative environment.<br><br>**Maury Rancio:** Wines that acquire a "Rancio" taste. |

| AOC | COLOR | GRAPE REQUIREMENTS | SPECIAL REQUIREMENTS |
|---|---|---|---|
| **Banyuls** | Red | Grenache Noir (min 50%), Grenache Gris, Lladoner Pelut | **Banyuls "traditionnels"**, aged for a few years in an oxidative environment<br>**Banyuls "Rimage"** Made in only great vintages. Wine undergoes a long maceration and bottled six to 12 months after harvest.<br><br>**Banyuls "Rimage" Mise Tardive,** elaborated on the same principle as the others, wines are matured from one to three years in tonneau or in full barrels. Analogous to Late Bottled Vintage Port. |
| | White | Grenache Blanc et Grenache Gris. | Banyuls Blanc |
| **Banyuls Grand Cru** | Red | Grenache Noir (min 75%), Grenache Gris, Lladoner Pelut | Oak aging for a min of 30 months. Made in the best years. |

# REGIONS

Five political *départements* make up the Languedoc-Roussillon. Four of these are wine regions: **Gard, Hérault, Aude, and Pyrénées-Orientales.** The fifth, Lozere, is known for its animal products.

**The Gard** starts at the left bank of the Rhône River and continues west. This region contains the famed rosé appellation of **Tavel** (AOC 1936)**,** well regarded appellations of **Lirac** (AOC 1947), **Costières de Nîmes** (1986), the white wine appellation **Clairette de Bellegarde** (1949), **Côtes de Vivarais** (1999), and several villages within the appellation Côtes du Rhône Villages. Wines from the Gard resemble those from other southern Rhône regions. Reds are generally Grenache-based, blended with Mourvèdre, Cinsault, Counoise, Carignan, and Syrah. Syrah is especially important in Costières de Nîmes. Whites are blends of Grenache Blanc, Roussanne, Marsanne, Viognier, Clairette, Bourboulenc and others. Rosé wines are famed in the region as well. Based on Grenache Noir, those from Tavel tend to be heavier in body than most. Rosés from other parts are usually lighter and based largely on Cinsault.

Moving west, into **Hérault** and centered on the hills encircling Montpellier is **Côteaux du Languedoc** (AOC 1985), which is itself broken down into thirteen named terroir-based sub-appellations, some of which contain named communes themselves. These sub-appellations are:

1. Grès de Montpellier
2. Pic St Loup
3. Terraces du Larzac (includes Montepeyroux and St Saturnin)
4. Picpoul de Pinet
5. Pézenas
6. Cabrières
7. La Clape (in the Aude department)
8. Sommières
9. St Christol
10. La Mejanelle

11. St Drezery
12. St Georges d'Orques
13. Quatorze (in the Aude department)

**Faugères** and **St. Chinian** (both 1982) are found in the Hérault, as well as three of Languedoc's four Muscat regions: **Lunel** (1943), **Mireval** (1959) and **Frontignan** (1936). Red wines in Hérault are almost always blends. Grenache Noir dominates, though it is being challenged by rapidly increasing plantings of Syrah and Mourvèdre. Carignan Noir is also found but is losing favor. Picpoul de Pinet is an appellation devoted solely to white wines made from the grape Piquepoul Blanc. Dry whites from other regions are blends, largely based on Grenache Blanc, Grenache Gris, Roussanne, Marsanne, and Bourboulenc. White wines from La Clape are required to contain Bourboulenc. Wines from the sweet Muscat regions are based exclusively on Muscat à Petits-Grains. The area near Aniane, in the hills northwest of Montpellier, is designated as a Vin de Pays zone. But, it has been proven that Cabernet Sauvignon thrives in the cool soils there, which goes into some superlative blends.

**The Aude** is the location of the fourth Muscat region **St. Jean de Minervois** (AOC 1949); also home to the region's well known **Minervois** (1985), **Minervois-La Livinière** (1998), **Corbières** (1985), **Corbières-Boutenac** (2005), and **Fitou** (1948). The sparkling wine region of **Limoux** (AOC 1981 for Blanquette and still white, 1990, Crémant, 2005, red) and the Atlantic-Mediterranean regions of **Cabardès** (1999) and **Malepère** (2007) occupy the Aude's northwest corner. Reds in Corbières, Minervois, and Fitou, like other parts of the Languedoc, are blends, with Carignan Noir assuming an especially large role, backed by Grenache Noir, Syrah, Cinsault and Mourvèdre. La Livinière and Boutenac sub-regions of Minervois and Corbières, respectively, tend to show less Carignan in favor of Syrah, Grenache Noir, and Mourvèdre. Cabardès, Malepère, and Limoux support, indeed require some percentage of Atlantic grape varieties such as Cabernet Sauvignon Cabernet Franc, and Merlot. The latter is a required component of Malpère reds. Limoux white is Chardonnay based, though Chenin Blanc and Mauzac are also permitted. Mauzac is the basis of Limoux's sparkling Blanquette, and must be a small part of the blend of its sparkling Crémant, Chardonnay and Chenin Blanc composing the rest. Whites in other parts of the Aude are blends of some combination of Grenache Blanc, Grenache Gris, Vermentino, Malvoisie, Macabeu, or others. Muscat à Petits-Grains goes into the sweet wines of St. Jean de Minervois.

**Roussillon** is synonymous with the **Pyrénées-Orientales**. **Côtes du Roussillon** (1977), **Côtes du Roussillon Villages** (1977), and **Collioure** (1971) produce mineral-laden, dry wines— red, white, and rosé. The area is also the home of the sweet wine centers **Rivesaltes** (1997) (including Muscat de Rivesaltes (AOC 1972), **Maury** (1972), and **Banyuls** (1972). Grenache Noir, Lledoner Pelut, and Carignan Noir dominate red blends in the Roussillon, though Syrah and Mourvèdre also find their place. Dry white wines are largely blends of Grenache Blanc, Grenache Gris, Vermentino, Malvoisie, or Macabeau. Of sweet reds from Banyuls, Maury, and Rivesaltes, Grenache Noir dominates. Muscat de Rivesaltes, the sweet white, is a fifty-fifty blend of Muscat d'Alexandrie and Muscat à Petits-Grains. Sweet Rivesaltes Blanc might be Grenache Blanc, Grenache Gris, Vermentino, Malvoisie, or Macabeau.

**Vin de Pays (IGP) wines are made in areas outside defined AOPs**. They are designated according to their place of origin. The most general designation is **Vin de Pays d'Oc**, which applies to wines from any part of the Languedoc-Roussillon. Wines originating from a particular département take the name of that département, for example, Vin de Pays de l'Hérault. Within each département are more particularly defined regions that can give their name to the local wine such as Vin de Pays Côtes de Thongue in Hérault.

## Vin Doux Naturel

As noted above, the Languedoc-Roussillon is the birthplace of naturally sweet, fortified wines. Called Vins Doux Naturels (VDN), the wines are made by a process called *mutage* that stops fermentation before the must's natural grape sugars have all been converted to alcohol. The process was patented in 1299 by the Catalan researcher Arnaud de Villeneuve in Montpellier.

The majority of VDNs are made from white Muscat. **Muscats du Languedoc**—a collective appellation for four Languedoc AOPs dedicated to the production of VDN, **Muscat de Mireval, Muscat de Lunel, Muscat de Frontignan, and Muscat de St. Jean de Minervois**—are made exclusively from the variety Muscat à Petits-Grains. Roussillon's Muscat de Rivesaltes is required to be a fifty-fifty blend of Muscat à Petits-Grains and Muscat d'Alexandrie.

In Roussillon, white VDN is also made from other grape varieties, including Grenache Blanc, Grenache Gris, Macabeau, Malvoisie du Roussilon/Tourbot and the two Muscats. Rivesaltes AOP makes the majority of these wines, though small quantities are made in Maury and Banyuls.

Maury and Banyuls are more noted for their red VDN. In both appellations, Grenache Noir dominates, potentially supported by Lledoner Pelut, Grenache Gris, Carignan, Mourvèdre and Syrah. Maury requires that Grenache Noir compose at least 75 percent of a blend, though pure Grenache Noir wines are not uncommon. Banyuls mandates a minimum of 50 percent Grenache Noir, 75 percent for Banyuls Grand Cru. Rivesaltes also makes red VDN.

Beyond simply colors, other categories warrant attention. Wines called *ambré* ('amber') are non-Muscat, though a percentage of up to 20 percent Muscat may be used in the blend, white VDN that have been oxidized in wood vats (*foudres*, *demi-muids*, barriques of various sizes) for at least two years. Wines might also be aged under the sun in round glass demi-johns called **bonbonnes** for a period of years.

Red wines can be aged in **reductive** or **oxidative** environments. Reductive wines are made in closed tanks and non-porous vats. Any time in wood is spent in completely-full barrels that prevent air contact. Depending on the AOP, they might be labeled **grenat** ('garnet'); **rimage** ('vintage' in Catalan); **mise precise** ('young bottled'); **vendage** ('harvest'); **récolte** ('harvest'); **vintage**; or from an obvious VDN appellation, simply, **rouge**.

Oxidative wines are made in conditions that facilitate the influence of air on wines. Wood vats or unsealed tanks are the norm, as well as aging under the sun in *bonbonnes*. Oxidized wines might be labeled **tuilé** ('tiled-colored'); **hors d'age** ('long-aged'); **rancio** (literally 'rancid,' but in the sense of 'well-ripened' rather than 'rotten'); or **traditionnel**. **Banyuls grand cru** is also aged in an oxidative manner.

Regardless of the style, grapes used for VDN are late harvested, at a minimum ripeness level of 252 grams of sugar/liter and a minimum potential alcohol level of 14.5 degrees (depending on specific AOP rules). After fermentation starts, a neutral grape spirit of 96 degrees, in a proportion of between five to ten percent of total must volume is added. This is usually done when the alcohol produced during fermentation reaches between four to ten percent—often four to six days after the start of fermentation. Must with sugars measuring 14.5 percent potential alcohol needs the addition of 10 percent of alcohol by must volume to stop fermentation. The higher the natural, potential alcohol in the must, the less alcohol must be added. The final alcohol level of a finished wine will be between 15 and 19 percent, the latter for some Banyuls and Maury. These figures are lower than the 20 percent level one finds in Port or Madeira wines, which are made in the same manner.

Fortification, *i.e.*, *mutage*, can be done in two ways: *Mutage sur jus*, that is, fortification to fermenting juice after skins have been removed, or *mutage sur grains*, fortification to must that is fermenting with skins still on.

*Mutage sur jus* (fortification on the juice) is used for white VDN, as well as some reds that are intended for consumption when young, especially wines labeled *mise precose* ('young bottled') from Banyuls or Rivesales *grenat*.

*Mutage sur grains* (fortification on the berries) is used for red VDN that are intended for aging. This process preserves some flavors and extracts tannin. From the 2010 vintage on, wines labeled **Rimage** ('vintage' in Catalan) must be fortified *sur grains*, though it has long been a common practice. Mutage sur grains might last as long as 30 days, or more, in order to maximize extraction of aromas.

The following are AOPs of Languedoc-Roussillon Vin Doux Naturel and categories within them.

## Muscat Appellations

Muscats du Languedoc is an umbrella term for the four recognized Muscat VDN producing AOPS within the Languedoc: Muscat de Frontignan (AOC 1936), Muscat de Lunel (AOC 1943), Muscat de Mireval (AOC 1959), and Muscat de St-Jean de Minervois (AOC 1949). Though each has a specific *terroir*, all require that only Muscat à Petits-Grains is used.

Dwarfing Languedoc Muscat production by a factor of three, is Roussillon's Muscat de Rivesaltes (AOC 1956). Required to be a fifty-fifty blend of Muscat à Petits-Grains and Muscat d'Alexandrie, Muscat de Rivesaltes must be aged at least until February 1 of the year following harvest. Two exceptions exist : **Muscat de Rivesaltes Hors d'Age** and **Muscat de Rivesaltes de Noël.** The former sees a minimum of five years age in oxidative conditions, though two decades normally pass before they are bottled. The term ***vieux muscat*** ('old Muscat') is sometimes found on bottles, but has no legal meaning. In contrast, Muscat de Rivesaltes de Noël is a *nouveau*-styled wine that, like Beaujolais Nouveau, is released the third Thursday of November following harvest As of this writing, no colorful posters announcing their arrival just in time for Thanksgiving dinner have been found.

## OTHER APPELLATIONS

Rivesaltes (AOC 1936). Rivesaltes Vins Doux Naturels are a rather diverse affair. Counting Muscat de Rivesaltes mentioned above, Rivesaltes produces 80 percent of all Languedoc-Roussillon VDN. Both white and red versions are made, the former being exclusively made in an oxidative style, the latter, in both oxidative and reductive styles. Because of its large size, the appellation overlaps with Maury in the northeast and Fitou to the southwest, which is in Languedoc rather than Roussillon.

Made from Grenache Blanc, Grenache Gris, Macabeau, Malvoisie du Roussilon/Tourbot, Muscat à Petits-Grains, Muscat d'Alexandrie, there is only one category of white Rivesaltes VDN: **Rivesaltes Ambré**. As the name indicates this is an amber-tinged wine that acquires its color from a minimum of 30 months in an oxidative environment. The blend may contain no more than 20 percent Muscat. **Rivesaltes Hors d'Age** is aged a minimum of five years, though over 20 years aging is the norm.

Red **Rivesaltes** VDN, whether ***Grenat***, produced in a reductive manner, or ***Tuilé***, made in an oxidative style, rarely reaches the acclaim of Banyuls or Maury noted below. But, both styles offer charming, occasionally profound drinking for lovers of sweet wines. *Grenat* wines are normally 100 percent Grenache Noir or Lledoner Pelut, though they might contain up to 10 percent supporting grapes Carignan, Cinsault, Syrah, or Listan. The wine must be aged a minimum of 12 months, three in bottle; or must be bottled a maximum of two years after harvest. They are analogous to Ruby Port. As its name indicates, Tuilé (tiled, i.e., tile red) is a tarnished red wine, made in an oxidative style. It must be composed of at least 50 percent Grenache Noir or Lledoner Pelut, and can be blended with black grapes Carignan, Cinsault Syrah, or Listan, and white grapes, Grenache Blanc, Grenache Gris, Macabeu, Malvoisie du Roussillon/Tourbat, or Muscat d'Alexandrie. The wines must be aged in an oxidative environment for a minimum of 30 months.

There are two other forms of oxidized wines. **Rivesaltes Hors d'Age** is aged a minimum of five years, though over 20 years aging is the norm. **Rivesaltes Rancio**, doesn't require a specific period of maturation, but, rather, has to acquire certain *rancio* characteristics, including nuttiness and a sweet-and-sour component. Both forms can be white or red wines, though they are decidedly amber or chestnut in hue.

**Maury** (AOC 1972): Considered with Banyuls as one of France's great sweet wine regions, Maury (like Banyuls) is home to fine white Vin Doux Naturel as well. White wines are blends of Grenache Gris and Grenache Blanc, Macabeu, Tourbat, and the Muscat d'Alexandrie or Muscat à Petits Grains. The Muscats cannot exceed 20 percent of the mix. White Maury can be made in reductive or oxidative styles and are aged a minimum of 12 months. Oxidative whites are referred to as *ambré*, but are rare as are Maury Hors d'Age.

Red Maury must be a minimum of 75 percent Grenache Noir, but with ninety percent of vineyards planted in the grape, the norm veers toward 100 percent. Other complementary grapes include Macabeu (a maximum of 10 percent), and Carignan Noir and Syrah, also for a maximum of 10 percent. Wines labeled *vendage*, *récolte*, or vintage are made in a reductive environment and are aged a minimum of 12 months. *Maury rouge* is made under oxidative conditions. Hors d'Age is aged a minimum of 5 years in an oxidative environment, though, like Rivesaltes, 20 years or more is the norm. *Rancio* wines are aged similarly, but take on a *rancio* flavor profile. Regardless of style, reductive or oxidative, Maury wines tend to maintain their red color (even if tarnished) over time better than most wines, including Banyuls. Some Maury producers, like others in Banyuls, keep impressively old stocks of wines, back to the 1920s or earlier, for bottling to order.

**Banyuls** (AOC 1972): Occupying the steep slopes where France and Spain meet on the Mediterranean, Banyuls is a dramatic place that makes dramatic wine. Some of its vineyards are so steep that cable-cars or donkeys must be used during harvest. Banyuls wines are very similar to those of Maury, though one might perceive more mineral characteristics from Banyuls, a reflection of its proximity to the sea.

White Banyuls is made from Grenache Blanc, Grenache Gris, Macabeu, Tourbat/Malvoisie du Roussillon, Muscat à Petits Grains or Muscat d'Alexandrie. The Muscats cannot exceed 20 percent of the blend. Wines are made in reductive or oxidative conditions. Prejudice toward the latter, leads winemakers to devote their better, potentially longer-aging grapes to the oxidative wines, called *amber*; but the fresh, reductive style has perhaps more general appeal— and is certainly better as an aperitif.

Rosé versions are made but are exceedingly rare.

Red Banyuls is made from a minimum of 50 percent Grenache Noir or Lledoner Pelut, as well as Grenache Gris and white varieties, Macabeu, Tourbat/Malvoisie du Roussillon, Muscat à Petits Grains or Muscat d'Alexandrie. In practice, white varieties are not widely used. Carignan Noir, Cinsault, and Syrah might also be added to the blend provided they do not exceed 10 percent. The wine is made in reductive and oxidative styles, the latter being most traditional.

Of the reductive wines the most widely found is **Banyuls Mise Precose**, made solely in stainless steel tanks to achieve a fresh, fruity style, suitable for early consumption. It is similar to, if fresher than, a Ruby Port.

**Banyuls Rimage** is made in excellent years and is always marked by vintage ('*rimage*' in Catalan). The wines undergo long macerations to extract aromas and tannin. In order to preserve the wine's fruit, freshness, and power, wines are bottled early, usually six to twelve months after harvest. Banyuls Rimage is the analog to Vintage Port.

**Banyuls Rimage Mise Tardive** is elaborated in the same manner as Banyuls Rimage, but rather than being bottled early, it is matured from one to three years in full *tonneau t*o round out tannin and flavors. It is Banyuls' equivalent of Late-Bottled Vintage Port.

Banyuls most common red VDN is **Banyuls traditionnel**. Aged in an oxidative environment it is a *tuilé* wine, tarnished a bit with dry fruit flavors and sweet acidity. It is similar to a non-age specific Tawny Port.

A common method for developing oxidation in Banyuls is to age wines in barrels or glass bonbonnes in plain air, unprotected from the elements.

**Banyuls Grand Cru** is a superior version of Banyuls traditionnel. It is made from grapes grown within a specified portion of Banyuls AOP (167 ha out of 898 ha) that are deemed exceptional afte*r mutage sur grains*. The blend must contain a minimum of 75 percent Grenache Noir and be aged for a minimum of 30 months in barrel. Far longer aging is common. Banyuls Grand Crus are analogous to age-specific Tawny Port. Styles that develop desirable *rancio* flavors can be labeled Rancio. The category of Hors d'Age exists, too, for wines aged a minimum of five years, but as elsewhere, the norm is often far longer.

## Sparkling Wines

Sparkling wine in the Languedoc has existed as long as it has anywhere in France. Indeed, the first written records of deliberately produced bubbly, dating to 1531, were found in the Abbey de Saint Hilaire in Limoux. Whether monks in the Languedoc were intentionally producing sparkling wine before anyone else remains a mystery, though local legend holds that Dom Pérignon of Champagne passed through Limoux over a century later while on pilgrimage to the Holy City of Santiago de Compostelles in Spain. After his return, so the story goes, he applied the knowledge acquired in Limoux in order to create the miracle that had him "drinking stars." As convenient as the story it for local Limoux producers, evidence shows that the blind Dom was interested doing quite the opposite—that is, avoiding residual carbonation in wine after fermentation— rather than intentionally creating liquid bubbles.

Whatever the veracity of the story, sparkling wine has been an established industry of Limoux for centuries. One of the early advantages Limoux producers had was their proximity to Catalan cork forests that provided reliable stoppers to trap carbon dioxide as wines fermented in bottles.

One of the region's indigenous grape varieties, **Mauzac** (aka **Blanquette**) provided the basis for Limoux's earliest sparkling wines. With its yellow apple and herbal flavors, Mauzac is distinctive, even to mild palates, esoteric. Locally, it is beloved. But, in order to accommodate more "international" tastes, growers in the 1980s started significant plantations of Chardonnay and Chenin Blanc, both of which excel in Limoux's largely limestone soils and relatively (for Languedoc) cooler temperatures. Increasing portions of these two grapes were blended into Blanquette de Limoux (AOC 1981) wines, to the disadvantage of Mauzac. Alarm over the possibility that Mauzac would become little more than a historic curiosity prompted locals to advocate for the grape to have an official place in the production of Limoux sparkling wines. In response, regulations adopted in 1990 stipulated the creation of three types of Limoux sparkling wine: **Blanquette de Limoux, Crémant de Limoux, and Blanquette de Limoux Méthode Ancestrale.**

**Blanquette de Limoux** must be made of at least 90 percent Mauzac, with allowances for a maximum of 10 percent of Chardonnay or Chenin Blanc. Wines are made using the *méthode traditionelle* (aka the *méthode champenoise*), and bottles must rest on their lees for a minimum of nine months before disgorgement and final corking.

**Crémant de Limoux** is also made in the *méthode traditionelle*, but the blend reverses the varietal requirements for Blanquette. For Crémant, there must be a minimum of 40 percent, up to 70 percent Chardonnay, and 20 percent, up to 40 percent Chenin Blanc. Together they can compose a maximum of 90 percent of the blend. The remainder could be filled by Mauzac (10 to 20 percent), or Pinot Noir, up to 10 percent. For Crémant de Limoux Rosé, Pinot Noir is an inevitable component of the blend.

**Blanquette de Limoux *Méthode Ancestrale*** is a tribute to the way sparkling wine used to be made, perhaps dating back at least to 1531 One hundred percent Mauzac, *méthode ancestrale* undergoes only one fermentation, which it finishes, if not starts, in bottle. After the base wine starts fermenting, it is held at a very low temperature to suspend fermentation until it is bottled during the waning moon at the end of March following harvest. Fermentation resumes, continuing until the yeast suffocates itself in the sealed bottle, leaving some residual sweetness. Never disgorged before serving, Blanquette *méthode ancestrale* is cloudy and is somewhat sweet. *Méthode ancestrale* wines are made in other parts of France under different names, such as Gaillac's *Mousseux methode gaillacoise*, or Jura's Bugey Cedron.

## HOT TOPICS

At present, the biggest issue facing the Languedoc-Roussillon is finalizing its appellation requirements and gaining final approval for its proposed Grand Cru system. Decisions are expected by the end of 2011.

France's largest wine region is also the most difficult to categorize. In the past, it was known as the source for vast quantities of cheap, indifferent wine. Some of those still exist, but a quality revolution in the past three decades has created justifiable excitement for wines that range from well-made international varietals to superb, world-class wines that hold their position against the best anywhere. Regulators have been trying to catch up to changes in the region, assessing, defining and demarcating new appellations in a meaningful way. And despite low expectations and the seemingly slow pace of reform, it seems there is reason to be optimistic in the future. Rather large appellations such as Côteaux du Languedoc are being broken down into smaller appellations that really give consumers an idea of what they might expect from a bottle.

# Southwestern France

By Jamal Rayyis

| Latitude | 43-44.5°N |
|---|---|
| Area Under Vine | 50,000 hectares (26,000 AOP, 24,000 IGP) |
| Volume Produced | 3,411,000 hectoliters/year |
| Red | 46% |
| White | 54% |
| Grape Varieties | Varieties grown here are extremely diverse. |
| Red | Fer Servadou (aka Mansois, Braucol, Pinenc), Tannat, Malbec (aka Auxerrois, Cot/Côt), Négrette, Duras, Jurançon Noir, Cabernet Sauvignon — Cabernet Franc (aka Branchy), Merlot, Syrah, Cinsault, Bordelais, Morterille, Chalosse, Mouyssaguès (Périgord), Manseng Noir, Courbu Noir, Mérille. |
| White | Petit Manseng, Gros Manseng, Len de l'El, Ondenc, Mauzac, Petit Courbu, — Arrufiac, Sémillon, Sauvignon Blanc, Muscadelle, Colombard, Chenin Blanc, Ugni Blanc, Listan, Lauzet, Camarelet, Cruchinet. |
| Climate | The climate is influenced by the Atlantic Ocean and features wet winters and springs, warm summers, and lengthy sunny autumns. Regions further inland are subject to higher temperatures. |

Le Sud-Ouest, land of D'Artagnan and the Three Musketeers, is about as swashbuckling as wine gets in France. From the southern and eastern-most edges of Bordeaux to the Pyrénées Basque country, Southwest wines are brash and bold, with a bit of nobility thrown in for good measure. It is here that some of France's heartiest reds are found: black and tannic, as well as wines elegant enough to be confused for Bordeaux. If you learn how to pronounce some of the Basque names, you'll be well ahead of the game.

Long in the shadow of Bordeaux, the wines of the Southwest have remained more obscure than they deserve. For generations, Bordeaux merchants controlled Southwestern access to waterways and ports to ensure that the then-pallid Bordeaux wines were sold first, before the competition could arrive. That is, except for heartier Southwest wines that would be used to beef up thinner ones from Bordeaux. Restrictions on transport were lifted at the time of the French Revolution (1789–1799). By then, however, Bordelaise winemakers had improved considerably their offerings to the world, and monopolized vital British markets.

Bordeaux had other influences on the wines of the Southwest. The northern portions of the Southwest—running alongside the Dordogne and parts of the Garonne rivers, which join to form the Gironde estuary to the Atlantic—produce wines made in the same style and from the same grape varieties as those produced in Bordeaux. Indeed, these regions, which include Bergerac, Buzet, Montravel and Côte de Duras, are often referred to as "Bordeaux satellites." Whether or not local pride is wounded by the inevitable comparison is debatable. But the association is surely helpful for producers and consumers alike; the latter because good quality Bordeaux-like wines is available for a non-Bordeaux price, the former, because they don't have to explain their wines to consumers.

But there is far more to the Southwest than the shadows of Bordeaux. Its Jurançon wines have inspired the seductions of the poet Colette; and its Cahors wines earned the infamous moniker of "black wine." Hosting France's largest collection of rare grape varieties, the Southwest produces idiosyncratic wines of every measure. Wines that seem light, but also impossibly tannic; wines that are heavy but have an unexpected delicacy; wines that are bone dry to unctuously sweet; and wines that are filled with wild herb and fruit, truffle and exotic spice flavors.

The inimitable qualities of the wines are well matched by the region's gastronomic legacy, one that almost defines French cuisine itself: foie gras, Roquefort cheese, *jambon de Bayonne*, Périgord truffles and cassoulet. For both the classic and adventurous wine drinker, the Southwest offers treasures to be explored and savored.

# HISTORY

The history of *Sud Ouest* (Southwest) wine could be cast as a soap opera. Land-grabbing Romans and Gaulish resistance; a period of barbarians eventually replaced by rising Church structures and libertine monks (some chaste ones, too). Followed by political turmoil between French and English monarchs (alternatively supported by Spanish royals), then religious wars between Protestants and Catholics. The French Revolution, the industrial revolution, the plague of phylloxera, revival, two world wars, terrible frosts, mismanagement, abandonment, and, finally resurrection. Within this weave of history, is found a parade of pious pilgrims, bands of troubadours, unscrupulous Bordeaux wine merchants, Huguenot refugees to Holland, liberating revolutionaries, dedicated cooperatives, mediocre bureaucrats, and visionary winemakers.

Winemaking in the Southwest started in the second century BC, in an area near the town of Gaillac. At the time, Gaillac was ruled by Romans from their Languedoc base at Narbonne. Logically, viticulture spread throughout the province eventually reaching other parts of the Southwest. After the fall of Rome in the early fourth century AD it took the Church a few centuries to organize itself, establishing monasteries and supporting their upkeep through winemaking throughout Europe. Inadvertently or not, the Church strengthened the fortunes of local winemaking when in 1189 Pope Alexander III declared the Galician town of Compostela a Holy City, in honor of the tomb of the apostle St. James (St. Jacques in French, Santiago in Spanish). The saint's body allegedly washed ashore in an oversized seashell over a millennium before. Compostela is located in far northwestern Spain, about 50 kilometers (30 miles) east of the Atlantic coast and 100 km (60 miles) north of Portugal

The spiritual equivalent of Rome or Jerusalem, **St. Jacques de Compestelle**, as it is called in French, attracted legions of pilgrims from all over Europe. Inevitably, large numbers of pilgrims from points north of the Pyrenees passed right through the Southwest, requiring board and lodging. Within a few years, their needs came to be accommodated by a growing network of monasteries and abbeys. Pilgrims also needed wine, which encouraged the planting of more vines. Moreover, as they made their way home from Spain, some pilgrims returned with novel varieties such as Listan (Palomino in Spain), Baroque, Alicante, and others, found on the other side of the mountains. Many of these were planted in the Southwest. Others, including indigenous Southwest varieties such as Cabernet Franc (though some evidence suggests it might have come from Spain, too), Merlot, and Sauvignon were spread to developing wine regions to the north, including Bordeaux and the Loire Valley.

Despite the supposed unity of the Catholic Church, competition for power—spiritual, economic, and political—wrenched the region over the next several centuries. England controlled parts of the Southwest, especially Aquitane in the twelfth and thirteenth centuries. This provided commercial opportunities between English merchants in search of easy accessible wine and English-ruled, French wine-regions, including Bergerac. In the fourteenth and fifteenth centuries, wars of succession raged between the English and French. Known as the **Hundred Years' War** (1337-1453), the conflict divided loyalties in the Southwest, which, depending on a specific region's position, permitted or restricted access for winemakers to markets abroad, especially Britain and the Netherlands. Power shifted back and forth. And, when a settlement in favor of the French crown was won in 1453, commercial relations to England were largely cut.

A restoration of relations between the French and English crowns in the sixteenth century revived trade somewhat; but even then conflict loomed—this time over religion. Several parts of the Southwest enthusiastically embraced the Protestant message of the **Reformation**, which split the Church into Roman Catholic and Protestant camps. During the sixteenth and seventeenth centuries wars raged between the (usually) Catholic French crown and independent-minded Protestants. The conflict devastated the region, though there were periods of tolerance and prosperity, too, culminating in the Edict of Nantes (1598) that assured freedom of worship. However, an assertion of Catholicism in the Southwest canton of Béarn in the early seventeenth century stirred revolts of **Huguenots** (French Protestants) that were harshly suppressed. Large communities of Protestants decided to immigrate to more hospitable countries, especially Britain and Holland. Refugees from the **Bergerac** went mostly to the Netherlands, taking not only their faith, but also a taste for the sweet wines of their native land. The Dutch-Bergerac connection remains to this day.

For centuries wine merchants in Bordeaux, located where the Garonne River meets the Gironde Estuary, controlled the transport of wine from regions upstream and enacted protectionist measures to favor then-poor quality Bordeaux wines. ***Haut-Pays*** ('high country,' essentially, upstream) wines were charged extortionist tolls for passage into the Gironde. From the fourteenth century until the start of the French Revolution (1789), the wines were prohibited from entering the port of Bordeaux until Christmas Day, thus assuring that foreign demand could only be satisfied by the local wines. The turmoil of the Revolution followed by the Napoleonic wars (1803 to 1815) delayed the advantages of the lifted restrictions.

Increased demand for wine during the emerging industrial period encouraged a planting boom in the Southwest; and the building of railroads in the nineteenth century made it easier for the region's producers to bring their wines to market. Of course, it made it easier for wines from competing parts of France such as the Languedoc, to reach markets, too. Moreover, railways, didn't reach every part of the Southwest. Even today, much of the southern reaches of the region remain without rail transport.

Like other French viticulture regions, phylloxera hit the Southwest hard. It was reported in Cahors in 1877 and spread to virtually every corner of the region. Since the Southwest was more intensely planted in vines than any other region in France (and possibly the world), the devastation had a catastrophic impact on the local economy. With few other sources of income, raising the money to replant on disease-resistant American rootstocks was impossible for many *vignerons*, forcing them to abandon their lands entirely.

By the beginning of the twentieth century, there was some recovery, particularly in areas such as **Madiran** that had been struck with phylloxera later than other areas. Producers there had been able to earn good incomes during the general wine shortage. When Madiran finally had to deal with the crisis, the vintners benefited from the experience others had combating the plague. Areas like Cahors took several decades to recover. And those areas able to replant sooner often did so using varieties prized for their resistance to disease and prolific production rather than quality.

A general rehabilitation of the Southwest wine industry didn't occur until after World War II, though efforts to do so started a couple of decades before. Syndicates and cooperatives were created to set standards for local production and to solicit recognition by the Appellation d'Origine Contrôlée (AOC) system. Though phylloxera no longer proved a significant problem in the second part of the twentieth century, other forces of nature did. Particularly disabling was a massive frost in 1956–1957 that killed large tracts of vineyards. Cahors particularly suffered. That Cahors, one of France's most storied wine regions, didn't receive full AOC recognition until 1971 indicates how slow the recovery was.

In the meantime a few regions were granted AOC status (e.g. Bergerac, Montravel, Côtes de Duras and Monbazillac in 1936–1937, Madiran in 1948). Others achieved recognition as **Vin Délimité de Qualité Supérieure (VDQS)** regions, establishing production limits, standards for wine quality, and codifying grape varieties. It is telling that despite the long history of proud viticulture in the Southwest, forty percent of France's VDQS appellations, essentially, France's minor wine-league, were located in the Southwest.

As many regions were renovations of an industry that had almost faded into memory, requirements became a sort of work in progress. Minimum barrel aging requirements in Madiran, for example, started off as thirty-three months when AOC status was granted in 1948, and grape production was limited to 25 hectoliters/hectare (1.7 tons/acre). Over time, aging requirements fell, and production limits rose. Today, the standards are 12 months in barrel and 55 hl/ha (3.7 tons/acre); requirements that can assure a reasonably high level of quality and character, but also make the enterprise of winemaking financially viable.

In the last decade, developments in the wine-world that demand well-made, international-style wines for low prices, call for powerful oak-fueled wines, and that appreciate expression of a particular regional identity, are being well served by Southwest producers. Large cooperatives, especially in the **Côtes de Gascogne** have proved astute in accommodating the desire for fresh, tasty but unchallenging, inexpensive wines. To accommodate the homogenizing tastes of international critics and the deep-pocket bourgeoisie that loves them, well-capitalized wineries in more famous appellations such as Cahors and Madiran have been making *prestige* wines bursting with ripe fruit flavors and lashes of new oak. And, small, dedicated producers, proud of a heritage that includes France's largest collection of indigenous grapes, are offering oenophiles wines that simply could not be made anywhere else in the world.

## CLASSIFICATIONS

The Southwest relies on the AOC classification system. From 2009 forward, wines that had been classified Appellation d'Origine Contrôlée (AOC) will be classified instead as Appellation d'Origine Protegée (AOP). Provided they are able to meet certain standards, regions that had been designated Vin Délimité de Qualité Superieure (VDQS) have been elevated to AOP status. The category Vin de Pays (VdP) has been changed to Indication Geographique Protégée (IGP). Wines previously designated Vin de Table will be without geographical designation and now are to be designated Vin de France. A departure from the past, these wines are permitted to note vintage and grape variety on their labels.

Unlike other large wine regions in France, for example, the Rhône Valley, the Southwest does not have an umbrella appellation that covers (most of) its wines. That is, whereas the Rhône Valley has the general Côtes du Rhône appellation, there is no "Sudouest" appellation, even as a VdP. The reasons for this seeming oversight are simple: one would be hard pressed to taste wines from different parts of the Southwest and say they have a whole lot in common other than the fact that all subject to the influences of the Atlantic Ocean and that most permit, in some measure (even if minimal) the use of Bordeaux grape varieties. Appellations closest to Bordeaux, of course, make the most use of Bordeaux varieties. Those on the outside edges of the Southwest use them less, if at all. While the physical boundaries of many appellations support both white and red grapes, made into dry and sweet wines, often, a specified appellation permits one type of wine, with other types labeled as a different appellation. Madiran AOP, for instance, must be a red wine. Defined by the same borders, Pacherenc du Vic-Bilh AOP must be white. Monbazillac AOP is a sweet white wine region. Dry whites produced there take the appellation Bergerac AOP.

## TERROIR

The Southwest is a large area, about 240 km (150 miles) north to south, and 400 km (240 miles) east to west. Its boundaries encompass the borders of thirteen *départements*: Pyrénées-Atlantiques, Haut Pyrénées. Haute-Garonne, Landes, Gers, Tarn, Aveyron, Corrèze, Cantal, Lot, Dordogne, Lot-et-Garonne and Ariège. Geographically it is defined by the Atlantic Ocean to the west, the Cévennes Mountains in the southeast, the Massif Central in the north and east, the Bordeaux estuaries north and west, and the Pyrénées Mountains to the south.

Understandably, it is impossible to generalize about the geology of the region. Millions of years ago, much of what we now call the Southwest was below the sea. After waters receded, the fossil remains of sea life formed a bed of limestone. The rise of the Pyrénées and the Alps in subsequent eras fractured this bed, creating, eventually, the river valleys that run through the region. Among these are the Dordogne and the Garonne, the Lot, the Gers, the Tarn, the Adour and others. The geological upheavals also created a pastiche of soil types, sometimes quite different within the boundaries of a single appellation. Within the Jurançon, for instance, one zone features clay with large, round stones, another, chalk with small pebbles, and a third, a combination of hard and soft rock, known as flysch.

Climatically, the Southwest is sunny and warm during the summer growing season, though, humid, too, due to influences from the Atlantic. Mountains trap this moist ocean air, also contributing to humid, if not damp, conditions. The sun's weakening influence to burn off ocean fogs in mid-autumn contributes to the development of *botrytis cinerea* that makes many of the region's sweet wines, especially at Monbazillac and Saussignac, so special. However, this oceanic influence is tempered somewhat by the Landes Forest that covers much of the western edge of the Southwest. The eastern parts of the Southwest, particularly Gaillac, receive warming **Autan** breezes from the Mediterranean, which are funneled from the adjoining Languedoc region. The benevolence of the Mediterranean is felt in some parts of Marcillac, Entraygues et Le Fel, Estaing, and Côtes de Millau, as well.

Eastern portions of the Southwest abut, and, indeed are the outer vestiges of the Massif Central plateau of central France. Cool, continental breezes that blow through that formation also have a strong influence. Altitudes that reach over 400 meters (1300 feet) and steep vineyard sites add other important dimensions. Vineyards that are stared down upon by the Pyrénées, especially in Béarn, Madiran, Jurançon, and Irouléguy, are not especially high in altitude; but they are heavily influenced by cool mountain air during much of the year— as well as precipitation, as clouds from the Atlantic run smack into the hills. From spring into early summer, heavy rainfall isn't uncommon. It should be noted, however, that in the middle of the growing season, warm, dry airs coming over the Pyrénées from Spain, mitigate the dampness.

So-called Bordeaux satellites, Bergerac, Montravel, and others are more or less continuations of the Bordeaux terroir they adjoin. Montravel is next to Côte de Castillon in Bordeaux; parts of Bergerac, next to Entre-Deux-Mers, as is Côtes du Marmandais. Côtes de Duras adjoins Ste. Foy de Bordeaux, and Buzet is upriver from Graves. It is no coincidence that wines from these regions so closely resemble those from Bordeaux, especially its Right Bank.

# Soil

| Region | Soil |
|---|---|
| **Bergerac** | Variable: clay, limestone, sand, gravel |
| **Monbazillac** | Sandstone, clay-limestone |
| **Saussignac** | Chalk-clay |
| **Pécharmant** | *Tarn:* Sand, gravel, clay, iron |
| **Montravel** | Clay with iron, clay and limestone |
| **Côtes du Montravel** | Greenish clay with fossilized oysters |
| **Côtes de Duras** | Marle and molassic soil with limestone or clay-limestone |
| **Côtes du Marmandais** | Varied, Marle and molassic soil with calcareous sandstone. Gravel and sand. |
| **Buzet** | Iron-rich fossil, sandy limestone and marl, |
| **Côtes du Brulhois** | Pebbles and sandy clay |
| **Cahors** | Varied: limestone, clay, gravel, sand, with iron deposits |
| **Gaillac** | Varied: Pebbles, clay, with chalky subsoil, sandstone, limestone. |
| **Fronton** | Varied: iron and quartz, sand, pebbles, *galets roulés* |
| **Côtes de Gascogne** | Varied: clay and limestone; sand; limestone |
| **St. Mont** | Sand and limestone |
| **Marcillac** | Red earth wand chalky pebbles. |
| **Entraygues** | Schist, granite |
| **Estaing** | Schist, granite |
| **Côtes de Millau** | Clay and limestone, some round stones. |
| **Madiran/Pecherenc** | Varied: clay; iron and magnesium, limestone, *greppe*; sand, clay, small pebbles; |
| **Béarn** | Predominantly clay and limestone. |
| **Tursan** | Sandstone, marl, limestone |
| **Irouléguy** | Red sandstone and chalky clay. |
| **Jurançon** | Varied: clay with large, round pebbles, chalk with pebbles. *Flysch* – soft and hard rock. |

# Varieties

So-called "Bordeaux" grape varieties— including Sauvignon Blanc, Sémillon and Muscadelle for whites, and Cabernet Sauvignon and Cabernet Franc for reds— have had such a long presence in the Southwest that they might well be considered a natural part of the region's viticulture. In appellations most proximate to Bordeaux, they are *the* local varieties. The Southwest, however, is home to over 40 indigenous varieties that are not much seen elsewhere. In many appellations, these grapes take the leading role in blends, supported—or sometimes "softened" to current tastes—by Bordeaux varieties.

# Red

**Fer Servadou**, often shorted to "Fer," finds its way into the wines of several Southwest appellations, albeit under different names. In Marcillac, where it absolutely dominates, the grape is called **Mansois**, though, the appellation's iron-rich soils ("fer" = iron), well reflected in the region's wine, suggest the general moniker is more appropriate. In fact, the name "Fer" refers to the vine's iron-strong stock. In Gaillac, it is called **Braucol**. The Gasconais and Béarnais call it **Pinenc**. Regardless of name, the grape is dark in color, violet, but bright, with full, yet not overwhelming tannin. Its flavor profile is one of spicy dark berries, especially black currants (cassis).

**Tannat** is most famous in Madiran. It is black in color, relatively high in acidity and potential alcohol, and, as one might expect from its name, notably tannic. While young it shows a mix of fresh berry flavors, leaning toward red, with some smoke. With age, tannins soften and the flavors evolve to baked fruit and spice. In Gascony, Tannat is sometimes called "Moustoun." Outside of France, Tannat is widely cultivated in Uruguay, where it also goes under the name "Harriauge." Uruguayan Tannat tends to be a bit less tannic with a flavor profile that evokes blackberries. It still produces hearty wines, though.

**Malbec** is also permitted (though not often seen) in the wines of Bordeaux. It is most well known in Cahors, where it is called **Auxerrois**. In other parts of the Southwest, it is often called **Cot** or **Côt**. "Pressac" is another name. The grape is typically dark ruby in color and full of appealing flavors such as cherries and dark fruit. Relatively low in acidity, though high in tannin, it ages well, developing more earthy flavors with time. The latter profile is favored by Southwest producers, though the success of Argentine Malbec has encouraged some winemakers to design early-consumption wines that emphasize the fruit flavors.

**Négrette** is a grape grown with passion in Fronton, storied for its especially dark skin, and, unusually dark juice. Legend has it that the grape was brought to the region from Cyprus by Templar Knights ($12^{th}$–$13^{th}$ centuries) returning from one of their Crusades to Palestine. In reality, it is probably related to Malbec and Tannat. It bears some resemblance to the latter, though its tannins are generally less challenging and its aromatics more flirtatious, bearing a bouquet of flowers, with blue and blackberries. Thin-skinned, Négrette is prone to mildew and rot, which keeps it from damper areas of the region.

**Duras** shares a name with the Southwest appellation Côtes de Duras, but has no other relation. Found almost exclusively in the Gaillac, Duras is deeply colored with an appealing bouquet. It ages well.

**Jurançon Noir** is widely grown and appreciated for its fruitiness, though is a bit crude.

**Abouriou** is an ancient grape in the Southwest, categorized for its heavy tannin and deep, almost black color.

Other red grapes include: Cabernet Sauvignon, Cabernet Franc, Merlot, Syrah, Cinsault, Bordelais, Morterille, Chalosse, Mouyssaguès (Périgord), Manseng Noir, Courbu Noir, Mérille.

## WHITE

**Petit Manseng** and **Gros Manseng** are almost synonymous with the wines of Jurançon. As one would expect from their names, the Petit has smaller berries and bunches, the Gros, larger. Both are thick-skinned and late ripening, tendencies that are ideal to avoid rot in Jurançon's humid climate, as well as to take advantage of warm autumns. Traditionally, the ability to ripen without malady into late autumn, sometimes past the first frost, privileges both Mansengs for sweet rather than dry wines. However, contemporary fashion prefers dry (and therefore, less expensive) wines, for which Gros Manseng is preferred since it ripens earlier with lower sugars while offering some exotic fruit flavors. Also, yields are higher and it can withstand machine harvesting, which keeps costs down, necessary for the economics of dry wine sales. Petit Manseng ripens later, and with higher sugars, making it attractive for sweet wines. Manual harvesting is the norm.

**Len de l'El** is an early-ripening Gaillac grape that is well suited to dry wines, but, also, sweet, since it preserves its acidity if left longer on the vine.

**Ondenc** also comes from Gaillac. It lost popularity because of its vulnerability to late frosts, but is regaining ground because its esoteric flavors such as heather honey and ginger add particular complexity to sweet wines.

**Mauzac** has its origins in the Languedoc's Limoux, but has been planted in the Southwest for centuries. Its apple and spice flavors are especially appealing in Gaillac's sweet and sparkling wines.

**Petit Courbu** is found in the southern, Basque regions of the Southwest, particularly Irouléguy and Jurançon, as well as Pacherenc, where it offers aromatic lemon blossom and honey flavors.

**Arrufiac** is widely grown in Pacherenc and, in some ways, plays the role Tannat does in overlapping Madiran. Its presence isn't required, but it shows an attractive minerality in dry wines. It sometimes goes by the name "Ruffiat" or "Ruffiac."

Bordeaux grapes **Sémillon**, **Sauvignon Blanc**, and **Muscadelle** are common in areas adjoining that region. Colombard, Ugni Blanc, and Folle Blanche go into many Vins de Pays, and are used for the production of Armagnac. Other indigenous grapes include **Lauzet**, **Camarelet**, **Cruchinet**.

| Appellation Name | Color | Grape requirements | Special Requirements |
|---|---|---|---|
| **Montravel** | Red | Merlot (min 50%), Cabernet Sauvginon, Cabernet France, Côt (Malbec) | |
| | White | Sémillon (min 25%), Sauvignon Blanc, Muscadelle | |
| | Sweet White | Sémillon (min 25%), Sauvignon Blanc, Muscadelle | Côtes du Montravel<br><br>Moëlleux style 8-54 grams residual sugar (r.s.)/liter<br><br>Haut-Montravel<br><br>Higher levels of r.s./liter. If infected by botrytis, might be called "liquoreux." |
| **Bergerac** | Red | Cabernet Sauvignon, Cabernet France, Merlot, Malbec, also permitted : Mérille, Périgord | Côtes de Bergerac, slightly higher minimum alcohol level (11% vs. 10.5%) |
| | White & White Sweet | Sémillon, Sauvignon Blanc, Muscadelle, Chenin Blanc. Odenc, Ugni Blanc allowed (max 25% if balanced by equal amount of Sauvignon) | |
| **Pécharmant** | Red | Cabernet Sauvignon, Cabernet France, Merlot, Malbec | |
| **Rosette** | Off-Dry White | Sémillon, Sauvignon Blanc, Muscadelle (latter two rarely used) | Normally a touch sweet |
| **Monbazillac** | Sweet White | Sémillon, Sauvignon Blanc, Muscadelle | Botrytis and two or more rounds of picking required. |
| **Saussignac** | Sweet White | Sémillon, Sauvignon Blanc, Muscadelle | Botrytis and two or more rounds of picking required. |
| **Entraygues et Fel** | Red & Rosé | Fer Servadou, Cabernet Franc, Cabernet Sauvignon, Gamay, Jurançon Noir, Merlot, Mouyssaguès, Négret de Banhars, Pinot Noir | |
| | White | Chenin Blanc, Mauzac | |
| **Marcillac** | Red | Mansois (Fer Servadou) (min 90%), Cabernet Sauvignon, Cabernet Franc; Merlot (10% max) | |
| **Côtes de Millau** | Red | Gamay, Syrah (each must be min 30% of grower's red vineyard), Cabernet Sauvignon (max 20%), Fer Servadou, Duras | |

| Appellation Name | Color | Grape requirements | Special Requirements |
|---|---|---|---|
| **Gaillac** | Red | Duras, Braucol (Fer Servadou), Syrah (min 30% plantings of some combination of the preceding), Gamay, Cabernet Sauvignon, Cabernet Franc, Merlot; | 60% of grower's vines must be of principle red varieties. |
| | White | Mauzac (min 60% of white grapes grown), Len de l'el, Sauvignon (15%, together, of planting) Muscadelle, Sémillon, Ondenc | Traditional and vin perlé style, the latter undergoes a second fermentation during bottling, offering a slight pricky sensation. |
| | Sweet White | Mauzac (min 60% of white grapes grown), Len de l'el, Sauvignon (15%, together, of planting) Muscadelle, Sémillon, Ondenc | |
| | Sparkling | Méthode Gaillacoise Traditionelle<br><br>Mauzac, Len d'El, Sauvignon Blanc, Muscadelle, Sémillon, Ondenc | « Traditional Method » aka méthode champenoise |
| | | Méthode Gaillacoise Ancéstrale<br><br>Mauzac | No secondary fermentation, no disgorgement, no dosage |
| **Fronton** | Red & Rosé | Négrette (min 50-70% of vineyard), Gamay, Mérille, Cinsault (together or alone max 15%), Côt, Fer Servadou, Syrah, Cabernet Sauvignon, Cabernet Franc (each max 25%), Sauvignon, Mauzac, (each phased out by 2012) | |
| **Lavilledieu** | Red | Blend of at least four varieties. Négrette (min 30%), Mauzac, Bordelais, Morterille, Chalosse (all, min 80% of vineyard); Syrah, Cabernet Franc, Tannat, Milgranet (max 25% each), Gamay (max 10%) | |
| **Côteaux du Quercy** | Red | Cabernet Franc (min 40%, max 60% of vineyard), Merlot, Gamay, Auxerrois (Côt), Tannat (no more than 20%) | |
| **Cahors** | Red | Auxerrois (Malbec or Côt) (min 70%), Tannat, Merlot (max alone or together 30%) | |
| **Côtes de Brulhois** | Red | Tannat (required), Cabernet Sauvignon, Cabernet Franc, Fer Servadou, Merlot, Côt | |
| **Buzet** | Red & Rosé | Merlot, Cabernet Sauvignon, Cabernet Franc, Côt | |
| | White | Sémillon, Sauvignon, Muscadelle | |
| **Côtes de St. Mont** | Red and Rosé | Tannat (min 60% of red vineyard), Fer Servadou (min 10% going to 20% by 2020), both obligatory in wine. Cabernet Sauvignon, Cabernet Franc, Merlot (not permitted after 2020) | |

| Appellation Name | Color | Grape requirements | Special Requirements |
|---|---|---|---|
| | White | Minimum 3 varieties: Arrufiac (min 20%), Petit Courbu (min 20%), Petit Manseng (min 20%), Gros Manseng, Clairette (not permitted after 2020) | |
| **Tursan** | Red | Tannat, Cabernet Franc (min each 30%), Cabernet Sauvignon, Fer Servadou (min 10% together) | |
| | Rosé | Tannat (between 10-30%), Cabernet Franc (min 50%, Cabernet Sauvignon and Fer Servadou (max 40% together) | |
| | White | Baroque (min 30%), Petit & Gros Manseng (max 50% together, max 20% Petit Manseng) Sauvignon (max 30%), Chenin Blanc or Cruchinet (max 20%) | |
| **Floc de Gascogne** | Rosé | Cabernet Franc, Cabernet Sauvignon, Cot, Merlot N. Tannat (max 50 %) | Made by fortifying unfermented grape juice with a young Armagnac spirit made on the same property. Fortification is to 16-18%. |
| | White | Colombard, Gros Manseng, Ugni Blanc (min 70 %, together, none more than 50 %); supporting grapes: Baroque, Folle Blanche, Petit Manseng, Mauzac, Sauvignon Blanc, Sémillon | |
| **Béarn** | Red and Rosé | Tannat (max 60%), Cabernet Sauvignon, Bouchy (Cabernet Franc), Pinenc (Fer Servadou), Manseng Noir, Courbu Noir | |
| | White | Gros Manseng, Petit Manseng, Courbu, Ruffiat, Lauzet, Camarelet, Sauvignon | |
| **Jurançon** | Dry and Sweet White | Gros Mansent, Petit Manseng, Petit Courbu; Lauzet, Camarlet (max together or alone, 15%) | Dry wines are labelled 'Jurançon Sec.' 'Jurançon' alone indicates sweet, moëlleux style. |
| **Irouléguy** | Red and Rosé | Tannat (max 50%), Cabernet Sauvignon, Cabernet Franc (max 50% alone or together) Petit Courbu, Gros Manseng, Petit Manseng | |

# REGIONS

The diversity of the Southwest defies standard regional categorization. Rather, it is best to understand the region as a collection of different zones that share certain sensibilities, including terroir, wine style, and history.

If not for the magnitude of its individual fame, Bordeaux would naturally be included in the Southwest. Appellations closest to Bordeaux are often referred to as "Bordeaux Satellites." Those to the east of Bordeaux include Bergerac, Montravel, Côtes de Duras, Saussignac, Monbazillac, Pécharmant and Rosette. The Bordeaux influence continues, but starts to fade, farther south in the Côtes de Duras, Côtes du Marmandais, Buzet and Côtes du Brulhois. Due east, in the

Lot Valley, are Cahors and Côteaux du Quercy— regions that are clear about their distinction from Bordeaux. Local pride strengthens as one moves even farther east, then south, into the steep terrain of Aveyron, home to Entraygues and Le Fel, Marcillac, Estaing, and Côtes de Millau. Sweeping back west, are the characterful regions of Gaillac and Fronton, the latter a virtual suburb of France's center of high tech, Toulouse. Gascogne, land of Armagnac, occupies a large portion of territory west of the city. On its southwest corner rests the land of brooding red wines, Madiran. Spreading southwest toward the Pyrénées Mountains are Béarn, Jurançon, and Irouléguy.

The **Bordeaux satellites** are natural extensions of the Bordeaux basin, defined in part by the rivers that run through them, the Dordogne and the Garonne. **Bergerac**, which flanks the Dordogne, is the largest of these appellations, so much so, that it contains within its borders, the superior red wine appellation, **Pécharmant**, distinguished by the iron content of its soil, and the sweet appellations of **Monbazillac** and **Saussignac**, whose botrytis-infected grapes are made into wines resembling Sauternes or Barsac. Provided certain standards are met, wines from these regions can take their own AOP, or, be declassified as regular Bergerac.

**Côtes de Bergerac** is not a separate region; rather it is an appellation that sets a slightly higher standard for the production of Bergerac wines. **Montravel**, too, sets a higher standard requiring that vine plots to be classified be claimed before harvest; and requiring that samples of wines be submitted for quality evaluation the spring following vintage. Wines that don't make the cut are declassified as Bergerac. **Rosette** is a tiny appellation dedicated to the production of light, slightly sweet wines.

Influenced more by the Garonne River are **Côtes de Duras**, **Côtes du Marmandais**, **Buzet** and **Côtes du Brulhois**. While Bordeaux-style wines are the norm in all of these appellations, Côtes du Marmandais enjoys the distinction of making several wines from the brash, indigenous grape **Abouriou**. Known for its notably dark color and heavy tannin, it makes wines that can rival Madiran in power. Realizing the advantage of creating a profile distinction separate from that of Bordeaux, the AOC now requires one-quarter of vineyards to be planted in Syrah, Malbec, Tannat, or Abouriou. Requirements for what has to go into the bottle are another matter entirely. **Côtes du Brulhois** requires that an unstated portion of Tannat go into every blend.

**The Lot Valley** is mostly appreciated by its famed appellation **Cahors**. Cahors, which defines what Malbec can be in France, has a storied history. At one point, Cahors earned the sobriquet "Black Wine." Contemporary wine romantics might imagine that the name was a laudation earned because of the especially dark color of Malbec; and nostalgically lament an "authentic" style now mournfully forgotten in the rush to satisfy pedestrian international tastes. There is some truth to the story, but praise was not a part of it. Indeed, "black wine" was essentially a wine made from grapes concentrated by boiling before fermentation, then, often fortified by a portion of neutral spirit. The wine concentrate was used to strengthen thinner wines, especially those from Bordeaux, which were regarded as pallid until viticulture improved in the eighteenth century. Today, this style of "wine" is no longer made, but Cahors, always red, does vary in style from easy drinking wines full of fresh fruit flavors, to nobler *vins de garde* designed for years in the cellar.

South of Cahors is **Côteaux du Quercy**, a chalk-rich appellation that requires 40-60% of appellation vineyards to be planted in Cabernet Franc.

The Southwest's inland, mountainous hinterlands within the département of **Aveyron** contain some of the region's most dramatic landscapes, where the Massif Central meets deep river gorges cut from the Cévennes mountains. As one might expect, the area supports some of the Southwest's most distinctive appellations. **Marcillac**, an area with striking red soil, was once a prosperous region that fell twice on hard times due to the double blow of phylloxera in the last part of the nineteenth century, and then, the closure of local mines in the middle of the twentieth. With no more than 23 hectares (57 acres) of vines planted in the mid-1960s, Marcillac was on the verge of extinction. But, local initiatives began a revival, both from stubbornness, as well as pride in the local grape **Mansois**. Though grown in other parts of the Southwest under different names (see above), Marcillac Mansois is distinctive due to region's iron-laden soils. It is typically dark in color, with flavors of forest berries, earthy spice, and full, yet soft tannin.

Nearby, the terraced vineyards of **Estraygues** and **Le Fel** produce aromatic wines on granitic and schistose soils, respectively. Similar wines are made at **Estaing**, the tiny appellation next door. Down the road is **Côtes de Millau**, which suffered from many of the same maladies as other Aveyron regions. Uniquely, though, its juicy wines are made from **Gamay** and **Syrah**. Some aromatic whites are made from Mauzac and Chenin Blanc.

**Gaillac** is the Southwest's oldest wine region, cultivated by Roman colonizers moving west from their Languedoc base at Narbonne, in the first century AD. It is an eccentric area, one that started a proto-appellation system by the sixteenth century AD, requiring the use of a distinctive symbol for Gaillac wines, forbidding imports of wines from other regions, and declaring that only pigeon guano could be used for fertilizing Gaillac vineyards. This last rule persisted until the nineteenth century.

Close to Limoux, the area credited for "inventing" sparkling wine in the sixteenth century, Gaillac developed an early sparkling wine industry of its own. Most of its bubbles, labeled **Gaillac mousseux**, and made using the *méthode traditionelle*, would tickle the palates of Champagne drinkers in familiar ways. More unusual is the sweet sparkler labeled ***méthode gallaicoise*** that is made through a single fermentation (rather than a double, as is done in Champagne) using indigenous yeast and the grape's natural sugars. In the winter when fermentation is arrested by cold temperatures, wines are bottled and sealed (usually by cork). When fermentation spontaneously resumes during the warmer days of spring, the carbon dioxide that is a natural bi-product of fermentation (another bi-product is alcohol) remains trapped in the bottle, creating bubbles. Limoux's Blanquette de Limoux Méthode Ancestrale is made in the same way, though grape requirements are different. Not really a sparkling wine, ***vin perlé*** is a lightly fizzy dry wine made by fermenting must at cool temperatures, then bottling immediately before all of the carbon dioxide ($CO_2$) left over from fermentation dissipates. If nothing else, it charms on a warm summer day. It can be made from any of Gaillac's white grapes.

Gaillac's dry red, rosé and white wines are of variable quality. Both are largely made from indigenous varieties and can be quite distinctive if made with care. The region's sweet wines are somewhat lighter and less saccharine than those from other parts of the Southwest. They are often delicious.

**Fronton**, formerly called Côte du Frontonnais, produces some of the Southwest's most distinctive red wines, based on the local grape Négrette. The wines are special insofar as they paradoxically seem heavy and refreshing at once, full of the perfume of violets, dark berries, and black licorice. With some notable variations in topsoil, the region's iron and quartz rich substrata assure a compelling element to Fronton's wines.

**Gascogne** is in many ways everyone's ideal of rural France. The province sits in the middle of the Southwest with green, rolling hills, small farms with weathered placards advertising artisanal foie gras, and charming houses from whose chimneys come the seductive waft of slow-cooking casseroles. This is also the land of Armagnac, the soulful brandy too long overshadowed by another *'gnac* up the road. Wine production here is overwhelmingly dedicated to supplying a base product suitably insipid for distillation. In the past couple of decades, however, efforts have been made to produce table wines, that if, not all that interesting, are at least well-made and modestly priced. Made from local and international grapes, white and red, the wines are classified as **Vin de Pays Côtes de Gascogne** (Now, IGP).

Occupying the southeast corner of Gascony that touches Madiran, **Côtes de Saint Mont** is very much under the influence of the Gascon cooperative Producteurs Plaimonts, which accounts for the large majority of Saint Mont production. But the grape varieties used are the same as those with neighboring Madiran and its white wine appendage Pecherenc du Vic Bilh: Tannat, Fer Servadou (locally called 'Pinenc'), and Cabernets Sauvignon and Franc for reds; Arrufiac, Petit Courbu, Petit and Gros Manseng for whites. Stylistically the wines carry the easy-drinking influence of Gascony, but reflect somewhat the substance of Madiran and Pecherenc.

If the wines from Côtes de Gascogne seem unimaginative, the same cannot be said of those from **Madiran** on Gascogne's southwest corner. Based on the hearty grape Tannat, Madiran wines are (in)famously powerful and tannic, and, historically require years of cellaring to soften. When Madiran first gained AOC status in 1948, thirty-three months of barrel aging were required before release. The required period has been reduced to one year, relieving some economic stress for producers, but also leaving many of the heavy tannins intact. Impatience, or perhaps pressure to market wines that can be consumed earlier, drove experiments to soften Madiran's tannin. In 1991, local enologist Patrick Ducournau invented the method of ***microbullage*** (micro-oxygenation), which polishes tannin and enhances fruitiness by adding controlled amounts of oxygen to wines during fermentation. *Microbullage* has been embraced by many in the region and has become part of the battery of techniques for winemakers throughout the world. **Pacherenc du Vic-Bilh** is Madiran's white wine appellation. Its boundaries are the same as Madiran's, though its historic center is in the clay-rich, western part of the territory. Dry Pacherenc wine are normally enjoyed young, but can age well. Sweet wines age beautifully.

The road west to the Atlantic passes minor regions **Tursan**, **Côteaux de Chalosse** and **Vins de Sables**. Production is dominated here by cooperatives.

**Béarn** marks the transition from Gascon to Basque cultures. The region is attached in two patches to Madiran, then again, about 20 miles (32km) southwest, next to **Jurançon**, lionized for its iconic dry and sweet whites. Conveniently, winemakers from both Madiran and Jurançon can use the Béarn appellation for wines not permitted in their own regions, rosés for those in Madiran, rosés and reds for the Jurançonais.

Climbing into the foothills of the Pyrénées, **Jurançon** is home to some of France's most unique white wines. Both dry and sweet styles are made. Climatically, the region is unique, even compared to other parts of the Southwest. Rain is common in spring and early summer, with warm, dry autumns and mild winters. Vineyards are planted on steep slopes, often hidden by forest. Growing seasons are long, extending to late autumn, especially for sweet wines. Botrytis cinerea is rare, which is perhaps fortunate considering the natural "funkiness" of the favored grapes, Gros and Petit Manseng. Dry wines, mostly based on Gros Manseng, are always identified with the word *sec* ('dry' in French). If the adjective doesn't appear, the wine will be at least a bit sweet, in the *moëlleux* style. Sweeter wines might be labeled "*vendage tardive*" (late harvest). Regardless of styles, Jurançon wines are universally herbal with exotic spice flavors such as cardamom, as well as dried fruit, all balanced by fresh acidity. Older, sweeter wines can be earthy and smoky.

The southernmost portion of the Southwest, in the unabashed *Pays Basque* region is **Irouléguy**. Most vines are planted on terraces skirting the Pyrénées, at elevations of 600 meters (2000 feet) or higher. Part of France since the seventeenth century AD, Irouléguy nonetheless, maintains its strong Basque identity, not the least of which through the Basque words on many of its wine labels. Relatively little white wine is made here, but they are usually made from *Izkiriota* (Gros Manseng), Izkiriota Ttipia (Petit Manseng) or *Zerratia* (Courbu). Reds and rosés are made from *Bordelesa Beltza* (Tannat — literally, Black Bordelais), *Axeria Haundia* (Cabernet Sauvignon) or *Axeria* (Cabernet Franc). It is claimed that the latter has its origins in the Basque country. Stylistically, whites and rosés are meant for early consumption; many reds, too, though those based on higher percentages of Tannat (over sixty percent) need some time to age.

Over sixty percent of wines produced in the Southwest have been classified as Vin de Pays or Vin de Table. Vin de Pays, which are being reclassified as IGP (see above), come from 21 demarcated zones, though ninety percent are from three larger regions: Côtes de Gascogne, Comté Tolosan and Côtes du Tarn. Côtes de Gascogne has been noted above. The designation **Comté Tolosan IGP** covers all areas of the Southwest that have no other geographical or other designation. Other IGP areas are the Agenais, Ariège, Aveyron, Bigorre, Côteaux de Glanes, Côtes de Condomois, Côteaux et Terrasse de Montauban, Gers, Haute-Garonne, Landes, Lot, Lot et Garonne, Pyrénées Atlantique, Tarn, Terroir Landais, Côteaux de Chalosse and Thézac Perricard.

## Hot Topics

Reforms in France's appellation côntrolée system have eliminated the category of VDQS. As a result, VDQS regions in Southwest have been promoted to full AOC/AOP status. Growers within various regions, notably Cahors and Montravel, have taken initiatives to create charters of quality that exceed appellation demands. While the efforts are worthy, all too often the wines that qualify for such distinction are those made from especially ripe-grapes and aged in new oak barrels, just like elite wines made in regions throughout the world. One might wonder, therefore, what the point is if adhering to higher standards simply makes a region's wine more like wines from other places. As time passes, though, one can expect that standards will be dedicated to showing what is special about a region rather than adhering to generic, international notions of elite quality.

## SPECIALTIES OF THE REGION

The Southwest is a veritable paradise for the gourmet. France's best foie gras, both duck and goose, is raised here, often elaborated with the region's famed black truffles, especially the *truffes de Périgord.* Other duck products, especially *magret de canard* are a local specialty. Roquefort cheese, which sets the standard for blue cheeses around the world, is made here. So, too, is the famed brandy Armagnac, which is distilled and aged in the heart of Gascony. Prunes from Agen, especially macerated in Armagnac, are prized as the world's finest. The *Jambon de Bayonne*, cured by dry air and local salt, is regarded as the best ham in France. Of local dishes, few are more celebrated than hearty cassoulet, which conveniently is the perfect foil to some of the region's brawnier reds.

The Southwest is perhaps the most difficult region in France to categorize due to the diversity of its terroirs and its large collection of indigenous grapes found nowhere else. But, it is a region that deserves attention on several accounts. Its so-called Bordeaux-satellites offer Bordeaux lovers the opportunity to enjoy very similar wines for markedly lower prices. The Southwest's most well-known regions, Cahors and Madiran are storied in history and distinction, and more outlying regions such as Marcillac and Fronton provide wines that are off the well-worn path of "international"-styled wines, yet offer immediate appeal

# BORDEAUX

| AREA UNDER VINE | 117,500 hectares |
|---|---|
| GRAPE VARIETIES | |
| RED | Cabernet Sauvignon, Cabernet Franc, Merlot, Malbec (Cot), Petit Verdot, and Carmenère |
| WHITE | Sémillon, Sauvignon Blanc, Muscadelle |
| CLIMATE | The climate is maritime, with warm, mild summers and falls, and occasional frost during winter and spring. The Atlantic Ocean, Gironde, Garonne, and Dordogne Rivers are Bordeaux's major climate moderators. |
| SOIL | The Left Bank is characterized by topsoils of gravel with a gravel base, or a base of sand with some limestone and clay. The Right Bank's vineyards benefit from clay soils with a limestone base. |

Bordeaux has long been a success in exporting wine because of its prime location on the Gironde and Dordogne Rivers. Bordeaux, reaching beyond its context, is a word even the most occasional wine drinker knows and has been *the* example for red wine producers everywhere. It stands, quite strongly, as a pillar to all in the winemaking—and drinking—world.

## HISTORY

Although organized viticulture probably arrived in Bordeaux after the Romans settled the Rhône Valley, there is mention by the Phoenicians and Greeks of grape vines as early as the 6$^{th}$ century BC. The marriage of Eleanor of Aquitaine and Henry Plantagenet (King Henry II of England) in 1152 marked the beginning of a period of British rule that would last for three centuries. At the end of the Hundred Years War in 1453, France reclaimed Aquitaine from British rule and stifled the thriving export market to England. During the 17$^{th}$ century, trading began instead with the influential Dutch, who built up the marshland (now called the Médoc) with levies. Until then all wines in the Bordeaux trade were from the Graves district.

By the 19$^{th}$ century, Bordeaux had established itself as *the* quality wine region, with its most well-known châteaux demanding the highest prices in the market. Yet in 1852 Bordeaux was struck with a disease called *oidium*, or powdery mildew, which decreased production by nearly half. In 1858, spraying sulfur in the vineyards was discovered to cure the mildew, only to be followed by the ravenous phylloxera louse. Phylloxera vastatrix devastated Bordeaux before moving throughout Europe and, later, South Africa, Australia, New Zealand, North America, and South America. Grafting vinifera vines to North American labrusca rootstock finally starved the pest. Just as winemakers and grape growers in Bordeaux dealt with the phylloxera louse, the vineyards were plagued by a case of downy mildew. Spraying the vines with *Bouillie Bordelaise*—a solution of copper, lime, and sulfur—soon cured this last set back.

The famous 1855 Classification took place, despite nature's attacks on Bordeaux, and the wines of the Médoc region were rated based on then-current market prices. At this time, the "Right Bank" was producing low quality wine. Only after World War II were Saint-Émilion and Pomerol finally recognized for their wines other than the well-established Châteaux of Cheval Blanc and Pétrus.

In the 1950s, modern technologies like stainless steel fermentation tanks appeared in Bordeaux, although many first growth châteaux refused to use them for several years. Nevertheless, modern technologies brought the bulk wines of Bordeaux to an overall higher quality level. In 1954, Saint-Émilion finally received its classification. Five years later, in 1959, the Graves district was classified with separate lists for red and white wines, which were all classified simply as Cru Classé. The exception here was Château Haut-Brion in Pessac-Léognan, which was classified as a first growth in 1855.

In 1972, châteaux bottling became compulsory in an effort to guarantee quality. This action was a solution to the growing number of *négociants* selling wine from the *midi* as Bordeaux wine. The following year, Château Mouton-Rothschild was elevated from a second growth to a first growth after years of petitioning for the promotion. This is the only promotion ever within the Médoc's 1855 Classification. In 1978, Robert Parker's first bimonthly publication of the *Wine Advocate* was circulated and brought a great deal of American attention to Bordeaux. Later, his enthusiastic review of the 1982 vintage resulted in a surplus of American interest in Bordeaux futures *(en primeur)*—the practice of buying of Bordeaux wines before they are bottled. The purchase of futures is still very much in fashion and vital to the production levels of many Bordeaux châteaux.

## QUALITY LEVELS, CLASSIFICATIONS, AND LAWS

**Generic** or **regional** wines are made from grapes grown anywhere in the region of Bordeaux. The following are generic Bordeaux AOCs: **Bordeaux, Bordeaux Supérior, Crémant de Bordeaux, Bordeaux Rosé, Bordeaux Haut-Benauge,** and **Bordeaux Clairet**.

**District** wines are made from grapes within the district stated on the label and only that district. For example, Haut-Médoc and Entre-Deux-Mers are districts. Such districts may include several communes.

**Commune** wines are from a specific commune within a given district, like Pauillac and Margaux within the Haut-Médoc. Châteaux themselves are not AOCs, but simply properties within a commune. For example, Château Latour is an estate within the **Pauillac AOC**.

## THE CLASSIFICATION OF 1855

The Classification of 1855 was devised to bring more attention to the quality wines of Bordeaux. Perhaps one of the better marketing ploys ever conceived in the wine industry, it established Bordeaux as an expensive, aristocratic wine region. In preparation for the Exposition Universelle de Paris, Emperor Napoléon III asked that the wines of Bordeaux be classified as a guide for visitors of the World Fair. The list of Grands Crus Classés was developed by the Chambre de Commerce et d'Industrie de Bordeaux based on the market price each château was demanding at the time. Sixty châteaux from the Médoc and one from Graves were classified for red wine as either a Premier, Deuxième, Troisième, Quatrième, or Cinqième Cru (First, Second, Third, Fourth, or Fifth Growth).

### THE FIVE FIRST GROWTHS

| Château | Current AOC |
|---|---|
| **Château Haut-Brion** | Pessac-Léognan |
| **Château Lafite-Rothschild** | Pauillac |
| **Château Latour** | Pauillac |
| **Château Margaux** | Margaux |
| **Château Mouton-Rothschild (added in 1973)** | Pauillac |

### SAUTERNES-BARSAC

Twenty-seven sweet white wines from Sauternes-Barsac were classified separately as Premiers or Deuxièmes Crus. Only one estate, Château d'Yquem, was classified as a Premier Cru Supérieur and is considered the highest quality wine in Bordeaux.

### THE 1954 SAINT-ÉMILION CLASSIFICATION

The 1954 Saint-Émilion Classification works uniquely within the AOC system and market value is not taken into consideration. In the Médoc, individual estates are rated, whereas in Saint-Émilion there is a separate AOC called Saint-Émilion Grand Cru with two sub-divisions—Saint-Émilion Grand Cru Classé (currently there are 55) and Saint-Émilion Premier Grand Cru Classé (currently numbering 13). Properties rated under this AOC are revised every 10 years with both promotions and demotions. In order to be considered for classification, an estate must meet certain requirements, including:

- The estate "must constitute a sufficiently large economic and viticultural unit and have cellars used exclusively for wine made on the estate"

- "At least 50% of the total vines must be able to produce wines entitled to Saint-Emilion Grand Cru status from vines over twelve years old"
- "Over the last ten years, the estate must have obtained the approval certificate for Saint-Emilion Grand Cru status for at least seven harvests"[6]

## THE CLASSIFICATION OF GRAVES

While the Graves' Château Haut-Brion was included in the 1855 Classification, the entire Graves region was not classified until 1953. This classification, which was revised in 1959, makes no attempt to rank the wines within the classification, instead it simply differentiates red from white and all properties have the right to use the Cru Classé terminology. Sixteen château are rated in total (with six of these being rated for both red and white wine), all of which are encompassed within the modern appellation of Pessac-Léognan.

## GEOGRAPHY, CLIMATE, AND SOIL

Bordeaux is considered one of the best places for growing grapes due almost solely to its climate and location. The Gironde River flows away from the city of Bordeaux and into the Atlantic Ocean. Up river, which looks like down river on any map of the region, there are two very important tributaries, the Garonne and Dordogne Rivers. The waterways split before they reach the ancient city and flow around the Entre-Deux-Mers district. The rivers of Bordeaux are responsible for the humidity levels in and around the region. The humidity level in Bordeaux, particularly in Sauternes and Barsac, is in turn responsible for noble rot or *pourriture noble*. Despite the fairly northern 45° latitude of Bordeaux, the three rivers and the Atlantic Ocean help maintain the region's temperate maritime climate. However, an occasional late spring frost during fruit set can cause *coulure* (the failure of grapes to develop properly after flowering), or a hailstorm at harvest can ruin a crop. Weather patterns like these demand knowledge of vintage qualities.

The soil in Bordeaux is very important as it plays a prominent role in dictating where certain grapes are grown. In the Médoc and Graves, the soil is predominantly well-drained gravel. Cabernet Sauvignon, which dominates the "Left Bank," needs such soil to efficiently ripen. On the "Right Bank" of the Gironde River, the soil is clay with a limestone base, which is better for growing the softer style Merlot grape. The few hillside vineyards are clay and limestone as well.

## VARIETIES

**Sémillon** is the predominant white grape and the major player in the sweet wines of Sauternes, because it is highly susceptible to *pourriture noble*, the magnificent condition caused by Botrytis cinerea. Sémillon brings a golden color and body to the wines of Sauternes.

**Sauvignon Blanc** is known for its acidity, especially when blended for Bordeaux's famous sweet wines. It must comprise a quarter of the blend in the Graves' dry whites; however, it is also produced as a still dry varietal wine. This is the only exception to the rule of blends in Bordeaux.

**Muscadelle** is perhaps a minor player in the production of sweet wines, but it is an essential aromatic component of the blend, lending floral and honey perfumes to these wines.

**Cabernet Sauvignon** is the "King of the Médoc" and certainly the most famous red variety in Bordeaux. It thrives in the gravel soil of the "Left Bank", where it is predominately found. However, it is a late ripener and therefore composes a smaller part in the blend in years when the weather prohibits it from ripening fully. It brings tannin and black currant qualities to the wine.

**Cabernet Franc,** or Bouchet, is grown primarily in Saint-Émilion where it possesses less tannin and acid than Cabernet Sauvignon. It can ripen in cooler climates and mature more rapidly.

---

[6] CIVB. (2006). *Saint Emilion Classification*. Retrieved November 11, 2010, from Bordeaux.com: http://www.bordeaux.com

**Merlot** is the most widely planted red grape in Bordeaux, dominating Saint-Émilion and Pomerol where it prefers the limestone soils. Merlot ripens earlier than Cabernet Sauvignon and has softer tannins.

**Malbec,** or Cot, is found mostly in the Bourg and Blaye regions. It produces early drinking reds possessing deep color and mellow acid levels, yet sufficient tannins.

**Petit Verdot** comprises a small portion of Bordeaux's blends; however, it brings a spicy character to the wine as well as tannin and color. It is grown mostly in the Médoc.

Historically there was also a sixth and seventh red grape of Bordeaux. Much of the **Carmenère** that was planted died in the particularly bad frost of 1956 and was never replanted. It is now one of Chile's signature grapes. The little known **Saint Macaire** died out in Bordeaux, but is now being used to make rare wines in Australia and California.

## Major Wine Regions

### The Left Bank

The **Médoc** and **Haut-Médoc** are together referred to as the "Left Bank," with the Médoc being home to only regional wines that are predominately **Cabernet Sauvignon**–based and grown in clay soils with fair amounts of gravel. The Médoc accounts for roughly 15% of Bordeaux's total wine production. The Haut-Médoc district is home to all of the 1855 Classification's First Growth wines, with one exception. It is known for its gravel soil and **Cabernet Sauvignon**–dominated wines. The Haut-Médoc consists of several commune appellations, which are listed below from north to south.

**Saint-Estèphe** is dominated by clay sub-soils with gravel surfaces. The **Merlot** grown here produces coarser, very tannic wines.

**Pauillac** is home to three of the five First Growth châteaux and fist-sized gravel in the most prestigious vineyards. A typical Pauillac wine is known for its longevity, power, and cedary bouquet from **Cabernet Sauvignon** grapes.

**Saint-Julien** is located in the center of the Haut-Médoc district and contains the highest number of classified châteaux. These wines, made from a traditional blend of **Cabernet Sauvignon** and **Merlot**, possess both the power of a Pauillac and the suppleness of a Margaux.

**Listrac** and **Moulis** are the two smaller communes in the Haut-Médoc. They are home to the smallest number of classified growths, yet they have the largest number of Cru Bourgeois. **Listrac** is the least favored of the six communes, in part because of its distance from the Gironde estuary. It has clay and limestone soils and is largely planted with **Merlot** vines. **Moulis** is the smallest of the Médoc communes, yet it has an interesting variety of soils including gravel, clay, and limestone. It also requires lower yields than Listrac.

**Margaux** is the southernmost commune in the Médoc, just north of Graves, and is known for elegant **Cabernet Sauvignon** wines. Its gravel and limestone soils produce wines with a velvety texture and enticing nose. Containing two thirds of all of the Grands Crus Classés, Margaux has more classified growths than any other communal AOC.

### Graves and Sauternes

**Graves** (meaning "gravel" in French) was known in the Middle Ages for its export of Claret to the British. The region has been a good quality producer of both red and white wines since its classification in 1959. In 1987 the commune of **Pessac-Léognan** was formed and consequently public interest in Graves as a district waned—the newly appointed appellation is home to Château Haut-Brion and all of the growths listed in the 1959 Classification of Graves.

**Sauternes** is a district known for its sweet white botrytised wines from the five communes of Sauternes, Bommes, Barsac, Preignac, and Fargues. The district's location near the Garonne and Cérons Rivers provides a unique microclimate with moist morning mists and dry, warm afternoons. The wines are made from **Sémillon**, especially fond of the botrytis fungus; **Sauvignon Blanc**, vital with its addition of acidity; and **Muscadelle**, which adds perfume, yet is often left out of the blend for its stubbornness in the vineyard.

Picking noble-rotted grapes by hand is very expensive and time consuming, but it is the only way. It is done in *tries*—the process of harvesting the botrytised grapes in a series of pickings, during which each individual grape is plucked from the vine when appropriate. This is essential, as each grape NOT each bunch rots at a different rate. The grapes must be delicately pressed and fermentation may take a very long time, as the juice is so rich with sugar that the yeast struggles to survive. Yeast cells usually die off when the must reaches about 13% alcohol, leaving enough residual sugar to approximate 6% alcohol if fermentation continued. These wines can be enjoyed fairly young, but will stand up to decades of aging, especially those from the only Premier Cru Supérieur, Château d'Yquem.

## Botrytis Cinerea

Botryitis cinerea is a fungus that attacks grapes by piercing tiny holes through their skins in order to remove the moisture inside, leaving the grape with high concentrations of sugar and tartaric acid. The reduction of water in the fruit naturally reduces the quantity of juice resulting from a crop. Sauternes is allowed a maximum yield of 25 hl/ha, although most châteaux yield between 18–20 hl/ha. Châteaux d'Yquem boasts yields of only 9 hl/ha. Botrytis-influenced wines are not only produced in Sauternes but in the Loire Valley, Alsace, Germany, Austria, and Hungary as well.

## THE LIBOURNAIS

The Libournais is the area known as the "Right Bank" and includes Saint-Émilion, Pomerol, and several satellite appellations surrounding the town of Libourne. The wine quality in this region was very low until the late 1950s when a devastating spring frost hit enough vineyards to justify uprooting and replanting the area with the better-suited Merlot and Cabernet Franc vines instead of Cabernet Sauvignon.

**Saint-Émilion** was a wine-producing region long before the Médoc although it was much less important commercially until the 19th century. Along the *côtes*, which are the slopes surrounding the village of Saint-Émilion itself, the soil is clay with a limestone base. Here **Merlot** dominates. Within Saint-Émilion there are several distinct sub-regions differentiated by their soils. Graves-Saint-Émilion is the area west of the village, featuring gravel soils planted with mainly **Cabernet Franc**, which is home to the First Growths Château Cheval Blanc and Château Figeac.

**Pomerol** is unclassified, but home to the most expensive wine in the world—Château Pétrus. Pomerol and Saint-Émilion have very similar soil types and variety plantings, so the differences in the wines are perhaps subtle. Nevertheless, Tom Stevenson writes in *The New Sotheby's Wine Encyclopedia*, "…the difference between St.-Émilion and Pomerol is like the difference between silk and velvet: the quality is similar, but the texture is not…."[7]

**The Côtes** are spread across all of Bordeaux and have certain similarities in their growing conditions. The soil of the Côtes is predominantly clay and limestone, and the vineyards are well exposed to the sun, facing south or southwest. The wines are highly underrated and not consumed enough and can be of excellent quality, especially for their low prices. The Côtes communes include: **Première Côtes de Bordeaux, Côtes de Bordeaux-Saint Macaire, Graves de Vayres, Côtes de Bourg, Côtes de Blaye, Première Côtes de Blaye, Côtes de Castillon,** and **Bordeaux-Côtes de Francs**.

**Entre-Deux-Mers**, literally translated as "between two seas," is bordered by the Dordogne River to the north and the Garonne River to the south. The district's varied soils, often containing clay, produce not only dry white wine but some very nice examples of medium-sweet white botrytised wines as well. These sweet wines from Loupiac, Sainte Croix-du-Mont, and Cadillac are not as highly regarded as the wines of Sauternes and are lighter in body and more expressively fresh with honey, fruity aromas. **Sauvignon Blanc** provides these wines with a healthy acidity that is complimented by the suppleness of its blend with **Sémillon** and aromas of **Muscadelle**. The Entre-Deux-Mers communes include: **Entre-Deux-Mers, Entre-Deux-Mers Haut-Benauge, Loupiac, Cadillac,** and **Sainte Croix-du-Mont.**

---

[7] Stevenson, T. (2007). *The Sotheby's Wine Encyclopedia*. New York: DK Publishing.

# Spain

| Area Under Vine | 1,160,000 hectares |
|---|---|
| Grape Varieties | |
| Red | Tempranillo, and Garnacha |
| | Monastrell, Graciano, Bobal, Mencía |
| | Carignan (Cariñena), Cabernet Sauvignon, Merlot, Syrah, Pinot Noir |
| White | Viura (Macabéo), Albariño, Verdejo, |
| | Moscatell, Palomino, Pedro Ximenez, Xarel-lo, Godello, Mazuelo |
| | Sauvignon Blanc, Chardonnay |
| Climate | Spain is unique with its many wine-growing regions often being characterized by drastic climatic conditions. With its both Atlantic and Mediterranean coastlines and many high altitude areas in both the cool damp northwest to the hot desert-like southeast-Spain's varying weather patterns lend to the production of many different styles of quality wines. Spain is also covered with several mountain ranges that help to moderate climate, including the Pyrenees and Cantabrian Mountains in the north, the Sierra Morena and the Bética range south of Madrid, and the Central Castilian Mountains to the capital's north |
| Soil | The key to Spanish soil is lime, and it is found throughout the wine regions. The northern regions in particular benefit from significant limestone in the soil. In Navarra, the soil is 25–45% "active" lime. In Rioja Alavessa and Alta, it blends with sandstone or calcareous clay. Soil in Rioja Baja includes ferruginous-clay or an alluvial silty-loam over the limestone base. Cava country offers a wide variety of soil including limestone-dominated clay, sand and chalk in Penedés. Priorato has an unusual blend of reddish slate and quartzite soil, the very unique and beautiful llicorela. |

In surface area, Spain is the second largest country in Europe, it is third in wine production and yet has the most land planted with nearly 1.2 million hectares under vine. Grapes are Spain's third largest crop behind cereals and olives. Vines are planted just about everywhere in Spain, even though a good portion of the country is so hot and dry that the vines can barely survive, so instead of wine making they are used for various Spanish staples which include Sherry vinegar, grape concentrates, marmalades, and of course grape alcohol used for the distillation of Spanish Brandy. The national average yield is only 23 hl/ha. Even the finest Burgundy estate usually sees yields of 30–35 hl/ha. This low figure is partly due to wider vine spacing in Spain. While the relatively recent legalization of irrigation in 1996 and better clonal selection has raised yields slightly in the last few years, the average is still remarkably low.

# History

As in many European countries, Spain's wine history is ancient, even prehistoric. Vines have been planted in Spain since 4000–3000 BC although serious cultivation began with the Phoenicians 3000 years ago. Recent evidence suggests that wild varieties flourished in Spain pre-dating man by millions of years. Although the Phoenicians and the Carthaginians both cultivated vines and traded wine, the Romans did the most to promote Spain's early reputation for the beverage. During the Punic Wars between the Romans and the Carthaginians, and Rome's subsequent occupation of Spain (100 BC–499 AD), Spanish wine was traded and sold throughout Europe. It was quite popular on its own and as a blending wine used to raise the alcohol content of wines from more northerly climates.

In 711, the Moors conquered Spain. Under their Islamic rule, wine was officially outlawed, but trade and production must have continued on, as wine was still taxed at that time. The Moors had a profound influence on Spanish culture and architecture, and they also perfected the art of distillation—originally for medicine, then later used for brandy. It has been theorized that they may have introduced fortification to Spain, without which Sherry would not exist.

Much to Spain's benefit, the mid-19th-century plagues of powdery mildew and phylloxera were late to arrive in the country. When phylloxera arrived in Spain, many of the great vineyards in the rest of Europe had already been seriously affected, and by the time the pest became a serious threat, the technique of grafting European vines onto American rootstocks had proven effective in stopping this nasty louse. Similarly, when powdery mildew posed a problem, French remedies were utilized to stop it. French wine makers (especially from nearby Bordeaux) were coming to Spain at this time in search of greener pastures (or vineyards) while theirs recovered. They brought their superior technologies and experience with them. Small barriques were used for fermenting and aging for the first time in Spain and quality was improved.

In 1872, José Raventós borrowed the *méthode champenoise* technology from the French and produced Spain's first sparkling wine at Codorniu, his family farm in Penedés. The Spanish had tried to recreate Champagne using the traditional Champagne grapes, but had failed. Raventós took a huge chance with his experiment using native Spanish grapes in a sparkling blend. The result was a wine that could be brought to market faster, was just as pleasing to the public as Champagne, and is now the largest selling sparkling wine style in the world having passed Champagne in 2001.

The Spanish Civil War in the 1930s, followed by World War II, resulted in the destruction and neglect of many of the country's vineyards. Spain's conflict with her Allied neighbors effectively severed all trade relations. After the wars, most small estates did not have the funds to replant their vineyards or rebuild their bodegas. Large cooperatives dominated and produced unremarkable wine. Franco's dictatorship was another important factor as most of the country was unable to modernize or move forward under his rule. After his death in 1975, the world had learned a valuable lesson and the Spanish gained. They had a wealth of native grapes that had been restricted to be pulled in favor of planting more popular varieties; in turn they also now had access to international money and were able to educate themselves on the world's progress in winemaking.

Spain joined the European Union in 1986 and in turn received a fiscal boost that helped rebuild its wine industry, which had been languishing for decades. International wine makers and non-indigenous varieties became an important part of the winemaking scene. Many private estates began bottling their own production instead of selling it to the local co-ops, rules became more defined and agriculture became more careful and studied. At long last, the improved image and quality enabled wine makers to command more attention and in turn higher prices for Spanish wines.

# WINE LAWS

The Instituto Nacional de Denominaciones de Origen (INDO) oversees the enforcement of Spain's wine laws at the national level. In 1925, Spain's first DO laws were established in Rioja. Jerez followed in 1933, and Malaga established its own regulations in 1937.

According to the last approved law on July 10, 2003, the levels of quality for Spanish wines are as follow:

## VINOS DE MESA

Vinos de Mesa is the most basic level. In VdM wine, grapes can be blended from various regions. The only designation permitted on the label is "Product of Spain." Most of these wines are unoaked and more often than not are consumed in Spain.

### VINO DE MESA DE _____
- It must come from a delineated area
- The area will have specified grape varieties and minimum alcohol percentage on the label

It is a level above Vino de Mesa and is used by many of the newest experimental producers to distinguish their wines from simple table wines. A general region may be indicated and a vintage date is allowed. Many of these wines are made from grapes not traditionally grown in the specified areas.

## Vino de Calidad con Indicación Geográfica - Vino de la Tierra de _____

- Grapes must come from that specific region
- Wines must be made and bottled in that specific region
- The quality of wines is controlled
- Wines come from a smaller, stricter, more distinguished area called VdlT
- After 5 years these areas will most likely apply for DO designation in the future

## Quality Wines - VCPRD
## (Vinos de Calidad Producidos en una Región Determinada)

Wines must have a regional character.

### Vinos con Denominación de Origen - DO

- 5 years minimum in the VdlT de \_\_\_\_\_ level
- Rules are imposed by their Consejo Regulador and then ratified by the national government (INDO), and finally by the EU
- Cava has the same rights as a DO although can come from any of the specified Cava regions within Spain
- There currently 70 DOs, but that number changes annually

### Vinos con Denominación de Origen Calificada - DOCa

- 10 years minimum in the DO level
- More rigorous quality control than DO

There are currently 2 DOCa: Rioja (DOCa) in 1991 and Priorat (DOQ) in 2000.

DOCa and DOQ are the same. Calificada en Castillian, Qalificada in Catalan. (Although, truthfully there are various dates that are claimed to be when Priorat received DOQ status—from various sources: 2000, 2001, 2002)

Ribera del Duero was set to gain DOCa status as well at the end of 2008, though it has yet to occur.

## Vinos de Pago

- Vineyard must show a different microclimate than the surroundings
- Limitations in size
- The name of the Pago must have being used for a minimum period of 5 years for a wine to acquire this designation
- If the Pago is within a DOCa, the wine will be called: Vino de Pago Calificado
- Wine must be made and bottled by the owners of the Pago, essentially creating a monopole

There are currently 10 Vinos de Pago, many of which are located within DO La Mancha. Finca Elez and Dominio Valdepuesa were the first two Pagos recognized in 2002.

Do not confuse the classification Vinos de Pago with the word pago. A pago is a viticulture term meaning parcel of land.

Vinos de Pago does not indicate "quality" per se; it is not a classification that exceeds the DOCa level, but merely a special designation.

## Age Designations

Spain has its own system of classifying wines by age. Traditionally, the finest wines in Spain were aged in the bodega and released when they were ready to drink. Wine makers often used American oak with its bigger pores and rich vanillin content to speed this process along. The international taste for younger, more fruit-forward wines has changed this somewhat. Wines are being bottled and released sooner, as it occurs in the rest of the Old World wine spectrum, and more French oak is being used, in order to achieve a more refined product.

This trend was started by traditional wineries which, in order to please the new niche of the international market, made special wines in a modern style. These wines are also known in Spain as *Vino de Autor* or *Vinos de Alta Expresión*, to differentiate them from the traditional ones.

The aging laws depend on the criteria of each DO. The well-known wine designations of Crianza, Reserva, and Gran Reserva only indicate age and not quality. Nevertheless, more and more winemakers are stepping aside from these designations. Why? Because they believe that they should control the time that a wine spends in oak and in bottle before it is released, and not the *Consejo Regulador* of the DO, they want to have the ability to release a wine when they believe it is ready. Of course economics plays a major role in this as well—the longer the wine remains in the winery the longer the winery has to wait to collect returns on the sale of the juice.

In the same manner, it is not always is worthwhile to age a wine. Depending upon the DO, the producer, the grape, the wine will have more or less aging potential due to the characteristics of that particular DO. Wines from some DOs have proved to have aging potential, for what make sense in those to use the terms Crianza, Reserva, and Gran Reserva. As an example of those DOs we have Rioja and Ribera del Duero, where the aging laws are as follows:

| Aging Designation | Oak Barrel | Bottle |
| --- | --- | --- |
| Crianza | 12 months | 12 months |
| Reserva | 12 months | 24 months |
| Gran Reserva | 24 months | 36 months |

As is the case with all of these categories, the minimum age requirements are often exceeded by many years. Although these designations are not official, *Joven or Tinto Joven or Tinto* refers to a wine that has spent no time in barrel or less time in oak than a *Crianza*. These are usually young wines meant to be drunk within the next year or two after the vintage.

## Geography, Climate, and Soil

There is some irony in the fact that while Spain is the largest wine-growing area in the world, as growing conditions throughout the country are far from ideal. Geologically, Spain is the most mountainous of the major European wine-growing countries, and these mountain ranges act as climate moderators for vineyards across the country. At the same time, Spain's arid conditions and lack of legally sanctioned irrigation (although it was practiced for some time) before 1996 made successful grape growing and wine making a challenge. This is why we did not see quality wine being produced in many areas of the hot south until after 1996. (Spain actually has a large national crisis with fresh water supply and they constantly suffer from drought.) Expanded technology, enhanced knowledge, and international influence, are a only a few of many factors in why there are many amazing, world-class wines now being produced and barrel aged all over the map of Spain.

Taking these demanding conditions and the country's spotty viticultural history into account, it is not surprising that the French theory of terroir has only recently gained a foothold in Spain. Nevertheless, the winemaking revolution that began in the 1980s and 1990s has pushed this development, and the results are evident through the acclaimed attention and fantastic wine revolution spreading rampantly through the Spanish countryside.

## Varieties

Spain boasts 600 grape varieties, although just 20 account for 80% of all vineyards planted. You've probably never heard of Spain's mostly widely planted grape, **Airén**, which is actually the most widely planted grape in the world, although 95% is grown in La Mancha. It is mostly planted in central Spain and is primarily used for distilling brandy. The international varieties of **Cabernet Sauvignon, Merlot, Pinot Noir, Chardonnay, Riesling,** and **Sauvignon Blanc** have become more prevalent in recent years, although some of these varieties have been planted in Spanish soil for more than 300 years. The following is a list of Spain's most important native varieties.

### Red

**Garnacha Tinta** (Grenache in French) is considered to be a native Spanish variety and is Spain's most widely planted red grape. It does well in the arid, windy conditions that are found so often in Spain. Garnacha is an important component of the Rioja blend and is the primary grape in the powerful reds of Priorato. Navarra, Campo de Borja and Calatayud are among the other key DOs where the juicy and spicy Garnacha grape can be found. In less distinguished areas where conditions are milder and yields higher, it is often used to produce rosados. Wines made from Garnacha often reach a natural alcohol level of 15%. Garnacha Tinta is not the same as **Garnacha Tintorera,** which has a colored pulp.

**Tempranillo** is the star grape of Rioja and Ribera del Duero. It is less alcoholic than Garnacha and ages well, when blended. It also thrives in cooler temperatures and requires more rainfall. There has been some speculation that Tempranillo is related to Pinot Noir, said to have been a gift left by the pilgrims, but this seems to be more analogy than fact. Although fine wines from Tempranillo share the finesse and age-worthiness of a great Pinot Noir, Tempranillo is much lower in acidity and benefits from blending with spicier, richer wines. There are actually many different aliases and clones of Tempranillo, but here are some of the important names it goes by:

| Region | Name for Tempranillo |
|---|---|
| Cataluña | Ull de Llebre |
| Toro | Tinta de Toro |
| Castilla La Mancha | Cencibel |
| Castilla y León, including Ribera del Duero | Tinto Fino, Tinta del País |

**Graciano** is the authentic indigenous grape of Rioja. Despite its low productivity and late ripeness, it is an essential component of Rioja blends. Its small, tough-skinned berries complement Tempranillo in Rioja blends, adding gorgeous aromatics, firm tannins and bright acidity. Due to this, its presence is growing, although it was not widely planted in the past. (It still only occupies approximately 0.4% of the total plantings in Rioja) It is frequently found planted in the fields of older vineyards amongst other varieties.

**Monastrell** (Mataró in Cataluña and Mourvèdre in French) is indigenous to Spain and widely planted in the Mediterranean Coast of the country. It does well in many different soils, has a high yield (by Spanish standards), and is resistant to disease. When well made, it produces wines of intense color and high alcoholic degree. It is most widely seen in the Southern DOs of **Jumilla, Yecla, Bullas,** and **Alicante**.

Monastrell is Castillan; Mataro is Catalan. Cataluña is Castillan Spanish; Catalunya (with a "y") is the very different Catalan language.

**Mencía** seems to be related to Cabernet Franc, but it is NOT (although it has some similarities). It can boast very rich and powerful wines, especially in **DO Bierzo** in Castilla y León and **DO Ribeira Sacra** in Galicia.

**Cariñena** (Carignan in French) is indigenous to Spain. This grape is mainly used in blends to raise alcohol levels and add structure. Cariñena is widely planted in Rioja, where it is called **Mazuelo** and blended with Tempranillo and Garnacha. It also used in larger percentages in the blends of Cataluña and is considered to be the true variety of Priorato—most often blended with Garnacha, Cabernet Sauvignon, and Merlot. Besides the name of a red grape, it is also the name of a DO and a town.

**Bobal** is a dark skinned grape that produces deep colored red wines and even grape concentrate in the Southern areas of Spain, particularly in the east around Alicante and DOES Utiel Requena. It retains better acidity and has lower alcohol than its more popular neighbor Monastrell. Recent increases in plantings and classified wine regions that permit the use of Bobal mean that we are just beginning to see interesting wineries pop up in the area.

## WHITE

**Albariño** (Alvarinho in Portugal) is the most important white grape of the **DO Rias Baixas** in Galicia. It produces fresh, mineral, whites with flower, citrus, or peach aromas for early drinking.

**Macabéo** (**Viura** in Rioja) is an important component of sparkling Cava and the main white grape of Rioja. In Catalonia, it is blended with **Parellada** and **Xarel-lo** to create the best Cavas. Outside of Catalonia, sparkling wines are often made with 100% Macabéo.

**Moscatel** (Muscat d'Alexandria in French) comes from Greece. It is one of the oldest cultivated plants known to man. It is the dominant white grape of Alicante and Valencia. In the southern tip of Spain, wine from the Moscatel grape is usually found in Jerez, fortified and aged in the *solera* system. DO Malaga is beginning to revive their sweet wine industry by creating beautiful sweet white Moscatels with peachy stone fruits and lush floral richness.

**Palomino** is the main grape of Fino and Manzanilla Sherries. It produces table wines of no particular distinction, but its ability to grow *flor* when exposed to air transforms it into something truly special in Andalucía.

**Pedro Ximénez** is historically a very important grape used for sweet Sherry. Although some traditionalists insist that it is the very best grape for this purpose, Pedro Ximénez plantings in Jerez have been steadily declining. On the chalky soils of Jerez, it tends to be a very low-yielding vine and is highly susceptible to disease.

**Verdejo** is native to the cool, damp region of Rueda. Traditionally, Rueda was made in an oxidized, fortified style to imitate Sherry. Today it is gaining popularity as a crisp citric grassy, refreshing white. Some note aromatic and flavor similarities to the Sauvignon Blanc grape with which it is sometimes blended.

**Godello** is indigenous to Galicia and produces wines of great quality and powerful aromas. Its best expression is reached in Valdeorras and Bierzo. It is perhaps the Spanish white grape with most potential to produce high quality wines with beautiful fruit and great minerality.

**Parellada and Xarel-lo** are used predominately in the blend of Cava and are rarely found on their own in Penedés, making bright, fresh and sometimes zippy still whites.

# MAJOR WINE REGIONS

Spain is most easily divided into seven regions that share similar climates, cuisine, and winemaking traditions. Each of these regions contains several sub-regions and DOs. Only the appellations most important to the international fine wine market will be discussed in detail.

## GALICIA

Galicia was originally settled by the same Celtic tribes that lived along Europe's western coast. The region's cool, rainy climate (50 inches annually) makes it quite different from the majority of Spain. As you drive along the Minho River through the rolling hills covered in lush green vegetation you realize Galicia is a picturesque landscape unique to itself. As you could imagine given its coastal location on the map, seafood of all kinds is Galicia's primary cuisine, and the crisp refreshing whites of the area complement it perfectly. The majority of the wines are fermented in stainless steel and bottled without oak treatment, although in recent years we are seeing some fantastic smaller production wines from Galicia with rounder textures and barrel aging. Of the five DOs within the region, **Rías Baixas** is the most well known.

**DO Rías Baixas** is located in the southwest corner of Galicia and forms the northern border of Portugal. Wines have been exported from this area to the rest of Europe since the 16th and 17th centuries. Unfortunately, after phylloxera ravaged the area in the 19th century, many of the native vines (including **Albariño**) were allowed to die out. In the 1970s, growers and producers were given government incentives to replant with the native grapes and invest in modern winemaking equipment. The result is the deliciously fruity and fragrant dry Albariños for which this area is justly famous. It is also common to blend Albariño with Loureira Blanca and Treixadura. The DO Rías Baixas is divided into 5 sub-regions:

- Val do Salnés
- Condado do Tea
- Soutomaior
- Ribeira do Ulla
- O Rosal

| Types of White Wines | Specifications |
|---|---|
| Blanco Rías Baixas Albariño | 100% Albariño |
| Blanco Rías Baixas Salnés | min 70% Albariño |
| Blanco Rías Baixas Condado do Tea | min 70% Albariño and Treixadura |
| Blanco Rías Baixas Rosal | min 70% Albariño and Loureira |
| Blanco Rías Baixas Ribeira do Ulla | min 70% Albariño |
| Blanco Rías Baixas Barrica | min 3 months in oak |
| Blanco Rias Baixas | min 70% main white grape varieties |

Godello, another native Galician grape, is found in its native **DO Valdeorras** (located just east of Rias Baixas), in the mostly red wine producing (Mencia grape) **DO Ribeira Sacra,** as well as in field blendings in the **DO Ribeiro,** where you will also find Treixadura planted. The other DO in southwestern Galicia is called **Monterrei** (bordering Portugal). There, like all areas of Galicia, you find a spattering of all these indigenous varieties.

## CASTILLA Y LEÓN

**Castilla y León** in north central Spain is a region dominated by castles and a proud, uniquely Spanish tradition. During the Renaissance, this was the seat of Spain's royalty and academic community. The most distinguished DOs of the region are **Bierzo, Toro, Ribera del Duero,** and **Rueda**, as well as the newly formed **DO Tierra del Vino de Zamora**

**DO Toro** has changed its wines from rustic and unrefined to rich, ripe, and powerful wines. The main grape is **Tinta de Toro**. Toro, due to its very sand soils and long distance between vines (up to 6 feet), was able to resist the devastation of phylloxera.

In **DO Bierzo,** the main white grape is Godello and the red Mencía. The slate in Bierzo soils makes reds from this region very minerally. The high altitude, which reaches 3,000 feet above sea level, enables a long grape maturation, giving high complexity to high quality wines in a region that is gaining popularity and therefore attracting investments from many great winemakers.

**DO Ribera del Duero** is situated along the Duero River (which becomes the Douro in Portugal). Its soil is light and sandy with some stones over clay, some limestone and chalky outcrops, which maintain lower acid levels in the high-altitude vineyards of the region. Although daytime temperatures in the height of summer can exceed 100°F, nights remain relatively cool. There is a small window of approximately 125 days a year where there is no danger of frost. These conditions are ideal for producing world-class wines, but attentive viticulture is essential. **Tinto Fino** (Tempranillo) is the grape of choice here. The famous estate of Vega Sicilia introduced **Cabernet Sauvignon** and **Merlot** to the area in the 1860s, but Tempranillo remains the backbone of their wine as well. Although Vega Sicilia has enjoyed worldwide acclaim for over 100 years, Ribera del Duero was not awarded DO status until 1982, and though it has been slated to receive DOCa status since 2008, it continues to be a DO. Its recognition as an important Spanish wine region has sparked explosive growth in the area and with the help of several back to back fantastic vintages (2004, 2005, 2006), Ribera del Duero has created some world class wines and has finally received the recognition it has been demanding for quite some time. The only white grape is called **Albillo**, although there aren't any DO Ribera del Duero whites, as it against the laws of the DO to label a WHITE WINE from DO Ribera del Duero. A white wine from this area would most likely be labeled Vino de la Tierra de Castilla y León.

**Rueda** is quickly becoming one of Spain's most highly regarded white wine regions, with its native **Verdejo** grape. Before phylloxera hit the area, Rueda wine was made in the oxidized style of Sherry. In the 15th century, the Moors' reign over Jerez made it difficult to supply the national and international taste for Sherry, and when it was discovered that wine from the Verdejo grape would also grow *flor*, the producers of Rueda stepped in to fill the need. The region's time as the world's Sherry supplier was brief though because Jerez regained the market when phylloxera hit Rueda. As a result, much of Rueda was replanted with the high-yielding Palomino grape that did not grow in the northern areas of Castilla y León as it did on the southern coast. Nevertheless, Verdejo would again put Rueda on the map in the 1970s, due to Francisco Hurtado de Amezaga y Dolagaray, the director of Marques de Riscal in Rioja. Paco, as he was known to his friends, thought Rueda's hot summers, cold winters, and limestone soil could produce a crisp, dry white fermented in stainless steel that was more suited to current tastes. He encouraged the re-plantation of Verdejo and introduced the sometimes similarly profiled **Sauvignon Blanc** to the region. The Viura grape is also used often in the blended wines of Rueda.

There are 3 types of young white wines, each with regulations on composition:

| Rueda Superior | 75% Verdejo |
| --- | --- |
| Sauvignon Blanc | 100% Sauvignon Blanc |
| Rueda Blanco | 40% Verdejo or Sauvignon Blanc |

Sparkling wines from Rueda are called DO Rueda Espumoso, not Cava. They must contain:

- 40% Verdejo for medium and medium-sweet
- 85% Verdejo for Brut and Brut Nature

Red (minimum of 50% Tempranillo) and Rosé (minimum of 50% red varieties) winemaking were approved in 2001.

# NORTH-CENTRAL SPAIN

Two mountain ranges protect north-central Spain: the Pyrenees in the north that creates its border with France and the Cordillera Cantabria in the northwest. These mountains buffer the region from the Atlantic rains of the Basque country and provide some higher altitude sites with good exposure and cool nights—perfect conditions for high quality red wines. Although the reputation of the **Navarra DO** region has been improving in recent years, and the **Cariñena DO, Campo de Borja DO,** and **Calatayud DOs** are exploding into the export market, **Rioja DOCa** remains the most famous and prestigious appellation of this area.

Please, note that the main grape in **DO Cariñena** is Garnacha Tinta and NOT Cariñena. Cariñena is also the name of a Spanish town.

One of the most special areas in North Central Spain is the Basque land where there are three coastal regions that produce wines called Txakoli. There are three DOs that produce Txakoli in Pais Basco, the most important being Getariako Txakolina (Txakoli de Getaria). It is in this region you find amazingly zippy, slightly effervescent wines made from indigenous Basque varieties—Hondarribi Zuri (white grape) and Hondarribi Beltza (red grape). About 85% of the vineyards are planted with Hondarribi Zuri. The Beltza is blended and crushed, and the free run must is used in the blend to Txakoli. The two other Txakoli producing DOs are DO Bizkaiko Txakolina and DO Txakoli de Avila. Txakoli style wines have become increasingly popular in the United States the past few years. They are amazing summer sippers with bright fresh fruits, beautiful minerality, brine, and crisp acid.

**Rioja** is a 120-mile long region located in the Ebro River Valley and is the most well-known and prestigious wine regions in North Central Spain. It is named for a tributary of the Ebro called the Oja or Rio Oja, hence Rioja. It is divided into three sub-regions: Rioja Alta to the west of the Ebro; Rioja Alavesa north of the river and extending into neighboring Basque country; and Rioja Baja to the south and east of the region, extending into Navarra. Rioja became Spain's first DOCa in 1991.

Rioja's red wines come in many styles: simple, fruity joven wine; elegant, traditionally cask-matured (often in American oak) crianzas, reservas, and gran reservas that are ready to drink upon release; and powerful reds with minimum cask aging or incorporation of heavily toasted new French oak, perhaps made to appeal to international tastes. Although in the past most Riojas were blended with grapes from all three Rioja Sub-regions, more boutique, smaller parcels and single vineyard estate bottlings are being developed by some of the most outstanding winemakers. These newer techniques are bringing surges of international attention to the wines of Rioja, but are also creating desire for the more "traditional style" of winemaking.

Rioja Alavesa: here, the climate is moderated in the north by the Sierra Cantabria, and in the south by the Ebro River. The important towns east to west are Labastida, Samaniego, Elciego, Laguardia, and Oyón. The soil in Rioja Alavesa is characterized by calcareous clay, which gives a deep, inky color to Tempranillo, in addition to finesse and rich fruit content.

Rioja Alta is composed of several sub-zones: La Sonsierra (town of San Vicente), east of Ebro River and similar to Rioja Alavesa; Oja-Tirón Valley (town of Villalba, Haro, and Briones), the heart of Rioja Alta; and Najerilla Valley (towns of San Asensio, Cenicero, and Fuenmayor). The soil here is also calcareous clay, with some ferruginous clay and alluvial soil.

The Oja-Tirón Valley has the most Atlantic climate, with frequent rains and cold winds. Wines from this area have high acid level and are apt for aging.

Rioja Baja: this area has more of a Mediterranean climate and is the hottest of the three. Although it offers wines with less complexity, because grapes ripe earlier, it is always a good source in cold vintages. The main grape is Garnacha Tinta and the soil is composed of ferruginous clay and alluvial deposits.

Rioja's whites are made from a blend of mainly **Viura** (Macabéo), combined with **Malvasia Riojana** for its aromatics, and a small amount of **Garnacha Blanca** for plumpness (especially in vintages in which Viura's natural acidity is particularly high). Whites are usually made in a fresh, crisp style but some from excellent vintages or older vines are oak aged and released as crianzas. Reserva and gran reserva whites are quite rare, but you will know them when you see them (and check them out), as they are rich and golden in color with high notes of oxidation—salted almonds, marzipan, and cheese rind. There are many bodegas that also make beautiful Rosados from the local red and white varieties, which are usually quite delicious and fresh. Rioja also has many towns that are permitted to make DO Cava.

Authorized white grapes in Rioja:

- Viura (Macabéo)
- Malvasía
- Garnacha Blanca

Authorized red grapes in Rioja:

- Tempranillo
- Garnacha Tinta
- Graciano
- Mazuelo (Cariñena)

# CATALONIA

Catalonia is a fiercely independent *autonomía* on the northern Mediterranean coast of Spain. Catalonia has always held itself apart from the rest of the country. It has its own language, and sided with France against Castilian Spain as recently as the War of the Spanish Succession (1702–1714). It was granted independence in 1932 and again in 1978 after the death of General Franco, who had refused to acknowledge Catalonia's autonomy. The region's independent spirit is evident in the diversity of wines produced within its borders. Catalonia is known for sparkling Cava, the brooding reds of Priorato, and everything in between. Although there are many DOs within Catalonia making quality wine, **Penedés, Priorato,** and **Cava** have made the greatest impact on the worldwide market.

There is a push to make it law that all wines produced in Catalunya must have the label printed in Catalan. Foreign varieties (Chardonnay, Cabernet, etc.) are usually spelled in their native language rather than being translated, with Syrah being the exception (Sirà). Priorat itself is a Catalan word (Priorato is Castillian) DOQ Priorat is the official name of the DOCa.

**Penedés** (or Penedès in Catalan) is an innovative wine region that has virtually reinvented itself within one generation. Until phylloxera arrived in 1887, the area was producing unremarkable semi-sweet fortified reds. When the vineyards were replanted, white grapes for making Cava were favored. In 1960 the mayor of the then-booming city of Barcelona, which has always been the region's best customer, issued a challenge to area winemakers. He offered cash to farmers willing to grow red grapes that would produce quality table wine. Another strong influence on the quality wine movement in Penedés was Miguel Torres, who is responsible for many "firsts" in the region. He established his brand in America during World War II and was the first to ship his wine to the States in bottle rather than in cask. Torres is also one of those responsible for bringing international varieties to the area, although the first was Jean Leon in 1963. Interestingly enough, Torres also maintains one of the largest experimental plots of native grapes. Torres also introduced temperature-controlled stainless steel tanks to the area. Many local producers have followed in his footsteps.

As a result, Penedés has some of the most modern winemaking facilities in the world and the diversity of varieties planted is truly remarkable. The unique geography of Penedés is partly responsible for the diversity of plantings—the region rises from the Mediterranean in a series of progressively cooler steppes.

Baix-Penedés (Bajo) is the lowest and hottest level of the three subzones. It is planted with hot climate grapes such as **Garnacha, Cariñena** (Carignan in France), and **Monastrell** (Mourvèdre in France). **Macabéo, Xarel-lo,** and **Parellada**—the three key white grapes for Cava—are also planted here.

Mitja-Penedés (Medio) sits at 1,600 feet above sea level and is protected from the water by a ridge of hills. All of the traditional Cava grapes are grown here with good results. Cooler weather reds such as **Cabernet Sauvignon, Merlot,** and **Tempranillo** grow successfully in the many microclimates tucked into the nooks and crannies of this subzone.

Alt-Penedés (Alta) is the highest, coolest level with conditions comparable to sites in Northern France. **Chardonnay** for Cava is planted here as the cool climate produces grapes with good acidity, as well as **Riesling** and **Gewürztraminer**. **Pinot Noir** and **Cabernet Franc** are also grown in sunnier spots.

# PRIORAT

Carthusian monks established Priorat in the 12th century after a shepherd boy from the area had a vision of angels descending from heaven via some sort of ladder. The monastery (or *priory*) was named Priorat de Scala Dei (heavenly ladder). The monks made powerful red wine from Garnacha and Cariñena in open earthenware vats, a production method that continued until the 1980s. In the mid-1980s a group of winemakers got together and bought eight plots of land in the town of Gratallops, high in the Siurana Valley. They planted the traditional **Garnacha** and **Cariñena** as well as the international varieties of **Cabernet Sauvignon, Merlot,** and even **Syrah**. As a group they committed to maintain extremely low yields and use the most modern techniques, including drip irrigation. All the wines used the naming convention "Clos _____" to distinguish them from the other wines in the region. Initially the group's unorthodox methods denied them DO status, but once the positive press and international medals started pouring in, they were granted the title of **Priorato DO**.

Priorato's soil and topography make it an ideal place for producing powerful, age-worthy reds. The dominant soil of the region is called llicorella, which is a mix of reddish slate and mica, with some schist in the highlands. This stony topsoil is ideal for retaining heat during the cool nights of this remote highland. It also forces the vines to dig deep into the schistose subsoil for moisture. The sun and wind make for thick grape skin—no matter what the variety—and many of the vines in the older vineyards are more than 100 years old.

A good substitute for the expensive Priorat wines is **DO Montsant**, which surrounds Priorat and also offers the llicorella soil and old Garnacha and Cariñena vines. Newly established in 2001, **DO Montsant** had originally been part of **DO Tarragona**, but applied for autonomy based on its geography, which envelops Priorat and shares many of its soils and terrain. The wines of Montsant share many characteristics of Priorat, except perhaps the price tag (for now).

**Cava** is not actually a DO. Its label says simply Denominación Cava. Although 95% of Cava is produced in Catalonia, and 75% of that is made around the town of San Sadurni d'Anoia, certain towns outside the region were making sparkling wine called Champaña before the term Cava existed. Spain's sparkling wine industry finally gave in to pressure from France to stop calling their wine Champaña or Spanish Champagne. Instead, they chose the name Cava (meaning underground cellar) to distinguish it from a bodega, which is usually above ground. Towns (and in some cases individual producers) wishing to be included in the new DO had to meet the requirements established by the *consejo regulador*, but did not have to be within a certain geographical region. This is most displeasing to the EU, and there has been pressure to define the limits of the DO; but remember, this is Catalonia.

San Sadurni d'Anoia is in the **Penedés DO** and producers of Cava take advantage of the progressively cooler steppes to create the right blend for their sparklers, using the three traditional Cava grapes—**Macabéo (Viura), Xarel-lo,** and **Parellada**. When the grapes are grown on the Baix-Penedés, they are high yielding, low in acid, and high in alcohol. They provide a creamy, powerful base for the blend. The same grapes grown at the Mitja-Penedés level have more structure and delicate aromatics. The Alt-Penedés is too cold for the traditional grapes to ripen fully but is perfect for the high-acid Chardonnay that gives the best Cavas finesse and elegance. As a whole, Cava is made in a less-acidic style than Champagne and is meant for early drinking. Cava made outside of Catalonia is usually comprised of **100% Macabéo (Viura)**.

## OTHER REGIONS

Other Spanish regions of note, whether for improving quality or sheer volume, are the **Levante** on the Mediterranean coast south of Penedés, and the **Meseta** in the desert-like center of Spain.

The **Levante** is beginning to produce some outstanding wines, exceeding its reputation for easy drinking table wines—particularly from **DO Jumilla**, an inland and elevated region that is by far the star of the Levante and has Monastrell showing at its best. In exceptionally high locations (4,000 feet above sea level), Cabernet Sauvignon and Syrah can be exceptional as well. Jumilla is unique in its growing conditions, being the hottest, driest, highest elevation wine growing region in Spain, where the temperature between night and day can sometimes fluctuate 60 degrees Farenheit. The thick boulder-like soil full of gravel and limestone that sometimes reaches up to 2 feet in depth before the soil begins adds great drainage and retention. Jumilla has entered into the market full force, producing slamming, powerful wines with high fruit, alcohol, and tannin levels all while maintaining great balance, elegance, and structure.

**DO Utiel Requena,** where Bobal grape is showing great potential to make quality reds.

**DO Alicante**, where international varieties such as Syrah and Cabernet Sauvignon are satisfactorily blended with the local Monastrell.

**DO Yecla** and **DO Bullas** are fast becoming contenders of the south, producing wines of similar profiles with both local and international varieties.

The **Meseta,** a vast desert-like flatland whose arid conditions made it impossible for many years to make quality export wines, is home to Spain's largest Denominación de Origen, **DO La Mancha**, as well as one of its most underappreciated—**DO Valdepeñas**. Valdepeñas has been making quality everyday wine for centuries but has been slow to make an impact on the international export market. This has been changing rapidly since irrigation became legal and the vines are being more sufficiently nourished. Alcohol and concentration levels are increasing, which in turn is allowing producers to better utilize oak and make bolder, richer wines—slowly moving away from the light oxidized style of the gran reservas.

**Andalucía** is one of Spain's oldest and most famous wine regions, but as it is primarily known for Sherry, it will be discussed in detail in the section focusing on fortified wine. This region is too hot for good quality still wines, although locals enjoy the light and fruity whites with the seafood from its coasts. In recent years, **DO Malaga** has resurrected the original clone of the Moscatel de Alexandria grape and has begun to produce beautiful dessert wines with lush peachy fruit and wonderful acidity thanks to its mountainous, coastal location. The grapes are sometimes even dried in the sun and raisinated to reach higher levels of natural sweetness. These wines are beautiful and should be sought out for dessert wines. If it gets too hot in the summer, sangria can be another alternative, and of course there is always beer.

# PORTUGAL

| GRAPE VARIETIES | |
|---|---|
| RED | Baga, Periquita, Touriga Nacional |
| WHITE | Arinto and Alvarinho (Albariño) |
| CLIMATE | The country boasts a Mediterranean climate, with significant influences from the Atlantic ocean. |
| SOIL | Soil varies considerably throughout the country. In the north, it is a patchwork of granite and schist. Regions further south, have loam soil, while inland areas such as Alentejo have soils ranging from cool, red clay to schist to volcanic soils. |

## HISTORY

This tiny country, which once owned half the world, has spent the 20th century largely cut off from it. On the positive side, this prolonged isolation has preserved many of the country's native grape varieties and styles of wine that are rarely seen elsewhere. However, the price of separation has been the fairly widespread use, until quite recently, of primitive viticultural and vinification techniques. Once a patchwork of individual growers making wine in whatever way they knew how, for the last 40 years Portugal's wine industry has been dominated by government-sponsored co-ops. Often volume was rewarded more than quality. Carefully produced, estate-bottled table wines that utilize the best of today's technology are just beginning to appear on the market. In the international wine scene, Portugal is still primarily known for Port, cork, and Lancers, but this too will change.

## LAWS

Portugal's wine laws were among the first to be established in Europe. In 1756, the Marquis de Pombal mapped the Douro and established regulations about Port wine production to ensure its quality and reputation. Several other regions were defined and regulated between 1908 and 1929. It is interesting to note that no other areas were added as Região Demarcada (RD) until 1979. Portugal's entry into the European Union (EU) in 1986 necessitated bringing its wine laws into line with its neighboring countries. The categories of wine follow:

**Vinho de Mesa** wine may be composed of fruit from several different regions and is not vintage dated.

**Vinho Regional** is table wine that is made entirely from grapes grown in a general region worth noting.

**Indicacão de Proveniencia Regulamentada** (IPR) is the level just below DOC. Some of these regions may attain DOC status in the future.

**Denominacão de Origem Controlada** (DOC) is the new name for Portugal's top wine regions that were designated as RDs before 1986.

## GEOGRAPHY, CLIMATE, AND SOIL

Overall, Portugal boasts a Mediterranean climate with cool, wet winters and hot, dry summers, creating an ideal environment for growing vines. Various climate moderators and soil types help influence the variety of wine styles in the country's different regions. For example, the light, crisp, effervescent Vinho Verde comes from a region with light, sandy soils and Atlantic breezes. Red wines from Douro, on the other hand, benefit from the region's more continental climate, near-perfect schist soil with some granite mixed in, and mountainous geography.

## VARIETIES

Portugal's native grape varieties are legion in number. Many vineyards are planted with several varieties that share space with grain, vegetables, and fruit trees. Since 1986, several EU-funded studies have attempted to establish which grapes have the most potential for quality wine in specific areas. Some of the varieties that are now gaining a reputation for quality, or have long been known to be between Portugal's finest, are mentioned here. This is by no means a comprehensive list of Portuguese wine varieties. Time and further study will tell which grapes are to become Portugal's most valuable players in the international scene.

**Arinto** is prized for its ability to retain its acidity no matter how hot the growing region. This has led to its wide plantation all across Portugal. Perhaps this white's best expression is in Bucelas, where it is required to comprise at least 75% of the blend.

**Alvarinho** (Albariño in Spain) is responsible for the new wave of longer-lived, higher alcohol, fruit-forward wines coming from Vinho Verde. Although these wines are not as spritzy as the traditional whites of the area, they are commanding previously unheard of prices in the world market.

**Encruzado** has been identified by the EU as a grape with great potential. It produces full-flavored, well-balanced wines in Dão that often have a distinctive nutty flavor.

**Muscat of Alexandria** is responsible for Muscat de Setubal, a vin doux naturel–style dessert wine with an interesting twist, that has been one of Portugal's most famous wines for some time. Like the Muscat-based VDNs of southern France, fermentation is stopped when the alcohol level reaches about 6% by the addition of a grape spirit. Setubal is then macerated on the grapes' skins for several months to obtain its unique flavor.

**Periquita** (Castelão Frances) is grown mainly in Dão where it produces full red wines with aging potential.

**Touriga Nacional** is thought to be the finest variety for Port, however, is now also being used as the base of some fine red table wines from the Douro and elsewhere.

**Alvarelhão** is starting to distinguish itself from the pack due to its relatively high acidity. When handled properly it can produce wines of great finesse. It is chiefly planted in the Douro, where it is thought to be something of a weakling. It is permitted for planting in Vinho Verde and Dão, both cooler regions where the grape may have a chance to shine.

**Baga** is Portugal's most widely planted red grape. In Bairrada, it makes up 85% of the blends. Most wine made from Baga grapes is very dense with intense, astringent tannins. The trend towards destemming and shorter maceration times may enable this grape to produce better wines that it is at present.

# Major Wine Regions

Portugal has a long, proud history of wine making. Its current place in the international wine market is unique, because thanks to its self-imposed isolation, many of the country's native winemaking techniques are still in practice and its library of indigenous varieties is sizable. The result is originality in a wine world that is increasingly uniform.

Portugal's most important wine regions are difficult to identify at this point in time. Some areas that were historically known to produce fine table wines, such as the three DOCs surrounding modern Lisbon, now barely exist, or their quality levels have fallen so significantly that their fame is no longer justified. (Some would say Dão falls into this category.) Other regions are just emerging as potential bright spots, or like Douro and Setubal, are areas that were once famous only for sweet wines but are now also producing equally good non-fortified wines.

**Vinho Verde** is one of Portugal's most internationally recognized regions for table wine. While Vinho Verde wines can be white or red, its name is most often associated with the light, acidic, often slightly sparkling white wine that has traditionally been its most famous export. A fizzy, acidic dry red wine with an alcohol level of around 10% actually represents about half of the region's production. The DO is located on Portugal's wet Atlantic Coast and is fairly densely populated. Limited space led to the practice of trellising vines on pergolas—granite posts rising as much as 15 feet above the ground. This vine-training method allows for other crops to be planted beneath the vines and reduces the risk of grey rot. The predominant grapes for white Vinho Verde are **Loureiro, Trajadura,** and **Arinto**. **Alvarinho** planted around the town of Monção on the Spanish border has recently created a stir by producing fuller, longer-lived, non-sparkling whites that have received some international recognition (i.e., higher prices). Varieties used for red Vinho Verde include **Vinhao, Azal Tinto,** and **Espadeiro**. True Vinho Verde wine is bone dry, but some are sweetened slightly for export.

**Dão** became an RD (now DOC) in 1908, attesting to its longstanding reputation as Portugal's finest region for red table wines. Quality was seriously depressed by the government-regulated co-ops that dominated the region's wine industry from the 1950s until 1989. Since the co-ops were disbanded, large privately held companies have invested significantly in the area, single estates are starting to flourish again, and quality is on the rise. Dão is located in north central Portugal where it is protected from the Atlantic rains by high, Granite Mountains. Its long, warm summers and well-drained sandy soils make it one of Portugal's most obvious areas for good wine. Two-thirds of the region's production is red. **Touriga Nacional** is believed to be the best grape for the area and it must comprise at least 20% of the blend. Other permissible red grapes include **Bastardo, Tinto Pinheira,** and **Tinta Roriz** (Tempranillo). **Encruzado** is making the best white wines of the area.

**Terras do Sado VR** on the Setubal peninsula of Portugal's southern Atlantic coast is emerging as a producer of good table wines. **Arinto, Esganacão**, and even **Chardonnay** are being grown on the hills, alongside **Muscat of Alexandria** that is used for the production of sweet, fortified Setubal. In the 1980s, California and Australian oenologists brought modern winemaking techniques and plantings of **Merlot** and **Cabernet Sauvignon** to the area. However, the native red **Periquita** is still the dominant grape of the region and is used to produce red, rosé, and sparkling wines. (Could the region be the next Penedés?)

**Douro** is adding to its worldwide reputation for Port by producing more and more quality table wines. In fact, the wines of the Douro DOC were originally unfortified. Alcohol was added only to wines destined for export in order to stabilize them for long sea journeys. Table wines from the Douro are most often made with the same grapes used for Port. Many of these varieties come from the low-graded *quintas*, which are located in cooler areas. These grapes often do not meet the standards to be used for Port, and therefore are used instead for table wine, as the cooler spots help preserve acidity in the finished wine. Grapes not permitted in Port (such as **Cabernet Sauvignon**) are now sometimes planted in these low-graded *quintas* for the express purpose of making table wine. These wines may not be labeled as Douro DOC but are allowed the designation of Terras Durienses VR instead.

Portugal is poised to become one of the world's great wine regions. It reemergence on the international wine scene is perfectly timed. The craze to pull up native varieties and replant with Cabernet Sauvignon, Merlot, and Chardonnay seems to be dying down. The quality standards of world wine making are starting to influence this sleepy country. This fact combined with Portugal's abundance of unique native varieties may produce some truly exciting wine in the not so distant future.

As appeared in Sante Magazine:

# AGED GRACE – BY ANDREW F. BELL

Port is finally receiving the recognition it deserves, but what a road it has traveled. As we enter the new century, one particular style—Vintage—has captured the imagination and purchasing zeal of American consumers and restaurant patrons. The days of low prices and ample inventories are now a distant memory, and on-premise beverage managers eagerly snap up new releases and search auction house offerings for venerable Vintage bottlings.

## PORT'S ROOTS/ROUTES

The development of the Port region is due to the establishment of trade routes and treaties by the British that date from the seventeenth century. Like most viticultural areas that arose prior to the establishment of reliable land transportation, Port relied on waterways to provide a vital link between the grapes' sources and their markets.

Port exploded on the international scene in the 1660s, as relations between England and France deteriorated, and France's wars on the continent disrupted her wine trade. England looked to Portugal as a resource to replace its stocks of French wine. British shippers also traded Port wine for Dutch cod and advanced a distribution system for Port throughout Europe.

The wine at this time was not the Port of today. Back in the early 1700s, Port was described as being strong, deep (elderberry juice was found to give the wine more color) and bright, with no mention of sweetness. Shippers added grape brandy to the 534-liter casks, called pipes, before shipping to insure that the wine arrived stable. One pipe would receive about 14 liters of spirit before shipping. Today, the same volume of fermenting Port receives 100 liters per pipe to stop fermentation. The arrival of sweet Port on the market is attributed to a move by British shippers to lower the cost of producing Port with the use of inferior spirit.

The earliest Ports came from the lower area of the Douro River, called Baixo (Lower) Corgo, where access to the major Atlantic trade routes was easiest. Today, Ports from this area constitute the lower quality blends; few Vintage Ports come from grapes grown here. The British took nearly a century before moving further upstream to the present Port-producing region, called Cima (Upper) Corgo, where most of the great Vintage Port growing areas are located. Growers planted vineyards on steep terraces along the Douro and its tributaries to increase sun exposure for riper, sweeter grapes.

## VINTAGE: PORT'S PRIZE

Of the many different Port types, Vintage Port, the flagship of the Port trade, receives most of the media attention and consumer interest in the U.S. Oddly enough, of all the Port styles, it may be the easiest to produce! Each shipper decides independently whether a particular year's grapes have reached the necessary ripeness to declare the wine a Vintage. On average, there will be three or four Vintage years per decade. For Vintage Port, the grapes are crushed and allowed to ferment for two days, fortified, then placed in large tanks (For reasons of hygiene, most wineries have switched from wood to stainless steel.) Bottling usually takes place during the second spring after the harvest. Prior to bottling, however, a sample must be submitted to the Instituto do Vinho do Porto (IVP) for tasting and approval. Until recently, IVP approval was considered a rubber stamp; it issued the *Selo de Garantia*, which is attached to the neck of every bottle, to all wines, including some that were clearly inferior. In 1994, however, several samples were rejected, and the government-run authority has begun to act as a guarantor of quality. According to the IVP, shippers have up to two years following harvest to decide whether to declare a vintage.

In the past ten years in the U.S., Port imports have swayed from a negligible amount to 3.43 percent of total Port production in 1998. This seemingly small percentage, however, represents the cream of the output. For the special categories of Port, including Vintage, the U.K. and the U.S. are the first and second export markets respectively.

## 1997: A VINTAGE YEAR

While very young Port Vintages are difficult to assess for longevity and ultimate greatness, 1997 is undoubtedly a very good year. Most Port houses and shippers declared a vintage, early reviews in the wine press have been positive, and sales have been brisk. "In America, we see a spike every time a vintage is declared," notes Willma Dull, former Brand Manager at Kobrand Corporation, which represents Taylor Fladgate and Fonseca in the U.S. Dull has seen a significant upward trend in Port sales since the early 1980s, an increase in imports of well over 600 percent across all categories.

Taking advantage of the hot market for Vintage bottlings, Port houses have held back a certain percentage of older Vintages for release once they are drinking well, not only as a way of aging them for the clientele, but also as a shrewd marketing ploy. As these Vintages arrived in the marketplace over the last five-to-eight years (e.g., the acclaimed 1963s, 1977s and 1985s), repeated buying surges occurred. Today, most of the 1963 stocks are depleted, even older Vintages are extremely scarce, and buyers with deep pockets must search the auction-house listings.

According to Dull, releasing both mature and current Vintage bottlings raises public awareness of Port, which translates into increased on-premise sales. "When a Vintage is declared, journalists are writing, and the more [that is written] about Port, the more consumers are likely to think of it during a dining experience." She also points to the rise in fine cigar sales and their association with Port, plus the continuing education programs sponsored by Kobrand and other importers as heightening Port's visibility on premise.

John Osbourne, Wine Buyer for Astor Wine in New York City and Home Liquors in New Jersey, believes that training your staff is the key to sales. "Making sure that they know the difference between LBV, Tawny and Vintage is a minimum. Giving your staff the tools for success--tastings and notes on food pairings--are necessary." In addition to importer-sponsored education programs, the Portuguese Wine Bureau, a division of the Portuguese Trade Commission (212-354-4610; www.portugal.org), has a wealth of useful information about Port, including an excellent video.

Osbourne also notes that sales across the board are on the rise, which he attributes in part to the impressive 1994s and 1997s, two Vintages that are currently being compared by many restaurant beverage managers. Traveling with sommeliers competing for the title of "World's Best Sommelier," I have had an opportunity to speak with them about the 1997 Vintage. Enrico Bernardo, a Milanese who is currently Le Cinque's Head Sommelier at the Hotel Georges V in Paris, is unimpressed. Having tasted through the majority of the offerings, he is happy to have invested so heavily in the 1994 Vintage. Bernardo explains, "The '97s are beautiful, they are easy to drink now, and they show delicious forward fruit. My fear is that there will be little wine in the bottle in ten years." In comparing the two Vintages, he offers, "The '94s are deeper in color and stronger in flavor than the '97s."

Jesper Boelskifte, Denmark's national champion sommelier and Co-Owner with his wife of Le Sommelier, a restaurant in Copenhagen, shares a similar position on the 1997s. "I am a big fan of young, fruit-forward Port. For this reason, the '97s are very appealing to me. I must admit, however, that the '94s are more complex."

Boelskifte's final words may offer the most suscinct summary of the last two Vintages of the 1990s and place the 1997s in their best light: "Ultimately the '94s will outlive the '97s qualitatively, but I am running through the 1997s out of sheer pleasure."

## Proffering Port at Manhattan's Most Majestic

America is in a unique position of developing a gastronomical culture at the young age of 224 years. Fine dining has never been more popular, and we are slowly seeing a move toward longer, less rushed meals. Nevertheless, promoting Vintage Port on premise presents some interesting challenges. The reasonable price of most Ruby-style Ports allows restaurants to offer them by the glass and still make a good margin, but in major cities, restaurant real estate is so expensive, that offering a glass of 1963 Dow's or Warre's at the end of a meal is not cost-effective. The front desk will have a server's head for tying up a table for another half hour to an hour when it could be seating another four-top, but substantial Port sales are possible at some high-end venues.

At Jean-Georges in New York City, where a month's advance booking, VIP status or one's eye teeth are necessary, Wine Director Kurt Eckert notes, "Port sales are good to very good, depending on the season." All of the Jean-Georges properties have a good selection of Ports by the glass, ranging from Graham's 6 Grapes Ruby at $9 to Fonseca 1963 Vintage at $75. Also available are 10-, 20- and 40-year-old Tawnies, an Osborne 1994 LBV, a Romariz 1963 Colheita and 1994, 1985, and 1977 Vintage Ports from Fonseca, Smith Woodhouse, Graham's and Warre's respectively. You also can indulge in an entire bottle, if you have the time and financial resources; a Taylor 1955 Vintage tops the half-dozen offerings at $900.

Eckert admits that without a smoking lounge, Ports tend to trail dessert wines, which offer ease of service and lower alcohol levels. To accommodate his regular Port clientele, Eckert suggests a move to Jean-George's smaller Nougatine lounge in the bar of the four-star restaurant to leisurely enjoy their glass of Vintage Port. This change of venue allows the dining room to accept the next table and prevents an interruption in the flow.

Even in such restaurants as the new Alain Ducasse in Manhattan's Essex House Hotel, where there is only one seating, Ports battle against the world of dessert wines that are available. Sommelier Peter Verheyde, recently relocated from Alain Ducasse, Paris, has witnessed Port finish third to Sauternes and Tokaji in New York City, but he maintains an extensive sampling for his clientele. He has noticed, however, a difference in consumption between Ducasse Paris and New York. "The French will have a glass of Port as an aperitif, while, so far, Americans seem to be looking for LBV, Vintage or Colheita toward the end of their meal." He offers Taylor 30-year-old Tawny, Graham's 1997, Broadbent 1994, Churchill 1982 for the Vintage crowd and Noval 1987 Vintage and 1968 Colheita. In addition, Ducasse New York offers eight different Vintage Ports dating from a Quinta do Noval 1937 Colheita to a Fonseca 1970 Vintage on their bottle list.

## Rating Vineyard Quality

Like Burgundy's, Port's vineyards, or quintas, have a complex hierarchy. In the 1940s, Alvaro Moreira da Fonseca devised a point system using twelve characteristics: altitude, locality, yield, soil type, vine training, grape variety, slope, aspect and exposure, soil, texture, age of vines, shelter and vine density. Each vineyard receives a negative or positive score that is set by the Instituto do Vinho do Porto (IVP) governing body for each of these characteristics, ranging from the impossibly low – 3,430 to a theoretical high of + 1,680. The classes are the following: A = >1,200 points; B = 1,001–1,199; C = 801–1,000; D = 601–800; E = 401–600; and F = <400. This rating system is used to determine how much grape must can be fortified to make Port. The total quantity allowed for each year, called the *beneficio*, is determined by the IVP according to market conditions and existing stocks. A vine must have a minimum age of 5 years; otherwise it must be used for dry wine.

The majority of vineyard sites for Vintage Port are found in Cima Corgo, where famous quintas, such as Bomfin (A), Bom-Retiro (A), Cavadinha (A), Noval (A) and Roriz (A), are located. There are two major vineyards in Baixo Corgo: Quinta Dona Matlide (B) and Quinta das Murcas (B). The third region is Duoro Superior; Vargellas (A), Vesuvio (A) and Val do Meao (A/B) are among the most revered quintas.

There are 25 grape varieties allowed for Port production. Over the years, however, five have risen to the top; in descending order of percentage of total plantings, they include Touriga Francesca (20%), Tinta Roriz (Spain's Tempranillo) (10%), Tinta Barroca (<10%), Tinto Cao (4%) and Touriga National (2%). Although Touriga National is considered the most noble of the grapes, its low yield and poor fruit set are reasons why it represents such a small overall percentage.

## A Century of Vintage Port

Outstanding Old Vintages (extremely rare) - 1908, 1927, 1931, 1935, 1945, 1948

Classic Vintages (very rare to rare, drinking beautifully) - 1955, 1963, 1970, 1977, 1983, 1985

Recent Vintages (somewhat rare to readily available) - 1991, 1992, 1994, 1997

# ITALY
BY ALESSANDRO BERNINI

| NORTH WEST | NORTH EAST |
|---|---|
| Valle d'Aosta | Veneto |
| Piedmont | Friuli Venezia Giulia |
| Liguria | Trentino Alto Adige |
| Lombardy | |
| **CENTRAL ITALY** | **SOUTHERN ITALY AND ISLANDS** |
| Tuscany | Campania |
| Umbria | Molise and Basilicata |
| Latium | Apulia |
| Emilia – Romagna | Calabria |
| The Marches | Sicily |
| Abruzzi | Sardinia |

## GEOGRAPHY

Italy is a peninsula separated in the north from the rest of the continent by the Alps, the highest-altitude mountain system in Europe. The Alps help create Italy's natural borders with France, Switzerland, Austria and Slovenia. Italy's territory is a little more than half the size of France, encompassed between the 47$^{th}$ parallel in the north and the 37$^{th}$ parallel that runs through the southern tip of Sicily. The country is about 1,000 miles long from north to south. Hills represent 42% of the land, 35% is mountains and 23% is flat (mostly in the area of the alluvial Padan Plain that runs along the Po River in the north of Italy and cuts through parts of the Veneto, Lombardia and Piedmont).

The peninsular part of Italy is characterized by the Apennines, an older, lower-altitude mountain chain that runs like a spine along the center of the country. The range stretches from the Alps in Liguria on the western coast of Italy down through Calabria (the toe of the "boot") and Sicily. These mountainous slopes are a major factor contributing to the high-acid white wines of Italy. The Apennines degrade east and west into smaller series of hills representing suitable arable land. The Mediterranean Sea contributes to Italy's mild weather, especially along the Tyrrhenian coast in the west. Some mountainous areas in the north are suitable for extreme viticulture. A number of soil types, rivers, lakes and three active volcanoes all shape Italy's viticulture by generating extremely varied microclimates. The specific geography and climate of each individual winegrowing region will be discussed in detail later in the chapter.

## HISTORY

Greek writers began to call the native inhabitants of the peninsula "Italian" in the 5$^{th}$ century BC, though it was not until 1861 that the Kingdom of Italy was officially born as a nation. The first documented cases of vines planted were from the Etruscans, predecessors of the Romans in what is now modern day Tuscany. The Greeks brought vines to southern Italy around the 8$^{th}$ century BC and planted widely through Sicily, Calabria, and Apulia. Later, the Roman Empire (27 BC-395 AD) was largely responsible for the widespread planting of vines not only throughout the country, but also the rest of Europe. Wine was a significant part of the Roman Army's diet (called *Centuriae*). Soldiers would carry vine buds with them and plant the grapes while setting up winter camps. This facilitated the spreading and mutation of many different varieties. Roman aristocracy consumed wine extensively, though those wines were very different from our modern perception of wine. They used to infuse honey and spices, possibly drinking it heated. Romans also helped to improve the conservation and transportation of wine by creating a clay vase called an *amphora* designed for long-distance shipping.

After the fall of the Roman Empire, viticulture was confined to monasteries until the 13th and 14th centuries. Around this same time period, the Mediterranean became more important in trade and a new intrepid merchant middle class began to populate small towns. These families, such the Frescobaldis and the Antinoris in Florence, used their wealth to establish vineyards.

After the emigrational period, Italy became a collection of different provinces run by local, weak governments who often sought support from foreign nations in order to maintain their own power. In general, Italian provinces (both then and now) tend to share little in common with each other in regards to clothing, food, and even language. With the unification of the Early Kingdom of Italy in 1861, efforts were made to publish unified production rules by Bettino Ricasoli in Tuscany and others in the Barolo area, though nothing ever materialized. However, a general improvement in viticulture processes and techniques materialized in the masked blessing of the phylloxera and oidium epidemics of the early 1900s. Winemakers were forced to replant their devastated vineyards and many chose to plant more noble varieties grafted to American rootstock. It was only after World War II, when Italy was proclaimed a Republic, that the country became organized in its modern way.

In the late 1970s and early 1980s, the first real push towards the production of quality wines was lead by the market abroad. Many European wine drinkers began to drink lower quantities of higher quality wine. As demand for higher quality wines grew, producers began to introduce significant new tools for improvements in the wine making process. Among these were temperature controlled fermentation tanks, roto-fermenters, new bottling technologies, elimination of the use of old barrels as well as trying to eliminate oxidation and overripe fruit in the finished product. This new generation of wine makers led the way towards a cleaner, more sophisticated style of wines. These Italian producers were among the pioneers of the international movement towards better production methods and technology—specifically in regards to white wine.

Today, thanks to Italy's 1000 indigenous grapes, its diversified soils and climates, both the enthusiasm and the capabilities of its producers, as well as a renewed focus on quality, Italy has the earned its place in the international competitive market for quality wine production. There are 220,000 wine growers in Italy that can be divided into 4 categories:

*Imbottigliatori* (bottlers) – Those that only bottle and label the wine with no growing responsibilities.

Small growers – Usually family run and estate bottled or they sell grapes to third parties.

Large estates – They can both grow their own as well as purchase grapes/juice, and can run vineyards under a lease.

*Cooperativa* or *Cantina Sociale* – Co-op producers whose members sell their grapes under a common label. They have some tax advantages but tend to be of lower quality unless the growers are rewarded for quality instead of for the volume of fruit sold. Sometimes the Government sponsors the creation of such entities.

*Consorzio di Produttori* – An association of single producers. Each individually owns, bottles and labels their own respective wines but join together as an association in order to promote their appellation and to determine standard rules of production.

# Wine Laws

While some wine production laws were drafted in the 18th Century and later in the 1930's, the first set of DOC rules that had effect on a national scale were not published until 1963. This is because the current nationalized system of government based on 20 delineated Regions (Regioni) was not set in place until 1961.

These regulations were further expanded upon after the controversial *Scandalo del Metanolo* in 1986. Wine laced with methanol was blamed for 26 deaths in the country, an event that severely damaged the acceptance of Italian wine on the International market. Methanol was being added to lower quality wines in order to bolster the body of the wine by increasing its alcohol content. After the scandal, regulators began promoting quality instead of quantity and reinforcing their application on a regular basis. Legal reinforcement from the government also tends to be higher than in other countries.

**Italian DOC Rules apply only to dry, sweet and sparkling wines.** Some fortified wines are covered (**Marsala** in Sicily) but some are not (**Vermouth** in Piedmont). **Grappa**, which is obtained by the distillation of pomace, is not covered, and neither is brandy (seldom called *Arzente*).

## The Pyramid of Italian Wines

In the early 1960s, Italy abandoned the sharecropper system, which had been the organizational model in the agricultural sector since the Middle Ages. This abolition initiated a shift towards major technological improvements and was in turn accompanied by the creation in 1963 of the controlled wine appellation system, known in Italian as **Denominazione di Origine Controllata (DOC)**. The original system included only 3 levels: Vino da Tavola (VdT), Denominazione di Origine Controllata (DOC), and Denominazione di Origine e Garantita (DOCG). Due to the sheer volume of geography as well as the large number of vines under planting, the original appellation system was rushed in implementation. The lawmakers based much of their determinations on traditional winemaking practices; many of which were outdated and unable to compete with modern wine making. Because these original delineations were not always clear and dependable concerning quality wine production, new laws was enacted in 1992 known as the Goria law. It was named after Giovanni Goria, the Italian Minister of Agriculture who pushed the law through. This law clarified the Italian scene considerably. It establishes, or rather tidies up, a pyramid of quality by adding a fourth level known as Indicazione Geografica Tipica (IGT).

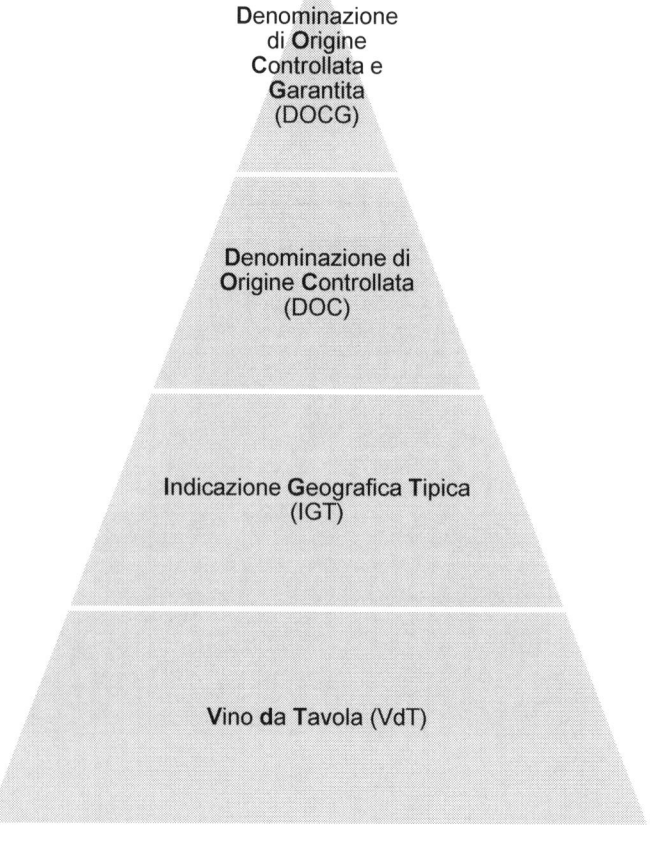

As of 2011, there were 332 DOCs, 60 DOCGs, and 119 IGTs. At least 60% of total production is at the IGT level or higher. The system works as a progression of restriction for production criteria that should lead to higher quality indication as the restrictions tighten. It also helps to give the consumer a better understanding of what they are purchasing as producers are required to express on the label what production level the wine was produced at.

**Vino da Tavola or VdT** (table wine) was introduced in 1960 and is the loosest term with which a producer can label his wine. The grapes can be sourced all from over the country and can also be blended without any restriction. There is also no indication of vintage or aging. It is usually labeled simply as *bianco, rosso,* or *rosato*. The majority of this wine is consumed locally.

**Indicazione Geografica Tipica or IGT** (Typical Geographical Indication) was introduced in 1992 as the latest addition to Italian regulation. This level was introduced by Minister Goria as answer to the existing gap between the DOC and the Vino da Tavola levels. At the time of the laws enactment, some of the most acclaimed Italian wines were still ignoring the DOC status due to ideological differences in winemaking. As a result of this, they were being forced to label their wines as simply VdT, even though they were of a superior quality (see also the chapter on *Supertuscans* in Tuscany). At this level, producers can still use a variety of grapes grown but the locality of the wines' production must be from within a given macro-area. The yields permitted are higher than that of a DOC but the vintage must be identified on the label. The wine may be labeled with a predominant grape or with a proprietary name. Originally, the areas of production were at minimum larger than a DOC and could cover an area as large as an entire region or even overlap two or more regions (IGT delle Tre Venezie). Today, sub-regions and specific sections of a region also apply.

Noteworthy exception: Piedmont and Valle D'Aosta do not have any IGT wines as the entirety of their respective grape growing territories fall under DOC or DOCG levels.

Denominazione di Origine Controllata DOC (Domain of Controlled Origin) was introduced in 1963.

At this level, producers must comply with a series of criteria:

- Sourcing of grapes from a delimited area
- More restrictive blending options
- Higher minimum alcohol levels
- Stricter acidity and extract levels
- Maximum yields
- Restrictions on winemaking techniques and aging
- Vintage specific

These restrictions will vary depending on the style of wine the regulation controls. With the early implementation of DOC law, blending options were less than optimal for quality wine making. Controls on percentage contributions for different varieties for blends were too loose and yields were set too high. Due to their initial rushed implementation, production areas also included unsuitable locations for growing the quality of fruit needed to make superior wines. With the laws enacted in 1992, obsolete restrictions and high yields were corrected, while subzones and single vineyards were introduced to identify distinctions in geography and topography. Though mapping and registering single vineyards remains a painstaking process to this day, the geographical delineations are much more accurate today. Wines must report a vintage on the label (with the exception of some sparkling wines) and must be bottled within the boundaries of the appellation. Chaptalization is never allowed but acidification is. Wood chips are not permitted and irrigation is allowed only in some areas and only in years declared a calamity. When a grape variety is quoted on the label, wine must be made with a minimum of 85% of the given variety. Finally, a tasting panel approves whether the wine is produced according to its specific DOC standards. There are currently more than 300 DOCs, but most of them are have multiple wines they can produce within the DOC so its real number is somewhere around 600 when counted individually.

There are other terns that may appear on the label which also help to identify qualities of the wine.

- **CLASSICO**, the grapes must be sourced from the original areas of the DOC. This area is often referred to as the "heart" of the DOC.
- **SUPERIORE** indicates that the wine is required to have a minimum alcohol level that is ½ to 1 degree higher and that yields are lower than the standard required for the DOC. The higher alcohol content, which helps to provide more structure and body for the wine, is generally obtained by postponing the harvest for several weeks.
- **RISERVA**, the aging requirements are longer still and the yields are lower. Traditionally, *Riserva* wines are the highest in terms of quality and are made only in good vintages. For all of these categories as well as those who are identify a *Single Vineyard* on the label stricter regulations are enforced.

Noteworthy exception: BOLGHERI SASSICAIA DOC is the only DOC with a proprietary brand name included in the DOC name. This DOC is also a monopoly, whose status is not reported on the label.

**Denominazione di Origine Controllata e Garantita DOCG (Domain of Guaranteed Controlled Origin)** was introduced in 1963 but did not become commercially available until 1980. The DOCG status is the highest level of wine quality in Italy. Its rules were taken so seriously that it was not until 1980 that the first DOCs (Barolo, Barbaresco, Vino Nobile di Montepulciano, Brunello di Montalcino and Chianti) were promoted to DOCG status. Controls are even stricter than a DOC, especially on the grapes used and their yields, which are much lower. To guarantee the wine, there are two tasting panels to guarantee that the wine is typical and it has produced according to the common criteria of the area. A DOC area must wait at least 5 years before it can apply for a DOCG. As of 2008 there are 44 DOCGs but their number grows every year.

Despite the restricted terms of production, at this level is possible that a wine would not be truly exceptional. Some DOCGs, such as Vernaccia di San Gimignano, Moscato d'Asti or Chianti can hardly be considered a remarkable wine on a global scale. The DOCG panel would not syndicate its quality but rather its adherence to the production criteria and the typicity of the area (whether those criteria have been met). Some of Italy's best wines (comparable to a First Growth in Bordeaux or Grand Cru of Burgundy) can be found at IGT and DOCG level but it all depends on the producer's ability to craft them.

In 2008, DOC and DOCG wines represent one third of the entire production with Veneto, Puglia, Emilia Romagna e Sicilia representing the main sources of quantity.

Some Italian winemaking terms:

- *Secco* = dry
- *Abboccato* = slightly sweet
- *Amabile* = semi-sweet
- *Dolce* = sweet
- *Ripasso* = a method of re-fermenting still wines in Veneto
- *Metodo Classico* = methode traditionalle in French
- *Frizzante* = slightly sparkling (3,5 atm of pressures)
- *Spumante* = sparkling wine (5 atm of pressure)
- *Passito* = wine made with dried grapes, usually sweet
- *Appassimento* = a method of drying grapes, common in Veneto
- *Vino Dolce Naturale* = Vin doux natural
- *Vin Santo* = a type of sweet wine common in Tuscany
- *Vino liquoroso* = fortified wine

- Vendemmia Tardiva = late harvest

# NORTHEAST ITALY

## PREDOMINANT VARIETIES

**Red:** Corvina, Rondinella, Molinara, Croatina plus Barbera, Bonarda, Oseleta (in Veneto), Teroldego, Schiava, Marzemino, Pinot Nero (in Trentino Alto Adige) Refosco, Schioppettino (in Friuli Venezia Giulia), Cabernet Sauvignon and Franc, Merlot (througout the region),

**Whites**: Mueller Thurgau, Sylvaner, Gewurztraminer, Nosiola, Kerner (Trentino Alto Adige), Tocai Friulano, Ribolla Gialla, Verduzzo, Picolit (Friuli Venezia, Giulia), Garganega, Trebbiano di Lugana, Torcolato and Vespaiolo (Veneto) Sauvignon Blanc, and Chardonnay (mostly Trentino Alto Adige and Friuli) Pinot Grigio and Pinot Bianco (everywhere in the region).

## SOIL

Very varied. Calcareous clay in Veneto, mountainous with gravelly soil and limestone in Trentino Alto Adige, limestone, sandstone and gravel (in Friuli Venezia Giulia)

## REGIONS

There are three regions that comprise Northeast Italy - Veneto, Friuli Venezia Giulia and Trentino Alto Adige. Collectively they are known as "Le Tre Venezie" (the three Venice). This is homage to the city of Venice, honoring the city's far-reaching cultural influence. As their diverse names suggest, these regions demonstrate a wide variety of cultural influences. In addition to the traditional Italian influence, the impact of foreign occupiers and the cultural exchange with their bordering nations can also be found. During the middle ages, this area was very important in the wine trade. This is an area known for its innovation, which coupled with the vast cultural exchange of bordering nations, has led to the adoption foreign grape varieties that are mainly from their neighbors Germany and France.

## VENETO

Veneto is a powerhouse of wine production, producing 20% of Italy's DOC wine. The region ranks 3rd in overall production. Gentle hills make this region suitable for intensive grape growing. Some years ago in this region, a cave drawing, dating back approximately 20 thousand years, depicts the planting of grapes for ancient wine production. The Etruscans, and then the Romans, intensified wine production in the region. Win production was devastated in 1800 when a majority of its vines had to be replanted due to a fungus. Veneto gained its independence from Austria and joined the Kingdom of Italy in 1866. The first DOC to reach its status was Lugana in 1967 followed by Bardolino, Soave and Valpolicella. The region is split into two halves. Northern Veneto is mountainous showcasing the picturesque Dolomites. Southern Veneto, following the course of the rivers Adige and Po, features flat, alluvial plains. Grapes for wine production grow in the hilly area in between the two, which offers calcareous soils. The climate is continental with great temperature dichotomy between day and night, abundant precipitation, and foggy winters. The Adriatic Sea and the Garda Lake temper the climate. The northwestern area is devoted to indigenous grapes, and the eastern part is mostly cultivated with international varieties such as Cabernet and Merlot. In this area, there is the large sparkling district of Conegliano, where Prosecco is produced. Here the experimental Viticultural Institute of Conegliano operates its laboratory and instructs soon-to-be winemakers in the best growth practices. The region is home of the largest wine companies operating in Italy.

Along highway A14, from Padua to Brescia (Franciacorta in Lombardy), several distinct growing areas are found: Colli Euganei, Colli Berici, Soave, Valpolicella, Bardolino and Lugana. Colli Euganei and Berici, located in Vicenza and Padua, are the largest of the hilly growing areas and produce a little bit of everything (red, whites, sparkling).

## SOAVE DOC

To the west lies the small hill top town of Soave, which is responsible for almost one third of all the DOC wines produced in Veneto. This white wine is made with the indigenous grape **Garganega** (min. 70%) with the possible addition of **Trebbiano di Lugana**, **Chardonnay** and **Pinot Bianco**. This very productive grape yields fine and delicate whites, with notes of lemon and almonds, good minerality and a great acidity. When made with 100% Garganega, this fresh and lively white is a true pearl. Due its success in the 1960s and 1970s, the area allowed tocarry the name Soave grew rapidly, and big companies began to mass-produce it and to dilute its characteristics. Since that time, production laws have been revisited extensively. A restricted SOAVE CLASSICO (DOC) area has been created. The inexpressive

Trebbiano di Toscana has been removed from the blend. A DOCG has been created carrying the name SOAVE SUPERIORE with an extra 1% alcohol obtained by postponing the harvest together with a SOAVE SUPERIORE RISERVA, aging the wine 2 years. The sweet dessert wine RECIOTO DI SOAVE (see below for description) made out of Garganega is the other DOCG of the area.

## Valpolicella DOC

Beyond Soave, a series of contiguous valleys, known as Valpolicella, punctuate the landscape. Valpolicella, translated from Latin, means "the valley of several (pluribus) cellars," attesting to its long tradition of vineyards. Valpolicella and its four neighboring valleys, Valpantena, Squaranto, Mezzane and Illasi form the VALPOLICELLA DOC. Valpolicella valley has been granted the CLASSICO DOC appellation. This region's winemaking tradition has produced some of the most exciting Italian wines based on indigenous grapes. The traditional blend is **Corvina, Rondinella** and **Molinara**. Of the three, Corvina has the largest percentage of the blend (up to 80%) and offers light, but fruity and aromatic wines with notes of almonds. Some successful experiments with this grape have been carried out under IGT labels. Corvina can also create an extremely effectual wine when produced from dried grapes, showcasing well the unique characteristics of wines from the Veneto. Rondinella and Molinara, the latter cultivated primarily for its high productive yield rather than its aromatics, contribute body to the blend. The law currently permits the use of **Bonarda, Barbera, Sangiovese** and **Cabernet** up to 10%.

## Valpolicella Superiore and Ripasso

Valpolicella can be made SUPERIORE by increasing its alcohol volume by 1% to a total of 12% and aging the wine one year in barrel. Alcohol content is increased using the traditional **RIPASSO** method. Ripasso means to "carry over again" and refers to a technique of re-fermentation that uses the dried, pressed grapes that are used for the production of **Recioto**. The wine vinified normally in September is passed over the lees (or the entire cluster) of dried grapes, causing a secondary fermentation that enhances the alcohol content and strengthens the body of the wine.

## Recioto

Recioto is a dessert wine produced in Veneto. Its name refers to the dialect term "Recie" (meaning ears). Corvina features big long clusters of berries, and farmers cut the external parts (or "the ears") in order to allow grape transpiration and to prevent the formation of mold within the bunch. Those clusters of grapes are put aside and dried on straw mats (or in plastic boxes) for at least four months. By February or March, the grapes have lost most of their water content and have higher sugar levels and concentration. Then they are pressed and fermented, leaving some residual sugar according to the desired sweetness. Grapes are monitored carefully during the drying process. Some producers welcome the formation of noble rot, while others try to avoid it completely. This technique is not an exact science, but in recent years, some ventilated "drying tunnels" facilities have been created in order to lower ambient humidity and to prevent botrytis from forming.

## Amarone

Amarone is one of the best-loved and most appreciated Italian wines in the world. Despite its growing reputation as the quintessential wine, it was created by chance, or more accurately, by mistake. Amarone translates to "big and bitter." During the production of Recioto, the wine would end up being fermented totally dry, and therefore, would not be sweet, but bitter (*amaro* in Italian). With the same process yielding to different results, in the early days, producers would mark the cask where sweet wine was produced with "recioto" and those casks with no residual sugar as "amarone." The second fermentation using dried grapes generates a bigger, more voluptuous wine whose alcohol content can reach 15% or more. Nowadays, vinification techniques are more precise and every producer exerts more control over the end result. Some shorten the "raisining" period, some use various oak barrels to impart a distinct flavor profile, and some keep the alcohol content within the 13-14% limit.

## Bardolino

The same blend of Valpolicella can me found in the Bardolino area. The area is named for the small town located on the Garda Lake bank. The wines from Bardolino are similar to the basic Valpolicella, but the lake's climactic influence makes them a little lighter and more acidic. The BARDOLINO SUPERIORE DOCG (12% alcohol requirement) is the highest appellation; there is a CLASSICO area here too. A lot of the production is released as *Rosé* and those wines, especially the so- called CHIARETTO DEL GARDA, are particularly appealing for their freshness and elegance. Some are called "vino di una notte" (translated to "one night wine"), because the maceration of the skins is only done for one night, allowing them to acquire a very pale color and some interesting cherry flavors. This area overlaps with the white production appellation BIANCO DI CUSTOZA DOC, which denotes more easy-drinking, everyday wines based on **Garganega**, **Tocai Fiulano** and **Trebbiano Toscano.**

## Lugana DOC

The Lugana appellation can be found to the south and west of the Garda Lake and within the boundaries of the Lombardy territory. Lugana DOC is made out of **Trebbiano di Lugana** (a clone variation of the very common Trebbiano). Its reputation is gaining ground thanks to the efforts of producers who are willing to limit the grape's productivity and to take advantage of the very favorable climactic conditions. Garda Lake and the Mincio River help to cool down the hot sunny days, allowing for healthy grape growth without rot and production of the necessary acidity. Lugana can be delicate and fresh and can offer interesting aromatics.

At the lake's northern banks, the Valdadige Valley gives way to the Alpine Mountain range with a steadily increasing altitude. The Adige River, one of Italy's longest, created this valley by carrying the melting Alpine waters down towards the Adriatic. Valdadige (The people of Alto Adige use to German term Etschalter) is a natural gateway to Trentino and Alto Agide. The larger part of its territory falls into this northern region. Here, a variety of grapes are grown. Whites (**Pinot Grigio**, **Pinot Bianco**, **Chardonnay**, **Sauvignon Blanc**, **Tocai Friulano**) thrive in the altitude, but the table wine **Schiava** grape and other French varieties are also found here. The whites usually offer nicer floral aroma with an even lighter body than the same grapes grown in the low land of Veneto.

On the east side of Veneto, the area of Breganze is renowned for international varieties. Indigenous grapes, such **Torcolato** and **Vespaiolo**, are more famous here for dessert wines made with dried grapes.

## Sparkling Wine: Prosecco

Most of the land in Veneto's eastern corner is planted with an indigenous variety called **Prosecco**, which lends its name to popular sparkling wine. Here vine growing and winemaking are separate processes. Small, specialized growers send their harvest to bottlers in the "bubble industry." Bottling requires large stainless tanks and filtering technologies.

Prosecco is a late ripening grape that was initially found in Friuli. Prosecco used to re-ferment in the spring; the first fermentation would be stuck during the cold winter nights, sometimes carrying residual sugar. The second fermentation sparked the idea of turning Prosecco into a full sparkling. In 1868, after graduating from the Conegliano Institute of Viticulture, Antonio Carpenè founded his company, Carpenè Malavolti. Carpenè introduced Italy to the industrial sparkling production method he learned from the Frenchman, Charmat. This industry now produces 250 million bottles annually. The second fermentation is carried out in large, temperature controlled and high-pressured tanks where the purchased grape juice is stored and where yeast is added. The final product is filtered and then bottled. Prosecco is drunk at every hour of the day, from North to South, as aperitif or with cocktails. The grape's fresh and lively quality, its low alcohol and its soft bitterness make it very popular. It is easy to drink. It can be made Brut, Extra Dry, and Dry according to the residual sugar. Proseccos are usually produced in a Non-Vintage style, though some wines produced with more sophistication and structure can be made in a Vintage specific style known as *Millesimat*. These wines are also given more structure and balance from the possible addition of up to 15% Chardonnay Most of the production is carried out between the towns of Valdobbiadene and Conegliano. The wider appellation is IGT Veneto, with these two DOCs (Conegliano and Valdobbiane) having a little better reputation for their quality. A select cluster of wine comes from Cartizze, a steep, low yielding 250 acres hill formation within Valdobbiadene, which is considered the CRU of the area. It produces is 8 million bottles.

## Friuli Venezia Giulia

Legend tells us that a local tribe, the Eneti, was cultivating vines between the 13$^{th}$ and 12$^{th}$ centuries BC During Roman times, the region was densely planted, but it was not until the Medieval period that wines became fundamental aspect of the common man's everyday life. The local grape RIBOLLA appears in official documents as early as 1307. French Count Theodore La Tour planted Merlot in 1869 on his property in the region. When phyllossera hit the area hard in 1888, farmers replanted most hectares with French varieties alongside the indigenous ones. Because of its long history, locals resist defining merlot as a foreign variety. The region was a battleground during both WWI and WWII, and fresh planting began in the late 1940s. Since the Middle Ages, this area functioned as a rich and important trade center. Friuli Venezia Giulia, considered to be culturally Italian, has been disputed territory for centuries, and ended up under the Austro-Hungarian Kingdom. During this time, Trieste served as the most important port on the Adriatic. Trieste and part of the Istrian peninsula were reassigned to Italy in 1954, the latest addition to the nation's territory. In 1968, Collio, meaning Colli Orientali or "eastern hills," became the first DOC. Domestically, the area is considered to be Italy's finest for white wines, but total production is split 50% with red wines. The northern part of the region is too mountainous and too cold for grape growing; production takes place in the hilly area in the middle of the region, alongside rivers Tagliamento and Isonzo and near the Adriatic Sea, where waters mitigate the harsh winters. Precipitation levels are high, and fog is common during the fall.

Pebbles are present in the soil of the Grave area's alluvial plains, and limestone is present in the soil of the CARSO DOC, located at the Slovenian border near Trieste.

The hilly areas of COLLI ORIENTALI DEL FRIULI DOC, and the COLLI GORIZIANI DOC, located at the Slovenian borders, are considered the best areas for viticulture. Within the soil, limestone is mixed with sandstone and marl. The steep hills drain allows for better water drainage, and there is less humidity. The two DOCS of the region, Ramandolo, grape **Verduzzo**, and **Picolit**, grape of the same name, are dessert wines obtained by drying local grapes (*passiti*). Once very famous for being the dessert wine of the court of Hapsburg, Picolit can be as delicious and as expensive as Sauternes. It has a rich texture, honeyed and floral nose, and crisp acidity with notes of apricot and peaches. Ramandolo is less fancy and tarter with citrusy notes.

Despite the prevalence of foreign varieties, including **Cabernet Sauvignon, Cabernet Franc, Merlot,** and **Pinot Grigio, Pinot Bianco, Riesling, Traminer, Sauvignon Blanc, Mueller Thurgau**, some indigenous grapes can be also found. The indigenous reds include **Pignolo, Tazzelenghe, Refosco, Schippettino**. The indigenous whites include **Ribolla Gialla, Picolit, Verduzzo,** and **Tocai Friulano.**

In 2006, Italy gave up the name **TOCAI FRIULANO** (the most widely planted white grape of the region) at the request of the Hungarian government. The Hungarian government sought to protect the Hungarian TOKAJ sweet wine appellation. Hungarian Tokaj is made with Furmint and Harslevelu. Apparently this grape is a clone of Furmint and was carried over from Tokaj, also the name of a Hungarian region, in the mid 1800s. Others suggest that in Alsace, *Tokai* is synonymous with Pinot Gris, or that it can be a minor clone of Sauvignon called *Sauvignonasse*. Producers have agreed to call this grape simply "FRIULANO."

In the 1970s, Friuli winemakers revolutionized white wine production. Rather than producing overripe, oxidized and highly alcoholic wine made by long skin contact, they introduced the stainless steel, refrigerated tank along with malolactic fermentation and soft press. A pure expression of grapes and soils, combined with lighter body, clean style and freshness could be found here before any other winery in Italy.

Reds have always had problems reaching full ripeness in this cold weather and were used mostly to supply the German market appetite for light bodied reds or to match salami and cold cuts. **Refosco** is the most widely planted among the local grapes and offers high acidity with a light body. Winemakers currently are attempting to produce in a more structured, bigger bodied fashion.

**Pignolo** and **Schioppettino** are ancient varieties that nearly became extinct, the latter being very difficult to grow. **Schippettino** has a curious name meaning "gunshot," named for the noises madeduring fermentation. It's a big red, tannic and spicy. **Pignolo** is believed to have the same potential as Sangiovese in Tuscany, offering black cherry flavors, tarry and tannic. Only three vineries are currently producing this variety, but it seems very promising.

## VARIETIES

- **Ribolla or Ribolla Gialla** (Robola in Grece) - light body, crisp with floral and cider aromas.
- **Tocai Friulano or Friulano** - light body, pale in color with floral to apricot notes.
- **Refosco** (Mondeuse in California) - late ripening, medium to full body with a lot of color- is acidic with aromas of plums and apricots.
- **Pignolo** - black cherry flavors, tarry and tannic.
- **Schioppettino** - big body, tannic and spicy
- **Verduzzo e Picolit** - used for dessert wines, with honey and apricot and cider notes.

# Trentino - Alto Adige

Leaving Veneto and following the Adige River towards its Alpine source, we enter in Trentino - Alto Adige. This territory has been under Italian control since 1919, following several centuries of Austrian rule. The region remains divided by a linguistic barrier between Italian and German.

The town of Magre, in the middle of the region, is Europe's southernmost German speaking village, separating the northern province and German speaking Bolzano (Alto Adige or South Tyrol) from the southern province, Italian-speaking Trento (Trentino). Its territory is completely mountainous. Its western mountain range climbs to 3,900 meters (12,400 feet). Grapes are grown between 300 and 600 meters on sea level. Grapes are grown on 14,000 hectares. 78% of its production has DOC status, the largest percentage in the country. It is Italy's northernmost point and its wine culture has strong a German influences. Since 1874 the Institute of Agriculture of San Michele all'Adige has operated in the region to promote productive farming techniques.

The soil contains gravel and limestone. The soil is the rockiest as its highest altitudes. Winds play an important role in determining the wide varieties of microclimates. It is a meeting point for cool air from the Alps and warm winds from the Garda Lake. As a result of Trentino-Alto Adige's altitude, it is known primarily for whites. Bolzano, however, is located in a humid valley and is one of the warmest cities in Italy during the summer, and 70% of its production is red. Most of its acreage planted with the **Schiava** grape, **Vernatsch** in German.

The most prominent local grapes are **Merlot, Cabernet Sauvignon, Cabernet Franc** and a cross of both called **Cabernet**. Other local grapes include plus **Pinot Nero, Marzemino, Lagrain, Malvasia (Nera), Moscato Rosa** (Pink Muscat) and **Teroldego**. Among the whites are **Chardonnay, Sauvignon, Pinot Grigio** and **Bianco, Nosiola, Kerner, Sylvaner, Muller Thurgau,** and **Gewurztraminer**. A total of 19 varieties are allowed in the TRENTINO DOC and 22 in the ALTO ADIGE DOC. Producers usually mention the grape in the label. One possible explanation is the fact that microclimates change dramatically from parcel to parcel.

Viticulture is also influenced by the presence of co-ops. Here co-ops are born spontaneously rather than government made. This is a significant distinction from the co-ops of Southern Italy. Of course some large co-ops are still focused on volume, but smaller ones have great models for rewarding members that provide quality grapes. These small co-ops are among Italy's best wineries and best-run wine companies.

## White Varieties - Trentino

Lower elevation vineyards are planted with **Chardonnay, Pinot Grigio, Pinot Nero** and **Bianco,** which supply a thriving sparkling industry. Some of Italy's best *spumante* are made here with *metodo tradizionale*. One producer ranks among the world top ten sparkling producers for quantity while still maintaining a remarkable quality. This sparkling production goes under the TRENTO DOC appellation. TRENTINO DOC, which is only for still wines, is a catchall appellation that can be made with 19 different grapes.

**Chardonnay** is impressive here for its fresher, fruitier style. **Sauvignon Blanc** has a peachy, citrusy note, without the body and warmth of New Zealand, for example. **Mueller Thurgau** is planted above 500 meters and harvested late, conditions under which other grapes would struggle. This German cross of Riesling and Sylvaner, created by Mr. Mueller, has strong exotic aromas, spice with petroleum-style body and apricots scents.

The local **Nosiola** is aromatic but almost bitter and is used to produce VIN SANTO.

## White Varieties - Alto Adige

At least 11 white varieties are cultivated in Alto Adige. Most labels are printed in both German and Italian. In addition to Sauvignon Blanc, **Pinot Bianco** is widely used by producers who relish its versatility and ability to be aged in oak. Some low yield examples, especially from single-vineyard, the suffix *–hof* usually refers to a single vineyard, present interesting nutty notes. The star is **Gewurztraminer**, which is believed to be originally from the city of Tramin, Termeno in Italian. The cinnamon, lychee nose and its rich profile of this wine make it sought after. Compared these with other German Gewurztraminer, these are surprising for their freshness and increased acidity.

**Sylvaner** and **Kerner** are also cultivated here. The latter is easier to grow. Some Gruner Veltliner can be found in the northernmost part.

## Red Varieties – Trentino

Reds produced here are generally light and are similar to the Schiava, mostly consumed locally or sold in the German market. The Schiava is a productive but not very expressive grape that can resemble young Pinot Noir. International varieties Cabernet and Merlot have ripening problems, not because lack of sunshine, but due to the fact that producers often harvest early to avoid September rains. Usually, they have a greenish, vegetal aroma with unappealing green bell pepper notes. Wines obtained from the **Teroldego** grape, cultivated mostly in the Trento province, that fall under the TEROLDEGO ROTALIANO DOC have received a great deal of attention recently. This grape has been cultivated since 1500 and grows well in the sandy and gravelly soils. It offers fruity, but not tannic, reds with a lot of color and intrigue. The other local grape, **Marzemino**, is produced less and less, but remains famous for its reference in Mozart's Don Giovanni. It is lively with good acidity and is sometimes slightly sparkling.

## Red Varieties – Alto Adige

This region, with its high altitude and gravelly terraces, offers Italy's best spot to grow **Pinot Noir**. **Lagrein** has been the most famous indigenous grape in this region since 1600. It grows very well, particularly in the hot valley near Bolzano where it can ripen fully. It offers dark color, funky spice and aromas of dark fruits. Sometimes is also made rosato, *Kretzer* in German.

# Northwest Italy

## Predominant Varieties:

**Red:** Nebbiolo (called Spanna in Northern Piedmont and Chiavennasca in Valtellina), Barbera, Dolcetto (called Ormeasco in Liguria), Grignolino, Bonarda, Vespolina (in Piedmont), Fumin, Petit Arvine, Petit Rouge (Valle d'Aosta), Rossese (Liguria), Pinot Nero (in Lombardy and Piedmont) Croatina (Lombardy) Syrah, Cabernet.

**Whites**: Cortese, Arneis, Erbaluce, Timorasso, Moscato (Piedmont), Pigato and Vermentino (Liguria, called Favorita in Piedmont), plus Chardonnay, Pinot Grigio (gris).

## Soil

Very varied. Calcareous marls and chalky soils in Piedmont, mountainous with terraces in Valle d'Aosta, terrace in Valtellina and Liguria, alluvial soil and clay.

## Regions

The Italian side of the Alps that borders France to the northwest and Switzerland to the north is home to some exciting wines. These wines are considered among the world's best, and that reputation is attributable to Barolo and Barbaresco. The region is defined to the south by the Apennines, a shorter and older mountain chain that begins here and goes down through the rest of the peninsula, dropping straight into the Ligurian Sea at this latitude. In the middle of the region, the largest Italian river, the Po, flows through the Padan plain en route to the Adriatic Sea. The region is predominantly mountainous and hilly with the exception of the low land of Lombardy. Milan—Italy's most industrialized area—is located within the low land of Lombardy. The climate is continental with cold winters hot summers. There is a significant difference between the night and day temperatures. There is a great deal of moisture, which generates fog. The maritime influence of the sea helps cool the summer nights. Wine is produced mostly in the rolling hills of **Piedmont**. Some extreme wine production is also carried out in the mountains of **Valle d'Aosta** and on the terrace vineyards of **Ligurian** Apennines or Valtellina, a mountainous district near the border with Switzerland. **Lombardy** is mostly renowned for Franciacorta—a small area specialized in sparkling wines.

## Valle d'Aosta

This tiny region is probably Italy's least contaminated wine country. It borders Switzerland to the north and shares with France Europe's tallest mountain (Monte Bianco or Mount Blanc, 4,810 meters or 15,700 feet). This is the smallest producing region in Italy with a mere 509 hectares under cultivation. Its high altitude and mountains make it very hard for producers to make a living by growing grapes. Some vineyards are at 1,000 meters above sea level, some 3,280 feet. Despite these prohibitive conditions, a few heroic wine makers have carved terrains and grow pergola style vineyards. At this altitude, most of the vines are pre-phylloxera. Wine regulators have created an all-comprehensive VALLE D'AOSTA DOC with subzones, basically coming back from the previous structure of different DOCs. Here **Nebbiolo**, locally called Picotener, **Dolcetto** and **Pinot Noir** are grown alongside local grapes such as the reds **Petit**

Rouge, **Fumin** and **Petit Arvine**. Delicious **Chardonnay**, **Muscat** and **Malvoisie**, or Pinot Gris, are made among the whites. TORRETTE (formerly a DOC) is the most renowned of all appellations. It uses Petit Rouge as main grape plus **Pinot Noir**, **Gamay** and **Fumin**. These wines are light in body with pale color and a sharp acidity and some spice. They resemble Beaujolais, and they match fondue or can be served in the summer. Fumin has a little more body, and it reminds the spiciness of Syrah. There are no Valle d'Aosta IGT wines.

## PIEDMONT

This region has a great significance in Italy's history. It was home to the Royal House of Savoy, the royal family that untied the country and served as the first Kings of Italy. The Savoy presence in Turin, briefly the first capital of the country, has had an impact on the history of winemaking. The court provided an audience for Piedmont's wines and a constant cultural exchange with bordering France. 43% of Picdmont is mountainous. Wine production is concentrated in the hills of **Monferrato** and **Langhe,** located south–southeast of Turin, around the towns of Alba and Asti. The soil is here is the most fertile of the region with clay-based marl and calcareous chalk. The region produces indigenous Italian grapes whose origins are uncertain and probably date before the Romans. Most widely planted reds are **Dolcetto, Barbera, Nebbiolo, Grignolino, Fresia**, and **Brachetto**. The most widely planted whites are **Moscato, Cortese,** and **Arnei**s. The region offers the greatest number of DOCGs (16) and DOCs wines (41) of all of the Italian regions. Despite producing 75% red wine, the DOC production is mostly white, due in large part to the productive MOSCATO D'ASTI DOCG (Frizzante) or ASTI DOCG (Spumante). These mass-produced, crowd-pleasing wines are generally sweet and widely consumed.

DOC production accounts for more than 60% of total output—Piedmont being the 6$^{th}$ largest region for quantity. In recent years, there has been a rediscovery of the white grapes thathas fallen out of fashion with producers, such as **Favorita**, **Erbaluce**, and **Timorasso**. Unlike what is happening in other regions, Piedmont does not have IGT wines since they did not believe in this newly created category. PIEDMONT DOC is an overall comprehensive appellation which is usually followed by the grape name (i.e., PIEMONTE BARBERA DOC). As the general use, when a variety is to be found on the label, there must be no less than 85% of the given variety.

Farmers in Piedmont historically have paid a great deal of attention to the individual plots of land where grapes are growing. In this respect, Piedmont resembles Burgundy for the ongoing "ratings" of best plots and the tradition of allocating the serious and age worthy Nebbiolo grape only to the best locations. Usually the best locations are the south facing hill slopes between 200 and 450 meters of altitude. The second best locations are allocated to Barbera and Dolcetto. These better sites are usually, as in Burgundy, divided among different families and labeled under different houses. Winemaking has always been taken very seriously, and vineyards are densely planted on these rolling hills. Nebbiolo was first cited by historians in the year 1303, while the single vineyard "*Cannubi*," which now if one of the most prized Barolo "Cru" or Single Vineyard, is cited around the year 1500 as a location that gives the best fruit year in and out. The widely popular **Vermouth** is made in Piedmont by adding generic wines with moscato d'Asti, spices, and aromatic herbs and can be made Bianco, Rosso, Dry, or "Secco". Vermouth is NOT a DOC wine.

Piedmont DOCs overlap according to what grape varieties are used to produce wine. We will discuss the region according to grape varieties rather than towns or regions.

**Nebbiolo** produces some of the finest red wines in the world. It is a difficult grape to grow. It has thin, multi-layered skin. It is a late-ripening variety and can vary greatly according to climate and soil conditions. When the conditions are right, it can produce long-lived reds with great acidity balanced by delicate aromatics, good tannins and firm structure. Unfortunately, hot weather can jeopardize its aromatics. The wrong practice in the cellar can produce over oxidation and result in a lack of complexity. Rainy seasons can dilute acidity and tannin levels.

Three different clones can be found, *Michet, Lampia* and *Rosé*. *Rosé* has been replaced recently, because it was not as well suited for high quality wine production. The name **Nebbiolo** seems to be derived from "*nebbia*"—Italian for "fog". The grape is prone to a grey mold—called "*pruina*"—that resembles fog. Winemaking techniques have improved significantly in the last 30 years in Piedmont. Before the 1980s, winemakers did not use rotofermenters or temperature controlled maceration. The maceration and fermentation were carried out spontaneously in open vats (containing 3,000 to 8,000 liters) and would last from 20 days to almost two months in order to extract the maximum of tannins and aromatics. Fermentation was dependant on outside temperature conditions, and sometimes, if the temperature dropped suddenly, fermentation would stop. The wine was later aged in large chestnut casks, called *botti*, whose capacity is anything between 2,000 and 10,000 liters. The wine was bottled on order. This practice seems to be fading, as producers have learned to bottle the wine when it is ready rather than when the order arrives. In recent years, improvements in the cellars have shortened the maceration time and have increased the extract. Small French *barriques* have introduced vanilla flavors and a much more approachable style. Now two styles, a more modern and a traditional one, can be found throughout Piedmont.

## BAROLO (DOCG SINCE 1980)

Known as the "King of wines and the wine of the King," Barolo has gained an international reputation. It was given its name by a small town that lies nine miles south of Alba. Its style changed dramatically when Giulia Colbert Countess of Barolo hired the French winemaker Louis Oudart to take care of the cellar. Before this happened, the wines from Barolo were produced in a sweet, sparkling style due to the fact that fermentation was stopped during the cool night temperatures in the cellar. Oudart helped to move the wine to its current reputation in style. The changes helped to make the wines the favorite of the Court of the Savoy and they are now exported on a large scale.

Barolo is made from 100% Nebbiolo grapes. According to the traditional law has to age at least 3 years, two of them in oak casks. The maximum yield allowed is 50 hl/ha. For the *Riserva*, the regulation calls for at least 5 years of aging. There are 12 communes (or villages) that are entitled to carry the Barolo name on the label. Critics have divided the area into two prevalent styles according to different soil composition. Wines from the western communes of La Morra and Barolo are usually softer, with grace and elegance as a result of the calcareous marl in the soil. They are younger, magnesium rich soils called Tortonian Marl. The towns of Monforte d'Alba, Castiglione Falletto and Serralunga d'Alba in the east lie on an older, poorer sandstone and iron rich marl called Helvetian Marl. These wines are more powerful, deeper and have more density that can usually sustain longer aging.

Since the 1980's, Barolo has been in the midst of an ongoing discussion between modernists and traditionalists. The modernists are producing more fruit forward, easy to drink wines made with shorter maceration, higher extract, and temperature-controlled fermentation with *barrique* aging. These are the characteristics that make wines more competitive in a world market where wine drinkers do not have the time or money to allow their bottles the long age times generally required of traditional Barolos. Traditionalists, on the other hand, insist on long fermentation and large oak. These producers still command a loyal audience as well. These controversies have been called the "Barolo Wars." There are also many possible variations that are a compromise of these two styles.

The traditional pale orange colored Barolos have a reputation for tart, ethereal wines with scents of truffle, chocolate and tobacco. Overall production of Barolo is around 10 million bottles, with 1,700 hectares under wine.

The "*CRU*" system follows a long tradition of viticulture and attention to soil types. Growers have determined which plots of land give consistent quality fruit. This had led to the crafting of "single vineyard" wines. These single vineyards are usually located in a North to South axis with Southern exposure necessary to receive the afternoon sunshine that allows grapes to ripen fully. Producer Renato Ratti was the visionary who took the time to meticulously map the Barolo area, giving a good "rate" to those parcels where snow melted first. Nebbiolo is usually planted mid-way on the hilltop. Barbera is usually planted at the bottom or at the top of the hill; where Nebbiolo is considered to not perform as well. Currently, producers have to register the single vineyard names in a specific index and the yields must be subsequently reduced. The evolution of the Italian law will soon establish a set of rules for this category of wines. The recurring "*Bricco*" or "*Bric*" is a local dialect term that stands for "hill-slope" or "vineyard." One may also see the term "*Sorì*" which means "a sunny plot." The following names are usually reported in the label and can command extremely high prices:

| Single vineyards names | In the commune of |
|---|---|
| Cannubi, Brunate, Cerequio | Barolo |
| Rocche dell'Annunziata | La Morra |
| Vigna Rionda, Francia, Falletto | Serralunga d'Alba |
| Ginestra, Bussia, Cicala, Colonnello | Monforte d'Alba |
| Villero, Rocche di Castiglione, Monprivato | Castiglione Falletto |

## Barbaresco (DOCG since 1980)

Another DOCG wine based on 100% Nebbiolo is Barbaresco, which is considered the "Queen" of wines versus the "King" Barolo. This is due to the more feminine approach style-wise. They have greater elegance and shorter aging requirements—2 years minimum with one in cask. It is 4 years obligatory aging for the *Riserva*. Some producers produce even more powerful, tannic wines that require aging of 15 to 20 years. Yields are kept at a maximum 50 hl/ha and wines can be sourced from the three communes of Barbaresco, Treiso, and Neive. Barbaresco is a smaller area than Barolo and has a little less than 500 hectares under vines. The average growing altitude is 50 meters lower than Barolo. The same discussion between modernist and traditionalist winemakers can also be found here. The more famous single vineyards are Asilii, Santo Stefano, and Rabaja.

## Roero DOCG

Roero is another small commune north of Alba on the other side of the Tanaro River. This new DOCG was established in 2005 and requires 95-98% Nebbiolo in the blend with the addition of Arneis. The yields are similar to Barolo and aging is 20 months, with 6 in oak. The soil is extremely chalky.

The white ROERO DOCG is made entirely with the Arneis grape.

## Ghemme DOCG and Gattinara DOCG

These appellations are Nebbiolo based and the local name for the variety is **Spanna**. Located in the northernmost corner of Piedmont, near the border of Lombardy, the DOCGs draw their names from the towns of the same names. These towns are located at the opposite sides of the Sesia River. The regulation calls for a possible blend of up to 14% of **Vespolina** and **Bonarda** in the case of **Gattinara** and up to 25% of **Vespolina** and **Bonarda** for **Ghemme.** The aging requirements are three years for Gattinara and four for the Riserva. It is also three years for Ghemme. It can be difficult for Nebbiolo to fully ripen at this latitude because of the high altitude so the resulting wines can be angular and acidic. The addition of Vespolina and Bonarda, with their fruity characteristics, helps to balance the acidity of Nebbiolo.

## Other Northern Appellations: Lessona, Bramaterra, & Carema DOC

**LESSONA DOC** is a Northern appellation made of 85% Spanna and 15% Vespolina.

**BRAMATERRA DOC** is an appellation that borders Lessona. They are also Spanna based wines (50-70%), with Bonarda and Vespolina (10-20%), and Croatina (20-30%) rounding out the blend. The aging requirement is 2 years. The generic appellation for these wines is COSTE DELLA SESIA DOC. At its west CAREMA DOC covers the Alpine foothills appellation (another Nebbiolo based appellation).

**BARBERA** is for Piedmont's producers the everyday wine that has to be enjoyed fresh. They usually reserve their second best plots in the vineyard to this variety due to the fact that Barbera is fairly productive everywhere and does not require the same arduous attention of Nebbiolo. It shares Nebbiolo's acidity but produces a wine with less tannin that tends to be much more fruit forward. It also tends to have high yields. BARBERA D'ASTI DOC and BARBERA D'ALBA DOC (the latter is a much smaller area) grow nearby the two towns of the same names and have the best reputation. BARBERA DELLE LANGHE DOC and BARBERA DEL MONFERRATO DOC are the wider appellations for this grape. In 2008, BARBERA D'ASTI SUPERIORE and BARBERA DEL MONFERRATO SUPERIORE were upgraded to DOCG status, and require both 14 months of aging (and of course a higher alcohol content).

Some producers have also successfully experimented in shortening the maceration time and then barrique-aging the wines. Asti can produce exceptional wines in this fashion but Alba has a more highly regarded, fruitier character when made in its honest, traditional way.

## Dolcetto Di Dogliani Superiore & Dolcetto Di Ovada Superiore DOCG

**DOLCETTO:** if Barbera was always relegated to the second best locations, Dolcetto had even a worst luck. Being a highly productive, early-ripening grape earned it its place on the least desirable plots of the vineyards. It has thick skin and is rich in pigments. A short maceration gives an intense purple color to the wine. Dolcetto, which in Italian means "small sweet," presents a sweet fruit at harvest that in reality is not sweet at all. Its residual sugar and potential alcohol are actually quite low. It has less acidity than Barbera and Nebbiolo and wine makers tend to prefer this wine for everyday, fresh, easy-drinking wines. DOLCETTO DI DOGLIANI DOCG and DOLCETTO DI OVADA DOCG are the areas where the grape gives its best. Both DOCGs are required to be a *Superiore* version. DOLCETTO d'ALBA DOC, DOLCETTO DI DIANO D'ALBA DOC, and DOLCETTO D'ACQUI DOC are also interesting versions of this grape.

Other notable red grapes of Piedmont are **Grignolino, Fresia, Brachetto, Palaverga** and **Ruché**. **Grignolino**. **Grignolino** gives a very pale, thin bodied but tannic wine that can be enjoyed chilled as refreshment for the hot summers. **Fresia** is also a naturally acidic, tannic wine that has a pale color. It can be made frizzante or still, offering sweet notes and a bitter aftertaste. **Pelaverga** is an ancient, almost extinct grape whose name refers to its supposedly aphrodisiac properties that is oftern reminiscent of a common Pinot Noir. **Ruché,** which is being planted less and less in the Monteferrato hills, is a plumy, tannic wine similar to Nebbiolo in aromatics. **Brachetto** can be made dry but is more successful when it is made sweet, slightly sparkling for dessert.

## White Wines of Piedmont

**ARNEIS** is probably the best expression of Piedmont's white indigenous grapes. It offers an abundance of aromatics with an almost nutty character. Its best vineyards are located in the chalky soils of ROERO, where the wine has a DOCG status. The soil helps to increase its acidity. Planted in other locations or if not consumed fresh, it can present flat.

**FAVORITA** – Cultivated in the hills of Cuneo, this naturally high acid grape is a close relative of Vermentino. It offers generous aromatics with greater acidity than that of Arneis, which can ensure longer aging.

**CORTESE** – As can often be the case, this less aromatic variety has gained a much stronger reputation thanks to the success of GAVI DOCG (or GAVI DI GAVI DOCG). This wine is clean, crisp, and very acidic. It is a great match for the fish dishes served in Genoa and Liguria during the summer. It is mostly planted within the province of Alessandria near the Southeast border of Piedmont. When harvest is slightly postponed, this wine can evolve and be well structured; offering good minerality with high potential for aging.

**ERBALUCE** – This ancient grape is cultivated in the Northern part of Piedmont and can have great acidity with interesting notes of citrus and flowers. ERBALUCE DI CALUSO DOC (also PASSITO) is the main appellation for this grape.

**TIMORASSO** – This is a cult wine for connoisseurs. When phylloxera destroyed most of its plantings, only a few producers replanted their vineyards with this grape. They preferred instead the easier and more productive Cortese variety. In the province of Alessandria, this grape makes a medium bodied, well-structured wine that offers good fruit aromas and floral notes.

## Sparkling Wines

Piedmont has a large industry of sparkling wines (one of the largest of the entire nation) based on the Moscato grape, especially near the town of Asti. MOSCATO d'ASTI DOCG and ASTI DOCG (this appellation was formerly known as ASTI SPUMANTE DOC and was renamed ASTI DOCG in order to try to improve its image in 1993) are made in the same villages in the province of Cuneo, though they differ a lot in their production. Moscato Bianco (a petits grains) is a naturally sweet grape with high residual sugar. MOSCATO D'ASTI is usually produced by small producers and is often estate bottled. These wines reach an average of 5% alcohol content and are released as *frizzante* (slightly sparkling, with 3 atms of pressure) as dessert wine. Its aromas are reminiscent of peach and apricot with some floral notes. Some producers achieve a fine expression of this grape. ASTI DOCG is mostly source from larger co-op cellars in the area and are made fully sparkling (spumante) using the Charmat method. They have an alcohol level that ranges from 7-9.5% with a fresh and vibrant character that can have notes of orange and honey.

## International Varieties

The rush to produce internationally recognized varieties has been less profound here than in other Italian regions, but the Piedmont climate has shown some welcome to foreign varieties such as **Pinot Noir, Chardonnay,** and even **Cabernet Sauvignon** and **Syrah**. Un-oaked style Chardonnay has gained popularity since the 1970s. Experiments with international varieties can now be labeled as LANGHE CABERNET DOC or PIEMONTE CABERNET DOC according to where the grapes have been sourced.

## Liguria

Liguria is a long stretch of hilly land compressed between France, The Apennines and the Ligurian Sea. It also touches Tuscany in the East. After Valle D'Aosta, it has the smallest production of wine in Italy. Those that make wine here have to struggle to carve terraces into the mountains that drop straight into the Ligurian Sea. When one sees images from Cinque Terre, it is quickly understood how winemaking can be difficult here. Liguria produces mostly whites, its *cousine* being oriented towards the sea with a touch of inland specialties; Pesto, for example, was born in Genoa, Italy's biggest port. Moreover, flocks of tourists that prefer light, easy drinking whites for the summer, have limited the capabilities of these producers to achieve anything better. 65% of production is white, mostly from **Vermentino,** which is cultivated both in the East and West Riviera, and **Pigato,** which is a Western Riviera grape. **Bosco** is a light bodied white that is found in the CINQUE TERRE DOC and SCIACCHETRA, along with Vermentino. They can be made dry, sparkling or sweet. Vermentino, thought to be of Spanish origins, can possess exotic aromatics and can offer good body with great acidity; helping to create a balanced wine. This is the same grape as in Sardinia, where it is called Rolle, as well as Piedmont's Favorita. It is also now being planted with success in coastal Tuscany. Some harvest it early to retain acidity while others prefer to produce it in a slightly overripe, almost oxidized style. Pigato is an older variety brought to Italy by the Greek. Many think it is genetically related to Vermentino. It has an herbal and sharp character with distinctive aromatics. Among the red grapes, **Ormeasco** is the local name of Dolcetto. **Rossese** is also an indigenous grape cultivated in the west bank, near the border with France. Rossese can create savory, dry reds reminiscent of wood. Some Sangiovese is cultivated near the border with Tuscany. Liguria has 8 DOCs. The COLLI DI LUNI DOC produces wines from Pigato and Vermentino and is a DOC shared with Tuscany. RIVIERA LIGURE DI PONENTE DOC and ROSSESE DI DOLCEACQUA DOC are also on the West Riviera, around the town of Dolceacqua.

## Lombardy

Despite being one of the largest and most densely populated regions, Lombardy (Lombardia) does not produce large quantities of wine. It has 3 major wine districts. Lombardy has Milan as its capital and is mostly industrialized and developed. Wine production is concentrated in the hilly slopes of Oltrepó Pavese, the narrow valley of Valtellina, and Franciacorta.

**Franciacorta** (DOCG since 1995) – this small appellation is the highest quality production of sparkling wines in Italy. The producers of this area were inspired to create wines that rivaled those of Champagne. Grapes allowed here are Chardonnay, Pinot Nero and Pinot Bianco. It is mandatory that the wines are produced *metodo tradizionale* (second fermentation obligatory in the bottle) with a minimum of 25 months of aging on the lees and 37 months for *Riserva*. This was a successful DOCG in the world market because it encompasses only the sparkling production of the wine. The dry table wines are still at DOC status. This has enhanced the reputation of the DOCG. Noteworthy: TERRE DI FRANCIACORTA DOC is only for dry wines made out the same grapes.

**Valtellina Superiore (DOCG since 2004)** is a high altitude, 40 km long narrow valley in the province of Sondrio. It is close to the border of Switzerland and runs along the Adda River. It is divided into 4 subzones: Grunello, Inferno, Sassella and Valgella. Wine production is made possible by the terraces in the rocks and by the pebbles that capture and retain daytime heat. Nebbiolo is locally called **Chiavennasca** and represents 80% of the blend. The other varieties allowed in the blend are **Merlot**, **Pinot Noir**, **Rossola** and **Vignola**. Minimum alcohol required is 12%. The resulting wines are tighter than Barolos and tend to be less forgiving than their Piedmont counterparts. They can be astringent, with less concentration than Barolos, but can offer interesting and ethereal aromas of tea, tar and tobacco.

**Sforzato Or Sfursat Di Valtellina DOCG** is a wine produced in a similar style to Amarones in which the grapes are dried and then pressed at the beginning of February. The raisination of Nebbiolo grapes offer some tarry, glycerin-like aspects with more savory and spiciness than Amarones tend to have.

**Oltrepó Pavese.** This appellation literally means "on the other side of the Po River" – looking from the Milan perspective. This area produces the largest quantity of both still and sparkling Pinot Nero in Italy. This area also produces wines made from **Riesling Italico** and **Moscato,** which can be made into deliciously sweet sparkling wines. The red production is concentrated mostly in the flat areas of land. It is based on **Barbera** and **Bonarda**, though this grape is actually **Croatina** and differs from the Bonarda used in Ghemme and Gattinara. The area is mostly renowned for quantity rather than quality.

**Lugana DOC.** This is Lombardy's easternmost appellation and is shared with the Veneto. Lugana is also a DOC on the other side of the Garda Lake. The Lugana DOC is made of **Trebbiano di Lugana,** which is a clone variation of the very common Trebbiano. Its reputation is gaining ground thanks to the efforts of some producers who are willing to limit the grape's potential over productivity and take advantage of the very favorable climate conditions. The lake and the Mincio River act as climate moderators, helping to cool down the heat of the sun during the day. This allows the grapes to grow healthily without rot and acquire necessary acidity. Lugana wines can be delicate, fresh and can offer interesting aromatics.

# Central Italy

## Predominant Varieties

**Red:** Sangiovese, Canaiolo, Malvasia Nera, Alicante (Syrah) (in Tuscany), Sangiovese, Montepulciano and Sagrantino (in Umbria), Lambrusco (Emilia-Romagna), Montepulciano (Abruzzo), Montepuciano and Sangiovese (Marches) Cesanese (Latium) plus Cabernet Sauvignon, Merlot, Syrah.

**Whites**: Vernaccia, Vermentino, Trebbiano Toscano, Malvasia Bianca, Ansonica (Inzolia), Moscato Bianco (in Tuscany), Grechetto, Procanico, Malvasia (Umbria), Trebbiano (Abruzzo) Trebbiano, Malvasia (Latium), Verdicchio (Marches) plus Pinot Grigio, Chardonnay and Sauvignon Blanc.

## Soil

Viniculture takes place at medium altitude hills and towards the coasts. Galestro and chalk rock in the Chianti Classico Area and Montalcino (Tuscany), sandy in Bolgheri, Scansano and sandy, clay in Montepulciano. Tufa, volcanic soils (in Latium), limestone, calcareous and clay soils (in The Marches and Abruzzi).

## Regions

## Tuscany

Tuscany began to build its cultural foundation in the Middle Ages. Florence later elevated this region's status on the world stage when it became the influence for the cultural Renaissance that began in the late 13th century. Tuscany today is no longer an influence from a commercial and cultural perspective but has retained its status as a renowned area for fashion and tourism. It is home to approximately 4 million people. The communes of Florence, Pisa, Siena, Lucca, and Arezzo are recognized around the world as beautiful examples of artistic towns that show unchanged medieval scenarios and still attract thousands of tourists each year. Equally beautiful is the countryside, where man and nature have now for centuries peacefully co-existed and gently shaped its postcard-like environment.

If Piedmont is similar to Burgundy in the way its wine industry is structured, Tuscany is more similar to Bordeaux. Here tradition is as equally important as innovation and noble families have the leverage of centuries of production experience. Red production is prevalent, but some whites are also produced. Tuscany together with Piedmont is considered to be Italy's top quality wine producer with a total of 8 DOCGs and 37 DOCs. Tuscany has 58,000 ha under vine and 50% of its production has achieved DOC status, making it 5th in total regional production of DOC wines.

## TUSCAN REDS

Tuscan red wines are mostly based on **Sangiovese**, a grape variety that is considered to be indigenous of Italy, possibly cultivated as far back as the Etruscans. The grape's name literally means "the blood of Jupiter". Sangiovese is Italy's most widely planted red grape, accounting for 10% of the total acreage, mostly in Central and South Italy. It is late to ripen, with thin skin and presents pale in color. It is aromatic, presents with great acidity and has good potential to age. It can however suffer in cool vintages when it struggles to ripen fully, creating wines that are too acidic or tannic. It is a highly terroir-expressive variety, articulating widely different characteristics depending on the wines place of origin. It is best suited for calcareous soils. There are at least two clones; Sangiovese Grosso and Sangiovese Piccolo. Sangiovese Grosso can be found in Montalcino (where it is called **Brunello**) and in Montepulciano and Lamole (where it is called **Prugnolo Gentile**). It is also known as Greve in Chianti. Sangiovese Piccolo can be found in Scansano, where is called **Morellino**. The main difference between the clones is the size of the clusters and berries. Currently there are too many clones to create a simple definition of the differences between them. In recent years, several projects, including the Chianti Classico 2000 Project, have been conducted in an attempt to identify the different varieties in order to replant the more prolific along with those that are more quality orientated. The grape has shown great improvements and producers are focusing on this local variety more and more.

| Name | Local name of Sangiovese | Blend (Sangiovese is always min.) | Aging | DOC /DOCG Year of creation |
|---|---|---|---|---|
| Chianti | Sangioveto | 75% Sangiovese 10% Canaiolo | 1 year for Riserva | 1967/1984 |
| Chianti Colli Aretini | Sangiovese | 75% Sangiovese 10% Canaiolo | 1 year for Riserva | 1996 |
| Chianti Rufina | Sangiovese | 75% Sangiovese 10% Canaiolo | 1 year for Riserva | 1996 |
| Chianti Colli senesi | Sangiovese | 75% Sangiovese 10% Canaiolo | 1 year for Riserva | 1996 |
| Chianti Classico | Sangioveto | 80% Sangiovese, Canaiolo, Colorino, Malvasia Nera | 2 years for the Riserva | 1996 |
| Brunello di Montalcino | Sangiovese Grosso Brunello | 100 % Sangiovese | 5 years 6 years for Riserva | 1966/1980 |
| Nobile di Montepulciano | Prugnolo Gentile | 70% Sangiovese 20 % Canaiolo max 10% Malvasia Bianca max | 2 years 3 years for Riserva | 1980 |

| Morellino di Scansano | Morellino | 85% Sangiovese<br>15% other red grapes max | 2 years Riserva | 2006 |
|---|---|---|---|---|
| Carmignano | Sangiovese | 45-70% Sangiovese<br>10-20% Canaiolo nero<br>6-15% Cabernet franc and/or Cabernet<br>+ other grapes max 5% | 3 years for Riserva | 1975/1991 |

## CHIANTI AND ITS SUBZONES (DOCG FROM 1980)

Chianti is world-renowned and has been produced in the hills between Florence and Siena since the Middle Ages. The name Chianti is probably of an Etruscan origin as they were the former inhabitants of the area. The first documents attesting to wine production can be found around the XIII Century. In the year 1716 the Grand Duke Cosimo III de' Medici in Florence issued legislation to identify the Communes of Greve, Radda, Gaiole and Castellina as the original production area. This instituted the first piece of legislation concerning how to produce, ship and sell wine under the Chianti label. In the 1870s, Baron Bettino Ricasoli, from Castello di Brolio, issued the official "formula" for the variety make-up of Chianti: a significant amount of Sangiovese, with **Canaiolo** or **Colorino** rounding out the blend. The latter two are blending grapes that help to round Sangiovese's sharp edges. A blend of white grapes was also allowed for those wishing to sell a fresher, easier to drink wine that could be produced in larger quantities. Following this recipe, the CHIANTI DOC was established in 1967 and became a DOCG in 1984. When it became a DOC, the percentage of white varieties allowed was up to 30%. Regulators changed this when it became a DOCG and again in 1996 and 2003; the purpose being to continually limit the percentage of white grapes in the blend until they are completely phased out. They have also begun to allow international varieties within the bend. Despite regulators early efforts, CHIANTI as a DOCG did not succeed in increasing the average quality of the wine because the area allowed to produce Chianti was too large. It included areas unsuitable for quality wine production that used maximum yields that were far too generous. Historical producers of the original area (Greve, Gaiole, Radda, Castellina) were frustrated, as they were not separately acknowledged as higher quality areas producing Chianti. In 1996, they managed to introduce a SUBZONE delimitation of CHIANTI CLASSICO together with CHIANTI RUFINA and CHIANTI COLLI SENESI. Later, CHIANTI COLLINE PISANE, COLLI FIORENTINI, COLLI ARETINI, MONTALBANO, and MONTESPERTOLI were added.

**CHIANTI CLASSICO DOCG**: Today the *galestro* soil, made of schist and crumbly marl, and the higher elevation of the hills (up to 500 meters) allow these areas to produce the best expression of Chianti. Since 2003, the allowed blend is a minimum 80% Sangiovese and the other 20% may be any allowed red grapes planted in the area such as Canaiolo, Colorino Merlot and Cabernet. 100% Sangiovese is also now allowed, and starting with the 2005 vintage, white grapes are no longer allowed. Here the yield is 55 hl/ha, which is lower than the other Chianti subzones. With 2 years obligatory aging the wine man be called **Riserva.** The areas of Panzano and Greve in the North, Castellina and Radda in the Center, and Gaiole and Castelnuovo Berardenga in the South differ stylistically according to elevations and expositions. Some of the producers still use the traditional method called *"Governo alla Toscana"* which calls for an addition of the pomace to the must to generate a second partial re-fermentation in order to mellow the astringency and round off the edges. This is similar to the Ripasso method in the Veneto, but to a lesser extent.

**CHIANTI RUFINA DOCG**: This small area North East of Florence has been the most successful in establishing its own reputation of being distinct from the other Chianti areas. Steeper hill slopes and the beneficial influx of the Pontassieve River help to make the wines a more rustic and angular yet enjoyable for concentration and flavors.

**CHIANTI COLLI FIORENTINI DOCG**: This is a large hilly area surrounding the South of Florence. Wines made here tend to be good, but light in style.

**CHIANTI COLLI SENESI DOCG**: The hills around Siena create the largest and most inconsistent production but the area goes from San Gimignano to Montepulciano.

CHIANTI COLLINE PISANE (PISA), COLLI ARETINI (AREZZO), MONTALBANO and MONTESPERTOLI are seldom exported since they are considered of a lesser quality.

Anywhere in Chianti with an additional year of aging the wine may be called ***Riserva*** and with an additional 1% alcohol content may be called ***Superiore.***

**VIN SANTO DEL CHIANTI (OR CHIANTI CLASSICO) DOC:** Throughout the Chianti area, a sweet wine is produced from grapes harvested and then left to dry on straw mats or hung to dry in lofts for about 4 months. The grapes are then pressed and put in small casks called *caratelli*, where they ferment slowly and obtain flavors from the lees of previous batches, known as "mother." These casks are not topped off which allows for a slow oxidizing process. Vin Santo, which literally means "Holy Wine," is then aged for a minimum of three years. With four years of aging it may be called Riserva. Most producers, however, release it only when they believe it is ready which means the wine may potentially age much longer. Vin Santo is usually made from the white varieties of **Trebbiano** and **Malvasia.** It can be made from red grapes including a minimum of 50% Sangiovese, in which case it takes the name of VIN SANTO OCCHIO DI PERNICE which literally translates as the "Partridge's eye." It is delicious when well made but generally commands much higher prices.

The DOCGs of Tuscany and their blend

**BRUNELLO DI MONTALCINO (DOCG since 1980).** Twenty miles South of Siena before approaching Mount Amiata, a small hilltop town is considered to produce the best and age-worthy wine in all of Tuscany, if not of all Italy. In Montalcino, a variety of Sangiovese with small berries and dark skin called *Sangiovese Grosso,* or simply *Brunello,* has evolved to be best suited to this very specific environment. Montalcino sits on top of a *galestro* and *albarese* rock at 560 meters above sea level. The lower hills surrounding the town with south exposure have alluvial topsoil with a calcareous and tuffau base, and towards the northeast the soil is more clay based. The climate is Mediterranean and Mount Amiata acts as a shield, protecting the vines from rain. Snowfall surpassing 400 meters in the winter is not unusual. The majority of the producers are concentrated midway on the hills where the drainage is better.

The first attempt to select a better clone of Sangiovese was made by Clemente Santi in the beginning of the 1800s. His grandson, Ferruccio Biondi-Santi was the first to replant his property with this clone. He labeled the wines Brunello di Montalcino with the 1888 vintage and this vintage is said to drink well even today. The recent success of Brunello in the world market happened only after WWII, but was so big that it was one of Italy's first red DOCG in 1980. According to the rules of production, the wine must be 100% Sangiovese and cannot be released for sale until the January of the 5$^{th}$ year following harvest (the 6$^{th}$ year for Riserva). Brunello must be aged for at least 2 years in oak and 4 months in bottle. Slavonian oak is the traditional choice for these wines.

The combination of diversified soils with the introduction of modern winemaking techniques makes Montalcino a very dynamic wine producing area. Wines from less favorable expositions can be labeled ROSSO DI MONTALCINO DOC which are 100% Sangiovese and require a minimum one year aging, which make for more ready to drink wines. International varieties also grow successfully here and can be sold under the SANT'ANTIMO DOC, which is the same territory as Brunello or Rosso. Montalcino also produces a white sweet wine from the Muscat family that is called MOSCADELLO DI MONTALCINO DOC. The grape for this wine is **Moscato Bianco** and can be made either still or sparkling.

**VINO NOBILE DI MONTEPULCIANO DOCG (DOCG from 1980):** east of Siena, the soil is clay based and sandier, the weather is warmer and the hills are less steep. A Sangiovese-derived local variety called *Prugnolo Gentile*, or "gentle plum," has adapted to suit the clay-based terroir here. It shows with rounder, more velvety and feminine characteristics in comparison with the more muscular and angular expression of Chianti Classico. This area has also proven to do well with international varieties such Merlot and Syrah. Some of the producers are experimenting with blending these foreign varieties with a Sangiovese base. The neighboring CORTONA DOC also produces Cabernet, Syrah and Merlot into single varieties wines. For the DOCG, which encompass the commune of the small town called Montepulciano, the wine must be at least 80% Prugnolo and at least 10% Canaiolo. This area has been long renowned for quality wine production. The name Nobile, or "Noble," refers to exactly to that and the name was attributed to the wine in the 1700s. Today its name does not evoke the same appeal as Brunello, and the wines are more moderately priced and a great value. The aging requirement is 2 years in oak casks. Producers often also release a declassified ROSSO DI MONTEPULCIANO DOC from the vineyards with less favorable expositions. VIN SANTO DI MONTEPULCIANO DOC is also particularly interesting.

**NOTE**: A common mistake is to associate the town of Montepulciano to the Montepulciano grape variety that grows in Abruzzi and Marches. As sometimes happens in Italy, similar names have different origins and the two things are not related.

**CARMIGNANO DOCG:** this small production area lies northwest of Florence, near the Monte Albano and on the other side of the Arno river. It was one of the original production zones regarded as a quality origin by Cosimo III. Since the 1700s Carmignano has grown **Cabernet Sauvignon**, called **Uva Francesca,** along with indigenous varieties. Completely surrounded by the CHIANTI MONTALBANO, its production was relegated as an inferior appellation with the 1960 regulation. It took the Italians another 15 years to award it a DOC status and finally DOCG status in 1990. The blend calls for 45-70% Sangiovese, 10-20% Canaiolo, 6-15% Cabernet franc and/or Cabernet Sauvignon with the addition of a maximum 5% of other allowed red grapes. One year of aging is required with 8 months being in oak. The requirement for *Riserva* is 2 years and at least 12 months in oak. The climate is cool, but low elevations help to make a wine that is full, long-lived and soft instead of the hard or tannic wine one might expect. In 1994, an entry-level qualification called BARCO REALE DOC was added for more accessible and fruit forward wines from Carmigliano made with a maximum of 15% Cabernet. This is one of the few examples of regulation that worked well in establishing an area reputation and then in turn increasing the average quality.

**MORELLINO DI SCANSANO DOCG** Scansano, with its own clone of Sangiovese locally known as Morellino, is Tuscany's most recently awarded DOCG. Established in 2006, the area is fairly extensive and goes from the coastal, sandy area of the Maremma to the more inland, hilly slopes, at a maximum 500 meters, of Scansano. The allowed blend for the area calls for at least 85% Sangiovese with the possible addition of **Alicante**. Alicante can either be a synonym of Grenache or a cross of Grenache with **Petit Bouschet** or other local red grapes. It does not have any aging requirement unless it is a **Riserva**, which is a minimum of 2 years. Lately this area has attracted a lot of investors, who have planted extensively throughout the area and brought investments in the technological advancements to the area. The wines are usually softer and rounder because rainfall is lower in this area when compared to other areas of Tuscany and should be drunk young.

## WHITES OF TUSCANY

**VERNACCIA DI SAN GIMIGNANO DOCG.** According to 2000 data, only 30% of wine produced in Tuscany is white. The abolition of white grapes in the Chianti blend has brought the total amount produced even lower. But Tuscany does have one white-wine only DOCG, designated in1993. **VERNACCIA DI SAN GIMIGNANO**, from the hilltop village in the province of Siena, lies west of Chianti. It has medieval origins documented since 1276 and was the first Italian DOC in 1966. The grape is **Vernaccia** and is a particularly dry, acidic wine with medium body. The name Vernaccia derives from Latin Vernaculum (means "local") and therefore is associated with other NON related grapes: there are Vernaccia di Oristano, Vernaccia di Cagliari (DOCs in Sardinia) and Vernaccia di Serrapetrona, a sparkling red DOCG in Marches, which have different origins.

White wines from Chianti producers made from **Trebbiano** and **Malvasia Bianca** have not given interesting results so far. They are mostly without personality or complexity and tend to be consumed locally in the summer. Some better results have been obtained in those areas by planting international varieties such as **Chardonnay, Pinot Grigio** and **Sauvignon Blanc.**

Even more interesting are the coastal wines from the peninsula of Argentario in the South obtained from **Ansonica**, which is known in Sicily as Inzolia. **Vermentino** on the Northwestern coast of Tuscany, under the umbrellas of the CANDIA DEI COLLI APUANI DOC and BOLGHERI BIANCO DOC, have also produced interesting wines. VAL DI CORNIA DOC also produces a wine that is a 50/50 blend of Trebbiano and Ansonica.

Going South, BIANCO DI PITIGLIANO DOC has a reputation that exceeds its actual quality, but has been made popular by Roman tourists who enjoy this fresh wine on their summer vacations in the area. The blend is 50-80% **Trebbiano Toscano,** with **Greco, Malvasia, Verdello, Grechetto, Chardonnay, Sauvignon, Pinot Bianco, Riesling Italico** rounding out the blend.

## SUPERTUSCANS AND THE CREATION OF BOLGHERI DOC

"Supertuscan" is not a term that was created by Italian regulation, but a term introduced by wine critics. Its origin derived from the frustration of some producers who were concerned that their reputation as fine wine producers was being compromised and wanted to challenge the wine regulations of the time. At the end of the 1960s, the wine from

Tuscany had a reputation of being everyday quaff wine often associated with the straw-covered Chianti *fiaschi*. Laws for the Chianti DOC in 1967 were not a great help because the early regulation called for a blend of at least 30% white grapes and the authorities were more concerned with quantity rather than quality. Two different areas of Tuscany showed interest in increasing their quality. The first was in Bolgheri, a small village not far from the Tyrrhenian coast of Livorno, where Mario Incisa della Rocchetta, a wealthy man and a great collector of Bordeaux, owned a plot of sandy, clay land covered with rocks with a maritime influence. In 1948, he decided to plant Cabernet Sauvignon and Cabernet Franc, buying the roots from Châteaux Lafite. The first commercial release was in 1968, and in 1985 Sassicaia, a proprietary brand name that literally means "a hill full of stones," was rated the World's best Bordeaux blend, soon becoming a cult wine. His success was quickly imitated by Incisa della Rocchetta's nephews, Lodovico and Piero Antinori, from the centuries old winemaking family. They began to blend international varieties in Tignanello, their estate in Chianti Classico. They later bought the Ornellaia and Guado al Tasso properties in Bolgheri, which create Bordeaux blends with Sangiovese. When Sassicaia was first released into the market it was labeled simply "Vino da Tavola" since that area had no previous wine regulation in place. In 1994, it was awarded the status of BOLGHERI DOC and BOLGHERI-SASSICAIA DOC. The DOC, which until recently was a monopoly, is also the only DOC in Italy which carries a proprietary name. Today Bolgheri is an acclaimed wine region that is home to very interesting projects and produces some of Italy's greatest red wines, attracting both consumers and wine critics.

Back in the mid 1970s in Radda (another of the communes of Chianti Classico), Sergio Manetti from Monte Vertine believed in the true potential of Sangiovese and produced a 100% Sangiovese wine, labeling it "Le Pergole Torte." It was originally placed in the Vino da Tavola category in 1977 because 100% Sangiovese wines did not qualify for the Chianti Classico DOC status. Since then, the scenario of Tuscan winemaking has changed dramatically. With the 1993 addition of the IGT category, better clone selection, the abolition of blending white varieties, reduced yields, the use of better technology, and the authorization to use international varieties in blends, Tuscany has seen a great shift towards a reputation for producing quality wines. Because of some confusion introduced by this new category of wine, most producers sell their *Supertuscans* or IGT wines as premium or superior selection. Some are capable of being truly great wines but others are not worth their tag price because they can lack the typicity of the Tuscan terroir or may be too over oaked and extracted.

Some examples of Supertuscans:

| Name | Producer | Area | Blend | First Vintage | Label |
|---|---|---|---|---|---|
| Cepparello | Isole e Olena | Chianti Classico | Sangiovese | | IGT |
| Flaccianello | Fontodi | Panzano in Chianti | Sangiovese | 1981 | IGT |
| Fontalloro | Felsina | Castelnuovo Berardenga | Sangiovese | 1983 | IGT |
| Le Pergole Storte | Monte Vertine | Radda in Chianti | Sangiovese | 1977 | IGT |
| I Sodi | Castellare | Castellina in Chianti | Sangiovese 85% Malvasia 15% | 1979 | IGT |
| Carbonaione | Poggio Scalette | Greve in Chianti | Sangiovese | 1992 | IGT Alta Valle Greve |
| Tignanello | Antinori | Mercatale Val di Pesa | Sangiovese 80% Cab. Sauv 20% | 1982 | |
| Siepi | Castello di Fonterutoli | Castellina in Chianti | Sangiovese 50% Merlot 50% | 1993 | IGT Toscana |
| Mormoreto | Frescobaldi | Chianti Rufina | 60% Cab Sauv 25% Merlot 15% Cab Franc | 1983 | IGT Toscana |

| Name | Producer | Area | Blend | First Vintage | Label |
|---|---|---|---|---|---|
| Vigna D'Alceo | Castello dei Rampolla | Panzano in Chianti | Cab Sauv 85% Petit Verdot 15% | 1990 | IGT Toscana |
| Sassicaia | Incisa della Rocchetta | Bolgheri | Cab Sauv, Cab Franc | 1948 – 1968 | Sassicaia DOC 1994 |
| Ornellaia | Tenuta dell'Ornellaia | Bolgheri | Cab Sauv 60% Merlto 35% Cab Franc 5% | 1981 | Bolgheri Doc |
| Desiderio | Avignonesi | Montepulciano | Merlot | | IGT |
| Masseto | Tenuta dell'Ornellaia | Bolgheri | Merlot | 1987 | IGT Toscana |
| Redigaffi | Tua Rita | Suvereto | Merlot | 1994 | IGT Toscana |
| Messorio | Le Macchiole | Bolgheri | Merlot | 1994 | IGT Toscana |
| Solaia | Antinori | Mercatale Val di Pesa | Cab Sauv 80% Sangiovese 20% | 1978 | IGT Toscana |
| Excelsius | Banfi | Tavarnelle near Montalcino | Cab Sauv, Merlot | | Sant'Antimo DOC |

## Umbria

Umbria is the natural extension of Tuscany on the west, with warmer weather, gentle hills and a beautiful countryside scenario. The region is landlocked, and its microclimate is moderated by the Bolsena and Trasimeno Lakes, as well as the Apennines to the west. The southeastern part, bordering with Latium, is a white wine production area of the ORVIETO DOC. This appellation is shared with Latium and calls for a blend of **Grechetto**, **Procanico**, the local name for Trebbiano, and **Malvasia**. Despite being quite famous, both Orvieto and Orvieto Classico usually sell moderately priced, simple table whites. Good examples of **Chardonnay** or **Pinot Grigio**, usually with medium to full body, can be found in this region. Going northeast, one finds some productions of **Sangiovese** and **Montepulciano**. The area also accommodates some interesting results with international varieties. **Merlot,** which is well suited to the climate, and sometimes **Cabernet Sauvignon** are blended in the IGT wines here. The Northern part of Umbria is predominantly red wine and is where Umbria's two DOCGs are located. The first is TORGIANO ROSSO RISERVA, a monopoly of the Lungarotti estate. It was awarded its status in 1991. Thanks to its efforts, this **Sangiovese** blend, made with a minimum 70% Sangiovese as as other allowed grapes in the region proves that regions beyond Tuscany can make distinctive, full character Sangiovese wines.

The most interesting grape is **Sagrantino**, which was awarded SAGRANTINO DI MONTEFALCO DOCG status in 1992. Sagrantino is an indigenous variety that arrived in Umbria in the early 1700's and mutated dramatically. The origin of the grape variety is still unknown. It grew in Montefalco, a typical medieval town located next to a monastery where perhaps some monks planted it after visiting other European abbeys. Its thick skin, dark color, and full and tannic flavor characteristics are unique among Central Italy's wines and it also has great potential for aging. Sagrantino DOCG must be aged for at least 30 months before release. A blend of Sagrantino, Sangiovese and Merlot is labeled as ROSSO DI MONTEFALCO DOC and has well balanced fruit, spice, and tannins, making it easier to drink.

## Latium

Latium is prevalently a white wine producer that contains tufa, volcanic soils, and has a climate with maritime influences. It shares the ORVIETO DOC with Umbria, as well as the classico area. There is also the quaff FRASCATI DOC. Italy's most curiously named DOC, EST! EST!! EST!!! is located here. These two DOC's are blends of **Trebbiano** and **Malvasia**, the latter with the addition of **Roscetto**. The same blend is found in CASTELLI ROMANI DOC in the south of Rome, which accounts for most DOC production in the region. Within the reds, **Cesanese** is the local and rare red variety that some producers are attempting to revitalize. Its strong acidity and tannins has proven it a difficult task to achieve greatnes. Recently, in 2008, **CESANESE DEL PIGLIO** from the province of Frosinone was granted the DOCG status (minimum of 90% Cesanese). Its *Riserva* version has to age at least 20 months.

Given the poor performances of the local grapes, most of the producers have turned their attention to international varieties such as **Merlot, Cabernet Sauvignon** and **Petit Verdot.** These varieties have been reputed to be very promising, given the potential of the soils here.

## Adriatic Coast

The following regions are all located on the east coast of Italy, bordering the Adriatic Sea.

### Emilia-Romagna

Emilia Romagna's only real merit is the creation of the first white DOCG - ALBANA DI ROMAGNA in 1987. It is a traditional quaff wine made with the variety of the same name. This wine can be dry, semi-sweet, sparkling or *passito*. Most of the alluvial plain of Emilia Romagna is covered by over-prolific grapes, such as **Sangiovese di Romagna**, that has a lighter body than the Sangiovese in Tuscany, and **Trebbiano di Romagna.** Both grapes are usually vinified by co-ops and sold as inexpensive table wines. **Lambrusco** is the most notable indigenous variety in Emilia Romagna and produces fresh, fruity, *frizzante* wines. Most of what is imported to the US is bulk wine, making it difficult for small, quality-oriented producers to sell Lambrusco, since the wine loses much of its freshness during long-distance shipment. It is to be enjoyed served chilled as a summer wine with simple food like cold cults. The DOCs of this region are LAMBRUSCO DI SORBARA DOC, LAMBRUSCO REGGIANO, LAMBRUSCO SALAMINO DI SANTA CROCE, and LAMBRUSCO GRAPSAROSSA di CASTELVETRO. Some encouraging results have been achieved in the western part of the region, with **Sangiovese** on the hillsides.

### The Marches

This region stretches between the mountains and the Adriatic Sea, where the hills and the Apennines footholds fall perpendicular to the east. The northern part of the region is good for white varieties, which grow well in limestone and clay soils. The grape **Verdicchio**, in particular, grows well here as an aromatic, delicate, and refreshing variety that is able to preserve a large amount of acidity. Verdicchio can produce high quality wines and is one of the Italian whites that has benefited from the improvements in the winemaking techniques in recent years. It is considered to be one of the most interesting grapes with a lot of potential and offers a medium body with distinctive aromas of pear and herbs. Two DOCs found in this region, VERDICCHIO DEI CASTELLI DI JESI DOC and VERDICCHIO DI MATELICA DOC, both benefit from the maritime influence. The latter is a little more inland and higher in altitude. Sometimes these wines are allowed to remain on the lees and age quite well and others are still produced in an everyday younger style. Directly south of the port of Ancona, the Conero massif shapes the landscape, allowing for more red varieties. This area is mostly planted with **Sangiovese** and **Montepulciano**. Montepuciano increases in acreage south towards the Abruzzi region. Montepuciano shares its name with the Tuscan town, but is not related. This productive, late ripening variety yields full colored, medium bodied reds with medium alcohol, extract and plum aromas. It cannot grow well in the north since it would not ripen fully. CONERO DOCG is a relatively new DOCG and is a blend of minimum 85% Montepulciano and 15% Sangiovese with two years of aging. This wine is more tannic and robust than the Montepulciano d'Abruzzo to its south. ROSSO CONERO DOC, known as its little brother and shares the same boundaries, reserves 15% of other allowed grapes. This makes for more generous yields and less alcohol in the final blend. ROSSO PICENO DOC, further south, is a catchall appellation which allows producers 35-70% Montepulciano and 30-50% Sangiovese, plus the addition of other permitted varieties.

The quite uncommon VERNACCIA DI SERRAPETRONA, a sparkling red with the DOCG status, is made out of red **Vernaccia Nera** and is NOT related to other wines made out of Vernaccia.

## ABRUZZI

Despite being located in the center of Italy only 50 miles east of Rome, Abruzzi has always been associated with southern Italy, historically part of the Southern Kingdom of Sicily. This view is also due to the lack of industrialism of this region, which is devoted to agriculture and is apparent in that the region ranks 13$^{th}$ in Italy in size, but only 6$^{th}$ for wine production. Almost two thirds of its land is mountainous with the remainder is calcareous clay hills rolling towards the Adriatic Sea. The climate is Mediterranean overall but becomes continental towards the rugged inland, where the altitude is higher. Several small rivers mark the terrain. Viticulture was practiced before the Romans but in 1890 local farmers began to grow and sell the local variety **Montepulciano**, the same variety as in The Marches but no relation to Montepulciano in Tuscany. Montepulciano has been the most exported Italian wine for many years, with all production aiming towards lower-end table wine. The predominant and almost sole white variety is **Trebbiano,** which produces a generous yield but is usually ordinary, chalky and acidic with light floral aromas. TREBBIANO D'ABRUZZO DOC covers the entire region. Some producers are experimenting with **Chardonnay** and obtaining interesting results.

MONTEPULCIANO D'ABRUZZO DOC also covers the entire region, including the recent introduction of subzones that have yet to make an impact on consumers. Quality-oriented producers benefit from the soils of the northern area of Abruzzi where the hills are steeper. The co-op producers prefer the southern area with flatter lands that maintain high yields. A handful of finer bottles of selected, oak aged Montepulciano with low yields can be found, attesting that the grape can also produce remarkable and age-worthy reds. Recently in 2003 a subzone in the Northern part of the region was granted the DOCG status. MONTEPULCIANO COLLINE TERAMANE DOCG calls for a blend of a minimum of 90% Montepulciano and an optional 10% Sangiovese, and at least 2 years of aging (with the first year in oak barrels).

CERASUOLO D'ABRUZZO DOC is a comprehensive appellation devoted only to *rose* wine and made with the Montepulciano grape. This grape is not to be confused with Cerasuolo di Vittoria DOCG, a red appellation of Sicily, as Cerasuolo is a common term derived from the Latin word for cherry.

## SOUTHERN ITALY AND THE ISLANDS

### PREDOMINANT VARIETIES

**Red:** Aglianico (in Campania, Molise and Basilicata), Cannonau (*Grenache*), Carignano (*Carignan*) and Monica (in Sardegna), Uva di Troia, Negramaro, Primitivo, Malvasia Nera (in Puglia), Nero D'Avola, Nerello Mascalese, Frappato (in Sicilia), Gagliopppo (in Calabria).

**Whites**: Fiano, Greco and Falanghina (Campania), Malvasia Bianca and Bombino (Puglia), Greco (Calabria), Grecanico, Inzolia, Cataratto, Zibibbo and Grillo (Sicilia) plus Chardonnay. Some Moscato is also produced.

## SOIL

Varied. Granitic, calcareous, alluvial and clay, sandy with quite a few volcanic areas (Etna in Sicily, Vesuvius in Campania and the plateau of high altitude Vulture in Basilicata).

## REGIONS

The southern peninsula of Italy and surrounding islands produce about 20% of the nation's wine but the percentage of DOC production is the lowest in the country. This area of Italy has been a wine country since the Greeks brought the grapes there, but its main market, aside from the local consumption, has always been other wine producing areas that buy high alcohol grapes or juice to give body to their cool climate wines, such as Piedmont, Tuscany, and France. With the sourcing restrictions imposed by the application of the DOC / DOCG regulations in northern areas, southern producers began marketing their products independently. Since that time, southern Italy has been regarded as the new frontier for quality wine production, as the land is inexpensive, which attracts investors, and because local grape varieties are rumored to have high potential. A few individual producers were attempting to establish their fine wine reputation as early as the 1980s by bottling superior selection, lowering the yields, limiting the external sourcing of grapes and introducing new winemaking technology. However, the bulk wine mentality and the presence of large co-op cellars that are making wines in the flatlands for volume and not quality have been hurdles to reaching a higher level of winemaking. Today, the combination of diversified soil types, the sunny, almost "African" weather, the presence of mountains, volcanoes, and the Mediterranean Sea influence, along with state-of-the-art winemaking technology, makes this part of Italy a great landscape for educated consumers to choose wines of value.

## CAMPANIA

Historically an important region, it is said that Etruscans and Greeks found grapes here that were already being cultivated by a local tribe of the Enotri, whose names suggest a close connection to wine. Romans did their part in the evolution of vinification, and documents remain that attest to the fact that wines from Campania were considered the best of the time. Phylloxera affected quality wine production and only after the 1960s did a new interest for it develop. Campania is the region of Italy known for offering coastal resorts dating back to the Roman era and 50% of its territory covered by hills. The Apennines Mountains plunge directly into the Mediterranean Sea at the Tyrrhenian Sea. This area has captured the imaginations of many from places such as Naples where culinary delicacies such as Pizza were born, to Capri and the Amalfi coast.

The area is renowned for its whites, which share the typical stainless steel, acidity, and freshness of food-friendly wines that pair well with pastas, vegetables, fish, and light meat.

**Falanghina** is the most common white variety planted in Campania and offers characteristic liveliness, aromatics, and acidity. Is was given this name from the word "Phalanges," which in Latin means "pole," since the grape originally was grown as a small tree and needed to be sustained. Throughout the region this grape is blended with indigenous non-aromatic varieties in various DOC wines, such as **Biancollella** in the COSTA D'AMALFI BIANCO DOC or Greco in the PENISOLA SORRENTINA BIANCO DOC. Also common from the area of Sannio, near the town of Benevento where FALANGHINA DEL SANNIO is a DOC. **Greco** has superior acidity, minerality and aromatics. As the name suggests, it is believed to have been introduced by the Greeks in ancient times. Greco is planted in Calabria and in other parts of Italy, where its name is turned into *grecanico* or *grechetto*, but the grape shows best in Campania. It does especially well on the volcanic hill slopes of the Vesuvius and the inland of Avellino. The growth in high altitude, minerality, and smokiness on the nose are intense and the flavors are persistent. Around the town of TUFO, meaning "*tuff*," the GRECO DI TUFO has DOCG status, and the soil is tufaceous rock with clay and sand.

**Fiano** is another white grape produced in the south that has one of the most intense aromatics. In Campania, especially on the gentle slopes of hills of Avellino and its 26 villages, FIANO DI AVELLINO has gained a DOCG status and it is the most refined, complex and worthy of aging wine. Its nose has intense spice, pine nut, and hazelnut flavors.

On the Mount Vesuvius slopes, a wine is produced under the peculiar name LACRYMA CHRISTI DEL VESUVIO BIANCO DOC, literally the "tears of Christ," as well as LACRYMA CHRISTI DEL VESUVIO ROSSO DOC. For these wines, an ancient and almost extinct grape variety **Coda di Volpe**, or "fox tail" given the shape of the grape, is used with the addition of **Verdeca**, **Greco** and **Falanghina**. The red is produced with **Piedirosso**, or "red foot," which is mostly a blending partner, and **Aglianico**. These white wines are very acidic and grapey, while the reds are tannic and hearty.

**Aglianico** is the most common red variety in Campania, especially around the city of Avellino and its communes, and produces some of most intense, hearty, and tannic wines of all southern Italy. This variety has been known since ancient times, as Aglianico means "Hellenic" or "Greek," although is it unclear as to where it was first grown. Aglianico is late to ripen but produces a medium- to full-bodied red wine that is earthy, ethereal, and capable of aging. Aglianico is widespread throughout the south, but is most successful in Campania where it produces the most intense and fine examples of all varieties. Many DOCs from the northern Falerno del Massico to the southern Cilento use Aglianico as the primary variety. Around the town of the same name, the very best example of 100% Aglianico is **TAURASI**, which is the only red wine DOCG of Campania and whose reputation is to be "the Barolo of the South." In this volcanic and calcareous marl and on steep hills, the tannins are tight and the wine is leathery and earthy. Its regulation requires at least 3 years of obligatory aging before release, with at least one year in oak barrels.

## MOLISE AND BASILICATA

These two tiny regions, bordering on the north and east with Apulia, each grow **Aglianico** grapes, but with different results. In Molise, the flat coastal lands give the grape mellow, rounder, and somewhat inexpressive characteristics. In Basilicata the high altitude plateau of volcanic soil called Vulture is home to the AGLIANICO DEL VULTURE DOC, which offers a perfect combination of sun exposure and cool nights. This environment advantageously results in a grape of cool climate that fully ripens. The omnipresence of co-ops makes the remaining Basilicata wines rather uninteresting. Molise also grows Sangiovese, Trebbiano and Montepulciano that are steadily improving in quality but remain everyday value wines.

## APULIA (PUGLIA)

Located in the heel of the "boot," Apulia is one of the few flat lands of the entire country and this has always had a reputation for producing high volume, poor quality viticulture. This trend began in 1890 when pylloxera hit other wine producing countries but did not affect Apulia's sandy soils and its bush vines. French producers then began buying a great amount of blending grape juice in bulk. Until recently few of the Co-ops had developed instruments that would require members to provide quality grapes rather than quantity. Grapes have been grown in this region since two millenniums before Christ, before the Phoenicians began trading with local tribes.

There are no DOCGs in Apulia and, until recently, only 2% of wine was DOC. Since the 1990s, technological advancements combined with a more serious approach to winemaking has been implemented and new DOCs have been created. Today there are 26 DOCs in this region, although some have had a difficult time establishing their name with consumers.

Since Apulia consists of a long stretch of land, the grapes varieties differ significantly from the north to the south. In the northern part of Apulia, the cultivated grapes are **Sangiovese, Uva di Troia, Montepulciano** and **Malvasia Nera**. The first noteworthy DOC from the north is the CASTEL DEL MONTE DOC, a red grape appellation, which is a blend of Uva di Troia, Aglianico and Montepulciano with 35% of allowed grapes.

Moving south and inland, in the area of Altamura, is a white wine appellation. The fresh and lively, dry wines here are of interest. This DOC is called GRAVINA and the grapes varieties are **Malvasia Bianca, Greco** with the addition of **Bombino Bianco** and **Trebbiano Toscano**. Most of the whites from Apulia, where Malvasia prevails, are not capable of reaching a good acidity and lack complexity due to the almost sweet aftertaste.

Around the area of Gioa del Colle are some of Apulian's more interesting red grape varieties: **Negramaro** and **Primitivo**. Negramaro, which translates into "dark and bitter," gives exceptionally colored, velvety and fruity red wines that can be appealing to the palate. Negramaro is usually part of a blend with Malvasia Nera, which allows it to obtain more acidic structure. Among the southernmost appellation, SALICE SALENTINO DOC and SQUINZANO DOC share the 80% Negramaro and 20% Malvasia Nera requirement. Here the soil is more calcareous and there is a traditional use of bush vines or pergola. After 2 years of obligatory aging, the wines can be labeled *Riserva*. Some Rosés from Negramaro are also produced with good results. COPERTINO DOC calls for Primitivo and Uva di Troia as well.

**Primitivo** is well known for being a grape with great potential for aging. It gives dark, plum, and spiced reds with enough acidity to be worthy of aging. This grape was initially found in the Dalmatian coast and seems to be genetically related to Zinfandel in California. Some of the more interesting wines are high in alcohol and grow in very old pre-phylloxera bush wines.

A DOC of note here is PRIMITIVO DI MANDURIA DOC.

**Aleatico** and **Moscato** grapes are widely produced throughout Apulia. ALEATICO DI PUGLIA DOC is a region-wide appellation with the possible addition of Negramaro, Malvasia, and Primitivo. It is a "vino dolce naturale" which develops into an orange-red, delicate, and velvety sweet wine. The minimum alcohol level is 15%, but when the grapes are slightly dried and the alcohol level reaches 18.5%, the wines are labeled "liquoroso."

MOSCATO DI TRANI DOC, grown around the town of the same name, is a golden-yellow color variety with characteristic aromas, and sweet and velvety "vino dolce naturale."

## CALABRIA

The Greeks called the inhabitants of Calabria Enotri meaning "people who cultivate grapes," since they used to cultivate grapes extensively. The Greeks improved viticulture practices and used Calabria to source large quantities of wine. With the onset of phylloxera, almost all vines were destroyed and the region fell behind in production. Less attention was devoted to wine production, and instead producers preferred to grow other agriculture products. Only in the past 20 years has a return to wine making been seen. Calabria is located on the tip of the Italian peninsula. It is an extremely coastal and hilly region with no consistency in altitude, exposition and soil type. Given these conditions, and with only 13,500 hectares under vine, the region is a far cry from its neighbors, Sicily and Apulia. Growers have been blessed with plentiful sunshine and more than 100 indigenous grapes, many of which are unknown to others outside the region. Among these are **Gaglioppo, Magliocco, Mantonico, Greco** and **Nerello Mescalese**. The best wines produced here are made out of **Gaglioppo**, the grape with most ha under vine. Gaglioppo presents several layers of skin and creates pale, light-body reds with good acidity and some saltiness. CIRO ROSSO DOC is the most appreciated appellation and is located in the eastern part of the region. The CIRO BIANCO DOC is made with 100% **Greco** grapes, which produce fresh, lively, and acidic whites that lack the minerality of the volcanic soil of Greco di Tufo, and is therefore good to drink when the wine is young.

## SICILY

Despite the fact that wines in Sicily have been made since 2000 years before Christ and were later improved by the Greeks, the area has always been an enormous producer of bulk wine. Sicily is the largest island in the Mediterranean Sea, being 25,708 square kilometers, and Italy's largest wine producer with 111,600 hectares under vine. The first documentation of its production was in 1773 for **Marsala,** when a cargo of Sicilian wine left the port of Trapani and was fortified in order to make the trip to England. Marsala is now a DOC produced from the indigenous white grapes **Grillo, Catarratto, Inzolia,** and the red grapes **Nerello Mascalese, Nero D'Avola and Pignatello**. It has a minimum 17% alcohol and is usually sold as *Secco, Semisecco* o *Dolce* according to its sugar content.

**Grillo**, **Inzolia** and **Cataratto** are vinified to create still wines that create fresh, acidic whites with some body. Among them, Catarratto is the most aromatic and can present itself, given low yields, with a nice complexity and good acidity. BIANCO D'ALCAMO DOC, with a minimum 60% of Catarratto, is a good example of the quality wines that can be produced using Catarratto.

Sicily has 1 DOCG and 22 DOCs, many of them completely unknown to the general public. Relative to its overall production, DOC wine consists of only 2% of total production andmost of the wine is found on the market as IGT Sicily. Because of its dimension, the region presents as 3 different set of soils: the hilly part on the East side is clay with schist and quartz, the central part is chalk and clay, and the western part is clay and limestone. From the landscape of Mount Etna to the east side of the island presents volcanic soils.

In the 1950's some producers started to use the Guyot method of training instead of bush vines. Historically, few illuminated producers had tried to produce better quality wine, demonstrating the potential of the native grapes, especially in the area south and southeast of Palermo. Over time a new generation of winemakers developed and the island attracted investors from the north who put capital and winemaking technologies into play. This increase in interest is due to the ideal condition for fruit ripeness, the decline of the bulk business, and the relatively inexpensive cost of land.

The main grape used is **Nero D'Avola**, also called **Calabrese,** which demonstrates its origin from Calabria. It is a spiced, full-bodied, and tannic red of dark color which ages well in oak and resembles Syrah to some extent. Most of the southwestern coast and the inland side of Palermo are planted with this grape. CONTESSA ENTELLINA DOC and SCLAFANI BAGNI DOC are the most renowned DOCs in this region due to the hills here that are steeper and cooler at night.

In recent years, producers in the northern, coastal area have begun planting international varieties such as **Cabernet**, **Syrah** and **Chardonnay** with good results.

In the southwest, the areas of Vittoria and Noto provide Sicily's best soil type. CERASUOLO DI VITTORIA is Sicily's only and recent DOCG that requires a blend of **Nero D'Avola** (50-70%) with **Frappato** (30-50%). Frappato is another local grape which offers bright fruit, delicate aromas, and light body, which helps to mitigate the more tannic Nero d'Avola. The soil here is limestone with sandy topsoil.

Moving north towards Messina, one finds the unique climate of the Mount Etna, an active volcano that is 11,000 feet, or 3,329 meters, above sea level. It possesses volcanic soil and it snows here during the wintertime. The ETNA DOC is the home of another white grape with much potential: the aromatic **Carricante. This grape** has racy acidity combined with strong aromatics and minerality, and is capable of aging well. The ETNA ROSSO DOC is made with **Nerello Mascalese** and **Nerello Cappuccio**, two cool climate grapes that produce light colored but alcoholic, cherry flavored wines that create hearty and smoky red wines.

Near Messina in the Northeastern corner of the Island, the FARO DOC is a recently discovered treasure based on a six-grape blend that is worthy of attention. The grapes allowed in the blend are **Nerello Mascalese**, **Nocera** and **Nerello Cappuccio** with **Nero d'Avola, Gaglioppo** and **Sangiovese**.

Given the hot weather in the region, Sicily produces a variety of desert wines. MALVASIA DELLE LIPARI, a DOC from the Aeolian Islands, is a very uncommon Malvasia, which can be *Passito, Passito dolce naturale* (minimum 18% alcohol) and *liquoroso* (minimum 20% alcohol).

MOSCATO DI NOTO DOC is made with the Moscato Giallo grape and must be at least 11.5% alcohol, and is sometimes made sparkling. MOSCATO DI PANTELLERIA DOC and PASSITO DI PANTELLERIA are produced with the ZIBIBBO grapes using the *passereillage* method or by drying the grapes after harvesting. This grape is a late-harvesting variety that produces small berries. Its ripeness quickly turns into dried bunches and it presents musky, aromatic character and fragrant nose (minimum 20° alcohol).

## SARDEGNA (SARDINIA)

Sardinia is another large island in the Mediterranean Sea, famous for its resorts and cork oak. At its center lays a mountainous complex that is hot and arid, therefore most wine production is carried out near the coasts. Vines were cultivated here by Phoenicians, although later the Romans complained of its scarce quality. A document from the year 1316 A.C. prohibits any new plantation of grapes for the purpose of not jeopardizing the market, which leaves the impression they were already cultivating enough grapes.

The sole DOCG wine produced here is **Vermentino di Gallura**, in the granite soil of the northeastern part and where the Mistral is able to cool the arid conditions of the region. It offers citrus, fresh pear, and hints of herb and grassy tastes. An all-comprehensive Vermentino di Sardegna DOC can also be found in this region.

The most popular white variety is **Nuragus**, which is believed to have been brought by the Phoenicians. Its name derives from the island's prehistoric stone towers known as nuraghe. Nuragus is the source of a modern dry white, clean and crisp, if rather bland in flavor.

In the South, the most typical white wine, though Sherry-like, is VERNACCIA DI ORISTANO DOC. It is made of the **Vernaccia** grape that grows in the sandy soil of Oristano and must be aged 2 years in oak casks before being released. It has minimum 15% alcohol and has an almond blossom nose with a bitter almond aftertaste.

In the warmer south, **Monica** is planted extensively and gives a spiced and fruity, but ordinary, wine. **Cannonau**, the Spanish Garnacha, is planted in the topsoil locations, which is mostly sandy with pebbles, and gives a rustic, full-bodied, and dry red with some aromatics. This variety is probably the best expression of red production.

CARIGNANO DEL SULCIS, or **Carignan,** is a DOC of the southwest where this difficult variety gives some astringent, tannic, and full-bodied wines.

## A Snapshot of Italian Wines

| GRAPE VARIETY | AROMA & STYLE | WINES | REGION |
|---|---|---|---|
| NEBBIOLO | **Aroma**: Violet, Rose, Tar, Gunpowder, Mineral, Raspberry, Pomegranate, Rhubarb, Licorice<br>**Style**: Full-body / Medium-High Alcohol / Tannic / Persistent / For Long Cellaring | Barolo<br>Barbaresco<br>Langhe<br>Nebbiolo<br>Roero<br>Gattinara<br>Gemme<br>Valtellina<br>Grumello<br>Sassella<br>Sforzato | Piedmont<br>Lombardy |
| BARBERA | **Aroma**: Red cherry, Red currant, Cloves, Red Flowers, Sap<br>**Style**: Full-body / Medium-High alcohol / Medium-High acidity / Soft Tannin / Early to Mid-Term Consumption | Barbera d'Asti<br>Barbera d'Alba<br>Monferrato Barbera<br>Colli Tortonesi Barbera<br>Oltrepò Pavese Barbera | Piedmont<br>Lombardy |
| DOLCETTO | **Aroma**: Black Plum, Black Currant, Beet Root, Fennel, Anisette, Violet, White Pepper<br>**Style**: Full-body / Medium Alcohol / Tannic / Low Acidity / Early Consumption | Dolcetto d'Alba<br>Dolcetto di Dogliani<br>Dolcetto Diano d'Alba<br>Dolcetto di Ovada<br>Dolcetto d'Acqui | Piedmont |
| MOSCATO<br>[White / Canelli] | **Aroma**: Pineapple, Rose, Peach, Passion Fruit, Musk, Sage<br>**Style**: Light-Body / Medium-Low Alcohol / Medium-Low Acidity / Aromatic / Persistent / Early Consumption | Asti Spumante<br>Moscato d'Asti<br>Loazzolo<br>Piemonte Moscato<br>Passito<br>Oltrepò Pavese Moscato | Piedmont<br>Lombardy |

| GRAPE VARIETY | AROMA & STYLE | WINES | REGION |
|---|---|---|---|
| CORVINA | **Aroma**: Red Cherry, Black Cherry, Cinnamon, Blue Flowers, Ginger spice, Cloves<br>**Style**: Medium to Full-body / Medium-High alcohol / Medium-High Acidity / Elegant and Spicy / Medium-long Term aging | Amarone della Valpolicella<br>Recioto della Valpolicella<br>Valpolicella Classico<br>Bardolino | Veneto |
| GARGANEGA | **Aroma**: Yellow Plum, Peach, White Flowers, Minerals,<br>**Style**: Medium-body / Medium Alcohol / Medium-Low Acidity / Rich Mouthfeel / Early Consumption to Mid-Term aging | Soave<br>Soave Classico<br>Gambellara<br>Recioto di Soave<br>Recioto di Gambellara | Veneto |
| PROSECCO | **Aroma**: Green Apple, Pears, Bergamot, Cedar and Citrus, Minerals<br>**Style**: Light-Body / Low Alcohol / High Acidity / Off-Dry / Early Consumption | Prosecco di Valdobbiadene<br>Prosecco di Conegliano | Veneto |
| PINOT GRIGIO | **Aroma**: Grapefruit and Ruby Grapefruit, Pears, Basil / Mint<br>**Style**: Medium-body / Medium-Low alcohol / Medium Acidity / Fruity / Early Consumption | Pinot Grigio<br>Veneto IGT<br>Trentino DOC<br>Valdadige DOC<br>Grave DOC<br>Venezie IGT<br>Isonzo DOC<br>Collio DOC<br>Colli Orientali del Friuli DOC | Veneto<br>Friuli<br>Trentino |
| VERMENTINO | **Aroma**: White Flowers, Herbs, Citrus, Minerals<br>**Style**: Light to Medium-body / Medium to Low-Alcohol / High Acidity / Refreshing / Aperitif / Early Drinking | Riviera Ligure di Ponente<br>Toscana IGT<br>Bolgheri Bianco<br>Vermentino di Gallura | Liguria<br>Tuscany<br>Sardinia |
| TEROLDEGO | **Aroma**: Violet, Blackberry, Spices, White Pepper, Fennel seeds.<br>**Style**: Full-body / Medium Alcohol / High Acidity / Persistent / Peppery-spicy Finish / Food Wine / Medium Term Aging | Teroldego Rotaliano | Trentino |

| GRAPE VARIETY | AROMA & STYLE | WINES | REGION |
|---|---|---|---|
| SANGIOVESE | **Aroma**: Violet, Red Cherry, Black Cherry, Guarrigue (Mediterranean Herbs), Meat, Leather, Earth, Cinnamon<br>**Style**: Full-body / Medium-High alcohol / Tannic / Persistent / Medium-Long Term Aging | Chianti – and its Subzones Brunello and Rosso di Montalcino Vino Nobile di Montepulciano Rosso di Montepulciano Morellino di Scansano | Tuscany<br>Marche<br>Umbria |
| VERDICCHIO | **Aroma**: White Flowers, Herbs, Stone-fruits (Almond), Citrus, Minerals<br>**Style**: Medium to Full-body / Medium Alcohol / High Acidity / Persistent / Medium - Long Term Aging | Verdicchio dei Castelli di Jesi Verdicchio di Matelica | Marche |
| SAGRANTINO | **Aroma**: Violet, Rose, Tar / Gunpowder / Mineral, Raspberry, Pomegrenate, Rhubarb / Licorice<br>**Style**: Full-body / Medium-High alcohol / Tannic / Persistent / Medium-long term aging | Montefalco Rosso Montefalco Sagrantino Montefalco Sagrantino Passito | Umbria |
| MONTEPULCIANO | **Aroma**: Black Cherry, Black Olives, Guarrigue (Mediterranean Herbs), Fur / Game<br>**Style**: Medium-Full-body / Medium Alcohol / Balanced Mouthfeel / Persistent / Medium-Long Term Aging | Rosso Conero Rosso Piceno Montepulciano d'Abruzzo | Marche<br>Abruzzi |
| NEGROAMARO | **Aroma**: Red Cherry, Black Cherry, Laurel, Dried Tomatoes, Leather, Cinnamon **Style**: Full-body / Medium-High alcohol / Soft Mouthfeel / Persistent / Medium-Long Term Aging | Salice Salentino Squinzano Brindisi Alezio Rosato Salento IGT Negroamaro | Apulia |
| NERO D'AVOLA | **Aroma**: Violet, Blackberry, Black Plum, Olives, Incense, Mint<br>**Style**: Full-body / Medium-High alcohol / Soft Mouthfeel / Persistent / Medium-Long Term Aging | Cerasuolo di Vittoria Sicilia IGT Nero d'Avola Contea di Sclafani Salaparuta | Sicily |

# Germany
BY CHRISTOPHER P. BATES

*Wine is sunlight, held together by water.*
—Galileo

## The world's best wines

Every German writer, it seems, loves to point to the status of German wines through history. As late as the end of the 19th century, the wines of Germany's great sites were coveted with equal—if not greater—enthusiasm as any wine in the world. Many texts cite that the wines of Rudesheim (Rheingau) were long worth more than the first growths of Bordeaux. The great sweet wines of the Rhein and Mosel were held in greater esteem than those of Sauternes and even Château d'Yquem. While such histories are interesting and even amusing, they fail to point out that the wines are still that good. It becomes an issue of perception, not potential. What's missing is us or, rather, our definition and understanding of "tasty." The world has long decided that sweet wines are for little girls and grandmas, yet as we profess this with the left side of our face, we gulp soda through the right. In a world where wine is more about perception than pleasure, dry wines are important (and manly). Why? Because.

In a world where wine needs to look tough to be accepted, Riesling's "happy-giving" properties are not welcome. That said, Tokaji may be the king of wines and the wine of kings, but Riesling is the wine of professionals. Ask any true wine professional (American journalists aside), what the best grape variety is, and Riesling will likely rank number 1 or 2. So be it. Drink and enjoy, because we professionals can at least still afford them.

Despite professional acceptance of Riesling the grape, many pros still have a hard time understanding Germany the wine producer. Rightly so: The words don't have the romantic air French or Italian, and they certainly are big. Keep an open mind—In a lot of ways, German *lingua vino* may look different but if you sound them out phonetically, they often sound familiar. Words like "halb" (half) and "Weiss" (white) aren't so challenging. A few other tricks will make you an expert in no time. Remember, in English, we make sentences, in German, theymakebigwords (see? no spaces). A word like "trockenbeerenauslese" may seem intimidating. When you learn to read the parts, however—"trocken (dry) Beeren (Berries) Aus (Out) Lese (Picked)"—it's not so bad. The following list should help with the upcoming sections.

# Translations

- Trocken–Dry
- Halb–Half
- Spät–late
- Lese–think of as "harvest."
- Einz–One of single
- Lage–Situation (site)
- Suss–Sweet
- Wiess–White
- Grau–Gray
- Rot–Red
- Burgunder–Pinot Varietal
- Oechsle–German equivalent of Brix
- Erzabfulung–Wines bottled by cooperatives
- VDP–**Verband Deutscher Prädikats und Qualitätsweingüter**: A self-regulated group of 190 of the best producers in Germany. Very Important Group
- Flurbereinigung-The restructuring of the vineyard slope to make them easier to work.
- AP Number–**Amtliche Prüfungsnummer**: This number is assigned to every bottle of QbA and QmP wine when it passes the tasting panel (an example is decoded below). It is typically on the front label at the bottom, and can be very helpful, especially in a cellar full of German Wine.
    - AP Nr. 2 576 537 9 06
    - 2=Examination Board Number
    - 576=Commune where the wine was bottled
    - 537=Bottles registered number
    - 9=In chronological order this is the 9th wine submitted for approval in the year of submittal.
    - 06-The year the wine was submitted for approval.

# History

Germany's winemaking history mostly likely dates back to the 1st century, with definitive evidence that by AD **340** the steep slopes of the Mosel were planted. Red wines are mentioned in Germany by AD **570**.

A Roman press was found in Piesporter Goldtropfchen (one of the great vineyards of the Mosel region) dating to AD **400**, and is the largest historic press found north of the Alps so far.

Charlemagne, ruler of the massive Frankish Empire in the 8th and early 9th centuries, is commonly credited with bringing viticulture to the Rheingau region through the spread of Christianity and the church.

A Benedictine abbey founded on the slope above Geisenheim in **1100** later became the Schloss Johannisberg estate.

In **1135**, monks from the Cistercian abbey Clairvaux in Champagne founded the Kloster Eberbach monastery.

**1318** Pinot Noir (Spätburgunder) was first mentioned in German vineyards

**1435** Riesling identified in Germans vineyards. Elbing and Silvaner were the most planted varieties at the time.

By **1500**, Germany's total area under vine was up to four times what it is today. Soon, however, vineyards began to decline. By the end of the Thirty Years' War in the **mid-1600s**, the wine industry was decimated.

In **1712**, the Kloster Eberbach began using a separate cellar built in **1245** for their best wines. This cellar was termed the Cabinet-Keller and is used to this day.

Tradition holds that in **1775**, a courier carrying the harvest permission destined for Schloss Johannisberg was delayed. During the two-week lag, the Riesling vineyards gave in to rot. When permission was finally received, winemakers set about trying to save something and harvested the rotten grapes. The highly concentrated sweet wines were termed **Spätlese**, which translates literally to "late harvest." The positive reception of these wines led to the practice of intentionally leaving the grapes to hang longer on the vine and develop rot prior to harvest. By **1787** a second ripeness level designation, **Auslese**, was in use.

The church controlled all vineyards for some time until Napoleon took them in **1805** over and divided them up. With Napoleonic inheritance in place (as in Burgundy), vineyards continued to be fragmented.

In **1845**, England's Queen Victoria traveled to the Rheingau and fell in love with the wines, coining the term "**Hock**" (after the village of Hochheimer) for German Reisling. The term is still in use today.

German wine has long been among the most sought-after of all wines. It is common, when reading old wine lists and auction offerings, to see German Riesling selling for the highest price. On one such **19th** century wine list, Bordeaux First Growth Château Latour cost 8 marks, while Mosel and Rheingau Auslesen cost 25 marks.

Germany's current wine scene has been largely determined by a post-war, attitude, even within Germany. In addition, a flood of cheap German wines to the U.S. during the **1960s** negatively influenced many people's perception of German wines. Lastly, modern trends have reduced the demand for what were historically the most sought-after styles—sweet wines.

# Classification and Regulation

## Regional Classification

The following was established by the reclassification laws of 1971.

- **Anbaugebiete**: there are 13 of these generic regional designations. They tend to be large, but unlike regional designations in many other countries, are based on geographical features, rather than quality or minimum/maximum production requirements.

- **Bereich**: These are large appellations within the Anbaugebiete, and allow for some region-specific blending. Due to their lack of recognition, these are rarely used, even less so by quality export producers. These days a consumer is more likely to purchase a wine labeled "Mosel" than "Burg Cochem."

- **Grosse Lage**: A category allowing producers to disguise regionally blended wine as single vineyard wines. This is potentially the largest mistake made by the 1971 Laws. These wines are labeled as to be indistinguishable from Einzellage, though they come from a considerably less-defined and less-distinguished vineyard area.

- **Einzellage**: *Einzel*=one or single, *Lage*=Vineyard, therefore this is the single vineyard appellation. These were defined by the 1971 law and were "simplified" and reduced in number from 30,000 to 2,600. In order to do this, multiple vineyards were combined. Typically the name applied was that of the most famous vineyard. In doing so, Germany diluted many of the most famous vineyard sites by combining them with wines from lower-quality surrounding sites.

Einzellage wines are labeled with two words, such as Graacher Domprobst. "Domprobst" is the Einzellage and, in theory, the name of the vineyard. That said, there are in fact many Domprobst vineyards in many Anbaugebiete. Therefore, the first word (in this case "Graacher") is very important in identifying which Domprobst vineyard this is. Graacher indicates that this wine comes from the town of Graach. So, when reading an Einzellage vineyard label, the first word will end in "-er" and will be the name of the town, the second word indicates which single vineyard in that town the grapes came from.

## Quality Classification

- **Wein**: Literally, "Wine." This represents the lowest quality wine.

- **Tafelwein**: Table wine, and grossly low on the quality scale.

- **Deutscher Tafelwein**: Similar to Tafelwein, but all of the grapes come from Germany. Must be Trocken (a term that indicates that a wine is perceptibly dry—discussed in depth later in this chapter).

- **Landwein**: Similar to Deutscher Tafelwein, though it does not have to be Trocken.

- **Qualitätswein bestimmter Anbaugebiete (QbA)**: These wines represent the beginning of the quality ascension. Wines in this category must meet minimum quality levels and certain practices must be adhered to during production.. These wines must be labeled with an Anbaugebiete designation, but may not carry a ripeness designation.

- **Qualitätswein mit Prädikat (QmP)**: These wines are labeled with one of six ripeness designations (see below), and a number of quality points must be reached. Among other requirements, a tasting panel must confirm that the wine conforms to region and quality standards. While it is rare for anyone to refer to a wine as being at the QmP level, the six ripeness levels within are often referenced. QmP wines may not be chaptalized. These wines can have *süssreserve* added.

NOTE: The laws define *minimum* ripeness levels for each of these categories, but no maximums. This allows producers to declassify wines that may qualify for a higher ripeness level. Additionally, these ripeness levels only indicate the sugars in the grapes at harvest and in no way define the level of residual sugar in the finished wines.

- **Kabinett**: This represents the basic level of QmP. These are ripe grapes with enough natural sugar to make a wine with reasonable sugar and alcohol.
    - 67-85 Oe /16.3-20 Brix/8.7%-11.4% potential alcohol
- **Spätlese**: Spat=Late Lese=pick = "picked late." Even though Spätlese literally translates to "picked late," the grapes used to make these wines have only a bit more ripeness than Kabinett level grapes, and the resulting wines are a far cry from New World late harvest wines. While these wines are often off-dry to somewhat sweet, they are not dessert wines.
    - 76-95 Oe/18.4-22.6 Brix/10.2%-13% potential alcohol
- **Auslese**: Aus= out, Lese=picked = "Picked Out." Wines made by picking out select grape clusters during harvest. Often largely botrytis-infected clusters, they can in fact be simply naturally dehydrated clusters as well. The resultant increase in sugar allows sweet wines to be made at this level, as well as dry wines with relatively higher alcohol levels. This category can be sweet enough to qualify as dessert wine, though not all are.
    - 83-105 Oe/19.9-24.8 Brix/11.3%-14.7% potential alcohol
- **Beerenauslese (BA)**: Beeren=Berries Aus= out, Lese=picked = "Berries Picked Out." As opposed to selecting the best clusters, only individual berries are selected. These are not only dessert wines, but can also become extremely expensive.
    - 110-128 Oe
- **Eiswein**: Somewhat the oddball in this group, Eiswein is its own style. Grapes are harvested when frozen and pressed as such so that the ice crystals remain behind, concentrating the juice that does drip out. Eiswein is similar to Beerenauslese in both sweetness and price. The flavors, though, tend to be less complex, but at the same time cleaner and more precise (an essence of wine, in a way).
    - 110-128 Oe
- **Trockenbeerenauslese (TBA)**: Trocken=Dry, Beeren=Berries Aus= out, Lese=picked = "Dry Berries Picked Out." Similar to Beerenauslese, except instead of selecting only botrytis berries, only fully dried berries are picked out. NOTE: in this case "Trocken" refers to the fact the grapes are dry when picked, not that the wine is dry. This is the *crème de la crème* of German wine, and represents the pinnacle of care. It is said to require an entire day's labor to harvest enough grapes to make one-half bottle, and then only if the vintage has produced the grapes for it.
    - 150-154 Oe

## ADDITIONAL LABELERS

**Trocken:** Wine with the perception of dryness, even if there is some residual sugar (RS). To be labeled trocken, a wine may contain up to 4 grams per liter of residual sugar, OR up to 9 grams per liter residual sugar as long as the RS is within 2 grams per liter of the total acdid. For example, if the titratable acidity or TA is 7 grams per liter, the wine can have *up to* 9 g/l RS and be considered Trocken. Sparkling wine can contain 17-32 g/l RS and be considered Trocken.

**Halbtrocken / Feinherb:** Like Trocken wines, this classification is dependent on the relationship of residual sugar and total acid in grams per liter. Feinherb wines may contain up to 12 grams per liter RS, OR up to 18 grams per liter RS as long as the RS is a maximum of 10 grams per liter higher than the TA. For example, if the TA is 8 grams per liter, the wine can have *up to* 18 g/l RS and be considered Halbtrocken.

**Capsules**: An attempt to further specify within each ripeness category (though only typically used for Auslese and up). If a winery makes more than one Auslese in a particular vintage from the same vineyard, they could designate which was the "best" via colored capsules. A Goldkapsel or gold-colored capsule was chosen designate that wine, with a longer capsule designating the best of several. The problem is some producers already use gold capsules and a variety of capsule lengths, muddying the classification. Another issue was that the longer capsule is only easily identifiable if you have all iterations from a specific winery on hand. In a store or wine cellar, it can be hard to determine weather a stand-alone bottle bearing a gold capsule is a "normal" Auslese or something special.

**Stars**: Some producers use an additional one-, two-, or three-star rating system to further pinpoint the ripeness level of the wine. The system is based solely on ripeness, not quality, and is used within the Prädikat system. A three-star Auslese is closer to a one-star Beerenauslese than a one-star Auslese.

**AP Numbers**: Some producers, Willi Schaffer in particular, will make multiple bottling of his various Auslesen. Schaffer's capsules are always gold, and he does not use stars. Instead, he differentiates only by AP numbers (see "Terms"), and prices his wines based on them.

**Classic** and **Selection**: Another attempt to fine-tune the classification system.

**Classic** is intended to be a step up from QbA, using varieties traditional to a region, made in a dry style with a maximum residual sugar of double the acidity, up to a maximum of 15 g/l RS.

**Selection** is essentially a Spätlese made from traditional varieties from a "selected" site. It must be dry.

**Charta** (karta): A Rheingau-only classification launched in 1983 by a group of producers, headed by George Breuer (Bernhard Breuer). This classification has much higher standards for quality than any other system, including three blind tasting panels. Charta wines must be on the dry side, with residual sugar no more than 3 grams per liter above total alcohol. Wines must be bottle-aged 12 months and bottled in tall brown bottles embossed with the double arches of the Charta. Charta-classified wines from approved Erstes Gewachs vineyards can be designated with a label depicting triple arches as opposed to the double shown here. They have lower yield restrictions must be hand-harvested and aged 18 months in bottle.

### Erste Lage, Grosses Gewächs, Erstes Gewächs

The concept of vineyard classification is a wonderful idea, especially since the 1971 laws made everything equal. Some producers like the idea of making the wines more "consumer friendly" by standardizing the style so the consumer can expect a dry wine every time. Others argue this practice reduces diversity and thus iconic flavors available to German wines.

*Note from the Editors: please refer to the VDP website for the most up-to-date information as major changes were implemented in 2012 (http://www.vdp.de/en/vdp-praedikat-wine-estates/).*

**Grosses Gewächs**: A term used to designate the Great Growths of all German wines, except Mosel and Rheingau. These are the "grand crus" of German vineyards. Wines labeled Grosses Gewächs must be dry and adhere to higher standards.

**Erstes Gewächs**: Similar to Grosses Gewächs, but only for the Rheingau.

**Erste Lage**: Wines from "grand cru" designated vineyards that can be made in any style and are designated by a Prädikat level.

# Terroir

## Geography

The vineyards of the Rheingau and the Mosel lie roughly on the 50$^{th}$ parallel, with the more northerly vineyard well above that. Being on the same latitude as the Okanagan Valley in British Columbia, it requires many special climate moderators allow fine wine to be made this far north. In fact, Germany is the world's northern-most "fine" wine-producing country in the world.

Moderators:

- The Atlantic Ocean and its warm currents
- The Vosges Mountains
- The Black Forest
- Extremely selective vineyard selections

# Varieties

| Total Vine / Ha | 102,340 | | |
|---|---|---|---|
| **Total White** | **65,114** | **% of White** | **% of All** |
| Riesling | 22,434 | 34% | 22% |
| Müller-Thurgau (Rivaner) | 13,721 | 21% | 13% |
| Silvaner | 5,236 | 8% | 5% |
| Grauburgunder (Ruländer) | 4,481 | 7% | 4% |
| Weißburgunder | 3,731 | 6% | 4% |
| Kerner | 3,712 | 6% | 4% |
| Bacchus | 2,015 | 3% | 2% |
| Scheurebe | 1,672 | 3% | 2% |
| Chardonnay | 1,171 | 2% | 1% |
| Gutedel | 1,136 | 2% | 1% |
| **Total Red** | **37,226** | **% of Red** | **% of All** |
| Spätburgunder | 11,800 | 32% | 12% |
| Dornfelder | 8,101 | 22% | 8% |
| Portugieser | 4,354 | 12% | 4% |
| Trollinger | 2,472 | 7% | 2% |
| Schwarzriesling | 2,361 | 6% | 2% |
| Regent | 2,161 | 6% | 2% |
| Lemberger | 1,729 | 5% | 2% |
| St. Laurent | 669 | 2% | 1% |
| Acolon | 478 | 1% | <1% |
| Merlot | 450 | 1% | <1% |
| Domina | 404 | 1% | <1% |
| Dunkelfelder | 352 | 1% | <1% |
| Cabernet Mitos | 320 | 1% | <1% |
| Cabernet Sauvignon | 288 | 1% | <1% |
| Frühburgunder | 252 | 1% | <1% |

While it may be easy to think of Germany as synonymous with **Riesling**, this is anything but the case, even in the quality world. **Pinot Noir (*Spätburgunder*)** is not only quickly on the rise in terms of quantity, but also in quality, a surprise to many. **Silvaner** finds its only true home in the world in Franken. And in the right hands even **Müller-Thurgau** is turning out some outstanding interpretations.

**Riesling:** With nods to Alsace and Austria, the Clare Valley and the Finger Lakes, Germany is still the home of Riesling. Not in history, but in brilliance, where it is produced in all styles, dry to sweet. German Riesling is both a pleasure-giving young wine, and capable of bottle aging perhaps better and longer than any other grape or unfortified wine in the world, with the exception of Chenin Blanc. Examples of the diversity of Germany's Rieslings abound: from light, friendly Kabinetts of the Mosel to the tense, nervous wines of the Saar; from the sheer breadth of styles from the Rheingau, to the balance of the Nahe and Mittlerhein; Delicate Kabinetts and QbAs, mouth-filling and savory Spätleses and Ausleses, all the way up to the mind-bending honey-and-apricot laden Beerenauslese and Trockenbeerenauslese; Federweisser (partially fermented and still-cloudy Riesling which must be sold in the fall) or a two-year-old wine screaming of fruit and sulfur, to the bottle-aged complexities developed over 20, 30, 50 or more years.

Riesling is a very "transparent" variety (as is Pinot Noir among reds). It has the ability to consistently taste of its place. The core flavors are there—apples and peaches (depending on ripeness), minerals (depending on soil), fruit blossoms, white flowers—but the site always leaves its own imprint. In the Mosel, for example, Rieslings are delicate, with high acid and green apple / unripe white peach notes. There is also, however, a definitive slate-like aroma, with a local red slate providing a more ruddy brown spice nose. Rieslings from Braunenburg where the soils is different, offer broad, earthy tones, and a less tense acid. Wines from the Saar and Ruwer seem almost "nervous," as if they ripened enough for picking only the morning of harvest, while the Rheingau Rieslings seem confident, saltier and more mineral in nature.

**Müller-Thurgau** is a high-yield, often neutral cross (Riesling x Madeleine Royale) from Switzerland. It has become a favorite of German vine growers, and the bane of German wine drinkers. Müller-Thurgau is well spread, being among the top three most frequently raised vines in each Anbaugebiete except the Ahr, Hessische Bergstrasse and Württemberg. The vines tend to over-crop naturally, and given that the best vineyard space is planted with more respected (and valuable) varieties like Riesling, Müller-Thurgau often is planted on overly fertile valley floors. As a result, the wines often end up simple at best, dilute and unpleasant at worst. Surprising examples do exist, when the grape is treated with respect. The result is wines exhibiting fresh, crisp fruits and a clear minerality. Typically dry in style, there are, of course, exceptions to the rule. Also known as **Rivaner**.

**Silvaner**, like Müller-Thurgau, is often abused. Given to the worst growers, and the worst lands, it seems to only be at home in one gebiete—Franken. The Silvaner grown in Franken manages to gain depth and body, showing intense minerality with floral and citrus fruits. The wines produced in the best vineyards are truly world-class dry wines. Typically dry, there are some enjoyable off-dry to sweet examples.

**Scheurebe** (also known as **Samling 88**) is another cross (Riesling with an unknown wild grape, once thought to be Silvaner). The grape was created in 1916 by Dr. Georg Scheu, probably trying to improve Silvaner. If Gewürztraminer is thought to be "forward," Scheurebe is downright promiscuous. Grapefruit peel, green grapes, tropical fruits, floral, black currant, raisins and honey sum up the wine's intoxicating aroma. When not fully ripe, it can show a bit too much aggressiveness. To avoid this, Scheurebe is generally fully ripened and thus most commonly used in sweet wines. More than half of Germany's 1,700 hectares of Scheurebe are planted in the Rheinhessen.

**Grauburgunder** (**Ruländer**) are local terms for Pinot Gris. The grape is planted primarily in Rheinhessen, Pfalz and Baden.

**Weissburgunder** is the local term for Pinot Blanc.

**Spätburgunder** is Pinot Noir, as it is known in Germany. With a German Pinot Noir winning the "Best Pinot Noir in the World" trophy from *Decanter Magazine*—beating out Burgundy, the U.S., New Zealand and Chile—Germany's Spätburgunder was thrust onto the international scene. Typically showing the lighter side of Pinot Noir (by world standards), the wines show brilliant balance, and a not-too-heavy a hand with oak for the moment. The Ahr and Baden seem to have shot ahead of the curve with Pinot Noir, though Assmannshausen in the Rheingau is its traditional home. In the Ahr, Pinot grows on steep slate hillsides similar to the Mosel and may be one of the most extreme terroirs for Pinot in the world. The wines here show a lighter fruit, and more mineral savory note. Baden—a region to watch—grows on a more classic landscape and produces riper, richer wines that can handle more oak.

**Frühburgunder** may not be important quantitatively, but is a true curiosity. Though mutation of Pinot Noir, which is interplanted in Burgundy (known as Pinot Noir Précoce), Frühburgunder is considered a separate variety, not a clone. It ripens earlier than Pinot Noir, helping it excel in cool climates where ripening Pinot Noir is challenging. Given its early bud break, it is also susceptible to frost. Wines tend to be a bit darker than Spätburgunder (most likely due to early ripening), and a bit bluer in flavor if not a bit coarser.

**Dornfelder**: Created by August Herold in 1955, Dornfelder is a cross of **Helfensteiner** (Frühburgunder × Trollinger) and **Heroldrebe** (Blauer Portugieser × Lemberger). Grown mostly in the Pfalz and the Rheinhessen, the grape has proven itself a workhorse, producing large quantities of moderate quality wine with minimal challenges. Considering the grape wasn't released until the 1970s, it is clear how quickly producers took it up.

**Blauer Portugieser**, known simply as **Portugieser** in Austria and **Kekoporto** in Hungary. It is grown mostly in Pfalz and Rheinhessen, and produces both Weissherbst (rosés) and basic table wines.

**Trollinger** is an ancient variety also known as **Schiava**. Currently grown mostly in Württemberg.

**Schwarzriesling** or Pinot Meunier (aka **Müllerrebe** and **Müller-Traube**), is grown mostly in Württemberg where is is also known as **Samtrot**, and produces **Shillerwein**—a dry, high-acid rosé. This is another early ripening mutation of Pinot Noir, though one that buds later as well, reducing frost and coulure risks.

**Regent** is a hybrid grape created in 1967 that shows a high resistance to most disease. Released for planting only in 1996, it now covers over 2,000 hectares.

**Lemberger** is a red grape also known as Blaufränkisch in Austria.

# REGIONS

## ANBAUGEBIETE

**Saale-Unstrut**: Germany's most northerly appellation. Along with Sachsen, the two appellations are alone in having been former DDR (Deutsche Demokratische Republik or East Germany) land. Small, but increasing in quality production, the region's top wines are expensive. Look out for Schloss Proschwitz. The region is planted largely with Müller-Thurgau and Weissburgunder and is situated on hillsides around the Saale and Unstrut Rivers.

**Sachsen** (Saxony): Planted largely with Müller-Thurgau and Riesling. The region is located along the Elbe River, with granitic and gneiss-based soils. Not all that different from the Wachau.

**Ahr**: The world's most northern red wine producing region, and one of the most interesting. The steep slate slopes and moderate climate contribute to some of the most sought-after Pinot Noirs in the world. The region follows the Ahr River from east to west, for a total of about 25 winding kilometers before the river spills into the Rhine. Soils are slate, basalt and greywacke sandy clay. Also home to Apollinaris mineral water (also called "the queen of table waters").

**Mittelrhein**: The third smallest Anbaugebiete, which has been shrinking for the last fifty years, and seemed, until recently, all but forgotten. That is changing, however. The extremely steep slate soils possess great sites for the production of exceptional Riesling. Look for Toni Jost's Bacharacher Hahn. The dominant grape is Riesling, though, a small production of Pinot Noir is known locally as "Dragon's Blood," from a story involving a slain dragon on one of the hillsides.

**Rheingau**: One of Germany's most famous and storied regions, where much of the progress has taken place in the German wine industry. Soils are quartzite and slate at elevation, with blue phyllite clays in and around Assmannshausen. Largely loess and loam soils, though a variety of other soils including chalk, sand and gravel make up the rest of the region. The region is dominated by Riesling, but do not overlook the Spätburgunder from the famous village of Assmannshausen.

**Rheinhessen**: The largest producing region, dominated by Müller-Thurgau, Silvaner and Riesling. Look for the wines of Gunderloch to try some of the best examples. Largely loess, limestone and loam soils produce large quantities of wines. As a result, variability in quality can lead to a great misunderstanding about potential. Often thought of merely as bulk wine producer, the Rheinhessen has amazing resources and produces wine on par with any wines produced in Germany, and the world.

**Nahe**: Along the river Nahe, this gebiete seems to be the Mosel's twin as a growing region. Wines are similarly structured and balanced, but the varied soils found on steep slopes along the river create more diversity. The soils of the Nahe are quite diverse, due to their volcanic origin.

The Nahe can be seen as three distinct areas. **The Lower Nahe** soil is mostly quartzite and slate as the Nahe enters with the Rheingau here. Wines include Riesling, Silvaner and Scheurebe as well as Weissburgunder. **Bad Kreuznach** consists mostly clay and loess-based soils. **The Upper Nahe**, currently the most sought-after area, has the most complex soils, including sandstone, slate, melaphyre and porphyry. Planted mostly to Riesling. While Dönnhoff may be the most sought-after producer here, a bottle of Hexamer should put you on the right track.

**Mosel**: Formerly the Mosel-Saar-Ruwer, the region's name was recently simplified and, as of the 2010 vintage winemakers in all three sub-regions can use the term "Mosel." One risk of this move may be that the wines of the Saar and Ruwer will fall into (greater) obscurity. As the Mosel River flows more or less south to north, it winds through extremely steep blue (mainly) and red slate soils. The wines here are light and pure expressions of place, typically balanced with residual sugar and acid. At the south end are two side valleys, the Ruwer and the Saar (on rivers of the same name) extending east to west. They are cooler than the Middle Mosel, and planted accordingly. Riesling is king in the Mosel. Along with the Rheingau, it is Germany's most famous region. The wines of Kerpen express typicity in the Middle Mosel.

**Pfalz**: Often called the Tuscany of Germany, as it is the warmest region (bordering Alsace) and the most diverse. A variety of red grapes can excel here, including Cabernet Sauvignon and Cabernet Franc. Even Chardonnay ripens here. Rieslings can be very powerful, and are typically dry or very sweet (with few in between).

**Franken**: Located on the Main River, the chalky soils here are the single greatest area for Silvaner in the world. The famous ***Bocksbeutel*** is the traditional shape of the best versions of typically powerful, dry Silvaner.

**Baden**: The southernmost region in Germany with the hottest spots, though the average temp is lower than in the Pfalz. Pinot varieties dominate.

**Württemberg**: A warm region known for its red wines like Dornfelder and Trollinger.

**Hessische Bergstrasse**: Germany's smallest region produces fine-tuned, dry Rieslings.

# AUSTRIA
By Matthew Wexler

| | |
|---|---|
| Latitude | 47° – 48° |
| Regions at the same latitude | Northern Burgundy, Alsace, Loire, Northern Washington State |
| Total area under vine | 45,908 hectares (2010) |
| Volume produced annually | 1,737,454 hectoliters (2010) |
| % White | 61% (1,064,709 hl) |
| % Red (includes rosé) | 39% (672,745 hl) |
| # Producers | Approximately 23,000 (2010) |
| Climate | Primarily continental with the eastern region influenced by Pannonian Plain |
| Average temperature | Summer between 68–95°F, Winter between 34–39°F |
| Hours of sunlight per year | ~1,900 hours of sunlight annually |
| Rain per year | 26 inches (660 mm) |
| Soil | Varied, including mineral-rich, loem, volcanic ash, gravel, limestone |
| Major cities | Vienna, Linz-Wels-Steyr, Graz, Linz, Salzburg, Innsbruck |
| Major geographical features | Alps, Pannonian Plain, Lake Neusiedl, Danube River |
| Primary Red Grapes | Zweigelt, Blaufränkisch, Blauer Portugieser |
| Primary White Grapes | Grüner Veltliner |
| Secondary Red Grapes | St. Laurent, Blauer Wildbacher, Blauburger |
| Secondary White Grapes | Welschriesling, Riesling, Müller-Thurgau, Sauvignon Blanc, Gelber Muskateller, Muskat-Ottonel, Traminer, Scheurebe, Weissburgunder, Chardonnay, Bouvier, Frühroter Veltliner, Furmint, Goldburger, Jubiläumsrebe, Sylvaner |
| Federal Governing Body | Austrian Federal Government |
| Local Governing Body | State wine authorities representing Niederösterreich, Burgenland, & Steiermark |
| Quality/rating system | 3 Rating Systems: National Classification, Wachau Classification, DAC Classification |
| Quality/rating levels | Wein, Landwein, Qualitätswein (subcategories: Kabinett, Prädikat) |
| Regions with DAC | Kremstal, Kamptal, Traisental, Weinviertel, Leithaberg, Mittelburgenland, Eisenberg |

# Introduction

If Maria von Trapp had strapped a bottle of Grüner Veltliner to her hip, her trek over the Swiss Alps might have been much more palatable. Von Trapp's free spirit and steadfast nature undeniably represent a certain je ne sais quoi found among Austrian people and their wine culture.

From as early as 700 BC to modern times, wine production has been an integral part of modern day Austria's tumultuous history, with the ebb and flow of viticulture correlating with who was in charge of the land. Around AD 800, Charlemagne (who then ruled an empire that consisted of much of Western and Central Europe) issued his "Capitulare de Villis"—a regulatory document that included wine laws, indicating a certain respect for viticulture. However, the subsequent Magyar invasion at the beginning of the 10th century resulted in a shift away from agriculture. By the early 1500s, Queen Maria of Hungary established an early form of Protected Designation of Origin, which helped to define the wine characteristics of the region, while the siege of the Turks during the 17th century, along with high taxation on wine and a greater interest in beer-brewing, discouraged wine consumption. So it went from century to century: planting, destruction and replanting anew.

Modern Austrian wine culture is embracing a movement toward small, handcrafted wines. Following the "antifreeze" scandal of 1985, when the illegal addition of diethylene glycol was discovered, the country has made concerted efforts to repair its image as well its production standards. By volume, it is still a blip on the international radar. Although Austria ranked seventeenth in global wine production in 2008 (as measured by metric ton), this represents a mere 1% share of the world wine production with no more than 25% exported. Even so, Austrians view viticulture as a vibrant part of their cultural identity and continue to promote and produce drinkable, accessible, and (at times) collectible wines.

Austria's gastronomy scene is highly complementary to its wine production, with traditional hearty dishes like goulash and wiener schnitzel providing backbone for the consumption of bright white wines or robust reds from the region. On a more delicate note, the Linzer torte, which dates back to the late seventeenth century, is the perfect accompaniment to a glass of local sweet wine.

Whether consuming wines made from the country's signature grape, Grüner Veltliner, or experimenting with the up-and-coming reds of Burgenland, Austrian wines often represent a renegade philosophy in flavor profile and attitude. Through the decades, Austrian producers have continued to make wines often implementing innovative viticultural techniques (such as *lenz moser*, a vine training system originating in Austria), while also combating late spring frosts and hail indicative of the region.

As of 2010, Austria's vineyard area is cultivated by 23,000 individual wine producers, of which 6,000 are bottlers. Although they may never reach expansive world popularity due to low yield and export, the wines exhibit century-old traditions as well as modern winemaking techniques.

# History

Austria has been, both literally and figuratively, at the center of European viticulture for close to 3,000 years. As early as 700 BC, there is evidence of grape pips throughout the region. Lower Austria yields further evidence of grape pips dating back to the Bronze Age and by 1 BC there is an indication of extensive plantings of grape vines and cultivation along and around the Danube River.

During the Roman Empire (27 BC to 476 AD), as the Roman forces moved north into what is now modern-day Austria, so began extensive planting and cultivation of grape vines. By AD 488, the Romans had relinquished governance of the Province of Noricum (a Celtic kingdom that included much of Austria and Slovenia). The subsequent mass migration of the Romans resulted in vast tracts of abandoned vines, as the remaining population struggled merely to survive.

Charlemagne's "Capitulare de Villis" in AD 795 offered detailed information on viticulture, vines and wine law, and an ownership map of the vineyards. This demonstrated respect for grape-growing and winemaking, coupled with the replanting of more beneficial grape varieties, suggested that the region was on track for a flourishing wine culture. The tenth century Magyar invasion destroyed this progress, as the tribe's means of survival relied more heavily on hunting and fishing. With limited knowledge of agriculture, the Magyars had little use for the vineyards.

Cistercians monks introduced Burgundian viticulture practices from the tenth through twelfth centuries, such as advanced training methods to promote vine growth and screw-driven presses for extraction. By 1359 a taxable industry was born as Duke of Austria Rudolf IV declared a 10% wine tax that favored landlords and allowed towns and territorial princes to charge for the transit and import of wines. The total area under vine in Austria reached a zenith by the mid-fifteenth century with cultivated vines found even within the city walls of Vienna. The first documented sweet dessert wines in Austria appeared in 1526 from the royal House of Esterházy family vineyards.

As a whole, the wine industry flourished from the fourteenth through the nineteenth centuries, although periods of religious conflict and the Napoleonic wars left their mark on the land. It is during this time that Riedel, one of the world's premier wine glass manufacturers, was founded. The business is still family-run in Kufstein, Austria, and represents eleven generations that span almost three hundred years.

In 1860, Baron August Wilhelm founded a viticultural and oenological school and research center in Klosternneuburg, just north of Vienna. As with most of the rest of Europe, the institute received a blow from Mother Nature in the last half of the 19th century when *Oidium* (powdery mildew), *Peronospora* (downy mildew) and *Phylloxera* decimated vineyard acreage. The institute was renamed the Höheren Lehranstalt für Wein- und Obstbau (Federal College of Viticulture, Oenology, and Fruit) in 1902, and continues to educate today as the world's oldest viticulture school.

It took several decades to recover from the devastation caused by these fungal diseases, but Austria's wine industry rebounded through more extensive planting of indigenous varieties like Grüner Veltliner, along with the creation of a new variety by Professor Friedrich Zweigelt. His cross of St. Laurent and Blaufränkisch yielded Blauer Zweigelt, which is currently Austria's most widely produced red variety. It can be found both as a varietal wine and is also often used as a blending grape.

In 1985, a scandal nearly destroyed what was quickly becoming a booming export industry. Diethylene glycol (found as a small percentage in antifreeze) was added by wine brokers in an effort to add sweetness and body to diluted, mass-industrialized wines. Once discovered, export sales plummeted. The Austrian Wine Marketing Board (*Österreich Wein Marketing GmbH*) was established to remedy the image and promote the sale of Austrian wine.

As Austria's wine culture continued to rebound, new wine laws were instituted to further classify wine producing regions as DAC (*Districtus Austriae Controllatus*). The first official wine displaying this classification from the 2002 vintage was the dry Weinviertel DAC Grüner Veltliner. The 2009 Austrian Wine Law contains further amendments in relation to the European Union wine laws. These include wine-making practices, classification, and control systems within the industry, among others.

Over the past twenty years, Austria has seen an increase in innovative wine architecture exemplified by architect Steven Holl's LOISIUM World of Wine—a unique "wine & spa resort." The property includes three integrated components: 900-year-old underground passages and vaults, a wine center and ramp connection, and a luxury hotel and wine resort. The project won the 2006 European Hotel Design Award for the Best Hotel Architecture Design Award (new build). Other recognized vineyards include the Arachon-Reifekeller winery in Burgenland designed by Wilhelm Holzbauer with Dieter Irresberger and the Leo Hillinger winery in Burgenland, designed by gerner° gerner[plus]. This design boom represents a rejuvenated confidence in winemaking and has been supported, in part, by the European Union through underwriting construction costs in "structurally disadvantaged regions."

Today, Austria's wine culture spans sixteen wine-growing regions and the dedicated winemakers who reside within them. As of 2008, Austria ranked as the seventeenth wine-producing country by volume and is poised to make an even greater impression as more Austrian wines become available on an international scale.

## CLASSIFICATIONS, QUALITY LEVELS, AND LAWS

Austrian wine has a national classification system that is based on the *Klosterneuburger Mostwaage* or Klosterneurburg Must Weight Scale (KMW), which measures the sugar content of the grapes at harvest in a way similar to the Öchsle scale. The Austrian national classification, which is based on the German classification, was implemented during World War II and revised in 1985. The KMW scale indicates the density of sugar in the grape as a percentage, for example:

1°KMW = 1% sugar = 1 gram of sugar per 100 grams of grape must

| Exact Conversion Formula KMW to Öchsle |
| --- |
| (0.022 x °KMW + 4.54) x °KMW = Öchsle <br> 1°KMW = approximately 5 °Öchsle |

There are four categories for wine classification that must meet the following standards*:

***Wein* (Wine)**, minimum must weight 10.6°KMW, no regional designation of origin is permitted.

***Landwein* (Wine with protected geographical indication)** refers to wines produced from the authorized 35 classified quality grape varieties and must derive from Weinland, Steirerland, or Bergland.

- Minimum must weight 14°KMW
- A more regionally specific declaration is *not* permitted

***Qualitätswein*** or Quality Wine, may only apply to wines produced from a single variety or blend of the 35 classified quality grape varieties, from a legally defined wine-growing area of a specific region (Quality Wine S.R.). The red-white-red banderole (typically a foil cap or cork enclosure) must be visible on the capsule of the bottle and also includes the producer's registration number.

- Minimum must weight of 15° KMW
- Minimum alcohol content of 9.0% volume

*Districtus Austriae Controllatus* (DAC) was implemented 2001 and is a subcategory of Qualitätswein (Quality wine). It is loosely modeled after the French Appellation d'Origine Contrôlée (AOC) system. Much like the *Appellation d'Origine Contrôlée* (AOC) in France and the DOC/DOCG *(Denominazione di Origine Controllata (e Garantita))* in Italy, the purpose of this classification is to highlight major varieties in each region, their appellation, and typical style. Regional committees abiding by European Union wine regulations oversee the system. They may opt to set higher standards for a particular DAC. They may also establish two quality levels: Klassik for a "standard" DAC wine, and Reserve for a DAC wine that fulfills slightly stricter or different requirements.

The goals of this classification encompass a more direct marketing strategy for the consumer, as well as maintaining a 'protected designation of origin' (PDO) to highlight the natural characteristics of the varieties and their geographical origin. There are currently seven designations with the following characteristics:

| DAC | First Vintage | Major Grape Varieties | Alcohol Level and Taste Profile | Region Highlights |
|---|---|---|---|---|
| Weinviertel DAC | 2002 | Grüner Veltliner (~ 50% of all plantings in Austria) | <u>Klassik</u>: Min 12% <br> <u>Reserve</u>: Min 13% | Signature aroma of Weinviertel's Grüner Veltliner is "pfeffrigen"—flavors of white, green and black pepper over a fruit-driven bouquet with refreshing acidity. Austria's first designated region-typical wine classification. |
| Mittelburgenland DAC | 2005 | Blaufränkisch | <u>Klassik</u>: 12.5% – 13% <br> Matured in stainless steel, traditional large neutral oak casks or used small oak barrels. <br> <u>Reserve</u>: Min 13% <br> Matured in large oak casks or small oak barrels. | The center of Austria's red wine culture. The heavy and deep clay dominated soils produce wines that are spicy and robust with full wild berry flavors. |
| Eisenberg DAC (red only) | Klassic 2009 <br><br> Reserve 2008 | Blaufränkisch | Klassik: <br> Min 12.5%, Max 13% <br> Little or no notable use of oak. <br> <u>Reserve</u>: Min 13% <br> Matured in traditional large oak casks or oak barrels. | In addition to Blaufränkisch, the area is known for the quirky wine specialty, Uhudler, a hybrid created during the phylloxera infestation. |

| DAC | First Vintage | Major Grape Varieties | Alcohol Level and Taste Profile | Region Highlights |
|---|---|---|---|---|
| Traisental DAC | 2006 | Grüner Veltliner (60% of planted varieties in region), Riesling | <u>Klassik</u>: Min 12%<br><u>Reserve</u>: Min 13%<br>No botrytis or oak notes in Grüner Veltliner or Riesling. | Grape pips discovered in Traisental dating back to the Bronze Age. |
| Kremstal DAC | 2007 | Grüner Veltliner, Riesling | <u>Klassik</u>: Min 12%<br>No botrytis or oak notes.<br><u>Reserve</u>: Min 13%<br>May show subtle botrytis and oak aging aromas. | Historic town of Krem is home to young winemakers, a wine co-operative and the famous Niederösterreich (Lower Austria) Wine Fair. |
| Kamptal DAC | 2008 | Grüner Veltliner, Riesling | <u>Klassik</u>: Min 12%<br>None or little (required) botrytis and no oak notes.<br><u>Reserve</u>: Min 13%<br>Subtle botrytis note or oak aging is acceptable. | Named after the river Kamp and home to Austria's largest wine-producing town, Langeniois. |
| Leithaberg DAC White | 2009 | Pinot Blanc, Chardonnay, Neuburger, Grüner Veltliner or a blend of these varieties | Min 12.5%<br>Max 13.5%<br>Little or no use of oak. | Famous for Ruster Ausbruch, the internationally renowned noble sweet dessert wine. |
| Leithaberg DAC Red | 2008 | Blaufränkisch (Min 85%, Max 15% St. Laurent, Zweigelt or Pinot Noir) | Min 12.5%<br>Max 13.5%<br>Must be aged in oak barrels. | Typically display consistent mineral characteristics and are relatively full-bodied. |
| Neusiedlersee DAC | Klassik: 2011<br>Reserve: 2010 | Klassik: Zweigelt<br>Reserve: Min 60% Zweigelt | Klassik: Min 12%<br>Reserve: Min 13% | Climate heavily affected by the nearby Pannonian Plain |

*Kabinett* is another subcategory of Quality wine that adheres to the following regulations:

- Minimum must weight of 17° KMW
- Harvested grapes may not be enriched or chaptalized

Note that unlike the German classification, Kabinett is not included in the *Prädikat Wine* category.

***Prädikat* Wines** are Quality wines with a designated level of grape ripeness at harvest. Just like Kabinett wines, chaptalization or enrichment is not permitted.

| Prädikat Style | ° KMW | Description |
|---|---|---|
| Spätlese | >19° | Made from fully ripe grapes. |
| Auslese | >21° | Only made from carefully selected and appropriate grapes. |
| Beerenauslese (BA) | >25° | Made from over-ripe and/or noble rot grapes. |
| Eiswein | >21° | Made from grapes that were frozen during the harvest and pressing. |
| Strohwein/Schilfwein | >25° | Made from completely ripe and sugar-rich grapes that were dried on straw or reed mats or hung for a minimum of three months prior to vinificaiton. |
| Ausbruch | >25° | Made exclusively from noble rot or naturally dried grapes. |
| Trockenbeerenauslese | >30° | Made from predominantly noble rot grapes that are severely dried. |

*Information provided by Austrian Wine Marketing Board*

## Sugar Content

Chaptalization, or the addition of sugar to grape must to increase alcohol content after fermentation, is permitted for Qualitätswein (not Kabinett or Prädikat wines) at the rate of:

- 1.4 kg of sucrose to 100 liters of grape must
- Maximum increase of 2% alcohol by volume

Another aspect that reflects the wine's classification is its residual sugar content:

| Residual Sugar | |
|---|---|
| Dry (Trocken) | Up to 4 g/l or up to 9 g/l if the acidity is not less than 2 g/l of the residual sugar value, e.g. a wine with 9 g/l residual sugar must have a minimum of 7 g/l acidity. |
| Off Dry (Halbtrocken) | Up to 12 g/l or up to 18 g/l if the acidity is not greater than 10 g/l beneath this value. |
| Medium Sweet (Lieblich) | 12 g/l and up to 45 g/l |
| Sweet | More than 45 g/l |

## Wachau Classification*

Although not part of Austria's official wine law, is an important part of the region's wine history. The classification, also known as the *Codex Wachau,* was created in 1983 by a self-proclaimed group of producers called the *Vinea Wachau*. The classification focuses on "natural wine production, guaranteed origin, and strict control" (from Vinea Wachau: Codex Wachau). Only dry white wines of the region are permitted for this three-tier classification, which is based on naturally-occurring must weight and alcohol content:

**Steinfeder®**, which refers to a delicate type of grass, is a light wine and may have a slight effervescence.

- Up to 11.5% alcohol
- 15–17°KMW

**Federspiel®**, which means falconry (to honor the pastime of the region), is typically derived from riper fruit.

- 11.5% to 12.5 % alcohol

- At least 17°KMW

**Smaragd®**, refers to a green-colored lizard indigenous to the region, has the highest sugar and alcohol content, and is the most in-demand wine of the region.

- Above 12.5% alcohol
- At least 18.2°KMW

# CLIMATE, GEOGRAPHY, SOIL

Austrian wine production relies on the presence of small, family-run vineyards that represent the character and nature of the regions in which they reside. Vineyards are concentrated in the country's east, primarily exhibiting cool and northerly weather conditions. Despite the fact that the entire country is smaller than the state of Maine, Austria exhibits varied weather patterns due to its central European latitude and diverse geography ranging from the central Alps in the west to the low-lying regions to the east.

The four major climate zones and their characteristics include:

## THE WEINVIERTEL

This area receives cool air from the northeast and is Austria's northernmost and largest region, stretching from the Danube in the south to the Czech border in the north. Microclimates abound in the Weinviertel, including the Mailberg Valley. Centered on the town of Mailberg, approximately six miles south of the Czech border, sheltering surrounding mountains make the valley dry and vines planted on the slopes get ample sunlight. The Manhartsberg mountain ridge in the west yields soils composed of clay and sand. The southeast of the climate zone is comparatively warmer, influenced by the Pannonian Plain and the blackwater Morava River that runs along the border of Slovakia.

## THE DANUBE AREA

Encompasses roughly the regions of Kamptal, Kremstal, Wachau, Traisental, and Wagram. Here, hot days and cool nights result in harvests through November. Weather patterns are also influenced by the Northern Alps, which stretch out south and west of the Danube climate zone resulting in low-pressure fronts and mild air streams.

## THE PANNONIAN AREA

Spans approximately two-thirds of the width of the country north to south. While the area runs the gamut in terms of climate and geography, in general it is one of the sunniest and warmest regions of Austria. The Pannonian Plain itself is a huge basin that covers the entirety of Hungary (to the east of Austria) and parts of surrounding countries. Millions of years ago it was home to the Pannonian Sea, and thus its soil can be rich in marine sediment. Loemy soils can be found in Mittelburgenland. Leithaberg exhibits cooler temperatures. Lake Neusiedl and its surrounding smaller bodies of water result in higher humidity, causing noble rot (Botrytis cinerea).

## THE STEIERMARK (OR STYRIA)

Vineyards abound in the Steiermark. The climate is said to be "Illyrian," named for the ancient kingdom that occupied the eastern coast of the Adriatic Sea. Here, it can be fairly humid with hot summers and a long growing season. The largely mountainous terrain offers steep slopes for vineyard plantings and occasional volcanic soil. As a northern extension of the Ilyrian forests, the Steiermark exhibits more forest coverage than any other part of the country.

## VARIETIES

As of 2010, there are 35 grape varieties authorized for the production of quality wines in Austria. White wines comprise 65.65% of production. Red wines comprise 34.35 percent—an increase from previous years. Major indigenous varieties as well as prominent international varieties are listed below.

| Variety | % of Total Vineyard Area (to nearest .5%) | Tasting Notes | Regions(s) Grown |
| --- | --- | --- | --- |

| Indigenous Whites | | | |
|---|---|---|---|
| Grüner Veltliner | 29.5%<br>13,518 ha | A recognizable mixture of apple and pepper (referred to as "pfeffrigen") with a wide spectrum ranging from young light-bodied wines to vintage dry wines. Very ripe styles such as the Smaragd have nuances of nut and dried fruit. | Weinviertel, Traisental, Kremstal, Kamptal, and Leithaberg, Wachau |
| Welschriesling | 8%<br>3,597 ha | Green apple and citrus aromas with a touch of dried flowers over mineral notes. | Weinviertel, Steiermark, and Neusiedlersee |
| Neuburger, Zierfandler, Rotgipfler, Roter Veltliner | | | |
| Aromatic Varieties | | | |
| Riesling | 4%<br>1,863 ha | Striking mineral aromas integrated with citrus and tropical notes. | Wachau, Kremstal, Traisental, Kamptal, Weinviertel, Wagram, and Vienna |
| Müller-Thurgau | 4.5%<br>2,102 ha | Fine aroma reminiscent of Muscat and delicate fruit. Soft acidity | Carnuntum, Neusiedlersee, Thermenregion |
| Sauvignon Blanc | 2%<br>933 ha | Thrives in southern Austria with notes of gooseberries and acacia coupled with a racy acidity. | Steiermark, Burgenland, Niederösterreich, Süd-Oststeiermark |
| Gelber Muskateller, Muskat-Ottonel, Traminer, Scheurebe | | | |
| Pinot Family | | | |
| Weissburgunder (Pinot Blanc) | 4%<br>1,995 ha | A restrained bouquet with soft acidity, often used in blending to bring out notes ranging from delicate floral to baked apple. | Leithaberg, Süd-Oststeiermark |
| Chardonnay | 3%<br>1,431 ha | A wealth of styles, depending on vinification. The chalky mineral-rich soil of Burgenland yields fruit with complexity and texture. | Planted in all of Austria's wine-growing regions but predominant in Leithaberg |
| Other Varieties | | | |
| Bouvier, Frühroter Veltliner, Furmint, Goldburger, Jubiläumsrebe, Sylvaner | | | |

| Variety | % of Total Vineyard Area (to nearest .5%) | Tasting Notes | Regions(s) Grown |
|---|---|---|---|
| **INDIGENOUS REDS** | | | |
| (Blauer) Zweigelt | 14%<br>6,476 ha | A cross between Blaufränkisch and St. Laurent. Pronounced cherry aromas and delicate spice. | Found in all of Austria's wine-growing regions, but most predominant in Carnuntum, Neusiedlersee |
| Blaufränkisch | 7%<br>3,225 ha | Deep aromas of cherry and herbal spice with high acidity. | Carnuntum, Mittelburgenland, Eisenberg |
| Blauer Portugieser | 3.5%<br>1,622 ha | Soft fruit characters, gently acidity and low tannins, meant to be drunk young. | Thermenregion, Weinviertel |
| St. Laurent, Blauer Wildbacher, Blauburger | | | |

*Statistics provided by the Austrian Wine Marketing Board, 2010*

# SUB-REGIONS

Austria has 16 wine-growing regions contained within three federal states:

1. Niederösterreich
2. Burgenland
3. Steiermark

*Wien*, or Austria's capital city Vienna, is often referred to as its own distinct region.

Of the 16 delimited regions, seven have attained DAC status.

# NIEDERÖSTERREICH (LOWER AUSTRIA) (27,128 HA)

With the largest vineyard area in the country, Niederösterreich contains eight wine-growing regions. Loess soil and more seasonal temperature extremes are indicative of the area.

## WACHAU (1,350 HA)

Wachau is the westernmost region along the Danube River. Home to Grüner Veltliner and Riesling, the region is known for mineral-rich soil, "Gföhl" gneiss (a composition of migmatitic granite gneiss, quartz, feldspar and mica), and the construction of terraces on steep inclines created by the Bavarian monasteries during the Middle Ages. Each single vineyard exhibits its own microclimate depending on its incline, sun exposure and cliff sides. Cool nights are common as a result of winds from the north and the large expanse of river.

## KREMSTAL DAC (2,243 HA)

Cool, humid northwest breezes combine with warm, dry eastern winds from the Pannonian Plain. The geology of the region includes primary rock soils in the west that result in mineral-rich wines like Riesling and Grüner Veltliner. Villages further east produce fuller-bodied versions of these wines in loess terraces. The town of Krems is known for Sandgrube 13, a modern wine school, cooperative, museum, and home to the Niederoesterreich Wine Fair.

## KAMPTAL DAC (3,802 HA)

Soil is particularly diverse in Kamptal, a hot and dry microclimate. The area of Heiligenstein (which translates to "hell-like") is known for a sandstone and volcanic soil dating back more than 270 million years, producing Riesling and Grüner Veltliner with aging potential. Loess and clay soils appear closer to Danube and offer growing conditions suitable for a larger number of varieties.

## TRAISENTAL DAC (790 HA)

Warm days and cool nights are a result of the cool breezes coming off the Alps combining with the warm air from the Pannonian Plain. Soil structure consists of calcareous gravel and limestone. More than 60% of vines from the region are Grüner Veltliner.

## Wagram (2,451 ha)

Deep layers of loess are consistent throughout the region, even though planting is bisected by the Danube. To the north is terrain that spans 30 km (18.5 mi), while the south is scattered among smaller villages. The loess gives wines from this region a spicy, robust quality, particularly the indigenous Roter Veltliner. It is also home to the country's largest privately owned winery, Stift Klosterneuburg, and the world's first viticulture and oenology school, Bundeslehranstalt für Wein- und Obstbau (Federal College of Viticulture and Pomology), founded in 1860.

## Weinviertel DAC (13,356 ha)

Located in the northeast corner of the country, Weinviertel is Austria's largest region in terms of wine production. Most of the land is flat with loess soils and a slightly cooler climate. Grüner Veltliner is the star attraction and even has a specific aroma indicative to the area. The "pfeffrigen" flavors of white, green and black pepper matched with a fruit-driven aroma form the criteria for the specific tasting profile of Weinviertel DAC—Austria's first designated region-typical wine classification.

## Carnuntum (910 ha)

One of the few regions in Austria known for red wine, Carnuntum's warmer weather patterns maintain relative stability due to the nearby large bodies of water, the Danube, and Lake Neusiedl. Its soil is composed of stony, dense loam and loess or sand and gravel, providing optimum growing conditions for Zweigelt and Blaufränkisch.

## Thermenregion (2,196 ha)

Southwest of Vienna, vines have been cultivated in this area for more than 2,000 years, although the region was officially formed as part of the 1985 wine law. The name originates from the nearby thermal, sulfuric water springs "Thermae Pannonicae." Hot weather and upward of 1,800 hours of sunlight annually contribute to grapes developing with thick skins and concentrated flavor. There are two major soil types: the western hills are composed of loam-rich clay and brown earth, providing optimum growing conditions for Zierfandler and Rotgipfler; the flat lands to the east are characterized by permeable limestone gravel and are better suited for Pinot Noir and St. Laurent.

# Burgenland (13,840 ha)

Red wines dominate Burgenland. The eastern area, with its high humidity and countless small lakes, encourages the development of noble rot, enabling the production of dessert wines.

## Neusiedlersee (7,649 ha)

Wine producers primarily concentrate on Welschriesling and Zweigelt throughout Austria's easternmost wine-growing region, capitalizing on the Pannonian climate. An extended growing period, Lake Neusiedl, seasonal fog, and high humidity also provide the perfect conditions for noble rot and high quality dessert wines.

## Leithaberg DAC (3,576 ha)

The Leitha mountain range contributes to one of the most diverse growing regions in Austria. The area is known for its *Alweibersommer* (Indian summer), when grapes are still ripening on the vine into the fall. Soil composition consists of crystalline gneiss and mica schist in the center and a layer of hardened limestone. The resulting wines have a spicy, tightly-woven quality. Leithaberg has also become a popular tourist destination, in part, due to the Weinakedemie (Wine Academy) in Rust.

## Mittelburgenland DAC (2,117 ha)

Blaufränkisch is the predominant grape variety of the region. Hills protect the warm, consistent climate from cooler, northwest breezes. This is coupled with a deep, clay soil to produce wines with a robust, full-bodied, signature style.

## Eisenberg DAC (498 ha)

The smallest wine region in all of Austria, Eisenberg is primarily composed of hobby winemakers, where the predominant grape is Blaufränkisch. The steep hills possess slate soils, while the low grounds have a high content of ferrous loam.

## Steiermark (4,240 ha)

Sauvignon Blanc and Welschriesling make their mark in Steiermark among the rolling hills to the west and the Vulkanland region in the south, known for its volcanic remains. The most abundant variety is Welschriesling. As of 2010, the region only accounts for 5% of Austria's wine production and does not have any DAC status.

## Süd-Oststeiermark (1,400 ha)

Pockets of densely packed vineyards appear along the mountainous slopes, exhibiting some of Austria's highest cultivated vines at 650 meters (2,130 ft) above sea level. Sand, basalt, loam, and weathered primary rock comprise the soil.

## Südsteiermark (2,340 ha)

Synonymous with fresh, aromatic white wines, the region is also represents one of Austria's most rigorous wine-growing regions to cultivate, as most vineyards are planted on steep inclines. Soil structure varies greatly, but the warm and humid Mediterranean climate encourages delicately fresh wines, from fruit-driven *Junker* (young) wines to the rich and opulent *Lagen* or reserve style of wines. The region is also home to the Silberberg College for Viticulture and Winegrowing, founded in 1895.

## Weststeiermark (500 ha)

Although it is the smallest wine-growing region in Steiermark, Weststeiermark has a history of viticulture dating back to the fourth century BC. Steep slopes and the undulating shape of the terrain protect the vineyards against prevailing winds, while gneis and slate soils predominate. Its claim to fame is Schilcher, a rosé made from Blauer Wildbacher, which accounts for more than 80% of plantings.

## Wien (Vienna) (612 ha)

Viticulture was present in the city center through the Middle Ages, and today, Wien is one of only two European capital cities to contain a major wine region (the other being Madrid). West of the city, mineral-rich limestone soils offer ideal conditions for Riesling, Chardonnay, and other white varieties. Traditional Viennese *Heuriger* wine taverns remain a popular attraction for tourists and locals alike, and the place to enjoy *Gemischter Satz* (Field Blend)—a single-vineyard wine comprised of a blend of plantings. The VieVenum, Austria's largest and most prestigious wine fair, is held bi-annually in Vienna and is a showcase for both established as well as up and coming producers.

# SOUTH AMERICA

## OVERVIEW

The fourth largest continent in the world also happens to be the second most significant wine-producing continent—after Europe. The most currently available statistics confirm that South America, with nearly 450,000 ha under vine, exceeds the total plantings of the United States, Australia, and New Zealand combined. The continent, which stretches 7,400 kilometers (4,600 miles) from north to south and spans 5,150 kilometers (3,200 miles) at its widest point, has been home to substantial wine producing regions for nearly 500 years. Though most modern wine consumers are just awakening to all that South America's wine industry offers, it should be noted that wine, for many inhabitants of the continent, has been an integral part of daily life since the age of the Conquistadores in the 16th century. Grapevines were cultivated by clergymen for Eucharistic purposes and laymen who yearned for the drink they had so enjoyed in Spain, their former homeland.

Ironically, given the overwhelming annual production of South American wineries, grapes grown for the production of wine occupy a just a fraction of the total land area on this continent. Indeed, out of the 13 nations that comprise South America, only nine produce wine, and of those nine, the major wine-producing nations number a mere four: Argentina, Brazil, Chile, and Uruguay. The remaining five—Colombia, Ecuador, Peru, Bolivia, and Venezuela—produce wine on such an infinitesimal scale that they scarcely garner any recognition or mention. One of the reasons for the scarcity of vineyard-friendly land (with the notable exceptions of certain portions of Chile, Argentina, and Uruguay) lies in the environmental conditions that dominate much of South America: tropical rain forest. South America is home to the Amazon Basin, which happens to be the largest area of tropical rain forest in the world. Tropical climactic conditions and wonderfully fertile soils may promote the proliferation of some delicious and desirable fruit, but grapes do not happen to be one of them. The tropical, humid climactic conditions that dominate some of the more northern interior regions, such as Brazil and Bolivia, can prove detrimental to the successful growth of wine grapes. Heavy rainfall is common and rot thrives in such an environment. Conscientious and innovative wine makers are, therefore, attempting to plant vines in areas with less potential for rot and harvest-season rainfall, but they are not easily found. Herein lies the challenge for many South American winemakers: They must combine the accumulated knowledge and expertise of nearly a half a century of traditional wine making with the innovation and creativity in wine production that the modern market demands.

## HISTORY

Although historical evidence strongly suggests the presence of indigenous varieties of vines in South America prior to the Spanish conquest, it is widely accepted that any grapes grown by the Incas, who then inhabited western South America, were not employed for the purpose of making wine. Initially, during the earlier decades of the Spanish conquest, wine was being shipped from Spain to the New World, in an attempt to alleviate some of the stress and strain felt by the new colonists, who were so far away from home. For obvious reasons, this proved to be an exercise in futility, as the wine that actually managed to reach the New World was often spoiled by the long and treacherous journey. Needless to say, this system would not sit long with the new colonists, and by the third decade of the 16$^{th}$ century, Spanish colonists, using imported Spanish vine cuttings, were becoming increasingly self-reliant regarding the production of wine. By 1536, Francisco Pizarro had essentially defeated the Inca Empire and established the Spanish viceroyalty of Peru, with its headquarters in Lima. With the indigenous inhabitants successfully subjugated or eliminated the ruling Spaniards were free to pursue the production of wine unfettered by interference from the resistant Incas. By the mid-16$^{th}$ century, Peru became the first region of the New World to establish viticulture on a systematic scale and rapidly grew to be the center of wine production in the New World. Colonial Spanish accounts reported that by 1560, Peru had 40,000 ha under vine, and was also incredibly influential in the dissemination of wine making to the other Spanish regions in South America, namely, Chile and Argentina.

At the close of the 16$^{th}$ century, the Spanish crown had decreed that wine production in New Spain (Central/South America) be severely limited. This decision was prompted by the protests of Spanish wine makers, whose hegemony over the colonial wine market, the crown was attempting to preserve. While the restriction on New Spain's production was significant in that it prohibited new vineyard development and plantings, it was also instrumental in securing Peru's already established position as the preeminent supplier of wine to the entire region—a fact of life that Peru would enjoy for centuries to come. The Spanish crown would, at the urging of colonial officials and farmers in the late 17th century, eventually lift the ban on new vineyard plantings. This would clear the path for New Spain to become a thriving producer of wine for the next four centuries.

Between 1810 and 1824, the movement toward independence for the colonies of New Spain, would invigorate the production and innovation in viticulture that had been rather stagnant under Spanish rule. Brazil, which would gain independence from Portugal in 1822, had attempted in the past to cultivate vineyards but with little success. However, once free from the constraints of the Portuguese crown, Brazil would join its neighbors, Peru, Chile, Argentina, and Uruguay in becoming a major wine-producing nation by the late 19th century. Each of these countries would begin to carve out its own niche in the world of viticulture, some with great critical success and acclaim, like Chile, and some with massive production abilities, like Argentina. Still others, like Bolivia, would come to the realization that their grapes could be more productively used to make brandy, while others would struggle, such as Peru, against the presence of the phylloxera louse.

# CHILE

| AREA UNDER VINE | 117,559 hectares |
|---|---|
| GRAPE VARIETIES | |
| RED | Cabernet Sauvignon, Pais, Merlot, Carmenère |
| WHITE | Sauvignon, Chardonnay, and Moscatel de Alejandria |
| CLIMATE | Chile's climate also varies considerably, but the key influences include the Andes Mountains, the coastal hills and, of course, the Pacific Ocean. Perhaps the biggest factor, however, is the Humbolt Current, which brings an Arctic chill to the country's vineyards. |
| SOIL | There are a vast variety of soils throughout Chile, although the best quality wines come from areas with a deep limestone. |

## OVERVIEW

With a remarkably narrow width and a length spanning 4,200 kilometers (2,600 miles) from Peru in the north to the southern tip of continent in the south, Chile occupies the entire southwest corner and coast of South America. From a critical standpoint, it is undoubtedly the continent's most important wine-producing nation that, for the last 15–20 years, has seen its standing in the international wine community grow substantially, both in terms of its products and the prices that they now command.

The most recent statistics show that Chile has approximately 118,000 hectares of vineyards that produce approximately 4,500 hl of wine each year. The country's essential claim to viticultural fame is its history of wine making free from the dreaded phylloxera louse, which has enabled Chile's wine makers to plant vines, many of which, are now over 100 years old, without having to graft any of them onto rootstocks. Chilean wine makers, who had imported Vitis vinifera vines from Europe prior to the phylloxera outbreak, now had the distinct advantage of producing wines made from original vinifera grape vines that were unaltered by new rootstocks or undesirable pesticides. This fact, combined with enthusiastic foreign investment and a nation in which per capita wine consumption is rather high (approximately 14 gallons, versus the United Kingdom's 12 and less than 2 in the United States), has offered Chile a wonderfully unique position with enormous potential in the world of wine: favorable climate, older vinifera vines, phylloxera-free vine cultivation, and substantial foreign investment in viticultural technology. It should be fascinating to see how Chile utilizes this essentially unparalleled position in the future.

## HISTORY

In essence, Chile's early viticultural history mirrors the experiences of the other colonies of New Spain. It is widely accepted that the first vinifera vines to be planted in Chile were brought in from Cuzco, Peru in approximately 1540. A priest, Father Francisco de Carabantes, is cited as having introduced the vines to Chile in 1548 in order for the new settlers to be able to celebrate the Eucharist and preserve their Christian communion tradition. Some of the original varieties mentioned in early historical accounts include **Muscatel, Torontél, Mollar**, and a grape later thought to be the incredibly prolific indigenous Chilean variety known as **Pais**, which is identical to California's Mission grape. In 1551, a conquistador named Don Francesco de Aguirre became the first recorded grape grower, as reports to the Spanish crown cited this fact among others, such as wine consumption was rising dramatically in Santiago, the colony's capital city. As was stated previously, in an effort to strictly regulate the production of wine in New Spain, as well as to protect the interests of Spanish wine exporters, by 1600 the Spanish crown had prohibited the plantings of new vineyards. However, in 1678 the colonial government in Chile strongly recommended lifting this ban on new production in order to simply promote general agricultural growth. The plea was eventually heeded, and by the 18th century, Chile was producing great quantities of inexpensive, unremarkable wine. In general, the wines were actually sweet, with dry juice being combined with boiled, concentrated grape must—a simplistic practice, perhaps even insipid by today's viticultural standards.

This style of wine would dominate the Chile's production for more than 100 years, essentially up until its achievement of independence from Spain in 1818. The fortunes of Chile's wine making industry would be forever altered in 1830, however, when an enthusiastic Frenchman, Claudio Gay, lobbied the government to establish the *Quinta Normal*, a nursery designed to study experimental botanical specimens. Naturally the study included grape vines, but specifically, European vines. This had an indelible impact upon the Chilean wine industry, since the *Quinta Normal* possessed and was studying European vines 50 years prior to the outbreak of phylloxera. The development of the *Quinta Normal* also marked the commencement of a lasting bond between Chilean and French viticulture. In 1851 a Spaniard, Don Silvestre Ochagavia Echazarreta, imported vine cuttings of "noble" French varieties—Cabernet Sauvignon and Merlot—in an effort to produce wines from varieties other than the ubiquitous Pais and Moscatel grapes. In addition, he also commissioned French oenologists to advise and consult on the proper cultivation of these "new" Old World varieties. It has been stated by some that Chilean wines often taste more like French wines than French wines actually do. Whether this is true or not is entirely a personal opinion, but one related fact is indisputable: Beginning in the mid-19$^{th}$ century Chilean wine making fell heavily under the influence of French oenologists and wine makers. It is a trend that continues to this day, with domaines such as Los Vascos, partly owned by Château Lafite Rothschild and Viña Aquitania, operated by one of the directors of Cos d'Estournel and the wine maker from Château Margaux.

In the late 19$^{th}$ century, Chile enjoyed the unique distinction of possessing the world's only healthy wine industry. Phylloxera had devastated vineyards throughout Europe, but Chile's geographical isolation served her well by protecting her vineyards from the louse. The Chilean wine industry had become healthy not only financially and viticulturally, but in reputation too, experiencing growing international prestige. With phylloxera diminishing the capacity for Europe's best vineyards to produce healthy wine, consumers turned to Chilean wine. In 1889, to the surprise of many, a Chilean wine even captured the Grand Prize at the Great Exhibition in Paris.

As the 20th century dawned, the Chilean wine industry was arguably the healthiest in the world. It was so healthy, in fact, that the government became concerned not only with some of the incredible profits amassed by the handful of families who controlled the wine industry, but with the rapidly escalating per capita wine consumption, as well. As a result, the government began to tax the wine industry much more aggressively than it had before. During the second half of the century, this stricter regulation, combined with decreased per capita consumption and the widespread political instability of the 1960s, dealt a severe blow to the wine industry. By 1970, nearly half of all vineyards had been uprooted, due to falling prices and dwindling consumer demand. In 1979, however, the tide would begin to turn slowly. Miguel Torres, the renowned Spanish wine maker, established a winery in the Curicó Valley. What was significant about this was that he was the first wine maker to employ modern wine making technology and techniques (stainless steel, cold fermentation tanks, etc.) in Chile, a country that had been producing wine for more than 400 years. Technologically speaking, Chile had lagged behind much of the rest of the international wine industry for some time. However, by the late 1980s, the focus of Chilean wine makers shifted from simply meeting domestic production levels to using new technologies and international noble grape varieties in order to compete in the quality export market. By 1995, 10,000 ha of vineyards were newly planted and new wine regulations regarding production guidelines and appellation controls were adopted. Both developments would aid Chile's wine industry in competing for the coveted center stage in the international market.

## Wine Laws

In 1985, legislation was passed that would regulate the contents of Chilean wine labels. According to this legislation, labels must state the following: an indication of the manufacturer, volume, alcohol content, and when relevant, if "table" grapes have been employed in the production. (Table grapes are grapes grown specifically for direct consumption and not for the production of wine.) In addition, Chilean regulations generally resemble those governing warmer wine regions. Chaptalization is not permitted, but acidification is.

In 1995, legislation was enacted with the goal of protecting by law the various regions and subregions of Chile. If a label offers the origin of the wine, this law stipulates the 23 grape varieties that may be utilized in the production. It should be noted that of these 23 varieties, the prolific indigenous Chilean grape, Pais, is not included. The 1995 legislation also governs so-called "variety" wines from specific origins and vintages. If a wine is labeled "Cabernet Sauvignon, 1995, Maipo Valley," for instance, it must, by law, contain a minimum of 75% of the named variety from the origin and stated vintage. Finally, regarding wines labeled with "Riserva" or "Gran Riserva" titles, they are permitted for wines where place of origin is indicated only. Interestingly, however, there are no rules pertaining to age or production that stipulate when a wine may be labeled with such titles.

# Geography, Climate, and Soil

It's natural that Chile's vineyards would spring up in its most populous areas. Santiago in particular has been the center of the country's viticultural heritage. The region confers such advantages as access to water for irrigation (in the form of runoff from the Andes), little threat from frosts, and low evening temperatures that bring acidity to grapes.

As wine makers have begun exploring other possible growing areas, they've discovered regions, such as Casablanca in the north (today being vigorously developed for wine making) and Bío-Bío in the south, that boast Mediterranean-style growing conditions better suited to viticulture. Vineyards in these areas benefit from their location on the rolling coastal hills, cool maritime breezes, and sufficient rainfall levels that eliminates the need for irrigation.

Other climate moderators that influence the country's terroirs include the low coastal mountain range that separates the Central Valley from the Pacific Ocean as well as the Andes that separate Chile from Argentina. Chilean vineyards are largely planted on flat, fertile land with predominantly alluvial and clay/limestone soils. Specific details for each region are described below.

# Varieties And Viticulture

Due to the country's naturally hot climate, irrigation is common and essential for approximately half of all Chilean vineyards. There is a plentiful supply of channel- and canal-based irrigation, made possible by the melting ice caps of the Andes Mountains. The irrigated vineyards are found mostly in the interior-situated vineyards of the Central Valley (Maipo, Rapel, Maule, etc.). Coastal regions such as Casablanca and Bío-Bío are generally afforded rainfall levels sufficient enough to negate any need for irrigation. Harvest begins at the end of February for early maturing varieties such as **Chardonnay**, continues through the end of April when **Cabernet Sauvignon** is generally picked, to well into May, when the ubiquitous **Pais** is ready for harvesting. Average yields for Chilean vineyards are approximately 70hl/ha, and various training and trellising methods are actually quite diverse, employing Spanish, Californian, and Australian practices. Chile's wine industry is truly a viticultural crossroads.

The most widely planted grape variety in Chile today is **Cabernet Sauvignon**, at approximately 40,800 ha. It recently supplanted the Pais, which has been stagnant for some time at about 15,000 ha under vine, as interest in quality export wine has grown. The principal white varieties, '**Sauvignon**' (approximately 8,900 ha under vine), **Chardonnay** (approximately 8,800 ha), **Moscatel de Alejandria** (approximately 6,000 ha), and the increasingly popular and prestigious '**Merlot**' (approximately 13,300 ha) compose the middle range of area under vine. **Carmenère** is the next most popular red variety at roughly 7,300 ha.

It should be noted here that 'Sauvignon' grapes planted in Chile are generally not the well-regarded Sauvignon Blanc, but other strains of Sauvignon, such as **Sauvignon Vert** (sometimes also called Sauvignonasse, and identical to Tocai Friulano). Grape identification is a relatively new science in Chile, and studies have shown that several grape varieties that have been labeled as one thing may in fact be another variety altogether. Sauvignon Blanc clones are, however, being planted with greater frequency these days, due to increased research into identification and consumer demand.

Interestingly, too, it has been discovered that much of what was thought to be **Merlot** vines were, in actuality, **Carmenère**, the rather ancient Bordeaux variety. With the increased interest in vine identification research, new interest has been sparked in creating a variety wine from Carmenère alone, as opposed to a hybrid wine labeled 'Merlot.' Many do feel that Chile may in fact be the successful home that Carmenère has had yet to find. The remaining major plantings in Chile, with over 1,000 ha under vine include **Syrah, Pinot Noir, Cabernet Franc, Cot, Sémillon**, and **Torontél**.

# Wine Regions (from North to South)

The northernmost wine producing region, **Atacama**, was awarded its status for reasons that seem to escape most experts. The Atacama Desert possesses one of the most arid climates on earth, with incredibly scarce rain and a generally hostile environment for wine grape growing. The region is known mainly for its production of table grapes and for its significant function as a producer of Pisco. First manufactured in the 1870s, Pisco is an oak-aged brandy, produced in the spirit of Cognac or Armagnac. Generally speaking, Pisco, whose production has been strictly regulated since the 1930s, is composed of grape varieties such as **Moscatel, Torontél,** and **Pedro Jiménez**. It is the national spirit of Chile and is mostly consumed neat after a meal or in aperitif form as the seductive Pisco Sour, essentially something of a "Sidecar" for South America.

Bearing a strong resemblance in climactic and environmental conditions to its northern neighbor Atacama, **Coquimbo** is a parched region known mostly for its production of table grapes and Pisco. However, there are parcels of vineyards in the cooler, Pacific-influenced areas of Coquimbo where export quality wine is being produced. The Limarí Valley, with steep slopes of mineral-laced terrain, has seen some success with the growth of noble varieties. The key factor to its limited degree of success, however, has been constant irrigation, something absolutely essential in this sun-drenched region. The grape varieties planted by its one registered winery, Viña Francisco de Aguirre, include **Cabernet Franc, Cabernet Sauvignon, Merlot,** and **Chardonnay**.

The northernmost of Chile's principal wine growing regions, the **Aconcagua Valley** is hot and dry—by far the warmest of the principal regions. Situated between Coquimbo and Santiago, valley temperatures in the summer often climb to 30°C (86°F) and the soil tends to be alluvial. As a result, the region is generally given over to the production of red grape varieties, primarily **Cabernet Sauvignon**. However, wineries situated in the cooler, breezy coastal site of **Panquehue**, have found some success with other red grapes, including **Cabernet Franc, Sangiovese, Nebbiolo, Syrah,** and even **Zinfandel.**

**Casablanca,** one of the newest, coolest wine regions in Chile, is officially part of the Aconcagua Valley, although its own microclimate creates a gulf of distinction between its own cool, coastal vineyard sites and the hotter interior vineyards of the Aconcagua. With an average altitude of 500 meters (1,640 feet) above sea level, cool morning fogs from the Pacific current, and a slow ripening season, prolonged by the constant presence of cloud cover, the grape varieties which thrive here tend to be white. Most prolific is Chardonnay, with more than 4,000 ha under vine. It should be noted that red wine is also produced in this small region, although most of the fruit is purchased from vineyards in the Maipo Valley.

The oldest and most famous wine region of Chile is **Maipo Valley**, situated in what is referred to as the Central Valley, just south of Santiago. Named for the Maipo River, it is not a large region, with about 10,800 ha under vine, and is dominated by **Cabernet Sauvignon** and **Chardonnay** vines. **Merlot** and **Sauvignon Blanc** play significant supporting roles in the vineyard composition of Maipo. Its annual average rainfall is a mere 300 mm (12 inches), prompting the widespread use of irrigation. The soil tends to be sandy and alluvial, enriched by calcium deposits from the Maipo River. The area's conditions generally favor **Cabernet Sauvignon**, the region's most prized variety. Given its proximity to the capital city, it is not surprising that many of the major Chilean wineries have been established here for some time now, which lends a heavy dose of prestige to this region.

With a reputation for producing full-bodied, long-lived red wines, the **Rapel Valley** has approximately 34,000 ha under vine, split between Cachapoal and Colchagua. Most of Rapel's vineyards are planted with **Cabernet Sauvignon**, with '**Sauvignon**' being the second most widely planted variety. The Rapel Valley enjoys sun-drenched summers with cool evenings, mild rainfall in the winter, and soils composed of rich clay and calcareous *Tuffeau*, all factors which together make Rapel one of the most potentially exciting wine regions in the world. Many wine makers share this sentiment, as investment in the region has exploded over the last decade.

Further south and situated more in the interior, the **Maule Valley** is Chile's principal wine region with the most area under vine, at approximately 31,000 ha. The influence of the Pacific Ocean makes this one of the cooler and cloudier regions in Chile and substantial rainfall in the western portion of the valley is a constant threat although the summer temperatures during the day can climb to a warm 32°C (88°F). However, temperatures generally drop significantly at night, enabling the grapes to achieve a relatively healthy balance between sugars and acidity. The indigenous, prolific **Pais** is the dominant grape variety, although wineries in the subregion of **Curicó** have taken advantage of the juxtaposition of day and night temperatures, along with clay soils, to plant more noble varieties. **Merlot** is considered to be the rising star of the Maule Valley, and some wineries have even begun to experiment with Burgundian styles of wines crafted from **Chardonnay** and **Pinot Noir**.

The southernmost principal wine region, **Bío-Bío,** possesses approximately 3,500 ha under vine, which are essentially divided between red and white varieties. Much of the wine produced in this cooler region is intended for domestic consumption and, therefore, constructed from varieties such as **Pais** and **Moscatel**. Substantial rainfall and decreased temperatures and sunlight make this region less of a target for wine makers to establish vineyards of noble varieties, but over the last few years, nearly 1,000 ha of noble varieties have been planted. These plantings, which include

**Chardonnay, Sauvignon, Cabernet Sauvignon, Pinot Noir,** and even **Gewürztraminer**, combined with an increasing reliance on modern viticultural technique, may spell the turning of the tide for this region.

# BRAZIL

This vast nation is the third most significant wine producing country in South America, with approximately 60,000 ha under vine. Of this total, a substantial 36,000 ha are devoted to the production of wine, with the remaining being earmarked for table grapes. Brazil's annual production generally hovers around 2.8 million gallons, a total output that has blossomed only as a national wine industry began to take shape over the last century. Brazil's viticultural history began many years ago, with Portuguese colonists planting vines in the 16th century. As was the case in many other former Spanish colonies, wine was produced initially by Jesuit priests for sacramental purposes. Following the destruction of the majority of the missions, most vineyards were uprooted in the 18th century, and Brazil's wine industry was essentially dormant until the middle of the 19th century. It was then that **Isabella**, a strangely aromatic, not particularly well-regarded American hybrid was planted, and it proved to be one of few grape varieties that could withstand the hot, humid, subtropical climate encountered in Brazil. In the final three decades of the 19th century, with an influx in Italian immigration, new grape varieties such as **Barbera, Moscato,** and **Trebbiano** were planted, reflecting the origin of Brazil's new settlers.

It was not until the 1970s, with substantial foreign investment from firms such a Moët & Chandon and Martini & Rossi did Brazilian viticulture begin to approach the modern era of wine making. The climactic and environmental difficulties remain today, however, Vitis vinifera grape varieties still struggle to gain footing in the humidity and incredibly fertile soil. American hybrids and Vitis labrusca still outnumber the more noble, more highly sought after vinifera varieties eight to one. A constant danger that farmers and wine makers face is diluted crops from overly fertile soils and substantial rainfalls. Much of the rain falls during the harvest and can reach levels of 1,800 mm (70 inches) per year. In an effort to alleviate this threat, grapes are often picked before precipitation levels are too high, the ironic result being grapes that are far too acidic for successful production into wine. Chaptalization or some other form of enrichment is almost always necessary as a result.

Viticulture is concentrated in the south, in the regions of **Serra Gaucha** (33,000 ha under vine) and the newer **Frontera** region, situated on the Argentina/Uruguay border, where rainfall levels are lower and optimism is higher for vinifera vines. Vitis vinifera vines account for approximately 25% of the total wine production each year, the vast majority of which is white wine composed of **Chardonnay, Sémillon, Riesling Italico,** and even **Gewürztraminer.** Red vinifera varieties include the ubiquitous **Cabernet Sauvignon, Cabernet Franc,** and **Merlot**. Despite substantial international interest and investment, the viticultural future of Brazil seems quite uncertain.

# URUGUAY

This nation is South America's fourth largest wine producer, with an annual production level of about 850,000 hl coming from approximately 10,000 ha under vine. Uruguay's viticulture history dates only to the late 19th century, when Basque and Catalan settlers introduced grape varieties to the country that reflected their origins, such as the thick-skinned **Tannat**, which is the most widely planted variety, and **Petit Manseng**. The vast majority of vineyards are situated in the south, where summers are warm and significant rainfall negates any need for irrigation, often reaching levels of 1,000 mm (nearly 40 inches) each year. Uruguay, just like Brazil, its neighbor to the north, also runs the constant risk of diluted crops, with yields climbing to 150 hl/ha. However, a recently formed national body, the *Instituto Nacional de Viniviticultura*, was created in 1988 to regulate the wine industry. The establishment of this organization combined with the adoption of modern techniques and viticultural technology suggests a real potential future for Uruguay's wine industry that few thought possible a couple of decades ago.

# Bolivia

Augustine missionaries introduced the grape vine to Bolivia in the 16th century. Currently, roughly 5,000 ha of land are under vine. The combination of phylloxera and humid, tropical climactic conditions have greatly hampered the growth and success of the Bolivian wine industry. Rain is concentrated in the early months of the year, which encourages fungal disease, and irrigation is necessary for much of Bolivia's largely alluvial soils. The great majority of the grapes harvested are used for the production of Singani, a Pisco-like brandy that is Bolivia's national spirit. **Muscat of Alexandria** accounts for about 80% of all white vinifera strains planted, however, other white varieties grown here include **Torrontés, Riesling,** and **Chenin Blanc**. Red vinifera varieties include **Cabernet Sauvignon** and **Merlot**, in rather minute quantities. A local wine made using ancient stomping methods and vinification in clay jars, named Patero, is also produced.

# Peru

Although Peru essentially introduced systematic viticulture to the colonies of New Spain in the 16th century, its own national viticulture was severely damaged by phylloxera in the late 19th century. As a result, the vineyards were employed primarily for grape growing for the production of Pisco, the national Peruvian spirit, which derives its name from the town and river of the same name. Today, there are approximately 12,000 ha planted with vines. Vineyards are concentrated around the central coast, generally around the town of Pisco, where the weather is warm, but rainfall levels are low. Irrigation channeled from the Andes is widely employed. Vine varieties currently being cultivated include **Alicante Bouschet, Barbera, Cabernet Sauvignon, Malbec, Moscatel, Sauvignon Blanc,** and **Torontél.**

# Colombia, Venezuela, Ecuador

The wine industry in **Colombia**, the largest of these three nations, is only about 80 years old. The country claims only about 1,500 ha under vine. There are about 20 wineries, which employ grapes grown in the **Cauce Valley**. Of the vinifera varieties planted, **Cabernet Sauvignon, Merlot,** and **Chardonnay** comprise the majority of the vines, with the peculiar American hybrid **Isabella** also finding a small niche. The majority of production is focused on fortified wines, brandies and wine-based aperitifs.

**Venezuela**, with approximately 1,000 ha under vine, enjoys the fruits of its tropical climate, with two full crops grown each year. Therefore, wine labels often reflect not only the vintage, but the month in which the grapes were harvested. Bodegas Pomar is the prominent winery, producing a Bordeaux-inspired **Sauvignon Blanc-Sémillon** blend, as well as a **Cabernet Sauvignon-Syrah-Tempranillo** blend.

**Ecuador** possesses the fewest vineyards of the South American nations, with only approximately 250 ha of indigenous plantings—**Nacional Negra** and **Moscatel Morado**—which can be found along the cooler coastal areas and interior mountain provinces. As is the case with Venezuela, Ecuador enjoys multiple crop harvests each year, due to its fertile subtropical climate.

# ARGENTINA

| AREA UNDER VINE | 228,575 hectares |
|---|---|
| GRAPE VARIETIES | |
| RED | Malbec, Bonarda, Cabernet Sauvignon, Syrah, Merlot, Criolla Grande and Cereza still hold significant dominance in the country's vineyards |
| WHITE | Pedro Giménez, Torrontés, Moscatel de Alejandria, Chardonnay |
| CLIMATE | Most of Argentina's vine-growing regions are concentrated in a narrow strip in the western half of the country. As in Chile, the Andes provide a key moderating influence, with numerous rivers offering additional influence (and irrigation) in the semi-desert wine growing regions. |
| SOIL | Argentina's soils vary considerably from sandy to clay. However, there is a common theme throughout the country of deep, loose soils that are alluvial and Aeolian in origin. |

## OVERVIEW

With more than 225,000 ha under vine, and an annual production level of approximately 14 million hectoliters (nearly 400 million gallons), Argentina is, needless to say, a giant in the world of wine production. The most recent statistics offer fascinating insight into the production capabilities of this nation; eight countries in the world have more acreage under vine, but a mere four produce more wine than Argentina. Similarly to Chile, the wine industry in Argentina has shifted focus relatively recently, from massive production goals designed to fuel the domestic market to more wine produced on an export quality level. Domestic per capita wine consumption has decreased in recent years from a staggering 92 liters in 1970 to 42 liters today. Along with this substantial decrease, there has been considerable interest on the international market in the potential of Argentina's wine industry, which has experienced something of a renaissance in just the last decade. Foreign investment from firms such as Moët & Chandon, Kendall-Jackson, Pernod-Ricard, and Allied Domecq have brought new technology, techniques, and use of the noble varieties into the mainstream of Argentina's viticultural environment. At this point, investment in new technologies and grape varieties, combined with a respect for some of the successful distinctive varieties, such as Malbec and Torrontés, could conceivably catapult Argentina to the forefront of the international wine market.

## HISTORY

As was the case in Chile, scholars generally believe that during the 1550s vines were introduced to Argentina by Peru. Historical records indicate that Jesuit priests constructed a vineyard at Santiago del Estero in northeast Argentina in 1557 to grow grapes for sacramental wine production. The city of Mendoza was founded in 1561, and commercial vineyards were established in the nearby province of San Juan from 1569–1589. The grape most commonly planted in the colonial era, and through the next 300 years, was **Criolla Chica**—the same variety as Chile's **Pais** and subsequently California's **Mission**. Jesuits and early wine makers generally found the most successful vineyard sites to be in the foothills of the vast Andes Mountains. Irrigation was a common practice during the colonial era, as a certain level of production was required to meet the demands of a growing population.

Independence from the Spanish Crown in 1822 brought a massive influx of European settlers to the fledgling nation, and as was the case with Chile, the lack of imperial controls provided a boon to the wine industry. However, what significantly altered the nature of Argentina's wine industry indefinitely was the completion of the railway from the wine-producing regions surrounding Mendoza in the west to Buenos Aires in the east. Wine could suddenly be transported across the country with great ease and expediency, thus further promoting the wines of the west in the ever expanding domestic market. In addition, the completion of the railroad meant that wine could now be shipped to Buenos Aires for export by ship.

In 1895, an Englishman named Edmund Norton, so enamored of the countryside of northwestern Argentina, constructed a winery in Mendoza. Bodegas Norton would be among the first to import vines from France for planting in Argentina, and by 1900, a second great influx of immigrants from Europe would instill even more vigor into Argentina's already thriving wine industry. By the 1920s, Argentina was the eighth wealthiest nation in the world, enjoying tremendous foreign investment and a successful export trade. The subsequent several decades would not be kind to Argentina, however. The global financial crisis of the 1930s caused Argentina's foreign investments to plummet and the demand for her exports wane. The political and social crises which would essentially envelop Argentina for the next five decades deflated investment in the wine industry to the point where most producers had abandoned goals of crafting export quality wine in favor of table wine that could be successfully sold and rapidly consumed by the domestic market. It was not until the late 1980s that producers began to experience the benefits of a stabilized political and economic situation, and started refocusing efforts to create export-quality wine. Wine makers also cooperated in a successful vine pulling scheme during this period, designed to reduce plantings and yields to more sensible and respected levels, thus creating the overall sense that export quality wine was again the overall goal for many of Argentina's best producers.

## Wine Laws

Argentina has neither a developed nor strict system of wine laws, although there is an official oversight bureau called the *Instituto Nacionale de Vitivinicultura* (INV). The primary purpose of the INV, however, is limited to controlling the production of grapes and wine exports. Argentina does not have specific laws about allowed grapes, the definition of wine areas, indications on cultivation of vines or specific procedures for wine making. In fact, the only rule concerns labeling. If a variety is stated on a label, the wine must be comprised of at least 80% of the named grape.

There have been attempts to set real and proper wine laws, but the idea has met with little success. One exception is in Mendoza, where wine makers have pioneered the concept of regulation for production of wines of specific origin in the quest to seek out the most advantageous terroir for each individual variety. The development and regulation of specific subregions began in 1993, in **Luján de Cuyo**, the first controlled viticultural area. Other specific subregions include **Maipú, San Carlos, San Raphael,** and **San Martín**.

## Geography, Climate, and Soil

Argentina's primary wine-making regions are concentrated in a narrow strip of high, semidesert land best described as having a continental climate. Vineyards are generally located 300–1600 meters (980–1,250 feet) above sea level, offering both intense sunlight as well as significant differences between daytime and nighttime temperatures. While rainfall is scarce (a mere 20–25 centimeters or 8–10 inches per year, spread mercifully throughout the growing season), Argentinean wine makers have developed strong irrigation systems that leverage runoff from the Andes so they never lack for water. Soils are sandy with clay/loam over a bedrock of gravel, limestone, and clay.

## Varieties and Viticulture

Even with the surge of interest in international noble varieties, thin-skinned pink grapes still dominate the plantings of Argentina. Varieties such as **Criolla Grande** and **Cereza** still account for half of all of the nation's plantings. **Pedro Giménez** is the most widely planted white grape variety and is most frequently found in Mendoza and San Juan. **Torrontés Riojano** is the second most-planted white variety with just over 9,000 ha planted, and Chardonnay comes in third with 6,000 ha. As was stated previously, **Malbec** is certainly the most prestigious and unique of Argentina's red grape varieties, and with approximately 26,000 ha under vine it is also the most widely planted. **Bonarda** (thought by many to be California's **Charbono**) ekes out Cabernet Sauvignon with approximately 19,000 ha under vine. **Cabernet Sauvignon**, a rising star in Argentina's portfolio, enjoys about 18,000 ha of plantings, a figure certain to increase in the near future. Adhering to its Spanish roots, Argentina contains a significant amount of **Tempranillo** (known as here as **Tempranilla**) plantings, whose wines have captured the fancy of many contemporary wine critics. Other red grape varieties in minuscule quantities include **Pinot Noir, Syrah, Sangiovese, Dolcetto,** and **Merlot**, which is often used as a blending agent in **Cabernet Sauvignon**–based wines.

Phylloxera, much to the relief of Argentina's wine industry, has never gained a significant foothold here. As a result, vines are generally ungrafted and planted on their own roots. Argentina's irrigation system, although dating back to the 16$^{th}$ century, is among the most successful in the world, as is evidenced by Argentina's massive production capabilities. Vine-training systems are widespread, especially the Parral training system, wherein vines rise to approximately two meters off the soil, making picking easier, and removing the stress of soil heat from the grapes. The harvest generally lasts about five months, usually commencing in February, although one of the functions of the INV is to set the harvest dates each year.

## Wine Regions (from North to South)

The three provinces of **Catamarca, Jujuy,** and **Salta** in the northwest corner of Argentina possess approximately 5,000 ha of land under vine. **Catamarca** claims the most land under vine of the three, with roughly 2,500 ha. **Jujuy** claims little notoriety for anything besides table wine. It is **Salta**, however, which has garnered the most prestige and respect for its wine production.

**Salta**, with nearly 2,200 ha under vine, actually produces almost 2% of the total annual output in Argentina. It lays claim to the vineyards with the highest altitude in the world, at 2,000 meters above sea level, and enjoys summer temperatures of 22°C (70°F) during the day and a brisk 12°C (54°F) at night. Controlled irrigation, permeable, sandy soils, and the climatic conditions of the area together allow for the successful cultivation of **Torrontés Riojano**, one of Argentina's most unique and important white grape varieties. This grape, when handled properly, can produce wines that are quite aromatic, almost **Muscat**-like, full bodied, and remarkably well balanced. **Cabernet Sauvignon** is the runner-up in Salta and is often so expressive in its character that wine makers may not employ any oak aging prior to bottling. Also planted are **Chardonnay, Chenin Blanc,** and **Malbec.**

South of Catamarca and northeast of San Juan lies **La Rioja**. With vines planted in 1591, it is the oldest continuous wine-producing region in Argentina, and it is considered to be the origin of the prized **Torrontés Riojano** grape. Besides these two facts, La Rioja's viticultural significance has waned in the last 50 years and currently possesses approximately 8,500 ha under vine. Its most noteworthy contribution these days tends to be wines produced from the **Torrontés** and **Moscatel** grapes. Problems with a steady flow of irrigation have made consistently successful wine production in La Rioja rather difficult in recent years.

As Argentina's second largest wine-producing region, **San Juan**, wedged in between La Rioja to the north and Mendoza to the south, contains approximately 49,000 ha of land under vine. The climate, to say the least, is hot. Temperatures in the summer frequently climb as high as 42°C (107°F), and rainfall amounts to little more than 150 mm (6 inches) annually. San Juan is known for production of wines that provide the foundations for Brandies and Vermouths. In addition, it also produces grapes that are used in concentrated must and Sherry-style fortified wines. The indigenous **Cereza**, a pink-skinned grape, thrives here, and is used mostly for blending, due to its high sugar content, or the production of table wines. It should be noted, however, that during the last few years, San Juan has become a region where winemakers are consciously lowering yields and production levels in pursuit of higher quality and more individualistic wines. Some of the new, experimental varieties being planted include **Chardonnay** and the warmer climate grapes **Syrah** and **Viognier**.

Nestled next to the eastern foothills of the Andes lies **Mendoza**, the largest most significant wine-producing region in Argentina. It produces approximately 75% of the nation's wine and is responsible for 95% of all exports. More than 1,000 registered wineries call Mendoza home. At present, the most recent statistics claim approximately 160,000 ha of land under vine, which is down substantially from the 1980 figure of 255,000 ha. The reduction is clearly a reflection of the overall national goal of reducing the sizes of vineyards and crop yields in favor of more focused, carefully crafted wines. The soil type in Mendoza is generally loose, sandy and alluvial. The climate is considered to be continental, with four distinct seasons and without the inherent disadvantage of extreme temperatures. Rain levels are moderate, with the annual average hovering around 200 mm (8 inches), but water supplies are plentiful, should a lack of rainfall necessitate irrigation. Summer temperatures do reach levels of 36°C (97°F), which is substantial, but grape growers take special pains to minimize the effects of sustained heat upon the fruit, with devices such as long rows of trees in the vineyards providing the grapes with relief from the sun. Many grape varieties are planted in Mendoza, the most important being **Malbec**, which is capable of producing long-lived, complex, and full-bodied red wine worthy of its renowned international reputation. Other varieties include **Chardonnay, Pinot Noir, Tempranillo** and **Sangiovese.**

While Mendoza is known for its increasing production of export quality wine, it is worth mentioning that approximately half of all plantings are of thinner-skinned pink grapes, such as **Cereza** and **Criolla Grande**, grown for the purposes of grape concentrate and inexpensive table wine production.

**Río Negro** and **Neuquén** lie to the south of Mendoza and the Colorado River. The region is significantly cooler than the higher yielding areas to the north and is home to vineyards with 4,400 ha under vine, essentially all in the eastern province of **Río Negro**. Traditionally, the region is known for being the fruit-growing center of Argentina, specializing in apples. The cool climate and chalky soils have encouraged the cultivation white grape varieties such as **Torrentés Riojano, Semillon** and **Sauvignon Blanc**, which thrive in cooler conditions. It is widely regarded as an up and coming region to watch.

# CALIFORNIA

| AREA UNDER VINE | 473,311 acres | 191,542 hectares |
|---|---|---|
| GRAPE VARIETIES | | |
| RED | Cabernet Sauvignon, Merlot, Pinot Noir, Sangiovese, Syrah, and Zinfandel | |
| WHITE | Chardonnay, Gewürztraminer, Pinot Blanc, Pinto Gris, Riesling, Sauvignon Blanc, Viognier | |
| CLIMATE | The climate varies from the southernmost winemaking regions to the areas far north. Understanding California's climate is not as intuitive as one would images. While the Pacific Ocean is a strong moderator for vineyards near the coast, the state's and numerous mountain ranges create a more continental climate for vines further inland. The northern wine-growing regions tend to receive more rainfall annually, while the yearly totals decrease as one moves south. Winter freezes rarely occur, while spring frosts pose the greatest threat to vineyards. | |
| SOIL | Soil types are as equally diverse as the climates in the grape-growing regions, although loamy soils are found throughout every major wine region. | |

# HISTORY

In the 18th century, Jesuit monks of the Franciscan Order, under the leadership of Father Junipero Serra, established Catholic missions all along the coast of what is now known as California. At that time the area was still a colony of Spain. The monks brought with them Vitis vinifera vines that descended from those of their mother country. The most widely planted grape was called **Criolla** by the missionaries. It is related most closely to the **Pais** of Chile, which is known simply as **Mission** in present day California.

In 1821, Mexico won its independence from Spain, and California became a province of Mexico. Under Mexican rule, the Franciscan missions were gradually secularized under the supervision of General Mariano Vallejo. Large land grants were parceled out by Vallejo—some to himself and his family and some to immigrants arriving in the area. A settler from Missouri named George Yount was granted land in 1836. He called the land Rancho Caymus, which is now the site of Napa Valley's most prestigious appellations.

A Frenchman and cooper named Jean Louis Vignes brought Vitis vinifera cuttings from his native Bordeaux with him when he settled near Los Angeles in the 1830s.

Many notable names arrived in the Golden State in the 1850s and 1860s, including Charles Krug (not related to the Krugs of Champagne), Joseph Schram (Schramsberg), Gustave Niebaum (Inglenook), and Hamilton Crabb, who established the famous To-Kalon vineyard and nursery that is now an important source for the Mondavi Reserve wines. One particularly colorful character to arrive on the scene at this time was the self-styled Count Agoston Haraszthy of Hungary. Haraszthy established the Buena Vista winery in Sonoma in 1856 after earlier attempts to grow grapes in Wisconsin and San Diego. Although his wines were soon winning prizes at the California State Fair, he insisted that California wine would never become truly great unless the Mission grape was replaced with more noble varieties. Haraszthy obtained a commission from the governor to tour Europe and study its vines and wine-making practices. The Count returned with 100,000 vines, however, many of them unfortunately did not survive the journey and those that did were hopelessly mislabeled. Haraszthy was also destitute from his extended trip, and he left California for Nicaragua to start a sugar plantation where he was devoured by an alligator.

Another arrival from the East arrived in California in the 1860s—the phylloxera louse. Phylloxera had withered all attempts to grow Vitis vinifera vines in the eastern United States. The pest was positively identified in 1873, but its impact was not truly felt until the late 1880s. Most producers were too busy supplying the increasing demand for their wines created by the newly laid transcontinental railway and the sharp decrease in European imports to worry about a little louse. The industry continued to expand during this time, and many famous estates such as Château Montelena, Mayacamas, Simi, Ridge, Christian Brothers, and Beaulieu were founded in the 1880s and 1890s. Once Phylloxera took hold, infested vineyards were replanted with vines grafted onto the native Vitis californica rootstocks recommended by agricultural specialists of the era. However, by the time it was discovered that this was not a resistant rootstock, the plague was in full swing. The St. George du Lot rootstock that had been developed in France was introduced in 1897, just in time to prevent total devastation. On the positive side, the Mission grape was rarely replanted. Instead **Zinfandel, Sylvaner, Riesling, Sauvignon Blanc**, and **Cabernet Sauvignon** among others took its place and were planted more densely, often wire-trained in the European manner. More care was also given to matching the grape varieties with areas with the proper climate and soil type. On the negative side, the major replanting was not cheap, and many smaller wineries went out of business as a result.

The industry began to be dominated more and more by the huge California Wine Association (CWA) trust that bought wine and grapes from all over the state and produced more sweet fortified wine than table wine. However, even the CWA could not survive the near-death blow dealt to the California wine industry by Prohibition, which was made a national law in 1920. Prohibition made the production, sale, and transportation of alcohol in the United States illegal until the law was repealed in 1933.

There was a loophole in the 18th Amendment, however, that allowed for the production of sacramental wine and wine used for "medicinal purposes" or for cooking. Many wineries converted their efforts to these kinds of wine to stay in business. Home wine making on a small scale was also allowed. California grapes were shipped all over the country, sometimes whole, but also in the form of wine "bricks" to supply the homes with wine grapes. The "bricks" were often shipped with a yeast tablet and a warning to avoid contact between the tablet and the grape must, as it could lead to fermentation (oops!).

The American palate and attitude towards wine was also damaged by Prohibition. Most bathtub gin tasted better than the crude wine produced in the average family basement. The low-quality grapes or wine bricks shipped from California made wine that was highly tannic and needed fortification to retain its sweetness. Cocktails, rather than wine, became the drink of choice in chic urban speakeasies. Following the repeal of Prohibition in 1933, many states chose to remain dry. (Mississippi repealed its prohibition on alcohol in 1966.) Most of them adopted complicated laws about liquor sales and distribution meant to control and discourage the industry that still exist today. The wineries that had survived were often in complete disarray. Barrels were rotten, pumps and tanks were rusty and infected with bacteria, and pocketbooks were stretched to their limit by years of limited or no revenue. America was also in the depths of the Great Depression, and outside investors with money for new equipment were scarce. A few estates such as Beaulieu and Inglenook had managed to hold on and released older vintages that were well received by those with the money to buy them. All but 212 of the newest wineries were out of business within four years, except for a few notable holdouts such as Martin Ray on Mt. Eden and for a time John Daniels at Inglenook. California wine was again dominated by the corporate giants that had money enough to weather the storm. Big distillers such as Seagram, Hiram Walker, Schenley, and National owned the majority of wineries in the 1940s. They recapitalized the industry but also strengthened the American perception of wine as booze.

E&J Gallo, which successfully grew grapes during Prohibition, and United Vintners, the marketing arm of a huge cooperative and the owners of the Old Italian Swiss Colony estate, dominated the industry in the 1950s and 1960s. Although originally producers of table wine, their production became more and more focused on fortified wines made popular by the "misery market". Gallo introduced Thunderbird—a white "port" flavored with lemon concentrate—in 1955. Gallo also produced "Hearty Burgundy" which, while it had little in common with wine from the Cote d'Or, was better than most table wine being produced on a large scale anywhere in the world. Other bright spots were the wines made by Andre Tchelistcheff at Beaulieu, particularly the Georges de la Tour reserve wines named after the founder of the estate, and the Charles Krug reds made by the Mondavi family, who purchased the Krug winery in 1943. Tchelistcheff remained at Beaulieu for 35 years and was a major force in the steady improvement of California wine until his death in 1994. The sons of Cesare Mondavi worked together at Krug until 1966, when a family dispute about the direction of their company resulted in Robert Mondavi being forced out of the firm.

In 1967, he built his own distinctive winery right on the main road of Napa Valley, creating not just another wine making facility, but a major tourist destination. Mondavi was not the only producer in the 1960s experimenting with French oak barrels, small lot production, and variety labeling in an attempt to make world-class wine in California. Robert Mondavi was the first to attempt it on a large scale. His sales and success at selling the "wine lifestyle" to America triggered a flood of wineries to join him in the 1970s and 1980s.

Many of these newcomers had made their money in corporate America and bought land in Napa and Sonoma as a tax shelter or a weekend retreat only to discover the remains of a pre-Prohibition winery or an overgrown vineyard on their property. Others were hippies and "back to the landers" looking for a simpler life. Most of them knew virtually nothing about making wine, and therefore they turned to the University of California at Davis for help. Maynard Amerine and Albert Winkler had been studying the winemaking process and the vineyards of California in their laboratory at U.C. Davis since the 1930s. In 1938, they created a **heat summation map** of the state that divided it into five regions, based on the number of **degree-days** between April $1^{st}$ and October $31^{st}$ in the area. (For further detail, see the section on major wine regions.) Winkler and Amerine admitted that it was a crude measurement in that it did not allow for factors like humidity, exposure, wind, fog, etc. Nevertheless, most producers used it to decide which grapes to plant in their vineyards. Producers also looked to Davis for advice about pruning and vinification. The university's advice tended to err on the side of increased production and highly controlled–wine making that produced sound, if not exalted wines. Even so, most of America's finest wine makers got their training at U.C. Davis and were soon joined by students from all over the world, including the sons and daughter of some of the most esteemed wine estates of the Old World.

Perhaps the biggest misjudgment made by U.C. Davis was its promotion of AXR-1 as a superior rootstock for grafting. Although it allowed for greater yields than the old St. George used prior to Prohibition, it proved to be less resistant to phylloxera, in particular Biotype B. In the late 1980s nearly everyone had followed Davis' advice to replant with AXR-1 and many vineyards were damaged. Although devastating for some small wineries, phylloxera again provided an opportunity for improvements. Replantation of the best sites was governed more by the nature of individual microclimates rather than by the current rage for Chardonnay or Merlot. Often vines were planted more densely to maintain the overall yield, but the yields of each vine were reduced to improve quality.

Better clones of the most popular grapes and experiments with lesser-known varieties have diversified California's vineyards, making them less vulnerable to widespread disease. Unfortunately, clonal selection has not been successful in combating another disease that is having an increasing impact in California. Pierce's Disease, named after Newton Pierce who discovered it had no cure in 1891, is a bacterium that damages the water-carrying structure of vines, causing them to die. The disease is carried by the insect known as the blue-green sharpshooter that is especially attracted to blackberry bushes and other brush that grow along rivers and woodlands. The insect feeds on the bushes and then infects vineyards. Young vines are especially susceptible, and the replantation brought about by phylloxera combined with a series of mild winters, may have added to the recent outbreak of Pierce's Disease. Experimentation with insecticides, clearing of nearby brush, and the plantation of evergreens are all being tried to combat this latest invader.

In the 1990s, world-class California wine became the rule rather than the exception. There are hundreds of boutique wineries—small and large—throughout the state, and prices on the world market have never been higher. The full, fruity early-drinking style that dominates California's production has been imitated all over the world and has influenced even some of the oldest and most esteemed wine regions. International joint ventures such as Opus One (Mondavi and Baron Philippe de Rothschild) and "flying wine makers" such as Michel Rolland, who hails from Bordeaux but is consultant in California and around the world, have become common. Hopefully, the internationalization of the wine community will not homogenize it, but instead will create a dialogue between traditionalists and proponents of the New World "California-style" that will prove beneficial to all.

# WINE LAWS

With the passage of the Homelands Security Act in 2002, the governing of wine laws was transferred from the jurisdiction of the Bureau of Alcohol, Tobacco, and Firearms (BATF) to the Tax and Trade Bureau (TTB) of the Treasury Department. The BATF's responsibilities with regards to firearms, explosives, arson, and criminal enforcement were transferred to the Justice Department.

In the United States, the American Viticultural Area (AVA) system was introduced by the BATF in 1978. Unlike the European AOC laws, the AVA system is not designed to ensure or even recognize quality. As defined by the BATF, an AVA is "a delimited grape growing region distinguished by geographic features, the boundaries of which have been recognized and defined." This departs dramatically from the appellation laws that exist in Europe. There are no laws that currently oversee yields, minimum alcohol levels, permitted grape varieties, etc.

Augusta, Missouri became the first AVA in 1980. All AVAs, which are also referred to as appellations, must be recognized and defined by the TTB. Anyone may petition the TTB for a rule change. Petitioners must show two things:

evidence that the name of the proposed viticultural area is locally or nationally known and evidence relating to the geographical features which distinguish the proposed area from surrounding environs.

Petitioning criteria requires that specific boundaries be shown on U.S. Government survey maps, plus information regarding climate, elevation, soil type, physical features, and similar growing conditions within proposed area. Boundary lines cannot be used.

## Labeling

The TTB laws that govern terms on California wine labels are as follows:

**Variety-labeled** wines must be comprised of at least 75% of the named grape. Prior to 1983, only 51% of the named grape was required. If a wine is an AVA specific bottling, the variety listed must comprise 85% of the blend.

**Estate-bottled** wines must be made by wineries that own or control all the vineyards where the grapes are grown. The winery and vineyards must all be located within the same AVA. The winery crushes, ferments, finishes, ages, and bottles the wine in a continuous process.

**Vintage-labeled** wines must be made from 95% of the wine from the vintage indicated.

**AVA-designated** wines must be made from 85% of grapes from the AVA indicated.

**Vineyard-designated** wines must be comprised of 95% of grapes from the specific vineyard listed.

Additional label requirements include the following:

- Every wine must be labeled with a brand name,
- The bottler's name and location must be named,
- Health warning must be listed,
- Pregnant women/birth defects warning listed,
- Machine operator/impaired motor skills warning listed,
- Sulfite content (10 ppm or more),
- Alcohol content stated with a tolerance of 1.5%, and
- The phrase "Table Wine" may be used for wine with a minimum 7%-14% maximum alcohol.

## Meritage (MEHR-ih-tihj)

For a wine to be designated a Meritage—a certification mark registered with the U.S. Department of Trademarks and Patents—it must meet the following standards:

- It must be a blend of two or more Bordeaux grape varieties. For reds—Cabernet Sauvignon, Merlot, Cabernet Franc, Malbec, and Petit Verdot—and for whites—Sauvignon Blanc, Sémillon, and Muscadelle.
- No more than 90% of any single variety may go into a Meritage wine.
- It must be the winery's best wine of its type.
- Its production is limited to a maximum of 25,000 cases per vintage.
- It must be produced and bottled by a U.S. winery from grapes that carry a U.S. appellation.

# Geography, Climate, and Soil

The State of California is, for the most part, a two-season Mediterranean climate with hot dry summers, mild winters, and loads of sunshine. What distinguishes the wine regions of California from the rest of the state is their many microclimates. A series of mountain chains running parallel to the coast creates valleys that trap the fog and cool breezes blowing in from the Pacific Ocean, while offering protection from rain and the strongest winds. These cool valleys are perfect for preserving acidity and aromatics in the grapes planted there. Varieties that need more heat and sunshine to ripen fully can be planted on the higher elevations above the fog line and still benefit from the cool evenings and long growing seasons of the mountains that add to their complexity.

An important (though not complete) descriptor of a region's climate is its **heat summation classification** based on the number of **degree-days** in each growing season. An area's heat summation classification is calculated by multiplying a month's average temperature above 50°F by the number of days in the month, x 7 (April-October). The five possible classifications are as follows:

| Region | Degree-days | Notes |
| --- | --- | --- |
| Region I | < 2,500 | Recommended for dry table wines with light to medium body and good natural balance |
| Region II | 2,500–3,000 | Recommended for dry table wines with light to medium body and good natural balance |
| Region III | 3,000–3,500 | Best for full-bodied dry table wines and sweet wines |
| Region IV | 3,500–4,000 | Best for fortified wines |
| Region V | >4,000 | Should only produce raisins |

The soil types in the various regions of California are quite diverse and will be discussed in connection with the specific wine-growing regions.

## VARIETIES

California wines are normally identified by grape variety rather than by style or region. California is home to many varieties which will be covered in greater depth when pertaining to a particular AVA. Listed below are some statistics regarding the more prominent varieties.

**Chardonnay** is the most widely planted white grape with 95,000 acres (38,500 hectares) under vine.

**Sauvignon Blanc** or **Fumé-Blanc** is the variety Mondavi capitalized on due to the market's familiarity with Pouilly Fumé from the Loire.

The first plantings of **Viognier,** the Rhône native, were in 1983 by Josh Jensen of Calera.

**Riesling** is made in a low-alcohol, residual-sugar fashion that has been defining the American palette.

Historically it turns out that California's early plantings of **Pinot Blanc** were in fact the **Melon de Bourgogne** grape or members of the **Muscadet** family.

**Pinot Gris** is found in California but it is made more successfully in Oregon in the Alsatian manner.

**Zinfandel** plantings are significant at 50,000 acres (20,000 hectares), and it is the closest thing to a native variety in California. It has been found to be genetically equivalent to the Croatian grape **Crljenak Kaštelanski**. Much of this acreage is used in the production of **White Zinfandel,** a semi-sweet "blush" wine that became the rage among wine drinkers in the 1980s.

**Cabernet Sauvignon** had just 600 acres under vine in 1961, but by 2000, the variety covered 76,000 acres (31,000 hectares) of land.

Though it seems like the **Merlot** craze has been going on forever, the grape is in fact a fairly recent arrival in California viticulture. Merlot's susceptibility to rot and frost made it unpopular with the oenologists at U.C. Davis, and for many years it was not recommended for plantation by the university. Louis Martini released the first varietyly labeled Merlot in 1969. As recently as 1986, there were only 2,881 acres planted, but by 1998, there were 38,000. Currently there are approximately 44,000 acres (18,000 hectares) of Merlot in California.

**Pinot Noir** has been an obsession for many California wine makers. It is highly revered and highly elusive. Unlike Cabernet Sauvignon that allows for a certain margin of error in the vineyard and the winery, Pinot Noir is sensitive to the slightest variation in climate, soil, and technique. It has been planted in California since the late 19th century.

It is unclear when **Syrah** arrived in California, as early plantings were sometimes mistaken for the only related Petite Sirah. In 1986 there were only 119 acres of true Syrah planted, but by 1997, that number had increased to 4,277. As of 2009 there was more than 19,000 acres (8,000 hectares) of Syrah planted.

**Petite Sirah** is most closely related to the Durif grape from France, which is a cross between Syrah and Peloursin. This unique variety has caused some confusion over the course of its long history in California. Many vines thought to be Petite Sirah were found upon further testing to be true Syrah, other Rhône varieties, and even Pinot Noir! Advanced DNA testing is helping to clear up the confusion, but many strains of what may or may not be Petite Sirah still exist in California.

**Grenache** historically has produced high alcohol–bearing wines that were nothing compared to their Rhône cousins, however in the last 30 years many wine makers in the hot, drier areas of the central valley have had great success with the grape.

**Mourvèdre**, also known as Mataro, is a favored booster for the Zins from Paul Draper's vineyards at Ridge. Some of the vines in California are older than any found in Bandol.

**Cinsault** and **Carignan** are usually used for blending.

Italian varieties (Cal-Italians) have also been in and out of fashion over the years. **Sangiovese**, **Nebbiolo**, and **Barbera** have all been grown and produced quality wines with varying success with consumers.

## MAJOR WINE REGIONS

All of the aforementioned climatic and geographical factors combine to create the many distinct wine regions that are beginning to be recognized by the American Viticultural Area system. County names such as **Monterey** or **Santa Barbara** will be used in this discussion to describe general areas, and significant AVAs will be covered in some detail within each county listing.

# Napa Valley
## The North Coast

| Area Under Vine | 45,275 acres | 18,322 hectares |
|---|---|---|
| Grape Varieties | | |
| Red | Cabernet Sauvignon, Merlot, Pinot Noir, Sangiovese, Zinfandel, Petit Verdot, Cabernet Franc, Petite Sirah, Syrah | |
| White | Chardonnay, Sauvignon Blanc, Pinot Gris, Viognier | |
| Climate | Warmer and rainier during the growing season in the north, cooler and drier as you travel southward, with several microclimates in between. Moderated by mountains and the Pacific Ocean, Napa has warm, sunny days and cool nights. Fog influences the climate closer to San Pablo Bay. | |
| Soil | Varied | |

Napa is both the name of a county and the regions included within the general **Napa Valley AVA**. This famous vineyard area is relatively quite small—the main valley (which contains most of the major growing areas) is 30 miles long and only 5 miles across at its widest point. Small as it may be, Napa is home to approximately 400 brick and mortar wineries and closer to 700 total producers (all producers do not necessarily own their own winery, but can rent space for production).

The Napa Valley is an uplifted ancient seabed that stretches from the mouth of the Napa River at the San Pablo Bay near San Francisco to Calistoga and Mount St. Helena in the north. Repeated flooding of this seabed over the course of millions of years has created a complex layering of sedimentary soils. Volcanic soil—that characterizes the still-active hillsides—has been carried down the slopes by tributaries to the Napa River, forming alluvial fans that add further interest and diversity to the valley's soil types, which number about 150. Temperatures rise as one moves to north in Napa, away from the fog and cooling breezes of San Pablo Bay; however, the warmer temps are mitigated somewhat by the higher elevations of the northern towns like Calistoga and the cool air that enters the northern part of the valley from the Russian River.

Napa represents 4% of California's total wine production. The region has more than 45,000 acres under vine, with the price of one acre starting at $150,000. Property can reach prices of $1 million per acre or more.

## Valley Floor Appellations

The 1990s saw a grower-supported movement to divide the valley floor into sub-appellations named after its major towns, reminiscent of Bordeaux's Haut-Médoc region. This effort was abandoned when replanting phylloxera-damaged vineyards became more pressing. Some regions became AVAs while others remain without the designation. Nonetheless, the town names provide a good basis on which to organize a discussion of the region.

Approved in early 2010 after years of deliberation and debate, **Calistoga** is the newest AVA in Napa Valley. The area around Calistoga can be 10–20°F warmer than the town of Napa during the day, though cool night air from the Russian River Valley helps extend the area's growing season and maintain enough acidity in the fruit to balance its ripeness. Gravelly soils of volcanic origin found here keep yields low and add interest to the **Cabernet Sauvignon** that dominates the vineyards. Calistoga produces particularly powerful and concentrated wines from Zinfandel, Syrah, and Petite Sirah, in addition to the aforementioned Cabernet Sauvignon.

**St. Helena** became an AVA in 1995. It is a few miles south of Calistoga on Highway 29. St. Helena is a touch cooler than Calistoga but is still primarily red grape territory. The AVA's wines are known for their elegance. **Zinfandel** and **Petite Sirah** do particularly well here, in addition to the Bordeaux and Rhône reds.

The next region to the south, **Rutherford**, received its AVA designation in 1993. Originally, Rutherford was to be divided into two appellations, Rutherford and Rutherford Bench. **Rutherford Bench** is an alluvial fan than runs along the western side of the valley and produces some of Napa's most prestigious wines. Although it is called the Rutherford Bench, this alluvial fan actually extends from St. Helena through Rutherford and Oakville into Yountville. Considered in its entirety, the Bench contains some of the most prized vineyards in Napa. Rutherford is a fairly large appellation that includes 6,800 acres surrounding the town, only 3,300 of which are planted with vineyards.

**Oakville AVA** is a large appellation south of Rutherford that includes sections of the Bench (Martha's Vineyard and To-Kalon) and sandier sections along the Napa River. Like its northern neighbors, Oakville is primarily **Cabernet Sauvignon** country, but the morning fog that lingers a bit longer and the occasional cool breeze that manages to reach the area from the San Pablo Bay enables good quality **Chardonnay**, **Sauvignon Blanc**, and **Sangiovese** to be produced here as well. There has been a movement among Oakville growers to designate an Oakville Bench along the lines of the Rutherford Bench, but so far nothing has come of it.

**Yountville** was designated an AVA in 1999 and encompasses roughly 8,000 acres of land, of which about 50% are planted to vineyards. This area is the historic heart of viticulture in Napa Valley, as George Yount planted the first vines here in 1836. Yountville is significantly impacted by the maritime influences of the San Pablo Bay. The region is considered somewhat marginal for **Cabernet Sauvignon**. **Chardonnay** does very well in this slightly cooler region and both **Crichton Hall** and **Domaine Chandon** are located within the Yountville district.

**Stags Leap AVA** sounds like it should be a hillside designation, but it is in fact located on the valley floor to the east of Yountville. The area earned its AVA status in 1989 and took its name from the rocky palisades of lower Atlas Peak that hang over the eastern part of the vineyards. These basalt palisades counteract the fog and cool nights typical of Napa's southern sections by reflecting heat onto the vineyards below during the day and retaining warmth through the night. As a result, Stags Leap can be up to 10 degrees warmer than Yountville to the west. This effect allows the **Cabernet Sauvignon**—for which the region is justly famous—to ripen fully.

**Oak Knoll District of Napa Valley** was granted its AVA designation in 2002. Located in the southern end of Napa, it encompasses 8,300 acres of land, including 3,500 acres of vineyards. Known as one the coolest AVAs in Napa, the appellation is gaining a reputation for **Cabernet Sauvignon, Merlot, Pinot Noir**, and **Chardonnay**. Due to low rainfall and substantial sunlight, the soil in Oak Knoll retains warmth well and allows for one of the longest growing seasons in the valley.

Established in 1983, **Los Carneros AVA** is shared with Sonoma County. In Napa it is the coolest, driest appellation and also the furthest south. Carneros is strongly influenced by the fog and cooling breezes coming from San Pablo Bay, and is well-known for Chardonnay, Pinot Noir, and some sleek Merlots.

**Wild Horse Valley** became an AVA in 1988. It lies on a plateau at about 1,000 feet above sea level, just to the east of Carneros. The appellation covers 3,300 acres in both Napa and Solano counties, though only about 100 acres are planted. Though still affected by moderating breezes from the ocean, Wild Horse Valley is warmer than its neighbors to the west. Cabernet Sauvignon, Sangiovese, and Chardonnay are the principal varieties here.

The most recent AVA in Napa Valley—**Coombsville**—was approved in late 2011 and made official in January 2012. The AVA is located at the southern end of the valley east of the City of Napa and encompasses just over 11,000 acres of land (approximately 1,400 of which are planted to grapes). Also influenced by the nearby San Pablo Bay, Coombsville is only slightly warmer on average than Carneros. Currently Cabernet Sauvignon is the most planted variety though Merlot, Cabernet Franc, Syrah and the cool-climate Chardonnay and Pinot Noir can also be found here.

## Mountain Appellations

The mountain ranges that flank the Napa Valley to the east and west are characterized by a longer growing season, cool days, and somewhat warmer nights. The volcanic soil near the top of the ridges lies on a base of bedrock that makes planting and irrigation difficult, keeping yields low. These conditions tend to create smaller berries than those found on the valley floor, and Napa's mountain wines can be quite tannic and intense. The Mayacamas ridge is more heavily wooded and receives more rainfall than dry, craggy Howell Mountain; the wines tend to be a little softer and lighter, though, from the best producers, just as ageworthy.

**The Mayacamas Range** runs along the western boundary of Napa County, separating it from Sonoma. From north to south it is divided into the several ranges.

**Diamond Mountain** became an AVA in 2001. The appellation covers 5,000 acres, with only 500 acres of land under vine. **Cabernet Sauvignon** and **Cabernet Franc** dominate plantings.

**Spring Mountain** earned its AVA designation in 1993. The appellation has approximately 1,000 acres under vine and encompasses a variety of microclimates, allowing a variety of grapes to be grown here—**Cabernet Sauvignon, Merlot, Zinfandel, Chardonnay,** and **Viognier** among them. In general, Spring Mountain is cooler than Diamond Mountain to the north.

**Mount Veeder** became an AVA in 1990 and currently has about 1,000 acres under vine. Vineyards are planted at altitudes ranging from 600–2,400 feet, meaning that many of them are above the fog line. The AVA has a Region I–II classification, with cool daytime temperatures and warmer nighttime conditions. **Cabernet Sauvignon** and **Chardonnay** dominate plantings (Cabernet Sauvignon accounts for nearly 65% of all vineyards), with smaller amounts of **Malbec, Merlot, Syrah, Cabernet Franc,** and **Viognier** (among others).

**Howell Mountain** became Napa's first nested AVA in 1984. Situated across the valley from Diamond and Spring Mountains, Howell Mountain was identified as an excellent site for red wines as early as the 19th century. The area receives significantly less rain than the Mayacamas Range and irrigation is common. The combination of the stony volcanic soil and cool weather keeps yields low. The vineyards in the AVA that are dry-farmed yield only about one ton of fruit per acre. Vines are planted at elevations ranging from 600–2,200 feet above sea level. **Cabernet Sauvignon** and **Zinfandel** dominate the plantings, but **Merlot** is becoming more prevalent. Some rather austere **Chardonnay** and Viognier are produced in the area as well.

**Atlas Peak AVA** lies south of Howell Mountain on the east side of the southern section of Napa Valley. The appellation spans 11,400 acres, with only 1,500 of these planted, and is home to only a few wineries.

The winery Atlas Peak, which is partly owned by Marchese Piero Antinori, is particularly committed to growing Sangiovese.

## Associated Appellations

When Napa Valley was designated an AVA in 1981, **Chiles Valley** and **Pope Valley** insisted on inclusion in the appellation because of the regions' history as grape growers from some Napa estates. The climatic conditions are quite different in the two eastern valleys, located on the other side of Howell Mountain and Atlas Peak. Chiles and Pope Valleys are hot regions because they are blocked from benefiting from cooling maritime influences of the Pacific Ocean. Both valleys have short growing seasons that are appropriate for only the heartiest red grapes, such as Zinfandel and Sangiovese.

# SONOMA COUNTY
## THE NORTH COAST

| AREA UNDER VINE | 60,300 acres | 24,400 hectares |
|---|---|---|
| GRAPE VARIETIES | | |
| RED | Cabernet Sauvignon, Merlot, Pinot Noir, Zinfandel | |
| WHITE | Chardonnay, Sauvignon Blanc | |
| CLIMATE | Sunny days and little rain during the growing season. Like Napa, moderated by maritime influence from the Pacific. | |
| SOIL | Varied | |

Sonoma County is one of California's largest coastal counties and contains many AVAs, which often overlap each another. In Sonoma, far more grapes are grown than in Napa County in much more diverse conditions. The region has always been made up of a patchwork of relatively small growers, many of them European immigrants, rather than a series of grand estates, like in Napa. Italian families, in particular, have a long history in the county and many Italian names like Sebastiani, Rochioli, and Foppiano are associated with wineries and vineyards to this day. Part of the legacy of these early settlers is the old-vine **Zinfandel**, **Carignan**, and **Petite Sirah** found in plots throughout Sonoma. The Russians were early settlers in the region as well, giving their name to the Russian River that flows through the northern portion of the county. Historically, many of these growers sold their wine or grapes in bulk to cooperatives in the Central Valley or to the Italian Swiss Colony at Asti. The practice of estate bottling and proliferation of large-scale producers are fairly recent phenomenon.

The **Sonoma Valley AVA** is situated in the historic heartland of Sonoma viticulture. The Franciscan's Sonoma Mission was located here, as was Count Agoston Haraszthy's Buena Vista estate. Unlike the Napa Valley AVA, which includes most of Napa County and is used almost interchangeably with the county name, Sonoma Valley is a 25 mile-long strip that is eight miles at its widest. The valley stretches across the center section of the southern half of the county and is separated from Napa by the Mayacamas Mountains.

Like in Napa Valley, breezes from the San Pablo Bay cool the southern sections of the region while temperatures rise to the north. The hottest sections of the Sonoma Valley are around Glen Ellen and Kenwood. The northernmost regions on the outskirts of Santa Rosa get some relief from the heat thanks to the Pacific breezes that flow through the Petaluma Gap. The soil types in this crescent-shaped valley—once known as Valley of the Moon—are quite varied and range from sand and gravel to shale and oceanic sediment. The appellation is home to about 30 wineries with wine makers and growers that produce the full gamut of wines.

**Sonoma Mountain AVA** is a 5,000 acre subappellation of the Sonoma Valley AVA.

The AVA applies to a section of the Sonoma Mountains that runs along the western side of Sonoma County. The lowest vineyards of Sonoma Mountain are planted at altitudes of 400–600 feet on the east side, with the majority of plantings between 1,200–1,600 feet on the west side. Higher elevations prolong the growing season and allow for more even temperatures than on the valley floor. **Cabernet Sauvignon** and **Zinfandel** do well above the fog line, as does **Chardonnay**. Like Napa's mountain appellations, grapes planted on the volcanic and gravel-rich soil of Sonoma Mountain often make well-structured age-worthy wines.

The **Sonoma Coast AVA** is an enormous region, covering 480,000 acres. The appellation includes not only all of Sonoma's coastal vineyards—from its border with Marin County in the south to Mendocino in the north—but also reaches into inland sites already included under other appellations. The AVA includes part of the following appellations: **Chalk Hill, Green Valley, Carneros, Sonoma Valley**, and **Russian River Valley**. Sonoma-Cutrer was one of the biggest supporters of the creation of this AVA, partially because it allowed them to use grapes from many areas and still label their wines as estate bottled. The Sonoma Coast AVA does contain some interesting sites that often are so cool that they barely qualify for Region I classification. Producers in Sonoma Coast claim that the region has the longest hang-time of any California appellation, enabling them to produce the very good quality **Chardonnay** and **Pinot Noir** that is coming out of the AVA.

Late in 2011 the TTB approved two new AVAs that are sub-AVAs of the much larger Sonoma Coast: Fort Ross-Seaview and Pine Mountain-Cloverdale Peak.

The most significant defining characteristic of the **Fort Ross-Seaview AVA** is its elevation, which at approximately 900 feet or higher places the vineyards *above* the fog line. At this altitude the grapes receive more sunlight and warmth than those in the lower surrounding regions that spend a significant amount of time under a blanket of fog. The appellation became official in January 2012.

**Pine Mountain-Cloverdale Peak AVA** overlaps Sonoma and Mendocino Counties. Here, the elevation is even higher than Fort Ross Seaview, with most grapes being grown at 1,800 feet or higher. This altitude has a big impact on climate factors from temperature to sunlight to precipitation and wind. Most vineyards are small and planted on steep slopes. The rugged terrain offers many different microclimates that in turn create a diverse array of wines.

**Northern Sonoma AVA** is an appellation covering areas throughout Sonoma County. The appellation was created at the behest of Gallo.

**Sonoma County AVA** is a 32,000 acre appellation that is part of the Russian River Valley. Due to its close proximity to the Pacific Ocean, the area has a very cool Region I classification. It is ideally suited for growing **Chardonnay** and **Pinot Noir**, which is used in sparkling wine production.

**Russian River Valley AVA** takes its name from the Russian River that runs through the northern portion of Sonoma Country. The river is named after the Russian fur traders who were among the first settlers in the area. There were approximately 200 wineries in the region by the late-19th-century, most of which did not survive the double blows of phylloxera and Prohibition. Most of the Russian River Valley AVA is fairly cool. The area has a Region I classification and experiences persistent morning fog. It is becoming well known for **Chardonnay** and **Pinot Noir**. However, the northern one-third of the AVA is warmer and therefore is planted with **Zinfandel** and other red varieties on its western side. The northeastern section of the appellation, Chalk Hill, has its own AVA, as does Green Valley, a small section in the south.

**Chalk Hill AVA** lies in the northeastern section of the Russian River AVA. Not surprisingly, Chalk Hill Winery was instrumental in the creation of this appellation. The strange thing about the AVAs name is that there is in fact no chalk on Chalk Hill. The soil does appear white, however, it is comprised of volcanic ash rather than limestone chalk. Vineyards on the hill are above the fog line and therefore warmer than those on the valley floor to the south, which have Region II status. **Chardonnay** dominates but **Sauvignon Blanc, Merlot**, and **Cabernet Sauvignon** are also grown in the area.

**Green Valley AVA** is located in the southwestern portion of the Russian River AVA.

The appellation is known for its high-acid **Chardonnay** and **Pinot Noir**. The acidity levels in the grapes are very attractive to sparkling-wine producers who have settled in the area.

**Dry Creek Valley AVA** lies to the north and west of the Russian River Valley.

It is a narrow valley that is protected from fog by coastal mountains. Overall the AVA is warmer than its southwestern neighbor, with Region II–III temperatures. Although its name would imply an arid climate, rainfall averages are slightly higher here than in other areas of the county, making dry farming an option. These features made Dry Creek Valley attractive to Italian immigrants who were growing grapes in the area before widespread irrigation came into practice at the end of the 19th century. Some of the **Zinfandel, Carignan**, and **Petite Sirah** they planted remain in production today. The region's soil, Dry Creek Conglomerate, predominates on the benchlands above the sometimes wet Dry Creek. It is a reddish, rocky soil that provides excellent drainage for the mostly red varieties planted in it. Some white varieties are grown here as well. **Sauvignon Blanc** and, less successfully, **Chardonnay** are planted on the fertile alluvial soils at the edge of the creek.

**Alexander Valley** became an AVA in 1988. It covers 76,000 acres, of which 15,000 acres is planted to vine. Named after Captain Cyrus Alexander, who planted the first grapes here after the valley was given to him in a land grant by

General Vallejo, the AVA is 20 miles long and 7 miles wide. The valley is minimally affected by fog and ocean breezes and is a warm Region III. The soils are fertile and yields must be kept in check to ensure quality fruit. Seventy-five percent of the total production is red, including significant amounts of Cabernet Sauvignon and Merlot, although white varieties, such as Chardonnay and Sauvignon Blanc, fare well at the higher elevations.

**Knight's Valley** received its AVA designation in 1983. It is a narrow valley that connects northern Sonoma to Napa Valley. The valley floor is quite hot during the day and hearty red varieties dominate. Nights are cooled by the breezes from the Russian River and make plantation of white grapes possible if not ideal. White and more delicate red varieties are having greater success at the upper elevations of the valley. **Chardonnay, Sauvignon Blanc**, and **Pinot Noir** do well in the volcanic soils of the hillsides at 1,100–1,800 feet.

**Rock Pile**, located in northwest Sonoma County, became an AVA in 2002. The appellation's name dates back to 1858 when Rock Pile Ranch was operating in the area.

The AVA covers 15,400 acres covered with rugged rock at elevations close to 800 feet.

The appellation overlaps with the northwest corner of Dry Creek. No wineries exist here, only vineyards constituted of 160 planted acres containing mostly **Zinfandel** with some **Petite Sirah** and **Cabernet Sauvignon**.

**Carneros AVA** covers an area of 8,000 acres, which includes parts of Napa Valley, Sonoma Valley, and Sonoma Coast. Although the region was first planted by relatives of General Vallejo, real development did not begin until the 1960s when Andre Tchelistcheff convinced Beaulieu to plant Chardonnay in Carneros. By the 1980s, Carneros was starting to appear as a designation on the labels of many North Coast producers, and during that decade sparkling wine producers such as Domaine Carneros, Gloria Ferrer, and Codorniu moved in to take advantage of the ripe but high-acid Pinot Noir and Chardonnay grown in the region.

Fog and cool breezes from the nearby San Pablo Bay make this a premium area for **Chardonnay** and **Pinot Noir**. The nearly constant wind that blows over the rolling hillsides helps to prevent springtime frosts that could damage the early-budding vines typical of the area. Some producers have conjectured that this wind also thickens the grape skins and adds complexity to the finished wine. Another advantage of Carneros is that rainfall is low year-round and virtually unheard of during the growing season, making irrigation necessary. The AVAs clay soil keeps yields in check and has led some to believe that the area might we well-suited to growing **Merlot** as well.

# Mendocino
## The North Coast

The mountains which separate Mendocino from its wine-producing neighbors to the south kept the region isolated until the early 20th century. Immigrants planed wine here in the 1860s but most of their produce was consumed locally. The Ukiah Railroad provided some access to outside markets beginning in 1910, but roads in and out of the area were still quite primitive. The area's extended isolation has delayed acceptance of the regional wines by America's mainstream wine-drinking population, however, it has also served to insulate the region from the whims of fashion.

Mendocino is one California's largest and most climatically diverse counties and has two distinct zones—east and west of the Coastal Range Its wine region is composed of a series of inland valleys that range in climate from barely Region I to high Region III. With the exception of the very cool Anderson Valley, Mendocino's valleys are too far inland to benefit from moderating maritime influences and have a more continental climate of hot summers and harsh winters. The best sites are planted on hilltop ridges where elevation can temper the extremes of the valley below. The area contains eight AVAs: Anderson Valley, Mendocino, Mendocino Ridge, Cole Ranch, Potter Valley, Redwood Valley, McDowell Valley, and Yorkville Highlands.

**Anderson Valley AVA** is a chilly, extremely narrow valley that has been formed in Mendocino's western side by the Navarro River that runs through it. The mouth of the Navarro meets the Pacific Ocean to the north of the valley, so unlike Napa and Sonoma Valleys, Anderson is cooler at its northern end. **Riesling** and **Gewürztraminer** get the most consistent results here. The high-acid **Chardonnay** and **Pinot Noir** grown in the upper end of the valley are perfect for producing sparkling wine. Producers, most notably Roederer whose scouts were looking for someplace in California with weather as miserable as Champagne, found it in the Anderson Valley in 1982. Further south along the Navarro towards Boonville, the maritime influence relents, allowing for warmer temperatures and the production of **Sauvignon Blanc** and **Merlot**. The hilltops on the eastern slopes of the valley are especially warm, and were given their own AVA of **Mendocino Ridge** in 1997.

**Mendocino Ridge AVA** covers 262,000 acres but only vineyards at or above an elevation of 1,200 feet are entitled to the appellation. It is the only AVA in the United States with noncontiguous growing areas. Here above the fog line, red varieties such as **Syrah, Zinfandel, Merlo**t, and even **Cabernet Sauvignon** are grown

**Cole Ranch AVA** is located just west of the main highway that follows the Russian River through the center of Mendocino. It is the smallest AVA in the United States.

The appellation is named for its only grower—the 61 acre Cole Ranch with its vineyards planted between 1,400–1,600 feet. The ranch's production is devoted to **Cabernet Sauvignon** but **Chardonnay** and **Riesling** are also grown.

**Potter Valley AVA** covers 27,500 acres. At an elevation of 1,000–2,000 feet, this inland valley's climate is decidedly continental with hot summers, cold winters, and the threat of frost in the spring and late autumn. Harvest rains can be a headache, but they can also introduce botrytis to the **Riesling** and **Sémillon** grapes planted here. **Chardonnay, Pinot Noir**, and **Sangiovese** are also grown. Interesting dessert wines have been this AVAs main claim to fame.

**Redwood Valley** received its AVA designation in 1997. Some oceans breezes do manage to make their way into the Region III area along the Russian River, providing just enough relief from the heat to allow Syrah and Italian varieties to retain their acidity. **Zinfandel**, **Cabernet Sauvignon**, and **Petite Sirah** also do quite well in the region.

**McDowell Valley AVA** lies east of the highway, south of Ukiah and not far from the northern border of Sonoma. The majority of the appellation's vines are planted on gravelly, volcanic benchland at 850–1,000 feet. Rhône varieties are a specialty of McDowell Valley Winery, the major player in the area.

**Yorkville Highlands** became an AVA in 1998. It is a new area that is home to only a few wineries across its 40,000 acres. The appellation is best for growing **Sauvignon Blanc** and Bordeaux varieties.

# Lake County
## The North Coast

Lake County is the smallest viticultural district in the North Coast. Until 1861, it was considered an extension of Napa County. Lake County is far enough inland to be virtually untouched by maritime influences. Its elevation of 1,300 feet and the presence of Clear Lake—California's largest lake that takes up half of the county's surface area—help to moderate the climate somewhat. All of the usual suspects are planted here, but so far **Sauvignon Blanc** has become its most distinguished produce.

The **Clear Lake AVA** winds around the shoreline of Clear Lake and contains 90% of vineyards planted in the county. Hot days and cold nights give this area a Region II–III classification. Relatively late bud-break makes for a short growing season. **Sauvignon Blanc** does the best here, but **Chardonnay**, **Cabernet Sauvignon**, and **Zinfandel** can hold their own as well.

**Benmore Valley AVA** is a small viticultural area encompassing a mere 170 acres at 2,400 feet. It lies on the border of Mendocino. The majority of the AVA is planted with **Chardonnay**.

**Guenoc Valley AVA** was established in 1981 at the behest of Orville Magoon, the owner of the historic Guenoc estate, which remains the only winery in the region, making this area a single winery appellation. The 400 acre AVA is located in the southern part of Lake County, only 15 miles north of Calistoga. Warm days and cool nights rank this area as a Region III. **Chardonnay**, **Cabernet Sauvignon**, and some **Sauvignon Blanc** are grown here.

# Sierra Foothills

The **Sierra Foothills** is both a large AVA and a region that runs through gold country. The AVA covers 2,600,000 acres spanning several counties with vines planted in Yuba, Nevada, Placer, El Dorado, Amador, Calaveras, Tuolumne, and Mariposa. Sixty wineries are scattered throughout the region but are located mostly in El Dorado and Amador Counties. This is a hot region in the summer, possessing a Region III–IV classification, but cold night air from the mountains above and a variety of exposures and elevations make it difficult to generalize about the climate. The vineyards are planted in the poor volcanic soil of the hillside at elevations of 1,000–3000 feet. Significant rainfall makes dry farming a possibility and yields are generally low. Although the area is best known as a "goldmine" for old vine **Zinfandel, Sauvignon Blanc, Cabernet Sauvignon**, and **Chardonnay** are the most widely planted grapes respectively.

**North Yuba AVA** is the northernmost appellation of the Sierra Foothills region. Its terraced vineyards on located on rocky hillsides at altitudes of 1,700–2,300 feet. A variety of grapes are planted here ranging from **Riesling** to **Cabernet Sauvignon**.

**El Dorado AVA** covers the foothills at elevations of 1,200–3,500 feet. Although the region is classified as a Region II–III climate, summer nights can dip into the 40°s F, and cool mountain air and substantial rainfall at its highest vineyards at 3,000 feet make this a good spot for **Sauvignon Blanc** as well as **Zinfandel**. **Cabernet Sauvignon, Chardonnay**, and **Syrah** are grown as well along with many others. El Dorado wines are known for their high acidity.

**Fair Play** became an AVA in 2001. It is a subappellation within the Sierra Foothills and is sometimes called South County. The vineyards are at altitudes from the 2,500–3,500, which is extremely high for California

**Fiddletown AVA** is a high-lying AVA just south of the El Dorado County line in Amador County. The vineyards are planted at elevations of 1,500–2,500 feet, and the lofty heights combined with an average of 40 inches of rain per year make the AVAs **Zinfandels** slightly less burnt and brawny than those from the hotter corners of Amador County. Zinfandel accounts for 10,000 acres of vineyard

**Shenandoah Valley-California AVA** has the state name appended to it to differentiate it from Virginia's Shenandoah Valley. The AVA is home of the Sierra Foothills's oldest surviving Zinfandel vineyard, Grandpére, which has been in continuous production since its plantation in the 1860s. While most of the region lies in Amador County, the northern tip crosses into El Dorado and contains the Sobon winery, which is the area's oldest winery still in production. **Zinfandel** reigns supreme here, but **Muscat, Sauvignon Blanc**, and Rhône varieties are also grown.

**Calaveras County AVA** is slightly cooler than its northern neighbors. The area's limestone outcroppings, found among its mostly volcanic soil, have made it a decent region for **Sauvignon Blanc** and **Chardonnay**.

# THE CENTRAL COAST

## SANTA BARBARA

Santa Barbara County, with its southern tip is just 100 miles from downtown Los Angeles, is gaining a reputation for its excellent Chardonnays, Pinot Noirs, and Rhône-style wines. Shortly after U.C. Davis identified it as a region with excellent potential in the 1960s, wine makers unable to pay escalating Napa and Sonoma prices or those just looking for cooler weather for more delicate varieties, began to flock here. The area has grown enormously over the last 20 years and now has 25 wineries located in two major growing areas: **Santa Maria Valley** and **Santa Ynez Valley**.

**Santa Maria Valley AVA** is a cool climate Region I and II. Of its 80,000 acres, only 7,500 acres are under vine. Cool breezes from the Pacific Ocean (just 10 miles west of town) blow freely into this east-west valley and summer fog can cover the vineyards until mid-morning. Spring frost is a threat, and occasional autumn storms can add a touch of botrytis to the ripening grapes. The soil is of marine origin with a high proportion of sand that helps to retain the afternoon heat. **Chardonnay** dominates the plantings followed **by Pinot Noir. Cabernet Sauvignon, Riesling, Sauvignon Blanc, Merlot**, and **Chenin Blanc** are also grown in the AVA.

**Santa Ynez Valley AVA**, which became an AVA in 1983, is mostly a cool Region II due to the cool ocean breezes. Of the AVA spans 76,800 acres.

In 2001, the **Santa Rita Hills AVA** was created in the western end of the region. Chardonnay dominates the plantings followed by **Cabernet Sauvignon, Riesling, Pinot Noir, Chenin Blanc Sauvignon Blanc**, and **Gewurztraminer**.

**Los Alamos Valley**, while not officially an AVA to date, has 3,000 acres under vine and is becoming known for its quality **Pinot Noir** and high-acid **Chardonnay**.

## SAN LUIS OBISPO

San Luis Obispo County is just south of Monterey and is part of the **Central Coast AVA**. There are 25 wineries in three main growing areas and one minor AVA, **Paso Robles**.

**Paso Robles** is a high Region II to Region IV AVA, divided north-south by Highway 101. The rugged landscape of the Santa Lucia Mountains on the west side of the highway allows for many pockets of diverse microclimates at varying elevations. The east side is comprised of a more uniform plateau and is generally hotter. It is not unusual for this area to have 50ºF nights and reach temperatures in the 100's F during the day. As of 2002, there were over 18,000 acres planted to vineyards. **Cabernet Sauvignon, Merlot, Zinfandel, Syrah, Chardonnay**, and **Sauvignon Blanc** are the top grape varieties grown in the region.

**York Mountain** is the only viticultural area within the Santa Lucia Mountains to be granted its own AVA at present. It is a distinct subregion that earned its AVA status in 1983 and is comprised of 9,360 acres on the mountain side of Paso Robles. It is only seven miles inland from the Pacific, and the cool air flowing through the Templeton Gap combined with altitudes ranging from 1,600–1,800 feet above sea level has put some vineyard sites firmly into the Region I category. **Pinot Noir** and **Chardonnay** are planted in the cooler vineyards, and **Zinfandel** and Bordeaux varieties are found in warmer spots

**Edna Valley** is also within the boundaries of San Luis Obispo County, but could not be more different from the high desert ruggedness of Paso Robles. The terrain instead is fairly flat and uniform and is highly influenced by the Pacific Ocean. Morning fog trapped by the Santa Lucia Mountains to the northeast and the San Luis range to the southwest often persists until just before noon. Afternoons can be quite hot in the summer, but are cooled down in the evenings by the breezes from Morro Bay to the northwest. Moderate rainfall and high humidity from the persistent fog can result in downy mildew in the growing season and botrytis during harvest. The soil is heavy in marine sediments. The climate and soil combination makes the region perfect for **Chardonnay**, which dominates the vineyards accounting for 69% of vines planted. Some **Pinot Noir** is also planted for sparkling-wine production.

**Arroyo Grande** is a subregion of Edna Valley that was granted its own AVA in 1990. The region, which occupies 42,800 acres of land, is just a little further from the coast than Edna Valley proper. The additional distance diminishes the cooling effects of wind and fog, permitting Pinot Noir to ripen more fully. Further east from the coast lies **Saucelito Canyon** that has warm enough sites to produce robust **Zinfandels**. **Chardonnay** is the most widely planted variety here followed **by Pinot Noir, Cabernet Sauvignon, Sauvignon Blanc**, and **Zinfandel**.

## MONTEREY

The Monterey region, including Monterey and San Benito Counties, is located in the Salinas Valley. U.C. Davis identifies the area as a Region I–IV with various microclimates. Aside from the Franciscans and the adventurous Frenchman who planted the Chalone vineyards in the late 19th century, wine makers have been slow to respond to the university's recommendation until quite recently. The Salinas Valley is 80 miles long and encompasses 36,000 acres. There are five AVAs in Monterey County: **Arroyo Seco, Carmel Valley, Chalone, San Lucas**, and **Santa Lucia Highlands**. There are five small AVAs in **San Benito County**.

**Carmel Valley**, which became an AVA in 1983, lies to the west of the Salinas Valley and is separated from it and the Pacific Ocean to its east by mountains. The AVA covers 19,000 acres but is home to only a few wineries. Fog and high winds are less prevalent here and allow for the full ripening of the Bordeaux varieties that dominate the Region I vineyards.

**The Santa Lucia Highlands AVA**, designated in 1992, is separated from the Salinas Valley–floor by a visible fault line. The area stretches for 22,000 acres along an 18 mile benchland on the fault's western side. The most widely planted grape is **Chardonnay**, while a variety of elevations and exposures are well-suited to the region's rising star **Pinot Noir. Merlot, Cabernet Sauvignon**, and **Pinot Blanc** are grown as well.

The **Arroyo Seco AVA** continues south along the Salinas Valley's western benchlands and then shoots to the west where the canyon walls created by the mouth of the Arroyo Seco River provide some protection from the high winds. The AVAs 18,240 acres are in places comprised of gravelly soil, producing grapes capable of high extract and acidity. Chardonnay is most widely planted variety. Vineyard sites in the protected western spur, such as Jekel's Sanctuary, allow for the plantation of red varieties.

**San Lucas**, which became an AVA in 1987, is at the southernmost end of the Salinas Valley. The region covers 34,000 acres, of which 8,000 are under vine. The AVA ranges from a Region III–IV classification and is quite hot but experiences cool nights. The area produces mostly bulk wines.

The **Chalone AVA** was named in 1982 for the Chalone Estate, which is located high in the Gavilan Mountains to the east of the Salinas Valley. The area's vineyards—some of which date back to the 1940s—are planted at altitudes from 1,800–2,000 feet above sea level. The vineyards' positions above the fog line and away from the valley winds mean they are usually warmer than sites near the valley floor. The increase in temperature is offset by cool mountain nights, preserving acidity in the grapes. Volcanic soils composed of limestone and granite are perfect for the **Chardonnay** and **Pinot Noir** planted here. Secondary grape varieties planted in Chalone **include Pinot Blanc, Chenin Blanc**, and **Syrah**. Yields are kept naturally low by the lack of rainfall and the near impossibility of irrigation in this remote site.

**San Benito County** covers less than 2,000 acres of land and contains five small AVAs:

- Mount Harlan
- Paicenes
- Lime Kiln
- Cienega Valley
- Pacheco Pass

The most notable AVA of the five is **Mount Harlan**. The AVA is comprised of 7,500 acres of land and is the coolest and highest viticultural area in San Benito County. The AVA is also home to Josh Jensen's Calera winery, which is planted high up in the limestone soil on the San Benito Valley side of the Gavilan Mountains.

The other four AVAs in the country were mostly owned by Almadén until its operations were moved to the Central Valley in 1987.

# THE BAY AREA
(SAN MATEO, SANTA CRUZ, SANTA CLARA, SAN FRANCISCO, SAN BENITO, ALAMEDA, AND CONTRA COSTA COUNTIES)

All the counties in the Bay Area, except Santa Cruz and San Benito, border the bay. There are 1,566,000 total acres in the area, spanning seven counties, with 6,000 acres of vineyards most of which are located in the **Livermore Valley AVA** which is a subappellation of the **San Francisco Bay AVA**.

**Livermore Valley** is one of California's oldest wine districts. It is 15 miles long and 10 miles wide. The cooling ocean breezes are blocked, giving the area a warm Region III classification. **Chardonnay** accounts for 50% of acres under vine. Urban sprawl has diminished the modern-day impact of the historically important vineyards in **Alameda, Contra Costa**, and **Santa Clara** Counties.

**Alameda County** is home to the Wente estate that is more famous for the clones of **Chardonnay** and **Sauvignon Blanc** developed there than for its wines today. Wente currently holds all of the best sites formerly owned by its historic competitors in Alameda's **Livermore Valley**.

**Contra Costa** was the original home of **Christian Brothers** and was an important part of the **Italian Swiss Colony** operation. Some extremely old patches of **Mourvèdre** and **Zinfandel** have managed to survive the crush of development from nearby Oakland and San Francisco.

**Santa Clara Valley AVA**, which covers 330,000 acres, includes the cities of San Jose, Sunnyvale, and Santa Clara. It is dominated by **Chardonnay** plantings and is home to more than 25 wineries. Santa Clara Valley is more commonly known today as Silicon Valley and contains more virtual vineyards than actual ones.

The small AVA of **San Ysidro**, located in the fog-influenced southern section of Santa Clara Valley, continues to hang on with a mere 520 acres of **Chardonnay** plantings.

The **Santa Cruz Mountains** are too rugged for large-scale development and have always been the enclave of visionary eccentrics. Some vineyards in the area almost reach the Pacific Ocean and have Region I and II classifications. Martin Ray used the profits from his deal with Seagram to establish his remote Mount Eden winery here in 1943. Paul Draper is the wine maker at Ridge, which is famous for their **Cabernet Sauvignon** from the old vines of Montebello Vineyard. Randall Graham, the often-quoted eccentric founder of the Rhône Ranger movement started his innovative Bonny Doon winery in these hills, as well. Some amount of vision is essential to produce wines in this remote, and rocky terrain. Low yields are a given, and the individuals that have persevered in spite of marginal profits have succeeding in producing some of California's most distinctive wines.

# THE SOUTH COAST
## LOS ANGELES, SAN BERNARDINO, SAN DIEGO, AND RIVERSIDE COUNTIES

With a few notable exceptions, the South Coast of California is of more historical than modern interest. The Franciscans in the 17th and 18th centuries, followed by Europeans in the early 19th century, such as Jean Louis Vignes and Charles Lefranc, planted their first vines here. By the mid 19th century, the area around Los Angeles and Anaheim was the heartland of California's mostly fortified wine production. The area fell victim to an outbreak of Pierce's disease in the 1880s that was more devastating to the region than phylloxera. However, Prohibition, suburban sprawl, and the trend towards table rather than fortified wines are mostly responsible for the area's decline. The region also includes parts of Orange County.

There are two AVAs in the South Coast that are home to approximately 20 wineries. **San Pasqual** is the smaller of the two viticultural regions. It is located in San Diego County and is home to no wineries. **Temecula** has about 3,000 acres under vine in Riverside County. Temecula is hot (Region III bordering on IV) but its saving grace is its altitude. The vines are generally planted at 1,500 feet above sea level and higher. Grapes predominately grown in the South Coast **include Chenin Blanc, Cabernet Sauvignon, Riesling, Merlot, Zinfandel**, and **Pinot Blanc**.

# OREGON

| AREA UNDER VINE | 19,400 acres | 7,850 hectares |
|---|---|---|
| GRAPE VARIETIES | | |
| RED | Pinot Noir, Cabernet Sauvignon, Merlot | |
| WHITE | Chardonnay, Pinot Gris, Riesling | |
| CLIMATE | Northern latitude, maritime breezes, and long hours of daylight helps to create warm summer days and cool autumns | |
| SOIL | Well-known for Red Jory Clay, Nekia, and clay loam called Willakenzie Alluvial soil | |

In 1979 a major blind-tasting competition was organized and held in Paris by *négociant* Robert Drouhin. There were over 600 entries from around the world, including David Lett's 1975 Pinot Noir from Eyrie Vineyards in Oregon's Willamette Valley. The industry was stunned when the Oregon wine placed second, beating numerous Burgundian houses. It was from this point on that Oregon was perceived as an ideal place to grow high-quality Pinot Noir that would rival the wines of Burgundy.

At present the state of Oregon is fourth in wine production in the country with more than 12,000 acres planted with vines. Presently there are about 250 wineries throughout the state.

## LAWS

Oregon has some of the strictest wine labeling laws in the United States. Variety labeled wines must contain 90% of the stated variety. The exception is Cabernet Sauvignon, which can have only 75% of the variety. Vintage labeled wines must contain 95% of grapes from the stated year. Appellation labeled wines must be made entirely (100%) of grapes coming from the named AVA. No generic names are permitted and chaptalization IS permitted.

## VARIETIES

### RED

**Pinot Noir** dominates in Oregon and it is the only region other than Burgundy where this variety rules. It requires a cool ripening period, and low yields are essential for maintaining quality. The best sites for Pinot Noir are those with soil consisting of <u>Red Jory Clay</u>, <u>Nekia</u>, and clay loam called <u>Willakenzie Alluvial soil</u>. Red Jory drains well and helps promote the bright cherry fruit quality of the variety. Nekia needs both drainage and irrigation, while Willakenzie soil is well drained with a low water holding capacity. Both Nekia and Willakenzie soils support Pinot Noir's black fruit qualities and a more tannic structure.

**Maréchal Foch** is an early ripening grape with good resistance to cold. It makes soft, sometimes smoky, jammy red wines. Oregon is one of the only places in the world that produces this grape in commercial quantity. The following quote pertaining to Maréchal Foch comes from a vine nursery description for the purpose of selling the vine to growers:

"This French hybrid grape yields juice that smells and tastes just like sweet cherries such as Bing. Foch also has a higher sugar content and better balance of acid than traditional juicing grapes like Concord. Hardy to about –25°F. Unique grape, excellent for making burgundy-type wines, requires little or no spraying.

Harvest up to 25 pounds per vine annually. Ripens in late August in Zone 5."

**Other red varieties** include Cabernet Sauvignon, Merlot, and Syrah.

### WHITE

**Chardonnay**, in terms of production, is the leading white variety. Its quality varies but better clones, such as Dijon, show great promise.

**Pinot Gris** is the grape proving to be the white variety of the state. Here fruit flavors and honey qualities shine through and provide a great alternative to the Chardonnay saturated market.

**Other white varieties** include Pinot Blanc, Sauvignon Blanc, Seyval Blanc, Riesling, Sémillon, and Folle Blanche.

# Climate

The state of Oregon is situated roughly between the $42^{nd}$ and $45^{th}$ parallels. Because of the Pinot Noir comparisons, there is a myth that Oregon and Burgundy are at the same latitude on the globe—do not believe it! The Côte d'Or in Burgundy is centered on the $47^{th}$ parallel, which is more comparable to the growing regions of Washington State.

Oregon's combination of northern latitude, maritime breezes, and long hours of daylight helps to create warm summer days and cool autumns, resulting in a long growing season with a gradual ripening of the grapes. Rainfall occurs primarily in the late fall and winter with the Willamette Valley experiencing less rainfall during its growing season than Burgundy. The majority of Oregon's wine production lies between the Cascade Mountains to the east and the Coastal Range to the west. This prolific pocket of land is protected from the effects of the Pacific Ocean by the Coastal Range.

# AVAs

Currently there are 16 AVAs in Oregon. As the industry has grown in the past 10 years, several sub-regions have proposed and gained AVA approval—six within Willamette Valley alone.

The three AVAs of the Columbia River Region, **Columbia Gorge, Columbia Valley,** and **Walla Walla Valley**, are located on the east side of the Cascade Mountains and lie mostly in the state of Washington. There are no wineries in these AVAs, only vineyards.

**Columbia Gorge and Columbia Valley** extend from west to east, thus the maritime air of the western region collides with the warm dry air of the east. The result is great variations of climate in short distances, making the region suitable for a growing a variety of grapes.

**Walla Walla Valley** experiences hot days contrasted with crisp, cool nights. The region receives a low amount of rainfall and is best known for its Bordeaux variety production.

**Willamette Valley** is Oregon's coolest wine appellation and is the source of most of the state's wine grapes. The valley runs north to south with its center lying approximately 50 miles east of the Pacific Ocean, which provides the region with its maritime climate. The vineyards are typically located on hillsides at the western edge of the valley. The AVA is known for its two major types of clay soil, which dominate the region—Red Jory Clay and Willakenzie Alluvial Soil.

Within Willamette Valley there are six sub-AVAs, all of which were established between 2004 and 2006:

1. Chehalem Mountains
2. Dundee Hills
3. Eola-Amity Hills
4. McMinnville
5. Ribbon Ridge
6. Yamhill-Carlton District

The **Southern Oregon AVA** encompasses Umpqua Valley, Rogue Valley, Red Hill Douglas County, and Applegate Valley.

**Umpqua Valley** is home to Hillcrest Vineyard, the first post-Prohibition winery to open in Oregon. Located just south of the Willamette Valley, the AVA extends west from the Cascades, through the city of Roseburg, toward the Pacific Ocean. The valley consists of many hillsides and river drainages known as the "Hundred Valleys of the Umpqua". The region is drier and warmer than the Willamette Valley, has more varied soils, and experiences a greater range between day and night temperatures. For these reasons a wide variety of grapes are grown here, such as Pinot Noir, Cabernet Sauvignon, Sauvignon Blanc, Chardonnay, and Riesling.

**Red Hill Douglas County** is a sub-AVA of Umpqua Valley and is distinguished by its higher elevation and deep Red Jory Clay.

**Rogue Valley** is Oregon's oldest wine region. The westernmost area, the Illinois Valley, is heavily influenced by the maritime climate of the Pacific Ocean and its vineyards feature the cooler climate varieties of the Pinot grape. The Rogue River sub-region, located south of Rogue Valley, is further inland and therefore more sheltered from the Pacific. The warmer, drier climate is suitable for the production of most Bordeaux varieties. Chardonnay is also grown throughout the appellation.

**Applegate Valley** is Oregon's newest AVA. The appellation separates the Rogue Valley into north and south areas. The AVA is recognized for its deep, well-drained soils and warm days and cool nights. The valley tends to produce intense, full-bodied reds. The climate is well-suited for growing Merlot, Syrah, Zinfandel, Cabernet Franc, and Cabernet Sauvignon.

**Snake River Valley AVA** is on the eastern border of the state and is shared with neighboring Idaho (it is in fact Idaho's only AVA at this time). With hot days and cool nights, the region can produce grapes with balanced acid and sugar levels.

# WASHINGTON STATE

| AREA UNDER VINE | 37,000 acres | 14,973 hectares |
|---|---|---|
| GRAPE VARIETIES | | |
| RED | Cabernet Sauvignon, Merlot, Syrah, Cabernet Franc | |
| WHITE | Chardonnay, Riesling, Sauvignon Blanc | |
| CLIMATE | The Cascade Mountains create a rain shadow effect. The western zone has a maritime climate, while the eastern zone is continental. | |

Although wine grapes were planted in Washington as early as 1825, and many French, German, and Italian immigrants pioneered early plantings, Prohibition forced a decline in production in the state in 1920. After Prohibition there were several small wineries scattered throughout the state, including Pommerelle and Nawico, which produced mostly Concord and other native varieties. These were among the first commercial scale plantings in the 1960s. Today these two wineries comprise part of one of the most famous and largest wineries in the state–Chateau Ste. Michelle.

The early efforts of the post-Prohibition wineries intrigued the wine historian Leon Adams, who recruited the famous enologist Andre Tchelistcheff to come work for Chateau Ste. Michelle. It was Tchelistcheff who guided the winery's early efforts and helped mentor early winemaking in the state.

Value, diversity, and, above all, quality characterize Washington's wine industry. The state is the nation's second largest producer of premium wines. In 1981 there were a mere 19 wineries in the state, but currently there are almost 240, sourcing and growing grapes from almost 30,000 vineyard acres.

Located at approximately 46 degrees north latitude (between Burgundy and Bordeaux), Washington's period of extended sunlight, many rivers and tributaries, close proximity to the Pacific Ocean, and mountainous landscape clearly separate this state from the rest. These many factors allow for great diversity in the grapes that are well suited for the area.

## WASHINGTON WINE QUALITY ALLIANCE (WWQA)

In 1999, the Washington Wine Quality Alliance was formed by a committee of wine industry members to spearhead development of industry standards in winemaking and labeling. Under WWQA guidelines, the nation's first definition of the term reserve was defined. In Washington State a reserve wine may represent no more than 3,000 cases or 10% of a winery's total production. The term reserve on a bottle indicates the winemaker's designation that the wine is of a higher quality than others from the winery.

Wines labeled Washington State must be made entirely from grapes from the state or the label must identify the percentage of grapes from each source. Variety labeling requires that wines contain at least 75% of the named variety. Additionally the use of Champagne, Burgundy, Bordeaux, and Chablis on labels is not allowed. Participation in the WWQA is voluntary, and wineries following the organization's guidelines are identifiable by the use of the WWQA logo. The regulations first went into effect with the 2000 vintage.

## Varieties

Washington produces a variety of grapes. Currently more red wine is being made than white—57% red to 43% white. The predominant varieties include Merlot, Cabernet Sauvignon, Syrah, Chardonnay, Riesling, Sauvignon Blanc, and Sémillon

## Reds

**Merlot** became a star in Washington around 1990. It is known for its sweet cherry and berry flavors plus its complex aromas such as spice, mint, and cedar.

**Cabernet Sauvignon's** fruity character develops slowly in Washington. The wines age well. It is generally used in Bordeaux blends. It features flavors of dark red fruits, leather, herbs, and chocolate.

**Syrah** in Washington is showing great promise. This Rhône variety produces big, intensely concentrated wines with aromas of black fruit and coffee.

**Other reds include** Malbec, Sangiovese, Pinot Noir, and Zinfandel.

## Whites

**Chardonnay** is Washington's most widely planted grape. The state's climate turns out crisp and delicate examples of this variety.

**Riesling** is generally fermented dry/off-dry, featuring a floral nose and prominent apricot-peach flavors. Noble rot enables the production of excellent late harvest and ice wines.

**Sémillon** wines when enjoyed young are full of crisp citrus and pear flavors. With age Washington Sémillon turns into a beautifully rich, honeyed, and nutty wine, that is luscious but light bodied. Late harvest wines are also produced.

**Sauvignon Blanc**, which is also labeled Fumé Blanc, possesses a distinct herbaceous and acidic character. A wide range of styles is produced.

**Gewürztraminer's** early success in Washington was due to its ability to withstand the cold. It is made in German and French styles, possessing zesty aromas.

**Other whites include** Pinot Gris, Aligoté, Chenin Blanc, Müller-Thurgau, and Viognier.

## Climate

The Cascade Mountain range divides the state into two very distinct climatic zones. The range is responsible for what is referred to as the "rain shadow effect". The Cascades create a barrier that traps moist air west of the mountains, preventing it from reaching the drier lands to the east. The western zone has a maritime climate, while the eastern zone is continental. In the west, the land is lush and green. It is heavily influenced by the Pacific and receives on average 48 inches of rainfall annually.

Irrigation is needed to help Vitis vinifera flourish east of the Cascades in the Columbia Valley where the average rainfall is about eight inches annually. The desertlike conditions, featuring warm days and cool nights, help to preserve the acidity in the grapes. Fortunately, the entire state due to its northerly latitude, receives more sunlight— almost 17.5 hours a day— which is more than two hours more than California receives daily.

It is also worth noting that Washington has never been affected by phylloxera or mildew thanks to its cold winters and sandy soils that were deposited by glaciers.

## AVAs

Washington currently has thirteen AVAs: Yakima Valley, Walla Walla Valley, Columbia Valley, Red Mountain, Puget Sound, Horse Heaven Hills, Columbia River Gorge, Wahluke Slope, Lake Chelan, Snipes Mountain, Rattlesnake Hills, Naches Heights and the most recent—Ancient Lakes of Columbia Valley.

**Puget Sound**, established in 1995, is the only AVA west of the Cascade Mountains. Nearly 35 wineries are located on a mere 80 vineyard acres. Annual precipitation averages between 15 and 30 inches and falls mostly during the winter.

Summers tend to be mild and dry. The AVAs semipermeable cemented subsoil enables vines to survive the end of summer's water deficit. The primary varieties are Madeleine Angevine and Müller-Thurgau. Plantings of Pinot Gris and Pinot Noir are on the rise. This region accounts for about 2% of Washington's wines.

**Columbia Valley** was established in 1984 and is Washington's largest AVA comprised of more than 11 million acres of which 17,000 acres are under vine. This vast area allows for many micro- and meso climates and receives an average annual rainfall of six to eight inches. Most vineyards are situated on southern facing slopes, increasing the vines exposure to the sun. Merlot, Cabernet Sauvignon, and Chardonnay are the most widely planted varieties. Riesling and Syrah also show great promise from the region. With the exception of Puget Sound, all of Washington's other AVAs are sub-regions within Columbia Valley.

**Yakima Valley** was Washington's first AVA. Established in 1983, it is the second largest in the state, encompassing approximately 11,000 acres under vine. Located within the Columbia Valley AVA, more than one-third of the state's vineyards are located within the Yakima viticultural area. The area receives on average about eight inches of rainfall per year, and silt-loamy soil dominates the vineyards. The Yakima River winds down eastward from the Cascade's foothills. The valley divides itself in half with the western portion being cooler than the east, which can be warm if not hot. The AVAs most widely planted variety is Chardonnay followed by Merlot and Cabernet Sauvignon. Riesling also does extremely well in the west. The first Syrah to be planted in Washington was in the Yakima Valley AVA.

The **Walla Walla Valley AVA** was established in 1984. This small viticultural area in the southeast corner of the state is shared with Oregon. The average annual rainfall can be up to 12.5 inches, so some vineyards in the AVA are dry farmed (irrigation is not used) due to the slightly higher precipitation. The soil is primarily comprised of loess. Cabernet Sauvignon is the most widely planted variety with Merlot, Chardonnay, and Syrah, in particular, on the rise. Merlot is particularly well-suited to the areas with loam soil.

**Red Mountain** AVA was established in 2001. Located in the eastern most tip of the Yakima Valley, the AVA receives six to eight inches of rainfall annually. The region is best known for its reds, including Cabernet Sauvignon, Merlot and Sangiovese, which shows great promise. However, the region also produces fine Sauvignon Blanc. What makes Red Mountain's wine distinctive is the region's topography. The vineyards are located at higher elevations and are planted on greater slopes, with cooling winds blowing in from the north. The resulting wines tend to be dark, dense, alcoholic, and tannic.

**Horse Heaven Hills** is bordered in the north by Yakima Valley and in the south by Columbia River. Temperatures are moderated by the presence of the river and high winds. Merlot and Cabernet Sauvignon grow well here.

**Columbia River Gorge** is located west of Horse Heaven Hills along the Columbia River. The area's soil is rich in volcanic bedrock as well as granite and schist. The region is fed by many tributaries. Chardonnay, Gewürztraminer, and Sauvignon Blanc thrive.

Wahluke Slope is found north of the Yakima Valley. Cold Creek Vineyard, which has one of the longest growing seasons in the Columbia Valley, is located in the area. The region is home to such diverse varieties as Chardonnay, Riesling, Cabernet Sauvignon, and Merlot.

**Rattlesnake Hills** is the most recent area granted AVA status by the state of Washington in 2006. This area has over 1,550 acres under vine and reaches altitudes of 3,085 feet, higher than any other surrounding AVA. The regions soils are much finer than the sandier soils found in neighboring AVAs, with a neutral pH. Chardonnay, Riesling, Cabernet Sauvignon, Malbec, Merlot and Syrah are all grown very successfully.

**Snipes Mountain AVA,** established in 2009, is entirely encompassed by Yakima Valley, but its rocky soils and elevation makes the region significantly different from the surroundings.

**Lake Chelan**, also established in 2009, is a subregion of Columbia Valley. The region is characterized by a longer growing season and more temperate climate—both due to the presence of Lake Chelan itself.

Approved in December 2011 and legally effective as of January 2012, **Naches Heights** is one of the newer AVAs in Washington State. With only two wineries and 37 planted acres (at the time of its establishment), Naches Heights is also the smallest AVA in the state in terms of vineyard area planted. The region has volcanic soils and is raised above its Yakima County surroundings at altitudes ranging from 1,200 to 2,100 feet.

In October 2012, **Ancient Lakes of Columbia Valley** became an AVA. This sub-AVA in the northern Columbia Valley grows mostly white grapes. The soils—laid down by the Missoula Floods approximately 15,000 years ago—are nutrient poor. Elvation ranges from about 550 to 1900 feet.

Other areas of note include Columbia Basin (where the Columbia, Snake, and Yakima Rivers converge. It is best known for its Sauvignon Blanc and Sémillon) Alder Ridge, Canoe Ridge, Zephyr Ridge, and Cold Creek.

# NEW YORK STATE

| AREA UNDER VINE | 33,700 acres | 13,600 hectares |
|---|---|---|
| GRAPE VARIETIES | | |
| RED | Cabernet Sauvignon, Merlot, Pinot Noir, Cabernet Franc | |
| WHITE | Chardonnay, Riesling, Gewürztraminer | |

The state of New York is presently third in United States wine production behind California and Washington, only recently losing the second place position to Washington. The state produces roughly 10% of all wine consumed in the U.S.

Commercially, one of the first important events in New York wine production came in 1860 when grapes were planted along Keuka Lake in the heart of the Finger Lakes region. This project eventually grew to become the large Taylor Wine Company, based in Hammondsport, NY. In the 1950s Gold Seal Winery hired Charles Fournier, a French Champagne master, to work for the company. About the same time, Dr. Konstantin Frank also settled in the Finger Lakes region to work at the Geneva Research Station, an internationally known center of viticultural experimentation. The two men worked together to grow Vitis vinifera grapes in the area, an achievement no one previously thought possible due to the harsh New York winters. However, Fournier and Frank proved everyone wrong by successfully growing both Chardonnay and Riesling. In 1976 New York passed the Farm Winery Act, which favored the establishment of family farm wineries. The legislation helped all four major wine regions in New York to flourish.

## LAWS

Wine labeled New York State must be made from at least 75% New York fruit. Variety labeling for wines made from vinifera must contain 75% of the stated grape, while labrusca wines must contain 51% of the variety named on the label.

## VARIETIES

Today, the predominant vinifera grape varieties produced in New York are Cabernet Franc, Pinot Noir, Pinot Blanc, Gewürztraminer, Riesling, and Chardonnay.

The labrusca grapes most often grown include Dutchess, Elvira, Niagara, and Noah for whites and Concord, Steuben, Delaware, and Catawba for red/blacks.

New York also produces several hybrid varieties. A hybrid is a variety produced from crossing two or more grape varieties from more than one grape species. Hybrids grown in New York include Ravat Blanc, Seyval Blanc, Vignoles, and Vidal Blanc for whites and Maréchal Foch, Baco Noir, and Chambourcin for reds. These hybrids, produced from native and European varieties, tend to be hardy enough to endure New York's climatic extremes from year to year.

While New York has in the past been known for its generic wines made from Vitis labrusca, in recent years, growers have been focusing more on quality and have been planting more Vitis vinifera.

## AVAs

There are five wine regions in New York: the Finger Lakes, Long Island, Lake Erie, the Niagara Escarpment, and the Hudson River Valley.

### Finger Lakes

The Finger Lakes region is centered on four lakes with American Indian names: Canandaigua, Keuka, Seneca, and Cayuga. There are three AVAs in the region, **Finger Lakes**, **Cayuga Lake,** and **Seneca Lake**. Cayuga Lake is recognized as its own viticultural area due to its unique geographical conditions. It is also the best-suited area in the lake region to plant vinifera due to its slightly warmer mesoclimate. There are more than 10,000 acres of land under vine with almost 60 wineries. The region's lakes moderate temperatures and the sloping hillsides on which the vines are planted aid in proper drainage. Seneca Lake, New York's newest AVA, is located entirely within the Finger Lakes AVA to the east of Cayuga Lake. Seneca Lake AVA has approximately 3,750 acres under vine. Specialties for the Finger Lakes include sparkling wines, Riesling, Pinot Noir, and ice wine.

### Long Island

Much of the state's premium wines hail from the Long Island region and its two sub-AVAs: **North Fork of Long Island** and **the Hamptons** (on the South Fork). The region has approximately 2,000 acres under vine—mostly vinifera—and about 30 wineries (only three of which are on the South Fork). The region is known for its long, cool growing season and well-draining, sandy-loam soils. Climate moderators for the region include the Atlantic Ocean, Peconic Bay, and the Long Island Sound. The area specializes in Bordeaux varieties such as Merlot, Cabernet Sauvignon, and Cabernet Franc, and the wineries in the area draw frequent parallels to its French counterpart. Both regions have maritime climates, and they are at similar latitudes. The **Long Island** AVA also grows Chardonnay, Riesling, Gewürztraminer, Vidal Blanc, and Vignoles. Vidal Blanc and Vignoles comprise the backbone of the area's acclaimed dessert wines.

### Hudson River Valley

The Hudson River Valley region is one of the oldest and most historic wine making areas in America. It is home to the oldest winery in the county, Brotherhood Winery, which has been in continuous operation since 1839. Presently, there is one AVA in the region, **Hudson Valley Region**. There are about 500 acres of planted land and more than 25 wineries. The Hudson River acts as a climate moderator as does the valley itself, which acts as a conduit of maritime air from the Atlantic. Today the region grows some vinifera varieties such as Chardonnay and Cabernet Franc as well as specializing in French-American hybrids such as Seyval Blanc and Baco Noir.

### Lake Erie

Within the Lake Erie region there is only one AVA, **Lake Erie**, which is shared with Ohio and Pennsylvania. Although frigid arctic air masses flow directly toward the Lake Erie region, by the time they arrive they have been warmed by passing over the Great Lakes. This warmer air is then trapped by the Allegheny Plateau—a ridge of hills running parallel to the southern shore of Lake Erie—that protects the vines from extreme temperatures. Much of the 18,000 acres of land are planted with the Concord grape, which is used for juice not wine, but there are some wineries producing vinifera and hybrid wines such as Seyval Blanc and Riesling.

### Niagara Escarpment

Niagara Escarpment is the most recent AVA in New York State (established in 2005), and has a counterpart just west of the border in Ontario. The region is moderated by Lake Ontario to the north, the Niagara River to the west, and the Niagara Escarpment to the south—the Escarpment is a limestone ridge that protects the vineyards by trapping air warmed by the surrounding water. Though the appellation covers approximately 18,000 acres of land, only about 400 of those are planted.

# VIRGINIA

Wine in Virginia dates back to 1609 and Jamestown. President Thomas Jefferson is considered by most to be the pioneer of American wine. His love affair with wine most likely started when he was the Ambassador to France. He was the first to believe the beverage had health benefits and encouraged his fellow Americans to drink it. In the 1760s he attempted to grow vitis vinifera, the vines did not take.

After a long and tenuous grape growing history, Virginia eventually grew vinifera varieties in the 1960s, and the state has been successful ever since. Here, as in other states, the Farm Winery Act of 1980 encouraged people to start wineries, and Virginia Tech helped to improve the palatability of the state's wines by implementing viticulture and enology programs.

Virginia is currently the mid-Atlantic region's top producer. About 75% of all vine plantings are vinifera. There are six AVAs in Virginia. From east to west they are **Virginia's Eastern Shore, Northern Neck George Washington Birthplace, Monticello, Shenandoah Valley, North Fork of Roanoke,** and **Rocky Knob**. Chardonnay is Virginia's most successful variety, with the Shenandoah Valley being one of its top producers. The Shenandoah Valley itself is more than 300 miles long and features several different microclimates due to the multitude of valleys and streams in the area. In addition to Chardonnay, the most common vinifera varieties grown in Virginia include Riesling, Cabernet Sauvignon, Cabernet Franc, Merlot, Pinot Grigio, Sauvignon Blanc, and Viognier among the vinifera. The French hybrids Seyval Blanc and Vidal are also grown. The red varieties Chambourcin and Norton are also gaining popularity today.

# TEXAS

Texas is the fifth largest producer of wine in the United States. The state's annual wine production is consistently more than one million gallons, most of which is consumed and sold within the state. Due to the state's size, there are almost as many climate and soil variations in Texas as there are in all of France.

There are 7 AVAs in Texas: Bell Mountain, Escondido Valley, Fredericksburg–Texas Hill Country, Mesilla Valley, Texas Davis Mountains, Texas Hill Country, and Texas Hill Plains. At 15,000 acres, Texas Hill Country is the largest AVA in the United States; however, only about 800 acres are actually planted with vines. Fredericksburg is a sub-region within Texas Hill Country. Bell Mountain—known for its Cabernet Sauvignon grown in sandy-loam soil—was the state's first AVA recognized in 1986. Generally the Texas Hill Country and Bell Mountain AVAs are producing Texas's higher quality wines.

There are approximately 34 wineries total in Texas, spreading across 3,400 acres. Irrigation is necessary and vinifera plantings dominate, except in East Texas where due to humidity, pest, and disease only the Muscadine grape flourishes. Advances in fermentation technology, mechanization, and irrigation techniques during the second half of the 20th century have all had a great impact on Texas, enabling the state to create and produce better quality wines.

# CANADA

Grape growing in Canada can be traced back to the Okanagan Mission, which was located in British Columbia in the 1860s. The country's commercial wine production started on Pelee Island in 1866, and by 1890 there were 41 commercials wineries in existence. Each Canadian province is overseen by its own liquor control board, which regulates sales and distribution. Canada's regulation and appellation system, known as the Vintners Quality Alliance (VQA) was created in 1988. The VQA regulates production, delimits growing areas, ensures quality, and oversees labeling laws. Ontario was the first province to adopt the system and it in turn asked British Colombia undertake a similar system, which it did in 1990. Appellations in the Canada are known as Designated Viticultural Areas (DVA). Each region maintains several unique rules and regulations that are specific to the area.

## LAWS

VQA Wine laws are applicable only in British Columbia and Ontario. The VQA has two categories, provincial and geographic. Vitis vinifera and French-American hybrids are allowed for the provincial designation for which 75% of the stated variety is required for a wine to be labeled as such. For geographic designation the laws are as follows:

Only Vitis vinifera varieties are allowed.

Wines must be produced from 100% Ontario-grown grapes or 100% from British Columbia.

Variety-labeled wines must contain at least 85% of the named variety and must exhibit the predominant character of that variety. If the wine is a blend, it must contain at least 10% of the second named variety.

When a vintage date is stated, at least 85% of the grapes must be from that year.

To designate the vineyard from which the wine is made, the site must be within the delimited DVA area and 100% of the grapes must come from that vineyard.

Wines described as estate bottled must be made from 100% of grapes owned or controlled by the winery in a viticultural area, and all aspects of production must be performed at the winery.

Minimum sugar levels are regulated for vineyard designation, estate bottled, dessert, and ice wine.

Wines are evaluated by an independent panel of experts. Only those wines, which meet or exceed the production and appellation standards, are awarded VQA status. A gold VQA medallion is awarded only to those wines that perform exceptionally well as judged by the tasting panel. Otherwise they receive a black VQA seal.

## DVAs

There are four growing regions in Canada: Ontario, British Columbia, Nova Scotia, and Québec. Collectively they have about 20,000 acres under vine; however, Ontario and British Columbia are the primary producing regions and will be discussed in greater detail. Nationally white wine production exceeds red—about 65% white and about 35% red.

### ONTARIO

The VQA recognizes four DVAs within Ontario: Niagara Peninsula, Pelee Island, Lake Erie North Shore, and Prince Edward County.

The **Niagara Peninsula DVA** is located in Southern Ontario at 43 degrees north latitude, which is the same as Chianti and Rioja. It is bound on the north by Lake Ontario, on the south by the shore of Lake Erie, and on the east by the Niagara River. The backbone of the peninsula is the Niagara Escarpment, which is a high ridge that influences the soil and creates microclimates. It is at the escarpment's base and first bench that wine growing is favored. The soils and the warm winds off Lake Ontario moderate winter temperatures and reduce the risk of spring frost. The escarpment extends along the entire Niagara Peninsula and influences the soil and creates microclimates. North of the escarpment is a flat plain rich with deposits of lacustrine clays, sands, and gravel.

**Pelee Island** is south of Canada's mainland in the middle of Lake Erie. The DVA has about 500 acres under vine and is home to Canada's southernmost vineyards. The area has a long growing season with a sandy loam and clay topsoil over limestone bedrock.

**Lake Erie North Shore** also has about 500 acres of vineyards that stretch along the shoreline of Lake Erie. The sunny region features soil ranging from gravelly to sandy loam.

**Prince Edward County**, officially recognized in 2007, is Ontario's most recent DVA.

## BRITISH COLUMBIA

In British Columbia, the VQA recognizes five DVAs: **Okanagan Valley, Similkameen Valley, Fraser Valley, Vancouver Island, and the Gulf Islands**. Just as in Washington State, the Cascade Mountains—with elevations as high as 14,000 feet above sea level—prevent the cooler and wetter weather systems from moving eastward. The rain shadow effect helps this wine region, once thought of as not suitable for the production of vinifera. The Okanagan and Similkameen regions lie to the east of the mountain range while the regions of Vancouver Island and Fraser Valley lie to the west.

**Okanagan Valley** is British Columbia's oldest and primary wine growing region. A multitude of microclimates are found in what is Canada's only desert, which is an extension of the Sonora Desert. With less than 10 inches of annual rainfall, irrigation is necessary. The water laden air currents often moderate local climate. The warmer areas in the southern part of the valley have sandy desert soils, while the cooler areas to the north have deep layers of topsoil and clay. The predominant varieties grown in the south are Chardonnay, Merlot, Cabernet Sauvignon, Pinot Gris, and Pinot Noir. In the north they are Pinot Blanc, Pinot Noir, Pinot Gris, Riesling, and Gewürztraminer.

**Similkameen Valley**, located west of the Okanagan Valley DVA, is a small wine-growing region. The vineyards lie on the shore of the Similkameen River.

**Fraser Valley** is British Columbia's southernmost wine-growing region. Its mesoclimate is ideal for growing Sylvaner, Pinot Noir, and Gewürztraminer.

**Vancouver Island** is located off the province's southwest coast and it has a small amount of acres under vine. **The Gulf Islands** is British Columbia's newest DVA.

## ICE WINE (EISWEIN)

Canada is probably most famous for its quality production of ice wine (spelled Icewine in Canada). It is one of three countries that follow very strict guidelines in the making of the sweet wine. The other two are Germany and Austria. In Ontario, Canada, the VQA's guidelines for producing Icewine include the following stipulations: the finished wine must have a Brix of 35 degrees or higher, the residual sugar level must be at least 125 grams/litre, and the wine's alcohol must come exclusively from the grapes' natural sugar.

The grapes for Icewine must be harvested while they are frozen on the vine. Cryoextraction, chaptalization, and the use of *Süssreserve* are not permitted in its production. The preferred varieties for Icewine are Riesling and Vidal Blanc. Vidal Blanc is the only hybrid permitted and must be sourced from VQA recognized areas.

# Australia
By Jim Clarke

## The Essentials

| | |
|---|---|
| Parallel (Latitude) | 34° - 43° S |
| Regions at the same latitude | Patagonia, Stellenbosch, Maipo Valley, New Zealand's North Island |
| Total Area Under Vine | 172,676 hectares |
| Volume Produced | 1.124 million liters |
| % White | 43.5% |
| % Red | 54.0% |
| % Sparkling | 2.5% |
| Volume Produced | 1,124 million liters |
| Volume Exported | 775 million liters |
| Top Export Markets | U.K., United States, Canada |
| # Growers | ~7000 |
| # Producers | 2,477 |
| Stats Related to USA | 21.4 million liters exported to U.S. in 2008, accounting for 27% the country's exports |
| Climate | Subtropical to Cooler Temperate, with arid conditions predominating |
| Average Temperature | New South Wales 71° F; Victoria 68° F; South Australia 72° F; Western Australia 76° F; Tasmania 63° F |
| Hours of Sunlight Per Year | New South Wales 2,480; Victoria 2,780; South Australia 2,770; Western Australia 3,200; Tasmania 2,165 |
| Rain Per Year | New South Wales 1,200 mm; Victoria 650 mm; South Australia 540 mm; Western Australia 850 mm; Tasmania 620 mm |
| Major Cities | Sydney, Melbourne, Adelaide, Perth, Hobart |
| Primary Red Grapes | Shiraz, Cabernet Sauvignon |
| Primary White Grapes | Chardonnay |
| Secondary Red Grapes | Grenache, Mourvedre |
| Secondary White Grapes | Semillon, Riesling, Sauvignon Blanc, Verdelho |
| Federal Governing Body | Australia Wine & Brandy Corporation |
| Local Governing Body / Committee | N/A |
| Regional Appellation Terminology | Geographical Origin (GI) |
| States with GIs | Queensland, New South Wales, Victoria, Tasmania, South Australia, Western Australia |
| Quality/Rating System | None |
| Quality/Rating Levels | None |

On the face of it, the one word summary for Australia's wine scene is "big." Big. Fruity. Alcoholic. Shiraz. Big companies: five companies make three-quarters of Australia's wine. Big appellations—the Southeastern Australia Geographical Indication (GI) encompasses 95% of the nation's vineyards. Big value—brands like Yellowtail made Australian wine synonymous with inexpensive, consistent bottles and introduced the world to the "critter label" phenomenon. One study showed that brands with an animal label consistently prosper in the market compared to their animal-free competitors. And big ambitions: in 1981 the government created **Wine Australia** (properly speaking, the Australian Wine and Brandy Corporation), to promote and regulate the industry. Building on their success in the 1980s, their **Strategy 2025** plan, introduced in 1996, aimed for annual sales of $4.5 billion by 2025…and succeeded twenty years early in 2005.

In each case, however, that's not the full story. Shiraz is the flagship grape, but a wide range of grape varieties are grown Down Under, and not all high-yield, high-alcohol, fruit bombs. Shiraz itself sees plenty of variety when terroir and climate are allowed to express themselves. It's also playing a part in southern Rhône-style blends known as GSMs (Grenache-Shiraz-Mourvèdre), adding another range of expression.

Winemakers are also exploring the range of Chardonnay, Australia's second most-planted variety. While over-the-top, opulent examples are easy to find, more restrained types are becoming increasingly common, as are light unoaked styles. Other white grapes like Semillon and Verdelho have gained reputations as varietal wines in Australia as well.

There are more than 2,300 wineries in the country, and a number of the smaller, boutique brands are becoming increasingly available in export markets. For that matter, the big companies that dominate Australia's production make a lot more than bag-in-a-box wines and supermarket brands. Southcorp, for example, produces Penfold's Grange, Australia's most expensive wine to date. The technological capabilities of even a modest Australian winery are typically state-of-the-art and their facilities are often significantly more sophisticated than those of many producers in the Old World.

**Australia's Geographical Indication (GI) system** isn't all broad, sweeping areas. The Southeastern Australia GI may include vineyards in four states, but those are further subdivided into **zones, regions**, and **sub-regions**—107 GIs in total, some home to just a handful of producers. In addition there are four other winegrowing states, although at this time only one, Western Australia, has been divvied up into zones, regions and sub-regions—twenty-two so far. Many producers are increasingly focusing on the smaller GIs to differentiate their wines from the low-price expectations that the broader state GIs have engendered.

The big plans have also hit a snag. Faced with a grape glut and low prices, many vineyards are no longer able to cover their costs; growers are ripping out vines even in well-known GIs like Barossa. Global climate change is also an increasing cause of concern in a country that already has some of the world's hottest growing regions. Water, too, has become increasingly scarce, a disaster for an industry dependent on irrigation. Australia's vinous future depends on how these issues are addressed, but the potential is not in doubt.

# History

The first vines in Australia were planted in 1788 in Sydney with vinifera cuttings brought by Captain Arthur Phillips from South Africa as part of the so-called First Fleet, charged with setting up the first penal colony in Australia. Within several decades Victoria, South Australia and even distant Western Australia had significant vineyard plantings. However, the "Father of Australian Viticulture" was James Busby, an ambitious Scot who emigrated from his home country in 1824. Convinced that Australia was a good place for wine grapes well before he had ever set foot there, he researched the subject in advance of his arrival and wrote a book about it during the journey. His biggest contribution was a large collection of vinifera vine cuttings from France and Spain, some of which include clones that are still well-regarded today.

Two changes affected the Australian wine industry in the second half of the nineteenth century: a move toward fortified wines and the appearance of phylloxera. Victoria was devastated by the latter, but most other states were largely spared thanks to quickly enacted, draconian quarantine regulations.

Fortified wines suited some of the warmer growing regions like Barossa and Rutherglen. Australia's winemakers were already looking toward the export market—they knew that fortified wines were much more likely to survive the long journey back to the United Kingdom.

Fortified wine remained the country's mainstay through much of the twentieth century, with South Australia and the Barossa Valley in particular dominating the industry. In the 1950s table wines began a return to fashion as Australian winemakers found more chances to taste European table wines (i.e., unfortified). The vintners imported technology that made fermentation temperatures and oxidation easier to control. Oxidation and hot fermentations are less detrimental to fortified wines and may even be part of the style, but generally don't play a part in table wine production.

1951 saw the first vintage of Penfold's Grange Hermitage—today known only as Grange—a Shiraz-based blend made with grapes from several South Australia areas (Barossa in particular) that has gone on to become the country's most highly regarded wine. The 1971 vintage won the Wine Olympics in Paris in 1979.

Another innovation, the introduction of varietal labeling, would make Cabernet Sauvignon and Chardonnay popular in the 1980s, with Shiraz lagging not far behind. In fact, the unorthodox Shiraz-Cabernet Sauvignon blend was developed so that Shiraz-based wines could ride the coattails of Cabernet's status among wine drinkers.

Wine competitions—typically at county fairs—played a role in separating the wheat from the chafe, and quickly proved influential, motivating winemakers to master a high level of technical excellence. Wines with even small faults were roundly rejected, so wineries needed an ultra-hygienic approach to take medals. This attention to technique, and with it, technology, led to innovations. Among others, the Australians introduced temperature-controlled fermentation for both whites and reds (arguably doing more to advance winemaking than anything else in the twentieth century) and, along with New Zealand, demonstrating the effectiveness of the screwcap as an alternative closure. Organizations like the **Commonwealth Scientific & Industrial Organization** (CSIRO) and the industry-owned **Australian Wine Research Institute** have had leading roles in advancing a technical understanding of viniculture and viticulture. The CSIRO is Australia's national science agency and conducts and finances scientific research. The organization has made relevant contributions in a wide range of areas including wine grape genetics, soil and water management, and supply chain optimization. The Wine Research Institute is funded by levies on wineries, with matching government support. It conducts research on everything from vineyards to packaging and distribution issues, while also providing commercial services (lab analyses, etc.).

Today, an Australian winery (even a smaller one) is typically a state-of-the-art facility replete with stainless steel and computers, often far more advanced than many of their peers in the Old World. An Australian winemaker has most likely attended one of the country's various wine colleges. There is some criticism that this institutionalization and a focus on technical excellence has led to cookie-cutter winemaking guilty of producing soulless wines that are incapable of expressing terroir. Nonetheless, Australian wine makers' techniques and advances have spread far and wide; taking advantage of the six-month gap between northern and southern hemisphere vintages, Australian "flying winemakers" took to consulting for European and North American wineries during their downtime, both learning and spreading Australia's high-tech innovations at the same time.

The 1970s saw the appearance of the bag-in-a-box wine—another Aussie innovation, euphemistically known as cask wine in Australia. Box wine remains the fate of more than 45% of Australian wine today. During the same period, however, boutique wineries also became a more prominent part of the landscape; but even today, 70% of Australian grapes are handled by just 14 producers. Ripe, fruit-forward, low-acid wines became the nation's calling card.

In the twenty-first century Australia became the premier source for budget wines in North America and the United Kingdom. The low average prices became increasingly unsustainable, however, and the country is struggling to raise its profile by focusing on regionality and terroir. Global climate change, water scarcity and a reliance on irrigation are also challenging vintners in a country with some of the world's hottest growing regions.

# CLASSIFICATIONS

The Australia Wine and Brandy Corporation founded **Australia's Geographical Indication (GI) system** in 1993. At the same time it also established the Geographical Indication Committee, a five-person board charged with establishing individual GIs. Aside from the broad Southeastern Australia "Super GI"— which encompasses more than 95% of Australian vineyards, omitting Western Australia and little else—and State designations (Western Australia, South Australia, Victoria, etc.), there are three levels to the indications:

1. Zones
2. Regions
3. Sub-regions

A **Zone** is defined as just an area of land, with no other necessary qualifications. A **Region**, unlike a Zone, must have some sort of homogeneity to its grape growing characteristics; the area also has to contain at least five independently owned vineyards of at least five hectares apiece and produce at least five hundred tons (50,000 kilos) of grapes, in most years. A **Sub-Region** is a single piece of land within a Region that is significantly differentiated from the rest of the Region, but has the same minimum requirements as a Region in terms of vineyards and production.

- For a GI to be used on the label 85% of the grapes used must have been grown within the GI
- Two or even three GIs may appear on a label, in which case 95% of the grapes must come from within those GIs as a whole, and at least 5% from each GI individually.
- On the label GIs must be indicated in agreement to their proportions in the wine.

The GI whose grapes make up more of the wine than those of other GIs must be listed first and in descending order from there. For example: a wine made with 25% Coonawarra grapes, 40% Barossa Valley grapes, and 35% McLaren Vale grapes would have to be labeled "Barossa Valley-McLaren Vale-Coonawarra, if the producer didn't want to use the broader South Australia designation.

**Variety Indications**: Whether a blend or single variety wine, the grape or grapes used must comprise 85% of the grapes listed on the label. In the case of blends, the grapes must be listed in order with their proportions in the wine, just as with GIs.

**Vintage**: If a vintage is given on the label, 85% of the grapes used must be from that vintage. However, a producer can list all the vintages used on the label, in which case 100% of the wine must be from those vintages and they must be listed in order with their proportions in the wine.

**Fortified Wines**: Must contain 15-22% alcohol, and may contain caramel.

**Alcohol**: Domestically, alcohol statements on table wines can vary up to 1.5% on table wines, or 0.5% for fortified wines.

Acidification, de-acidification, and enrichment are permitted, but chaptalization is not.

As of September 1, 2011 Australian producers were no longer able to use many names associated with European wines, including many popular with Australia's fortified wine industry. For example, Port, Sherry, Fino, Oloroso and Champagne will be off-limits to Australian producers for use as names on their products.

The **Label Integrity Program** assigns responsibility to growers, wineries, retailers, and exporters for truthfulness in all statements regarding wine styles, grape sources, varieties used, and vintages; previously this responsibility rested solely on the shoulders of wine producers. The intent is to ensure that accuracy can be confirmed at each step of the production and sales chain.

## TERROIR

The great majority of Australian wines are made with grapes from broad regions, so *terroir*, in the sense of expressing the character of a given vineyard in a wine, is relatively rare. Even Penfolds Grange, the country's most expensive wine, is made with grapes from several vineyards quite a distance apart. However, more producers are working at focusing on the terroir of individual vineyards, or, at the very least, regions.

Quality winemaking lines the southern coast of the country, with a few isolated regions further inland. The northern half of the continent is too hot for quality winegrowing, and even many of the southern states depend on elevation or maritime influence to moderate temperatures. Excessive rainfall is rarely a problem; in fact, most vineyards rely on irrigation. Drought in the first decade of the twenty-first century has put pressure on the water supply for some areas, as has the threat of global climate change.

Aside from Victoria, most of the country fought off phylloxera with extremely aggressive quarantine and isolation regulations. Many vines are still planted on their own, ungrafted roots.

Generalizing about the soils of an entire continent is impossible, so see the descriptions of individual regions for details. The most famous soil is the **terra rossa** of the Limestone Coast in South Australia, a limestone base covered by red clay topsoil.

Climate change and ongoing drought problems have also led to increasingly high salt levels in the water table of some regions—the inland Murray River Basin centered in northwest Victoria, in particular—which can interfere with grape quality or demand aggressive irrigation for dilution. Winegrowers are also making an effort to locate cooler growing sites, primarily via maritime influence (Mornington Peninsula and the Yarra Valley, for example) or higher elevations (Adelaide Hills, Granite Belt).

## VARIETIES

### REDS

**Shiraz** is the country's most popular variety—known as Syrah in most of the rest of the world—with more than 43,000 hectares of vineyards in 2010. It, along with Grenache and Mourvèdre, were long used for fortified wines. Many of today's Shiraz table wines are still aged in American oak, a practice dating to the 1940s, when the Australian Wine Board began encouraging its importation, stating that the French oak being imported was of inadequate quality. American oak can give wine distinctive coconut and dill notes, though French oak has become more common in the past decade. Australian Shiraz tends to be fuller-bodied, with more fruit, red or dark, than the Syrah-based wines of the Rhône Valley, and is often tinged with notes of chocolate in lieu of peppery spice.

Shiraz can be found in most of Australia's winegrowing regions, but its most noteworthy homes are in South Australia. Hunter Valley and Margaret River also produce some notable examples.

Some producers, following the Northern Rhône model, blend a small percentage of Viognier into their Shiraz. Other common blending partners include Grenache and Mourvèdre—known as a **GSM**— or, less traditionally, Cabernet Sauvignon.

**Cabernet Sauvignon** is more associated with premium wines than Shiraz, perhaps owing to its popularity when Australian wines were attracting attention in the export market in the 1970s. In fact, the demand created led to the Shiraz-Cabernet Sauvignon blend as a means to expand marketable production while keeping the Cabernet name on the label. As of 2010 there were about 26,000 hectares planted—Margaret River, McLaren Vale, and Coonawarra being the most highly-regarded homes for the grape. Many age-worthy examples are produced, often full, with dark blackcurrant aromas and often a minty touch.

**Grenache** is mostly used in GSM blends with Shiraz and Mourvèdre, aside from a few old vine bottlings. On its own, Australian Grenache is typically very fruity, high in alcohol, and only lightly tannic. There were about 1,800 hectares planted as of 2010, in mostly the same regions as Shiraz.

**Pinot Noir** is mostly used for sparkling wines. Boutique wines in Tasmania and parts of Victoria (Mornington Peninsula, Yarra Valley) are producing some impressive still examples, as are producers in the Adelaide Hills. Most of Australia's developed wine regions are too warm for the grape. Red fruit aromas are typical, though some darker, more powerful and earthy wines are appearing as vines mature.

**Merlot** is on the decline, with about 10,000 hectares as of 2010, but often found as Cabernet Sauvignon's junior partner in blends. Varietal renditions from South Australia tend toward a plummy fruitiness, while examples from Margaret River and other cooler areas are typically firmer and earthier.

**Mourvèdre** often appears in GSM blends, with the occasional varietal wine. As of 2010 there were about 700 hectares planted.

Other Reds: Many producers are exploring **Tempranillo**, which does seem to be well-suited to the warm, dry climate, but currently there are only about 600 hectares planted. Some remarkable wines from **Sangiovese** and **Nebbiolo** are also being made.

## WHITES

**Chardonnay** is Australia's second-most planted grape, with 28,000 hectares in 2010. It's vinified in a wide range of styles, from light, crisp, and citrusy (and increasingly, unoaked) in cooler areas like Tasmania and the Adelaide Hills, to richly oaked and tropical in warmer areas— Riverland, Margaret River, and the like. The latter style has been fading in popularity as winemakers move toward a more restrained style.

**Sauvignon Blanc** is sometimes blended with Semillon, particularly in Margaret River; as a varietal wine it tends toward a more tropical expression, though growers are seeking out cooler areas with hopes of replicating the New Zealand, gooseberry-and-grass style, which is very popular with Aussie wine drinkers. Yarra Valley and Adelaide Hills are prime spots for the grape. There are about 7,000 hectares planted.

**Semillon** has been a signature wine for several decades—particularly that of the Hunter Valley. Unoaked and crisp, with moderate alcohol, it develops handsomely with age, taking on toasty, honeyed aromas, and a firm, dense mouthfeel. There are about 6,000 hectares planted.

**Riesling**, historically, has been heavily planted; but today there are only about 4,600 hectares, mostly in Clare and Eden Valleys, Great Southern, and Tasmania. Typically vinified dry, many examples show the minerally, petrol aromas normally associated with well-aged Riesling when still young; lime and grapefruit notes are also typical, while Tasmanian examples tend to be more floral.

**Pinot Gris** is generally labeled under its French name in sweeter examples, but **Pinot Grigio** when dry. With the popularity of the latter, this variety has been enthusiastically planted in recent years, almost tripling from 1,300 hectares in 2006 to 3,500 hectares in 2010. Mornington Peninsula, Tasmania, and Great Southern are the biggest producers.

**Viognier**, **Marsanne** and **Roussanne** are seeing more attention, especially Viognier. There are about 1,500 hectares planted. Sometimes small amounts are blended into Shiraz in accordance with practices in the Northern Rhône, but varietal bottlings are becoming more common in areas like Eden Valley and McLaren Vale.

**Verdelho** was originally planted for making fortified wines, but producers in Hunter Valley and Western Australia are making some nutty, dry examples. About 1,600 hectares are planted.

Other white grapes: **Muscat Gordo Blanco** (elsewhere known as Muscat of Alexandria) and **Sultana** are used in some fortified wines, and **Colombard** is heavily planted in some warmer regions for its ability to retain its acidity; it typically disappears into boxed wines and other blends.

Sparkling wines make up just 2.5% of Australia's production. Many producers work with the classic Champagne varieties Pinot Noir, Chardonnay, and to a lesser extent, Pinot Meunier. Tasmanian sparklers have led the way in terms of critical praise, but many of Victoria's cooler regions (Yarra Valley) are producing notable examples. Australian law permits both traditional and Charmat methods for producing sparkling wines, which can be vintage or non-vintage blends.

Australians have been making sparkling Shiraz for about 150 years as well. Often on the sweet side, these full-bodied red sparklers are usually intended for festive drinking, but a few have developed more serious followings. Many are made from Barossa fruit, though multi-region blends are quite common.

Sweet fortified wines—known as "stickies"—once the mainstay of the Australian wine scene, remain a small (1.5%) but important part of Australian production. Muscat is the primary variety (but several varieties may be used), typically harvested late, fortified with neutral brandy and then aged extensively.

Tokay's are produced much the same way from the Muscadelle grape. As of 2009 the Tokay name began to be phased out over ten years to comply with EU regulations; the name "Topaque" will take its place. Australian Sherry took on the name "Apera" in 2010 for the same reason.

Producers use red varieties—Shiraz, Grenache, Mourvèdre, or Cabernet Sauvignon, most commonly—for the Tawny and Vintage styles (formerly called Port). Tawny is a multi-vintage blend; Vintage uses grapes from a single harvest.

Many regions made fortified wines in the past. Today Rutherglen dominates Muscat and Tokay production; the neighboring regions of Glenrowan and Beechworth also make some notable examples. Tawny and Vintage fortified wines can be found in several regions, with some outstanding examples coming from the Barossa Valley in particular.

# Regions

## Queensland

Queensland is a hot and unlikely place for winegrowing, but there are a few noteworthy areas; enough to support about seventy wineries, in fact. There are currently about 1,500 hectares (3,700 acres) planted. The **Granite Belt**, nestled on the border of New South Wales, is the state's most highly regarded GI; soils, as you'd expect, are generally granitic, and its high elevation of 2,600–3,300 feet (800–1,000 meters) makes it cool enough even for Riesling, with Shiraz and other grapes also finding homes there. On the whole the wines have a reputation for a lighter, crisper character than those from other Australian regions.

A few other GIs dot the coast north of the Granite Belt, most notably **Darling Downs, South Burnett**, and **North Burnett**. In general these are newer regions, with Chardonnay leading the way amongst a mix of other varieties.

## New South Wales

**Hunter Valley**, most notably, is an unusual spot for quality wines; subtropical and rainy, it gives plenty of things for the winegrower to worry about. But its whites—crisp Semillons that age into honeyed complexity, in particular, but also elegant Chardonnays—are highly regarded. It's also home to quality, earthier Shiraz. Vintage variation is endemic, given the climate. The Lower Hunter, closer to Sydney, is the historical center of the action, and one of Australia's first regions to focus on table wines and French grape varieties. The drier Upper Hunter is all about Chardonnay, and dominated by one producer, Rosemount.

**Mudgee**, farther west, is cooler at 1,500 foot (450 meter) elevation, and noted for Chardonnay and Cabernet Sauvignon along with the ubiquitous Shiraz. An older region, it was often neglected until wine tastes changed. Growers seeking out cooler climates gave it a second look. With about 160 growers and 40 wineries, today it's still home more to boutique producers than big players.

The same might be said for **Orange**, though the focus is more on red varieties; even Pinot Noir is finding a hospitable home here. These regions enjoy the moderating benefits of altitude at 1,500–1,700 feet (450–600 meters).

**Canberra,** farther south, does well with Shiraz and Pinot Noir from its higher elevation vineyards. Riesling and Chardonnay are the region's important whites.

The inland **Riverina** region is hot, dry, and reliant on irrigation, but actually grows more than half the grapes in New South Wales. Chardonnay, Semillon, Cabernet Sauvignon, and Shiraz are the most planted varieties. Most grapes are destined for cheap, multi-regional blends and bulk wine but Riverina's botrytis-affected Semillon has given the area a point of pride as well.

# Victoria

The smallest and coolest state in mainland Australia, Victoria is also the most viticulturally diverse, with more than twenty regions and 850 wineries. A Gold Rush brought immigrants to the area in the second half of the nineteenth century, and with them a wave of vineyard plantings that were then aggressively uprooted in an attempt to stamp out an epidemic of phylloxera. Victoria was hit first and more aggressively than other states, and the state government failed to isolate the aphid or support the replanting with grafted, resistant rootstocks. The policy changed in 1906, but for most regions that was too late to revive the industry. Serious replanting didn't begin until 1966. On the plus side, restarting from scratch has allowed growers to incorporate new ideas regarding clonal selection, canopy management, and other viticultural advances, which has given Victoria a leg up in establishing a reputation for quality wines.

**Murray Darling** overlaps into New South Wales and grows much the same grape varieties as Riverina, for much the same wines. The calcareous soils of the area encourage high yields; but extensive irrigation and water management efforts have created areas with salinity problems. The Murray River is a prime source of water for winegrowing irrigation in this region and elsewhere.

The **Grampians**, especially under their former name Great Western, were known for their sparkling wines, though today Shiraz is getting increasing attention; while cooler than some areas associated with Shiraz, long, dry autumns have made a ripe and spicy style possible. Those two possibilities come together in the form of Sparkling Shiraz, and the region makes some Riesling and Cabernet Sauvignon as well.

**Henty**, a cooler region reaching from the Grampians south to the coast, is also doing well with Riesling and sparkling wines.

As one moves through the regions stretching northeast from the Grampian— the **Pyrenees**, **Bendigo** and **Heathcote**— the climate becomes warmer. Shiraz and Cabernet Sauvignon dominate, although Bendigo does make a significant amount of Chardonnay.

The **Goulburn Valley**, at the end of this northeastern arc, is more fertile and hot; it is also home to Australia's oldest Marsanne plantings, which yield some impressive wines.

The cluster of regions to the east of Goulburn Valley includes **Rutherglen**, the source of Australia's most noted fortified wines, made from **Rutherglen Brown Muscat** (a dark clone of Muscat à Petits Grains Rouge) or Muscadelle for white wines.

Neighboring regions like **Glenrowan** and **Beechworth** make some "stickies" (as Australians call their sweet wines) and weighty Shiraz; but cooler, higher-elevation vineyards in Beechworth also yield some of the country's most elegant Chardonnays.

The winegrowing regions that encircle Melbourne generally enjoy the cooling, moderating influence of the Port Philip Bay or Bass Strait. **Geelong**, the **Yarra Valley** and **Mornington Peninsula** all take advantage of the maritime climate to make some of the country's best Pinot Noir. Chardonnay is also popular, as are Shiraz and Cabernet Sauvignon. However, the latter two must be planted and grown with care in Yarra Valley and Mornington Peninsula to insure proper ripening. Most Cabernet Sauvignons there are blended with significant amounts of the earlier- ripening Merlot or Cabernet Franc. Pinot Gris is also popular in Mornington Peninsula, and has become the area's signature grape in the domestic market.

# Tasmania

This island state is quite cool, and the only state producing premium wines without any regional GIs. There are several unofficial regions on the north and southeast coasts, most notably **Tamar Valley** and **Pipers River**. The west coast is considered too wet for viticulture. Pinot Noir and Chardonnay dominate the island's vineyards, vinified both still and sparkling. Other aromatic white varieties like Sauvignon Blanc and the so-called Alsatian varieties also do well here. Production is still quite limited, but higher-end; while the state makes less than one percent of Australia's total by volume, it accounts for six percent by sales.

# South Australia

The state of South Australia occupies the middle third of the continent's southern half, but the wineries are all clustered in the southeastern corner alongside Victoria. Some of its vines are among the oldest in the world, spared—due to their remote location—by the phylloxera that plagued Victoria. South Australia's regions and sub-regions are among the most recognized names in Australian wine. By volume, almost half the country's production takes place here. The state is home to all the major research and trade organizations.

## THE LIMESTONE COAST

South Australia is also one of the only states with a signature soil type— **terra rossa** soils, a layer of red topsoil over a limestone base. The limestone lends its name to this zone, the state's southeast corner. Within the zone the **Coonawarra** region was the earliest to be singled out. First planted in 1890, Coonawarra saw growth spurts in the 1970s and again in the 1990s. It's the most southerly, and therefore cooler—cooler, in fact, than Bordeaux—but with a long growing season well-suited to Cabernet Sauvignon, which makes up almost 60% of its vines. The region also produces some notable Shiraz. There are only 17 wineries here, but many outside producers make grapes with fruit from the area.

**Wrattonbully** and **Padthaway** stretch north from Coonawarra and focus on much the same varieties; the latter is a bit warmer but has more of a reputation for Chardonnay. The terra rossa soils drain very well, making for concentration and intensity in the wines. When not blended with grapes from other regions, this can be one of Australia's few examples of terroir-driven wines.

Some of Australia's most well-known regions run in a line just east of Adelaide. The state's northernmost region, **Clare Valley**, is most noted for its Rieslings; dry, with lime and grapefruit notes and often showing the petrol notes associated with older Rieslings, at a young age. Shiraz and Cabernet Sauvignon also do well there.

The **Barossa Valley** is probably the country's most famous region, particularly for Shiraz. This variety accounts for more than half the region's vines and the acreage planted with Shiraz continues to grow. Winegrowing here dates back to 1842. The area is home to many historic wineries, typically founded by Silesian immigrants who left Prussia after facing religious persecution there; many are still operating and highly-regarded today. In some cases the vines are over 100 years old (ungrafted vines live longer than their grafted counterparts). Old vine vineyards are responsible for many of the region's flagship wines.

The area's Chardonnay, Semillon, Cabernet Sauvignon and other varieties are also well-regarded, and GSM blends are common. Soils are varied, encompassing a range of sandy and clay-based types, and the hilly terrain makes for a variety of aspects and sun exposure. The area is hot and dry, so irrigation is a necessity.

The **Eden Valley** lies alongside Barossa, but is cooler because of its higher elevation of 1,300—1,650 feet (400–500 meters). Riesling and Shiraz are the region's two most planted and critically acclaimed varieties.

If there is an area in Australia that might take on the New Zealanders when it comes to their signature grape, Sauvignon Blanc, it is the **Adelaide Hills**, where the grape tends toward a citrusy, floral style. Higher elevations from 1,300 to 2,300 feet (400–700 meters) provide the coolness the grape enjoys. Chardonnay and Riesling have also done well there. A few reds are made, too; the Adelaide Hills are considered the best spot for Pinot Noir in South Australia. This row of wine regions reaches Gulf St. Vincent at **McLaren Vale**, a region of varied soils, exposures, and even elevations at its border with the Adelaide Hills. The ocean has a cooling influence, and the region is known for its old vine vineyards—South Australia's first vines were planted here in 1838. Cabernet Sauvignon is the area's calling card, often full and rich, though Shiraz and Grenache do well along with some Sauvignon Blanc.

Nearby **Langhorne Creek** is also one of the state's oldest growing regions, situated along Lake Alexandrina rather than Gulf St. Vincent. Winds off the lake have an even stronger cooling effect, so grapes here typically ripen later than in McLaren Vale. While Langhorne Creek rarely appears on the label, its grapes make an important contribution to many South Australian Shiraz and Cabernet Sauvignons.

## WESTERN AUSTRALIA

Western Australia is the country's largest state, but its winemaking activities are confined to the cool southwest corner and comprise less than five percent of the country's production. Premium wines make up a large proportion of production, and relatively little of Western Australia's wines are destined for cask wine or budget bottles.

The state's oldest vineyards are in the hot, dry **Swan District** north of Perth; viticulture there dates back to 1829. The region makes some well-regarded Chenin Blancs and Verdelhos, and Chardonnay and Shiraz plantings are increasing. Unlike the other regions of Western Australia and despite its historical significance, however, most of the Swan District's grapes find their way into bulk wines.

Western Australia's most famous region, **Margaret River**, occupies most of the broad peninsula that juts out south of Perth. The area is relatively young, with its first significant plantings coming in 1967; but by the end of the 1970s it had made its name with elegant Cabernet Sauvignon. Chardonnay followed in its wake as a signature white. Shiraz and Semillon-Sauvignon Blanc blends have also proven to do well here. Today there are more than 120 producers (mostly smaller, boutique wineries) in the region; while they account for just 3% of Australia's overall production, they produce 20% of the country's premium wines.

Margaret River's soils are varied, but there are some spots of infertile, gravelly loams that are particularly valued. The terrain is mostly rolling hills, leading to cliffs overlooking the Indian Ocean. Being surrounded by water, the region's temperatures are quite stable year-round. In fact, growers occasionally have problems with vines not getting the hint when winter comes and failing to go into dormancy, which can disrupt budding and flowering in spring. Winds are also a problem; they temper the heat but intense breezes in spring can sometimes interfere with flowering.

Moving eastward off the peninsula the climate becomes more continental. The **Geographe** and **Blackwood Valley** regions do well with much the same varieties as Margaret River, but in somewhat warmer conditions.

**Pemberton**, to the south, is cooler than Margaret River, with enough rainfall so that some growers don't need to irrigate. Chardonnay is the most planted variety, often showing a rich but structured style. There is a fair bit of Merlot and Cabernet Sauvignon planted as well. There is some interest in Pinot Noir among the region's growers, but results have been inconsistent so far.

The **Great Southern** region is quite large, and makes 37% of Western Australia's wine grapes. It enjoys some cooling maritime influence, which fades into a more continental climate inland. There are five officially recognized sub-regions: **Denmark** and **Albany** on the coast and **Frankland River, Mount Barker** and **Porongurup** inland. Soils are extremely varied. Denmark in particular has some very fertile loams that call for careful vine management if quality is to be achieved. Rainfall and humidity are problems in some areas. The region is known for its crisp, lean Chardonnays and Rieslings, as well as spicy Shiraz and dense Cabernet Sauvignons and Merlots.

## SUMMARY OF STATES, ZONES, REGIONS & SUB-REGIONS

| State/Zone | Regions | Sub-regions |
|---|---|---|
| QUEENSLAND | South Burnett | |
| | Granite Belt | |
| SOUTH EASTERN AUSTRALIA | (Super Zone including the entirety of New South Wales, Victoria, and Tasmania as well as parts of South Australia and Queensland) | |
| NEW SOUTH WALES | | |
| Northern Slopes | New England | |
| Northern Rivers | Hastings Rivers | |
| Hunter Valley | Hunter | Pokolbin |
| | | Broke Fordwich |
| | | Upper Hunter Valley |
| South Coast | Shoalhaven Coast | |
| | Southern Highlands | |
| Central Ranges | Mudgee | |
| | Orange | |
| | Cowra | |

| State/Zone | Regions | Sub-regions |
|---|---|---|
| Southern New South Wales | Canberra District | |
| | Hilltops | |
| | Gundagai | |
| | Tumbarumba | |
| Big Rivers | Riverina | |
| | Perricoota | |
| | Swan Hill (extends into Victoria) | |
| | Murray Darling (extends into Victoria) | |
| Western Plains | | |
| AUSTRALIAN CAPITAL TERRITORY | | |
| VICTORIA | | |
| Gippsland | | |
| North East Victoria | Alpine Valleys | |
| | Beechworth | |
| | Rutherglen | |
| | King Valley | |
| | Glenrowan | |
| Central Victoria | Upper Goulbourn | |
| | Strathbogie Ranges | |
| | Goulbourn Valley | Nagambie Lakes |
| | Heathcote | |
| | Bendigo | |
| Port Phillip | Yarra Valley | |
| | Mornington Peninsula | |
| | Sunbury | |
| | Macedon Ranges | |
| | Geelong | |
| Western Victoria | Pyrenees | |
| | Grampians | |
| | Henty | |
| North West Victoria | Swan Hill (extends into NSW) | |
| | Murray Darling (extends into NSW) | |
| TASMANIA | | |
| SOUTH AUSTRALIA | | |
| Adelaide | (Super Zone including Mount Lofty Ranges, Fleurieu, and Barossa) | |
| Limestone Coast | Mount Gambier | |
| | Wrattonbully | |
| | Coonawarra | |
| | Padthaway | |
| | Robe | |
| | Mount Benson | |
| Lower Murray | Riverland | |
| Barossa | Eden Valley | High Eden |
| | Barossa Valley | |

| State/Zone | Regions | Sub-regions |
|---|---|---|
| Mount Lofty Ranges | Adelaide Hills | Lenswood |
| | | Piccadilly Valley |
| | Adelaide Plains | |
| | Clare Valley | |
| Far North | Southern Flinders Ranges | |
| Fleurieu | Langhorne Creek | |
| | Currency Creek | |
| | McLaren Vale | |
| | Southern Fleurieu | |
| | Kangaroo Island | |
| NORTHERN TERRITORY | | |
| WESTERN AUSTRALIA | | |
| Eastern Plains, Inland, & North of Western Australia | | |
| South West Australia | Great Southern | Albany |
| | | Porongurup |
| | | Mount Barker |
| | | Denmark |
| | | Frankland River |
| | Manjimup | |
| | Blackwood Valley | |
| | Pemberton | |
| | Geographe | |
| | Margaret River | |
| Central Western Australia | | |
| Greater Perth | Peel | |
| | Perth Hills | |
| | Swan District | Swan Valley |

# HOT TOPICS

Beginning around 2005, a grape glut has led to pricing problems for Australia's winegrowers. Cheap, easily drinkable wines were no longer providing enough of a return to keep many producers in business. In 2007 Wine Australia rolled out **Directions to 2025**, an industry-wide plan intended to address problems related to unsustainably low grape prices, water demands, and global competition. The goal is to restore the industry's health by focusing on regionality and terroir and the promoting of premium wines so sustainable, profitable pricing can be maintained. Australian winemakers have discovered they need to convince foreign markets that they are more than just a source of well-made but undistinguished budget wines if they are to stay in business.

Market forces are not the only problems to plague the Australian wine industry; global climate change and competition for irrigation water are also forcing many to rethink their viticulture practices. In 2006 the industry established a national **Drought Management Taskforce**, focused on managing water allocations across the industry and finding more efficient means of water use for winegrowers. Sixty percent of Australian wine production relies on irrigation water from the Murray River Basin, which is shared by three states. Recurrent droughts have created conflicting demands for water use, and population growth in cities like Adelaide compete for some of the same allocations. Some producers are even ripping out vineyards, leaving them destined to lie fallow or used for other agricultural endeavors. Even prized regions like the Barossa Valley have not been immune. Negotiating the dynamic between these more challenging conditions and the need to convince consumers to spend more for a bottle (or box?) of Australian wine will very likely keep the industry occupied through 2025 or perhaps longer.

# New Zealand

By Jim Clarke

## The Essentials

| | |
|---|---|
| Parallel (latitude) | **36°-45° S** |
| Regions at the same latitude | Patagonia; Victoria and Tasmania, Australia |
| Total area under vine | 31,964 hectares |
| Volume produced | 205.2 million liters |
| % white | 76% |
| % red | 24% |
| Volume produced | 205.2 million liters |
| Volume exported | 112.6 million liters |
| Top export markets | Australia, United Kingdom, US |
| # growers | 1,128 |
| # producers | 643 |
| Stats related to USA | 22.181 million liters exported to U.S.; 223.666 million NZ$ |
| Climate | Subtropical to Cooler Temperate |
| Average temperature | North Island 60° F, South Island 48° F |
| Hours of sunlight per year | 2000+ |
| Rain per year | Most winegrowing regions receive between 800 and 1,600ml of rain annually |
| Major cities | Auckland, Wellington, Christchurch |
| Major geographical features | Maritime influence; central mountain range rain shield |
| Primary Red Grapes | Pinot Noir |
| Primary White Grapes | Sauvignon Blanc, Chardonnay |
| Secondary Red Grapes | Merlot, Cabernet Sauvignon, Syrah |
| Secondary White Grapes | Pinot Gris, Riesling, Gewurztraminer |
| Federal Governing Body | New Zealand Food Safety Authority |
| Local Governing Body | N/A |
| Appellation terminology | Geographical Origin (GI) |
| Regions with GIs | Northland, Auckland, Waikato/Bay of Plenty, Gisborne, Hawkes Bay, Wairarapa/Martinborough, Nelson, Marlborough, Canterbury/Waipara, Waitiki Valley, Central Otago |
| Quality/rating system | None |

*New Zealand is not a small country but a large village.*

–Peter Jackson

On the face of it the New Zealand wine scene looks fairly straightforward. Signature white: Sauvignon Blanc. Signature red: Pinot Noir. Some other miscellaneous international varieties. The climate is all about maritime influence, except for Central Otago. Done and next.

This is certainly the way many New Zealand wine exports have been marketed, but it's hardly the whole story. The country's two islands stretch almost 1,000 miles (1600 km) north-to-south, making it substantially longer than California. Climates range from sub-tropical north of Auckland to the chilly side of temperate (think British Isles) in the south. While the Pacific Ocean does exert a moderating effect on most of the winegrowing regions, their climates are quite varied and grape planting choices have to be made accordingly.

The range of grape varieties planted and wine styles produced belies New Zealand's relatively small output, which accounts for less than one percent of the world's wine. The South Island is home to Pinot Noir, Sauvignon Blanc, Chardonnay and other aromatic whites; once you cross Cook Strait to the North Island, Syrah and red Bordeaux varieties begin to infiltrate the mix, becoming more predominant as you head north. The cool climate areas also lend themselves to sparkling wine, and several Champagne producers have invested in sparkling wine production here.

Rain and rich soils are two challenges for New Zealand winemakers, and vigorous vine growth has to be restrained if wine quality is to be achieved. It is no accident that most of the maritime wine regions are on the east coast— rain typically moves from west to east across the islands, and the mountain ranges that run down the center of both islands afford the vineyards some protection from precipitation.

Due to its southerly location and clean air, New Zealand's UV levels are significantly higher than in other wine-producing countries; as much as fifty percent more than in continental Europe. Some observers think that the additional UV exposure encourages the development of phenolics in the grapes (which contribute flavor, color, mouthfeel, and perhaps even health benefits) that otherwise wouldn't develop in the cool climate. The 1980s saw the introduction of canopy management techniques (trellising, pruning, etc.) to manage the amount of sunlight that reaches the leaves of the vine and the grape bunches themselves. These techniques help to take advantage of the sunlight and also help to control overabundant vine vigor.

New Zealand's biggest export customer is their large neighbor three hours to the west, Australia, followed by the United Kingdom and then the United States. While large vintages like 2008 sometimes put downward pressure on wine grape prices, the country has been fortunate to maintain a high average bottle price in the export market.

# History

New Zealand's first vines date to the beginning of the nineteenth century. James Busby, considered the father of Australian viticulture, actually made wine in the Northland (the region north of Auckland) in the 1830s, which he sold to British troops. This area continued to be the focus of winemaking activity on the North Island for most of nineteenth century, spurred on by a flow of immigrants from Dalmatia (now part of Croatia) who worked in the Kauri gum fields there. The British settlers up to that point had been more interested in brewing beer.

Many of New Zealand's modern wine companies have Dalmatian roots including Nobilo —Nikola Nobilo was part of the second generation of Dalmatian immigrants, arriving in 1937 and planting his first vines in 1942— and Babich, whose founder Josip Babich arrived in 1910 at the age of 14 and began making and selling wine under the name Babich Brothers in 1916. Winegrowing was picking up in cooler regions to the south as well; much like California, Central Otago experienced a Gold Rush in the 1860s, some former gold diggers subsequently turned to winegrowing. One pioneering figure, a Frenchman named Jean Desire Feraud, won the country's first wine medal in competitions in Sydney and Melbourne in 1879.

For the bulk of the twentieth century the wine industry went through a number of ups and downs, largely driven by changes in government policy. At the beginning of the century domestic wines made up about a quarter of the domestic market, which was otherwise dominated by Australian imports. An active temperance movement failed to impose a prohibition in the 1910s; but by the end of the decade mounting restrictions—limiting on-premise service to the hour between 5 and 6 p.m. during the workweek, for example, which led to a tradition of sixty minutes of heavy drinking known as the "Six o'clock swill"— hamstrung the industry, as did the subsequent global economic depression of the 1930s.

Industry choices also affected wine quality. Most notably, the planting of hybrid varieties as a way to address the phylloxera epidemic instead of grafting vinifera vines onto rootstocks from American grape species like Vitis Aestevalis— the more successful answer developed elsewhere. Isabella, an American hybrid, was still the country's most planted variety as late as 1960. Müller-Thurgau (the Riesling-Madeleine Royale cross) also became popular for its high yields and was used to make an innocuous white wine, often sweetened with *sussreserve* (the adding of unfermented, fresh grape juice to sweeten wine).

After World War II the government installed significant industry protections that helped stabilize the industry, but it wasn't until 1979 that the Montana Wine Company (now Brancott Estates) introduced vintage- and variety-labeling, thereby allowing Marlborough Sauvignon Blanc to take the place of generic blends and unleashing a style and expression that has proved next to impossible to replicate elsewhere. They began exporting the following year; but it was Cloudy Bay (founded in 1985 to make Sauvignon Blanc specifically) that exported aggressively to the U.S., U.K., and Australia, and garnered critical raves abroad. Around the same time Martinborough and then Central Otago began to turn heads with their Pinot Noirs, sealing the country's sterling reputation for these two cool-climate grapes.

Two priorities have dominated New Zealand wine in the first decade of the twenty-first century. Firstly, some high-yielding vintages have growers concerned about a wine glut that could threaten the strong price point that New Zealand prices have enjoyed; the industry as a whole is leery of becoming seen as a producer of budget wines to the detriment of premium wine sales. The other priority has been expanding the market for varieties other than Pinot Noir and Sauvignon Blanc. Plantings of the aromatic, "Alsatian" varieties (Riesling, Gewürztraminer and Pinot Gris) are growing, and some experts say the latter will be New Zealand's next cash cow. North Island Syrah, most notably from Hawke's Bay, but also from Waiheke Island, is also receiving more attention from critics; the wines' black pepper spice and structure distinguishing them from most of the Shiraz being produced by Australia. Merlot has also surpassed Cabernet Sauvignon in the past decade; its ability to ripen earlier may finally put the end to a reputation for greenness that haunts the country's Bordeaux varietal wines and blends.

Today there is only one thing as emblematic of New Zealand wine as Sauvignon Blanc: the screwcap. Marlborough's producers first turned to the alternative closure in 2001 due to increased frustration with the quality of corks they were receiving, and producers in other regions have followed suit. **The New Zealand Screwcap Initiative** did much of the groundwork in researching the closure's potential, and perhaps more importantly, in marketing the idea to consumers so that the screwcap would gain public acceptance internationally. Eighty-five to ninety percent of the country's wines are now sealed with screwcaps; nearby Australia has also taken to them and screwcap wines are becoming more popular (or at least accepted) by producers throughout the winemaking world, New and Old.

## CLASSIFICATIONS

**New Zealand's Geographical Origin system** is quite simple, with few regulations outside of vintage, grape source, and grape variety. Although passed in 1996, the regulatory system was not introduced until 2007 (with revisions in 2004 and 2006). The regulations are minimal compared to the strict regulations of many European appellation systems, with no restrictions on yields or on which grape varieties are grown (though regulations do specify how the varieties are listed on the label). The New Zealand Food Safety Authority is the governing body, so accurate labeling is more a priority than any deeper concern with wine style or quality.

The latter, however, are the concern of New Zealand Winegrowers, an association founded in 2002 by the older Wine Institute of New Zealand. The association funds research, advocacy, and global marketing, and is supported by a levy on grape and wine sales. All New Zealand wineries and winegrowers are automatically members.

**As of the 2007 vintage, the number to remember for New Zealand's wine regulations is 85%:**

- If a vintage is stated on the label, the wine must consist of at least 85% grapes from that year.
- If a grape variety or blend of grape varieties is stated on the label, 85% of the grape or grapes used must be of those varieties. Grape varieties in blends must be listed in descending order in accordance with their amounts in the wine.
- If a wine indicates an area of origin, it must contain 85% grapes from that area.
- A wine label cannot state a percentage of a grape variety, vintage, or area of origin if there is another grape variety/vintage/area of origin in the wine of greater percentage that is not stated on the label.

In 1995 New Zealand Winegrowers rolled out a sustainability program, which today operates under **the Sustainable Winegrowing New Zealand (SWNZ)** moniker. The program has proved very popular, with over 90% of producers participating. Organic production is also on the rise.

## TERROIR

The standout element of terroir in New Zealand is the cooling, moderating influence of the Pacific Ocean; the resulting maritime climate holds true for all the country's winegrowing regions aside from Central Otago. The latter has a continental climate but is still quite cool given its southerly location. High UV levels also contribute greatly to ripening and flavor development; vineyards in New Zealand can receive up to 50% more UV exposure than those in the Old World. This increased UV exposure encourages the development of phenolics in the grapes, necessary for aroma, mouthfeel, and color, which otherwise could struggle to develop in the cooler regions.

New Zealand's soils are varied, with some volcanic areas as well as sand and clay. A few winegrowing areas like the Gimblett Gravels in Hawke's Bay stand out— in that case for its gravel, of course. On the whole the soils tend to be nutrient-rich and controlling vine growth is important in making quality wine. **Canopy management**—trellising vines, leaf plucking, and otherwise manipulating the vine to control sun exposure, ripening, and disease—is vital in this regard. Dense vine spacing and **clonal/rootstock selection** (matching the clones and the rootstocks the vines will be grafted onto to the terroir) are also extremely important.

Rain is also common in most of New Zealand, but on the whole the wine regions are on the eastern side of the islands and protected from the usual west-to-east weather patterns by a spine of mountains that runs north to south down the western side of both islands, including the South Island's picturesque Southern Alps (one-fifth of the North Island and two-thirds of the South are mountainous). These peaks create a rain shadow effect, with clouds dumping the bulk of their precipitation on the western side of the mountains; aside from the most northerly, New Zealand's wine regions are generally well-insulated from rainfall during harvest, receiving between 800 and 1600ml of rainfall annually. Most vineyards are planted on flat or gently sloping hills, with some steeper vineyards in Central Otago.

## VARIETIES

### WHITE

**Sauvignon Blanc** is New Zealand's signature grape, grown throughout the country but really defined by Marlborough. As of 2009 Sauvignon Blanc represents 53% of the nation's vineyards with 16,200 hectares planted. Noted for grassy or asparagus notes alongside tart fruit— gooseberry, passion fruit, grapefruit —with refreshing acidity. Sauvignon Blanc can sometimes be vinified with a touch of residual sugar in budget styles, or as a riper, more tropical wine with some new oak in higher-end bottlings.

**Chardonnay** was the country's most planted variety until Sauvignon Blanc surpassed it in 2002; now it makes up about one eighth of the plantings with 3,900 hectares planted as of 2009. Planted throughout the country, and vinified in a variety of styles ranging from lean, unoaked examples to rich and opulent.

**Pinot Gris** plantings have been on the rise in the past five years, expanding from 300 hectares in 2003 to 1,500 in 2009 and thereby making up five percent of vineyards. Styles vary, with some rich, honeyed examples along with a number that seem to look toward the market for Pinot Grigio, albeit often with a freshness and tropical quality to distinguish them.

**Riesling** is mostly grown on the South Island, and made in dry, off-dry, and dessert styles.

**Gewürztraminer** is generally vinified dry and medium-bodied, though some examples from the North Island can get quite opulent; can have a phenolic bitterness in poorly balanced examples.

## Red

**Pinot Noir,** with 4,800 hectares as of 2009**,** makes up 15% of plantings, mostly on the South Island; however, Martinborough's earthy, sometimes gamey Pinots were among the first to receive critical attention. The styles can range from intense and powerful, to a lighter, red fruit-toned wine, all typified by structure and focus rather than lushness.

**Merlot** is the preferred red wine grape of the North Island, generally well-structured and ripe; used as a varietal wine and in blends; there were about 1,400 hectares planted as of 2009.

**Cabernet Sauvignon** is occasionally made as a single varietal wine, but most often used in Bordeaux-style blends. Prone to greenness in the lower half of the North Island when not planted in the best sites; as the variety it can have trouble ripening in cooler spots. As of 2009 there were 500 hectares planted.

**Syrah** is noted for its black pepper spice and structure while rarely sacrificing fruit notes and body. There are only 300 hectares planted, mostly in Hawke's Bay and Waiheke Island, but the wines have received a disproportionate amount of critical attention.

## Regions

There are twelve wine regions designated by the Food Safety Authority in New Zealand: the two broader, self-explanatory appellations, North Island and South Island, and the other, more specific regions.

## North Island

**Northland**: While the Northland region gave birth to winegrowing in New Zealand, its subtropical climate doesn't lend itself to quality production; humidity and rainfall are winegrowers' biggest challenges. Most vineyards are planted on gentle hills and alluvial flats, with sandy clay and volcanic soils. Only a dozen or so wineries operate here, producing mostly Cabernet Sauvignon, Merlot, and Chardonnay for local consumption, supported by a popular tourism scene.

**Auckland**: Most winegrowing here takes place on **Waiheke Island,** as urban sprawl has put pressure on the wineries on the mainland**,** which increasingly source their grapes from regions farther south. Bordeaux varieties—this is probably New Zealand's best place for Cabernet Sauvignon—bottled both singly and as blends make up most of production along with some Syrah. There is no mountain range to provide a rain shadow, so rain is a problem for winegrowing here. The island's soils are mostly argillaceous (clayey), with a thin topsoil of fine silt.

**Waikato/Bay of Plenty**: A small but growing region southeast of Auckland focused on Chardonnay, Sauvignon Blanc, and Cabernet Sauvignon; clay soils predominate. Rain and dampness make this area a difficult home for wine grapes, so most wineries here bring in grapes from elsewhere for at least part of their production.

**Gisborne**: Home for many of the box wines in the 1970s (made from Müller-Thurgau and Muscat, primarily), when it was the country's largest wine region. Today Gisborne is noted for its Chardonnay, which makes up half its vineyards, filled out by Gewürztraminer and some other white varieties; less than a tenth of the vineyards are planted with red varieties. Gisborne's soils are primarily silt loams and clay.

**Hawke's Bay**: Well-protected from rain, Hawke's Bay is home to some of the country's most highly-regarded Syrahs, Chardonnays, and Bordeaux-variety wines. Cabernet Sauvignon can struggle in cooler years, so Merlot is becoming a more dominant part in many blends, though this varies with the vintage. The Syrahs are complex, full with fruit but structured and spicy, and the Chardonnays are typically full but focused.

The **Gimblett Gravels** area stands out within Hawke's Bay. This 800 hectare area was created by the Ngaruroro River, which has changed its course on multiple occasions (most recently after an earthquake in 1867) and left behind fields of gravel. These provide better drainage and heat retention than the fertile loam that is more typical to Hawke's Bay. The former riverbed was long thought to be useless property, but winegrowers discovered the gravels' virtues in the 1980s; these days almost every hectare is planted with vines. **As New Zealand law has not provided for defining sub-regions for wine production**, wineries and wine growers with property in the Gimblett Gravels area have trademarked the name to protect its use.

**Wairarapa/Martinborough**: Wairarapa is divided into three regions, **Masterton, Gladstone** and **Martinborough,** but only the latter receives any extra distinction on wine labels. Significantly cooler than other North Island wine regions, Wairarapa's focus is Pinot Noir. Winegrowing pioneers like Neil McCallum and Larry McKenna singled out Martinborough for its geographic and climatic similarities to Burgundy in 1979, and by the mid-1980s several small wineries were demonstrating the region's potential. Chardonnay, Riesling, Gewürztraminer, and Pinot Gris are other notable varieties in the region. The area continues to produce some of the country's best Pinot Noir, despite increasing competition from Central Otago.

The town of Martinborough is situated on an escarpment that limits further vineyard plantings, but with gravelly soils that offer superb drainage for what is already the driest winegrowing area in the country; dry autumns in particular mean winegrowers are rarely rushed to bring in the harvest. In terms of production, the region remains a small player, making about one percent of the country's wine (from three percent of the vineyards), but as the home to a number of small, artisanal producers it punches above its weight in terms of quality and reputation. While not a source for budget wines, Martinborough's meaty Pinots have maintained a high standard.

## South Island

**Marlborough**: With almost four times the planted vineyards of its nearest competitor Hawke's Bay, Marlborough is the center of the New Zealand wine scene, appropriately located on the strait where the two islands look across from each other. It is home to the Sauvignon Blanc that put New Zealand wine on the map and also to some remarkable Pinot Noir, Pinot Gris, and Chardonnay. The Pinot Noirs tend toward a round, fruit-forward character but without becoming overly lush or alcoholic. The bulk of the country's sparkling wines also come from Marlborough.

Marlborough is also home to most of the production of New Zealand's sparkling wine. It is made in the traditional method from Pinot Noir and Chardonnay. Many are quite good and comparable to Champagne for smoothness of mousse and complexity, but they are rarely found in the export market as they are very much in demand domestically.

Recently producers have become more interested in the division between the two main areas of Marlborough, the Wairau and Awatere Valleys.

The Wairau River cuts through the mountains (the northern end of the Southern Alps) and the resulting **Wairau Valley** broadens as it approaches Cloudy Bay. The valley accounts for most of Marlborough's vineyards. Most lie on stony, alluvial soils south of the river; these are generally well-drained, and younger vines often need irrigation to survive until their root structure reaches deep enough into the water table. The Wairau area enjoys wide diurnal temperature variations courtesy of sunny days and the cooling maritime influence of the Marlborough Sound; that evening chill helps moderate ripeness and freshness, and the Sauvignon Blancs tend toward tart tropical fruit expressions. The **Southern Valleys** in the hills south of the larger Wairau Valley were the first to be planted in the 1970s, but the valley floor was easier to work; today winegrowers are re-discovering the potential of these hillside vineyards, where Pinot Noir seems to do particularly well.

### SUMMARY OF REGIONS NORTH TO SOUTH

| Region | Sub-region |
|---|---|
| **NORTH ISLAND** | |
| Auckland | Waiheke Island |
| Waikato/Bay of Plenty | |
| Gisborne | |
| Hawke's Bay | Gimblett Gravels |
| Wairarapa | Gladstone |
| | Masterton |
| | Martinborough |
| **SOUTH ISLAND** | |
| Nelson | |
| Marlborough | Wairau Valley |
| | Awatere Valley |
| Canterbury/Waipara | |
| Waitaki Valley | |
| Central Otago | Wanaka |
| | Lowburn |
| | Gibbston |
| | Bannockburn |
| | Bendigo |
| | Alexandra |

The **Awatere Valley** lies over a small ridge of hills to the south. Vineyard soils here tend to be more fertile, so site selection becomes more important to avoid high yields and flavor dilution. On average the area is a few degrees cooler than in Wairau, and the green, grassy and capsicum notes are more typical to the sub-region's Sauvignons. While not part of the officially recognized Certified Origin system, producers are increasingly using the valley names on their labels.

**Nelson**: While some of New Zealand's largest wine companies call Marlborough home, the two dozen or so wineries of Nelson are small, family-owned affairs. Over a mountain range about two hours north of Marlborough, the area sees a bit more rainfall and has more fertile soils, so site selection and controlling yields is essential to wine quality. The mountains create an amphitheater of alluvial slopes leading down to Tasman Bay, with clay and loam soils predominating. Slightly cooler than Marlborough, it grows mostly the same grape varieties, with Sauvignon Blanc, Pinot Noir, Chardonnay, Riesling and Gewürztraminer among the most common.

**Waipara Valley/Canterbury**: These two adjacent regions are focused on Chardonnay and Pinot Noir—the latter being the focus of critical attention so far—with Riesling and Sauvignon Blanc filling out much of the remaining vineyards. Canterbury is closer to Christchurch, and Waipara is an hour to the north; both areas enjoy long, dry, sunny growing seasons, but are cool enough that ripening can be difficult in some years. Soils, drainage, and aspect among Waipara's vineyards are quite varied, and producers there are very keen to explore and exploit site-specific terroir in their wines.

**Waitaki Valley**: New Zealand's newest wine region, first planted in 2001; the main draw for winegrowers is the limestone soils, so reminiscent of those in Burgundy. Located on the border of Canterbury and Otago, Pinot Noir, Pinot Gris, Riesling and Gewürztraminer dominate plantings.

**Central Otago**: The world's most southerly wine region at 45° latitude, and the only one in New Zealand to enjoy a truly continental climate; hot, dry summers with cool nights are the rule. It also has the country's highest vineyards, between 650 and 1,300 feet (200–400m) in elevation, all in a pocket wedged into a valley in the middle of the mountains. Here the vineyards must be planted on north-facing hillsides to maximize sun exposure and limit the threat of frost. Given the latitude, diurnal temperature variations can be substantial.

Pinot Noir makes up 70% of Central Otago's vineyards and is the area's claim to fame. The typical Pinot Noir here shows a mix of red and darker fruits with wild herb and floral touches, focused and lean, but less powerful and full than those of Martinborough. Chardonnay, Pinot Gris, and Riesling are also planted; winemakers are exploring dry and off-dry styles of the latter.

**Central Otago has six sub-regions. Wanaka**, the most northerly, was the first to be planted, and sees some extra protection from frost due to the vineyards proximity to its eponymous lake. Centrally-located **Bannockburn** is the warmest and most heavily planted; **Bendigo**, a bit farther northeast, is also relatively warm. **Lowburn** lies between the two and remains relatively undeveloped so far. **Alexandra**, to the south, and **Gibbston Valley** to the west are generally cooler; most of the quality vineyards are planted on north-facing slopes.

## Hot topics

The industry is very wary of becoming thought of as a value/budget wine producer and losing their relatively healthy price point in export markets; as a small wine-producing nation New Zealand does not want to be put in the place of competing with Australia or Chile, nor do they want to hamstring their premium brands and bottling or become a Sauvignon Blanc-based one-trick pony. In Marlborough large fluctuations in annual yields have tended to create temporary wine gluts that push grape and wine prices down, causing tension in the market and threatening the above-average price point the region's wines (and those of other New Zealand regions) have enjoyed. **A government-supported campaign called Complexity** was launched in 2010 to help increase awareness of the nation's vinous diversity and premium wine styles.

Grown in several regions, Pinot Noir may be the grape that allows New Zealand to demonstrate its regional variety and terroir differences. Bordeaux varieties remain a challenge, but the shift toward earlier-ripening Merlot-based wines may shed the country's reputation for greenness.

Among whites, Chardonnay remains popular domestically, but internationally remains a drop in the bucket; so far only a handful of producers have distinguished themselves. Pinot Gris continues to appeal to producers; needing no lengthy barrel-aging, it's a quick turn-around grape that does well in many regions of the country. Diversity is central to New Zealand's efforts to maintain and develop its reputation; whether it does it stylistically via different expressions of one variety, most likely Pinot Noir, or by promoting a shopping bag of different varieties—Sauvignon Blanc, Chardonnay, Pinot Gris, Pinot Noir, Syrah— remains to be seen.

# SOUTH AFRICA

| AREA UNDER VINE | 101,000 hectares |
|---|---|
| GRAPE VARIETIES | |
| RED | Cabernet Sauvignon, Pinotage, Merlot, Cabernet Franc, and Shiraz |
| WHITE | Chenin Blanc (Steen), Sauvignon Blanc, Chardonnay, Muscadel, Colombar |
| CLIMATE | South Africa generally has a mild Mediterranean climate, with coastal areas experiencing cooler temperatures and higher annual rainfalls than inland vineyards, which can reach Region V levels. |
| SOIL | The coastal plains possess a range of soils ranging from gravel to sandstone, shale, and granitic loams. River valleys have deep alluvial, sandy soils. |

## HISTORY

The first vines were planted in South Africa in the 17th century in an experimental vineyard owned by the Dutch East India Company situated in the shadow of Table Mountain. It was not until the arrival of Governor Simon van der Stel in 1679, however, that wine making began in earnest. Van der Stel created Groot Constantia, an excellent estate on the flanks of Table Mountain, where he passed his wine making skills on to the burghers settling around Stellenbosch. From 1688–1690, about 200 Huguenots arrived in the country, and they were granted land in the region, particularly around Franschhoek (French Corner). Although only a few of the Huguenots had actual wine making experience, they gave the fledgling wine industry new impetus. For a long time, Cape wines were not in great demand and most grapes were used for producing brandy, but the industry received a large boost in the early 19th century when war between France and Britain gave South Africa the opportunity to fill much of Britain's wines needs.

It was in the 1800s that Cape wines became well known in Europe, most notably the sweet Constantia, requested by Napoleon and the tsars of Russia. But in the latter half of the century, South Africa's wine industry began to suffer due to several factors including phylloxera, the Anglo-Boer War, and replantation and overproduction despite lack of demand. The creation of the Kooperative Wijnbouwers Vereniging (KWV) in 1917 alleviated much of the industry's troubles at that time. Although the KWV kept the industry afloat for years, inevitably, isolation led to inertia and failure to keep up with world trends.

Because South Africa—by virtue of its failed apartheid policy—isolated itself for so long, its wine industry has been out of touch with most state-of-the-art production methods and contemporary trends. Since the country's return to "normal" trading with the world markets, international demand has initiated a change in the direction of the nation's wine making, shifting the focus from white to red grapes with a greater concentration on noble varieties.

In 1999, South Africa ranked eighth in worldwide production, with just less than 800 million liters of wine produced, equaling 2.8% of the world total. Presently South Africa is making great efforts to increase its exporting by moving out of the bulk and fortified wine markets and into that of high-quality vinifera table wines. The shift poses several inherent challenges to the country, which has a population with a per capita consumption of only three gallons of wine per year, a 15 year waiting period imposed by the government that delayed availability of new plants to farmers, a warm climate that produces grapes with low acidity, the tendency for farmers to plant high-yielding vines, and a historic political situation that resulted in sanctions on virtually all for a significant period of time.

## LAWS AND LABELING

The **Kooperative Wijnbouwers Vereniging** (KWV) was instituted in 1917 to address problems that faced South Africa's wine industry. The primary mission of the KWV was to issue licenses for growing grapes, to set official quotas for production, to create marketable products, and to stimulate demand. Today, the KWV still acts as administrator for the wine industry, but independently of the country's government. It no longer controls production with quotas, allowing growers to plant vineyards and varieties at will and compete in a free market. The current KWV also functions as a wine company, operating vineyards and producing and selling wine, mostly internationally.

In 1973, the **South Africa Wines of Origin System** (WO) was adopted, applying government rankings to regions, districts, wards, and estates, in ascending order of specificity. Under the system, the South African government issues a sticker indicating the origin of a wine. Until fairly recently, neck labels on table wines were color-coded to indicate levels of quality, but this labeling approach has been abandoned. The country's highest quality wines, which formerly received gold neckbands, are tasted and approved by a government-appointed tasting panel.

In 1998, South Africa introduced the **Integrated Production of Wine** system (IPW), an initiative aimed at encouraging environmental responsibility amongst producers. A joint venture of the Agricultural Research Council's *Infruitec-Nietvoorbij* and the wine industry, the IPW covers not only grape growing but also harvesting methods, transportation of grapes, use of equipment, wine making processes, cellar practices, and waste management. Currently, 98% of the South African grapes are grown according to IPW guidelines and 95% of wine cellars adhere to its principles.

South African wines—for domestic consumption—that are varietyly labeled must contain at least 75% of the stated variety and if labeled with a vintage, 75% of the named vintage. If the wines are meant for export, the proportion of variety and vintage used increases to 85%.

## GEOGRAPHY, CLIMATE, AND SOIL

Situated at the southernmost tip of Africa, the Benguela current from Antarctica makes the Cape cooler than its latitude would suggest. Long, hot summers are moderated by cold, wet, blustery winters, with snow in the mountains. Late frosts are rare, as are unseasonably heavy summer rains.

Temperatures often exceed 75°F in February and March during the harvest. In the summer, temperatures can easily reach 100°F. For this reason, cooler mesoclimates are constantly being searched for. Most of the wine regions would be classified as Region III sites on the Winkler scale, equivalent to Oakville in Napa Valley. However, some newer growing areas experience cooler conditions, comparable to a Region II site.

Climatic conditions and soil types in the growing areas vary as dramatically as the landscape. In Stellenbosch alone, more than 50 soil types have been identified. However, nearly all soils have low PH levels, requiring acidification to achieve good levels of acidity in the wines. Irrigation is usually necessary, particularly in the hot river valleys.

## VARIETIES

Grape varieties in South Africa are known as **cultivars**. White cultivars dominate the vineyards, accounting for about 85% of planted areas.

### RED

**Cinsaut** (spelled without the "l" in South Africa) used to be known as Hermitage—the name reflected only in its offspring, Pinotage. Plantings of this grape are decreasing steadily.

**Pinotage** is a 1920s cross between **Pinot Noir** and **Cinsaut**. It became unfashionable in the 1980s, but now has some international success. It is made in a variety of styles, from simply fruity to well oaked. Acres under vine are on the rise.

**Pinot Noir** is now being produced in South Africa, especially as the use of the BK5 champagne clone wanes. The wines are usually matured in wood and are typically pricey.

**Cabernet Sauvignon** is used for pure variety wines as well as blends where it is combined with a wide range of other varieties such as **Cabernet Franc, Merlot, Shiraz,** and **Pinotage**. Vineyard plantings are steadily increasing.

**Merlot** is a classic blending partner for cabernet Sauvignon. Variety wines are also increasingly common.

In 1997 less than 3,400 acres were planted with **Shiraz** (Syrah); today there are almost 20,000. The South African approach to the grape falls between the ripe, full-blown Aussie style and the more elegant, mineral and meaty style of the Rhône.

Small plantings of the following grapes also exist: **Grenache, Cabernet Franc, Carignan, Malbec, Mourvèdre, Nebbiolo, Petit Verdot**, and some Port varieties.

## WHITE

**Chenin Blanc** (known as **Steen** in South Africa) is planted more widely here than in even France's Loire Valley. It is used in South Africa for everything from generic dry whites to ambitious sweet wines to brandy. There are few table wine successes in a "sea of mediocrity". Vineyard space is declining quickly.

**Colombar** (spelled without the "d" in South Africa) is one of the mainstays in Cape production. Colombar is used for numerous variety and blended wines, ranging from dry to sweet. It is seldom wooded. Acreage is peaking currently.

The small acreage devoted to **Sémillon** is now quite different from the early 19$^{th}$ century when the grape represented 93% of all Cape wines. It now occupies less than 1% of all vineyard areas.

**Viognier** is increasingly fashionable and is showing promise in a lightly wooded style.

**Muscadel** is the name used in South Africa for **Muscat Blanc à Petits Grain** and **Muscat de Frontignan**. It is the grape associated with the famous Constantia dessert wines of the 18$^{th}$ century. Today is used chiefly for dessert and fortified wines.

**Sauvignon Blanc** is usually made in a dry style, but some sweet wines are produced. It is sometimes wooded and is then referred to as Fumé Blanc.

The demand for **Chardonnay** is increasing and so is its acreage. The wines are made in a array of styles and quality levels.

In South Africa, when mention alone, **Riesling** refers to **Cape Riesling**, a much inferior grape properly known as **Crouchen**. It is mostly used anonymously in blends.

**Rhine Riesling**, which is the German Riesling variety, is also grown and vinified in an off-dry style, with some noteworthy botrytised dessert wines being produced.

Small plantings of Ugni Blanc, Clairette, Gewürztraminer, and Muscat of Alexandria (known as Hanepoot) are also found.

# REGIONS

There are three main wine-growing regions in South Africa: **Coastal Region, Boberg Region**, and **Breede River Valley Region**. However, there are many other wine-growing areas/WO that are located outside of these three groupings, and some are discussed here.

## COASTAL REGION

**Constantia** is a ward within the Coastal Region umbrella on the eastern gradients of the Cape Peninsula. It is summer-cooled by the south easterlies from False Bay. A premier viticultural area, Constantia has been producing wines since the earliest days of South Africa's fine wine–production period. It is particularly noted for producing excellent **Sauvignon Blanc** as well as **Chardonnay** and **Cabernet Sauvignon**.

**Durbanville** is a coastal ward in transition, poised between rustic tradition and headlong development. Some of the earliest land to be planted with vines; Durbanville is now beginning to come out of the shadow of bulk wine production. Quality factors include deep moisture-retaining soils, cooling summer night mists, and climate moderating influences from Table and False Bays. It is recognized for its **Sauvignon Blanc** and **Merlot**.

**Stellenbosch** is actually a town with an intensely-farmed wine-producing area surrounding it. To many, it is the most highly regarded wine-producing area in South Africa, known primarily for its reds but offering first-class whites and sparkling wines as well. Key quality contributors include cooler mountain slopes, varied soil types, and breezes off False Bay, which moderate temperatures. Smaller designated wards within the district include Jonkershoek Valley, Simonsberg-Stellenbosch, Bottelary, Devon Valley, and Papgaaiberg. The region is known for its **Cabernet Sauvignon, Merlot, Shiraz**, and **Pinotage**, but it also produces some fine **Sauvignon Blanc** and **Chardonnay** as well.

**Swartland** is traditionally associated with big, booming reds. However, this sunny, previously neglected wheat and tobacco area north of Cape Town has shown it can make top-notch white wines too. The ward of Groenekloof, near the cooling Atlantic, and the more established ward Riebeekberg, are places to watch. There are plans to demarcate the area around Darling as a district as well.

**Cape Point** is an exciting new cool-climate district situated on the western ridges of the Cape Peninsula Mountain spine. (The Constantia vineyards are on the opposite side.) The area was quickly noticed when the first and as yet, sole producer, Cape Point Vineyards, was awarded a SAYWS championship trophy.

## BOBURG REGION

Inland, scenic **Tulbagh**, is situated north of Paarl and to the east of Swartland. With its mountain-skirted vineyards, the region has in the past concentrated on white varieties but there now seems to be movement toward reds.

**Paarl** possesses many different mesoclimates and soil types and thus correspondingly offers a wide range of wine styles. Paarl is known for its **Shiraz** and as of late for its excellent **Viognier** and **Mourvèdre** grown on warmer slopes. The ward of Wellington is now offering some promising wines, especially reds, from properties mostly on higher grounds. The other ward in the district, Franschhoek, was founded by the Huguenots in the 17th century and excels with **Sémillon** and **Chenin Blanc**. Agter-Paarl, located to the west of Paarl Mountain, is not yet an officially recognized appellation but is producing some very exciting high quality wines.

## BREEDE RIVER VALLEY REGION

**Robertson** though situated in a warmer area, it benefits from cooling late afternoons, southeastern winds during the summer, and limestone soil. The region that is typically known for white wine is now turning out some promising reds as well, especially with **Shiraz** and **Cabernet Sauvignon**. The region is most recognized for its white wines made with **Chardonnay** and **Colombar** plus its sparklers too.

**Worcester** is the nation's largest wine area, with more than 60 million vines planted, comprising 20% of the national total. The region's grapes are used chiefly for brandy. The rest of the fruit goes to merchants, with the exception of very small quantities that are bottled under wine makers' own labels. These wines, while few, are known to be good values. Traditionally, vineyards were sited in fertile alluvial soils, but now they are moving into the hills. Worcester is recognized for its fortified **Muscadel** and **Hanepoot**.

## OTHER REGIONS

Since the 1980s some of the Cape's most popular wines have come from **Walker Bay**, a maritime area southeast of Cape Town. The ward is located within the Overberg WO district. The area is recognized for its **Pinot Noir**, aromatic **Pinotage**, and **Chardonnay**.

**Little Karoo,** also known as **Klein Karoo,** is a semi-arid scrubland that is ideal for ostrich farmers. Additionally, the region poses something of a challenge for wine growers who rely heavily on irrigation for their vineyards. The climate is similar to that of the Douro Valley in Portugal and this comparison has inspired some vintners to apply their efforts to making Port and other fortified wines.

**Elim**, with its maritime-influenced vineyards, is situated around the old mission village of Elim near Cap Agulhas, Africa's southernmost point. It is a tiny ward that shows a great deal of promise. At present, its production is 65% red and 35% white.

Quality wines are now being produced in **Olifants River**, a cooler upland region, which includes the vineyards of Cedarburg. Piekenierskloof, a ward for just three years, is one of the region's most promising areas. Its production is currently 26% red and 74% white. **Shiraz, Pinotage, Merlot, Chenin Blanc**, and **Colombar** are being grown here.

**Northern Cape** is the hottest, northernmost Cape wine-growing area. It is the fourth largest, with more than 15,000ha under vine. Overwhelmingly a white grape area, reds varieties are quickly growing in number.

# Summary of Growing Areas

*From Wines of South Africa (http://www.wosa.co.za/)*

**Geographical Unit: Western Cape**

| REGION | DISTRICT | WARD |
|---|---|---|
| Breede River Valley | Breedekloof | Goudini |
| | | Slanghoek |
| | Robertson | Agterkliphoogte |
| | | Bonnievale |
| | | Boesmansrivier |
| | | Eilandia |
| | | Hoopsrivier |
| | | Klaasvoogds |
| | | Le Chasseur |
| | | McGregor |
| | | Vinkrivier |
| | Worcester | Aan-de-Doorns |
| | | Hex River Valley |
| | | Nuy |
| | | Scherpenheuvel |
| Cape South Coast | Cape Agulhas | Elim |
| | Overberg | Elandskloof |
| | | Elgin |
| | | Greyton |
| | | Klein River |
| | | Theewater |
| | Plettenberg Bay | No ward |
| | Swellendam | Buffeljags |
| | | Malgas |
| | | Stormsvlei |
| | Walker Bay | Bot River |
| | | Hemel-en-Aarde Ridge |
| | | Hemel-en-Aarde Valley |
| | | Sunday's Glen |
| | | Upper Hemel-en-Aarde Valley |
| | No district | Herbertsdale |
| | | Napier |
| | | Stilbaai East |

Continued Next Page…

**Geographical Unit: Western Cape**

| REGION | DISTRICT | WARD |
|---|---|---|
| Coastal Region | Cape Point | No ward |
| | Darling | Groenekloof |
| | Franschhoek/Franschhoek Valley | No ward |

| | | |
|---|---|---|
| | Paarl | Simonsberg-Paarl |
| | | Voor Paardeberg |
| | | Wellington |
| | Stellenbosch | Banghoek |
| | | Bottelary |
| | | Devon Valley |
| | | Jonkershoek Valley |
| | | Papegaaiberg |
| | | Polkadraai Hills |
| | | Simonsberg-Stellenbosch |
| | Swartland | Malmesbury |
| | | Riebeekberg |
| | Tulbagh | No ward |
| | Tygerberg | Durbanville |
| | | Philadelphia |
| | No district | Constantia |
| | | Hout Bay |
| Klein Karoo | Calitzdorp | No ward |
| | Langeberg-Garcia | No ward |
| | No district | Montagu |
| | | Outeniqua |
| | | Tradouw |
| | | Tradouw Highlands |
| | | Upper Langkloof |
| Olifants River | Citrusdal Mountain | Piekenierskloof |
| | Citrusdal Valley | No ward |
| | Lutzville Valley | Koekenaap |
| | No district | Bamboes Bay |
| | No district | Spruitdrift |
| | | Vredendal |
| No region | No district | Cederberg |
| | | Ceres |
| | | Lamberts Bay |
| | | Prince Albert Valley |
| | | Swartberg |

## Geographical Unit: Northern Cape

| REGION | DISTRICT | WARD |
|---|---|---|
| No region | Douglas | No ward |
| | Sutherland-Karoo | No ward |
| | No district | Central Orange River |
| | | Hartswater |
| | | Rietrivier FS |

## Geographical Unit: Eastern Cape

| No region | No district | St Francis Bay |

**Geographical Unit: Kwazulu-Natal**

| No region | No district | No ward |

**Geographical Unit: Limpopo**

| No region | No district | No ward |

**Boberg Region: For use in respect of fortified wines from Paarl, Franschhoek, and Tulbagh**

# BEER

## HISTORY

Beer has been around longer than most people realize. Throughout recorded history there are mentions of "beer-like" beverages. It can be traced back to 6,000-year-old Sumerian tablets as well as vessels found along the "Silk Route" through historic Persia. The Book of the Dead written in Egypt about 5,000 years ago also makes mention of a barley-based beverage that was buried with royalty to quench their thirst during the journey to the after-life. The Chinese made a beverage called *Kiu* about 4,000 years ago, which is derived from barley, wheat, millet, and spelt.

It is thought that monks in monasteries made beer due to religious law. Since food could not be consumed during periods of fasting, beer was originally produced for consumption to obtain nutrients at these times. The royal courts in medieval times, as a means of revenue, assumed the rights of brewing policies in their countries. Most private brewers and farmers produced beer for their own taverns and local pubs. Bavarian monks discovered bottom-fermenting beer, which became known as lager. The discovery occurred by chance when they decided to store fermenting beer in cool cellars. They noticed that by doing this the yeasts sank to the bottom of the barrel and fermented slower than top-fermenting ales.

In 1842, Josef Groll, a brewer in the town of Pilzen, Bohemia, today's Czech Republic, created the first almost clear lager beer called Urquell. Today the same brewery still creates the original pilsner, Pilsner Urquell.

## LAWS

There are few laws that pertain to the production of beer. The most notable is the German purity law passed in 1517 called <u>Reinheitsgebout</u>. The law states that beer can only be made from **water, malted barley, hops,** and **yeasts**. An exception is made for wheat beers.

## GEOGRAPHY

Beer is typically produced in cooler, more northern climates than where wine is normally produced. This is due to the fact that barley—a major ingredient in beer—usually does not thrive in the warmer climates known for growing Vitis vinifera. However, there are some areas where the crops overlap. Historically, the world's great brewing centers have been Belgium, Germany-Austria, the United States, and Japan.

## INGREDIENTS

Beer is made from four ingredients:

- Grain
- Yeast
- Hops
- Water

# GRAIN

Brews of old used many cereals to make beer, but barley was preferred because it was easier to malt and produced more sugar, which in turn produced more alcohol. Typically malted barley is used today, although wheat can be used too. Malting is the process by which grains of barley are partially germinated (allowed to sprout), then roasted. This process allows the natural sugars in the barley to be transformed into a fermentable form. The degree to which the grains are dried or roasted contributes directly to the flavor of the beer being produced. Brewers use the Lovibond scale to rate the color of the roasted grains—the higher the number, the darker the product. Below is a chart listing some common types of roasted malt and their Lovibond scale rating.

| Malt Type | Degrees Lovibond |
|---|---|
| British Pale Ale | 3 |
| Vienna Malt | 5 |
| Crystal Malt | 10-120 * |
| Chocolate Malt | 350 |
| Black Patent | 540 |
| Roasted Barley | 550 |

*\* Crystal Malt is the style of malt that is most often used; therefore it has the widest scale of color variation. Each brewer uses a specific degree of coloration in his brew.*

# YEAST

Yeast is a are microscopic organism that converts fermentable sugars found in grain into alcohol. There are two major species of yeast used in the brewing of beer: ale (*Saccharomyces Cerevisiae*) and lager (*Saccharomyces Carlsbergensis*). Each of these yeasts has numerous subspecies that can be specific to a particular brewery. **Ale yeast** *(Saccharomyces Cerevisiae)* for centuries was the only style of yeast used to make beer. The yeast rises to the top of the vessel during fermentation producing a foam or cap of bubbles. All true ales and most wheat beers are fermented with a derivative of this strain of yeast. **Lager yeast** *(Saccharomyces Carlsbergensis)*, now classified as *S. uvarum*, is a bottom fermenting yeast that works at lower temperatures than ale yeasts.

# HOPS

Hops are an essential part of the brewing process. The cone-shaped flower of the hop vine serves two purposes in brewing. It imparts a bitter flavor and aroma onto the brew and it acts as a preservative. There are many varieties of hops, the most notable being noble hops. *Hallertauer Mittelfrueh* has a delicate aroma, while Spalt is very complex in character. The Czech *Saaz,* which is low in bitterness but has a pleasant scent and flavor, is the most delicate with a flowery aroma. Fuggles and East Kent Goldings are primary British examples that produce British ales with mild and rounded flavors. Cascade, grown in the United States, adds a strong floral note to brews.

## BITTERING HOPS

Bittering hops have a high level of bitterness but add less flavor and aroma to beer than noble hops. Varieties include Northern Brewer, Brewer's Gold, Cluster, and Willamette, which is US grown.

# WATER

Water is often the most overlooked ingredient in beer, but the quality of the water has a direct effect on the final taste of the beer. Hard water high in mineral content will yield a much different tasting beer than one made with soft water with a low mineral content. Many breweries have developed their recipes to directly compliment the style of water found near the brewery, such as Bass, while other breweries have based their advertising on the kind of water they use, like Coors.

# PRODUCTION OF ALES

After the grains have been selected and roasted, the brewer places the grains in a mill where the outer husk of the barley is stripped away and placed in a mash tun—a stainless steel tank with a slotted floor. The grains are repeatedly sprayed with water and then drained. Once the water raises the temperature of the grains to about 190°F, the sugars that were created during malting are ready to be released. The resulting liquid, now called <u>wort,</u> is placed into a brew kettle for the next steps.

Hops, appropriate to the style of the particular ale, are introduced and the wort is boiled. These hops tend to add more of the bitter flavor to the beer and not much aroma, since the part of the hops that adds aroma tends to break down quickly when boiled. Additional hops for aromatic purposes can be added in the last few minutes of the boil.

There are five reasons for boiling wort:

1. Sterilization
2. Excess water evaporates
3. Volatile materials, which appear naturally in barley and hops, are lost through evaporation
4. Insoluble substances are made soluble by the heat, otherwise known as Hot Break
5. As the sugars boil they caramelize and add an amount of color to the brew

After boiling, the wort is transferred to fermentation vessels and cooled. Once the brew has cooled to a temperature of 68–78°F, yeast is then "pitched" into the wort to start the fermentation process.

The initial stage of fermentation, which lasts 5–8 days, will yield a thick cap on the top of the fermentation vessel thus protecting the new beer from the influence of any airborne contaminants. Once this stage is completed, the beer is racked to a storage container where it will undergo a secondary fermentation and possibly fining. Finally, it will be carbonated either by adding additional sugar or through $CO_2$ inoculation.

## PRODUCTION OF LAGERS

The process begins the same way as it does for ale, but once the wort has been cooled and the yeast added, different procedures must be followed since lager yeasts sink and don't develop a protective cap. Lager must be placed in an airtight secondary fermenter and kept cool, since the strain of yeast does not survive well in temperatures above 50–55°F. The length of time it takes to ferment a lager is considerably longer than that for ale due to the colder temperature. Lager takes 2–3 weeks to ferment.

## STYLES OF BEER – LAGER (FROM LIGHT TO FULL)

| Style | Description | Examples |
|---|---|---|
| Mass Market | Pale Golden Color, light body, mass appeal and refreshment. Modeled after Pilsner. Usually made with adjuncts. | Coors, Budweiser, Miller |
| Pilsner | Eastern European Beer style–pale to yellow-gold color, light body with distinctive crisp poppy flavor. | Pilsner Urquell, Amstel, Beck's, Warsteiner |
| Amber Lager (Red & Nut Brown are sub-categories) | Style associated with the US. Copper/amber color, medium body, and a good helping of hops. | Harp, Sam Adams, Brooklyn Lager |
| Bock | A classic German beer style– traditionally heavy, strong and dark. Brewed in the winter for consumption in the spring. | Ayinger Celebrator, Spaten Optimator (true German Bocks have the ending "ator") |

## STYLES OF BEER – ALES (FROM LIGHT TO FULL)

| Style | Description | Examples |
|---|---|---|
| Wheat Beers | Summer Beer made with malted wheat replacing some or all of the barley. White to pale gold in color. Traditionally these beers are cloudy due to the suspended yeast cells. | Paulaner Hefe-Weizen, Spaten Wheat, Ayinger Export Weissbier |
| Lambic | Made with up to 30% malted wheat and always with wild yeasts. These beers can have fruit added to them for additional flavor. (Note: Not all Belgian Fruit beers are Lambics.) | Lindemans (Kriek, Framboise, Peche) |
| Pale Ale | The classic English Ale. Deep gold to copper in color. Full-flavored, malty with moderate bitterness. | Sierra Nevada Pale Ale, Bass |
| India Pale Ale (IPA) | An extra hoppy version originally sent to English troops stationed in India. | |
| Trappist Ale | Beer brewed in one of the five remaining Trappist Monasteries in Belgium (Chimay, Orval, Rochefort, Westmalle, Westvleteren). Amber to brown with high alcohol content. | Chimay, Orval |
| Abbey Ale | Any beer brewed in a similar style to a Trappist beer but made in a secular brewery. | Duvel, Affligem, Corsendonk |
| Amber Ale Brown Ale | Named for the color. Darker due to the use of heavier malts. Can be less hoppy than Pale Ales. | Newcastle, Brooklyn Brown Ale Samuel Smith's Nut Brown Ale |

| Style | Description | Examples |
| --- | --- | --- |
| English Bitter | ESB - Extra Special Bitter | English Bitter Fuller's ESB |
| Porter | Reddish-Black in color. Strong but not as strong as Stouts. | Samuel Smith's Taddy Porter, Whitbread, Catamount |
| Stout | The darkest of brews, creamy full head, toasty, chocolate. | Guinness, Murphy's |
| Imperial or Oatmeal | Imperial Stouts originally made in England for export to the Russian court. Oatmeal Stouts replace barley with Oatmeal | Samuel Smith's Imperial Stout<br><br>Samuel Smith's Oatmeal Stout |

# SAKE

BY JIM CLARKE

*"It is the man who drinks the first bottle of Sake. The second bottle drinks the first. Finally it is the sake that drinks the man."* — Japanese toast

## INTRODUCTION

Japan's rice wine is the alcoholic beverage most associated with the island nation, but it is not the most popular domestic alcoholic drink. That honor goes to beer, which surpassed sake in the 1960s. Today there are approximately 1,800 sake breweries, down from 2,500 in 1990. However, sake quality has been on the rise, as brewers address the domestic decline in popularity by becoming increasingly artisanal in their production. Properly speaking, the term "sake" refers to any sort of alcoholic beverage, and the Japanese have traditionally called it *"Nihon-Shu"* or *"Seishu"*.

Within a given region a distinct brewing style can be found because a Toji, or master sake brewer, is assigned to train brewers within a given prefecture, or area. A collection of brewers' guilds called the Toji Seido oversee the training. There are currently 25 in existence. In recent years, brewers have been communicating with each other more broadly across the country. As a result the impact of regionality has become less essential; nonetheless, sake brewing culture is quite conservative and remains aware of local tradition. There are about 1,800 sake brewers in Japan today; all are members of the Japan Sake Brewers Association. The production and sale of sake and other alcoholic beverages in Japan are overseen by the Tax Bureau. Unlikely as it might sound, the National Research Institute of Brewing operates under their umbrella.

The term "rice wine" is itself misleading. The starch in rice must be converted into sugars before yeasts can turn them into alcohol. So sake is brewed, like beer, and not simply fermented like wine. "Rice beer" has other connotations, however. Japanese beers, such as Sapporo and Hitochino, are brewed from rice (just as sake is) but are unique in the minds of brewers and consumers.

A typical sake is about 15-16% alcohol, far above most beers, and even higher than most wines. It's traditionally served in small (approximately 2 ounce) ceramic cups or, more commonly these days, glasses. These small glasses are ideally suited to Japanese ritual, with drinkers courteously and constantly topping up each others' drink. The tradition is less common in restaurant settings, so many establishments use larger glasses. Traditional cups are also poorly suited for analytical tasting: There is no headspace to contain the sake's aromas, and swirling is impossible. Many tasters instead use a tulip-shaped wine or cordial glass for this purpose.

Western drinkers are often taken with the idea of hot sake, but high-quality sake is best served chilled to 40-50° F. More delicate sakes will lose much of their prized aromas at warmer temperatures, and richer sakes can become cloying when not refreshingly chilled (heating can also help hide the flaws in lower quality sakes). Weightier, earthier sakes are more amenable to being served hot or at room temperature (60-70° F). When served too chilled, these sorts of sakes can taste astringent or grainy. At room temperature those aspects smooth out, integrating with the rest of the sake. Thus, it becomes important to understand the nature of specific sakes, in order to offer them up under ideal circumstances.

Sakes that benefit from being served hot can be served at temperatures as high as 125° F, though 105° F is more typical. Ideally, sake should be heated by pouring it into a pewter or ceramic sake flask, placing the flask in a saucepan of water and gently heating it on the stove to the desired temperature. Many Japanese microwaves come with a pre-programmed sake-heating button, where restaurants and bars often use specially designed heating units.

Tasting sake follows roughly the same steps as wine tasting. First, the sake should be examined for clarity and impurities and then for color. Aromas follow, then taste, including aromas on the palate, mouth feel, and finish. Persistence is not necessarily considered a sign of quality; long and short finishes are both acceptable.

## HISTORY

The first mention of Japanese sake actually appears in Chinese documents from the 3rd century BC. Records from following centuries from within Japan itself mention the use of mold in making sake, and a 10th century legal treatise called Engishiki spells out production in more detail. However, sake in this period was difficult to produce and primarily consumed by the Imperial court or in ceremonial use. The latter use led to Buddhist and Shinto religious centers becoming primary production centers for sake, and it was these producers who in the following centuries developed and codified many of the techniques that would characterize sake production up until the beginning of the 20th century: mashing, lactic acid (via bacterial fermentation) as a preservative, koji inoculation, etc..

By the 16th century, polished rice previously used exclusively for growing the koji, was being used for the entire brewing process. Additionally, the development of larger wooden vats made sake production more accessible in the 17th century. Finally, the practice of pasteurization in this period made the sake more stable. Sake recipes up until the 19th century called for much smaller additions of water – as little as 50% in comparison to what is used today. This suggests that sake was a sweeter, heavier drink than it is now.

The Meiji Restoration, which restored Imperial rule at the end of the 19th century deregulated sake production and raised taxes on it. However, it also inaugurated modern research on the subject with the founding of the National Research Institute of Brewing in 1904. The Institute has been essential in modernizing sake production with innovations like classifying the yeast strains used in brewing, encouraging the shift to more hygienic ceramic-lined tanks instead of wood vats and introducing the addition of lactic acid as a preservative. The other major change in the 20th century was brought about by rice shortages during and after World War II. While small amounts of added alcohol had been used previously for stylistic reasons, brewers now began using large amounts of added alcohol to increase yields.

Competition from beer, wine and liquor has dampened sake's popularity in Japan over the past several decades. Exports, however, are at a record high: over 14 million liters (3.7 million gallons) in 2011, up from just over 7 million liters in 2000 (according to the Japanese Ministry of Finance). About 27% comes to the U.S., where sake is no longer confined to Japanese restaurants. Innovative importers have made a concerted effort to create more accessible labels, branding sakes with easily remembered English names. In addition, there are now sake producers in several other countries, most notably across Asia and the Americas. So far none have achieved the sophistication and depth of Japanese sake, but it is hard to argue anything stands in their way besides experience.

# How Sake is Made

Just as beer begins with barley, sake begins with rice. As there are many different varieties of grapes used in winemaking, there are many different varieties of rice used in making sake. Most sake is made using a single rice variety but blending is possible.

Rice requires a lot of water to grow. Irrigation and flooding are a common part of rice growing. Once snows have receded and the fields are wet from spring rains, the grower will cultivate seedlings in a greenhouse. These seedlings are usually planted in May. Water is especially important at this point. Flooding is used to drown competing weeds and to encourage the rice to grow. This is very different from winegrowing, where excess moisture is often considered an invitation for rot and mildew. The grains grow throughout the summer. In August, the grains begin to brown and harvest typically occurs in September. In most cases today, planting and harvesting are done by machine.

While different rice strains favor different environments, there is little to no sense of terroir from the rice. Similarly, there is not significant vintage variation. If a certain harvest varies in some way from the norm, brewers typically adjust their brewing process to make that year's production consistent with previous years'. In this regard sake is again more like beer than wine.

## Milling (Seimai)

Rice needs to be milled to remove (at the very least) the brown outer coating. This coating is high in fats and proteins that can interfere with brewing and add earthy, unwanted "off" aromas. Just performing this minimal milling process reduces the grains to about 70% of their original size, leaving a kernel of more-or-less pure starch. Further milling results in a change of aromatic character, generally making the end product fruitier, more floral, cleaner and more "pure". It is important to note that the fundamental basis for sake classifications is based on how much the rice is milled, rather than rice variety. Milling must be done gently to avoid cracking the grains or creating too much heat, which would hamper the grain's ability to absorb moisture.

## Washing, Steeping, Steaming (Senmai, Shinseki, Jomai)

After milling, the rice must sit to re-absorb moisture lost during the milling process; otherwise, the rice grains can be brittle and might break or crack, resulting in an uneven fermentation later. The rice is then washed to remove any remaining rice powder from the milling and steeped in water. Rice milled to 70% takes approximately one hour to steep but more refined rice absorbs the proper amount of water in just a few minutes. Following the steeping, the rice is steamed to make it soft enough for the starter (koji) and yeast to work on it.

## Koji (Koji-Zukuri)

Creating the *koji* (starter) is vital and unique to sake brewing. About 20% of the rice is set aside in a warm, humid room and wrapped in cloth to prevent it from drying out. Koji mold (*Aspergillus oryzae*) is sprinkled on the rice that had been set aside. As it begins to grow, the rice is stirred to distribute the koji mold evenly. Koji mold's spores provide the enzymes necessary for **saccharification** (the conversion of starch into sugars). The enzymes will ferment when yeast is added. Other non-fermentable sugars are also created, providing additional body and mouth feel.

## Yeast (Moto)

The resulting koji (now the mold and the rice within it) is inoculated with yeast and used to grow the yeast starter. At this point, lactic acid is added to the mix of koji, water, and yeast to help prevent bacterial infection. The yeast strain used is very important and has a dramatic effect on the overall character of the sake. More steamed rice is added (as needed) to encourage the growth of the koji and yeast. The whole batch is placed in a cool room in order to slow down the fermentation caused by the introduction of the yeast. The koji continues to spread and saccharify the additional rice. The temperature is raised and lowered repeatedly over the next few days to allow the koji to continue its work. At the same time the yeast begins fermenting the sugars that are already available. Building the starter typically takes about two weeks.

## Mashing (Moromi)

Once the starter is going strong, it is mixed with the remaining steamed rice and water in several stages to continue this process of saccharification and fermentation. This process is called **mashing**. The whole batch then ferments in an open-top fermenter at a low temperature (typically below 48° F) for at least 18 days and possibly as long as one month. It is important to note that the conversion of starches to sugars (the work of the koji) and sugars to alcohol (that of the yeast) actually overlap in time; this is called, rather grandly, "**multiple parallel fermentation**." More importantly, the slow feeding of sugar from the koji to the yeast accounts for the high alcohol of the finished sake (19-20%). If the yeast were confronted with all the sugar upfront, the yeast would peter out and the resulting sake would be sweeter and lower in alcohol.

The finished sake may have some residual sugar or be completely dry depending on the yeast used and the mix of sugars the koji was able to convert from the rice starch. Some sugars, such as dextrins, may be too complex for the yeasts to ferment. In beer, residual sugars often result for this reason. This is often not the case in winemaking because the pure glucose in grapes is much more readily consumed and fermented.

## Finishing (Joso)

Following fermentation, the sake is gently pressed to remove the rice and *koji* solids. It is then left to sit and settle in a tank for a few days. Finally, the sake is ready to be racked (which will remove most remaining sediments), filtered, and pasteurized. See below for exceptions such as unfiltered and unpasteurized varieties. The brewer may opt to mature the sake for several months, which will help round out its mouth feel. Traditionally, sake was brewed and pasteurized in the winter months, because the cold weather made bacterial infection less likely. It was then aged through the summer for release the following autumn. Today refrigeration allows for year-round brewing.

Before bottling and sale, sake is diluted with water to the desired alcohol level – typically bringing it down to around 15-16% from 19-20%. This step, reminiscent of the water added to Scotch whisky to bring it down from "cask strength," helps create a balanced product.

## Ingredients

### Rice

Sake rice is typically large-grain rice and more expensive than rice that is intended for eating. There are around 60 kinds of rice traditionally used for brewing, but nine varieties dominate production today. While different varieties generally grow best in particular regions, rice is easily transportable and brewers source rice from all over the country.

### VARIETIES OF RICE USED IN SAKE PRODUCTION

| RICE VARIETY | CHARACTERISTICS |
| --- | --- |
| **Dewa San San** | Yields sweeter, complex sakes. Typically grown in the northern half of the main island. |
| **Gohyakumangoku** | Dry and smooth; the most-used sake in terms of quantity. Grown in central and northern Japan. "Gohyakumangoku" translates to "five million bags of rice," a reflection of its dominance in sake production. |
| **Hatta Nishiki** | Less aromatic, earthy. Grown in Hiroshima. |
| **Kame No O** | Rich, full-bodied sakes. Grown in the north part of the main island. |
| **Miyama Nishiki** | Noted for its elegant mouth feel; tends to yield off-dry styles. Grown throughout the northern half of Japan's main island. |
| **Omachi** | Large-grained, and yielding earthier, less aromatic sakes; used for a wide range of styles. Grown primarily in the south. Very popular among sake drinkers. |
| **Oseto** | Earthy and rich. Grown on the north part of Shikoku Island. This produces distinctive sake which a moderately experienced taster could pick out from a line-up. |
| **Tamazakae** | Soft and round, yet also rich and full-flavored. Only grown in a couple small prefectures on the south third of the main island and considered "artisanal." "Amazake" is an unrelated low-alcohol rice drink, not unlike eggnog, made from Amazake rice. |
| **Yamada Nishiki** | The premium rice variety, used for most of the country's **Daiginjo**-level sakes (the most premium category; see below). Quite aromatic. Generally grown in the southern parts of Japan. |

## WATER

Water is added to sake at several steps in the brewing process and is vital to a sake's character. Historically, the major brewing centers sprung up around good water sources. Hard water (i.e., water with lots of mineral content) encourages a more complete fermentation and therefore drier sake. Soft water is better for slow-fermenting, sweeter sakes. Water with high iron content creates off flavors in sake and is undesirable.

## YEAST

There are 15 yeast strains officially designated for use in sake production by Japan's Central Brewers Union. Several of these are no longer used however because they generated a marked, undesirable level of acidity. The Union isolated the desired yeast strains in the early 20$^{th}$ century and now supplies them to breweries throughout the country. Yeast **#15** is highly prized for its aromatic complexity; **#7** is the most used. Yeast **#9** is used for many ginjo sakes (sakes made with minimally milled rice and added alcohol). Variations on these basic strains are often proprietary to the specific brewery that developed them. As unprocessed rice offers no sugars to yeast, the rice grains do not carry wild yeasts into the brewery with them, so inoculation is necessary for a reliable fermentation.

## CLASSIFICATIONS

For premium sake there are two basic categories, ***Honjozo*** and ***Junmai***. Junmai, made with 100% rice, and is produced as described in the section above. Honjozo sake has small amounts of distilled alcohol (typically sugar cane-based) added after pressing – by law not more than 10% of the total weight of the polished rice used in the batch. It is not higher in alcohol, as it is still diluted back to the usual 15-16% at bottling. Generally the brewer has chosen to make Honjozo for stylistic rather than economic reasons. Quality Honjozo sake is typically dry, smooth and mineral-driven.

Premium sake encapsulates 20% of total sake production. The rest is **Futsuu-shu**—"normal" or everyday sake—which may contain much larger amounts of added distilled alcohol. Essentially analogous to jug wine, it can be quite drinkable nonetheless. Adding alcohol became common during World War II as a way to extend rice supplies, but has since become a standard part of the brewer's toolkit.

Beyond the fundamental division of Honjozo and Junmai, premium sake is then classified based on how extensively the rice is milled. There are three categories (or six, once you include Honjozo and Junmai versions of each):

| No Alcohol Added (Junmai) | | Alcohol Added (Honjozo) | |
|---|---|---|---|
| **Junmai** | Pure rice sake (i.e. containing no added alcohol); Rice grains must be milled to 70% or less their original grain size. Typically fuller-bodied, with some earthier notes. | **Honjozo** | Contains some added alcohol. Rice grains must be milled to 70% or less of their original grain size. Light-bodied, minerally, and dry. |
| **Junmai Ginjo** | Pure rice sake. Rice grains must be milled to 60% or less of their original grain size. Light to medium-bodied, fruity, and refined. | **Honjozo Ginjo** | Contains some added alcohol. Rice grains must be milled to 60% or less of their original grain size. Light, aromatic, and fruity. |
| **Junmai Daiginjo** | Pure rice sake. Rice grains must be milled to 50% or less of their original grain size. Light, aromatic, and complex. Often with a mix of fruit and floral aromas. | **Honjozo Daiginjo** | Contains some added alcohol. Rice grains must be milled to 50% or less of their original grain size. Light, complex, and aromatic. |

Note that the higher grades of Honjozo sake are not explicitly designated as such on the label. A brewery must specify no alcohol was added, by using the term Junmai. Thus, a sake label will identify a Daiginjo sake as "Junmai Daiginjo," if no alcohol was added, but only "Daiginjo" if it is a Honjozo Daiginjo. In export markets there is a perception that Honjozo sakes are of lower quality, which is not necessarily the case. It does mean that fewer high-quality examples of Honjozo sakes are exported, as they are difficult to market.

On a similar note, it takes more rice to make the same amount of (Honjozo or Junmai) Daiginjo compared to a Ginjo or Junmai. More milling means more rice lost in the process. Consequently, a Daiginjo is inherently more expensive to make, and that cost is passed on to the consumer. Many consumers therefore assume this to be a quality designation. Brewers are aware that their most expensive Daiginjo sake is under pressure to be worth its price. However, it would be more accurate to consider these categories as stylistic rather than quality designations. A drinker who prefers fuller, earthier sake is likely to be disappointed with a Daiginjo, regardless of its steeper price.

There are other designations that may appear on the label, some indicating particular brewing techniques or styles, and others that are less specific:

**Tokubetsu**: Best translated as "reserve" or "special." However, there is no single or legal definition as to what this means in terms of brewing. Used with the Honjozo and Junmai categories, a Tokubetsu may be more finely milled than a brewery's regular Honjozo or Junmai, or may have been made using special techniques (perhaps it's a kimoto, for example); if the latter, the label must indicate which.

**Namazake**: Unpasteurized sake. As such, it still contains active enzymes and yeast, is very prone to spoilage, and must be kept refrigerated during transport and storage. Historically Namazakes were released in spring and only available in the brewery's immediate area, but modern refrigeration has changed that. These sakes are typically light and fruity, with some green or grassy notes and more perceptible acidity. Namazakes are becoming increasingly popular in the U.S., and are often sold as seasonal products.

**Kimoto**: Brewers used the traditional, labor-intensive kimoto method for centuries until discoveries at the beginning of the twentieth century led to more straightforward, "quick-fermenting" approach. The koji, rice and water are mashed up for hours with long poles, eventually forming a paste or purée. The indigenous lactic bacteria thrive in low-oxygen environments like this paste, and some of these bacteria produce lactic acid, eventually creating enough to stabilize the sake. For a long time the mashing was thought to be a necessary step to develop the lactic acids and mix the koji; only in 1911 did brewers discover they could simply add lactic acid rather than developing it in the mash. Kimoto sakes are typically complex and often earthy and rich, with a clear touch of acidity.

**Yamahai**: Similar to a Kimoto, a Yamahai sake is defined by how the yeast starter is made, and, in a way, was a transition to the practice of simply adding lactic acid. In 1909 Kinchiro Kagi, working at the National Institute for Brewing Studies, discovered that with slightly warmer temperatures and some additional water, airborne, indigenous lactic bacteria and koji enzymes would develop in an open-top fermenter on their own, without labor-intensive mashing. As with Kimoto sakes, the various microbes add complex, earthy aromas, body, and a perceptible streak of acidity to the sake. Yamahai process is slower, adding a month to the brewing cycle, and can be harder to control, so most brewers choose to use more modern methods. Yamahai sakes account for less than one percent of the world's sake.

**Genshu**: This is undiluted sake. As no water is added before bottling, these sakes are stronger, ranging from 17% up to even 20% in some cases. They are full-bodied, often with some perceptible heat on the nose and/or finish.

**Koshu**: Most sake is sold fresh and intended to be drunk within a year or less, but Koshu, or aged sake, has deep historical roots. It was much prized until the Meiji era (1868-1912), during which the government began taxing sake based on when it was *produced* rather than when it was *sold*. Brewers suddenly had a motivation to move their product more quickly. Today many brewers are re-examining the category. After seven or eight years, sake deepens in color and takes on Madeira-like notes similar to those of a tawny port or amontillado sherry. Aging can be in tank (stainless steel) or in bottle; sake madeirizes more quickly than wine would in these environments. Note that some brewers age their sakes for shorter periods—a year or two—at near freezing temperatures to smooth out the sake's texture, similar to how lager beers are aged. However these sakes are not considered Koshus.

The term Koshu includes sakes aged at the brewery and sold as "koshu," as well as sakes aged in bottle by consumers after purchase. Earthier styles like Yamahai and Kimoto sakes age well, as do Namazakes if they are kept in a cold enough environments to avoid spoilage.

**Kijoshu**: Kijoshu sake is fortified and aged. Finished sake is added to a batch in mid-brew to elevate the alcohol level and stop fermentation, just like Port. It is typically (though not necessarily) aged for several years in stainless steel tanks, taking on the deeper color and characteristics of a Koshu, albeit richer and sweeter.

**Nigori**: Cloudy and white, Nigori sake (also called a Cream Sake in the U.S.) contains sediment of rice and koji. The bottle should be shaken before opening and pouring to evenly mix the sediment in the sake. Nigoris are typically fruity and sweet, though there are some elegant dry examples. Store in a refrigerator after opening, and consume the remainder within a few days, as spoilage can be rapid.

## REGIONALITY

Regionality in sake has always been largely a matter of brewing practices. While historically brewers might be somewhat limited by the character of the local water or rice variety, generally they had enough flexibility to make a sake that suited the local cuisine. Many of those traditions still hold true.

Broadly speaking, sake from brewers nearer the coast favor lighter, drier, more delicate sakes complementing the saltwater fish caught fresh from the ocean. Cuisine further inland was more reliant on the stronger flavors of freshwater fish and preserved foods, so sakes from these areas are accordingly fuller and more powerful.

Climate was a historical factor before the days of air-conditioning and refrigeration, and sake from the warmer areas would be fuller and richer, owing to a warmer fermentation. Thanks to modern technology there are plenty of exceptions these days.

## HOT TOPICS

Sake production remains an area of experimentation and innovation, with new pasteurization techniques, for example, helping to raise the quality level across the board. However, the real battleground for innovation lies in marketing. English names on labels are one example, but a few producers have stripped away the wine-like lingo and instead market themselves more like spirits, with distinctive colored bottles, branding, and celebrity sponsorship. Some also encourage the use of sake as a cocktail ingredient or have introduced fruit-flavored, sparkling, and low-alcohol sakes.

In the U.S. sake is moving out of the Japanese restaurants and into venues focusing on other cuisines, or bars. Sake-focused retail outlets have also appeared in New York and San Francisco.

The earthquake, tsunami, and subsequent nuclear disaster in March, 2010, was devastating to a number of breweries in the affected area, but did not impact exports, which continued to grow. Most of the breweries have been repaired or rebuilt, and have been able to source safe, raw materials uncontaminated by radiation either locally or from other provinces.

# Spirits, Dessert & Fortified Wines

## Cordials and Liqueurs

The historical distinction between cordials and liqueurs is that liqueurs were produced on the European continent in France while cordials were produced in Great Britain or another part of the world. This distinction has blurred in modern times. The sweet after-dinner drinks are now produced around the world and the terms are interchangeable.

## Production

Most cordials and liqueurs are made by **infusion** or **maceration**. The **infusion** method entails the steeping of a fruit or flavor in brandy for an extended period of time, usually a year. After one year, the mixture is strained and sweetened with sugar syrup, then bottled. The **maceration** method entails the steeping of herbs in brandy for a couple of days and then distilling the entire mixture. The final distillation is sweetened and bottled. Fruit liqueurs are usually made using the infusion method while herbal liqueurs are made by the maceration process.

Following are some brief looks at various cordials and liqueurs.

## Ricard and Pernod (Absinthe)

In the mid-19th century, Absinthe was the most popular liqueur in the world; however, by 1919, it had been outlawed by every nation except Spain and Portugal. Spain continued to make the drink under the name Absenta until 1985. Absinthe and its substitutes are made by the maceration method using wormwood, hyssop, lemon balm, anise, Chinese aniseed, fennel, coriander, and other roots and herbs. Brandy serves as its base. It is important to note that wormwood is not used in Absinthe-substitute products such as Ricard and Pernod because the substance is illegal. It is distilled at 130 proof, and is a popular aperitif.

## Galliano

Galliano is an herb liqueur based on brandy made by the infusion method with vanilla flavoring. It is most popular as a flavoring in cocktails.

## Amaretto di Saronna

Amaretto di Saronna is dominated by almond and apricot flavors and is one of the best known of the Italian liqueurs. It is usually consumed after a meal or as a part of many cocktails.

## Maraschino

Maraschino is a sweet, clear liqueur made from cherries and cherry pits. It was a popular ingredient in early punches and cocktails and is almost never consumed straight.

## Sambuca

Sambuca, with its anise-based licorice flavor, is the most widely used of all Italian liqueurs. It is a popular after-dinner drink often taken with coffee.

## Brandy

The term brandy can be used specifically to refer to the distillates of grape wine, or to spirits distilled from a fermented mash of grapes or other fruit. The generic term that can be applied is *eau de vie*, which is French for water of life. The word brandy comes from the Dutch word *brandewijn* meaning burnt wine. These brandies are aged in oak casks, and usually bottled at either 80° or 84° proof.

Brandy is broken down into three basic categories: **grape, pommace,** and **fruit brandy**. **Grape brandy** is brandy distilled from fermented grape juice and is aged in wooden casks. **Pommace brandy** is made from the pressed grape pulp, skins, and stems that remain after grapes are processed for wine. This type of brandy rarely sees wood and Italian grappa and French marc are the best examples. **Fruit-flavored brandy** is brandy that has been flavored with the extract of another fruit. Some fruit liqueurs are labeled as brandies, but since they are not actually distilled from fruit, they are not true brandies. Calvados, the apple brandy form Normandy is the best-known type of fruit brandy.

Brandy can only be called Cognac when produced in its delimited growing area in France. Similarly, Armagnac hails from Gascony in the southwest of France. Spanish brandy is produced mainly in Jerez and is either distilled from Sherry or from Spanish wine. California is the main producer of brandy in the United States and by law must be aged in wood for a minimum of two years and may be distilled by either method.

## Quality Levels

There are three levels of quality that are recognized for brandy: V.S (very superior), V.S.P (very superior pale), and Three stars; followed by V.O (very old) or V.S.O.P (very superior old pale); and finally XO (extra old), Napoleon, or Extra, which is considered the best type of brandy in the world. The United States does not use quality designations.

## Armagnac

Armagnac has been produced in the region of Gascony in Southwestern France since the 15th century.

Armagnac has four designations:

<u>Armagnac:</u> sandy soil type, general region

<u>Bas-Armagnac:</u> sandy soil type, specific region

<u>Haut-Armagnac:</u> chalky soil type, specific region

<u>Tenareze:</u> clay soil type, specific region

Ninety-nine percent of the Armagnac that is exported carries the designation of Armagnac or Bas-Armagnac. To be called Bas-Armagnac, which is acknowledged to be the best designation, the brandy must be blended and stored in warehouses separate and distinct from any other Armagnac designation. The lesser designations, Tenareze and Haut-Armagnac, produce brandy that is course and is often sold in bulk as the base for liqueurs, which is an important aspect of the trade.

## Production

The variety Saint-Emilion (also known as Ugni Blanc and Trebbiano) is the primary grape used in the production of Armagnac. Other minor grapes used include Picpoul, Jurançon, and Plant de Grec. The grapes are picked before they are fully ripe and mature to insure high acidity levels, a key component to the finished product. The low alcohol liquid (9–10%) is immediately distilled in a continuous still. (See spirits section for detailed information.) All distillations must be completed by April 30th of the spring following the harvest. Armagnac is aged in oak that comes from the local Gascon forest, which is black, sappy, and not very porous. The element of oak is just as important as the grapes or the soil in producing the distinctive flavor that makes Armagnac unique. It may or may not be vintage dated. It may also be blended. If it is both vintage dated and blended, then the vintage indicated will denote the youngest year in the blend. Three star requires at least two years in wood, V.S.O.P. at least four years in wood; and Extra at least five years in wood. The key element of Armagnac is not the vintage date but the time it is aged in wood.

## Cognac

The area of Cognac overlaps the departments of Charente in the east and Charente Meitime in the west in the south-central part of France. The town of Cognac is about an hour's drive north of Bordeaux. Cognac was first distilled sometime after 1600, after other brandies were being produced in France.

Cognac has six districts:

<u>Grand Champagne:</u> produces the best and most expensive cognac of finesse and elegance, requiring 15–20 years to mature, represents 14.65% of total vineyard area

<u>Petite Champagne</u>: produces cognac similar to Grand Champagne but less so, maturing more quickly, represents 15.98% of total vineyard area

<u>Borderies</u>: produces cognac of the greatest body, represents 4.52% of total vineyard area

<u>Fins Bois</u>: 37.82% of total vineyard area

<u>Bons Bois</u>: 22.19% of total vineyard area

<u>Bois Ordinaires</u>: 4.83% of total vineyard area

It is the percentage of chalk in the soil composition that determines the quality of the cognac produced in the six districts. Grand Champagne has the highest percentage, and so on down through Bois Ordinaires.

## PRODUCTION

Like Armagnac, the most common grape variety in cognac is Saint-Emilion. Other grapes used include Colombard and Folle Blanche. As in Armagnac, the wine produced is highly acidic and low in alcohol. The wine goes through a double distillation process in an Alembic or pot still. Unlike the continuous still used to make Armagnac, there is a definite beginning and end to cognac's distillation. The first and last parts—"headings" and "tailings"—of the distillation are removed, leaving only the middle or *Brouilli*. In the second step of the distillation, only the Brouilli is used and again the headings and tailings are removed. What remains is the raw cognac to be aged. Cognac is aged in porous Limousin oak from the Limoges Forest or Troncais oak from trees ranging in age from 80–100 years old. Because the oak is porous, a portion of the cognac is lost due to evaporation during the aging period. This loss is romantically known as the "angel's share." Unlike Armagnac, blending is the rule rather than the exception in Cognac. Each stage of blending is carried out slowly so that the flavors of the Cognac may marry properly. Rectification, which is the addition of distilled water, is carried out to bring the blend to its final bottling strength. Vintage cognacs are very uncommon. Cognacs labeled as three-star have approximately five years of barrel age. V.S.O.P. Cognacs average 20 years of age.

## SPANISH BRANDY

Spanish brandy and Sherry come from the southwest area of Spain. The heart of this area is the town of Jerez de la Frontera, which is surrounded by vineyards. Spanish brandies, like Cognac, are made using an Alembic or pot still. What differentiates the production of Spanish brandy from both Armagnac and Cognac is that it is aged using the *solera* system and not in individual casks. (You will recall this is the same system used to age Sherry.) Spanish brandies that spend a mere three years in a *solera* system achieve the same aging results as brandies that spend 15 years in individual casks.

## SPIRITS

### PRODUCTION

A spirit is distilled alcohol. Most are made from fermenting fruit or grain-based solutions also known as "cereal". There are four main steps in the production of spirits: **malting, fermentation, distillation,** and **rectification**. In order to ferment grains, malt must be present. **Malt or malting** is the process of soaking barley is in water, allowing the grain to sprout. It is then dried. This step is also referred to as germination. The malt is now able convert grain starch to sugar. **Fermentation** occurs next by adding yeast and water to the malted grain. The yeasts convert the sugars in the grain into ethyl alcohol and carbon dioxide gas. After the gas evaporates, the mixture contains a low level of alcohol that will be extracted and concentrated through distillation. **Distillation** is the process that uses heat to extract the alcohol from a liquid that contains both alcohol and water. Alcohol vaporizes at a lower temperature (172°F) than water (212°F), and when heated it turns into a gas and rises, leaving the water behind. As the vapors cool, they condense back into a liquid as concentrated alcohol. This process takes place in a still. Basically, a still extracts alcohol from a fermented liquid by boiling it. The alcohol content in a spirit can be increased by distilling it more than once to further concentrate the alcohol and reduce the total volume of liquid. Following distillation, one is left with a neutral spirit or ethyl alcohol. **Rectification** is the process of removing undesirable components, such as congeners and volatiles from the distillate. This is done to purify the alcohol. Commercial distilleries purify alcohol by filtering it through activated carbon.

## Types of Stills

There are two types of stills that are used to distill alcohol. The first called a **pot still** or **Alembic still.** It is an enclosed vessel that narrows into a tube at the top, where the alcohol vapor collects while the fermented contents are being boiled. The tube then bends downward, from the top and runs through a bath of cold water. This allows the vapor to condense back into liquid and drain into a container at the end of the tube. This process is usually repeated more than once, and the main portion of the resulting product, called "the heart" is bottled and sold. Although considered inefficient, the pot still continues to be considered better for spirits such as brandy, whiskey, or those with distinctive flavors. The shape of the still can be either tall and thin or short and stout. The taller stills produce lighter spirits, while the shorter produce the heavier varieties. Most pot stills are made from copper.

The second type of still has several names. It can be referred to as a **column or reflux still**, or a **continuous** or **Coffey still** as well. This still has two enclosed stainless steel or copper columns. The fermented liquid is slowly fed down into the top of the first column while steam is sent up from the bottom. The rising steam strips the alcohol from the descending liquid and carries it over to the second column where it is recirculated and concentrated to the desired percentage of alcohol. The column is considered more efficient because it requires only a single distillation, which is done in a continuous operation. Column stills are thought to be more efficient for neutral flavored spirits such as vodka, gin, and white rum. All spirits are clear when they run off the still. If a spirit is colored, it is done so later. Some spirits are stored and aged in oak casks or barrels that help them mature and impart some flavor and color.

Spirits are measured by alcohol content. Here, in the United States, the proof scale is used in measurement, with the proof of a spirit being double the **alcohol by volume (ABV).** For example, a spirit that is 50% ABV is 100° proof. (It is customary for a degree symbol to be used when expressing proof.) Other countries use ABV ratings, such as the **Gay-Lussac System**, which expresses the alcohol content as a percentage of the total liquid volume of the beverage. If a spirit's ABV is 50%, it contains 50% alcohol.

Spirits are classified as gin, rum, tequila, vodka, brandy, and whiskey. Each type of spirit will be discussed briefly.

## Gin

The word gin is derived from the English word Genever, which means juniper in Dutch. Gin originated in Holland but it was in England that it developed into its popular style. Gin's origins lie in a juniper/spice based medicinal spirit that was promoted as a diuretic in 1650. In the 1660s it was used to cure colic, however during this time it also started to be consumed as a beverage that was fancied by English soldiers fighting on the continent.

### Production

Gin is distilled from grain, and its flavor and aroma come from juniper berries and other botanicals like anise, cinnamon, orange peel, and coriander to name a few. Gin makers have their own recipe of botanicals, the number of which can range from as few as four to as many as fifteen. Top gin producers flavor their product in a unique way. It is during the final distillation that the flavor is truly imparted to the spirit. The alcohol vapor passes through a chamber that has suspended juniper berries and other botanicals in it. It is here that the aromatics and oils are extracted from the botanicals by the vapor before it moves on to the condenser.

Most gin is colorless, though some brands may have straw-yellow hue because of aging in barrels. Even though most distillers age their gin, they cannot make aging claims for the product. Most gin is sold at 80° proof, although the Brits tend to be higher, around 90°. American gins are referred to as soft gins while the English counterpart is referred to as hard. There are a few classifications of gin, however one style is dominant, London Dry Gin. This is the gin style produced in the United Kingdom, the United States, and Spain. The other types are Plymouth Gin, Old Tom Gin, and Genever. Plymouth gin has a fuller body than London Dry, slightly fruity and very aromatic. Old Tom Gin is an example of the 18th century gin that was typically produced. This is slightly sweet and produced in minuscule quantities. Genever is the Dutch style of gin. It is distilled from a malted grain mash similar to that of whiskey. These style gins are produced in Holland, Belgium and Germany.

The following drinks contain gin: Martini, Martinez cocktail, and Gin and Tonic.

## Rum

The Moors from Malaga are credited with first producing. Sugarcane, the primary ingredient in rum, has its origins in what is present day Indonesia. The Chinese were the first to spread its cultivation, and the Arabs brought it to the

Middle East and present-day Europe. The Spanish and Portuguese transported sugarcane to the Canary Islands and what is now the Caribbean and Brazil. Barbados is home to Mount Gay Distillery, which is the oldest producer of rum in the world. Brazil is known for its unaged cane spirit called Cachaca. Puerto Rican rum gained popularity in the Spanish colonies during the 17th century. By the mid-19th century, Puerto Rico started to produce rum on a commercial basis, and is now the largest producer of the spirit in the world.

## Production

Rum's production starts with raw sugar cane, which is pressed to extract juice that is boiled and clarified. It is then exposed to centrifugal force to separate the crystallizing sugar from the molasses. The molasses is then reboiled, and the residue is mixed with water and yeast and allowed to ferment. The process can take about 24 hours for light rums, and up to several weeks for fuller varieties. Light rums are rectified and produced in column or continuous stills, while the heavier ones are distilled in pot stills. Some are made by blending both types of production in a manner similar to Armagnac. All rums come out of the still as clear, colorless spirits. It is generally aged in uncharred oak barrels to add a degree of smoothness, and very little color is imparted to the spirit. Carmel is usually added to dark rums for color and taste. Most rums are blends of several aged rums, which are selected for their special aroma, flavor, and color.

There are four classifications for rum. The first is **white or dry, light-bodied rums**, which are usually clear with a subtle flavor. Puerto Rican and Nicaraguan rum are good examples for this type. The **golden or amber, medium style rums** spend several years in American oak casks, which impart a smooth mellow taste to the drink. Barbados is the best producer of this type. **Dark or rich, full-bodied rums** are traditionally carmel-dominated and show superbly from Jamaica. They are frequently aged in oak casks for extended periods of time. Finally there is **aromatic rum**, which can be distilled in more than one way, aged or not, with or without oak. These rums can range from light to full-bodied. Batavia Arak and the East Indies are the best producers. The subtle differences in rum relate directly to the growing area from which the sugarcane comes from because all aspects of weather and soil type have a direct affect on the plant.

Rum can be blended with almost any mixture and generally is. Popular drinks with rum include: the Cuba Libre (rum and coke with a lime), Daiquiri (any flavor), Mai Tai, Pina Colada, and Zombie.

## Tequila

Tequila was North America's first distilled drink. The natives in pre-Hispanic times fermented sap from the maguey plants and created a drink known as *Pulqe*. In the early to mid-1500s, after the Spanish conquest, "Mezcal wine" was produced in what was New Galacia, which is now the town of Tequila. Tequila is the name of the spirit, town, and the valley in the state of Jalisco, Mexico. The product from Jalisco—mezcal of Tequila— became known as tequila the same way that brandy made in a certain region of France became known as cognac. Don Pedro Sanches de Tagle is the father of tequila and opened the first tequila distillery around 1600. Mexico underwent there its own prohibition from 1785–1792. This was due to favoritism toward Spanish wines and liquors of King Charles III. It was at this time that the agave was brought underground to be baked, which is still a process used in making some tequila, but is always used for making mezcal.

### Types of Tequila

The Tequila Regulatory Council oversees the standards and quality of a distiller's production. All 100% agave tequilas must be bottled in and labeled, "*Hecho en Mexico*" (Made in Mexico). Only "*mixto*" tequila is allowed to be sold in bulk and bottled outside of Mexico. The Declaration for the Protection of Denomination of Origin (DOT) states that tequila is an alcoholic beverage made with agave and grown in the allowed villages and states to be labeled as such. The states include Jalisco, Tamaulipas, Nayarit, Michoacan, and Guanajuato. No agave, outside of these regions, including other countries, can be labeled a product known as "Tequila". Mezcal is made outside the delimited growing areas but still in Mexico.

There are four officially recognized types of tequila according to Mexican regulations. *Blanco* (silver) is bottled immediately after distillation or held for no more than 60 days in steel tanks, but never on wood. *Reposada* (rested) must be aged in oak barrels for 2–12 months before bottling. *Anejo* (aged) must be stored and aged in oak barrels for more than one year before being bottled. *Oro* (gold) is almost the same as blanco, but it contains flavoring and coloring ingredients, which are added to make it appear aged. This is typically done with *mixto* tequilas.

### Production

Tequila is distilled from the *pina* (roasted center) of the blue agave plant, also known as "maguey". Originally, the plant was thought to be a member of the cactus family but it actually belongs to the lily family. The agave plant must be eight years old before it can be considered for fermentation. Some growers allow it to grow for up to 12 years. Once ripened, the leaves are pruned to encourage growth of the *pina*. At harvest time, the pina is cut from the stalk and transported to the factory, where it is quartered or halved before being baked. This precook is done to rid the plant of external waxes and solids that can create a bitter juice. Traditional distillers allow the pina to soften either in steam rooms or ovens for 50–72 hours. This process allows the agave to process its natural juices and keeps it from caramelizing. Baking retains more of the natural flavors. <u>Mezcal is baked in underground pits, rather than steamed.</u> The pinas are then cooled for a 24–36 hour period; they are then mashed to separate the pulp from the juice, although some distillers keep them together. Once the juice is strained, it is mixed in large vats with water, creating wort. Yeast is then added to the wort. The must is then left to ferment in wood or steel tanks for 7–12 days. Once fermentation has subsided, the must may be left for up to 12 hours to richen the product and allow it to settle before distillation. It is then distilled twice either in an Alembic still or in modern stainless steel column stills. Distillation takes 48 hours to complete.

Tequila is clear after distillation. If it is to be sold as *blanco* it may be bottled immediately or remain in the steel tanks until bottling. *Reposada* and *anejo* will be stored in wooden oak casks. The most prized tequilas are placed in bourbon barrels to age; however, Sherry, whiskey, and cognac barrels can be used. They are then stored in bodegas. The color of tequila does not reflect either quality or age. To create a consistency of aroma and taste, most tequila is blended with other barrels of similar age. The end result is then bottled or tanked for bulk shipment.

Drinks which include tequila include: the Margarita, Teqini (similar to a Martini), and Tequila Sunrise.

# VODKA

Vodka is considered the most versatile spirit. It was originally used to describe grain distillates that were used for medicinal reasons. Its name comes from the Russian word *voda*, meaning water. Polish vodkas are mostly made from rye mash. Those from Russia used to be made from potatoes, but today are made mostly from wheat. Swedish and Baltic distillers use wheat mashes, while the United States uses a wide variety of base ingredients. Vodka is sometimes classified by the number of distillations it undergoes. In Poland, it is graded according to degree of purity: *zwykly* (standard), *wyborowy* (premium), and *luksusowy* (deluxe). In Russia, labels classify vodka in two ways. It can be *osobaya* (special) of superior quality and may be exported. *Krepkaya* (strong) denotes an over proof vodka of at least 56% ABV. The United States Government identifies vodka very generally as a distilled neutral spirit that is treated after distillation with charcoal or other materials. It should have no aroma, taste, color, or distinctive character.

## PRODUCTION

Vodka is a non-aged neutral spirit that can be fermented from anything fermentable. Most are made from cereals. Rye is most often used, followed by wheat, oats, barley, and potatoes. Wort is made from the grain or potatoes and then is heated, to convert starches into fermentable sugars. The wort is then fermented and becomes wash. It is then distilled. Continuous stills are most efficient for producing vodka. Since higher purity and alcohol levels are desired, most vodkas are double or triple distilled. It is then filtered, usually through charcoal. Other materials such as sand or even coagulants may be used for filtration. The subtle difference in taste is due in part to the grain chosen and the filtering process employed. Vodka is not aged; it is colorless, virtually odorless and tasteless. The exception is flavored vodkas, which were originally produced to mask the actual flavor. Now they are seen as a mark of a distiller's skill.

The list of cocktails containing vodka is long but some of the most well-known include, the Moscow Mule, Martini, and Bloody Mary.

# WHISKEY

The word whiskey comes from the Gaelic word *uisgebaugh*, (pronounced wys-ger-baw) which means water of life. Whiskey is made from grain, but it is the type and proportion of grains used and the aging process that determines a whiskey's style and flavor. Whiskey has two spellings depending on the area from which it comes. Irish and American whiskeys keep the "e", while others drop it.

## PRODUCTION

All whiskey undergoes a similar distillation process. Grain is ground into a product that is known as grist. Water is added to the grist and is cooked, allowing the starches to be released. Malt is then added to convert the starches into sugars. The grist is then removed and the remaining liquid, the wort, is inoculated with yeast and allowed to ferment. The liquid produced is known as beer. The beer is then distilled and the end product is whiskey. Whiskey is then watered down and aged in various types of barrels. The barrel selection depends on the type of whiskey being made. When placed in barrels to age, the whiskey is clear. It is during the aging period that whiskey obtains its color, aroma, and flavor.

## TYPES OF WHISKEY

**American whiskey** was at first made from rue, barley, and corn. Now it is also made from wheat and rye. Straight whiskey is a simple term that denotes bourbon. Any straight whiskey must be distilled from a 51% base of a single grain. Blended whiskey contains a minimum of 20% straight whiskey, and may be mixed with a grain spirit or light whiskey. It may also contain Sherry, peach, or prune juice. American whiskey is usually aged in charred oak barrels. Light whiskey is made from a high percentage of corn and aged in uncharred or used casks. Rye whiskey must be made from a mash consisting of at least 51% rye. Tennessee whiskey as previously discussed must be made in Tennessee. Corn whiskey must be comprised of at least 80% corn and be aged in uncharred or old casks. Wheat malt and rye malt whiskey must contain 51% of their respective grains to be labeled and sold as such. Bourbon must be distilled from a mash of at least 51% corn. It must be distilled through a column still and aged in new charred barrels. After use, the casks must be discarded and not used for bourbon again. They are generally sold to the Scot's for aging their single malt scotches. Sour mash is a style of bourbon that differs from other whiskey because mash from a previous distillation is used in the production process.

**Irish whiskey** is generally distilled three times in a pot still and is blended with a whiskey from a continuous still. Whiskey used for blending can be made from unmalted barley, corn, rye, wheat, or oats. Single malt whiskies are made purely from malted barley. Irish whiskey is generally aged in used Sherry casks for a minimum of five years.

**Canadian whiskey** must be produced from cereal grain, such as rye, barley, wheat, and corn. Canadian law does not specify the actual percentages of grain which must be used, but generally rye is the implied grain when referring to Canadian whiskey. The column still is primarily used for distillation. Though not regulated, most are aged from 2–6 years.

The word **scotch** identifies a whisky that is made in Scotland. The most sought after of these whiskies is **single malt scotch**, which is made entirely from malted barley. Very simply, the barley is soaked in water and sprouted. The malted barley is then toasted over a peat-fueled fire, enabling the smoke to come into contact with the barley and impart flavor upon the grain. The malt is then mashed with warm water and the starches change to sugar. The liquid, or wort, is then strained and yeast is added. Fermentation occurs and alcohol is produced. The fermented wort is then distilled at least twice in a pot still. The resulting scotch is placed in old Sherry or bourbon casks for aging. By law, it must remain in cask for at least three years, but most producers age their scotches for longer, even up to 25 years.

Single malt scotches are quite unique and are greatly affected by their individual production. The type of water and peat used, the surrounding air during maturation, the shape of the pot still, and the casks in which they are aged all impact the final product. Single malt scotches are produced in four regions of Scotland: the Highlands, the Lowlands, Islay, and Cambletown.

Some scotch whiskies are **blended**. They are comprised of a both a portion of a single malt scotch plus some whisky produced in a column still from unmalted barley or corn. Another type of scotch whiskey is a **vatted malt** scotch, which is a blend of single malt scotches from various distilleries.

Cocktails that include scotch include the Rob Roy, Rusty Nail, and Manhattan. Single malts are best drunk neat, usually with a glass of water on the side.

# FORTIFIED WINES

Fortification is defined as the addition of a spirit (usually, but not always distilled from grape must) to fermenting or fermented wine. The addition of this spirit raises the alcohol level of the finished wine, ensures microbiological stability, and arrests fermentation. The earlier the spirit is added in the fermentation process, the more residual sugar there will be present in the finished wine. *Vins de liqueur* (VDL) such as Pineau des Charentes (produced near Bordeaux) have barely started fermenting when they are fortified and therefore are quite sweet. By comparison, Sherry is usually fermented to dryness before fortification.

Fortified wines are produced in practically every warm wine region of the world, though the largest consumers of fortified wines tend to be from countries with cooler climates. Fortified wine is made to be exported and its history and profitability are highly dependent upon global trends, politics, and economies. Although there are many styles of fortified wine, only those that have made the most impact on the world market will be described here in detail.

# SHERRY

Sherry comes from the **Jerez DO**, a region of Andalucia in southwest Spain. The Moors occupied Andalucia longer than any other region of Spain, and it is thought that they introduced the practice of fortifying wines to the area. After Spain's unification in 1492, Andalucia became a major center for trade, creating a thriving market for Sherry in England and the New World.

The soils of Jerez include sand, clay, and chalk. Chalk soil, called albariza, produces the best grapes for dry Sherry. Grapes used for the blending of sweet wines are often grown in clay or sand. **Jerez Superior** is considered the best area within the region, and the soil is almost entirely chalk. It is located in and around the only towns legally allowed to ship Sherry: Jerez de la Frontera, El Puerto de Santa Maria, and Sanlúcar de Barrameda.

## SHERRY VARIETIES

The three most important grapes for Sherry are **Palomino, Pedro Ximénez,** and **Moscatel**. Palomino is the most widely planted grape of the region. Its neutral flavor profile provides good raw material for the *solera* process (see below). Pedro Ximénez is naturally high in sugar and produces the best sweet wines of the region. It is less hardy and prolific than Palomino. Moscatel (also known as Muscat of Alexandria) can be made into a wine on its own or used as a sweet blending wine.

## SHERRY PRODUCTION

The Sherry Process is what truly defines the wines of this region. After the harvest, grapes are crushed and the must is fermented into a dry wine with 12–13% alcohol. The best lots are then fortified with *aguardiente* (distilled grape must) to about 14.5% alcohol. The fortified wine is then put into a cask. By Spring some casks will have grown a film of yeast on the top of the liquid known as *flor*. *Flor* absorbs any traces of residual sugar, lowers the glycerol and volatile acids in the wine, and adds the esters and acetaldehyde that give Sherry its unique aroma. Casks that develop a healthy *flor* are classified as fino Sherry. Those that fail to develop *flor* are classified as oloroso (see "Styles of Sherry" below). *Flor* only survives in wines with an alcohol level between 14.5–16%. Casks with the most significant *flor* are fortified to 15.5% to encourage continued growth. Oloroso casks without *flor* and casks with only a thin layer of *flor* are fortified to 17.5%. Once the Sherry has been classified as fino or oloroso, it may be kept as *añadas* (vintage), but it is more often blended with older Sherries of its type in a *solera*.

The *solera* system is used to blend wines of many vintages into a single Sherry. The barrels that contain Sherry from the oldest vintages are known as the *solera*. Several *criaderas* (or nurseries) feed each solera. As wine from the solera is drawn off and bottled (up to 33% yearly), the casks are replenished with slightly younger wine from the first *criadera*. The first *criadera* is replenished with wine from the second *criadera*, and so on. The final *criadera* is topped off with the wines of the most recent harvest. Younger soleras may have three or four *criadera*s. Well-established soleras may have as many as 14 *criadera*s. Although a solera is commonly depicted as layers of barrels stacked on top of one another, *criadera*s are often grouped separately, sometimes even in different buildings. A fino solera that is consistently refreshed can support *flor* growth for 8 to 10 years. The *solera* system creates a consistent product thereby establishing Sherry's reputation throughout the world.

## STYLES OF SHERRY

Styles of Sherry range from fino-type sherries which are light, dry and crisp to oloroso-type sherries which are fuller-bodied, darker in color, and sometimes sweet.

**Amontillado** is an aged fino Sherry with a distinctive nutty aroma. A true amontillado is bone-dry.

**Manzanilla** is a fino Sherry from the town of Sanlúcar de Barrameda. Finos produced in this cool, seaside town grow a thick *flor* that protects them from oxidation while enhancing aromatics. Some say that you can taste the salt air in a Manzanilla. These are delicate wines that do not travel well. A true Manzanilla is best enjoyed locally.

**Palo Cortado** is a fino that produced *flor* initially but lost it before it reached amontillado status. It is officially classified as an oloroso, but its flavor is somewhere between that and a young amontillado.

**Cream Sherry** is an oloroso blended with sweet wine. Sweet wines made from Pedro Ximénez grapes produce the most distinguished cream sherries, but many are sweetened with wines made from Palomino and Moscatel, or even with *arrope*, a sweet syrup made from reduced grape must.

# MADEIRA

Madeira comes from a small volcanic, subtropical island of the same name. Only 375 miles off the coast of Morocco, Madeira is nonetheless a province of Portugal (530 miles northeast). The island is a geographical and climatic composite of rough terrain and searing heat. Since temperatures on the coasts can be very hot, most grapes for Madeira are grown in the higher altitudes at the island's center. Vineyards are often planted on steep slopes and require terracing and harvesting by hand.

Madeira's key location along many historical trade routes has spread the fame of its wine throughout the world. It was especially popular in America during colonial times. At one point, 80% of the island's wine production was exported to the States. Powdery mildew was especially damaging to Madeira. Production dropped 99% over a four-year period in the 1850s. Phylloxera followed close on the heels of the mildew crisis, and many of the best Vitis vinifera vines for Madeira were lost. Because of these difficulties during the mid-19th century, desperate farmers sometimes planted and cultivated American vines and hybrids instead of using them only for grafting. Nearly one-half of the island is still planted with these non-vinifera vines. Portugal's entry into the European Union in 1986 made it illegal to use these vines in the production of Madeira.

## MADEIRA VARIETIES

Four traditional noble grapes make the highest quality Madeira: **Sercial, Verdelho, Bual,** and **Malvasia**. Wines must contain at least 85% of one of these varieties to be bottled under the name of the grape.

**Sercial** is planted on the cool northern side of the island and produces the driest (0.5–1.5% residual sugar) of the variety Madeiras. Sercial was once thought to be related to Riesling, but is in fact the same grape as **Esganacão** on the Portuguese mainland. This grape is known for its high acidity. **Verdelho** is also grown on the northern side of the island but is lower in acidity than Sercial and is used to produce "medium" Madeira (1.5–2.5% residual sugar). **Bual** (or Boal) is grown on the warmer, southern side of the island and is significantly lower in acid than Sercial. Bual grapes, which are sometimes eaten as table grapes, produce a fairly sweet (2.5–3.5% residual sugar), deeply colored dessert Madeira. **Malvasia** is also grown on the south side of the island and makes the sweetest (3.5–6.5% residual sugar), longest-lived Madeira. The English sometimes refer to it as Malmsey.

About 90% of Madeira wine is made not made from the four noble varieties but from **Tinta Negra Mole**. This grape is a prolific, disease resistant variety that produces somewhat bland wine. Up until the early 1990s, this blandness was an asset. Skillful wine makers used Tinta Negra Mole planted at various altitudes to simulate Sercial, Verdelho, Bual, and Malvasia styled wines. However, the EU put a stop to this practice in 1993. Now for a wine to be labeled Madeira, it must contain 85% of one of the four noble varieties.

## MADEIRA PRODUCTION

The unique flavor of Madeira is the result of oxidation and cask aging at warm to hot temperatures. Early Madeiras were fortified to help them survive long journeys at sea. It was discovered that the sun's heat and the movement of the ship improved the wine's flavor and, consequently, *vinho da roda* (round trip wine) became more popular than the *vinho canteiro* aged in casks on the island. An alternative system of heating Madeira had to be created when the cost of aging it on ships became prohibitive and the intense demand outpaced the supply of ship-aged wines.

*Estufagem* has been a controversial, yet widely practiced technique since its introduction in the late 18th century. After fermentation, the wine is fortified with *aguardiente* to 17% and then heated in an estufa (heated tank) to a maximum of 55°C by running hot water through pipes inside the wine vat. Ninety days (the legal maximum) in an estufa is equivalent to two years spent aging in cask. However, wine that is heated too quickly or too long can develop unpleasantly stewed, burnt qualities. High quality variety wines are never heated in an estufa. After fermentation they are fortified and then aged in American oak casks stored in warm but not artificially heated facilities. Moderate temperatures and the gradual integration of oxygen allowed by cask aging create the complex, long-lived wines that represent the best of Madeira.

## STYLES OF MADEIRA

Styles of Madeira are determined by the variety used and by the length of aging.

Finest Madeira is a blended wine that has usually been heated in an *estufa* and then aged for a minimum of three years, usually in a tank rather than wood.

Reserve Madeira is a five-year old blended wine that was likely heated in an *estufa*. Some of the blend may have been aged in wood casks.

Special Reserve Madeira is a blend of at least 10-year-old wines, usually aged in casks and not heated in an *estufa*. It usually contains higher percentages of the four noble grapes. Special reserves that contain at least 85% of any one noble variety may be labeled as such.

Extra Reserve Madeira is a blend of wines that are at least 15 years old. Like the special reserves, they are dominated by the noble varieties and are not heated in an *estufa*.

Superior Madeira is at least 15-years old and must be made with only the noble varieties.

*Garrafiera* translates loosely as "vintage" Madeira. Most of the wine in a *garrafiera* Madeira comes from a single vintage. The wines must be aged for at least 20 years before bottling and 2 years after bottling, but most shippers keep the wines in cask much longer. Wine kept in cask reduces and concentrates the volume significantly over time. Very old vintage Madeira that has not been bottled can become almost solid, and is extremely alcoholic. For this reason, younger wine is sometimes added to the oldest casks, although it is not officially allowed.

Solera-aged Madeiras were introduced after phylloxera. Because Madeira is so long lived, many shippers had very old casks of Madeira in their storehouses but only very young vines to produce new vintages after powdery mildew and phylloxera. The young Madeiras were added to the older casks fractionally through the solera system, stretching the stock without significantly diminishing the quality of the shipper's offerings.

## PORT

Port comes from only one place in the world, Portugal's Douro River Valley. The Douro River begins in Spain, northeast of Madrid (where it is known as the Duero River), then moves westward across the border into Portugal, toward the eastern coast, before washing into the Atlantic Ocean at the city of Oporto. Interestingly, the name port derives from the fact that these wines historically were shipped out to sea from the Port of Oporto.

The Douro River Valley is one of the most unforgiving viticultural regions in the world. The hillsides are composed of extremely steep banks of schist and granite. These hardened rock slopes originally contained so little soil that more had to be manually transported in over the generations. The presence of schist and granite is extremely important because both drain water well, allowing the vines to burrow deeply into the soil and become stable enough to survive the summer's heat.

### PRODUCTION OF PORT

To make Port, a neutral grape alcohol is added to the wine partway through fermentation. Arresting fermentation at this point generally preserves the wine's residual sugar level at 9–10% and boosts the alcohol level to 18–20%. The wines are then generally shipped from the Douro Valley across the river to the town of Vila Nova de Gaia where the aging process begins in lodges (warehouses).

### VARIETIES AND TYPES OF PORT

While there are several types of Ports, there are four basic categories: vintage, ruby, tawny, and white. There are many grapes that can be used for red (vintage, ruby, and tawny) Ports but the main ones are **Tinta Barroca, Tinta Cão, Tinta Roriz (Tempranillo), Touriga Francesa,** and **Touriga Nacional.** White ports are made from the following white grapes: **Esgana-Cão, Folgasão, Malvasia, Rabigato, Verdelho,** and **Viosinho.**

Vintage Ports are made from grapes of a single vintage and are bottled within two years. They tend to be regarded as the best Ports and are typically the most expensive.

Ruby Ports are made from lower-quality batches of wine, which are aged in wood for about two years. Ruby Ports are generally the least expensive.

Tawny Ports are made from a blend of grapes from several different years. They can be aged in wood for as long as 40 years and are tawny in color and ready to drink when bottled.

White Ports are made in the same way as red Ports except different grapes are used. (See listing of grapes above.) Often producers will create a drier style white Port to be consumed as an aperitif.

# Vin Doux Naturel

*Vin doux naturel* (VDN) implies that this type of wine comes by its sweetness naturally, but it is actually another type of fortified wine. A neutral spirit is added to the fermenting grape must when it reaches 6% alcohol, preserving unfermented sugar and the aromatics of the partially fermented wine. Although the spirit used to arrest fermentation is more concentrated than that used in Port, it constitutes only 5–10% of a finished *vin doux naturel*. In Port, the spirit makes up to 20% of the finished wine. *Vin doux naturel* is typically 15% alcohol by volume, quite low for a fortified wine.

The two grapes most often used for VDN are **Muscat** and **Grenache**. Both grapes have full, fruity flavors and complex aromatics.

The two most famous areas for *vin doux naturel* are the Côtes du Rhône and Roussillon. In the Côtes du Rhône, one finds **Muscat de Beaumes-de-Venise** made from **Muscat** and **Rasteau** made from **Grenache**. Roussillon has several appellations for *vin doux naturel* and is actually the birthplace of the technique. Roussillon's ruler, the King of Majorca, granted a Catalan alchemist attending Montpellier University the patent for the process in 1299. The most notable appellations for VDN in **Roussillon** are **Rivesaltes** (who's best wine **Muscat de Rivesaltes** is made from 100% **Muscat**), **Banyuls**, and **Maury**. The two latter regions are well known for their **Grenache-based** wines.

# Appendix A: Latitude

## Northern Hemisphere
(By Continent & Roughly North → South)

## North America
### United States of America

#### Washington

| | |
|---|---|
| Growing Regions | 45.5-48.0°N |
| Seattle | 47.6°N |
| Yakima | 46.5°N |

#### Oregon

| | |
|---|---|
| Growing Regions | 42.0-46.0°N |
| Portland | 45.5°N |
| Salem | 44.9°N |
| Eugene | 44.0°N |
| Roseburg | 43.2°N |
| Grant's Pass | 42.4°N |

#### California

| | |
|---|---|
| North Coast | 37.5-40.0°N |
| San Francisco | 37.8°N |
| Napa Valley | 38.0-38.5°N |
| Calistoga | 38.6°N |
| Yountville | 38.4°N |
| City of Napa | 38.3°N |
| Sonoma County | 38.0-39.0°N |
| Healdsburg | 38.6°N |
| Santa Rosa | 38.4°N |
| City of Sonoma | 38.3°N |
| Petaluma | 38.2°N |
| Central Coast | 34.5-38.0°N |
| Monterey | 36.6°N |
| Paso Robles | 35.6°N |
| Los Angeles | 34.1°N |
| San Diego | 32.7°N |

#### New York

| | |
|---|---|
| Growing Regions | 40.5-43.0°N |
| Rochester | 43.2°N |
| Buffalo | 42.9°N |
| Albany | 42.7°N |
| Riverhead, Long Island | 40.9°N |
| New York City | 40.7°N |

#### Virginia

| | |
|---|---|
| Growing Regions | 36.5-39.0°N |
| Winchester | 39.2°N |
| Richmond | 37.5°N |
| Danville | 36.6°N |

### Canada
#### British Columbia

| | |
|---|---|
| Growing Regions | 49.0-50.0°N |
| Vernon | 50.3°N |
| Kelowna | 49.9°N |
| Penticton | 49.5°N |

#### Ontario

| | |
|---|---|
| Growing Regions | 42.0-44.0°N |
| Toronto | 43.7°N |
| Windsor | 42.3°N |

## Europe
### Germany

| | |
|---|---|
| Growing Regions | 47.5-51.5°N |
| Dusseldorf | 51.2°N |
| Frankfurt | 50.1°N |
| Strasbourg | 48.6°N |

### Austria

| | |
|---|---|
| Growing Regions | 47.0-48.5°N |
| Vienna | 48.2°N |
| Rust | 47.8°N |
| Graz | 47.1°N |

# France

## Champagne

| Growing Regions | 48.0-49.0°N |
|---|---|
| Reims | 49.2°N |
| Épernay | 49.0°N |
| Bar-Sur-Seine | 48.1°N |

## Alsace

| Growing Regions | 47.5-48.5°N |
|---|---|
| Strasbourg | 48.6°N |
| Colmar | 48.1°N |
| Mulhouse | 47.7°N |

## Loire

| Growing Regions | 46.5-48.0°N |
|---|---|
| Orléans | 47.9°N |
| Tours | 47.4°N |
| Nantes | 47.2°N |

## Burgundy

| Growing Regions | 46.0-48.0°N |
|---|---|
| Chablis | 47.8°N |
| Dijon | 47.3°N |
| Beaune | 47.1°N |
| Macon | 46.3°N |
| Belleville, Beaujolais | 46.1°N |

## Jura

| Growing Regions | 46.0-47.0°N |
|---|---|
| Arbois | 46.9°N |
| Château-Chalon | 46.8°N |
| St. Amour | 46.3°N |

## Bordeaux

| Growing Regions | 44.0-45.5°N |
|---|---|
| Lesparre-Medoc | 45.3°N |
| Libourne | 44.9°N |
| Bordeaux | 44.8°N |
| Langon | 44.5°N |

## Rhône Valley

| Growing Regions | 43.5-45.5°N |
|---|---|
| Vienne | 45.5°N |
| Montélimar | 44.6°N |
| Nîmes | 43.8°N |

## Provence

| Growing Regions | 43.0-44.0°N |
|---|---|
| Avignon | 43.9°N |
| Marseille | 43.2°N |
| Toulon | 43.1°N |

## Languedoc-Roussillon

| Growing Regions | 42.5-44.5°N |
|---|---|
| Nîmes | 43.8°N |
| Montpelier | 43.6°N |
| Carcassonne | 43.2°N |
| Perpignan | 42.6°N |

# Italy

| Entire Country | 37.0-47.0°N |
|---|---|
| Venice | 45.4°N |
| Florence | 43.8°N |
| Rome | 41.9°N |

## Piedmont

| Growing Regions | 44.5-45.5°N |
|---|---|
| Torino | 45.1°N |
| Asti | 44.9°N |
| Alba | 44.7°N |

## Tuscany

| Growing Regions | 42.5-44.0°N |
|---|---|
| Florence | 43.8°N |
| Siena | 43.3°N |
| Montalcino | 43.1°N |
| Scansano | 42.8°N |

# Spain

| Entire Country | 36.5-43.0°N |
|---|---|
| San Sebastian (Basque) | 43.2°N |
| Logroño (Rioja) | 42.5°N |
| Pontevedra (Galicia) | 42.4°N |
| Barcelona (Catalonia) | 41.4°N |
| Madrid | 40.4°N |
| Malaga (Andalucia) | 36.7°N |

# SOUTHERN HEMISPHERE
(By Continent & Roughly North → South)

## AUSTRALIA & OCEANIA

### AUSTRALIA

| Entire Country | 10.0-40.0°S |
|---|---|
| Growing Regions | 27.0-43.0°S |

### NEW SOUTH WALES

| Growing Regions | 29.0-36.0°S |
|---|---|
| Sydney | 33.9°S |
| Canberra | 35.3°S |

### WESTERN AUSTRALIA

| Growing Regions | 31.0-35.0°S |
|---|---|
| Perth | 31.9°S |
| Bunbury | 33.2°S |
| Albany | 35.0°S |

### SOUTH AUSTRALIA

| Growing Regions | 33.0-37.0°S |
|---|---|
| Clare | 33.8°S |
| Adelaide | 34.9°S |
| Coonawarra | 37.3°S |

### VICTORIA

| Growing Regions | 36.0-38.0°S |
|---|---|
| Melbourne | 37.8°S |

### TASMANIA

| Growing Regions | 41.0-43.0°S |
|---|---|
| Devonport | 41.2°S |
| Hobart | 42.8°S |

### NEW ZEALAND

| Entire Country | 35.0-46.0°S |
|---|---|
| Auckland | 36.8°S |
| Wellington (Martinborough) | 41.3°S |
| Christchurch (Canterbury) | 43.5°S |
| Dunedin (Otago) | 45.9°S |

## SOUTH AMERICA

### CHILE

| Growing Regions | 30.0-38.0°S |
|---|---|
| La Serena | 29.9°S |
| Santiago | 33.4°S |
| Curicó | 35.0°S |
| Concepción | 36.8°S |

### ARGENTINA

| Growing Regions | 22.5-42.0°S |
|---|---|
| Salta | 24.8°S |
| La Rioja | 29.4°S |
| Mendoza | 32.9°S |
| Neuquén | 38.9°S |

## AFRICA

### SOUTH AFRICA

| Western Cape | 31.0-35.0°S |
|---|---|
| Lutzville | 31.5°S |
| Cape Town | 33.9°S |
| Cape Agulhas | 34.8°S |

# Appendix B: Grape Page

## CABERNET FRANC

Skin: Medium/Thick
Acid: Medium

*Co parent to Cabernet Sauvignon*

OLD WORLD: Raspberry, cherry, blackcurrant leaves, herbaceous, tobacco, dark spice, red licorice, graphite

NEW WORLD: Cassis, tobacco, black and red currants, spicey (can be stemmy and green bell peppery if picked under ripe)

REGIONS: Loire, Bordeaux, California, New York, Ontario, Italy, New Zealand, Australia, South Africa

PAIRING: With rich tannins and varying degrees of fruit expression, dishes with higher fat and protein content work well. Given its ability to express soil and origin, gamier dishes can also work.

## CABERNET SAUVIGNON

Skin: Medium/Thick
Acid: Medium/High

*Born from Cabernet Franc and Sauvignon Blanc*

OLD WORLD: Cassis (blackcurrant), blackberry, black raspberry, cedar, earth, spice, tobacco

NEW WORLD: Ripe jammy blackberries, plum, earth, cedar, chocolate, eucalyptus, mint

REGIONS: Bordeaux, California (Napa, Sonoma, Paso Robles), Washington State, Australia, Chile, Argentina, South Africa, Italy

PAIRING: The acid profile of Cabernet Sauvignon is often higher than that of Franc. The fruit profile can tend towards a juicier expression as well. The amount of juiciness is related to overall heat in the region or vintage and winemaker preferences. Pairs well with richer fattier dishes from beef to pork to roasted fowl and fattier fish can go with softer Cabs.

## GRENACHE

Skin: Thick
Acid: Low/Medium

OLD WORLD: Black pepper, spice, tar, black olives, leather, black cherry, strawberry, raspberry

NEW WORLD: Strawberries and raspberries, spice, black pepper and olives, tar, potential for high alcohol

REGIONS: Spain (Priorat, Rioja, Navarra), Southern Rhône, Provence, Languedoc, Australia, California (Central Valley), Sardinia

PAIRING: Will depend on the style and blend of the wine. Purely from a 100% varietal wine persective, the spice and the tannin can handle gamier dishes. If you are drinking a Grenache blend, use the percentages of other grapes to influence your pairings

## MALBEC

Skin: Thick
Acid: Low/medium

OLD WORLD: Red currant, black currant, prune, liquorice, raisin, tobacco, meaty, rustic, tannic

NEW WORLD: Violet, plum, soft, ripe, lush, rich, juicy

REGIONS: Southwest France (Cahors), Argentina, Loire, Bordeaux, California

PAIRING: Usually spiced with reasonable to high alcohol, bigger dishes can stand up to this grape. Think *flavor* spice in your dish before *heat* spice! If you are getting a dish with heat spice, check the alcohol level of your Malbec. Higher alcohol will help soften spice if the wine is balanced with a ripe fruit profile.

## MERLOT

Skin: Medium/Thick
Acid: Low/Medium

Old World: Plums, soft, round, velvet, violets

New World: Figs, prunes, chocolate, coffee, smooth, lush

Regions: Right Bank Bordeaux, Northern Italy, California, Chile, Argentina, Australia, New Zealand, South Africa, New York

Pairing: Owner of the "plum family" aromas and initial flavors. Vineyard yield and wood use changes the profile dramatically. Old world examples can be massive and powerful, yet elegant. For these, think game, beef, venison. For new world Merlot, where there might be a riper profile of plums, think salmon, swordfish, tuna. Remember that the specific expression of the wine you're drinking, plus your palatte and the sauce with the dish will help deteremine which way to go.

## NEBBIOLO

Skin: Thin/Medium
Acid: High

Old World: Tar, roses, cherry, black chocolate, black cherry, leather, spice, herbs, licorice, dried fruit, truffle

New World: Tar, dark berries, spice, big tannins

Regions: Italy (Piedmont, Lombardy, Valle d'Aosta), Argentina, California, Virginia, Washington, Australia

Pairing: Game in all its forms

## PETIT VERDOT

Skin: Thick
Acid: Medium

Old World: Violets, tannic, inky blackcurrant, blackberry

New World: Violet, Black berries, leather, earthy, earthen, animal

Regions: Bordeaux, California, Chile, Australia, Spain, Italy, South Africa

Pairing: Game, wild meats and fowl! Similar to Petit Sirah, this inky black wine with fruit and earth requires structure in its food.

## PINOT NOIR

Skin: Thin
Acid: High

*Know your clones; this changes all aspects of expression*

Old World: Cherry, wild strawberry, raspberry, light earthiness, violets, cabbage, beet

New World: Wild, spiced and Bing cherry, wild strawberry, rhubarb, wild raspberry, sweet beets, clove, baking spices

Regions: Burgundy, Loire, Jura, Oregon, California, New Zealand, Champagne, Australia, Chile, Argentina, South Africa, Germany, Italy (near everywhere)

Pairing: From fish to meat, everything is on the table (literally) the style of a house or winemaker massively influences each clone's expression. One of the few grapes where knowing the producer trumps loving a region or appellation.

## SANGIOVESE

Skin: Thin/Medium
Acid: High

Old World: Herbs, cherry, violets, tea, spice, cinnamon, earth notes, slight animal, cranberry

New World: Bright cherry, strawberry, spice, cranberry, earthy

Regions: Italy (Tuscany), Argentina, California, Australia

Pairing: Sangiovese is a base in most Tuscan wines, but becoming increasingly seen as a stand alone. Look for blending percentages to assist in food accompaniment. The spice and earth go well with pasta (all sorts and textures; it can even handle spicy meats with pasta). Steak, fowl and game pair well relative to blending grapes.

## SYRAH (Shiraz)

Skin: Thick
Acid: Medium

Old World: Blackberry, blackcurrant, game, leather, smoked meats, tar, pepper, earth, violets

New World: Blackberry, blueberry, smoke, tar, black pepper, chocolate, spice

Regions: Northern and Southern Rhône Valley, Languedoc-Roussillon, Australia, South Africa, California, Washington State, Spain, Chile, Argentina

Pairing: Syrah is often confused with Cabernet Sauvignon! Its black fruits and silky smooth texture belies massive structure. The barnyard and smoked meats sets it apart. Dishes with a dense consistency (i.e., venison, pigeon, wild boar), forest floor and mushroom flavors, in addition to smoked meats and root vegetables fare well.

## TEMPRANILLO

Skin: Thick
Acid: Low

Old World: Strawberry, black cherry, raspberry, tobacco, leather, dill and coconut (if newer American Oak is in use)

New World: Figs, jammy, coffee, dried fruit, chocolate, earth

Regions: Spain, Portugal, Argentina, California

Pairing: A dense rich earth driven wine in which tannins abound. Here, richer meats and root vegetables work especially well.

## ZINFANDEL

Skin: Thick
Acid: Medium

*Zinfandel is genetically the same as Primitivo from Italy and Crljenak Kastelanski from Croatia*

Old World: Blackberry, pepper, smokey, spice

New World: Juicy blackberry, strawberry, raspberry, pepper, plum, prune, date, raisin, spice, cedar

Regions: California, Italy (Puglia), Croatia

Pairing: Relative to the expression, the juicier the wine, the bigger the spice in the dish can be; the earthier the wine, the gamier the dish can be, as a general rule.

## ALBARINO

BODY: Medium
ACID: High

OLD WORLD: Apple, white flowers, peach and apricot skin, highly aromatic, zesty

NEW WORLD: Ripe white peaches, honey, exotic fruit

REGIONS: Spain (Galicia), Portugal, California (Edna Valley, Santa Ynez Valley)

PAIRING: Usually clean aromatic and steely in style, the opulence and rich expression of fruit can accompany many dishes inlcluding ceviche, grilled fish, crustaceans and light meats.

## CHARDONNAY

BODY: Medium/Full
ACID: High

OLD WORLD: Apple, pear, quince, keen sense of place from limestone soil. Slightly smoked as quality increases with increased use of new oak

NEW WORLD: Ripe apple, pineapple, melon, tropical fruit

REGIONS: Burgundy, California, New York, Washington State, Australia, South Africa, Italy, New Zeland, Chile, Argentina (similar to Pinot Noir, Chardonnay can be found throughout the world of *Vitis vinifera* vineyards)

PAIRING: The sky is the limit! Here, as with Pinot the production and yield tell a story far greater than grape and region necessarily. Fish and shell fish, white meats and light red meats, fowl not game.

## CHENIN BLANC

BODY: Full
ACID: High

OLD WORLD: Apple, pear, honey, wet wool, bee's wax, linoleum (if you're old enough to remember that aroma)

NEW WORLD: Peach, apricot, pineapple, quince, guava, honey

REGIONS: Loire Valley, South Africa, California (Central Valley), Argentina, New York (Long Island: one producer)

PAIRING: In addition to range of aromas and flavors, Chenin can be bubbly, bone dry and crazy sweet! Therefore the food pairing opportunies are limited only by your imagination.

## (GEWURZ)TRAMINER

BODY: Full
ACID: Medium/High

OLD WORLD: Rose, lychee, spice, honeysuckle

NEW WORLD: Melon, peach, lychee, apricot, baking spice (often off-dry)

REGIONS: France, Germany, Australia, Austria; California, Canada, Australia, New York, Oregon

PAIRING: Varying degrees of Residual Sugar will assist in determining interesting pairings here. The more sugar in the wine, the greater the need for spice or texture in the food. Drier versions are beginning to appear, adding complexity to the profile of this grape.

## GRUNER VELTLINER

BODY: Medium/Full
ACID: High

OLD WORLD: White pepper, grapefruit, great mineral expression, zesty, electric texture, angular (usually made in stainless steel)

NEW WORLD: California (beginning to see experimental plantings)

REGIONS: Austria (all along Danube)

PAIRING: the combination of mineral, acid and spice allows for significant leeway in pairings. Fat and protein in dish is a great place to start!

## PINOT BLANC

SKIN: Medium
ACID: Medium/High

OLD WORLD: Spicy, pear, apple, honeycomb

NEW WORLD: Apple, pear, peach, apricot

REGIONS: Alsace, Germany, Austria, Italy, California, Oregon, Wahington State, Canada

PAIRING: With attributes similar to Chardonnay, coupled with producers lowering yields and increasing attention paid to winemaking, the properties of Pinot Blanc are developing annually! Deeper richer expression allows for pairings including rich fish in sauce, shellfish, and roasted meats to veal!

## PINOT GRIS (or GRIGIO)

SKIN: Medium
ACID: Medium

OLD WORLD: Honey, grapefruit, baked apple, quince, floral, rich texture

NEW WORLD: Pear, apple, mango, honeysuckle

REGIONS: France, Italy, Germany, New Zealand, Oregon, Canada, California, Washington

PAIRING: From the lighter side of Italy: seafood, shellfish, crudités. As the body increases: higher fat fish, more protein in a dish. When sweet: bitter chocolate and Asian spices in a dessert fare well.

## RIESLING

BODY: Medium/Full
ACID: High

OLD WORLD: Apricot, peach, green apples, aromatic, petrol and honey with age

NEW WORLD: Apricot, ripe peaches, pineapple, ripe lime

REGIONS: Germany, Austria, Alsace, Australia, New Zealand, California, New York, Washington State, Canada, Chile, Argentina (and increasing)

PAIRING: Similar to Chenin Blanc, this variety has the ability to be bubbly, bone dry and layered with late harvest to noble rot sweet. With this array of expression, one could pair salted port dishes with sauerkraut, to dried sausage; roast pork to shoulder to roasted chicken with mushrooms. Do not hesitate to experiment with the expression of your Riesling (you won't be disappointed).

## SAUVIGNON BLANC

Body: Medium/High
Acid: High

OLD WORLD: Grapefruit, peach, apricot and gooseberry (apple and pear are possibilities as well). Chalky and often confused with Chardonnay when from Kimmeridgian Clay.

NEW WORLD: Pink grapefruit, passionfruit, kiwi peach, apricot skins

REGIONS: France, New Zealand, Chile, South Africa, Languedoc-Roussillon, California, New York, Italy Bordeaux, Australia

PAIRING: Can be a stand alone and often blended with Semillon. Steely fruit with pithy notes of stone fruit makes this awesome for many dishes. Think: steely high acid requires fat and protein from salmon to monkfish to scallops (pay attention to sauce and preparation). Increase the age of vine and add oak and/or blending grapes, the white meats come into play.

## TORRONTES

Body: Medium
Acid: High

OLD WORLD: N/A

NEW WORLD: Aromatic, floral, grapefruit, (muscat contribution: orange flower water and blossoms, rose petal)

REGIONS: Argentina (where it is considered a cross between Criolla Chica and Muscat d'Alexandria)

PAIRING: Salted fish and Ceviche are places to start relative to the aromatic profile and how much Muscat comes through vintage to vintage. Milder dishes with soft spices are best.

## VERMENTINO (Rolle)

Body: Medium/Full
Acid: Medium

OLD WORLD: lemons, nuts, unctuous, rich and round, oily in texture (not Riesling petroleum)

NEW WORLD: somewhat richer fruit profile and weightier in alcohol

REGIONS: Italy (Tuscany, Sardinia), France (Languedoc-Roussillon, Provence), California

PAIRING: The mouth feel alone implies that a bigger fish dish with meatier fleshier fish are needed (not sole) white meats and pork, veal. There is an elegant power to this wine so the dishes should have character, but not overwhelm.

## VIOGNIER

Body: Medium/Full
Acid: Medium

OLD WORLD: Apricot, acacia, jasmine, aromatic, peach

NEW WORLD: Sweet apricot, peach and melon, lilies and freisa (floral, as with new wood, is avoided)

REGIONS: Northern Rhône Valley, Pays d'Oc, Languedoc-Roussillon, Australia, California, Oregon, Virginia

PAIRING: Think light fare to start if the expression is floral and light bodied. If the profile is richer meatier and your wine may have some barrel aging, richer meats and fattier fish can pair well.

Made in the USA
Middletown, DE
03 March 2017